Marriage and Family Interaction

The Dorsey Series in Anthropology and Sociology

EDITOR
ROBIN M. WILLIAMS, JR.
Cornell University

ARGYRIS *Understanding Organizational Behavior*

HSU (ed.) *Psychological Anthropology: Approaches to Culture and Personality*

BELL (ed.) *The Sociology of Education: A Sourcebook*

HAGEN *On the Theory of Social Changes: How Economic Growth Begins*

BELL *Marriage and Family Interaction* rev. ed.

BARNOUW *Culture and Personality*

GOTTLIEB & RAMSEY *The American Adolescent*

JACOBS *Pattern in Cultural Anthropology*

JOHNSON *Crime, Correction, and Society*

SALISBURY *Religion in American Culture: A Sociological Interpretation*

BREER & LOCKE *Task Experience as a Source of Attitudes*

WILSON *Sociology: Rules, Roles, and Relationships*

SHOSTAK *Sociology in Action: Case Studies in Social Problems and Directed Social Change*

MARRIAGE and
FAMILY INTERACTION

ROBERT R. BELL

Temple University

1967 · Revised Edition

THE DORSEY PRESS

Homewood, Illinois

Revised Edition

First Printing, March, 1967

Library of Congress Catalog Card No. 67–17037

PRINTED IN THE UNITED STATES OF AMERICA

To

my wife, *Phyllis*

and our daughters,

Marta Lee and Robin Ann

PREFACE

In planning the revision of this text, I considered the possible inclusion of a number of new topics, as well as the possibility of alternative ways of presenting and interpreting data. But I decided that any major shift in orientation would result in a book quite different from the first edition. Therefore, in deciding what approach to take toward the revision I held to the definition presented in the Preface of the first edition; "[this text] is primarily a functional text for marriage and family courses, but the orientation is not functional in the 'how-to-do-it' sense." I continue to hold firm to the belief that any contribution I might make to the student is as a sociologist of the family and not as a prescriber of behavior.

The most common suggestion I received for this revision was to include more cross-cultural data. However, to do that with any degree of comprehensiveness and sophistication would mean a basic reorientation and rewriting of my text. Where appropriate, I have presented brief cross-cultural summaries that provide a general base for comparing our American culture with those of other countries. However, the main changes have been bringing the first edition up to date with new and relevant research findings, expanding and developing a number of new sections, and writing one essentially new chapter.

I have received opinions from a number of teachers who have used this text, as well as from many students who have studied from it. I am greatly indebted to them for both their favorable comments and their critical reactions. I have tried to respond objectively and examine all suggestions, but I am fully responsible for the content of both the original and the revised edition.

I want to particularly thank for their perceptive and valuable comments both Robert S. Pickett, Syracuse University; and Ira L. Reiss, State University of Iowa. As always, I am most indebted to my wife for her interest and for the significant contributions she makes to my work.

Dresher, Pennsylvania   ROBERT R. BELL
January, 1967

TABLE OF CONTENTS

PART I. BACKGROUND

PART II. DATING-COURTSHIP

Table of Contents xi

PART 1

Background

THE STUDY OF MARRIAGE
AND THE FAMILY

With few exceptions, all who read this book have had the experience of being a member of a family. As a matter of fact, most Americans will be members of three different, but related, families: the family of *orientation,* in which the role is that of the child, and the primary relationships are to parents and siblings; the family of *procreation,* in which the role is that of husband or wife, and the primary relationships are to the spouse and children; and the *in-law* family, in which the role is that of an in-law, and the primary relationships are to parents-in-law and siblings-in-law. Because of these common, personal experiences, the individual often sees himself as an authority on the family—and he is, as regards his own, personal family relationships.

The individual moving through his own families of orientation and procreation develops the characteristics of becoming social, and the acquisition of these social skills enables him to contribute to the perpetuation of society. As Arensberg has pointed out, the families of orientation and procreation are two families in "a repetitive succession of like social organisms, families, endlessly transmitting cultural and social experience."[1] That is, they are constantly making the individual social and—by doing so—they are at the same time perpetuating society.

This book will attempt to move its readers from their personal understanding of the family to a broader, more generalized understanding of marriage and family relationships in contemporary America. An individual may react to portions of the discussion with, "I know that from my own experience." Certainly much that will be said about the family will correspond to everyone's experience, because of cultural patterns common to American society. However, the social scientist often studies what people *think* they already know

---

[1]Conrad M. Arensberg, "The American Family In the Perspective of Other Cultures," in Eli Ginzberg (ed.), *The Nation's Children* (New York: Columbia University Press, 1960), p. 54.

in order to provide evidence about the accuracy of those assumptions. And sometimes the results of such studies indicate that what we "know" is not, in fact, true.

This book is based on the belief that disciplined thought and controlled research are the best means of providing knowledge and understanding of marriage and family relationship. This is not to say that an individual, with skillful uses of his senses and intelligence, cannot give an insightful picture of marriage and the family. He can, and does—as, for example, the able novelist does—but he is restricted for the most part to his own, always limited observations. The social scientist, on the other hand, draws upon the disciplined analysis of many observers to provide a general picture of marriage and the family.

STUDYING AMERICAN MARRIAGE AND FAMILY

A number of different approaches to an academic analysis of marriage and family relationships exist. No one approach can—or at least it rarely does—claim absolute jurisdiction, but each sees the family within the confines of its specific orientation. A single text cannot possibly incorporate, in a meaningful way, the orientations and findings of all the many different approaches that are concerned with marriage and the family. For example, the various "personality" approaches (for the most part ignored in this book) study and treat the individual and his family experiences from or "through" the individual personality. But while "personality" findings are of great significance, they do not always lend themselves to analysis within the *social* framework of a book such as this.

The study of the family in this book centers around a sociological and a social-psychological approach. These two interrelated approaches are the theoretical orientations followed by many sociologists in studying marriage and the family. Social scientists usually focus on one, or combinations of four interrelated sets of family characteristics: first, the formal nature of family relationships, such as kinship ties; second, the demographic or population factors related to the family; third, the cultural approach, which looks at the family in relationship to the specific culture of which it is a part; and fourth, the social-psychological relationships[2] of which the family is a part. All of these points of emphasis will be used to some ex-

---

[2]Ernest W. Burgess and Harvey Locke, *The Family* (New York: American Book Co., 1953), p. 7.

tent in discussing marriage and family relationships; however, this book primarily follows the social-psychological approach.

The following definition of the family, taken from Burgess and Locke, indicates the basic conception of the family used in this book: "The family is a unit of interacting and intercommunicating persons enacting the social roles of husband and wife, mother and father, son and daughter, brother and sister. The roles are defined by the community, but in each family they are powerfully reinforced by sentiments, partly traditional and partly emotional, arising out of experience."[3]

Later in this chapter, more will be said about the theoretical approach to be taken, but at this point it is more germane to discuss the nature of research in the marriage and family area. Social scientists accept the need for empirical research as a basic tenet of their discipline. In studying marriage and the family, particular research problems emerge because of the nature of the subject matter. While individuals frequently react with little personal emotion to an economist studying consumer behavior or a political scientist analyzing voting behavior, they will often react strongly to the sociologist studying an area of marriage and family that is of interest and importance to his discipline. For example, the study of sexual behavior is one of the most important areas in sociological research—yet it has been, at the same time, probably the most sensitive study area as far as the general public is concerned.

Research Problems

Behavioral studies of premarital sex have had the effect of forcing many adults to recognize that the behavior of the young unmarried population does not correspond to society's values. Because their personal assumptions are thus questioned, many Americans feel threatened by these behavioral studies; as a result, many react to them with great moral indignation, thereby implying that human sexual behavior would be better left unstudied. Disbelief is another common reaction when people are faced with behavioral information that indicates not everyone behaves in a prescribed manner. People prefer to cling to an idealized, nonfactual interpretation of human behavior, rather than accept the unidealized, documented version presented by the social scientist. Sometimes a person will react by saying, "Maybe the rest of the world is that way, but not the part I live in." The rest of the world may be perceived as different

---

[3]*Ibid.*, p. G.

without discomfort, but not the part identified with by the individual himself.

Further, because the human being functions in a social setting, he often feels that he knows as much about general human behavior as the social scientist. Yet the social scientist, with all the limitations and problems he encounters as a result of the complexity of his data, presents a far more accurate picture of human behavior than does the untrained individual. Some of the assumptions and controls followed by the sociologist illustrate this greater reliability. First, he believes that all areas of human behavior can be made the focus of study, though he recognizes that some areas are much more complex and difficult to study than others. "There is an honesty in science which refuses to accept the idea that there are aspects of the material universe that are better not investigated, or better not known, or the knowledge of which should not be made available to the common man."[4]

Second, a basic tenet of all science is that scientific knowledge is open to all, rather than reserved for a select few. Thus, in a democracy, the individual has the right of access to knowledge and the choice of its use, within the limits of legal and social sanctions. In a totalitarian society, on the other hand, few such rights exist and little or no social science exists, because human behavior is determined and explained by political dogma. People in a democracy do not assume a single dogmatic explanation of human behavior; rather, they recognize a pluralistic explanation. For example, the scientific, the religious, the artistic, and the philosophical points of view all have an equal right to be heard and evaluated.

Third, the scientist makes every possible attempt to control biases in his investigations. The greater the degree of control over biases, the closer research findings will be to the scientific ideal of objectivity. Because scientific research seeks unbiased, empirical evidence, the results of scientific inquiry may go counter to accepted social beliefs. Hence, the scientist must be constantly aware of the dangers of bias or vested interest. No study can be called scientific if the results have not been arrived at objectively, or if the results are altered to fit some predetermined value assumptions.

Fourth, a distinction must be made between a moral and a scientific interest in right and wrong. The moralist believes certain human behavior to be right; evidence showing that many people do

---

[4]Alfred C. Kinsey, Wardell B. Pomeroy, Clyde E. Martin, and Paul H. Gebhard, *Sexual Behavior in the Human Female* (Philadelphia: W. B. Saunders, 1953), p. 9.

not function accordingly does not repudiate his moral definition. He continues to believe that certain behavior is right and that this is a prescription for human action, even if it is not a description of actual behavior. The scientist, then, views right and wrong only as values and attitudes to be studied and considered in his investigations. His findings attempt to describe and explain behavior as he finds it, not according to what he thinks it should be. It is important to keep in mind that science cannot provide a system of morality, not even a rational morality, because "moral values cannot be scientifically proven; they must be chosen."[5]

Even without such problems, however, the researcher interested in the family in America does not study all areas of marriage and family, nor is the amount of his research always determined by some measurement of significance. In general, family research has been most concentrated on dating and courtship, sexual behavior, and the socialization of the child. By contrast, much less has been done on various aspects of marriage relationships, and particularly on the older person in marriage and family relationships.[6]

The focus of research so far has been influenced partly by the researcher's particular interests, and often by the high cost of many types of research. Costs not only influence what will be studied, but often the method of study and the particular populations studied. The most extensive, and usually the methodologically most sophisticated, studies have been done when large grants were available and "team research" was possible. The comprehensive studies on sexual behavior and family fertility are illustrations.[7]

Many marriage and family research studies have used samples of only several hundred; extending the findings to larger populations must be done with caution. For example, the family researcher is often accused of studying the "college sophomore." The charge contains a great deal of truth, and implies that he should be studying some larger and more representative population sample. The researcher would agree, except that often his choice is to study the small group, or none at all. Even the small groups studied provide at least some empirical evidence for an understanding of marriage

[5]Ira L. Reiss, "Personal Values and the Scientific Study of Sex," in *Advances in Sex Research,* (New York: Harper & Row, Pubs., 1963), p. 8.

[6]Nelson N. Foote, "New Roles for Men and Women," *Marriage and Family Living,* November, 1961, pp. 325–29.

[7]See Kinsey, *op. cit.*; Ronald Freedman, Pascal K. Whelpton, and Arthur A. Campbell, *Family Planning, Sterility, and Population Growth* (New York: McGraw-Hill Book Co., 1959); and Charles F. Westoff, Robert G. Potter, Jr., Philip Sagi, and Elliot G. Mishler, *Family Growth in Metropolitan America* (Princeton, New Jersey: Princeton University Press, 1961).

and the family. In this book, many such small studies will be quoted. The tentative and restricted nature of the findings should always be kept in mind; but the findings should be recognized as providing at least some empirical evidence more reliable than individual experiences or nonempirical arm-chair speculation.

AMERICAN MARRIAGE AND FAMILY

Man, with his specialized ability to use symbols, has the ability to create a vast variety of complex and often different social systems. "Marriage and the family in human society are what they are because man, although biologically conditioned, yet has a capacity for creativity so that repeatedly he invents something new and unexpected."[8] Uniformities, as well as many cultural variations, are usually found in families of different societies. Furthermore, a function performed by the family at one point in time may, at another point, be taken over by other agencies of society. Some functions performed by the family are often interpreted as being functions that can *only* be performed by the family. Yet, given different cultures or variations within any one culture, probably all functions that are traditionally the family's have been performed on some occasions by other social agencies. For example, Reiss suggests that the family institution is a small, kinship-structured group that *generally* performs the key function of nurturance. This is usually provided by the parents, although there is nothing inherent in the function itself that requires that it be done by the biological parents, or even by a female or an adult.[9] The *only* requirement is that the nurturant function be performed by some socially functioning individual.

The American family has been historically characterized by change and the loss of many traditional functions. As a result, the family "has become a more specialized agency than before, probably more specialized than it has been in any previously known society."[10] For example, the American family has partly relinquished to other social agencies such functions as: economic unit of production, formal teaching of offspring, protection, care of the aged, and recreation. The result, of course, as Dager suggests, is that however

---

[8]Arnold S. Nash, "Ancient Past and Living Present," in Howard Becker and Reuben Hill, *Family, Marriage and Parenthood* (Boston: D.C. Heath & Co., 1955), p. 85.

[9]Ira L. Reiss, "The Universality of the Family: A Conceptual Analysis," *Journal of Marriage and Family*, November, 1965, p. 449.

[10]Talcott Parsons and Robert F. Bales, *Family, Socialization and Interaction Process* (Glencoe, Illinois: The Free Press, 1955), p. 9.

functional these changes may be for the larger society, they are be-coming increasingly nonfunctional for individuals. "Symbolic of this nonfunction is the increasing reliance by families upon many sec-ondary agencies: social security, industrial retirement programs, care of the aged, a plethora of welfare agencies, care for the young in the form of day nurseries, play schools, nursery schools, pre-kinder-gartens, and baby-sitting, fringe benefits, and so on."[11]

Parsons and Bales have pointed out that, as a result of these changes, the American family now has only two basic functions: "first, the primary socialization of children so that they can truly be-come members of the society into which they have been born; sec-ond, the stabilization of the adult personalities of the population of the society."[12] But even though these two functions are primarily as-signed to the family, other agencies of society are also involved. For example, the extending of formal education in nursery schools down to younger ages means that the educational institution is entering the socialization of the child at an earlier age than ever before. The non-family influences on adult personalities are recognized by Parsons and Bales when they write that "adult members must have roles other than their familial roles which occupy strategically important places in their own personalities."[13]

In line with the two functions suggested by Parsons and Bales, another primary basic function, especially in the middle class, cen-ters around the satisfaction of ego-needs through marriage and fam-ily relationships. By *ego-needs* is meant the desire of the individual to achieve emotional satisfaction from the giving and receiving of meaning and importance in interaction with another person. Ego-needs extend to many social relationships outside of the marriage and family setting. However, our main interest is in the family, where the basic ego-needs center in the emotional give and take be-tween husband and wife, parents and children, and siblings.

If the contention that ego-need satisfaction is a basic function is true, then the contention that the American family is disappearing is not true. The American family has certainly lost many of the im-portant functions it performed in the past. However, if Americans no longer believed in some significant marriage and family functions, the motivations for marriage and having children should, logically,

---

[11]Edward Z. Dager, "Socialization and Personality Development in the Child," in Harold T. Christensen (ed.) *Handbook of Marriage and The Family* (Chicago: Rand McNally & Co., 1964), p. 776.

[12]Parsons, *op. cit.,* pp. 16–17.

[13] *Ibid.,* p. 19.

have decreased—but exactly the opposite is the case. For example, the proportion of the adult population in the United States that was married increased far more between 1940 and the mid-1960's than in any other comparable period for which data are available, and the proportion has continued a slight but steady increase to the present day.[14] Furthermore, the birth rate has been very high over roughly the same period of time.

The high divorce rate in the United States offers still further support as to the importance of ego-need satisfaction. Many individuals get a divorce because they failed to find satisfaction with the person they had married. Apparently, however, they were not disillusioned with marriage in general, but rather with a specific marriage, as attested by the very high remarriage rates of the divorced. Often the divorcee enters the second marriage hoping to find a satisfying ego-need relationship that did not exist in the first marriage.

The ego-need factor in marriage and family relationships is one of the major themes of this book. The reader may assess the validity of the argument after he reads the book; that is, after evidence supporting the theme has been analyzed throughout discussion of the various facets of marriage and family interaction.

One other general characteristic of the American family should also be kept in mind: In at least one important respect the family as a social institution is very different from other social institutions; it is in the family setting that the individual usually spends the greatest number of years in his most pervasive interpersonal relationships. Because the individual often has a strong emotional commitment to certain family roles and role relationships, he may be "used" in his family roles to meet the needs of other social institutions. This point can be illustrated by the example of the relationship of family roles to illness as it is controlled by medical institutions.

Often the family's responsibility in taking care of their sick members is seen as primarily meeting the needs of medical institutions, and only in a secondary way is there any concern with how the family's care of its sick members may affect the family itself. For example, the home-care movement in the United States is supported by funds from agencies with an interest in increasingly facilitating their own beliefs about the care of the ill. Some of these home-care agencies' assumptions about the family's role are illustrated by their hope to return mentally ill persons to their families. Vincent writes that

---

[14]Paul C. Glick and Hugh Carter, "Marriage Patterns and Educational Level," *American Sociological Review*, June, 1958, p. 295; *Statistical Abstract of U.S.*, 1966, p. 31, No. 29.

"the family is expected to adapt to the return of its mentally ill or emotionally disturbed members, just as it was expected to adapt to the return of the parolee member of the family several decades ago. The family will also be expected to adapt to the intrusion of the mental health personnel concerned with the rehabilitation of the patient, just as it has adapted to the intrusion of the parole and probation officers, the judge of the juvenile court and the social worker."[15] Given the emotional involvement of family members with one another, it is not difficult to persuade them of their "responsibility." As Vincent puts it: "Given the mores of our society, how could the family maintain its ideological image if it refused to accept one of its members convalescing from mental illness or rehabilitating from crime or delinquency."[16]

There are institutions besides those of health care that may use the emotional commitment of family members to one another. For example, institutions of education, or of government, or of religion. This is not to say that the "use" of the family is necessarily undesirable, but simply to point out that the special emotional nature of the family makes it susceptible to being persuaded that it is serving its members, while in fact it is at the same time meeting the needs of another social institution.

SOCIAL CLASS

The complexity of marriage and family relationships in the United States today is great. To talk about "American marriage and the family" is to state a generality that stresses common patterns. However, anyone who studies the family quickly realizes that, within American marriage and family, many significant variations exist. For example, there are significant differences by social class, religion, ethnic, and racial background. The decision to concentrate in this book primarily on modern middle-class marriage and family relationships was made for several reasons. First, the middle class is increasing in size and significance in the American society. If any marriage and family pattern is emerging as typical of American society, it is that of the middle class. Second, the great bulk of empirical research has been done with middle-class subjects. Therefore, middle-class orientation provides the best opportunity for showing what is known through research. Third, the vast majority of readers of this

---

[15]Clarke E. Vincent, "Familia Spongia: The Adaptive Function," *National Council on Family Relations,* Toronto, Canada, October, 1965, p. 13.

[16]*Ibid.,* p. 13.

book either are in or will be in the middle class. An academic analysis may contribute to a greater understanding of the nature of middle-class marriage and family, allowing the reader to better "see" the family relationships he has experienced and will experience at various stages of marriage and family interaction.

Meaning

Social class, as a variable of social analysis, is of increasing significance in describing, explaining, and predicting many facets of social thought and behavior. Lloyd Warner, one of the pioneers in the sociology of social classes, writes "recent scientific studies of social class in the several regions of the United States demonstrated that it is a major determinate of individual decisions and social action; that every major area of American life is directly and indirectly influenced by our class order; and that the major decisions of most individuals are partly controlled by it."[17] This statement does not suggest that social class is an absolute variable, but rather that it is more reliable than many other variables in distinguishing significant variations in social thought and behavior.

One problem, still far from being resolved in the study of social class, is determining the number of different classes in the United States. The number has been estimated at anywhere from two to twelve. However, six class levels will be used here. As Bergel suggests, "on a nationwide basis the six categories are preferable—scale provides an excellent working proposition ('statistical' classes) and fairly depicts the actual situation ('social' classes)."[18]

The six classes are:

> Upper-upper class
> Lower-upper class
> Upper-middle class
> Lower-middle class
> Upper-lower class
> Lower-lower class

Differing social classes should be considered as a conception of "ideal types," or models that describe hypothetical social class positions. A hierarchy of "ideal types" makes it possible to relate, order, and compare the fit of social reality. Persons or families might be placed, for example, in the upper-middle class because they more

---

[17]W. Lloyd Warner, Marchia Meeker and Kenneth Eells, *Social Class in America* (New York: Harper Torchbooks, 1960), p. 6.
[18]Egan E. Bergel, *Social Stratification* (New York: McGraw-Hill Book Co., 1962), p. 259.

closely approximate that "ideal type" than any of the others; but few will "fit" exactly. The use of "ideal-type" social classes is essentially the same as the method used in medicine to diagnose a health problem. The physician catalogs as many of the patient's determinable variables as possible, and then "names" the patient's medical problem as that which most closely approximates one of his medical "ideal types." Analagously, in the study of social class one can rarely be absolutely sure of diagnoses because cases rarely fit the "ideal type," and because "ideal types" are never complete or absolute empirical models.

How Social Classes Differ. Most Americans can and do make crude distinctions between themselves and others on the basis of social class, whether they are aware they do or not. Such frequently heard expressions as "We have nothing in common," "They live differently," or "They are not our kind" often imply social class distinctions. However, the characteristics which show social class differences are more numerous and complex than the casual observer generally recognizes.

Social scientists have used several approaches to distinguish social classes.[19] By what may be called the *subjective* approach, individuals rate themselves or rate others in their community. Self-ratings often produce great distortion; for example, as many as nine out of ten Americans identify themselves as middle class.[20] Ratings of individuals by other individuals are more reliable but require a community where many individuals are known to each other.[21] In a second approach, which may be called the *objective,* ratings according to certain variables (education, income, etc.) are made either singly or through the use of multiple correlation scales. In general, the objective approach is more reliable than the subjective.

Individuals in a given social class share both the same general degree of a certain variable and common values. Social-class value orientations "usually combine aspects of *ought* (value) and aspects of *is* (existential beliefs about reality)."[22] The sharing of social class values is related to differential social interaction; that is, because most significant relationships occur between individuals of the same

---

[19]For a good discussion of the various theories and methods used in the study of social class see: Leonard Reissman, *Class in American Society* (Glencoe, Illinois: The Free Press, 1959).

[20]Bergel, *op. cit.,* p. 260.

[21]Warner, *op. cit.,* p. 6.

[22]Joseph A. Kahl, *The American Class Structure* (New York: Rinehart & Co., Inc., 1957), p. 185.

social-class level, at least some values, qualities, and skills common to the particular social class are inculcated and cultivated.

The family is the most important agency, at least initially, in determining the differential social-class associations of the individual. The family is important because the children of a family, at least until they grow up, have the social class position of their parents. Norms and values differ from one social class to another, but whatever they are, they help guide social interaction and provide some of the standards an individual uses in making evaluations. The family initially provides the norms and values which must be socially acquired. Because various values related to social-class position are acquired during the formative years, they often seem "natural" to the individual. Furthermore, these values are often reinforced by nonfamily associates, since the individual usually interacts with persons of similar social-class background. The very fact that the person feels at ease and has a sense of naturalness with others like himself tends to drive a wedge between his "world" and those in different social-class "worlds."

The lines between the different social classes cannot be sharply drawn or held to be absolute. Some familys will fall between two adjoining social classes and not fit one more than the other. American society is complex and contains a variety of hierarchies of social values and variables. Therefore, an individual may fall into one social class according to a number of different criteria, but into a different class according to other criteria, making his overall social-class position difficult to determine. But, even recognizing the problems of classification, significant general differences between the social classes may still be observed. The various classes should be seen as having average, but not absolute, differences.

The Middle Class

The old middle class in the United States represented the rather small percentage of the population that had its economic base in the ownership of small, independent property. Since about the time of the Civil War, however, a new and much extended middle-class, occupationally centered around technical-managerial, professional, and clerical employees, has emerged.[23]

The percentage of the American population in the middle class cannot be estimated accurately, but Bergel's estimate of about 40

---

[23]Lewis Corey, "The Middle Class," in Reinhard Bendix and Seymour M. Lipset, *Class, Status and Power* (Glencoe, Illinois: The Free Press, 1953), p. 375.

percent of the population will suffice for our purposes.[24] Of this estimate, about 15 percent are in the upper-middle class and the other 25 percent in the lower-middle class. Bergel further estimates that, by annual income, the bulk of the middle class falls into the range of $5,000 to $15,000, with $7,500 roughly dividing the upper-middle class from the lower-middle class.[25] By occupation, clerical and sales workers constitute the bulk of the lower-middle class, while professionals, proprietors, and managers characterize the upper-middle class.[26] By education, the lower-middle class usually has no more than a high school education, while the upper-middle class has at least some college. The variable used to distinguish the two middle classes are admittedly crude, but provide a general picture. While the broad middle class will often be discussed, the *upper*-middle class is the more common focus in this book.

The three values briefly discussed next provide a broad framework for understanding some areas of middle-class marriage and the family. These values often overlap, of course, and have varying influences on each other.

Social Mobility. A common belief, handed down as part of the American democratic tradition, has supported the idea of the "rugged individualist" who could attain upward social mobility by hard work and perseverance. In part, this belief still prevails, but upward mobility is more often believed to be best achieved today by proper preparation, particularly through the use of extended formal education.

An outstanding characteristic of contemporary mobility aspirations is that the values are instilled by the parents early in the child's life. Middle-class parents feel that they must at least help their children solidify their social-class position and, if possible, improve it; thus, one common middle-class value is the parents' conscious concern for their children's social mobility.

That upward social mobility is possible is shown by the fact that individuals do move up from their parents' social class. However, social mobility as a value often leads to problems. For example, what happens to the individual taught to be socially mobile, but who is unsuccessful? While some individuals reassess their mobility aspirations in light of their experience, many who have accepted the values probably feel at least some sense of frustration. Myers and Roberts

---

[24]Bergel, *op. cit.*, pp. 274–77.
[25]*Ibid.*, p. 269.
[26]*Ibid.*, p. 272.

found mobility frustration highly correlated with mental health problems. The patients they studied were under constant tension because of their mobility efforts and felt extremely frustrated by their lack of success.[27]

Even those who are successful may have problems. Ironically, parents who help their children move up in the social class hierarchy often find that their children's new values and way of life make strangers of them. Successfully mobile children may also be insecure in their new position and have to make a constant effort to present a correct "front." Goffman writes, "commonly we find that upward mobility involves the presentation of proper performances and that efforts to move upward and efforts to keep from moving downward are expressed in terms of sacrifices made for the maintenance of front."[28] Max Lerner vividly illustrates the nature of mobility anxiety when he writes: "They (the middle class) form a loose collection of occupational strata, probably more anxiety-ridden than the rest of the culture, dominated by the drive to distinguish themselves from the working class, uncohesive, held together by no common bond except the fact that they are caught in a kind of Purgatory between the Hell of the poor and weak and the Heaven of the rich and powerful."[29]

Success. Closely related to the belief in social mobility is the belief in success; but success, like mobility, has a different meaning today than it had in the past. In theory, the sky was the limit for personal success in the past; today, the kind and degree of success is stressed. "Not economic security alone but a whole psychic security syndrome is involved"[30] in middle-class success. Many times the successful young man is one who enters an occupation that provides only a limited possibility for individual achievement but gives him the security of having a place, of belonging. William H. Whyte, Jr., in *The Organization Man,* argues that the business world commonly believes that the driving individualist is no longer needed; rather, the kind of man needed for every kind of job "is a practical, team-player fellow who will do a good shirt-sleeves job."[31]

Thus in the middle class, success and security have become inter-

[27]Jerome K. Myers and Bertram H. Roberts, *Family and Class Dynamics in Mental Illness* (New York: John Wiley & Sons, Inc., 1959), p. 252.

[28]Erving Goffman, *The Presentation of Self in Everyday Life* (New York: Doubleday Anchor Books, 1959), p. 36.

[29]Max Lerner, *America As A Civilization* (New York: Simon & Schuster, 1957), p. 488.

[30]*Ibid.,* p. 692.

[31]William H. Whyte, Jr., *The Organization Man* (New York: Simon & Schuster, 1956), p. 152.

related. The individual sees himself in competition with an amorphous "they"—those he wants to move away from through social mobility. On the other hand, he sees his social-class peers in much less of a competitive sense because he doesn't want to *compete* with them, but rather *be* one of them. Therefore, security becomes an important criteria of individual success. In effect, middle-class "success" is often the movement from one group to another, where the measurement of personal achievement is acceptance in and a sense of belonging to the achieved group.

Happiness. Both mobility and success are also closely related to what may be the main goal in life for the middle class—the seeking of happiness. Happiness is reflected in the seeking of ego-need satisfaction by many individuals; if their ego-needs are met, they feel "happy." Not only is it believed that happiness can be achieved by all, but also that every person has a natural right to happiness.[32] Because of the importance of ego-needs, happiness is defined as being accepted by others as a significant person. Acceptance is sought in the close relationship of marriage, and also in work and leisure-time associations. Thus, social success is often determined by being accepted by those held to be significant, which in turn gives to the individual his belongingness—his happiness.

A great concern with being liked and accepted is an important part of the socialization process of the middle-class child. He is often reared under a reward-and-punishment system based on parents giving and withholding love and approval for his behavior. When he conforms, he is often loved, but when he deviates he may find the love withdrawn. Thus, there is a close relationship between love and approval—of having others show through approval that they love you or like you.

The same value system often operates in the schools. Henry writes that "mental docility achieved in middle class schoolrooms is not based on authoritarian control backed by fear of corporeal punishment, but rather on fear of loss of love. More precisely it rests on the need to bask in the sun of the teacher's acceptance."[33]

A popular belief is that one achieves happiness when he is accepted, and acceptance is defined as belonging. Therefore, a personality cult emerges, revolving around a mutual admiration society in which the group members approve of each other because they are

[32]Lerner, *op. cit.*, p. 693.
[33]Jules Henry, "Docility, or Giving the Teacher What She Wants," in Robert R. Bell, *The Sociology of Education: A Sourcebook* (Homewood, Illinois: The Dorsey Press, Inc., 1962), p. 345.

essentially alike; by approving of the others, each thereby approves of himself. Whether this is really happiness is left to the philosopher to determine, but the fact that many in the middle class believe it is happiness tends to determine behavior and perpetuate the belief.

These general values of mobility, success, and happiness permeate many middle-class thoughts and patterns regarding marriage and the family. However, these same values, since they are not clearly defined and are often contradictory, contribute to some of the problems and frustrations of middle-class life. The interest of this book is not in the "right" or "wrong" of these values, but rather in how they are reflected in middle-class courtship, marriage, and parent-child interaction.

THE INTERACTIONIST APPROACH

One last introductory area remains to be discussed—the theoretical approach that will be followed in the analysis of marriage and the family. Theory provides a framework for giving order and relationship to what otherwise may seem a series of unrelated areas. Theory also guides research, gives it direction, and attempts to provide some logical consistency. A theory or consistent approach need not be developed in extensive detail in a book that is primarily "functional" in approach, as this book is. But the theoretical assumptions made by the writer, as well as some explanation of the concepts that will be used, do need to be stated.

The approach in this book is that of symbolic interactionalism, which has its historical roots with John Dewey, Charles Cooley, Robert Park, and, particularly, George Herbert Mead. Its modern development and application can be read in the texts of Coutu, Lindesmith and Strauss, Rose, and Shibutani.[34] The interactionist approach is a social-psychological theory that centers around two major problems: "The first is that of socialization: how the human organism acquires the ways of behaving, the values, norms and attitudes of the social units of which he is a part. The focus here is on development—that which happens over time in the human neophyte.

---

[34]See: Walter Coutu, *Emergent Human Nature* (New York: Alfred A. Knopf, Inc., 1949); Alfred R. Lindesmith and Anselm L. Strauss, *Social Psychology* (New York: The Dryden Press, 1956); Arnold M. Rose, *Human Behavior and Social Processes* (Boston: Houghton Mifflin Co., 1962); and Tamotsu Shibutani, *Society and Personality* (Englewood Cliffs, New Jersey: Prentice-Hall, Inc., 1961). For a discussion of symbolic interaction related to the study of the family see: Sheldon Stryker, "Symbolic Interaction as an Approach to Family Research," *Marriage and Family Living*, May, 1959, pp. 111-19.

The twin of the problem of socialization is that of personality: the organization of persistent behavior patterns."[35]

Certain basic assumptions made by symbolic interactionists must be clearly understood in order to understand the direction and emphasis of the theoretical approach. First is the belief that man is unique and must be studied, not merely by comparing him to other forms of life, but on his own level; therefore, the position is anti-reductionist. Second, the belief is that one can better understand the social behavior of individuals by studying society. Third, the belief is that the newborn infant is asocial but has the potentialities for social development. The final assumption is that the human being is an actor as well as a reactor and does not simply respond to stimuli occurring outside himself.[36]

The basic unit in social interaction, the *social act,* refers to the relationship between two people. The action is social because when one individual acts, the other reacts with reference to the first actor. "Thus every social act implicates at least two individuals, each of whom takes the other into account in the processes of satisfying impulses."[37] The life of the social being is made up of an unlimited number and variety of social acts. Because new social acts influence the individual's social life, it is constantly in process and never in equilibrium; therefore, the individual is constantly adapting and functioning in a world of ever-changing social relationship.[38] Stryker suggests that by using the concept of *social act* as the starting point of analysis in symbolic interaction "an articulation between sociology and social psychology [is permitted] which alternate frameworks can forge, if at all, only with great difficulty.[39]

Of basic importance to the interactionist approach is man's ability to use symbols. Man's social world achieves its meaning because of man's use of symbols. Symbols refer to all conventional signs of human symbolic activity, and language is *more* than merely a system of symbols because it is "the activity of using and interpreting symbols."[40] So, in order for man to react socially to his environment, his use of symbols must always be involved. Even a physical gesture or expression has no meaning for the individual, unless he interprets

---

[35]Stryker, *op. cit.,* pp. 111–12.
[36]*Ibid.,* p. 112.
[37]*Ibid.,* p. 113.
[38]Rose, *op. cit.,* p. ix.
[39]Sheldon Stryker, "The Interactional and Situational Approaches," in Harold T. Christensen (ed.), *Handbook of Marriage and The Family* (Chicago: Rand McNally & Co., 1964), p. 135.
[40]Lindesmith and Strauss, *op. cit.,* pp. 56–57.

it through language. For example, a husband arrives home at the
end of the day and before he says a word, his wife knows he
has had a bad day. She can "read" her husband—she knows from past
experiences how to symbolically interpret his facial expressions, his
walk, his bearing.

Interpretation through language always occurs between the stimulus and response in human behavior.[41] The symbolic nature of man
means that he lives in a symbolic world and can be stimulated to act
by symbols.[42] When a man says "I love you" to a woman, the words
convey a vast variety of meaning and very often drastically influence
her future behavior. The importance of the symbol becomes obvious
if we imagine the reaction of a woman who had never before heard
the word "love." The word itself is not important, but rather the
meaning attached to it by individuals who share in their general
agreement of symbolic meaning. Hence, the social world of the individual is circumscribed by the limits of effective communication.[43]
For example, the lower-lower class has a more restricted world of
communication because the development of language is often much
more limited than in the middle class.

Symbolic interaction implies both action and reaction. For instance, through the use of language one person says something that
is meaningful to a second person, who—in turn—is often stimulated
by the other's verbal action to respond with a verbal reaction. Furthermore, the patterns of interaction frequently follow a predictable
pattern, not usually in a long-range sense, but in some accurate anticipation of how the other person will react. If one uses the symbols
of friendship, he does not expect the symbols of hostility in return.

Symbolic interaction does sometimes involve anxiety, however,
when a person is unable to or insecure in predicting responses. For
example, a child may be "anxious" in asking his parents' permission
because he knows the reaction he wants, but is not sure exactly what
he is going to get. But, most symbolic interaction involves a generally accurate prediction of action-reaction. Exchange has a routine
of standardized quality.

Role is another concept of basic importance to the interactionist
approach. The concept of *role* refers to the expected behavior attached to a social position. "These expectations are social in the
same sense symbolic behavior is always social: the ultimate meaning

---

[41]Herbert Blumer, "Society as Symbolic Interaction," in Rose, *op. cit.,* p. 180.
[42]Rose, *op. cit.,* p. 5.
[43]Tamotsu Shibutani, "Reference Groups and Social Control," in Rose, *op. cit.,*
p. 136.

of the positions to which these expectations apply is shared behavior. They are social in another and most important sense, namely, that it is impossible to talk about *a* position without reference to some context of *other* positions: one cannot talk about the behavior of father except with reference to the positions of mother, child, and so on. Thus every position assumes some counter-position, and every role presumes some counter-role. To use the term 'role' is necessarily to refer to an interpersonal relation."[44]

To say that a role refers to expected social behavior does not mean that it is rigid or that the individual has no flexibility in filling the role. A role carries general rights and obligations; so long as the individual stays within the limits of the socially defined role expectation, he is adequately filling it. For example, a man in the role of father has a number of approved alternatives in dealing with the discipline of his child; however, he cannot go beyond a certain point without being socially punished.

The fact that roles have meaning only in relation to other roles gives order and some predictability to many social relationships. In addition to general knowledge, part of a young woman's knowledge of how to fill her new role as wife is based on predicting how the man she marries will fill the counter role of husband. The individual is often confused when he enters a new role and is unsure of his, and the related, role requirements. For example, someone not used to handling children but put into a role of supervising their activities may not be sure of how he should act or of how the children will act or react.

Role performance involves a number of possible sources of conflict. First, the individual may find that the demands of the role conflict with his self-interests. An example would be the father who is expected to provide for his children but doesn't want that responsibility. Second, the individual may define his role differently than someone in a related role defines it: the husband may want to make all the decisions in a marriage, while his wife thinks he should consult her. This points out the interrelationship of related roles: each individual involved must define not only his own, but also the related role. Third, different role demands being filled by the same individual may conflict. For example, a working mother may on occasion find the demands of her role as mother and her role as employee occur at the same time so that it is impossible to satisfy both. Fourth, a role definition may be confused—what is expected is not

---

[44]Stryker, *op. cit.,* p. 114.

clear. Many modern women are faced with a wife-mother role different from the traditional role; this lack of clarity in social definition results in role confusion.

The extent to which the sources of conflict are minimized determines the efficiency of role relationships in various social settings. Therefore, an important question in analyzing roles "becomes one of the congruence of definitions, situation, role and self, of the interacting persons. Congruence permits efficient, organized behavior."[45]

The importance of role learning can be seen in the process of socialization. "The child becomes socialized when he has acquired the ability to communicate with others and to influence and be influenced by them through use of speech."[46] The newborn infant starts life with the capacity for social development, but for a time remains unsocialized because his elder's symbols as such have no influence on him. As the infant's awareness of language, self, and others increases, his social world develops.

The development of the *self* in the youngster means a development of social self-awareness. With time, he learns to respond to himself as he responds to other people, "by naming, defining, classifying himself."[47] The self is "defined in terms of socially recognized categories and their corresponding roles. Since these roles necessarily imply relationships to others, the self necessarily implies such relations. One's self is the way one describes to himself his relationships to others in a social process."[48] The development of the self in the child is a slow and continual process; with time, the self becomes more complex as the child finds himself in more social relationships. The child is increasingly called upon to relate himself to a variety of different role situations. The child moves from the relatively limited relationships of the parental home into expanded relationships with other adults and other children, and he does this within the different social settings where those relationships occur.

An important part of the "self" development in socialization is determined by *role-taking*. Role-taking "refers to anticipating the responses of others associated with one in some social act."[49] For instance, from previous parental discipline the child often disciplines himself through role-taking. He decides on an action by tak-

---

[45]*Ibid.*, p. 117.
[46]Lindesmith and Strauss, *op. cit.*, p. 160.
[47]Stryker, *op. cit.*, p. 114.
[48]*Ibid.*, p. 115.
[49]*Ibid.*, p. 115.

ing his mother's role and anticipating her reaction to the possible behavior. If he anticipates that the behavior will make her angry, he may then decide against it. While role-taking may involve anticipating the reactions of a specific "other," it frequently involves "the anticipation of response of what Mead called the 'generalized other.'"[50] *Generalized other* means that "one is taking the related roles of all the other participants rather than the role of just one other person."[51] This does not refer to an actual group of people but rather an abstract "they," and may represent the individual's conception of abstract moral standards.[52]

Role-taking also has an important dimension in planning and learning of future roles. By imaginative participation in the behavior of others, the youngster lays the foundation within himself for playing these roles later in life. The play world of the child is a good illustration of role-playing related to future roles. The little girl playing house is playing the role of the mother and imitating many of the traits of the woman's role in the home as she has observed them in her own mother. When she reaches the age of marriage, she will have partially learned through role-playing the role she is entering. Role-taking may also serve as a powerful force in striving to achieve a role. Through a positive identification with some future role behavior, an individual may work with great energy and effort in the process of achieving the role.

Of course not all "others" will be of equal influence on the individual as role models. Symbolic interactionists refer to the role models the individual considers important as *"significant others,"* because "others" are differentially viewed by the individual as having significance for his thoughts and behavior. For example, the eight-year-old boy may view the ten-year-old as a "significant other" and desire to act like him and be accepted by him as an equal; but compared to another boy twelve years old, the ten-year-old becomes less significant. In this way the perceiver may rank order or place "significant others" on a continuum, which will vary with time and social setting.[53]

The use of the terms *role* and *role-taking* are sometimes falsely interpreted to connote some kind of artificial behavior. On the contrary, roles are usually behavior patterns which the individual accepts and which meaningfully influence his behavior. But role-

---

[50]*Ibid.,* p. 115.
[51]Lindesmith and Strauss, *op. cit.,* p. 394.
[52]*Ibid.,* p. 394.
[53]Stryker, *op. cit.,* p. 115.

playing by the individual often does have a "theatrical" quality, which may arise from the "taking the role of the other." That is, the individual does not always act publicly as he wants or feels, but as he thinks others want him to act.

Goffman points out that "there is hardly a legitimate everyday vocation or relationship whose performers do not engage in concealed practices which are incompatible with fostered impressions."[54] So role-playing often involves the element of *front,* the concern with giving an impression to the audience that may or may not accurately reflect the role player. In dating, "front" is very common. Because neither the boy or the girl has a commitment from the other both will often try to mask their "true" selves. Young people are often aware of the use of "fronts" in dating, and therefore enter and continue the relationship with caution and, sometimes, suspicion.

Because "front" has a contrived nature, the individual must constantly be alert. Frequently in dating and courtship, a person becomes upset when the other's behavior seems inconsistent. Inconsistency can occur either when the actor lets his "true self" show through or the other person defines as inconsistent what the actor feels is consistent role-playing. For instance, the male, who has been putting on a "front" of great consideration for the desires of the female, may do something she defines as inconsiderate. His action may actually be a revealing slip on his part, or may only be defined by the female as inconsistent with his "front."

The intent of this discussion has not been to develop the symbolic interactionist theories comprehensively, but rather to provide some useful concepts for studying marriage and the family. The reader should keep in mind the suggested concepts, as well as the assumption that many middle-class family relationships have an ego-need focus, for these are the basic conceptual orientations used in this book's study of marriage and family interaction.

Chapters 2 and 3 constitute the rest of the introductory section. Chapter 2 provides a historical contrast to the contemporary middle-class family, and Chapter 3 shows some family variations within today's American society. Marriage and family relationships are ongoing processes; in the aggregate, individuals are at all points in the process at a given point in time. Chapter 4 begins the common procedure of entering the process at the dating-courtship stage. Succeeding chapters follow the life cycle of marriage and family interaction until they have been discussed at all stages.

---

[54]Goffman, *op. cit.,* p. 64.

SELECTED BIBLIOGRAPHY

BERGEL, EGAN E. *Social Stratification.* New York: McGraw-Hill Book Co., 1962.

COUTU, WALTER. *Emergent Human Nature.* New York: Alfred A. Knopf, Inc., 1949

GOFFMAN, ERVING. *The Presentation of Self in Everyday Life.* New York: Doubleday Anchor Books, 1959.

HOLLINGSHEAD, AUGUST B. *Elmtown's Youth.* New York: John Wiley & Sons, Inc., 1949

KAHL, JOSEPH A. *The American Class Structure.* New York: Rinehart & Co., Inc., 1957.

LERNER, MAX. *America As A Civilization.* New York: Simon & Schuster, Inc., 1957.

LINDESMITH, ALFRED R., and STRAUSS, ANSELM L. *Social Phychology.* New York: The Dryden Press, 1956.

MEAD, GEORGE H. *Mind, Self and Society.* Chicago: The University of Chicago Press, 1934.

PARSONS, TALCOTT, and BALES, ROBERT F. *Family, Socialization and Interaction Process.* Glencoe, Illinois: The Free Press, 1955.

REISS, IRA L., "The Universality of the Family: A Conceptual Analysis," *Journal of Marriage and Family,* November, 1965, pp. 443–53.

REISSMAN, LEONARD. *Class in American Society.* Glencoe, Illinois: The Free Press, 1959.

RIESMAN, DAVID; GLAZER, NATHAN; and DENNEY, REUEL. *The Lonely Crowd.* New York: Doubleday Anchor Books, 1953.

ROSE, ARNOLD M. *Human Behavior and Social Processes.* Boston: Houghton Mifflin Co., 1962.

SHIBUTANI, TAMOTSU. *Society and Personality.* Englewood Cliffs, New Jersey: Prentice-Hall, Inc., 1961.

STRYKER, SHELDON. "Symbolic Interaction as an Approach to Family Research." *Marriage and Family Living,* May, 1959, pp. 111–19.

STRYKER, SHELDON, "The Interactional and Situational Approaches," in HAROLD T. CHRISTENSEN (ed.), *Handbook of Marriage and the Family,* (Chicago: Rand McNally & Co., 1964), pp. 125–70.

WARNER, W. LLOYD; MEEKER, MARCHIA; and EELLS, KENNETH. *Social Class in America.* New York: Harper Torchbooks, 1960.

WHYTE, WILLIAM H., JR. *The Organization Man.* New York: Simon & Schuster, Inc., 1956.

CHAPTER 2

THE PURITAN FAMILY

The roots of today's American family go back to many cultural influences—particularly, in the Western World, to the early Hebrew, Greek, and Roman families. From those early family systems came many of the patterns and values found in marriage and family interaction today.[1] The focus in this chapter is not on the entire historical development leading to the modern American family, however, but rather on one specific early American family system— the Puritan family.

Historically, the American family extends back to about the start of the seventeenth century, and therefore is less than 400 years old. The early American colonists brought with them to America the family systems of the cultures within which they had been reared, but the American colonial family that emerged was not simply a European institution transplanted to the new continent; it had many new and original developments, though these were usually within the framework of the old country family system.

The old system was altered in part by the need to cope with the environment of the New World. Furthermore, because of distance and restricted transportation, as well as limited communication with the old culture, the influence and reinforcement important to the maintenance of the old-country values in the New World was limited. While originally the colonists may have desired to transplant the old-country family system complete, its maintenance became impossible, and so with time it was gradually altered in the various colonies.

Because the early colonists came from different cultures and settled in different locations with different environmental demands, the family systems varied in the different colonies. For example, the problems of acquiring food in New England were more difficult than those in the Southern colonies. With communication and contact between the early seaboard colonies very restricted, exchange be-

---

[1]See: Willystine Goodsell, *A History of the Family as a Social and Educational Institution* (New York: The Macmillan Co., 1919); and Edward Westermarck, *The History of Human Marriage* (New York: The Allerton Book Co., 1922).

tween them was also limited, resulting in some degree of autonomy for each. Exchange was further restricted by the tendency of individuals in one colony to view individuals in other colonies as culturally different and as "foreign" in their behavior patterns, even though all were settlers in the New World.

Traditionally the early colonies have been divided into three geographical groups: New England, from Maine to New York; the Middle States, from New York to Maryland; and the South, from Maryland to Georgia. While the family systems of the three geographical regions had many similarities, they also had many differences.[2] Finally, the fact that "the United States was settled by isolated farm families rather than by village communities as in Europe determined in great measure the distinctive characteristics of American family tradition."[3]

The description in this chapter of the early New England Puritans and their family system is included to provide the reader with some understanding of *one* early American family system that may, by contrast, make clearer some areas of family change that have developed over time in the United States. Often, the individual is so much a product of his culture that he is unable to realize that what seems natural to him has not always been the "normal" way of doing things. An historical contrast, and some variations in the modern family (as discussed in Chapter 3), may also serve to remove the reader from his middle-class orientation to a more objective view of that family system.

The Puritan family was selected, rather than another early colonial family system, because "the culture of Puritan New England had more to do with the shaping of our national culture than did that of any other colonial region or that of any subsequent immigrant group."[4] Many values felt to be basic to contemporary American society have their origins with the New England Puritans. For example, the Puritan beliefs in thrift and hard work continue to be values highly respected in theory, if not always in practice. The term "puritanical," which is frequently used as a synonym for prudery, refers to behavior often attributed to the early American Puritans. Social historians disagree on what the Puritans were *really* like, but

---

[2]See: Arthur W. Calhoun, *A Social History of the American Family: Colonial Period*, Vol. 1 (New York: Barnes & Noble, Inc., 1960).

[3]Bernard J. Stern, *The Family Past and Present* (New York: Appleton-Century-Crofts, Inc., 1938), p. 186.

[4]Manford H. Kuhn, "American Families Today: Development and Differentiation of Types," in Howard Becker and Reuben Hill, *Family, Marriage and Parenthood* (Boston: D. C. Heath & Co., 1955), p. 134.

more important than these academic disagreements is the fact that values attributed to the Puritans continue to be influential in the American middle class.

PURITANISM

Historically, Puritanism developed out of a desire for liturgical reform and as a corrective movement aimed at "purifying" the established church from "popery." It emerged as a hard-headed and sometimes frightening religion built upon the theological assumptions of human depravity and predestination. "Eternal damnation was certain for many, and thus fear of the hereafter, coupled with a sense of personal guilt before God, became a constant element within the Puritan conscience. Mundane pleasures, though good and right as far as they went, were suspect. Health, beauty and the natural body appetites were to be enjoyed—but here was the snare—only provided that they were no encroachment upon the supreme good and were kept always subordinate. The very fact that man desired such pleasures made them suspect."[5] Therefore, the "good" Puritan often rejected sensate pleasures in order to give proof that he was good. The same logic applied to Puritan thinking about punishment and justice. "If an accused person standing before the court is scheduled to spend eternity in hell, it does not matter very much how severely the judges treat him, because all the hardships and sufferings in this world will be no more than a faint hint of the torments awaiting him in the hereafter."[6]

Puritanism meant the belief in the supreme sovereignty of God and, since the fall of Adam, the totally sinful and corrupt nature of man; this basic human depravity was believed to extend even to the newborn infant. The Puritan was caught in a personal trap in reference to predestination for himself. If he lived an exemplary life on earth it might be an indication that he was one of the "chosen"—but it was no guarantee. So he might give up all of the pleasures of life on earth for the next life and yet never be sure that he was going to be one of the "chosen."

One of the best ways for a person to try to convince others (and possibly himself) that he was truly saved was to become totally devoted to the church and completely loyal to the state. Erickson points out that the Puritan ministers were not suggesting that outer con-

---

[5] Eric J. Dingwall, *The American Woman* (New York: Signet Books, 1957), p. 32.
[6] Kai T. Erickson, *Wayward Puritans* (New York: John Wiley & Sons, Inc., 1966), p. 190.

formity was necessary to *"earn* salvation, but they seemed to be saying that outer conformity was a convenient way to *prove* salvation."[7]

The Puritans in England were subjected to severe religious persecution, and one of their chief motives in coming to America was their search for religious liberty. However, the fact that the Puritan colonists came seeking religious freedom did not mean that they were tolerant or accepting of other religious faiths. By the very nature of their religion the Puritans *knew* they were right, and those who believed differently were wrong. Thus, the Puritans left the old country where they had suffered religious persecution, and came to the New World where, in many cases, they then became the persecutors of those who would not accept Puritanism.

The Puritans who colonized America were a selected group with strong clerical leadership. Their initial purpose was not primarily to develop the New World, but rather to accomplish what they had been prevented from accomplishing at home, a Puritan society.[8] Their colony was planned as a legal extension of the old country, one where all the wrongs that existed at home would be corrected. "It was to be a 'heavenly translation' of Puritan theory into a living community of saints, a blueprint for the City of God."[9] The Puritan colonist was completely dedicated to his religion. He was characterized by an intense zeal to reform and to order everything in light of God's demand upon him.[10] The all-encompassing nature of the Puritan religion must be kept in mind in looking at the Puritan family. The great importance and control of the church is shown by the fact that "in 1635 a law was passed in Massachusetts making church attendance compulsory, and in 1638 every resident was taxed for the ministry, whether church member or not."[11]

Puritan values prevailed for almost three quarters of a century in New England and during that time were, in effect, the laws of the land. The period of greatest Puritan strength and influence ran from the first settlement in Massachusetts established in 1630 to the loss of the old charter in 1691. Erikson suggests that the end of the Puritan experiment in Massachusetts in 1692 resulted from more than the original charter being revoked and a Royal Governor being appointed by the King. The Puritan experiment ended in 1692 "be-

[7]*Ibid.*, p. 86.
[8]"Puritanism," Vol. 18, *Encyclopaedia Britannica*, 1962, p. 779.
[9]Erikson, *op. cit.*, p. 43.
[10]Encyclopaedia Britannica, *op. cit.*, p. 777.
[11]Herbert W. Schneider, *The Puritan Mind* (New York: Henry Holt & Co., 1930), p. 75.

cause the sense of mission which had sustained it from the beginning
no longer existed in any recognizable form, and thus the people of
the Bay were left with few stable points of reference to help them
remember who they were."[12] Under the leadership of Jonathan Edwards in the 1730's, an attempt was made to reconstitute the old Puritan order on a new basis, but it was generally not successful.[13]

The relatively long period of Puritan success in New England was
due in great degree to their success in maintaining nearly absolute
control of their religious ideals. But as the number of colonists with
different religious backgrounds increased, the Puritans began to
have difficulty controlling not only the other religions, but also their
own younger generations. A strong economic force also contributed
to a weakening of Puritan control. Schneider writes, "The Puritans
of their own strength might have kept New England holy, but in
order to keep it at all, and to give it the necessary footing, they were
compelled to invite outsiders by adopting a new liberal land
policy."[14]

Lastly, changes in the demands of life eased the strength of Puritanism. "Social life became freer and more pleasure-loving throughout the colonies. The severest phases of the struggle for existence in
the new land were past and even in New England the harsh Puritan
spirit was gradually becoming softened."[15]

The discussion that follows is limited to the time when the Puritans were a dominant force and exerted strong controls over their
family life. Over time, the Puritan values have been diffused, but
they have never completely eliminated. Therefore, a description of
the Puritan family during its period of greatest strength provides a
contrast with the modern American middle-class family, indicating
both differences and some of the Puritan values that continue to
operate. The areas of marriage and family interaction are discussed
in the same order for the Puritans as they are in the rest of this book
for the contemporary middle-class family.

COURTSHIP

The Puritan family was patriarchal, with the male's authority
derived from the patriarchal values of the religion. In mate selection,
as is almost always the patriarchal case, the parents, and particularly

---

[12]Erikson, *op. cit.*, p. 155.
[13]*Encyclopaedia Britannica, op. cit.*, p. 777.
[14]Schneider, *op. cit.*, p. 79.
[15]Goodsell, *op. cit.*, pp. 363–64.

the father, play a dominant role in arranging their children's marriages. The Puritan father, even if he did not actually select the mate, made the ultimate decision as to marriageability. Because an important value in the patriarchal system is the strong obedience of children, Puritan offspring generally accepted the decision of the father without question. To go against him was rebellion against the family and, even more important, against the accepted religious beliefs.

While the parents exerted strong control over mate selection, the young person did have a degree of freedom. Calhoun argues that some freedow was given to the young because in a "new country, needing population, it was natural that pious authorities should frown upon any discouragement of legitimate increase. The interests of the community took precedence over the private interests of parents, guardians, and masters."[16] Many social factors that later served as barriers to marriage in the United States did not exist in the early Puritan colonies. Because the early Puritans were alike in many of their social characteristics, the likelihood of choosing a partner who was significantly different was minimized. With time, the economic factor became increasingly important, and as a result, courtship was increasingly permeated by economic considerations.[17] Thus, even when the marriage was successful, "happy husbands were ready to sue their father-in-law if he proved too tardy or remiss in the matter of the bridal portion."[18]

Courtship interaction between the young couple was very limited because of several factors. First, discovering the personality of the future mate was not important, and even if it were considered, discovery would come after marriage. The Puritans believed that one did not marry for love, but that love was found in all good Puritan marriages. Married love did not mean to the Puritans what it means to us today; the Puritans believed that it was God's will that a husband and wife love each other. Therefore by definition, if one were a good Puritan, one loved his spouse. Second, there was little time for courtship; survival and material attainment demanded excessively long hours of work for all able-bodied Puritans. Furthermore, where distance separated the colonists, the opportunities for the social interaction of extended courtship were limited by the restricted means of transportation. Therefore, young people often had neither the time nor the energy to pursue an extended courtship.

---

[16]Calhoun, *op. cit.*, p. 55.
[17]*Ibid.*, p. 59.
[18]*Ibid.*, p. 59.

Third, the pleasurable aspects of courtship, as we know them today, rarely existed for the Puritans. The sharing of recreation and pleasure would have violated the Puritan ban on such activities. Modern courtship also implies some degree of privacy for the couple, but the Puritans—believing that man must constantly fight against his basic depravity—would have viewed privacy for a young unmarried couple as playing into the hands of the devil. (A Puritan could be suspect not only in action, but also in thought; unmarried privacy would certainly be highly tempting to immoral thoughts, if not actions.)

These courtship restrictions are suggested as general norms governing the behavior of the Puritans. However, it is questionable whether any society, even with a system of severe punishments, can achieve complete control over the personal behavior of all individuals. Many historical reports indicate some degree of deviancy from the Puritan norms; the strength of the norms may, therefore, be more accurately assessed in terms of relative, rather than absolute, control. For example, it cannot be assumed that romantic love was never found among the Puritans. "But it was obviously hampered by the habit of driving hard bargains which, in turn were traceable partly to the narrow margin of survival and partly to the stern code of Puritanism."[19] In other areas of deviation from the norms, Hunt points out that "the court and church records of early New England are filled with case histories of men and women who gamed, swore, fought, and got drunk—but who were Puritans."[20] Some of the Puritans must be recognized as individualists for going against norms which carried such severe punishment for those who were caught. The internal controls of the Puritan conscience did not always seem to work either, because some of the Puritan deviants do not seem to have been greatly bothered by feelings of guilt.

PREMARITAL SEXUAL BEHAVIOR

Unlike those adherents of many other patriarchal systems, the Puritans believed in the premarital chastity of both male and female. Calhoun writes that "the Puritan emphasis on sexual restraint was of a piece with the general gospel of frugality so appropriate among a class of people trying to accumulate capital in an age of deficit. Urgent economic interests furthered the novel virtue of male chas-

---

[19]Stuart A. Queen, Robert W. Habenstein, and John B. Adams, *The Family in Various Cultures* (Philadelphia: J. B. Lippincott Co., 1961), p. 278.

[20]Morton M. Hunt, *The Natural History of Love* (New York: Alfred A. Knopf, Inc., 1959), p. 232.

tity. The necessity of accumulation led the Puritan to reprobate all unprofitable forms of sin including licentiousness, that prodigal waster."[21] For those strongly influenced by Puritan theology, premarital sexual behavior was interpreted as succumbing to the temptations of the flesh—behavior not found among the "chosen." Thus, the strength of the premarital chastity norms was derived from both economic and religious beliefs. However, the high value set by the Puritans on premarital chastity was not the same as that placed on virginity by the Roman Catholic Church. The Catholic Church had set up the ideal of virginity and it forbade the marriage of its priests. But the Puritans had no ideal of virginity as such; they encouraged marriage at an early age, and their ministers usually married.[22]

Yet, even with their strongly supported norms against premarital sexual experience, a number of Puritans clearly deviated. The church records suggest a degree of deviancy from the norms that seems very alien to the traditional picture of Puritanism. The records of the Groton church show that of 200 persons owning the baptismal covenant there from 1760 to 1775, 66 confessed to fornication before marriage.[23] In all types of disciplinary cases mentioned in the records of Massachusetts churches, a plurality of them concerned fornication. "It was, in other words, the most prevalent and most popular sin in Puritan New England."[24]

Several explanations may be suggested. First, the barrenness and economic dearth that oppressed the first settlers helped to reduce life to elemental levels.[25] Even with stern religious restrictions on pleasures, the early Puritans' lives were so restricted that sexual encounters were sought partly because there were so few other opportunities for "pleasure." Second, where wealth was scant, questions of legitimacy and inheritance were less urgent.[26] Therefore, premarital chastity norms were not always given strong support by economic values. Third, Calhoun suggests that deviations may partly have been due to a morality that did not allow for a class of recognized prostitutes.[27] When sexual deviancy occurred, one of the Puritan women had to be the partner in the act. In contrast, many patriarchal societies protect the sexual purity of their women by providing a group of prostitutes to meet the sexual needs of a large number of

[21]Calhoun, *op. cit.*, p. 39.
[22]George R. Stewart, *American Ways of Life* (New York: Dolphin, 1964), p. 164.
[23]*Ibid.*, p. 133.
[24]Hunt, *op. cit.*, p. 235.
[25]Calhoun, *op. cit.*, p. 134.
[26]*Ibid.*, p. 134.
[27]*Ibid.*, p. 135.

men. The pattern of premarital sex for the Puritan and today's middle-class female may be similar. That is, few women today are sexually promiscuous, but a number may have sexual experience with only one male, resulting in a large number having premarital sexual experience—since a large number do have such experience.

For the Puritan, the risks of engaging in premarital intercourse were great, especially for the female. "The matter of fornication before marriage was given shameful notoriety. Groton church records show that until 1803 whenever a child was born less than seven months after marriage a public confession had to be made before the whole congregation."[28] Hunt points out that the Puritans punished more sex sinners than the courts and "employed a public form of confession far more painful than the Catholic confessional they had repudiated."[29]

Puritan repression of pleasures in general, and of sexual pleasure in particular, has been offered as a causal explanation of many personal and social characteristics of the Puritans. Hunt writes that sexual repression "undoubtedly played a part in the two outbreaks of witchcraft hysteria in New England; the earlier one began in 1647 and resulted in the execution of fourteen witches in Massachusetts and Connecticut while the Salem frenzy of 1692 brought about the execution of twenty persons and two dogs."[30] In light of present psychological knowledge, such strong sex repression along with other restrictions of pleasure must clearly have had a strong influence on the Puritan personality. One can also speculate that personal guilt and trauma must have been very great for those who sexually deviated but were otherwise strong Puritans.

Bundling. Historically, bundling was a means of courtship utilized on the American frontier, but it was also found at an earlier date in New York, Pennsylvania, and some of the New England colonies. Bundling, according to Calhoun, prevailed to a very great extent in New England from a very early time. *Bundling* refers to the practice of allowing a young couple to get into bed together so they could talk in privacy without using the candles that would be necessary if they stayed up. The couple were not completely trusted: they often entered the bed fully clothed and, in some cases, a wooden bar was put on top of the coverings to make sure they stayed apart.

In some situations bundling had nothing to do with courtship. Many of the early dwellings consisted of only one or two rooms, and

[28]*Ibid.*, p. 132.
[29]Hunt, *op. cit.*, p. 234.
[30]*Ibid.*, p. 230.

members of the family occupied all available beds. However, a friendly wayfarer had to be accommodated, if only with half a bed.[31] When this happened, there seems little evidence that the husband moved his wife out of his bed and shared it with the male stranger. Either he had confidence in another female family member as a bed partner for the stranger, or simply was not willing to disturb his routine of sharing a bed with his wife.

The practice of bundling was found among the Puritans, but it provoked a great deal of controversy. Over a period of time, the practice was extended beyond its original intent and, at last, was viewed as such a scandal that the church felt forced to suppress it. "Jonathan Edwards attacked it on the pulpit and other ministers, who had allowed it to go unnoticed, joined in its suppression."[32] By 1800 the practice survived only in very few places, although in 1804 the New York Supreme court ruled, in a seduction case, that since the girl's parents had permitted her to bundle they had no right to complain of the consequences which "naturally followed . . ."[33]

MARRIAGE

For the Puritans, marriage was a very important relationship based upon religious, social, and economic values. A man needed a wife and children so as to survive and to prosper. Today, children are often an economic liability because they contribute little or nothing to the family's economic worth, but in the Puritan society, children even at very young ages were an economic asset.

As is almost always the case in a patriarchal society, the woman had little choice of adult role other than that of wife-mother. The inevitability of the Puritan girl's marriage was supported by her upbringing and by the religious values that saw the woman's natural adult state as that of wife-mother. A few women chose an adult role other than marriage, though they were often widows or women unable to acquire a marriage mate. For the vast majority, marriage was the only adult status.

The male had equally strong motivations to marry. "Each man urgently needed a wife to satisfy imperative needs—clothing, food, medical care, companionship, sex, and, not least of all, status."[34]

---

[31]Calhoun, op. cit., p. 129.
[32]Ibid., p. 131.
[33]Ray E. Baber, Marriage and the Family (New York: McGraw-Hill Book Co., 1953), p. 32.
[34]Hunt, op. cit., p. 238.

Religious values also made marriage a highly desired state for the
Puritan male. Patriarchally oriented, he needed a wife to provide
him with economically important children. Given the great importance attached to marriage, "it was common for a man to meet a girl,
appraise her, propose to her, and publish the bans all within a few
weeks or less."[35]

Marriage, once accomplished, was not treated lightly by the Puritans. Both husband and wife had a moral obligation to function as
completely as possible according to the religious and social expectations for marriage. Calhoun writes that "so important was proper
family relations that persons living apart from their spouses were
sometimes ordered to get their partners or clear out. The well-being
of the community was conceived to depend on rigid family discipline
and if a man had no family he must find one."[36] Today's concern
with happiness in marriage was not of great importance to the Puritans, particularly if the stability of the marriage was threatened. But,
since individuals did not go into marriage expecting great personal
happiness they therefore had no such expectations with which to
compare reality.

The Puritan definition of marriage as secular contradicts their
strong religious values until it is viewed against their rebellion
against the Catholic church. The Puritans, and others in New England, called a halt to the growing tendency to make marriage an
ecclesiastical function. "Marriage was declared to be a civil contract,
not a sacrament, and to require no priestly intervention."[37] Over the
years, the Puritan contention has prevailed, and marriage in the
United States has been secularized and brought under the control of
civil law. Even today, a minister performing the marriage ceremony
is legally acting as an agent of the state and not in his religious capacity. The Puritans had no prescribed marriage ritual; any appropriate words might be used. And in the earliest years, marriages were
not performed in the church but, customarily, took place at the
bride's home. In line with Puritan thought, marriage was viewed
with seriousness and there was little festivity or celebration.[38]

Because the Puritans took a matter-of-fact view of marriage, and
because the courtship period was of little importance, the early Puritans entered marriage at young ages. Girls often married at 16 or
under, but there is no evidence that the child marriages, so common
in England at that time, were ever permitted in America.

---

[35]*Ibid.*, p. 239.
[36]Calhoun, *op. cit.*, p. 71.
[37]*Ibid.*, p. 60.
[38]Queen, Habenstein, and Adams, *op. cit.*, p. 279.

Social and religious values for marriage were so strong that old maids were ridiculed or even despised. "A woman became an 'ancient maid' at twenty-five. Bachelors were rare and were viewed with disapproval. They were almost in the class of suspected criminals. In Hartford solitary men were taxed twenty shillings a week."[39] Because failure to marry was counter to the norms supported by both religious and social values, a person refusing to marry was seen not only as defying the values of his religion, but also as an economic threat.

The demands of the New World and Puritan theology made colonial New England a man's world. "Life conditions allowed a type of patriarchism that found affinity in the Old Testament regime. The Puritan views, as expressed and followed by the men, as to proper relations between husband wife, parent and child, or between man and maid before marriage, came directly from the scriptures."[40] The father's authority could not be openly questioned without implying a questioning of basic religious tenets.

The father's role within the family and within the church were often closely interwoven; frequently, the requirements of the church took precedence over the requirements of the family. The fathers adopted the maxim that "families are the nurseries of the church and the commonwealth; ruin families and you ruin all."[41] The maintenance of family religion was universally recognized in early New England as a duty and was seriously attended to in most families. The scriptures were read and worship was offered to God daily.[42]

While the husband had nearly absolute authority over his wife and children, some restrictions were placed on him. Since the wife and children were expected to be obedient, he could punish them for disobedience; but he was expected to act within reason. His reasonableness arose from practicality: every last individual was needed to cope with the harsh environment of the New World. To be too severe in the physical punishment of a family member would have been to deprive himself and the community of the individual's contributions. The father was also expected to take care of his family according to his financial ability. Goodsell writes, "The husband must maintain his wife in accordance with his means, whether or not she brought him property at marriage."[43] Furthermore, the man

Willystine Goodsell

---

[39]Calhoun, *op. cit.*, pp. 67–68.
[40]*Ibid.*, p. 83.
[41]*Ibid.*, p. 75.
[42]*Ibid.*, p. 76.
[43]Goodsell, *op. cit.*, p. 347.

was not expected to add to his prosperity by depriving his family members of their rightful due.

There is some evidence that the woman's subordinate role under the Puritan patriarchy was somewhat different from that under earlier patriarchal systems. While still subordinate to her husband, the wife often had a relationship with him which drew upon her as an individual personality, and not just as a worker and bearer of children. In general, Puritan women were supposed to be good companions to their husbands. "Puritan writers stressed the importance of emotional harmony between man and wife."[44] The Puritan wife role seems to fall somewhere between that found in traditional patriarchal societies and that of the modern middle-class family with its emphasis on husband-wife companionship.

The Puritan woman also made some gains over her old-country counterpart in the area of legal rights. For example, women began to receive some legal protection over their property interests. "In 1646 the consent of the wife was made necessary to the sale of houses or lands. Massachusetts (1647) allowed the widow one-third of her husband's estate as dowry."[45] As a further example, "In Puritan New England a women whose husband beat her could win legal separation and sometimes divorce; in the Southern colonies, where the influence was Anglican and Cavalier, the law made no such provision."[46] While the woman attained some rights, she continued for the most part to be controlled, both in person and in property, by her husband, whom she was bound to serve and obey under the English private law which became the "common law" of the colonies.[47] However, the oft-described "rigidity" of the Puritans should be recognized as an easing of traditional values, for in some practical ways, woman's status was improved under the Puritans.

A universally severe problem faced by women in all societies, including the Puritan, was the burden of interminable childbearing. Among the Puritans, large families were the rule. "Families of ten and twelve children were very common. Families of from twenty to twenty-five children were not rare enough to call forth expression of wonderment."[48] Puritan social and religious values placed importance on large families, and even if individuals had desired to limit the number of their offspring, the knowledge of how to do so was very restricted.

---

[44]Hunt, *op. cit.*, p. 236.
[45]Calhoun, *op. cit.*, p. 95.
[46]Hunt, *op. cit.*, pp. 251–52.
[47]Goodsell, *op. cit.*, p. 345.
[48]Calhoun, *op. cit.*, p. 87.

Continuous childbearing took a heavy toll of Puritan wives. Great numbers died at childbirth, and the number and close spacing of births, plus the harsh nature of the environment during the early days of settlement, brought about old age and death long before it was chronologically due. The mother also had to live with the expectation of losing many of her children. "With freezing homes, bad diet, and Spartan treatment it does not seem strange that a large proportion of seventeenth century children died in infancy. This was the case even in the most favored families; thus of Cotton Mather's fifteen children only two survived him and of Judge Sewall's fourteen only three outlived the father."[49]

The life of the Puritan wife-mother was highly restricted and almost wholly bounded by the interests of maintaining the home. Her social life was often no more than a weekly visit to church on Sunday and a religious "lecture" on Thursday.[50] During the earliest period, demands on the woman were great, but they eased off over time, particularly in the more economically successful families. Calhoun writes:

But the impression that the colonial dame performed Herculean labors is a myth. These *tours de force* were rarely performed by a one-woman household. The wife bore and reared children and superintended the house; but she did not do the heavy work if there was need of her services in other lines. Some families had numerous trained and capable servants. In the country daughters not needed at home worked in neighbor's households until married. Many families in town and country took bound children to raise for the return of their labor . . . The commonest helpers were the unmarried sisters of husband or wife. Moreover, most of the large families of earlier times were the offspring of at least two mothers, and the later wives had fewer children. The first wife would get quickly six or seven children and die exhausted by maternity and labor. The next wife, young and sturdy, would take hold and bring up the family, some of whom were likely old enough to be of help. She would have three or four children, perhaps at longer intervals.[51]

What little personal life the Puritan wife achieved was often in her relationship to her husband. While he was in theory the unquestioned authority, no doubt a number of Puritan wives were able to make their feelings felt, and influence or even manipulate their husbands. For even with the unemotional nature of courtship and marriage, real affection probably existed between many Puritan husbands and wives. But demonstrations of such affection had to be very private; it was not prudent for the Puritan to be publicly demon-

[49]*Ibid.*, p. 106.
[50]Goodsell, *op. cit.*, p. 352.
[51]Calhoun, *op. cit.*, pp. 97–98.

strative. Calhoun relates that "Captain Kemble of Boston sat two hours in the public stocks for his 'lewd and unseemly behavior' in kissing his wife 'publicquely' on the Sabbath upon his doorstep when he had just returned from a voyage of three years."[52]

Even though the Puritan woman had the generally low status common to women in patriarchal societies, she nevertheless played a significant part in the history of the New England Puritan era. Erikson, in his recent study of deviancy in Puritan society, traces three major "crime waves." Of particular interest is that in all three women played major roles. The first, in 1636, was a theological argument involving Mrs. Anne Hutchinson. The fact that one of the disputants was a woman must have added to the elder's sense of irritation.[53] The Puritan view as to the intellectual capacities of women is reflected in a statement by John Winthrop "that a woman of his acquaintance had been mentally ill as a result of reading too many books."[54] The second "crime wave" was the Quaker persecutions of 1656 to 1665, and the first open indication of this trouble was when two Quaker housewives were arrested on ship in Boston Bay. They were taken to jail, stripped of their clothing and searched for markings of witchcraft.[55] The third Puritan "crime wave" was the Salem Witchcraft outbreak of 1692. In the period that followed, a number of girls and women were accused, tried and found guilty of witchcraft.[56] In all three of these major historical events women made their presence strongly felt in the Puritan community.

One common stereotype is that the Puritans were against sex. However, for all their emphasis on the sinfulness of fornication and adultery, the early Puritans can not be said to have been against sex as such. "Not only did they breed large families and take pride in so doing, but their spiritual leaders praised married sex and roundly condemned the 'Popish conceit of the excellency of virginity.' "[57] An example of the value placed on marital sex is given in an account by Hunt: "At the First Church of Boston, the congregation considered action against one James Mattock for several offenses, one of them being, of all things, sexual abstinence. Mattock, it appeared, had denied his wife conjugal relations for two years on the grounds that he was punishing himself for his sins; the congregation voted this

[52]*Ibid.*, p. 92.
[53]Erikson, *op. cit.*, p. 82.
[54]Quoted in: *ibid.*, p. 82.
[55]*Ibid.*, p. 115.
[56]See: *ibid.*, pp. 141–53.
[57]Hunt, *op. cit.*, p. 234.

was unnatural and unchristian, and expelled him from membership in the church."[58] The evidence indicates that the Puritans were not so totally against sex—at least in marriage—as many have believed. However, they may have suffered a severe conflict because sexual satisfaction, even in marriage, might indicate a weakness to "things of the flesh"—negative evidence of the possibility of being one of the "chosen."

Sexual relationships outside of marriage *were* severely condemned, however. No distinctions were made in the Puritan laws between men and women concerning adultery and both were supposed to suffer the same consequences. As it happened however, female offenders were generally more severely punished than male offenders.[59] In 1707, in Plymouth, a couple were tried for adultery and the woman was sentenced to be set on the gallows, receive thirty stripes upon her naked back, and forever after to wear the Capital A (for *adultery;* cf. Hawthorne's *The Scarlet Letter.*) The man was acquitted with no assignment of reason.[60] Yet not all Puritan men escaped punishment. For example, in 1661, the first civil divorce case occurred under the colonial legislature and the court "granted a divorce to Elizabeth Burge on the ground of her husband Thomas's adultery—a crime of which he was sentenced to be severely whipped."[61] Adultery not only countered religious values, but was also seen as threatening to family and community beliefs.

CHILDREN

Calhoun writes that "colonial childhood is largely hidden in obscurity."[62] The letters and diaries that provide records of the Puritan's life rarely mention children except for the records of their births, illness, and deaths. "Children were 'to be seen not heard,' and not seen too much either."[63] Children had no legal rights, and the father was the sole guardian of the offspring of his marriage. He alone could determine important questions concerning the education, religious training, preparation for life-work, and marriage of his children.[64]

---

[58]*Ibid.,* p. 234.
[59]*Ibid.,* p. 234.
[60]Calhoun, *op. cit.,* p. 138.
[61]Nelson M. Blake, *The Road to Reno* (New York: The Macmillan Co., 1962), p. 35.
[62]*Ibid.,* p. 105.
[63]*Ibid.,* p. 105.
[64]Goodsell, *op. cit.,* p. 346.

Subservience

Children were expected to obey the will of their parents without question; in some cases of disobedience, punishment permissible under the laws was unbelievably severe. The Piscataqua colony had the following law: "If any child or children above 16 years old of competent understanding, shall curse or smite their natural father or mother, he or they shall be put to death unless it can be sufficiently testified that the parents have been very unchristianly negligent of the education of such child . . . if any man have a rebellious or stubborne son of sufficient years and understanding, viz., 16 years of age or upwards, which shall not obey the voice of his father or the voice of his mother, yet when they have chastened him will not harken unto them . . . such son shall be put to death, or otherwise severely punished."[65] Even in day-to-day activities, the discipline of children, by today's standards, was very severe. In some households the children were made to stand through meals, eating whatever was handed to them. They were taught that it was sinful to complain about food, clothing, or their lot in life. The parents, particularly the father, insisted upon courtesy of a very formal and subservient nature.[66]

Industry

Puritan children were not given personal freedom or allowed a "childhood world." They had to work from an early age. In Puritan ethics, idleness was a serious sin, and the child with no work to do was highly susceptible to temptation. In addition, the economic factor was important; Puritan child labor was "fundamentally a response to a condition rather than to a theory. It was a compliance with the exigencies of the case. The rigor of the struggle for existence in early New England made impossible the prolongation of infancy that marks high civilization."[67]

Religion

Children were in no way exempted from or given special privileges easing the harshness and pervasiveness of Puritan religious dogma. Because of the depravity of human nature, it was necessary to seek infantile conversion. Starting in the earliest years, children were constantly confronted with the terrors of hell and told that they

---

[65]Calhoun, *op. cit.*, p. 121.
[66]Queen, Habenstein, and Adams, *op. cit.*, p. 280.
[67]Calhoun, *op. cit.*, p. 127.

could only escape by following what they were being taught about religion and by rejecting almost everything they might naturally as children want to do.

Cotton Mather wrote: "I took my little daughter Katy (aged four) into my study and there told my child that I am to dy shortly and she must, when I am dead, remember everything I now said unto her. I set before her the sinful condition of her nature and charged her to pray in secret places every day. That God for the sake of Jesus Christ would give her a new heart . . . I gave her to understand that when I am taken from her she must look to meet with more humbling afflictions than she does now she has a tender father to provide for her." (This was thirty years before he died.)[68] The excessive nature of the fears of hell and damnation directed at children must have greatly disturbed the personality balance of many youngsters.

The lot of Puritan children was obviously not an easy one. It contrasts sharply to the benevolent treatment of children common today. Within the limits of the Puritan value system, the children who managed to survive infancy were probably loved as much by their parents as children are today, but "they were denied all the normal sources of joy and happiness."[69] Because a set pattern for all children was accepted, "a pert child was generally thought to be delirious or bewitched."[70] The give-and-take companionship of parents and children often found in today's middle-class family was almost totally absent among the Puritans. It is hard to imagine any parent-child "democracy" among the Puritans, when children's manners were so formal that parents were often addressed as "esteemed parent" or "honored sir and madam."[71]

DIVORCE AND REMARRIAGE

When the Puritans came to the New World, they brought English law with them; but they parted from it in respect to divorce by adopting, as they thought, the Rules of the New Testament. According to Calhoun, "By following what they construed to be the spirit of the book, rather than the letter, they spread out from adultery and desertion as the only causes of divorce. Dissolution of the marriage bond was freely granted for a variety of causes, such as de-

[68]*Ibid.*, p. 108.
[69]*Ibid.*, p. 111.
[70]*Ibid.*, p. 111.
[71]*Ibid.*, p. 111.

sertion, cruelty, or breach of vow. Generally, though not always, husband and wife received equal treatment at the hands of the law."[72] However Goodsell states that "Although far more generous treatment was accorded wives, in respect to divorce or separation than was conceded in the other colonies, discrimination in favor of men very generally existed."[73] (For example, the husband could and did obtain divorce on the single ground of adultery, whereas in the vast majority of cases the wife could not.) In the new colonies, it was the Puritans who took the lead in developing a liberal civil divorce policy. About 40 Massachusetts divorce cases have been discovered for the years up to 1692; there may have been more; the records are incomplete. Ignoring ecclesiastical law, the Massachusetts magistrates granted either absolute divorce or none at all."[74] Two important factors contributed to the liberality of divorce views in New England. First, the Puritans were openly rejecting the sacramental theory by making marriage secular, and following logically from this came their liberal, secular views about divorce. Second, in many cases, wives had been left in the old country and could or would not come to the colonies. Because the new life was very difficult without a wife, and because population increase and family life were felt to be so important, it was necessary to allow the acquisition of new spouses. The more liberal attitudes of New England were not found in the colonies of the Middle States or the South, the primary reason being that the New England colonists did not hesitate to go counter to English law and practice in regard to the dissolution of marriage, while the other colonists did.

In the case of the death of a husband or wife, remarriage among the Puritans was often very quick. "The first marriage in Plymouth colony was that of Edward Winslow, who had been a widower only seven weeks, to Susanna White who had been a widow not twelve weeks."[75] One particular case vividly illustrates the amount of remarriage in one family. "Peter Sargent, a rich Boston merchant, had three wives. His second had had previously, two husbands, who had three wives. His father had four, the last three of whom were widows."[76] Widows were obviously of great value on the marriage market, often much more so than the younger single woman. Calhoun suggests that the principal reason was that the widow often

---

[72]*Ibid.*, p. 146.
[73]Goodsell, *op. cit.*, p. 379.
[74]Blake, *op. cit.*, p. 36.
[75]Calhoun, *op. cit.*, p. 69.
[76]*Ibid.*, p. 70.

had some wealth from her previous marriage to take into the re-marriage.[77]

Life was full of dangers, and the chances of early death were great among the colonists. A man's life was constantly endangered by his day-to-day dealings with the environment, a woman's by extensive childbearing, and both men's and women's by the limited control over disease and the primitive state of medical knowledge. These factors, combined with the strong social and religious values placed on marriage, usually moved individuals into a new marriage as soon as possible.

SIGNIFICANCE OF THE PURITAN FAMILY FOR TODAY

As we said at the beginning of this chapter, the purpose in discussing the Puritan family is twofold: first, the Puritan family system is enough different from today's middle-class family to provide a better understanding of what *is* as contrasted with what *was;* second, enough puritan values continue to prevail to make the Puritan family historically significant.

It is true that many areas of Puritan family activity were quite different from what is held to be right and proper for middle-class marriage and family interaction today. Little interpersonal interaction occurred between a Puritan couple prior to marriage. Marriage was entered into not because the couple were in love, but because it was the religious and economical thing to do. Furthermore, the personal demands of courtship were few because in most cases the parents did the important arranging. When the Puritan couple entered into marriage, they entered a formal status relationship. The success or failure of the marriage was not usually determined by the personal ego-satisfactions achieved from the marriage, but rather by how the marriage conformed to the well-defined expectations of the Puritan community. Thus, the frustration of personal expectations often found in today's marriages were not apt to be found in the Puritan marriage. The greatest contrast between the Puritan and today's middle-class family, however, is probably in the relationship of parent and child; complete subservience and obedience of children is a concept almost totally alien to most modern middle-class thinking.

On the other hand, there are some close similarities between the Puritan family and the middle-class family of today. For example, the Puritan concept of the wife being a companion to her husband

---

[77]*Ibid.,* p. 70.

has a very modern sound. And the acceptance of the rights of marital sex for both the husband and the wife, while probably not a common norm, seems to have existed in some Puritan thinking. Another similarity is the acceptance and encouragement of remarriage, although today that involves more divorced than widowed persons, since there are more divorcees and fewer widows than in the past.

Without question, many Puritan values have been transmitted to today's society. However, the values have altered since their origin several centuries ago. To attribute to the Puritans all of the qualities found under the popular heading of "puritanical" is not historically accurate. Daniel Bell argues that there has long been a *legend* in the United States about the "puritan" culture. Bell suggests that this legend has arisen out of a mistaken identification of the protestant ethic with the Puritan code. "Puritanism and the 'New England mind' have played a large intellectual role in American life. But in the habits and mores of the masses of the people, the peculiar evangelicism of Methodism and Baptism, with its high emotionalism, its fervor, enthusiasm, and excitement, its revivalism, its excesses of sinning and of high-voltage confessing, has played a much more important role."[78] The "puritanism" that has been handed down is, thus, in many cases the product of influences developed much later in American history. The Puritans were no doubt strict and harsh in many areas of family life, but they are certainly not "guilty" of all they have been accused of.

SELECTED BIBLIOGRAPHY

CALHOUN, ARTHUR W. *A Social History of the American Family: Colonial Period,* Vol. I. New York: Barnes & Noble, Inc., 1960.

DINGWALL, ERIC J. *The American Woman,* chap. ii. New York: Signet Books, 1957.

Encyclopaedia Britannica, "Puritanism," Vol. XVIII, pp. 777–80. Encyclopaedia Britannica, Inc., 1962.

ERICKSON, KAI T. *Wayward Puritans* (New York: John Wiley & Sons, Inc., 1966.)

GOODSELL, WILLYSTINE. *A History of the Family as a Social and Educational Institution,* chap. x. New York: The Macmillan Co., 1919.

HUNT, MORTON M. *The Natural History of Love,* chap. vii. New York: Alfred A. Knopf, Inc., 1959.

QUEEN, STUART A.; HABENSTEIN, ROBERT W.; and ADAMS, JOHN B. *The Family in Various Cultures,* chap. xiii. Philadelphia: J. B. Lippincott Co., 1961.

---

[78]Daniel Bell, *The End of Ideology* (New York: Collier Books, 1961), p. 113.

SCHNEIDER, HERBERT W. *The Puritan Mind.* New York: Henry Holt & Co., 1930.

STERN, BERNHARD J. *The Family Past and Present,* chap. vi. New York: Appleton-Century-Crofts, Inc., 1938.

STILES, HENRY REED. *Bundling.* New York: Book Collectors Association, Inc., 1934.

WESTERMARCK, EDWARD. *The History of Human Marriage.* New York: The Allerton Book Co., 1922.

WRIGHT, LOUIS B. *The Cultural Life of the American Colonies.* New York: Harper Torchbooks, 1962.

CHAPTER 3

SOCIAL CLASS VARIATIONS IN MARRIAGE AND THE FAMILY

As stated in Chapter 1, this book's focus is the contemporary middle-class family in the United States. The Puritan family discussed in the previous chapter provides both contrast and background for an analysis of the modern middle-class family. In this chapter, the upper and lower social class levels are analyzed to provide contemporary contrasts with the middle-class family.

A number of other contemporary family types with particular social characteristics—based, for example, on religious, racial or ethnic variations—could also be used to provide contrast with or show variations within the middle class. Our choice was made for several reasons. First, the analysis of various other social-class families is categorically consistent with this book's focus, the middle-class family. Second, social class as an analytic tool for studying variations in social behavior is one of the most fruitful and important approaches available to the social scientist. Third, many Americans are increasingly aware of and interested in social class, as illustrated by the common use of a social-class focus in various areas of mass communication. Finally, some insight into social-class variations may give the reader a greater understanding of the marriage and family characteristics of his own social class, and of the relativeness of certain family characteristics he may have formerly assumed were universal in the American culture.

THE LOWER CLASS FAMILY

Lower class as used here is often referred to as the lower-lower class, to distinguish it from the upper-lower class which has more of the traits and values of the middle class. The lower class to be discussed includes roughly 5 to 10 percent of the total American population. For purposes of discussion, certain arbitrary decisions have been made in defining this lower class. To go into all of the variations of lower-class life, as related to rural-urban, geographical, migrant-nonmigrant, racial, and ethnic factors, would demand a number of chapters or possibly another book. Therefore, the description of the lower class that follows refers for the most part to *a* white, urban lower class.

Some common social characteristics of this lower class are: (1) A formal education of eight years or less. (2) The male's occupation is almost always semiskilled or unskilled, and his work pattern is often sporadic, with long periods of unemployment. There is also a strong probability that the woman works in unskilled or service occupations. (3) The total income of the male is rarely over two or three thousand dollars a year, and the families make up a large number of those on the public assistance rolls. (4) Their place of residence is found in the slum areas of the city, often in old homes and buildings converted into small apartments. The ratio of persons per room is often three or four to one, and frequently as many as 20 people share the use of a single toilet.

In looking at the values and behavior patterns of the lower class, we must be careful to avoid imposing middle-class evaluations. The language used to describe lower-class patterns can convey to the reader an interpretation. It should not. Rodman writes, "It is little wonder that if we describe the lower-class family in terms of 'promiscuous' sexual relationships, 'illegitimate' children, 'deserting' men, and 'unmarried' mothers, we are going to see the situation as disorganized and chock-full of problems."[1] Such words "promiscuous" and "illegitimacy" are often evaluations made by middle-class observers and are frequently not a functional part of the language used by the lower class for describing and assessing their own behavior. (The very term "lower class" itself may sound interpretive.)

Some middle-class people believe that because the lower class has a low commitment to many middle-class values, this suggests a lower-class tolerance for different values and behavior patterns. However, studies have found that while the lower-middle class was at least forgiving of "conventional morality—i.e., heterosexual misconduct, drunkedness and swearing," it was "most harsh in condemnation of other sorts of deviants; the atheist, the homosexual, the 'un-American,' the radical, the artist-intellectual."[2]

Related to lower-class conservatism toward deviant behavior is the conservatism of their views of roles they feel most at ease with.

---

[1]Hyman Rodman, *Marriage, Family and Society* (New York: Random House, 1965), p. 223.
[2]Albert K. Cohen and Harold M. Hodges, Jr., "Characteristics of the Lower-Blue-Collar-Class," *Social Problems,* Spring, 1963, p. 321.

Cohen and Hodges write that "one of the clearest outcomes of this study is an image of the lower-lower class as one reluctant to meet new people and new situations, to form new social relationships, and above all to initiate interactions with strangers. On the contrary, he values and seeks out, more than anybody else, the routine, the familiar, the predictable."[3] Within the same context, and for the same general reasons, Cohen and Hodges also found that "role relationships are more likely for the lower-lower class to be defined in terms of somebody responsible for carrying them out."[4] Such research suggests that when the lower class are compared with the middle class they prefer fewer role involvements and they want their role-sets to be clearly defined in terms of power.

The lower class philosophy of life is also reflected in the following beliefs or ways of seeing the world around them. _Luck:_ What happens in the world is determined primarily through forces external to the individual. "One may be spared unpleasantness by good fortune, one may be 'lucky,' but one cannot be personally successful against difficulty."[5] Luck is closely related to lower-class _fatalism_. Lower-class individuals often see the world around them as confusing and chaotic; they do not feel that they understand it, and they feel that what goes on is essentially unpredictable—up to fate. Many attempt to explain or rationalize the chaos and lack of control over their own destiny by blaming it on an abstract "they," a scapegoat which often materializes as individuals seen as "powers"—the police, employers, city hall, and so forth. And because lower-class life tends to focus on the present, the time dimension in life is _the present,_ with a tendency to forget the past and ignore the future. Because the problems of the present often seem overwhelming, lower-class individuals view the future as beyond their control and, in consequence, rarely plan ahead.

Another important influence on lower-class life patterns is the constant fear of "getting into _trouble,_" a major concern of male and female, adults and children. Miller writes, "For men, 'trouble' frequently involves fighting or sexual adventures while drinking; for women, sexual involvement with disadvantageous consequences."[6] "Trouble" is not a concern over the moral or legal implications of behavior, but rather over the possible consequences.

---

[3] _Ibid.,_ p. 316.
[4] _Ibid.,_ p. 320.
[5] Lee Rainwater, _And the Poor Get Children_ (Chicago: Quadrangle Books, 1960), p. 52.
[6] Walter B. Miller, "Lower Class Culture as a Generating Milieu of Gang Delinquency," in Marvin E. Wolfgang, Leonard Savitz, and Norman Johnson, _The Sociology of Crime and Delinquency_ (New York: John Wiley & Sons, Inc., 1962), p. 268.

The concept of *fun* is also important to many lower-class individuals. Many middle-class "satisfactions with achievement" are not available or are of little interest to the lower class. The stress on the present, rather than the future, implies a seeking out of immediate pleasures. This interest in fun is also related to the fear of trouble, because trouble implies the pressure of forces that will curtail the amount of fun. Fun also implies some personal modification of the fatalistic attitude in that the individual can seek out the pleasurable and thereby he can determine some aspects of his own life.

Family relationships are often important to lower-class individuals because they are not "joiners," and, being suspicious of formal agencies, will turn to relatives or a few friends when help is needed. A study of lower-class migrants found that "family, kin and close friendship have much deeper personal roots for migrants into the urban community than might have been anticipated. This seems to be true for both recent migrants and for those who were older and more settled."[7] When the world around is viewed as hostile and confusing, it becomes natural to seek out those who live in the "same world" with the same kinds of problems. Another reason that the lower class often turn to relatives for help is that they frequently have relatives handy to them. One study of the lower class found that about half, as compared to about one-tenth of a middle-class sample, said they had close relatives living within a four-block radius of their own dwelling.[8]

These general values of the lower class will serve as a background for a discussion of some of the characteristics and values found in courtship, marriage, and the family. A few comments on the world of the lower-class adolescent precede this discussion. Miller points out that the worlds of both boys and girls are the *one-sex peer unit* rather than the two-parent family unit.[9] Because lower-class home life is often limited by absent parents and crowding, children at very young ages move out onto the streets. There, they usually interact and identify with their age-sex groups. The interaction across sex lines is often limited, in contrast to middle-class interaction, because the lower-class adolescent generally lacks the verbal skills needed for extended boy-girl social interaction. Also his age-sex peers provide him with what sense of identification he has, and they frequently act as a one-sex group or gang.

The importance of the age-sex peer group, particularly for the

---

[7]Leonard Blumberg and Robert R. Bell, "Urban Migration and Kinship Ties," *Social Problems,* Spring, 1959, p. 331.
[8]Cohen and Hodges, *op. cit.,* p. 310.
[9]Miller, *op. cit.,* p. 273.

adolescent boy, is illustrated by the following description of what it is like for a boy to grow up in the lower-class culture. "A boy spends the major part of the first twelve years in the company of and under the domination of women. He learns during that time that women are the people who count, that men are despicable, dangerous, and desirable. He also learns that a 'real man' is hated for his irresponsibility but is considered very attractive on Saturday night. He learns, too, that if he really loves his mother, he will not grow up to be 'just like all men' but that, despite her best efforts, his mother's pride and joy will very likely turn out to be as much a 'rogue male' as the rest. In short, he has sex-role problems."[10] The boy's adolescent associations with his age-sex peers is the process whereby he attains his independence and masculinity, and acquires all of the characteristics his mother had told him were undesirable about men.

The values the lower-class boy accepts and the roles he tries to fill center around activity defined as masculine; his focal concerns are trouble, toughness, smartness, excitement, fate, and autonomy.[11] Miller suggests that "the genesis of the intense concern over 'toughness' in lower class culture is probably related to the fact that a significant proportion of the lower class males are reared in a predominantly female household, and lack a consistently present male figure with whom to identify and from whom to learn essential components of a 'male' role."[12] In one respect the lower-class boy is effectively socialized by the lower-class man—the boy imitates the man's rejection of the home as well as his high involvement in all-male groups.

Lower-class adolescent girls value being attractive to the males, even though they are reared by the same mothers as the boys and have been told the same negative things about men. That men are irresponsible and frequently mean, the girls have often observed for themselves in their own fathers and other men. Regardless of what they have been told and have seen, the girls often see relationships with boys as adventurous and romantic, especially in contrast to the life they are leading. Many of them are quite romantic in their thinking and tend to believe what they have heard and seen is true for men in *general*, but not for the *particular* man they will find for themselves.

---

[10]David J. Bordua, "Delinquent Subculture: Sociological Interpretation of Gang Delinquency," *The Annals*, November, 1961, p. 129.
[11]*Ibid.*, p. 128.
[12]Miller, *op. cit.*, p. 220.

Dating and Courtship

In most cases, lower-class adolescents follow a pattern of early and steady dating. A "significant other" is often needed and may be acquired through the agreement of "going steady." This, in addition, partially protects the girl, because if she dates randomly, she is not identified with any one boy and may therefore be subject to strong sexual pressures. Probably, too, the lower-class youngster so desperately seeks adult status that the semipermanent relationship of "going steady" gives him the illusion of engaging in adult behavior. This early, steady dating pattern often results in sexual laxities, unplanned pregnancies, and early marriages.

Lower-class adolescents do very little shopping around through random dating for the eventual marriage partner. Rainwater writes that "many in the lower class give the impression of having just drifted together—they do not seem to have regarded themselves as active choosers of a mate but are inclined to think simply that it was about time to get married."[13] Drifting together reflects the lower-class value of stressing the present not the future. The pattern of thinking and planning needed in seeking out the best mate and planning marriage is often alien to the lower class. Rainwater goes on to point out that members of the lower class rarely show enterprise in seeking or choosing marriage partners. "Rarely do they express strong feelings about the decision to marry. Resignation, a feeling that fate is dictating what is happening, and a lack of much elaboration in conscious planning and consideration are frequently reflected in the use of such phrases as 'it was just time,' 'somehow it was settled' or 'we just did it'."[14]

When compared with the middle class, dating and "going steady" in the lower class are different relationships, characterized by a lack of planning and, often, a desire to escape from role frustrations rather than enter new roles through anticipation. Stress on immediate satisfactions and time restriction to the present often make dating and courtship in the lower class less of a process leading to marriage and more of a series of day-to-day events frequently having little logic or pattern to provide overall continuity. As a result, when marriage does occur, it just happens; it is not seen as the meaningful end result of a dating-courtship process, as it often is in the middle class.

---

[13]Rainwater, *op. cit.*, p. 62.
[14]*Ibid.*, p. 63.

Premarital Sex.　Attitudes about premarital coitus are more commonly permissive in the lower than in the middle class. It should not be assumed, however, that lower-class attitudes toward sex in general are more liberal. While premarital intercourse is often viewed as normal, and visiting prostitutes is acceptable, such sexual expression as heavy and extended petting and masturbation are strongly condemned and often viewed as perversions. What is accepted is the sexual act as related to actual coitus with little foreplay or variations in technique and procedure.

Permissiveness about premarital coitus is reflected in the lower-class male's preoccupation with sex. The male sees sexual conquest as a strong sign of his masculinity, and in a world where other signs are often unavailable, the sex sign takes on great significance. By seeing sex as conquest, he gains a sense of personal achievement. Restricting sex to the act, without frills, also means that the sexual act is to satisfy only the male, thereby providing him with an activity considered exclusively male. Even when the female achieves satisfaction from sexual relations, the male interprets that as a sign of *his* sexual ability.

Miller suggests that "a concern over homosexuality runs like a persistent thread through lower class culture."[15] This may be due to the early female dominance in the boy's life and because of the few achieved activities that give him a sense of his masculinity. Any indication of homosexuality is threatening to his sexual prowess with girls, which is so important to his sense of masculinity. Middle-class boys will kiddingly call one another "queer," but in the lower class this is taboo.

The literature on the lower class lacks certainty as to the importance of female virginity from the male's point of view. In some lower-class areas, virginity has an important value, as was the case in Whyte's study of lower-class boys of Italian background. Whyte found that the codes of those boys strongly prohibited sexual relations with virgins. The boys defined a good girl as one who "submitted to a limited amount of kisses and caresses without compromising her reputation. She must not be a 'teaser' (one who attempts to excite the man as much as possible without granting him sexual access). The virginity of a 'teaser' is thought to be only a technicality, and if she is raped it serves her right. Otherwise a girl's virginity must be protected."[16] The lower-class boys made a further

---

[15]Miller, *op. cit.*, p. 270.
[16]William F. Whyte, "A Slum Sex Code," *American Journal of Sociology*, July, 1943, p. 351.

distinction between "one-man" girls and "promiscuous" girls. Whyte says it was difficult to distinguish between these two types of girls "because the promiscuous girl usually tries to pass herself off as a one-man 'lay' and one-man girls are constantly slipping into the lower category."[17] The boy perceived and treated the two classes of girls in different ways. He would talk freely about the "promiscuous" girl and was quite willing to share her with his friends, but he talked much less about the "one-man" girl and treated her with more respect.

While Whyte's study referred to a specific ethnic group in the lower class, the male's attitudes about the nonvirgin probably reflect common lower-class attitudes. The male has no respect or concern for the promiscuous girl because she only functions as a sex outlet, while the "one-man" girl not only provides a sexual outlet, but also can satisfy his ego-need for masculinity through personal conquest and sexual exclusiveness. Because of respect, many of the "one-man" girls are married by the boy if they get pregnant. This appears to be common because the number of lower-class girls pregnant at the time of marriage is high. Hollingshead and Redlich in their study of a broadly defined lower class found that 40 percent of the girls were pregnant before marriage.[18] When all unmarried pregnancies are taken into account, probably over half of all lower-class women are pregnant at some time prior to marriage. However, the pregnant girl does not necessarily have either the inclination or the ability to get the father to marry her.

"One-man" girls probably provide only a small part of the total premarital sexual experience of the lower-class male. The much higher frequency of premarital experiences for the male than for the female suggests that prostitutes and "promiscuous" girls account for a large majority of his premarital sexual experiences. Kinsey found that in the 16- to 20-year-old group with an eighth-grade education or less, the frequency per week of premarital coitus for the male was 1.6 times as contrasted with 0.3 times for the female. In contrast, among the college population coital frequency for the male was 0.2 per week and the female 0.1.[19] By educational level, the differences among the females was not great, but among the males it was very great. It may also be noted that the less-educated female has a

---

[17]*Ibid.*, p. 352.

[18]August B. Hollingshead and Frederick C. Redlich, *Social Class and Mental Illness* (New York: John Wiley & Sons, Inc., 1958), p. 126.

[19]Alfred C. Kinsey, Wardell B. Pomeroy, Clyde E. Martin, and Paul H. Gebhard, *Sexual Behavior in the Human Female* (Philadelphia: W. B. Saunders, 1953), p. 78.

slightly higher frequency of premarital coitus per week than does the college-level male.

The lower-class girl's decision as to premarital coitus is obviously difficult. She may feel that virginity is one of her strongest weapons in acquiring a husband. Yet because of the male's great desire for sexual conquest, he may not be willing to continue a relationship with her without sexual relations. In many cases, rather than lose him the girl will engage in premarital coitus. However, if she does this with more than one or two boys, she may find herself defined as "promiscuous" and have her chances of marriage greatly reduced. If the girl gets pregnant, no great personal or social pressure is put on the boy to marry her, and she may find herself an unmarried mother, with marriage even more difficult because of the baby.

Thus, in the lower class, premarital sex frequently centers around "exploitation." The boy seeks sexual conquests without personal commitment as an expression of his masculinity, while the girl tries to use sex to move the male into marriage. In the lower class, neither the male nor the female generally believe that sex has any great personal satisfaction for the female. Therefore, to say that the lower-class female "uses sex" is accurate in the sense that she frequently gets no personal satisfaction from it. Then, too, when a girl has premarital coitus and gets pregnant, she often says it is really not her fault, but the fault of the man. The view is that men, because of their sexual insistence, are responsible for the pregnancy, but that the girl must "pay" for the man's sexual desires.

Marriage. To say that a lower-class couple are married does not always imply the same thing it does in the middle class. Lower-class "marriage" may mean simply that a couple are living together; whether they are legally married may be of little importance. A woman may be "married" a dozen times in her lifetime and have children from a number of different "husbands" in that in any given relationship the woman may define herself as being "married." The temporary nature of numerous "marriages" does not usually stop the woman from entering new "marriages." In part this reflects the fact that the lower-class woman expects little from a "husband." Rainwater points out that the lower-class woman is often quite willing to settle for some permanence in a not-too-happy relationship because she feels nothing better is to be gained from a man; indeed, she feels lucky if he will just stay around.[20] Marriage may offer little

---

[20]Rainwater, *op. cit.*, pp. 72-73.

to the lower-class woman, but she nevertheless sees it as better than nothing.

Women in the lower class frequently enter marriage at a young age because they feel somewhat lost when they outgrow the status of daughter and they look forward to establishing themselves, in what often seems the clear-cut status of wife and mother.[21] As officially recorded, the average age for first marriage of lower-class women cannot be reliably used because the records do not include the many who enter a "marriage" relationship without being legally married. Eighteen years of age would seem a reasonable average for the lower-class woman's first marriage.

Studies show that the age difference between husband and wife is greater in the lower than in the middle class. In the Hollingshead and Redlich study, 32 percent of the husbands were six or more years older than their wives.[22] The age differential may be due to the male resisting marriage and the female seeing the older male as somewhat better marriage partner.

Entering into marriage for the lower class calls for little celebration and often little significant change in role behavior. Life continues after marriage as it did before, except that the couple define themselves as married. Marriage may mean little more for the male than complete sexual rights, and for the female than that the husband probably will contribute something to their living expenses. At the start of marriage, the lower-class couple often do not set up any kind of home of their own. Hollingshead and Redlich found that 77 percent of the newly married couples move into homes of relatives, in-laws, or friends; whereas 23 percent move into their own "rents." None own their own homes.[23]

The values of companionship and sharing so important in middle-class marriages are often absent from the marital interaction of lower-class couples. A necessary condition for effective husband-wife interaction is that both have the ability and the motivation to communicate with each other. Komarovsky found in her sample that while little marital communication was characteristic of only 12 percent of the high-school educated wives she studied, it was descriptive of 41 percent of the less educated women.[24] However, it may be that many in the lower class *expect* little communication

[21]*Ibid.*, p. 72.
[22]Hollingshead and Redlich, *op. cit.*, p. 126.
[23]*Ibid.*, p. 127.
[24]Mirra Komarovsky, *Blue-Collar Marriage* (New York: Random House, 1962), p. 144.

between husband and wife and, therefore, don't find its absence too important. This appears to be the case in the Komarovsky study, where 59 percent of the high-school educated spouses believed that a lack of conversation in marriage was a genuine problem, but only 26 percent of the lower-educated spouses gave the same assessment.[25]

Leisure time is usually not pursued by the lower-class husband and wife in a paired relationship. This is reflected by their having few friendships as a couple with other couples, and also because they seldom go out as a couple for an evening's entertainment. Komarovsky found that "about one-fifth of the couples never visit with another couple apart from relatives. An additional 16 percent do so only infrequently, a few times a year."[26] When the lower-class male is at home, he usually wants to be let alone—not bothered with family demands. When he goes out, he generally goes with other men and his destination is often neighborhood bars that are for the most part all-male hangouts. Yet there is some evidence that while many lower-class men function as a part of all-male groups, they do not develop close friendships with any one man. The male's low interpersonal involvement, when compared to that of the woman, seems to hold true both in and out of lower-class family relationships. For example, Komarovsky found that while about 60 percent of the wives had close friendships outside the family, only about 20 percent of the husbands did.[27] But even though the lower-class male has few close friends, his all-male social groups are important to him because that masculine world contributes to his personal sense of masculinity.

The wife's social life often centers around relatives or friends of the same sex. The husbands of these friends are absent for the same reasons as her own is. With her husband often not functioning in a close role relationship, the lower-class wife frequently turns to others for a significant role relationship. Komarovsky found that "two-thirds of the wives have at least one person apart from their husbands in whom they confide deeply personal experiences. In 35 percent of the cases the wife not only enjoys such intimate friendships but shares some significant segment of her life *more fully* with her confidants than with her husband."[28]

The generally low family involvement of the lower-class male often means there is no great difference in his behavior patterns

---

[25]*Ibid.*, p. 119.
[26]*Ibid.*, p. 311.
[27]*Ibid.*, p. 215.
[28]*Ibid.*, p. 208.

before and after marriage. If he gives some of his earnings to his wife, he often defines himself as being a good husband. Since neither his marriage nor his job contribute very much to his sense of masculinity, the maintained interaction with his sex peers therefore continues to be important. Unlike many middle-class males, he rarely has any positive identification with his occupation. In fact, in the lower class, the aim is often to escape from thinking of the job. In his perceptive article "The Myth of the Happy Worker," Harvey Swados writes, "The worker's attitude towards his work is generally compounded of hatred, shame, and resignation," and adds that the kind of work done is degrading "to any man who ever dreams of doing something with his life."[29] Thus, to gain at least some assurance of significance, the male turns to the world of other males like himself, putting aside home demands and the demanding nature of his job.

Some disagreement exists between the lower-class man and woman as to what constitutes a "good husband." Rainwater writes, "Men tend to give first importance to being a good father, but few women do. Instead, women are more likely to want their husbands first of all to be either good providers or good lovers. Three-fifths of the lower class women in our sample ranked being a good lover first or second in importance for a good husband, yet less than 5 percent of the lower class husbands ranked this role as high, and three-fifths of them put it in the 'least important' category."[30] Many lower-class women see a "good lover" as extending far beyond sexual relations to the much broader desire for some consideration of them by their husband. On the other hand, the husband probably ranks "good lover" low because he also sees it as meaning he should give his wife emotional consideration, which he is often not willing to give because it is not "masculine" behavior.

The primary role of the woman centers around her being a mother, rather than a wife. She often has the responsibility not only of caring for the children, but also of meeting the day-to-day needs of the family. A study by Olsen found that "responsibility taken by husbands—both alone and jointly with their wives—is greatest in middle status families and less in high and low status homes."[31] Rainwater found that lower-class men "sharply restrict the defini-

---

[29]Harvey Swados, "The Myth of the Happy Worker," in Maurice R. Stein, Arthur J. Vidich, and David M. White, *Identity and Anxiety* (Glencoe, Illinois: The Free Press, 1960), pp. 199, 202.

[30]Rainwater, *op. cit.*, p. 67.

[31]Marvin E. Olsen, "Distribution of Family Responsibilities and Social Stratification," *Marriage and Family Living*, February, 1960, p. 65.

tion of a good wife to the mother-housekeeper components."[32] For many middle-class women there is often a strong personal desire to fill roles besides the traditional ones of wife and mother. But for lower-class women there appears to be little personal frustration related to any low evaluation of the traditional roles of wife, mother and housekeeper. Komarovsky found there was hardly a trace of any feeling of low prestige attached to being housewives by working-class or lower-class wives.[33]

Marital Coitus.   Many of the middle class values regarding marriage interaction are either totally absent or modified in the lower class. The lower-class marriage is of a patriarchal nature when there is a husband present. The male tends to be patriarchal in his assumed rights of authority, but not usually in his obligations. The patriarchal pattern is limited because most of the time the male's world centers around other men; therefore, such values as sharing and mutual ego-satisfaction common to middle-class marriages are often totally absent from lower-class marriages.

The absence of "sharing" is further illustrated by lower-class attitudes about marital sex. While marital sex is an important part of lower-class life, particularly for the husband, actual knowledge about sex is restricted. "The typical lower class pattern among men includes at most the knowledge that men and women have sexual intercourse, and that contraception can be effected with a condom."[34] Rainwater goes on to point out that lower-class women generally have even less information about sex and methods of birth control than do men.[35] Thus, in the lower class, sexual satisfaction is basically for the male. "Both husbands and wives feel that sexual gratification for the wife is much less important, so that, consciously at least, wives seem generally content if intercourse results in the husband's pleasure even if not their own."[36] Sexually satisfying her husband indicates to the wife that she continues to have the sex "weapon" in dealing with him. The fact that marital sex may be so viewed is reflected in the male view that marital coitus is a "getting-on-getting-off" experience. "It is a good idea to get away from the woman as quickly as possible—to run or to retreat into oneself—in order to avoid consequences and possible demands."[37] Marital sex is often, therefore, a constant battle, with the male "getting" but try-

---

[32]Rainwater, *op. cit.*, p. 67.
[33]Komarovsky, *op. cit.*, p. 49.
[34]Rainwater, *op. cit.*, p. 63.
[35]*Ibid.*, p. 64.
[36]*Ibid.*, p. 94.
[37]*Ibid.*, p. 81.

ing not to give, and the wife "giving" and hoping to get something in return.

A number of studies have indicated a positive relationship between sexual satisfaction and overall adjustment in marriage. But Komarovsky points out that this relationship may vary with social class. She writes, "Because some of our less-educated women expect little psychological intimacy in marriage, and their standards of personal relationships are not demanding, they were able to dissociate the sexual response from the total relationship."[38] This also suggests that marital sex is less apt to be a part of a broader interpersonal intimacy in the lower class than it often is in the middle class.

The lack of importance attached to marital sex by the lower-class wife is reflected in the lack of sexual satisfaction she achieves. Rainwater found in his sample that only about 25 percent of the lower-class women indicated some measure of personal enjoyment in sexual relations, and "about 40 percent of the lower-lower class women indicate a real rejection of sexuality."[39] Further evidence is found in the Kinsey study of the female, by education, and achievement of orgasm in marital coitus. For example, for those females with eight years of education or less, 28 percent had never achieved orgasm even after five years of marriage, as contrasted with 17 percent with "some high school" and 15 percent with "some college."[40] Generally, a "good" wife in the lower class is not expected to show any great interest in, or satisfaction with marital sex. Being interested in sex, even with her husband, may raise questions about her "goodness." This is reflected in the belief that "good women stay at home and are not too interested in what goes on in the outside world. Bad women, of course, are mainly interested in sex, and are to be found mostly in bars and hotel rooms."[41]

It logically follows from the attitudes of the lower class that extramarital relations are acceptable for the male, but severely condemned for the female. Whyte writes, "The wife is expected to be completely faithful, and even the slightest flirtations are seriously regarded."[42] But for the male, extramarital adventure is not barred, though he may try to keep it separate from his married life. In most respects, the married man sees his potential world of sexual outlet in the same way as he did when he was single. A common rationali-

---

[38]Komarovsky, *op. cit.*, p. 349.
[39]Rainwater, *op. cit.*, p. 121.
[40]Kinsey, *op. cit.*, p. 401.
[41]Rainwater, *op. cit.*, pp. 79–80.
[42]Whyte, *op. cit.*, p. 357.

zation is used by both men and women to explain the husband's philandering—"that's the way men are." The greatest threat to the lower class wife from her husband's philandering is often not her "ego" loss, but the implied loss of the use of marital coitus as a means of control or influence over her husband.

Children. The attitudes and behavior patterns of the lower class in regard to sex are closely related to some of the attitudes about having children. The woman who both desires and has children is strongly approved in the lower class because having children is seen as the woman's primary reason for being. Rainwater says: "The woman who wants only one child is condemned . . . emphatically for being a bad person, for going against her nature—and the woman who wants no children is beyond the pale, she should not have married at all."[43] The lower-class woman who accepts these values not only wants children, but wants a number of them. Her own experience of growing up in a large family with poverty around her does not deter her from moving into the same situation. In part, this reflects her inability to relate past experience to the present in realistically anticipating the future. The male's interest in children often centers around his own ego needs, rather than around interest in the children. "Since they (the males) tend to feel ineffective and weak in relation to their world, fathering a string of children comes to represent a kind of defiant demonstration that they are real men."[44] They see getting their wife pregnant as one of the few signs of their masculine effectiveness.

Given the woman's strong desire for children, and the man's view of his wife's pregnancies as a sign of his masculinity, attempts to control pregnancy are obviously often limited and ineffective. Even when there is a feeling of having enough children, wishfulness often substitutes for action; that is, lower-class limitation of family size is often "a subject for fantasy and tentative goals, but not one in which concerted effort is devoted."[45] As a result of lack of interest or ability in controlling family size, the lower-class wife expects to have a large number of children and, in general, is more likely at any age to become pregnant.[46] Couples in the middle class who exert increasingly efficient rational control over pregnancy sometimes find it hard to understand the frequency with which lower-class couples have large

---

[43]Rainwater, *op. cit.*, p. 55.
[44]*Ibid.*, p. 85.
[45]*Ibid.*, p. 59.
[46]See: Paul H. Gebhart, Wardell B. Pomeroy, Clyde E. Martin, and Cornelia B. Christensen, *Pregnancy, Birth and Abortion* (New York: Harper-Hoeber, 1958), p. 87.

numbers of children. A partial explanation is the "fatalistic" attitudes toward pregnancy that restrict motivation toward or any interest in contraception.

Often, even when the lower-class woman wants to practice contraception, she gets little help or understanding from her husband. In Rainwater's study, 65 percent of the women claimed that contraception was noneffective for them because the husband was impatient and demanding. "Such men feel that having sexual relations is their central right in marriage and that their wives are duty-bound to make themselves available on demand. The husbands are therefore highly impatient with the interferences which contraception represents."[47]

Another attitude among lower-class women that limits the effectiveness of contraception is stated as, "He's the one that always wants it, let him worry about the protection."[48] Thus, the woman leaves it to the male to take the responsibility by using a condom. But the male is not often willing to take responsibility because contraception interferes with his sexual rights. The title of Rainwater's book accurately describes the result of these attitudes: *And the Poor Get Children.*

An interest in contraception does not usually develop, if it ever does, until after the lower-class woman has had several children. Initially the woman sees children as her primary means of attaining personal significance. So long as the children do not interfere with the husband's "rights," the mother controls the children's lives—the notion of shared parental roles being largely absent in lower-class families. The mother sees the children as her property and her responsibility, "and it is through them that she expects to fulfill herself and her potentialities; if her children love her now and in the future, she feels she has gained the only really important gratification which her world allows her."[49] However, as indicated by the son breaking away from her in his early adolescence, and the daughter entering marriage in her late teens, the mother does not, for long, maintain importance for her children.

The father's role is often sporadic and may last only a short period of time. The father's reaction to his children—when he is around them—is generally determined by his mood. He can be indulgent if he feels like it, because he does not concern himself with the rearing of the child. When the father is home, the home is often

[47]Rainwater, *op. cit.*, p. 240.
[48]*Ibid.*, p. 241.
[49]*Ibid.*, p. 86.

father-centered, not child-centered as is often the case in the middle class. Because the father has a strong sense of his "rights" in the home, he is not apt to brook violation and interference from either the wife or the children. With physical punishment and even violence common in the lower class, the male can and does make sure of his "rights" through his greater physical strength. The depressed nature of the home setting often spurs on the male's feelings of frustration and suspicions of self-inadequacy, so that he is apt to strike out in any direction at what may seem slight provocation by his wife or children. If his negative feelings become strong enough, he may walk out and disappear.

It appears that many lower-class males want to be *seen* as being influential and possessing power with regard to their families, but not necessarily to *function* accordingly. The male may judge the respect given to him in his husband and father roles on the basis of the amount of compliance by his wife and children to his wishes, but this does not mean he will attempt to run the household; he will leave that to his wife.[50] Rainwater points out that the lower-class husband's being tangential to family functioning is also often what the wife prefers. "That is, in spite of the worrying she may do about the possibility of her husband straying away from home and thus depriving the family of its source of support and measure of respectibility, the lower-lower class wife seems to find handling the family on her own to her liking, or at least consistent with what she has learned to expect from living in her particular social world."[51]

Child-rearing practices in the lower class, as followed by the mother, often show a mixture of permissiveness and authoritarianism. For example, lower-class mothers, often more permissive in feeding, weaning, and toilet training their children than are middle-class mothers, lack the compulsiveness to "move the child along," possibly for several reasons. The mother does not concern herself with the future, and therefore has no great interests in leading the child into anticipated stages of development; time and order have less importance in the thinking of the lower class than the middle class, and it does not matter if something is done now or later; and finally, there is not the middle-class stress on neatness and cleanliness and, therefore, the need for such learning as toilet training does not loom as important. In other areas, the mother may be very authoritarian and arbitrary and punish the child with little rhyme

---

[50]Cohen and Hodges, *op. cit.*, p. 327.
[51]Lee Rainwater, *Family Design* (Chicago: Aldine Publishing Co., 1965), pp. 59–60.

or reason. This may be due to the acceptance of physical expression, the inability to verbalize, the sense of personal frustration, and the lone parent responsibility of the lower-class mother.

As previously mentioned, there is evidence to suggest that children are very important to the lower-class woman because she has few other adult roles that give her personal satisfaction. Yet the problems of rearing a child in the lower class may cut down on the satisfactions she can achieve through the mother role. One study found that about one-fifth of the low social class parents studied said their children gave them more trouble than pleasure and this was about five times the rate found for the high social class respondents. This finding "seems a direct contradiction of the popular statement that the pleasure of the poor is in their children, that this is their form of 'wealth'."[52]

As mentioned in Chapter 1, a high aspiration level for her children is an important value to the middle-class mother. The lower-class mother, on the other hand, because of the reality of the world and the feeling of inability to influence the future, often has very limited expectations for her children. Continued education seems both hopeless and useless. The lower-class mother may hope for nothing more than that her children will stay out of trouble and be decent to her in the future. Hoping that the child will be able to move out of the lower class is completely outside the frame of reference—the realm of possibility—of lower-class thinking. When the mother does have expectations for the child's upward social mobility, it generally means that she has a membership in the lower class, but has taken on at least some middle-class values as her reference. Such a mother is in, but not of the lower class.

Marriage Instability. By social-class level, divorce and desertion rates are highest in the lower classes. But the official records say little about the many relationships that are named as "marriages" by the couple and then end after a period of time. A rough overall estimate would suggest that probably no more than one third of the number of marriages in the lower class are permanent. When contrasted with other social classes, a lower-class marriage is much more apt to end through desertion or divorce than death. Hollingshead and Redlich found that the ratio of widows and widowers to separated and divorced in the lower class was 1 to 1.3.[53]

---

[52]Thomas S. Langner and Stanley T. Michael, *Life Stress and Mental Health* (New York: The Free Press of Glencoe, 1963), p. 341.
[53]Hollingshead and Redlich, *op. cit.*, p. 126.

After one marriage relationship ends, the individuals often move into new marriage relationships, either legally or illegally. For example, legal records show that "a fourth of the recently married persons with no high school education had been married twice or more, whereas only a tenth of the college graduates has been remarried."[54] When unofficial marriages are added to official marriages, then the "serial marriage" of the lower class is very frequent. The social pattern of "remarriage" seems to be about the same as first marriage in that the male expects exclusive sex rights, expects the woman to cook for him, and expects "to be let alone." The female wants some financial help and some indication that the husband cares for her. Because the partner's sets of expectations are seen as contradictory, the relationship is often ripe for ending almost as soon as it is started.

Out of the series of "marriages" comes a large number of children, and with the large number of broken marriages and remarriages, lower-class children often experience marriage breakup and stepparents, almost always a stepfather. The Hollingshead and Redlich study found that 41 percent of the children in the lower class under 17 years of age lived in homes that had been disrupted by death, desertion, separation, or divorce.[55] Mayer estimates that at the lower class level, 50 to 60 percent of the families with adolescent children have been broken, often more than once.[56] Since parents are important role models for marriage, many lower-class children obviously grow up seeing marriage as a series of transitory relationships with a variety of partners.

Although some writers romanticize the lower class, the actual situation in regard to their family life does not justify it. The picture of the lower lower-class family presented here is a dismal one, both from a social and personal point of view. However, the picture presented has been a general one, and there are of course exceptions to all that has been said about lower-class attitudes and behavior.

THE UPPER CLASS FAMILY

Compared to the many studies done on the middle class, the discussion of the lower-class family drew upon a limited body of empirical research. Empirical research on the upper class is even more

---

[54]Paul C. Glick and Hugh Carter, "Marriage Patterns and Educational Level," *American Sociological Review,* June, 1958, p. 296.

[55]Hollingshead and Redlich, *op. cit.,* p. 124.

[56]Kurt B. Mayer, *Class and Society* (New York: Doubleday and Co., Inc., 1955), p. 51.

limited. The works of Baltzell and Hollingshead are the main sources in the discussion that follows.[57]

Upper class as used in this discussion refers to the social class level that has sometimes been referred to as the upper-upper class. Two variables are important in defining the upper-upper class: First, the family has money. How much money is difficult to say, but the amount must at least be adequate for maintaining an upper-class style of life. Second, the family must have had its money for at least two generations, and very frequently for three or more generations. This second point distinguishes the upper-upper class from the lower-upper class (or *elites,* in Baltzell's terminology). In many cases, the lower-uppers may have more money than the upper-upper class, but they do not qualify as upper-uppers because their money is first generation.

Of all social class levels, the upper class is by far the smallest, probably including less than 1 per cent of the total American population; however, in wealth, power, and influence, members of this class are an extremely significant part of the population. To the rest of the social-class hierarchy the upper class may be unknown, vaguely recognized, held to be a "different world," or, for the upper-middle or the lower-upper represent the class level for mobility aspirations that will rarely be reached.

Having had wealth for at least two generations is important because of what it has meant in the socialization of the upper-class individual. Growing up without financial problems produces a socialization process different from one in which money problems are serious considerations. When money is not a problem, one grows to accept that which is presented to him; the fact of the money itself is of little significance. For example, the youngster in the upper class is provided with the care, education, and privileges that money will provide, with little conscious awareness that money is involved. This is in contrast to the mobility-oriented middle class where the child grows up with aspirations for things that must be achieved. In the upper class, the child is reared in a family with no sense of social striving because they are already at the top. He is taught the values of a social position he acquired at birth, and social anxiety is not a part of his socialization process.

---

[57]E. Digby Baltzell, *Philadelphia Gentlemen* (Glencoe, Illinois: The Free Press, 1958), and Hollingshead and Redlich, *op. cit.* The writer is greatly indebted to E. Digby Baltzell for providing many insights into the upper-class family through private conversations, as well as through speaking to the writer's Marriage and Family classes on the upper-class family.

The values and way of life in the upper class are based upon the family *not* striving; the symbols of class position are not important because they do not *have* to be shown. The fact that they are there is known by those who matter, their fellow members of the upper class; recognition by the lower social classes is generally of no importance. The upper class believes in being inconspicuous; the compulsion to show material wealth in conspicuous ways often gives away the elite (lower-upper) class. As Hollingshead and Redlich point out in their study, for the upper-upper class, "pretense is a cardinal sin; to pretend is as vulgar as an attempt to buy one's way."[58]

Clearly, the family is the basic unit in the upper class, and various families through interaction with one another define upper-class attitudes and behavior. Baltzell writes, "These families are at the top of the social class hierarchy; they are brought up together, are friends, and are intermarried with one another; and finally, they maintain a distinctive style of life and a kind of primary group solidarity which sets them apart from the rest of the population."[59] The distinctive style is illustrated by Baltzell by the speech of the upper class. The following illustrates upper-class as contrasted with middle-class usage: "The upper class *live* in a *house, employ servants* to *wash* the *curtains* and clean the *furniture,* including a *sofa;* they use the *toilet,* the *porch, library,* or *playroom.* The middle classes *reside* in a *home, hire help* or *domestics* to *launder* the *drapes* and clean the *house furnishings* which include a bedroom *suite* (like suit) and a *davenport;* they use the *lavoratory,* the *veranda, den,* or *rumpus room."*[60]

To summarize, the basic values of the upper class are: one, respect for familism and lineage; two, a belief that money is important, but *only* as a means to achieve ends; three, contempt for pretense, striving, and conspicuous consumption. It will be seen that these values are reflected in a number of ways in the upper-class marriage and family patterns.

Dating and Courtship

The world of the upper-class adolescent is tightly circumscribed by his social class because many of his activities are determined by the family or by peer groups that tend to reflect upper-class parental values. Upper-class adolescent life is usually much more formalized

---

[58]Hollingshead and Redlich, *op. cit.,* p. 84.
[59]Baltzell, *op. cit.,* p. 7.
[60]*Ibid.,* p. 51.

than that of the middle class because the basic values of formality, important both for the present and the future, are being transmitted. The very fact that almost all of the important social activities of the adolescent are with the family or with the children of other upper-class families provides a situation where strong homogeneous values can be transmitted and reinforced. The upper-class adolescent follows a way of life which stresses what he is and will continue to be by virtue of his birth. By contrast, the middle-class adolescent is being prepared for a somewhat unknown future that he is to achieve.

Dating in the upper class, especially for girls, is restricted to persons within the same class level. For most upper-class girls, dating outside the social class is limited simply because they do not come into contact with boys in other social classes. Upper-class girls' contacts with boys are more closely watched than are those of middle-class girls; furthermore, they are often going through a finishing-school process preparing them for their adult roles. Reflecting the patriarchal tradition which continues to prevail in the upper class, the girl is carefully watched and protected. At home the family is in control; and in school the authorities are usually very restrictive. Protection is not usually through force, but rather through socialization where little contact with males from other social classes makes the girl's class-limited relationships seem perfectly normal. However, the woman is not expected to deviate from the upper-upper class values, and if she does, she may be severely punished.

The upper-class boy is also socially controlled, but not to the same degree as the girl. A patriarchal tradition implies that males will have more freedom, and while boys may be allowed to interact with girls on a different social class level, it is expected that the relationships will be casual. If the boy gets too serious with a girl from the lower social classes, the family can and does exert strong social pressure to bring him back into line. Although the family may not always be successful, their success rate far exceeds their failure rate.

During early adolescence, many boy-girl relationships are encouraged because of the need for both sexes to be taught approved patterns of upper-class behavior, such as the acquisition of social graces. As the children grow older, and nearer the age of mate selection, the family exerts many kinds of pressures to move mate selection into the proper channels. This does not mean that romance is absent from the upper class, but as Baltzell points out, "Where romantic love is a reason for marriage it is deftly channeled within a relatively coherent subcultural circle, and the informal sanctions of relatives and friends are strong."[61] Rarely is correct behavior forced on the young people, but rather its acquisition reflects an effective socialization process.

It has generally been assumed by family sociologists that mate selection in the upper class is tightly controlled, resulting in few young people marrying outside. Recently Rosen and Bell undertook a study using the Philadelphia *Social Register* for 1940 and 1961 to determine how many marriages in those years were between upper-class individuals. In their study, the upper class was limited to those listed in the *Social Register* (the method used by Baltzell). They found that in 1940 in only 31 percent of the marriages were *both* spouses listed in *the Register,* in 29 percent only the groom was listed and in 40 percent only the bride. In 1961, in only 21 percent of the marriages were *both* the bride and groom listed in the *Social Register,* in 39 percent only the groom was listed and in 40 percent only the bride was listed.[62] On the basis of this study, upper-class rates of homogamy were not high.

However, Rosen and Bell suggest that the potential marriage market for upper-class individuals may be thought of as consisting not only of those listed the *Social Register,* which constitutes a small group (A), but also a larger group (B) consisting of a contiguous white Anglo-Saxon Protestant population, and, last of all, (C) the great majority of the American population. Ideally, the upper class is encouraged to marry a partner from (A), or from (B) where the outside individual can through his marriage be easily absorbed into the upper class. It appears uncommon for the upper-class individual to marry into (C), and when one does he may drop or be dropped from the upper class (the *Social Register*).[63]

Premarital sex. Empirical information on the premarital sexual behavior of the upper class is completely absent. The stated attitudes for the most part reflect the patriarchal tradition. A girl is expected to be a virgin at the time of marriage, but the male is often assumed to have had some sexual experiences. (In acquiring sexual experiences, the male is expected to be very discreet so that no scandal will occur to damage the family.) The actual sexual experiences of the upper-class female are difficult to assess. The upper-class social group is almost impossible to study, and impressions given in the mass

---

[61]*Ibid.,* p. 161.

[62]Laurence Rosen and Robert R. Bell, "Mate Selection in the Upper Class," *Sociological Quarterly,* Spring, 1966, p. 162.

[63]*Ibid.,* pp. 165–66.

media are unreliable because of the power of the upper class to keep information about its personal behavior from becoming public.

Marriage

Upper-class marriage extends the family line and binds together upper-class families, in contrast to the middle-class marriage that centers around the ego-needs of the individual. Because of the effectiveness of the upper-class socialization process, it seems likely that most young people accept the value of family importance in mate selection and do not enter marriage primarily for ego satisfaction. This is not to say that upper-class marriages do not provide personal satisfactions, but rather that they are achieved within the context of a family, rather than a personal, orientation to marriage.

The great importance of marriage is reflected in Baltzell's findings that upper-upper class women are almost twice as likely to be married (64 percent) as the elites. (37 percent)[64] The high percentage married is due to a very low divorce rate, and to the fact that very few upper-class women reject marriage for a career.[65] The high marriage rate reflects upper-class patriarchal values, which continue to give the highest recognition and status to the woman in the wife-mother role.

Marriage in the upper class does not imply the creation of a new and autonomous conjugal family, but rather an addition to the extended family relationships of the past and the present. While each new family created through marriage usually maintains a separate household, they do not conceive of themselves as a unit apart from the larger kin group.[66] Obligations to the extended family almost always take precedence over nonfamily social demands, and this importance is reinforced through continued close interaction with the extended family.

Acceptance of the extended family by the new conjugal marriage unit has a practical economic side. The upper-class way of life, to which the couple has been completely socialized, is often dependent, at least for some time after marriage, on the extended family. Hollingshead writes, "Usually a number of different nuclear families within a kin group are supported, in part at least, by income from a family estate held in trust."[67] This may be true of both the hus-

---

[64]Baltzell, op. cit., p. 161.
[65]Ibid., p. 162.
[66]August B. Hollingshead, "Class Differences in Family Stability," in Reinhard Bendix and Seymour M. Lipset, Class, Status and Power (Glencoe, Illinois: The Free Press, 1953), p. 286.
[67]Ibid., p. 286.

band and wife's families. "Because of the practice of intermarriage it is not unusual for a family to be beneficiary of two or more estates held in trust."[68] Thus, the internal forces of the upper class have great power through socialization, economic control, and intermarriage.

The role of the husband is in part determined by the values of a patriarchal system. Baltzell points out that the "patriarchal nature of the upper class family is shown by the fact that the college attended by the wife (if any) is *never* listed in the *Social Register.*"[69] Formal education has no prestige significance for the upper-class woman; the males are the ultimate arbiters of acceptability and of membership definition in the upper class. For example, in Philadelphia, "an annual invitation to the hallowed Assembly Balls is still the best index of first family status in the city. Unlike many such affairs held elsewhere in America, which are usually dominated by women, the Philadelphia Assembly has always been run by men"[70]

The upper-class male's occupation does not have the same ego significance as it does for the middle-class male, because he chooses his occupation according to his own or his family's feelings about how he will occupy himself in his adult years. A large number of upper-class men enter the world of finance because of the need to handle and, if possible, add to the family wealth. Many upper-class men are able to choose an occupation because it interests them, or even to pursue *no* occupation other than leading a "gentlemanly" life. Except for personal satisfaction, the male is usually not occupationally seeking or striving in the middle-class sense; the upper class male often *enters* an occupation; he does not *pursue* one.

The primary role of the woman centers around having children, running the household, and participating in a variety of social activities. Generally the mother does not devote a great deal of time to rearing her children because others handle their day-to-day care. This allows her to enter the many social activities important to the upper class.

The husband-wife relationship in the upper class of course varies a great deal with different couples. The very fact that the great stress on ego-needs that is found in the middle class is usually absent makes it probable that upper-class individuals demand and expect less of each other in marriage. Also, because family lines are of great importance, the personal nature of marriage is somewhat less important.

---

[68]*Ibid.*, p. 286.
[69]Baltzell, *op. cit.*, p. 27.
[70]*Ibid.*, p. 163.

The upper class has the money and the knowledge of many areas of interest to enable them to pursue a way of life that makes them less dependent on the marriage relationship. In the middle class, one's spouse is usually the most important "significant other," while in the upper class, the partners may have a number of other "significant others."

Only speculations can be offered as to the sexual nature of the upper-class marriage. Because less importance is attached to ego-need satisfaction in marriage, the upper-class couple may be less apt than the middle-class couple to seek personal reassurance through their sexual relationships. This is not to say that being significant as a sexual partner is unimportant, but rather that significance lies within a less extended psychological context. Second, the possession of money and power means that with a minimum of difficulty some in the upper class can and do seek sexual satisfaction outside of marriage.

An extramarital relationship, carried out with discretion, is not usually a reason for ending an upper-class marriage because the exclusiveness of the marriage relationship was not the prime reason for entering or maintaining the marriage.

Children. That children are important follows from upper-class patriarchal values. Family lines perpetuate themselves through the children and, thus, having a son is of particular importance. Baltzell found that the upper-upper class family had more children (2.66) than the elite family (1.62).[71] Conditions are favorable for having larger families because upper-class women can have the best in medical care and relief from the demanding burdens of child-rearing.

To say children are important to the upper class does not mean that the family is child-centered. The upper-class home tends to center around adult living; the children live within the adult world, their activities often restricted to their segregated section of the home or to peer associations outside the home. The adult world of the home is important to the socialization of the children because they are expected to learn to interact according to adult standards in dress, manners, and behavior patterns. They participate in adult activities as "young adults," not as children. One implication of this type of socialization is pointed out by Mills when he writes, "Adolescent boys and girls are exposed to the table conversations of decision makers, and thus have bred into them the informal skills and

---

[71]*Ibid.,* p. 162.

pretensions of decision makers. Without conscious effort, they ab-
sorb the aspiration to be—if not the conviction they are—the Ones
Who Decide."[72]

In the upper class, many values and patterns of behavior are
taught by highly specialized agencies. Baltzell says that the private
school and college are a kind of surrogate family.[73] "The private
educational institutions serve the latent function of acculturating
the members of the young generation."[74] Attendance at the right
private school is so important that Baltzell says it "is the best index
of ascribed upper class position, even more indicative than neighborhood, religion, or social register affiliation."[75] As it becomes more
difficult for the family to maintain direct control over the children,
the school is used more and more as the means of "correct" socialization.[76]

Divorce. Because of the minimum importance of ego-need satis-
factons in marriage and because of the great importance of the extended family, the upper class has a low divorce rate. Hollingshead
and Redlich write, "Divorce is avoided if possible; when it occurs
the entire family looks upon it as a disgrace, if not a scandal."[77] As
an indicaton of the low rate of divorce, Hollingshead and Redlich
found, in their study of the upper class, that the ratio of widows and
widowers to divorced persons was 27 to 1.[78]

The dominant values of the upper class regarding marriage and
family relationships may be summarized as wealth, the importance
of the family, and the patriarchal nature of family relationships.
The socialization of the children into the upper class is the key factor in understanding how the upper class maintains itself. As long
as socialization is controlled, the upper class can maintain itself and
determine the admission of new members.

The discussion of the lower and upper classes in this chapter provides contrasts with middle-class marriage and family relationships.
The lower and upper classes, though at the opposite ends of the
social class hierarchy, *share* certain values in regard to marriage and
the family that are not usually a part of the middle-class family's
values. Both lower and upper class lack, for example, the mobility
interests which are so common in the middle class. The lower class

---

[72]C. Wright Mills, *The Power Elite* (New York: Oxford University Press, 1956),
p. 69.
[73]Baltzell, *op. cit.,* p. 293.
[74]*Ibid.,* p. 293.
[75]*Ibid.,* p. 295.
[76]*Ibid.,* p. 293.
[77]Hollingshead and Redlich, *op. cit.,* p. 77.
[78]*Ibid.,* p. 77.

tends to see social mobility as beyond them; the upper class is already at the top.

The similarities, as well as the differences, between the lower and upper class should be kept in mind in the chapters that follow, in order to distinguish many areas in marriage and family relationships peculiar to the middle class. The differences to be shown between social-class levels do not indicate the superiority of any one set of class values over another, but rather that many of the values accepted as natural must be seen within the context of a particular socialization experience.

SELECTED BIBLIOGRAPHY

BALTZELL, E. DIGBY. *Philadelphia Gentlemen.* Glencoe, Illinois: The Free Press, 1958.

BLUMBERG, LEONARD, and BELL, ROBERT R. "Urban Migration and Kinship Ties," *Social Problems,* Spring, 1959, pp. 328-33.

BORDUA, DAVID J. "Delinquent Subculture: Sociological Interpretation of Gang Delinquency," *The Annals,* November, 1961, pp. 119-36.

COHEN, ALBERT K. and HODGES, JR., HAROLD M. "Characteristics of the Lower-Blue-Collar-Class," *Social Problems,* Spring, 1963, pp. 303-34.

HOLLINGSHEAD, AUGUST B. *Elmtown's Youth.* New York: John Wiley & Sons, Inc., 1949.

HOLLINGSHEAD, AUGUST B., and REDLICH, FREDERICK C. *Social Class and Mental Illness.* New York: John Wiley & Sons, Inc., 1958.

KAHL, JOSEPH A. *The American Class Structure.* New York: Rinehart & Co., Inc., 1957.

KOHN, MELVIN L. "Social Class and Exercise of Parental Authority," *American Sociological Review,* June, 1959, pp. 352-66.

KOMAROVSKY, MIRRA. *Blue-Collar Marriage.* New York: Random House, 1962.

MAYER, KURT B. *Class and Society.* New York: Doubleday & Co., Inc., 1955.

MILLER, WALTER B. "Lower Class Culture as a Generating Milieu of Gang Delinquency," in Wolfgang, Marvin E., Savitz, Leonard, and Johnson, Norman, *The Sociology of Crime and Delinquency,* pp. 267-76. New York: John Wiley & Sons, Inc., 1962.

OLSEN, MARVIN E. "Distribution of Family Responsibilities and Social Stratification," *Marriage and Family Living,* February, 1960, pp. 60-65.

RAINWATER, LEE. *And The Poor Get Children.* Chicago: Quadrangle Books, 1960.

ROSEN, LAURENCE, and BELL, ROBERT R. "Mate Selection in the Upper Class," *Sociological Quarterly,* Spring, 1966, pp. 157-66.

WARNER, LLOYD W.; MEEKER, MARCHIA; and EELLS, KENNETH. *Social Class in America.* New York: Harper Torchbooks, 1960.

WHYTE, WILLIAM F. "A Slum Sex Code," *American Journal of Sociology,* July, 1943, pp. 24-31.

PART II

Dating-Courtship

CHAPTER 4

THE DATING-COURTSHIP PROCESS

In contemporary American society it is expected that adolescent boys and girls will interact in a variety of social settings. The trend is for less segregation of the sexes, and often the relationships between boys and girls are approved and encouraged by middle-class adults. This is true for two reasons: (1) dating and some aspects of courtship are a part of the social and personal patterns of behavior associated with adolescent entertainment and recreation; (2) dating and courtship are ultimately related to the important business of selecting a marriage mate.

Dating and courtship may be thought of as a process made up of stages—with transitions from one stage to the next. For many individuals the process is through the stage of dating, to the stage of going steady, to the stage of engagement, to marriage. Each of the stages is dynamic for the individuals involved. For example, in going steady the relationship is altered as the two individuals develop their own common experiences. The relationship of two individuals starting to go steady is not the same as the relationship between them after having gone steady for a period of time. The stages do not necessarily mean the same thing for all people going through them or even for the individuals in any given pair. For some individuals, going steady may be a more serious commitment than it is for others.

Experience with at least some aspects of dating and courtship is common to almost all middle-class Americans. The experiences range from a single date with a person to the mutual exclusiveness and commitments of formal engagement. The discussion that follows moves from the primarily ego-centered stage of dating, through going steady, to the paired commitment stage of engagement. The emphasis in this chapter is on some patterns common to dating-courtship in the American middle class.

DATING
Emergence of Dating

In the past, in most cultures—including the American—the relationships between the unmarried boy and girl were carefully circumscribed. Traditionally, during adolescence, the period primarily associated with dating, social relationships between the sexes were limited. This was true for several reasons: (1) Sex roles were more clearly differentiated than they are today. As adulthood was approached the individual learned a sex role primarily related to his future adult role. This was usually taught to him by older members of his own sex. The young man was prepared for his future occupational role by his father or other male adults; the young woman was taught her future occupational role of wife-mother-housekeeper by her mother or other female adults. (2) There was less leisure time than today and, when it did exist, it was often pursued within one's sex group or within the family setting. (3) The selection of a marriage partner was not achieved through extended emotional interaction between two individuals, but was often arranged by parents or other adults in the society.

From such a system of limited premarital social interaction for young people, the American society developed a system at almost the opposite extreme. There are few other societies where the kind of adolescent-young adult cross-sex interaction has developed to the degree that it has in the United States. (There is, however, some evidence that the American system is beginning to influence that of other countries of the world.[1])

In most societies the needs of the individual were achieved as part of the overall needs of the family unit. When a young person reached the age of marriage the selection of a mate was primarily determined by factors important to the family and the values stressed were often economic. In contrast, today in the United States the needs of the individual are believed to be the crucial elements in mate selection. Whether the person will achieve happiness and need-satisfaction in the person they choose as a mate is often *the* crucial question. This change is in part due to the shift of the American family from a rural setting with extended patriarchal values to an urban one with conjugal democratic values. As the value stress moved from the family to the individual, a decrease in parental con-

---

[1]See David Mace and Vera Mace, *Marriage East and West* (Garden City, New York: Doubleday & Company, Inc., 1960).

trol was inevitable. The individual was increasingly oriented to make a marriage choice that would meet his own psychological needs, the assumption being that this would lead to greater personal happiness. Thus, the emphasis was placed on emotional factors of need-satisfaction rather than the more practical factors related to the broader needs of the family unit. This transition from parental control to individual decision-making in mate selection is not absolute, however, because the parents, in varying degrees, continue to influence their children.

Along with the shift away from family control over mate selection, an increasing amount of time spent in premarital social relationships also emerged. For the young adolescent, dating may have only an indirect relationship to future mate selection, but the relative privacy it affords is important because it contributes to the belief that mate selection is a private decision.

The increasing privacy of the paired relationship was influenced by the movement out of the home to satisfy leisure-time recreational needs. In the past, recreation centered around the family unit either in the home or in the family's participating together away from home. But commercial recreation has developed to such an extent that the amount of entertainment centered around the home is minimal for most young people. Furthermore, commercial recreation has developed around specialized appeals to specific age groups. Even when young people pursue recreation at home it often centers around friends of their own age and activities focused around their own age interests.

Another contributing factor, along with freedom from the parents, has been the increasing freedom of the American female. The stress on individuality in dating and courtship could not have been achieved if freedom had been given only to the male. As women acquired the right to enter more occupations, to extend their education, to attain greater legal equality with the male, and to have more freedom in social relationships, a demand for greater freedom in premarital activities also occurred. In many areas of life the female still has only second-class citizenship, but in dating and courtship she has achieved near equality with the male; she has basically the same rights as the male in seeking satisfaction from dating and in making the important decision of mate selection. This is not to say that the girl is no longer affected by special role requirements of being a female. The rights and obligations for the roles of male and female are different, but the opportunities to pursue sex roles of near equality in dating and courtship are available to both.

None of the influences of the past have completely disappeared, however. The parents still exert influence; the family unit is still viewed as having some importance; the female is not completely equal to the male; and, all leisure time is not spent completely beyond the influence of parents. The transition has not been complete, but the direction of change has been consistent—moving in the direction of individual need-satisfaction.

A *date* is an end in itself, with no further commitment. (In this discussion we will use "date" to refer to the event, the person one goes out with as the "person dated.") A date is viewed primarily as recreational and it lasts for a short period of time. When a boy picks up a girl at her home at eight o'clock on a Saturday night, their commitment to one another starts; it ends when he leaves her at her home at the end of the evening. Even if he makes another date with her for the following Saturday night, there is no commitment on either of their parts between the end of the first date and the start of the second. If there is a commitment (for example, an agreement not to go out with any other person), they are no longer dating but have moved into a new relationship. *Lack of commitment* is the crucial element in defining dating, whether it be the first or the tenth time the two individuals have gone out together.

Some Functions of Dating

Through the process of dating, certain functions are performed for society as well as for the individual. Dating serves recreational ends while at the same time providing the means through which a mutual commitment to marriage may arise. Whether or not it is the most effective means for both goals, it is the procedure followed by most Americans. A discussion of some main functions of dating in the United States follows.

Learning of Sex Roles. For the first three or four years of life, generally not much attention is directed at sex differences among children. A young boy is just as apt to choose a little girl as a best friend as to choose another boy. However, from age four to eight a sharp awareness of the sex differences between the boy and the girl usually develops. This age period may be seen as one of strong sex identification, particularly on the part of the boy. Then, from the ages of ten to twelve, there is usually a tentative movement back in the direction of the opposite sex. From this point on the stress in the middle class is increasingly on the paired nature of sex roles in a vast variety of social activities.

From the initial tentative movements of interest in the opposite sex on through adolescence, the facility for filling one's sex role and relating it to the opposite sex generally improves. Initially the contacts are awkward and the youngsters are often unsure of how to interact. For example, the preadolescent boy may treat a girl in about the same way he treats a boy of the same age. He may punch her on the arm or throw snowballs at her. While his behavior may seem inappropriate, it does represent a change from when he was a year or two younger and simply ignored girls. For the preadolescent girl, the relationship may not be quite as awkward because she has probably not rejected boys to the same extent. She can also focus her interest on a boy a year or two older than herself, one who has started to move out of the fumbling, awkward stage of the exclusive male world.

Many times the initial adolescent social relationships with the opposite sex are made a little easier through group dating. In this situation the youngsters support and fortify one another in the new and tenuous dating relationship, but as some degree of sophistication and confidence is achieved the tendency is to move in the direction of the paired relationship.

From the hit-or-miss, trial-and-error initial relationships, important role learning takes place. An increasing awareness of the self as a boy or girl emerges and the significance of the role played by the individual is greatly determined by the related role played by an age peer of the opposite sex. That is, one important aspect of adolescence is dating—and dating means a pair-relationship. This is the start of a relationship that most individuals will participate in for the rest of their lives—the close role-relationship to a member of the opposite sex. Role learning also provides an opportunity to develop one's personality, and to see more clearly some of the facets of role playing in relationship to a "significant other." Dating provides an understanding of self-role and significant-other role that is basic for socialization to adult roles. The adolescent through dating is extending his world of "significant others" and having his attitudes and behavior shaped by their influence.

Pleasure and Recreation. When adolescents go out on a date, it is usually to engage in behavior of a pleasurable nature. It should be remembered that in most cases adolescents decide what they are going to do on a date. So, within limits, they will choose doing what they find enjoyable. In this sense dating is quite different from more serious relationships, because in dating the realities of life can often be ignored. This may explain why many older people look back with nostalgia to their dating days—days of relative irresponsibility. Pleasure is also involved in the satisfaction achieved by the girl in being chosen for a date and for the boy in being accepted. Success in dating also implies success in the peer-group value system.

For many adolescents the actual time spent on dates may be only a few hours a week, but its influence on their interest may take up many hours of the week. There may be daydreaming and anticipation about the date already arranged and time consuming recollections of the date after it has occurred. Because middle-class adolescents tend to be highly vocal about their dating interests, they do not have to restrict their thinking to themselves. They have friends more than willing to discuss dates, both past and present, their own and the friends'.

Prestige. Related to the recreational function of dating is that of receiving prestige. To be successful in dating is to meet the standards of the peer group. For many youngsters it is not just meeting the standards, but also of competing with one another. Sometimes prestige is achieved by the sheer frequency of dating different individuals. This may be seen as popularity of a quantitative dimension. There may also be a qualitative dimension where prestige is determined not by numbers but by the prestige of the individuals dated. One person may have far fewer dates than another but be given higher prestige by the peer group. In high school, a date with captain of the football team may be worth five dates with boys having no particular prestige qualities.

The prestige element in dating is not limited to the young adolescent. A number of dating studies of college students have been made since the classic dating-rating study of Waller, and one such study indicates that prestige is not limited just to *dating* for college students, but is found at all stages of the courtship process.[2] While the prestige stressed varies in different types of colleges, there seems little question that it is an important factor. For college students, it may be related to desirable values in a future marriage partner. In the writer's university, coeds place much higher prestige on dating young men from the professional schools than those from the undergraduate schools. This is not simply a question of age differences between the two possible dating groups; it is attributable to the higher prestige of the male continuing his education beyond the undergraduate degree. (However, this is not true of all graduate training—for example, there is much less prestige in dating a young man going into academic than there is in dating a young man training for the highest prestige profession, medicine.)

---

[2]Everett M. Rogers and Eugene A. Havens, "Prestige Rating and Mate Selection on a College Campus," *Marriage and Family Living,* February, 1960, p. 59.

Mate Selection. That dating during the younger years has, at the least, an indirect relationship to future mate selection is important enough to restate. As the individual enters late adolescence and the early adult years, dating becomes more directly related to mate selection. With time, dating provides the opportunity for developing an awareness of one's own needs and how they are related to the needs of others. Even the blind date that turns out to be a complete flop may have some value as a learning experience, indicating as it does the lack of desire for a relationship to develop between the two indivduals.

As dating occurs for the older person, it becomes increasingly important. In American society almost the only way to reach the more commited stages of courtship leading to marriage is through the initial experience of the date. The individual realizes that to go beyond dating he must continue to date until he finds a person to move on with to succeeding stages. College students, particularly upperclassmen, increase the number of dates they have with different individuals. As marriage becomes more important, college students are inclined to spend less time checking out one individual by dating them a number of times. Rather, they tend to make faster assessments and move on to the next individual. This may be most true of an older coed feeling the pressure of being at the age of marriage and soon about to leave the large college market of potential marriage mates. The writer found that female seniors in college had on the average two more dates per month than did coeds in the three lower classes.[3] While pleasure continues to be important in dating for the older girl, it tends to become secondary to mate selection.

Ultimately the proof of dating success lies in whether the individual feels it has been adequate for finding the kind of mate he wanted. While the opportunities for dating vary greatly for different groups of individuals, it seems to be successful for the majority. However, the high marriage rates of Americans should not be taken as complete evidence that the dating system provides sufficient contacts. It would seem adequate in at least providing the opportunities to find a person to marry, but we have no way of knowing whether the person chosen was a limited, "forced" choice or a "free" choice selected from a large market. This is a hypothetical point because even the person who has dated many different individuals might have selected someone else if they had dated a few more. It may be

---

[3]Robert R. Bell, "Some Dating Characteristics of Students in a Large Urban University," unpublished.

suggested that the fewer individuals dated, the greater the probability of "forced" choice in mate selection.

There is some evidence that the dating process is believed to be successful for college girls. In a study of 235 unmarried coeds asked to make an assessment of their dating experience, it was found that 52 percent had about as many dates as they wanted; 30 percent sometimes wished they had more dates; 15 percent often felt they had not had enough dates; 3 percent said they rarely had enough dates.[4]

Some Elements of Dating

The previous discussion centered around the functions or purposes of dating. In this section we will discuss some of the elements that shape dating behavior in the American middle class.

Role of the Parents. We have suggested that over the years the influence of parents upon the premarital behavior of young people has decreased. Yet, parents maintain a strong interest in the dating of their youngsters and continue to influence them both directly and indirectly. Parents are interested because of their emotional involvement with their children and their desire for them to be successful as adolescents and adults. Parents know that a part of success centers around their children's ability to date. However, parents realize that the values of dating they believe to be important are not necessarily the ones their children accept and they sometimes find their own values about dating in conflict with the peer-group values accepted by their children.

Parents can exert various kinds of influences on dating. They can set the time and frequency. They can often give or withhold the financial assistance important for successful dating— children's allowances, buying of the clothes they want, providing an automobile, and so on. Most parents probably do not use this kind of direct control over dating if they can avoid it. Even if this kind of control is used, it becomes less effective as the young person grows older and has the means of achieving his own financial base for dating.

A more important parental influence on dating, as well as on eventual mate selection, is indirect. The parents have reared the child and have had the opportunity of instilling in him certain values they as parents feel are important. When their child reaches dating age his selection of a person to date and his behavior during

---

[4]Robert R. Bell, "Some Factors Related to Coed Marital Aspirations," *The Family Life Coordinator*, October, 1962, p. 42.

the date will be a reflection of the values his parents have passed on to him. Yet, the ultimate effectiveness of the parents' training will be to a great degree influenced by the values of the peer group.

Peer Group. The age-peers the adolescent associates with quite often constitute his most important reference group. His identification with the peer group makes him highly susceptible to their reward and punishment system. In many situations the values of the family and of the peer group are in essential agreement and tend to reinforce one another, thereby minimizing the possibility of conflict between the youngster and his parents. However, in other cases values may differ significantly and the youngster may find himself in a position of role conflict. In order to satisfy his role expectations as a son, he may not, at the same time, be able to meet the role expectations of his peer group. And if he chooses the expectations of his peer group, he is not able to meet the expectations held by his parents. Many times the youngster evades a role conflict by keeping his role in the peer group separate from his role of son and not allowing his parent's to see his different behavior in the peer group. While this happens in many areas, it is of particular relevance in dating behavior. Many youngsters allow their parents to believe the parents' role definition is accepted, but in actuality they perform according to peer-group definitions. As a consequence, many aspects of dating behavior are determined by the peer group—individuals to be dated, where to go and what to do on a date, degrees of intimacy, and styles of dress. Dating behavior in the peer group context is very important to the adolescent because it is often symbolic of adult behavior and therefore provides one of the initial footholds in the climb to adult status.

Exploitation. One other element important to dating is the possibility of exploitation. Dating is ego-centered, rather than pair-centered, and the individual has a minimum of responsibilty to the person dated. For many individuals the selection of the person to go out with is determined by an estimate of what the person dated can contribute to his need-gratification. This may center around prestige, or it may be more psychologically oriented in the direction of ego-fulfillment.

Whatever factor is uppermost, the individual tends to ignore the needs of the person dated. Oftentimes this leads to exploitation; but the exploitation is not always one way. Frequently the two on a date will contest which one is going to exploit the other. This is of course well illustrated in the area of sexual behavior. The boy may try to enhance his self-esteem as a male by pushing the sexual relationship as far as possible. The girl, on the other hand, may be less interested in the sexual aspect and more interested in getting an emotional commitment from the boy which can provide her with control over the situation and enhance her self-esteem as a love object. Because the two sets of needs are often incompatible, exploitation frequently *results* if one scores a decisive victory.

One factor that may influence possible exploitation results from the feelings of the individuals toward the other at the end of their first date. During adolescence girls may be more involved than boys at the end of a first date, but as girls move in to the early adult years they may become more critical of their dates than do boys. Older girls are more marriage-oriented and therefore less inclined to want to spend their time in casual dating. Coombs and Kinkle found that after a first dating situation men "were more prone to be satisfied with her personality, physical appearance, and popularity standing and to think it possible to be happily married to such a person."[5] By contrast, the women were more critical and rejecting of the men dated. They would therefore, with less commitment, appear to be less prone to exploitation than the men.

Whatever the specific situation may be, exploitation is always of potential significance in dating because of the lack of commitment to the other person. This is not to say that all dating is a constant and conscious struggle for personal gain. The struggle may not emerge unless there is some significant need difference between the two individuals; when there is, the wants of the individual usually take precedence because the individual cares directly about himself and often only indirectly about the other.

Ability to Date

Given the importance of dating as both a recreational end and as a means of eventual mate selection, the opportunities and abilities for dating take on great significance. Because dating ability varies a great deal among young people, it is necessary to look at some of the factors which affect success in dating.

Age. The phenomena of dating had hardly began to be common to college students in the 1920's when it slowly began to reach down into younger age groups. Burchinal suggests that it was during the late 1930's and the 1940's that dating moved to the high-school

---

[5]Robert H. Coombs and William F. Kenkel, "Sex Differences in Dating Aspirations and Satisfaction With Computer-Selected Partners," *Journal of Marriage and Family*, February, 1966, p. 66.

level.[6] Several studies provide information as to the age at which young people start dating. A study done in the 1940's found that during "the thirteenth year, 20 percent of the girls and 15 percent of the boys had their first date."[7] Another study carried out in the late 1950's found the mean age of the first date for 250 college girls and 160 college boys was 13.3 and 14.1 years, respectively.[8] A recent study of adolescents found that they started dating at young ages with "45 percent of the boys and 36 percent of the girls saying they began dating in the fifth grade or at ages ten and eleven."[9] The available evidence indicates that over the last few decades the trend has been to start dating at younger and younger ages.

The evidence also suggests that girls start dating at slightly younger ages than boys. This is due to the age differential of the male-female relationship that shows itself even at very young ages. We also know that romantic interests appear at younger ages for girls than for boys. In a recent study of youngsters in the age range 10 to 13 it was found that "girls were far more romantically oriented than boys although they were at about the same level in terms of actual heterosexual interaction.[10]

Many of the dates of the young adolescent are probably lacking in the privacy and emotional involvement that goes with somewhat older-age dating. The early period may represent an initial transition to an emotional commitment to a member of the opposite sex that will not reach a high degree of involvement until later in adolescence. "It is significant that children under sixteen seldom name another boy or girl as the one they love best. Their attachments to their parents are still the strongest of all."[11]

There is also evidence that starting to date at younger ages than their age peers may have some implications for girls in their future dating, courtship and marriage behavior. Burchinal found "that girls who married while still in high school had begun dating earlier, dated more frequently, dated more boys, had gone steady

[6]Lee G. Burchinal, "The Premarital Dyad and Love Involvement," in Harold T. Christensen (Ed.), *Handbook of Marriage and The Family* (Chicago: Rand McNally & Co., 1964), p. 624.
[7]Ernest W. Burgess and Paul Wallin, *Engagement and Marriage* (Philadelphia: J. B. Lippincott Co., 1953), p. 106.
[8]Robert R. Bell and Leonard Blumberg, "Courtship Intimacy and Religious Background," *Marriage and Family Living*, November, 1959, p. 357.
[9]Carlfred B. Broderick and Stanley E. Fowler, "New Patterns of Relationships Between the Sexes Among Preadolescents," *Marriage and Family Living*, February, 1961, p. 28.
[10]Carlfred B. Broderick, "Social Heterosexual Development Among Urban Negroes and Whites," *Journal of Marriage and Family*, May, 1965, p. 203.
[11]Burgess and Wallin, *op. cit.*, p. 113.

earlier, and felt that they had been in love with a greater number of boys than [had] a control group of girls."[12] Lowrie, in a recent study, found "no significant relationship between the age at which brides had their first dates and premarital pregnancy."[13]

Frequency. Not only do girls start dating at a younger age than boys, but when age is held constant they have dated more frequently and more different individuals.[14] The writer found the estimated number of different individuals dated by college women and men with a mean age of 20 years was 53 and 43, respectively. In a study in which respondents kept records over a 28-day period, the average girl went out on dates seven times and the boy five times. During the same period the number of different individuals dated was 3.3 for the girls and 2.5 for the boys.[15] These figures indicate that for many college students the frequency of dating is high.

Because the getting of dates is a problem to be solved by the young person, certain institutionalized procedures have developed. The young person is highly dependent on the peer group for the getting of dates and tends to get dates within the peer-group system, either through personal contacts or through peer-group friends. Table 4-1 shows that—in one study—the getting of dates through a

TABLE 4–1
HOW A COLLEGE SAMPLE MET DATES (PERCENT), BY SEX*

	Male	Female
Blind date	28	35
Through friend	15	19
At college	16	15
Party or dance	16	12
In high school	10	6
Other sources	15	13
	100	100

*Bell, Robert R., "Some Dating Characteristics in a Large Urban University," unpublished.

friend or through a "blind date" accounted for 43 percent of the college boys' and 54 percent of the college girls' dates. It is of interest to note that the help of the family in arranging dates was found to be numerically insignificant. With friends so important in arranging dates, the peer group can exert strong control over dating behavior. Thus, the peer group not only contributes a great

---

[12]Burchinal, *op. cit.,* p. 630.
[13]Samuel H. Lowrie, "Early Marriage: Premarital Pregnancy and Associated Factors," *Journal of Marriage and Family,* February, 1965, p. 52.
[14]Bell, "Some Dating Characteristics of Students in a Large Urban University."
[15]*Ibid.*

deal to the desire for dating and provides the "contacts" that influence who is dated, but it also affects dating patterns.

The sex-role patterns for the attainment of dates is generally clearly defined. With few exceptions the girl is expected to wait until she is asked by the boy. This places different ego demands on the two sexes. The choice rests with the boy as to whether the initial step will occur. The girl can not usually initiate directly the request for a date, although there are methods of letting the boy know she is interested in going out with him. The girl must usually wait for the phone call—that may or may not come. She does have some advantage in the contest of relative commitment, however, because the boy shows his interest in her by asking for the date. This initial one-way commitment of interest makes it difficult for some boys to ask for a date because of the possibility of being rejected. This may in part explain the popularity of the "blind" date where both individuals start with an equal *non*commitment. It might be speculated that boys sensitive to the ego-commitment of asking for a date would be most satisfied with "blind" dates and girls most desiring ego-commitments by the boy least satisfied with "blind" dates.

Dating Problems. We have suggested that a crucial dating problem centers around the ability and opportunity to date. As a person grows older, and nears the age of mate selection, dating becomes increasingly important. Studies agree that age is the most important variable influencing the frequency of dating, with frequency of dating increasing with increased age.[16]

Given the great importance of dating, both as an end in itself and as the means for entering the courtship process, one potentially important problem centers around the individual's ability to enter and participate in dating. It seems clear that a strong majority of middle-class young people initially begin dating while in high school. Yet Reiss has estimated that for the high-school age group about one third of the boys and one fifth of the girls are *not* involved in dating.[17] Even those who are dating may be dissatisfied with the frequency of their dating or with the individuals they are able to date. One study of high-school students found that one fourth of the males and one third of the females felt that they were failures in dating and courtship.[18] With reference to making the

---

[16]Burchinal, *op. cit.*, p. 629.

[17]Ira L. Reiss, "Sexual Codes in Teen Age Culture," *The Annals*, November, 1961, p. 60.

[18]M. J. Williams, "Personal and Social Problems of High School Youth and Their Bearing Upon Family Education Needs," *Social Forces*, 27, 1949, p. 280.

acquaintance of members of the opposite sex in early adolescence, another study reported 11 percent of the males and 14 percent of the females stated "difficulty" and the rest stated "some difficulty."[19]

Studies indicate that the problems of dating become less severe for the young adult in college. Kirkpatrick and Caplow found that only 6 per cent of the men they studied reported no dating, with the corresponding figure for the women at 3 percent. This and other studies would indicate that at least some dating is found for the vast majority of college students. The findings indicate that 65 percent of the males and 59 percent of the females in college felt the opportunities to meet members of the opposite sex had been adequate.[20]

It is possible that a new problem is emerging in middle-class dating related to different levels of significance attached to dating by boys and girls. It may be that middle-class boys are increasingly beginning to identify at younger ages with their future adult role of occupation, especially as this hinges upon their educational preparation. This is suggested by Henry in his finding that twice as many girls as boys worry about dates and twice as many boys as girls worry about their studies and their careers. Thus, during late adolescence "boys ruminate about their place in society and girls ruminate about boys."[21] Therefore, the dating which is highly important to the girl has much less significance for the boy and this difference may increasingly represent an area of potential conflict.

Problems related to the ability to date have both personal and social implications for the individual. Burgess and Wallin point out that "the evidence from personality tests given to college youths shows that those who do not date are disposed to be socially retiring but with only a slight tendency toward emotional maladjustment. Evidently the majority have found more or less satisfactory compensation for their lack of association with the other sex."[22] Inability to date or inadequacy of dating may have more serious consequences for the individual as he nears the age of marriage. As mentioned, limitations on the individual often have the ultimate effect of narrowing the market of mate selection. Some may have to make a "forced" choice because, when marriage becomes of increasing importance, the desire to find a mate intensifies. This may mean that

[19]Clifford Kirkpatrick and Theodore Caplow, "Courtship in a Group of Minnesota Students," *American Journal of Sociology*, September, 1945, p. 116.
[20]*Ibid.*, p. 114.
[21]Jules Henry, *Culture Against Man* (New York: Random House, 1963), p. 169.
[22]Burgess and Wallin, *op. cit.*, p. 125.

a particular choice might not have been made if more dating opportunities had been available. The choice may be determined by a strong desire to marry rather than through the impact of a specific individual.

The nature of the college world generally provides students with extended opportunities for meeting a variety of different individuals for dating. However, this is not always true for the many individuals of the same age who are not in college. Since very few approved agencies exist in the United States through which young people can meet, they are often left to their own devices, which may be inadequate. The person with limited dating contacts may suffer severe frustration. For some, so few dates may come along that any person who seems reasonably satisfactory will continue to be dated. While dating is a basic requirement for mate selection, the social opportunities out of college for meeting a variety of potential mates are often inadequate.

Although dating patterns in contemporary middle-class America present many problems as related to the overall courtship process, they are still functionally related to our present marriage system. Furthermore, the major values of dating and courtship have remained relatively consistent over the past few decades. Burchinal argues that changes "that have occurred over the long run have strengthened those aspects of the dating and courtship system which should contribute to increased competency in marriage. Modern youth, it seems, acquire more experience in heterosexual association before engagement and marriage than was true for youth several generations ago."[23]

GOING STEADY

Almost all Americans eventually make the move from the non-committed and ego-centered relationship of dating into a premarital relationship of some commitment to another person. This may be either through going steady or engagement. Going steady may be defined as an agreement between two people that they will not date any other individual. In our discussion of going steady a distinction will be made between the older and the younger age groups. The older refers to late adolescence and the early adult years and the younger to under 16 or 17 years of age.

Older. Going steady for individuals entering and in the marriage-

---

[23]Burchinal, *op. cit.,* p. 635.

able ages has been a part of the American dating-courtship system for some time. Generally, if the relationship lasts over a period of time, it will move into the greater commitment of engagement or marriage.

During adolescence there is often a great deal of pleasure in the adventurous qualities of dating—that is, the sense of excitement associated with the anticipation of each new date. But with increasing age the sense of adventure with regard to random dating decreases. Burchinal found that "students gradually become disenchanted with the competitive dating world of the first several years of college and replaced this 'whirl' with more individualized pair activities."[24]

Studies of going steady for college students give some evidence as to the age and frequency of going steady among the older group. One study of college students with an average age of 19 years showed that 68 percent of the females and 72 percent of the males had gone steady at least once.[25] Another study of a similar age group found 69 percent of its respondents had gone steady.[26] In the former study, of those college students who had gone steady the males had gone steady 2.2 times, the females 1.6 times.[27] In the latter study, where no distinction was made by sex, 45 percent of the respondents had gone steady one or two times and 24 percent three or more times.[28]

In the Bell and Blumberg study, of those who had gone steady, the average age of first going steady was 17 years for the females and 17.2 for the males.[29] In the Burgess and Wallin study, of those who had gone steady, 67 percent of the males and 87 percent of the females had gone steady for the first time before they were 18 years of age.[30] The two studies indicate that by the time the young person has reached college age he has had, in the majority of cases, at least one experience with going steady.

Younger. Going steady in the lower age groups is probably an American phenomenon which has developed since the end of World War II. For the younger groups, going steady has only a limited and indirect relationship to marriage. The middle-class 16-year-old going steady does not usually perceive the relationship as one that will move into marriage in the near future. In one study of high-school students, two types of going steady were distinguished. "One was

[24]*Ibid.*, p. 634.
[25]Bell and Blumberg, *op. cit.*, p. 358.
[26]Burgess and Wallin, *op. cit.*, p. 127.
[27]Bell and Blumberg, *op. cit.*, p. 358.
[28]Burgess and Wallin, *op. cit.*, p. 127.
[29]Bell and Blumberg, *op. cit.*, p. 358.
[30]Burgess and Wallin, *op. cit.*, p. 127.

marriage-oriented, and the dating of students with this view represented courtship. The other type implied no thought of marriage and represented a relationship maintained for recreation, fun, education, or other reasons."[31] The frequency of going steady in the younger ages is difficult to estimate. The Burgess and Wallin data show that of those who had gone steady, 30 percent of the boys and 46 percent of the girls had gone steady before they were 16 years of age.[32] In the middle class, going steady is probably an experience for at least half before they reach 17.

We defined going steady as an agreement between two people that they will not date any other individual. For young adolescents this agreement may sometimes be given little more than lip service. Henry found that among the younger adolescents there were differences in the commitment of boys and girls to the general norms of going steady. He found that if, while going steady, a girl "makes eyes at another boy in her steady's group, both boys will drop her. Within the girls' group, however, a steady is not taboo, and a girl's readiness to steal the best friend's steady fits the predatory interpersonal pattern of girls' culture."[33]

The discussion that follows focuses on some of the reasons for and problems related to going steady in the younger age groups. Special notice is given the younger age groups because early going steady seems to be the most significant recent development in the dating-courtship process. The younger age groups have taken over a behavioral relationship from the older groups and emerged with a relationship that is in some ways quite different.

Some Reasons for Going Steady

The increase in going steady for the younger adolescent has many causes, and the following sections will suggest some of the pressures that are being exerted. It should, however, be recognized that adolescent behavior varies in different parts of the United States and by social class. The suggestions made here are for the urban middle-class youngster.

Security. Sociological literature is full of empirical material illustrating the modern American stress on security. In the adult world, particularly since the depression of the 1930's strong emphasis has been placed on the achievement of psychological, social, and

---

[31]R. D. Herman, "The Going Steady Complex: A Re-Examination," *Marriage and Family Living*, 17, 1955, p. 38.

[32]Burgess and Wallin, *op. cit.*, p. 120.

[33]Henry, *op. cit.*, pp. 154–55.

economic security. The values of the adult world permeate the adolescent world and may be taken up in totality or with various modifications.

For many youngsters, going steady provides a form of security. In the discussion on dating, some insecurity aspects for the individuals who must compete in getting dates in sufficient number and adequate prestige were suggested. The young person going steady is assured of a date for "important" occasions and does not have to compete openly, with the consequent possibility of being rejected or of not being asked.

A concern with security in the boy-girl relationship seems to have emerged since World War II. In the period between the two World Wars, dating popularity was based on having as many different partners as possible. Ehrmann points out that that popularity trend "was manifested even at dances with the stag lines and the custom of 'breaking in,' whereby success and failure were measured by the frequency of changes of partners during a single dance and in the course of an evening."[34] The values of dating competitiveness are different from the values of going steady frequently found today. Henry argues that for American boys and girls today the "steady" is the answer "to the instability, emptiness, and anxiety inherent in other types of boy-girl relationships, and becoming 'steadies' sometimes gives the boy-girl relationship solemnity, dignity, and meaning."[35] Yet, the security provided by going steady may in the long run be dysfunctional because it removes the adolescent from learning experiences easier assimilated during adolescence than during adulthood.

The increase in going steady may also be related to the rise in the status of the female. With dating often having highly exploitive qualities, the girl may feel less inclined than in the past to stay with noncommitted dating and instead to seek out the more emotionally satisfying relationship of going steady. If other dating opportunities are available, she realizes that at any time she may break a relationship that does not meet all her needs and can move on until she finds one that does.

Insecurity. The possibility of insecurity resulting from going steady can occur in several ways. First, the adolescent is in a transitional role between that of child and adult. He often places great

---

[34]Winston Ehrmann, "Marital and Nonmarital Sexual Behavior," in Harold T. Christensen (ed.), *Handbook of Marriage and The Family* (Chicago: Rand McNally & Co., 1964), p. 594.

[35]Henry, *op. cit.,* p. 154.

importance on the peer group and gains acceptance by living up to its norms and values; therefore, he is anxious to do what will make him acceptable. If the values of the peer group stress going steady, going steady becomes important in gaining group acceptance. A premium is placed on the ability of the individual to meet the expectations of the peer group; inability to do so may lead to individual frustration.

Second, the transitional nature of adolescence may have an influence in another way. Many times the adolescent is anxiously striving for adult status, and this striving intensifies the importance of what he defines as the symbols of adulthood. Going steady may appeal to many adolescents because it implies an adult relationship and achievement of some adult status. Very often, adults fail to recognize the great significance of adult symbols for the adolescent. Adults simply do not see the role insecurity of the adolescent resulting from being neither an adult nor a child and not having a well-defined adolescent role.

There is also some evidence that going steady contributes to the adolescent's emancipation from his parents. Going steady provides a highly important "significant other" and often serves to shift away from the parents some of the adolescent's emotional commitment and involvement. One study found that serious dating was more significant for males than for females in their emancipation from parents.[36]

While we have been primarily interested in the increase of going steady among adolescents, it should also be pointed out that there may be a counter-trend away from the interpersonal commitments of going steady. A recent study by *Newsweek* of a nationwide sample of 775 teenage boys and girls reveals that "now the going is 'steadily' because socially mobile teen-agers are wary of entangling alliances and increasingly convinced that a relationship depends on what emotions its partners invest in it, not on what term they agree to call it."[37] Going "steadily" is a compromise between the low interpersonal commitment of random dating and the high emotional involvement of going "steady."

Parent's Influence. Many parents have strong objections to youngsters going steady. But many times they find themselves almost powerless to do anything about it because they are in opposition to

[36]Charles W. Hobart, "Emancipation From Parents and Courtship In Adolescence," *Pacific Sociological Review*, 6, 1958, pp. 25–29.

[37]*Newsweek*, "The Teenagers," March 21, 1966, p. 60.

the adolescent reference group. Parents then find themselves in a dilemma. They want their children to be successful and popular but this may mean the youngster feels he must go steady or be unpopular. So the parents may accept what they feel to be the lesser of the two evils—going steady.

Research on the relationship of the young person going steady to his parents would be valuable. Many adolescents may seek an emotional satisfaction through going steady that they do not have with their parents. Almost all human beings at all ages need to be significant to some "other." If the young person feels that he is not significant to his parents, the emotional relationship of going steady may be felt to meet this need.

Problems of Youthful Going Steady

It is difficult to make a positive case for going steady during early adolescence. A discussion of some of the problems should illustrate why this is so. To begin with, a psychological examination of those who go steady would probably find some basic personality problems for at least some of the individuals. Nimkoff and Wood found that young adolescents who started going steady at an early age against their parents' desires and had four or more steadies tended to be socially aggressive and emotionally maladjusted.[38] Going steady excessively may in some cases be symptomatic of important personality problems.

Limited Dating Experience. The longer an adolescent spends in going steady, the less time he has to date different individuals. The young person going steady is not acquiring a variety of experiences with different individuals. If we assume that a variety of dating experiences allow the adolescent to learn more about himself and how his needs are related to others, then frequent going steady limits the variety of experiences important to mate selection.

It might be argued that instead of having superficial experiences with a variety of different individuals he will have had extensive experience with a few, and this will enable him to have interpersonal experience in greater depth. However, it may well be that it is more valuable to learn something about a broader variety of personalities before moving into a depth relationship with one person. Early emotional relationship may be moving the young

---

[38]Meyer F. Nimkoff and Arthur L. Wood, "Courtship and Personality," *American Journal of Sociology,* January, 1948, p. 269.

person into an intense involvement before he is familiar with the variety and choices of possible relationships.

In the American society, where ultimate mate selection rests primarily in the hands of the young person, any social mechanism that restricts the opportunity for the best preparation possible may contribute to later problems. Therefore, extended dating with a variety of different individuals is generally needed if the system of mate selection is to function most efficiently.

Making Adult Decisions. The adolescent is in the process of reaching adult status. Generally, the younger the adolescent, the less apt he is to be an adult physically, psychologically, and socially. While some older adolescents are coming close to adequate fulfillment of adult roles, the younger adolescents are not. And going steady often places the younger adolescents in a role position that in many ways has adult dimensions.

The young adolescent may be required to make adult decisions about the closeness of a relationship that he is not as yet equipped to make. The area of sexual behavior provides probably the most vivid illustration. The young adolescent is physically capable of indulging in adult sexual behavior, but not necessarily psychologically or socially mature enough to make an adult decision about a sexual relationship. A person of 15 is about as sexually capable as he will be at 20, but he is not socially ready to make decisions that he should be adult enough to make at age 20. Thus, going steady may force adult decision-making on the individual before he is ready.

Premature adult decision-making can also be a problem in other areas of the going-steady relationship. The nature and the degree of the emotional commitment, for example. Many of the feelings that develop are adult in nature but unadult in their application. The young person may behave irrationally because he has not developed the ability and lacks the experience necessary to function in a fashion defined as socially mature.

Many of these criticisms of social immaturity may also be directed at the older adolescent or even the adult; however, it seems logical that the younger the age, the greater the probability of immaturity. Therein lies what is probably the most crucial problem of youthful going steady.

Going steady a number of times at various ages may have significance for future adult behavior. Since going steady is generally not a permanent commitment and often involves a series of "steadies," the individual must learn to get over the "old" and move into the "new" relationships. From such learning may emerge an awareness that one may be in love a number of times. The phenomenon of going steady a number of times may also help socialize the individual to the possibility of future divorce and remarriage.

ENGAGEMENT

The final stage in the process of dating and courtship for a majority of middle-class Americans is engagement. When compared with going steady, engagement is a more serious paired commitment. It has the explicit end of moving into marriage, and may be viewed as the most exclusive pair commitment outside of marriage in the United States. But, when compared with marriage, engagement does not carry the same rights and obligations.

Engagement is a social ritual developed and utilized by almost all societies. Waller and Hill have pointed out that the common usage of engagement by societies is due to at least two common human needs: the need for facilitating the transition from the adolescent to the adult status of marriage and parenthood—the transfer from single irresponsibility to married responsibility; and, because the transition is important, the need for socially developed group sanctions related to the roles that go along with the assumption of mature adult responsibility.[39] Therefore, engagement is important both to the individuals involved and to the society.

Engagement Characteristics

Engagement is highly developed in the American middle class and is felt to be a necessary prelude to marriage. With the lowering of age at marriage for Americans and the increased number going on to college, both engagement and marriage are now common occurrences for college students. One study of college students found that the average age of first engagement was 19.1 years for females and 21.7 years for males.[40] The findings of the Burgess and Wallin study indicate that engagement for college students occurs after a fairly long acquaintanceship. In the study's group of unbroken engagements, 66.6 percent of the individuals had an acquaintance of 18 months or more prior to their engagement.[41] The Landis findings,

---

[39]Willard Waller and Reuben Hill, *The Family* (New York: The Dryden Press, 1951), p. 143.
[40]Bell and Blumberg, *op. cit.*, p. 359.
[41]Burgess and Wallin, *op. cit.*, p. 286.

that the time from first date to engagement was one year or more for 47 percent of their respondents, are in essential agreement.[42]

The Burgess and Wallin study also shows that among engaged couples a stronger interest when "first aware" of the other was shown by the male. First interest when they were strangers was stated by 46.2 percent of the males and 33.8 percent of the females. The rest of the males and females stated first interest when they were either acquaintances or friends.[43] These findings indicate that initial physical attraction, even in a relationship leading to engagement, is common, and particularly for the male.

Symbols of the Engagement. Two symbols of engagement with a long historical heritage are still found in the American middle-class: the engagement announcement and the engagement ring. Historically, the function of the announcement is to inform the community that the couple are to be married. The announcement is made because marriage of individual members is of importance to society. But as the American culture developed in size and complexity, the announcement lost its importance as a statement of marriage intent to a responsive community, and probably its most important aspect today is the prestige it may give to the individuals involved. Such prestige may be secured through the engagement party to which friends and relatives are invited and at which the engagement is announced, or through an announcement carried in local newspapers. Society-page editors usually determine the amount of space given to an engagement announcement on the basis of the news value it is assumed to have. A girl coming from a prominent family will be given more space for both story and picture than a girl coming from a less socially important family. This stress on prestige aspects is also shown by the information presented in the engagement story. The social prominence of either set of parents, as well as membership in organizations and the schools attended by the engaged pair, will be mentioned. Very often a chief concern of the engaged couple and their families is the amount of space given the announcement.

The ring is a symbol for all who care to observe that the girl is "chosen," and in many cases the ring is also a prestige symbol. The engagement ring is generally a diamond and often the belief is, the bigger the better. The size (cost) of the diamond indicates that the

---

[42]Judson T. Landis and Mary G. Landis, *Building A Successful Marriage* (New York: Prentice-Hall, Inc., 1953), p. 178.

[43]Burgess and Wallin, *op. cit.*, p. 160.

girl has not only been successful in being chosen, but that she has been successful in being chosen by an affluent male. The cost of diamonds seems to be an area of knowledge common to most young women.

Many times the cost of the ring may mean an expenditure of money the couple might better have used in other ways. But many girls may not really feel engaged unless they have a ring, and the need for one is often supported by friends and relatives. Sometimes when the boy does not have enough money for an appropriate ring, his family will buy it for him. They want to see the fiancée with an acceptable ring because an unacceptable one casts a poor reflection on their son and on themselves. Although the engagement ring actually has little or no functional value, in a society characterized by prestige symbols, it will probably retain its importance.

The Importance of the Female. For a large number of American women, the period of highest personal prestige is during engagement, reaching its peak on the wedding day. The engaged girl in the United States is often a symbol of happiness and beauty. (Not long after she marries, her personal glamor leaves her and she enters the unromantic ranks of married women.) While engagement is a period of high prestige for the girl, it is not equally prestigeful for the male. The girl has the symbol of engagement—the ring. There is no observable symbol for telling the world that the young man is engaged. Second, most engagement parties are for the girl. She has showers given for her and she participates in the planning of the wedding to a far greater extent than the male. Many times the prime duty of the male seems to be to serve as a chauffeur for his fiancée— and her mother. In fact, during engagement and at the wedding the girl's mother may be the second most important figure. (Some young engaged women have suggested she is *the* most important figure.) Generally, the girl and her mother share in most of the activities of engagement and planning the wedding; the engaged male's role is much, much less significant.

The Process of Engagement

Falling in lose is a prerequisite to engagement for most Americans. Once the couple decide they are in love, then the natural development is to become engaged, with marriage in the near future. The development of love is discussed in Chapter 5, but it should be pointed out here that the dating and going-steady relationships move (with possible ups and downs) toward the awareness of love. The forces and processes that draw the couple together are many and varied, but they must usually occur before love and engagement develop for the individuals.

Pair Identification. The process of dating and courtship is one of moving from ego-centered interests to increasingly pair-oriented involvement. Many of the factors of pair-identification occur prior to engagement and are important contributing factors to engagement. Waller and Hill describe the pair development as follows:

> A boy and girl have a date and they hear some particular song, or sing it, and that is their song from then on. They soon develop a special language, their own idioms, pet names, and jokes; as a pair they have a history and a separate culture. They exchange rings or some other articles as soon as possible, striving to make tangible and fixed that elusive something between them.[44]

Through the social mechanism of pair-identification, the two individuals see their relationship as being of such a special nature to them that it becomes important to further solidify it—through engagement and marriage.

The result of pair-identification is a sense of exclusiveness. If the relationship is to continue, the individuality of the two members must, to a certain degree, be subordinated.[45] The degree of subordination may be taken as a rough measure of the exclusive paired nature of the relationship. If the individuals function primarily in response to their own personal needs, the relationship is less an exclusive bond than a working partnership for the ego-satisfaction of individual desires. That is to say, the exclusiveness of engagement demands a minimizing of individuality, at least on many occasions.

The exclusiveness found in the paired relationship of engagement may lead to trouble. "The obvious fact that the dyad is composed of two and only two individuals limits the placement of blame and responsibility for errors and mistakes."[46] Any trouble that arises within the relationship must be resolved within it. In more extended relationships, praise and blame can be spread out, but in engagement, where the couple has cut itself off from the rest of society, there is no available third party on whom to displace hostility and blame.[47] Under such circumstances, one technique is to use individuals outside the pair relationship as scapegoats even though they had little or nothing to do with the problem. Transference of blame allows the couple through rationalization to maintain the purity of their relationship.

---

[44]Waller and Hill, *op. cit.*, p. 189.
[45]*Ibid.*, p. 239.
[46]*Ibid.*, p. 232.
[47]*Ibid.*, p. 232.

For many engaged couples, the experience of an intense pair relationship probably leads to rational and honest understanding. The awareness of one another and satisfaction with the privacy of the relationship exists in a world where the dyad is recognized as only one small part. It seems reasonable to assume that this understanding develops in those engagements and marriages that achieve some degree of success. The very fact of achieving some degree of success would indicate the integration of the private paired world with the large public world of which it is a part. Burgess and Wallin felt that in the population of engaged couples they studied there was good evidence for the assumption that excessive idealization in courtship or marriage was not widespread.[48] No doubt, the degree and the duration of exclusiveness in the love relationship varies with different couples, but it probably rarely extends at a high pitch very long into the marriage relationship.

Expression of Love. Closely related to the pair-identification aspect is the importance of engagement as a period of time for expressing and receiving love. The giving and receiving of love is a socially conditioned need that reaches a high level of expectation during engagement. While many individuals have been in love before engagement, the notion of love takes on greater importance during engagement because it is love for the person to be married. Therefore, this love is seen as mature adult love and the individual often approaches it with seriousness and possible apprehension.

The means of expression and the intensity of love demonstration sometimes leads to disagreement by the couple. The expression of love as related to sexual involvement is discussed in Chapter 12; the concern here is with the broad demonstration of love. Psychological and sociological factors both contribute to different attitudes about the demonstration of love. The psychological factors refer to the differences of various personalities in their need to give and receive love. The sociological factors refer to the differences by sex in the giving and receiving of love. In the American culture the female is more apt to be inhibited. While engagement provides a socially approved setting for some display of affection, there may be significant differences in what is seen as acceptable by the female as contrasted with the male.

Burgess and Wallin found among the engaged couples they studied that almost half of the men and women did not always agree on display of their love. They found the most common disagreement re-

---

[48]Burgess and Wallin, *op. cit.*, p. 237.

sulted from one desiring more than the other was willing to give.[49] This reaction is not surprising when it is realized that during engagement love is very tenuous and one or both of the individuals may desire frequent reassurance of the love of the other. The insecurity of engagement is vividly illustrated by the Burgess and Wallin findings of the engaged couples' feelings about the future marriage. They found that 41 percent of the males and 48 percent of the females felt some hesitation about marrying their betrothed.[50]

Final Testing. Under the assumption that a broken engagement is less personally and socially disruptive than a broken marriage, engagement is often seen as a final testing period prior to marriage. This reflects the belief that engagement allows the couple to become closer and to gain more insight about each other and thereby discover some problem areas that might make marriage difficult. Kuhn writes, "In our society the main purpose of the engagement is to facilitate, by allowing a certain intimacy and privacy, the testing of personalities in order to see how well suited the mates are to each other."[51]

TABLE 4–2

FEELINGS ABOUT ENGAGEMENT, BY SEX*

	Wished Had Not Become Engaged		Contemplated Breaking Engagement	
	Male	*Female*	*Male*	*Female*
Never	80.2	77.6	88.3	77.2
Once	9.6	7.6	11.8	13.4
More than once	10.2	14.8	4.9	9.4
	100.0	100.0	100.0	100.0

*Adapted from: Burgess and Wallin, *Engagement and Marriage* (Chicago: J. B. Lippincott Co., 1953), p. 181.

While some severe problems may emerge that end an engagement, it can not be assumed that the only alternative is the feeling that the relationship is perfect. In most engagements there is probably some feeling of insecurity because of the highly emotional nature of the relationship. Table 4–2, taken from the Burgess and Wallin study, shows that 19.8 percent of the men and 22.4 percent of the women wished on at least one occasion they had not become engaged. Fur-

[49]*Ibid.*, p. 249.
[50]*Ibid.*, p. 180.
[51]Manford H. Kuhn, "The Engagement: Thinking About Marriage," in Howard Becker and Reuben Hill, *Family, Marriage and Parenthood* (Boston: D. C. Heath and Co., 1955), pp. 288–89.

thermore, they found that 16.7 percent of the men and 22.8 percent of the women had contemplated breaking the engagement.[52]

Some Engagement Problems

An important part of a successful engagement is the meeting and handling of problems that arise.

Pair Disagreements. The very nature of their close new role relationships means that the engaged couple must develop an understanding and working agreement around areas of importance. It is unrealistic to assume that engaged couples agree on everything; in fact, it can be argued that some disagreement is basic to a better understanding of the self and the "significant other." One set of empirical findings indicate that nearly four fifths of the engaged couples studied report disagreements in one or more areas. Only 1.7 per cent state they "always agree" on all areas.[53]

While disagreements are common and sometimes contribute positively to the relationship, there may be danger if the disagreement is extended in intensity and scope beyond the specific areas of difference. There may also be danger when the couple argue for the sake of arguing. Unless the two individuals differ in an area that has significance for both of them, argument can probably be eliminated or held down. This seems to be a tendency in successful engagements. Burgess and Wallin found the group of couples that tried to avoid arguments is represented in 77 percent of the unbroken and in 68 percent of the broken engagements.[54]

One area that often has high emotional impact for many engaged couples is any discussion of old boy friends or girl friends. The mention of a past love may threaten the security of one member of the couple as to the exclusive personal commitment of the other in the present love relationship. This sensitivity may be a little greater for the male than for the female because of his somewhat greater possessive feeling. Burgess and Wallin found that 31.4 percent of the men and 23.4 percent of the women reacted with feeling to the mention of past boy friends or girl friends.[55]

Parents. One very common source of difficulty for the engaged couple centers around the parents' reactions to the fiancé (e). The conflict may center around incongruity in defining the young person's role—the engaged person feeling that mate selection is his own

---

[52]Burgess and Wallin, *op. cit.*, p. 181.
[53]*Ibid.*, p. 247.
[54]*Ibid.*, p. 294.
[55]*Ibid.*, p. 267.

choice, with his parents having little to do with it, and the parents feeling they should play an important part in their offspring's selection of a mate. The conflict may also revolve around the idealistic romantic beliefs of the young person and the more realistic values of the parent. It is probable that girls, because of close ties to their mothers, are more willing to listen to their parents and to be influenced by the parents' wishes. That how to deal with the parents is a major controversial issue among engaged couples is evident by the finding that one out of four men and women disagree occasionally or more often on this matter.[56]

Even though young people want to think that engagement is almost entirely their own concern, their parents may influence them either directly in ending the relationship, or indirectly contribute to its end by pointing out the faults and dangers of the relationship. The Burgess and Wallin findings show that when the parents disapproved of the engagement, 21.6 percent were unbroken but 78.4 percent were broken. When the parents approved of the engagement, 42.7 percent were unbroken—and 57.3 percent were broken.[57]

Broken Engagements. All individuals who have any experience in the dating-courtship process have had the experience of ending a relationship. When a person dates an individual on only one occasion, the emotional commitment is not great and the ending of the relationship rarely carries any great difficulties. However, as the stages of courtship are entered into, the emotional commitment increases and it becomes more difficult to deal with and adjust to the ending of the relationship. More personal pain will probably be associated with a broken engagement than with the ending of going steady, and more pain over a broken marriage than a broken engagement. Regardless of the emotional pain involved, the broken engagement is relatively common in American culture. While we have indicated that parents may play a part in breaking engagements, the more important fact is that individuals select their love objects with a strong desire for happiness and ego-satisfaction. An engagement lacking these qualities is a prime candidate for dissolution.

The best empirical material on broken engagements is to be found in the excellent Burgess and Wallin study. These two investigators made extensive comparisons of broken and unbroken engagements according to a number of social variables. They found some evi-

---

[56]*Ibid.*, p. 250.
[57]*Ibid.*, p. 289.

dence that length of acquaintance is related to successful engagement. In 66.6 per cent of unbroken engagements, as contrasted to 50.4 percent of the broken engagements, the couples had been acquainted for 18 months or longer.[58] Their evidence also indicates that increasing amounts of time spent together is related to successful engagement. For the unbroken engagement couples, 74.3 percent, as contrasted with 60.2 percent of the broken engagement couples, averaged 13 or more hours together per week.[59]

The Landises found the most common reasons given for broken engagements were loss of interest by 45 percent of the men and 38 percent of the women; separation by 20 percent of the men and 18 percent of the women; parents by 9 percent of the men and 11 percent of the women; incompatibility by 9 percent of both sexes; and, other reasons by 17 percent of the men and 24 percent of the women.[60]

Because of the high emotional involvement, adjustment to a broken engagement often takes time and an emotional toll. Many persons become "gunshy" after a broken engagement and are in no hurry to enter into a new relationship.[61] Often it is more difficult for the girl to get back into dating circulation than it is for the boy. The boy can re-enter the dating-courtship process by actively seeking out dates, while the girl must usually wait until word gets around that she is again in circulation. In addition, the girl is not perceived as datable for some time because she often goes through a period of "mourning." Girls probably take longer to recover from a broken engagement than boys because of the greater significance the female attaches to love. Because there is a common belief that love is more deeply felt by the girl, boys may be hesitant to ask the ex-engaged girl for a date because of the fear that she is still in love. A girl seems to accept a date from the ex-engaged boy with less fear.

Given human recuperative powers, individuals recover from the broken engagement and eventually almost all move back into the dating-courtship process. Going back and starting all over again with dating may be difficult for many, but go back they do—often wiser and more careful. With love and marriage so important to most Americans, the period of remorse and mourning tends to be intense, but short. Because love and marriage are so personally and socially important, the individual must recover from the broken engagement

[58]*Ibid.*, p. 286.
[59]*Ibid.*, p. 288.
[60]Landis and Landis, *op. cit.*, p. 185.
[61]Burgess and Wallin, *op. cit.*, p. 301.

and start again the forward march through the dating-courtship process.

The dating-courtship process provides for many young people in the middle class the socialization necessary for moving into the marriage relationship as well as other adult relationships. Dating and courtship contribute to a familiarity and ability to enter the "paired world" of the adult man and woman. The behavior of adult models is often supported by peer group values that give great importance to cross-sex interaction. The individual is thus socialized to the skills of "relating" and "belonging" which are so important to the middle class in a wide variety of social settings.

SELECTED BIBLIOGRAPHY

BABER, RAY E. *Marriage and the Family,* chaps. iv and v. New York: McGraw-Hill Book Co., 1953.

BELL, ROBERT R., and BLUMBERG, LEONARD. "Courtship Intimacy and Religious Background," *Marriage and Family Living,* November, 1959, pp. 356–60.

BRODERICK, CARLFRED B., and FOWLER, STANLEY E. "New Patterns of Relationships Between the Sexes Among Pre-Adolescents," *Marriage and Family Living,* February, 1961, pp. 27–30.

BURCHINAL, LEE G. "The Premarital Dyad and Love Involvement," in HAROLD T. CHRISTENSEN (Ed.) *Handbook of Marriage and the Family* (Chicago: Rand McNally & Co., 1964), pp. 623–74.

BURGESS, ERNEST W., and WALLIN, PAUL. *Engagement and Marriage,* chaps. iii-x, and xiii. Chicago: J. B. Lippincott Co., 1953.

EHRMANN, WINSTON. *Premarital Dating Behavior.* New York: Henry Holt & Co., 1959.

KEPHART, WILLIAM M. *The Family, Society and the Individual,* chap. x. Boston: Houghton Mifflin Co., 1961.

KIRKPATRICK, CLIFFORD. *The Family,* chap. xii. New York: The Ronald Press Co., 1955.

KIRKPATRICK, CLIFFORD, and CAPLOW, THEODORE. "Courtship in a Group of Minnesota Students," *American Journal of Sociology,* September, 1945, pp. 114–25.

KUHN, MANFORD H. "The Engagement: Thinking About Marriage," in Howard Becker and Reuben Hill, *Family, Marriage and Parenthood,* pp. 276–303. Boston: D. C. Heath & Co., 1955.

LANDIS, JUDSON T., and LANDIS, MARY G. *Building a Successful Marriage,* chaps. iv, v, and x. New York: Prentice-Hall, Inc., 1953.

NIMKOFF, MEYER F., and WOOD, ARTHUR L. "Courtship and Personality," *American Journal of Sociology,* January, 1948.

REISS, IRA L. "Sexual Codes in Teen Age Culture," *The Annals,* November, 1961, pp. 53–62.

Rogers, Everett M., and Havens, Eugene A. "Prestige Rating and Mate Selection on a College Campus," *Marriage and Family Living*, February, 1960, pp. 55–59.

Waller, Willard, and Hill, Reuben. *The Family*, chaps, vi-xii. New York: The Dryden Press, 1951.

CHAPTER 5

LOVE

The interest in this chapter is with the love of men and women leading to and resulting from marriage. This focus on love shall be called conjugal love and it may be defined as a strong emotion directed at a person of the opposite sex and involving feelings of sexual attraction, tenderness and some commitment to the other's ego-needs. In the American middle class, conjugal love places a great stress on each individual's varied ego-needs being satisfied by the other. In this chapter we will look at various facets of love, including the influence of romantic love, the psychological and cultural nature of love, and some theories about love.

Conjugal love, with its stress on ego-needs, is probably more important and more basic to the American culture than to almost any other culture of the world. To be unloved in the United States is to be more than unwanted; it is to lack importance in the eyes of a "significant other"—it is to be unchosen. This is often extremely upsetting in a culture in which being chosen is often equated with having social worth as a human being. Furthermore, love is important both as a condition for marriage and for marriage satisfaction.

One important historical influence which has been handed down over the centuries in the Western world, and which has contributed to contemporary American beliefs about love, has been the notion of romantic love. A brief historical description of the origins of romantic love and how it has been altered over time and ultimately incorporated into the values of American society follows.

ROMANTIC LOVE

The Greeks developed two concepts of adult love: *Eros,* which was a carnal love associated with the sensual, physical, and sexual; and *agape,* a spiritual love associated with the more "pure" human emotions. Originally neither of these types of love had anything to do with marriage, because love was not related to mate selection or the relationships of husband and wife. The main reason for marriage

111

was reproduction; having children, particulary sons, was of great importance to the Greek man, but love between husband and wife was usually not.

Love among the Greeks stressed physical beauty, but the Greek male did not often feel that beauty could be found in the female, and certainly not in a wife. Actually the status of the female was so low that she was often felt to be unworthy of idealistic love; furthermore, as a female she was incapable of returning the love. The ideal Greek love tended to be homosexual, between an older man and a younger boy. It was based on the belief that the essence of beauty and therefore the realization of love could be found by the male in the male. It is an ironical historical fact that love as it is viewed today, with the exchange of deep emotional commitment between members of the opposite sex, had partial roots in male homosexuality.[1]

The next great historical influence on romantic love was early Christianity. The Church began a strong fight against the temptations of the flesh and, as often happens with social reaction, its objection took a position at the extreme. For the early Christians, the highest achievement of man was as complete a rejection of his body as possible while still retaining life. The priesthood represented the highest level of achievement because it resisted as completely as possible all things sensual. Because priesthood could not be the state for many, marriage was tolerated, but even here the highest form of marriage was one of physical continence.

At the root of all evil were women. Women were believed, simply because they were women, to possess evilness and therefore were to be distrusted, watched, and controlled. The highest state for the woman was in the glory of everlasting virginity. "Reasoning ran something like this—in Paradise Eve was a virgin. Virginity, therefore, is natural; hence wedlock only follows guilt."[2] This historical period was characterized by severe ascetic attacks against the inherent evilness and implied witchery of women. The following passage, written by Saint John Chrysostom in A. D. 370 to a friend who had said he was in love with a young woman and wanted to marry her, provides a vivid picture of the woman:

> The groundwork of this corporeal beauty is nothing else but phlegm and blood and humor and bile, and the fluid of masticated food . . .: If you consider what is stored up inside those beautiful eyes, and that

---

[1]Morton M. Hunt, *The Natural History of Love* (New York: Alfred A. Knopf, Inc., 1959), p. 8.

[2]Isabel Drummond, *The Sex Paradox* (New York: G. P. Putnam's Sons, 1953), p. 8.

straight nose, and the mouth and cheeks, you will affirm the well-shaped body to be nothing else than a whited sepulchre: . . . Moreover, when you see a rag with any of these things on it, such as phlegm, or spittle, you cannot bear to touch it even with the tips of your fingers, nay you cannot endur' looking at it; are you then in a flutter of excitement about the store houses and repositories of these things?[3]

During the rise of Christianity, the Church struggled constantly against the sensate behavior of the people. As a revolt against the rigid dictates of the Church, a movement based on the Romantic Ideal emerged in Europe. This movement had its origins in southern France near the end of the 11th century; it emerged from, and for the most part stayed with, that group with enough power to oppose the Church—the upper class of noblemen. Some contradiction and disagreement exists among historians as to the degree of sexual behavior in the romantic movement. Probably, the early romantic movement was clandestine and idealistic, and involved a great deal of sexual frustration because it was often pursued in a highly erotic setting, but presumably with no sexual intercourse. Knights and their ladies were sometimes put nude into bed together and making love was expected so long as intercourse did not occur.

This was a kind of "adventure" and "courage was associated with love of adventure and the glorification of war. Their [the knights'] religion was apt to be a mere formality. Their courtesy was for the ladies of the castle, not the women of the cottages."[4]

A large part of court behavior developed to mock both religion and the prevailing system of marriage. Love practiced by the troubadours was devotion to little more than an inanimate object; "the lady was an inert, icon-like figure."[5] It must be stressed that courtly love had nothing to do with mate selection, because marriages were arranged and the basis for arrangement was usually economic. The ideal of chivalry and its particular definition of love was more important than marriage or reproduction. Marriage was one point on which the romantics and the ecclesiastical were in agreement—it was a duty rather than a pleasure.[6]

The long historical period from the rise of Christianity, through the age of Chivalry and into the Renaissance was generally one of hatred and contempt of women. Drummond points out that it was during the "dark age" of woman that the doctrine of the immacu-

---

[3]*Ibid.*, p. 110.
[4]Stuart A. Queen, John B. Adams, and Robert W. Habenstein, *The Family in Various Cultures* (Philadelphia: J. B. Lippincott Co., 1961), p. 232.
[5]Hunt, *op. cit.*, p. 151.
[6]Queen, *op. cit.*, p. 237.

late conception arose.[7] To compare the status of women during that "dark age" with their status in modern American society is to illustrate a great and significant social change.

Over the centuries, the influence of romantic love varied greatly. Morton Hunt argues that three general influences emerged. (1) a greater emotional relationship between men and women, which meant an uplifting in a part of the woman's status; (2) sexual fidelity to a single partner (even though, during the early period this meant fidelity within the framework of adultery); (3) the idea that love must be mutual, which also contributed a great deal to improving the status of women.[8] The adulterous flirtation and illicit infatuation of the Middle Ages were the very instrument that began to enhance woman's status, and hence, eventually to alter marriage."[9]

Over time, many influences and changes developed around the concept of romantic love. Today it has a variety of meanings and must be viewed as a loose collection of beliefs and customs. Hunt writes that "as it passed down the centuries, some [ideas and customs] were continually sluffed off and others added; it is something like the philosopher's much darned socks, the fabric of which was eventually altogether changed, but which never lost their identity as a specific pair of socks."[10] Hunt further points out that "it is therefore a paradox of no mean order that modern love began with Greek love and owes so much to it, although the forms and ideals of Greek love are considered immoral, and to a large extent, illegal, in modern society."[11]

Over the centuries when the notion of love was being altered and assimilated in the Western world, no equivalent process occurred in most Eastern countries. The Maces[12] point out that "it is a rigid principle of Eastern life that the stability of the family, and the maintenance of the social order always come before the happiness of the individual. Romantic love is an unruly emotion, which out of control can do as much damage as uncontrolled anger."[13] But in many countries of the Eastern world the traditional patterns are now beginning to break down and romantic love is being accepted by the younger generation primarily because of the increasing infil-

---

[7]Drummond, *op. cit.*, p. 8.
[8]Hunt, *op. cit.*, p. 171.
[9]*Ibid.*, pp. 171–73.
[10]*Ibid.*, p. 299.
[11]*Ibid.*, p. 16
[12]David Mace and Vera Mace, *Marriage East and West* (Garden City, New York: Doubleday and Company, Inc., 1960), p. 121.
[13]*Ibid.*, p. 124.

tration of Western ideas. However, there is some evidence that a romantic approach to marriage is not being quickly assimilated. A recent study, using Indian, Burmese, and Singapore Chinese respondents, found that although they were from the segment of their societies most subject to Western influences, they did not show an acceptance of the American-type romantic orientation to marriage.[14] Nevertheless, the influence of romantic love is of a far-reaching nature and must be assessed as having world-wide implications.

From the rich and often contradictory historical tradition of romantic love, some ingredients may be found in American society today. Although no list could be complete, certain elements may be suggested as important to many Americans when they think of romantic love.

Idealization—the placing of the love object on a pedestal, untouched by the commonness and coarseness of the everyday world. A high degree of selective perception on the part of the lover is often involved. He sees only what he wants to see—often in an exaggerated fashion—and ignores the love object's human frailties. Generally, this idealization has a strong positive influence on the loved one because most of us thrive on esteem and can not help being responsive to the one who esteems us.[15]

Fantasy—the tendency to withdraw into a world of make-believe and to create images of what should be in a most perfect-of-all-worlds with the most perfect-of-all-individuals. As with idealization, fantasy suggests ignoring what may go counter to the imagined.

Highly Emotional—the wish to "feel rather than think." This ideal is often held to be so strong that it defies rational understanding or analysis; in fact, to attempt either would be to destroy it.

Exclusiveness—the stress on the privacy and singular nature of the love experience. The belief is that in true romantic love neither person can really care about anything or anyone else. The couple live in a world of their own and, when it is necessary to move out and deal with the world at large, the overriding desire is to return to the exclusiveness of the private world as soon as possible.

The above ingredients are not found in all love relationships of a romantic nature, nor necessarily in quite the fashion described. Rather, they describe a few beliefs that exist and affect some people. What might be called the American folklore of romantic love, which

[14]George A. Theodorson, "Romanticism and Motivation To Marry In The United States, Singapore, Burma and India," *Social Forces*, September, 1965, p. 27.
[15]Hunt, *op. cit.*, p. 98.

is often found in mass-media productions and is frequently presented as being necessary to "real or true love," further illustrates the influence of romantic love in today's society.

American Folklore

Soulmate. The belief in a soulmate is that in this great wide world exists one person, and only one, meant for each of us. This belief is very ego-satisfying because it suggests that each of us is so special that only one person can meet our needs, and that one person has been created especially to do so. It also implies an adventurous quality, because adolescence and the early adult years can be devoted to a search for the soulmate.

While many young people may say they do not believe in a soulmate, their actions often indicate they do. Many find it psychologically difficult to accept the idea that they could fall in love with any one of many different individuals, particularly when *they* define themselves as being in love, because it seems to them impossible to imagine loving someone else. Being in love, therefore, often reinforces the soulmate idea because once a loved one has been found it is psychologically reassuring to believe, that there are no other possibilities. The writer once had a coed tell him the most "fantastic" event: Her family had been going to their cottage at the shore every weekend, as was their custom. Early in one week, her mother became ill and the family thought they would have to postpone their usual weekend trip. However the mother made a rapid recovery so that they *did* go to the shore, and on that *Saturday* night she had a blind date who turned out to be HIM. "Just think," concluded the coed, "we almost stayed in Philadelphia, and if we had I never would have met him and my life would have been incomplete." When it was suggested that if she had stayed in Philadephia, she might have met *another* HIM, on a blind date there, the reaction was one of indigant disbelief.

A person frequently enters the romantic maze and, after many a false start and dead end, finds his way to the "bait" at the exit. But because of the exclusive nature of the "bait" he mistakenly thinks it was the only "bait" at the only exit of the maze. He has no way of knowing what other exits with their various "baits" he might have reached.

Love-at-first-sight. This love is found "across the crowded room"—their eyes meet and they know they are meant for each other. When love at first sight occurs, it can be based on little more than physical attraction. Like the belief in a soulmate, it too has an adventurous quality. Part of the belief is that when the couple meet they will really *know* it: something dramatic and earth-shaking—an exchange laden with cosmic meaning—will occur between them. All other individuals will become only vague shadows in the background of the newly discovered exclusive world. And the clincher will be the first kiss—an event during which some believe the world observes 30 seconds of silence.

College students—even college students—are influenced by a belief in love-at-first sight. In one study, the Landises asked 735 college students if they believed in "falling in love at first sight"; 39 percent of the men and 34 percent of the women said they did.[16] A measurement of when love-at-first-sight actually happens would be useful in checking the belief. People telling when they fell in love are usually describing something that *has* happened, not what *is* happening, which may influence their willingness to believe in love-at-first-sight. A favorite argument between young lovers is which one knew he loved the other one first. When remembering, however, each tends to move back the time when he said to himself he was in love. Unable to remove himself from the intervening experiences and emotions, he sees the past event not as it was, but in the light of what he has experienced since.

Some dangers are involved for the individual who believes in love-at-first-sight. The highly significant first meeting may never occur; love doesn't always follow the folklore script. Thus, he may never experience "real" love or may feel frustrated in a love relationship which developes over time, because the first meeting lacked a dramatic quality.

Overcoming Frustration. An important component of the American folklore of true love is that it should be put to a test. If it passes the test, it is true love; if it doesn't, then it may not be "real" love after all. Many popular mass-media magazine stories have as their theme a couple overcoming the frustrations confronting their love: boy meets girl, obstacle enters, and when they surmount the obstacle, they live happily ever after. Only the nature of the obstacle ever seems to vary. Typically, the girl wants a career instead of marriage, the boy thinks he is in love with someone else, or the parents have strong objections. If the story has a happy ending, as it generally does, the great love which has resolved the problem is proved "real."

---

[16]Judson T. Landis and Mary G. Landis, *Building A Successful Marriage* (New York: Prentice-Hall, Inc., 1948), p. 45.

For young people who have been reared with the belief that "true love never runs smooth," problems may arise in their own love affairs. They may search for obstacles to be conquered and for an opportunity for the virtue of love to win out over the evil of obstruction. Some may exaggerate a situation into an obstacle, or even dream up an obstacle. Others who face no obstacles may feel that something is lacking, that their love has not been put to a true test, and so they can not be sure it "really" is love.

Love Conquers All. With love conquering all, romantic love becomes paramount—with it nothing in the world is unattainable. This belief may cause several reactions. Individuals may put aside the realities of life and retreat into the protective cocoon of love. They need not then worry about such mundane, unromantic problems as housing or food, because love will find a way. When they discover all the world doesn't really love the lover, the romantic pair may be somewhat jolted.

Cues of possible interactional difficulty in the relationship may also be ignored. Idealization often means ignoring certain qualities in the other person that may lead to future difficulty. What may be even more dangerous is to recognize faults, but believe that love can overcome them. The writer once talked to a woman who had just divorced her alcoholic husband. Her husband had previously been divorced for the same reason. When asked if she knew he was an alcoholic when she married him she replied, "Yes, but I believed that my love would straighten him out."

In one respect, a belief in love helping to conquer many difficulties has some truth. Many newly-married young couples, facing rather severe role adjustments and often with limited financial support, find their love involvement helps them over rough spots and may even make enjoyable what without love would be unpleasant. When this happens, love is not a replacement for reality, but rather a positive force in helping to deal with it.

Assessment of Romantic Love

The reader may feel that the preceding picture of contemporary American romantic love is unfair and exaggerated. If the description of romantic love has been extreme, consider it as one end of a continuum. The other end might be called "rational mate selection." A picture of the opposite end of the continuum will describe the selection of a mate on extremely rational or objective grounds.

Imagine that a girl looking for a husband wants to use objective, rational criteria for making her final choice. She will try to control emotional influences—other than possibly some feeling of physical attraction, which would have some significance for her future sexual adjustment. She meets a physically attractive young man and must decide if he is the man to marry. To be purely rational and objective, what could she theoretically do? First, she could turn him over to a board of psychologists and psychiatrists. They could probe his psychological make-up, and measure his intelligence, motivation, aspirations, and the overall strengths and weaknesses of his personality. His potential as a husband and father and provider, his mental health and stability might also be assessed. Second, she could turn him over to a group of biologists and medical experts. His family background could be thoroughly examined to determine possible genetic skeletons in his family closet and possible positive genetic contributions he might make to their children. The state of his physical health and some estimate of possible life expectancy might also be established. A third test would subject him to a variety of new social experiences, with the results used to analyze his ability to adapt and adjust adequately. As a final test, he might be followed day and night for at least six months by a competent private detective agency

This purely rational, objective approach is the extreme at the other end of the continuum. In life, very few individuals make their choice at either extreme on the continuum (romantic or rational), but rather at points in between.

Since romantic love is an important part of the social fabric, to exclude it completely from the love relationship is to ignore social reality. Most individuals in love probably find a satisfactory middle ground between the romantic and the rational. The romantic emphasis may be stronger during courtship and the early stages of marriage because of the newness of the experience and because emotional ties are the primary bases for the new relationship. But through the common experiences of living together, a new relationship often emerges, one that replaces some of the romantic emotionality of the earlier relationship. We will have more to say on the changing nature of love later in the chapter.

LOVE IN CONTEMPORARY AMERICAN SOCIETY

While romantic love is an important and dramatic part of the American love ethos, it is not all of it. A marital love pattern can be distinguished from the romantic love complex. Goode suggests that under the love pattern "love is a permissible, expected prelude to marriage, and a usual element of courtship. There is also the ideological prescription that falling in love is a highly desirable basis of courtship and marriage and love is strongly institutionalized."[17] These aspects of the conjugal love pattern have been borrowed from the romantic love complex, but should not be viewed as synonymous with it.

For the vast majority of Americans, love and marriage go together; an important, and recent, social invention is that love is the reason for marriage. This change is closely related to the shift of emphasis from the family members as a group to the family member as an individual. When the family group had greater control in choosing the marriage partner, premarital love was not usually important. The predominant values stressed in the selection of a mate satisfied the needs of the family unit, not the ego-needs of the individual getting married. But with mate selection increasingly determined by the person getting married, love came to be the important factor in choosing a mate. Loving and being loved satisfied the ego-needs of the two individuals involved. The anthropologist Stephens suggests that the *notion* of romantic love, used as a rationale for marriage, emerged to fill an ideological vacuum caused by the disappearance of arranged marriage.[18]

Most, but not all, Americans believe love to be a necessary prerequisite to marriage. In the Burgess and Wallin study of engaged couples, 12 percent of the men and 15 percent of the women thought one could marry when not in love.[19] The answer of these respondents should be interpreted to mean that they feel marriage without love may be justified in some cases; the actual number who marry without being in love is probably much less.

Most Americans not only believe that marriage must be preceded by love but also that the only satisfactory consequence of being in love is to marry. If two people in love cannot marry for some reason, it is generally viewed as a tragedy by the individuals and as unfortunate by society at large. American literature is full of stories of individuals who have a led a life of misery and unhappiness because they could not marry their beloved. The reaction of society to unfulfilled love varies according to the reason marriage did not occur. If a woman chooses against love and marriage and pursues a

[17]William J. Goode, "The Theoretical Importance of Love," *American Sociological Review*, February, 1959, p. 42.

[18]William N. Stephens, *The Family In Cross-Cultural Perspective* (New York: Holt, Rinehart & Winston, Inc., 1963), p. 206.

[19]Ernest W. Burgess and Paul Wallin, *Engagement and Marriage*, (Philadelphia: J. B. Lippincott Co., 1953), p. 394.

career, she receives little sympathy from society and her basic "womanliness" is often subject to question. However, if she does not experience love because she must care for an ailing or aging parent, she is usually treated with respect and sympathy.

SOME THEORIES OF LOVE

In American society there is no shortage of theories or definitions of love. Ranging from the simple to the complex, theories have been developed by social observers of various types and interests. One of the briefest definitions of love was made by H. L. Mencken when he called it "a state of perpetual anesthesia."[20] After extensive study of the various theories of love, Morton Hunt came to the conclusion that "most of the learned people who write about love seem to equip themselves in advance with a special theory; with this as a kind of butterfly net, they then sally forth and attempt to capture cases to prove or exemplify their point."[21]

Most definitions suggest that love is a strong emotion between two individuals which involves and satisfies the need of giving and receiving. This implies either the reality or the expectation of emotional, physical, and intellectual exchange.[22] Based on this general statement, the following sections will examine some common love components, as well as love as a process.

Love Components

The ingredients to be suggested should not be seen as a check list for determining whether or not love exists. Rather they are characteristics, without set manner or degree, that are often, but not always, associated with love. As with romantic love, *idealization* contributes to the extent that the loved one is seen as having some special qualities for the lover. Often a somewhat exaggerated notion of qualities felt highly desirable compensate for those qualities not so highly prized. This is often idealization within rational limits. *Respect* for the loved one as an individual, in what he does and how he thinks and feels, is also an important quality. The individuality of the two is never completely destroyed by the paired relationship. *Sexual attraction* enters when the other person is a meaningful and

---

[20]Hunt, *op. cit.*, p. 5.

[21]*Ibid.*, p .8.

[22]See: Earl L. Koos, *Marriage* (New York: Henry Holt and Co., 1957), p. 111; Robert F. Winch, *The Modern Family* (New York: Henry Holt & Co., 1952), p. 337; and, Ira L. Reiss "Toward a Sociology of the Heterosexual Love Relationship," *Marriage and Family Living*, May, 1960, pp. 139–45.

satisfying physical counterpart. Although almost everyone needs physical satisfaction, the need varies greatly among different individuals. Particularly for the female, the sexual act becomes meaningful through love and often only with the loved one. *Companionship* indicates that the couple find satisfaction in being and doing together, but not to the complete exclusion of others or the destruction of the identity of each in the relationship. Rather, some experiences are shared, with the amount depending on the changing needs of the individuals.

Selflessness suggests that the individual can move outside himself and attempt to meet the other's needs. Sometimes personal preferences and desires are put aside for the fulfillment of the other person, and this is often reciprocated. Selflessness recognizes that on some occasions individuality may temporarily have to give way to the basically interdependent nature of the pair relationship. A final ingredient, *maturity*, refers to the ability and motivation to accept adult rights and obligations in a variety of adult role relationships. Adult responsibility entails attempting, as sincerely as possible, to deal with all contingencies. For example, the young wife who turns to her mother for support after an argument with the husband is not socially mature in her adult fulfillment of the wife role.

Love Process

Love is not generally assumed to be there today and gone tomorrow, but to last over time. American cultural values generally suggest that love should be retained through periods of strain and not disappear without just and sufficient cause. While the ideal is that love will continue for the rest of the individual's life, many love relationships probably do not realize this ideal.

Some writers like to characterize love as growing, but it may be more accurately described as changing. Growing implies maintaining what has existed and adding to it. But elements important early in love relationships may, over time, be discarded and replaced by new ones. For example, early idealization may be replaced by a feeling of interdependability based upon the cumulative experience of the pair relationship.

No discussion of the ingredients and process of love should be considered final or authoritative. Love affairs differ in the strength of each ingredient. For example, some individuals feel that sexual attraction is of great significance, but others may limit its importance. One writer argues that only one thing really matters: no element should be missing.[23] This argument, that love is not really love if some ingredients are absent, seems arbitrary and questionable. The best that can be said is that many love relationships contain these ingredients. A related point is that not any list of ingredients should ever be viewed as complete. The elements of human emotions, the variety of individual responses, and the differential impact of cultural values are not well enough understood to make arbitrary decisions on exactly what constitutes real love. That is why mass magazines that provide check lists for determining *whether your husband really loves you* are misleading, dishonest, and sometimes dangerous. Some professional social scientists contribute to the illusion that love is exact. One writer tells her readers that "seven qualities give strength to love that is good enough for marriage."[24] While that kind of authoritarianism may be reassuring to some readers, it is nevertheless misleading. Such writers rarely provide any empirical research to substantiate the ingredients they are selling as "real" love.

Infatuation vs. Love

Many family writers like to distinguish between love and infatuation. Most believe the two emotions are different, but no one is quite sure in what way. Infatuation is generally viewed with suspicion—a kind of ersatz love that will lead the follower down the path of disillusionment. Infatuation is often described as being on a lower level than love and unworthy of marriage.[25] Rarely, however, does the individual involved define a current emotional experience as infatuation. Kephart points out that "whenever individuals speak of their infatuation it is nearly always in past tense. Very few individuals report themselves as being currently infatuated, yet at a given time a fair number considered themselves to be in love."[26]

Apparently, when individuals are going through the emotional relationship they call it love; when it is over, they often call it infatuation. By calling past love affairs infatuations, the individual maintains the uniqueness of love so that, when he falls in love at some future time, the term *love* will refer to the new, not the used.

---

[23]Robert O. Blood, *Anticipating Your Marriage* (Glencoe, Illinois: The Free Press, 1955), p. 100.

[24]Ruth S. Cavan, *The American Family* (New York: Thomas Y. Crowell Co., 1953), p. 117.

[25]*Ibid.*, p. 117.

[26]William Kephart, *The Family, Society and the Individual* (New York: Houghton Mifflin Co, 1961), p. 322.

Many individuals, however, will admit to having been in love on several occasions. The concept of infatuation seems to be of little analytical value for anyone trying to understand love. Because of its *ex post facto* nature, it is useful only for categorizing past love relationships, not for understanding present or future ones.

This section has suggested a list of ingredients often found in love. That the ingredients should not be taken as absolute, either in conclusiveness or degree of existence, has been stressed. Furthermore, little is known about the interrelationship of ingredients other than they operate as part of a total package, no doubt affecting and affected by each other. As examples, idealization may be minimized by strong sexual attraction; different personalities will relate to the ingredients of love in different ways; or two self-sufficient personalities in marriage may have less need for companionship than a couple who both need personality reassurance.

CULTURAL INFLUENCES ON LOVE

The previous section concentrated primarily on the psychological elements of love for the individual and in his relationship with a loved one. This section will consider cultural factors. Ego-need love is not a universal found in all cultures at all times. While it prevails for most members of the American culture today, it is not the common pattern in many other cultures of the world nor was it the common pattern in the American society of the past.

Love is clearly a learned behavior. People are born with the capacity for all kinds of social learning, including the capacity for love, but they must learn to love as they must learn, for example, to hate. This section is concerned with the cultural factors that contribute to the individual's learning a love that is meaningful to himself and in his relation to a "significant other."

The American culture regards some form of love relationship as an ideal for all periods of a person's lifetime. The newborn infant will, with socialization, presumably enter into a love relationship with, at least, his parents. Most social scientists believe the effectiveness of this love is crucial to the child's emerging personality. Since the socialization of the child affects his preparation for future adult love relationships, early participation in and learning of love becomes a significant cultural factor. If young children are conditioned to marriage as a future adult expectation before they learn of love as the prerequisite to marriage, it may be because marriage and marriage roles are easier to identify with and grasp than the more abstract concept of love. Children often perceive love and marriage as a basic characteristic of adult status. They learn to believe that these values are as natural to their future as growing to adult height.

As children enter adolescence, the part that love plays in their lives increases. They hear others telling about their love experiences (often imaginary), and begin to anticipate the experience for themselves. Because love is thought of as "grown-up" and because adolescence is a period of age-role insecurity, love is yearned for as proof of attaining adult status. Indicating these pressures, Kirkpatrick writes: "Young persons of dating age fully expect that sooner or later they will be caught in the magic spell of love and experience the pangs and delights which seem as inevitable as growing older or being mortal. It is well-known that cultural expectations produce real results."[27]

To what extent adolescents seek out love for its own sake, and to what extent for its symbolic adult attributes, is hard to say, but no doubt both influences are operating. Another pressure is added if the mode of the peer group is to fall in love. Few other groups in American society demand as much conformity as the adolescent subgroup. Thus, the adolescent is simultaneously reaching for and being pushed into a new role. Oftentimes when the adolescent feels he has found love, his new self-image becomes very important to himself and to others who care to observe it. As Morton Hunt puts it, the "jaunty step, new-minted optimism, and smug contentment of the adolescent in love means that he has found two things to be of great value—his beloved, and himself."[28] He has attained that which society has taught him to seek and attain.

Cultural conditioning is often so effective and efficient that the adolescent, and many times the adult, believes that when he has fallen in love he has discovered something distinctly unique, discovered by few others, past or present. When the individual who has fallen in love thinks his experience is unique, mysterious, and without precedent, his culture has usually taught him to so think.[29] He has so well internalized external cultural values that he has come to believe they originated within himself.

As the young person reaches late adolescence and enters the early

---

[27]Clifford Kirkpatrick, *The Family As Process and Institution* (New York: The Ronald Press Co., 1955), p. 273.

[28]Hunt, *op. cit.*, p. 374.

[29]Willard Waller and Reuben Hill, *The Family* (New York: The Dryden Press, 1951), p. 115.

adult years, various pressures that help propel his internalized value of finding love increase. Because marriage is of great importance in the American society—especially for the girl—love must be encouraged to develop so that marriage can and will occur during the accepted age period. Goode argues that because love, as related to marriage, is so important to society, it must be controlled before it appears.[30] Therefore, the constant early emphasis on love values is closely related to future marital choice. Parents often increasingly pressure the young person to fall in love; more specifically, they try to direct their children to fall in love with the "right kind of person." When parental pressure starts early in adolescence, parents are often able to control the children's choice of a love partner. Parents "threaten, cajole, wheedle, bribe and persuade their children to go 'with the right person,' during both the early love play and later during courtship phases."[31]

The peer group can support or undercut parental influence, depending on whether the general values of parents and peer groups are alike or different. When the values are essentially the same, the individual will, presumably, suffer only minimal conflict finding a proper kind of love partner. But when parents and peers differ, the potential for conflict is great, depending upon the influence and meaningfulness of each of the pressure groups for the individual.

Pressures intensify during the age period when increasing numbers of the individual's age peers are finding love and marriage. The peer group splits sharply between the "chosen" and the "unchosen." Increasingly concerned with a negative, "unchosen" status, both the individual and his parents may actively try to wipe out the stigma.

At this age stage rather sharp differences occur, determined by the sex of the young person. Girls are generally much more preoccupied with thoughts of marriage than boys of the same age because love and marriage usually mean more for the future adult roles of the girl than of the boy. It is our contention that the most important adult role for most American girls is still that of wife-mother; and to achieve this role she must first fall in love. For the boy, the most important adult role is probably his occupation, the achievement of which is not dependent on love. In fact, the boy may view love as a threat to occupational achievement, fearing that marriage and parenthood may restrict his occupational education or the chance of directing his full energies toward successful job fulfillment. Thus,

---

[30]Goode, *op. cit.*, p. 43.
[31]*Ibid.*, p. 45.

girls and boys, especially those in college, often view marriage differently: the former see it as something to be achieved as soon as possible, the latter as something that should be at least temporarily postponed. A college boy will frequently explain that his break-up with a girl was due to her "getting too serious." On the other hand, resistance to marriage is obviously not true for a large number of young college men. Largely because college and marriage were combined by the GIs of World War II, a pattern of college marriage has continued to prevail. This trend has been strengthened by parental encouragement and financial aid. In view of the girl's stronger marital interest, it would be interesting to discover whether financial aid comes most often from the girl's parents.

While the girl generally sees marriage as important, she also tends to remain somewhat idealistic about the love that leads to marriage. One study of college girls entering marriageable ages found that 98 percent of them desired marriage. Yet, with marriage so important, only 16 percent said they believed "all is fair in love."[32] A note of interest is that those who were or had been in love took a less idealistic view than those who had never been in love. A parallel contrast was discovered between older and younger coeds. Seemingly, as the culturally specified time for love and marriage draws closer, the means may become somewhat less idealistic.[33]

LOVE AS A NAMING STAGE

The process nature of love has been suggested—each individual must be taught to love, prepared for love, and then given the chance for it to occur. As the male-female relationship develops an emotional awareness of the self and the "significant other," each of the individuals reaches a point when he defines himself as being in love with the other person. Until the naming occurs, love does not exist for the individual, either as a conscious self-awareness or as a determinant of action. The process and the ingredients contributing to a conscious awareness of love will vary with different individuals. Awareness may come as a gradually emerging consciousness for some, but may just happen, without any emerging consciousness, for others. But the consequence is the same—the individual honestly and consciously believes himself to be in love.

Evidence indicates that many people can recall at least the general

---

[32]Robert R. Bell, "Some Factors Related to Coed Marital Aspirations," *The Family Life Coordinator,* October, 1962, p. 92.
[33]*Ibid.,* p. 92.

point in time when they first defined themselves as being in love. In one study of engaged couples asking "at what point in their association they first felt they were in love, all but a few were able to answer with considerable certainty. Most individuals specified the exact day, week or month."[34]

To argue that people can say they are in love but are clearly not is to imply that the evaluator knows what love is and the person being evaluated doesn't. However, an axiom of sociological research is that if a man defines situations as real, they are real in their consequences. Hence, if a person believes he is in love, insofar as this belief contributes meaningfully to his behavior, he is. Therefore, love as a naming stage has two aspects: (1) the self-definition of being in love, and (2) the consequent action resulting from that self-definition. For example, since love is a prerequisite to marriage, the person defining himself as in love will commonly move in the direction of marriage.

Some observers mistakenly assume that the existence of love can be determined by actions. Actions may occasionally, but can not universally, be applied as determinants. On the one hand, a valid determination presupposes knowledge of action patterns related to love and lack of love applicable to all individuals. For example, one might say, "He doesn't show her respect, therefore he doesn't love her." But the individuals in a particular relationship may not perceive respect in the same way as the viewer. On the other hand, the needs of love vary for different individuals and different couples. If the needs of the individuals in a pair-relationship differ drastically, problems may emerge. However, the couple may work out a compromise that to an outsider seems inadequate, but to them is quite adequate. Thus, any attempt to assess or predict actions for all people in love is highly questionable.

In most cases of love, many of the ingredients will be found and they will develop, through an emergent process, to the naming stage. Kirkpatrick's "component-package" theory amplifies this statement.[35] Kirkpatrick's theory simply suggests that different ingredients, in different degrees, operate for different individuals who define themselves as being in love. His theory further indicates that the statement that love changes for the individual over time means that the person continues to define himself as in love, but that the component parts of his love may be altered, reshuffled, or changed.

---

[34]Burgess, *op. cit.*, p. 128.
[35]Kirkpatrick, *op. cit*, pp. 275–76.

The naming stage can also be applied to falling out of love. When a person consciously ceases to define himself as being in love, he ceases to be in love. When the individual no longer perceives the object as a loved one, his actions are usually influenced. Even if his actions do not greatly change, his emotional involvement with the person is bound to be affected. The married individual who no longer defines his feelings as love may continue to treat his partner in essentially the same way as before, because of other important relationship values, but his emotional attachment will have been altered.

FREQUENCY OF LOVE

For a large number of Americans, the romantic notion of a single, everlasting love is not a reality. Many people fall in and out of love on a number of occasions, as a number of empirical studies have shown.

By the time a college student has finished his undergraduate years, he will usually have experienced love at least once. In one study, 96 percent of the males and 97 percent of the females, mean ages 22.0 to 21.9 years, had had one or more important love affairs.[36] In another study—of coeds only—74 percent of those 19 years of age and under, and 85 percent of those 20 years of age and over had been in love at least once.[37]

Of the college students who had experienced love, many had experienced it more than once. In fact, a large number of college students experienced love before they entered college. Burgess and Wallin report that 84 percent of the college girls in their sample had been infatuated or in love between the ages of 12 and 20; and that 50 percent had been infatuated or in love five or more times between ages 12 and 18.[38] A study by the writer found that for those coeds who had been in love, with a median age of 19 years, 53 percent had been in love on two or more occasions.[39] Based on a large sampling of college students, Kephart speculates that the average college student has somewhere between six and ten romantic experiences prior to marriage.[40] Although the findings of these studies differ widely, and although many of the relationships were

[36]Clifford Kirkpatrick and Theodore Caplow, "Courtship in a Group of Minnesota Students," *American Journal of Sociology*, September, 1945, pp. 114–15.
[37]Bell, *op. cit.*, p. 94.
[38]Burgess, *op. cit.*, p. 120.
[39]Bell, *op. cit.*, p. 91.
[40]Kephart, *op. cit.*, p 323.

not defined as love, the evidence clearly indicates that love relationships are common among college students and that a majority experience love more than once.

The various romantic experiences that young people have during the process of dating contribute later to the love that ends in marriage. Yet terminal love affairs have many of the same characteristics as those that move into marriage. "The action tendencies generated in early love affairs are of the same kind as those which later lead to mating, but they fail because they are counter-poised by other attitudes."[41] When an individual has been in love before, he probably recognizes and contrasts a new love relationship with previous ones—and may think of marriage after a relatively short courtship. Burgess and Wallin suggest that "couples who fall in love and decide they wish to marry tend to achieve this stage with moderate rapidity, in an interval ranging from about six months to a year after they first begin to date."[42]

Platonic Relationships

A complete discussion of cross-sex interaction must consider the possible kinds of love relationships that are free from sexual desire. A platonic relationship between a male and a female involves neither romance nor sex. The writer has found that a majority of college students believe platonic relationships can exist, but when they are asked to describe the nature of the relationship, their illustrations almost always fall into specific categories such as the following: *Dating rejects*—The individual was dated at one time but is no longer viewed as datable for various reasons. *Pseudo-family*—The individual has grown up with the person in a close, "brother-sister" type relationship. *The committed*—The friend is going steady, is engaged or married, and is therefore not a dating possibility. *The different*—The person is of a different race, religion, age, etc.

These categories are essentially *safe* relationships in which the platonic friend is not perceived in the role of a possible love interest. It is always possible that the safe factor may be destroyed if the individual starts to define the friend in a romantic light. But essentially, the friend is usually defined as platonic because it is believed that he can't be a romantic figure.

"Safe" platonic relationships are probably common among students only when the institutional framework permits them. It is

---

[41]Waller, *op. cit.*, p. 128.
[42]Burgess, *op. cit.*, p. 169.

much more difficult to have even a "safe" friendship in other institutional settings. Furthermore, with few exceptions, close paired friendships are restricted to the unmarried person. Once a person is married, friendships are either between members of the same sex or between married couples. In American society, a close friendship between a married man and a married women is viewed with suspicion. What the couple may view as a platonic friendship will often be viewed as romantic or sexual by others. The implications are twofold: by the early adult years, the person must, in most cases, exclude members of the opposite sex from close personal paired friendship; the importance of the loved one intensifies because he must satisfy most of the needs of the other for cross-sex involvement.

LOVE AND MARRIAGE

The importance of marital love to roles and role relationships in marriage will be discussed in a later chapter. However, a few comments on marital love are necessary here for a logical development of premarital love. As mentioned earlier, romantic love is probably most emphasized during courtship and the first year or two of marriage. Later in marriage, the relationship increasingly depends on the realities of the partners' accumulated shared experiences.

Some brief suggestions on ingredients commonly found in enduring marital love follow.[43] *Physiological*—All kinds of bodily and sexual attractions. Courtship love differs from conjugal love: in the former, physical interest is often based on the unknown and the mysterious elements of the other as a sex object; after marriage the satisfactions often come from what is known and learned through marital interaction. *Psychological*—Various sentimental and affectional feelings. The psychological satisfactions result from the emotional interaction between the two personalities in the marriage. *Sociological*—The many adjustments which make the man and woman companionable and interdependent upon each other. Role-playing abilities, as well as the relating of the various facets of marriage roles, are developed.

An important part of marriage and love is the changing nature of love from the premarriage through the marriage period, but one must be careful in measuring love over time as if it were a quantifiable item. As Folsom has suggested, there is no constant quantity

---

[43]Harold T. Christensen, *Marriage Analysis* (New York: The Ronald Press Co., 1958), p. 225.

of love in general. So far as we know, love does not have its own special budget of bodily or mental energy.[44]

There is good reason to believe that those satisfied with their marriages have the insight and ability to perceive the changes in their relationship and to assess their love within the context of change. What they currently have in their marriage they often feel to be more important than what took them into the marriage. In many marriages characterized by disillusionment and unhappiness, the partners probably tend to look back on the ego-exciting elements of courtship and the early stages of marriage and feel deprived because those elements are gone. If nothing has developed to replace the old excitement, then the marriage is in trouble.

A study by the writer attempted to get at some views of love by the college-educated wife.[45] The average length of marriage for the wives studied was five years. Eighty-three percent were satisfied with their husbands' romantic treatment and 14 percent were dissatisfied; 3 percent said it was unimportant. When asked to compare the husband's romantic treatment now with that when they were first married, 35 percent said it was greater, 47 percent said it was about the same, and 18 percent said it was less. The wives were probably defining romantic love differently than they did when they were first married, but the findings indicate that the majority of college-educated wives studied were generally satisfied with the romantic aspect of their marriages.

The wives were also asked to contrast other respects of their love now to that when they were first married. When they were asked to compare their love for their husbands now and when they were first married, 67 percent said they now loved their husbands more, 28 percent said—about the same, and 5 percent said—less. Asked to evaluate the love of their husbands for them now with that when they were first married, 62 percent of the wives felt their husbands now loved them more, 32 percent said—about the same, and 6 percent said—less. The findings suggest that over 90 percent of the wives studied felt no decrease in love either by their husbands or by themselves.

Since love is a prerequisite to marriage for most Americans, it follows that the failure of love in the marriage raises serious questions about continuing the marriage. When one or both of the married pair no longer defines himself as in love, the marriage be-

---

[44] Joseph K. Folsom, "Steps in Love and Courtship," in Howard Becker and Reuben Hill, *Family, Marriage and Parenthood* (Boston: D. C. Heath & Co., 1955), p. 208.

[45] Robert R. Bell, unpublished research.

comes difficult, if not intolerable. But while many couples may no longer define themselves as in love, they often continue their marriage for a variety of reasons. Many times the reasons are seen in a negative rather than a positive sense: for example, concern with what ending the marriage will do to children, relatives, and friends; the fear of social criticism; financial difficulties; and so forth. Therefore, many marriages continue even though the love doesn't. Yet the common ideal is that when love ceases so should the marriage. When Burgess and Wallin asked their engaged couples what they thought a married couple should do when they were no longer in love, 80 percent of the men and 84 percent of the women felt the couple should either separate or get a divorce.[46]

MASS MEDIA AND LOVE

The impact of mass communications on beliefs about love is difficult to assess, but it can not be denied that the images presented are important indications of what is believed, or assumed to be believed, about love in the American society. The mass media teach or support many people's attitudes toward love, and because of the increasingly strong role they play in the ongoing socialization of the individual, it is important to recognize this influence. Mass media includes radio, television, movies, popular novels, and mass circulation magazines and newspapers.[47]

In his study of the 1,224 most popular songs from 1890 to 1950, Norman Charles found that almost two thirds dealt with love.[48] The most frequent theme was the lonely or disappointed lover, and, in number, these far exceeded those written about satisfactory love affairs. The second most frequent theme concerned situations in which love had not yet been fulfilled, but presumably soon would be. Charles also points out that the themes rarely question marriage as the logical and inevitable outcome of every love affair, nor do they assume that the love will ever die.

Here are some images about love which are implied in many mass media presentations:

1. *Romantic love belongs to the young.* The general picture of romantic love is associated with the young and the immature. While

---

[46]Burgess, *op. cit.*, p. 395.

[47]R. W. England, Jr., "Images of Love and Courtship in Family-Magazine Fiction," *Marriage and Family Living*, May, 1960, pp.162–65. Also see Betty Friedan, *The Feminine Mystique* (New York: W. W. Norton & Company, Inc., 1963).

[48]Norman Charles, "Values and Themes in Popular Song Lyrics (1890–1950)" Ph.D. dissertation, University of Pennsylvania, 1958), pp. 93–118.

older people may love one another, their love is expected to be sedate, private, and unromantic. While all the world may love a lover, it is the young lover they love, and if an older person behaves as do the young, he is criticized for being in his second childhood. With an increasing percentage of the population in the older age groups, and with increasing rates of remarriage, the emphasis on youth as a prerequisite to love and marriage is partially unrealistic for today's American society.

2. *The female "understanding" of love.* As popularly pictured, the male is *allowed* to believe he is the aggressor, while in reality he is being manipulated by the shrewd female. Women are assumed to know more about love and to be best qualified to deal with questions of the heart. In matters of love, it is implied that women really know what is best for the man and because right must win out, they bring the man around to their way of thinking.

3. *Love conquers all.* There is no problem or situation that true love can't conquer. If love isn't the panacea for all social ills, it will do until something better comes along.

4. *The female as the romantic sex.* A common picture is the never-ending battle between the sexes, resulting from the woman's lofty, idealistic notion of love and the male's predatory, sexual lust. The woman always wins and "tames the beast" because her understanding of true love—which always emerges victorious—is correct.

5. *The pathetic loveless.* Without love, the male becomes an unhappy, cynical bachelor and the female a sour, frustrated spinster. Without the experience of romantic love, individuals are considered lacking as basic human beings, and their lives are perceived as incomplete and empty.

Mass media images probably present some truth, but their tendency to exaggerate is dangerous. The ultimate balance that seems to be important in love lies somewhere between the idealistic and the realistic. When a balance can be achieved, the individual may be able to relate the pleasures of emotion with the satisfactions of reality and achieve a level of happiness satisfying to the self and the loved one.

SELECTED BIBLIOGRAPHY

BURGESS, ERNEST W., and WALLIN, PAUL. *Engagement and Marriage,* chaps. iv, v, and xiii. Philadelphia: J. B. Lippincott Co., 1953.

DeRougemont, Renis. *Love in the Western World.* New York: Anchor Book, 1956.

ENGLAND, R. W., JR. "Images of Love and Courtship in Family-Magazine Fiction," *Marriage and Family Living,* May, 1960, pp. 162–65.

FRIEDAN, BETTY. *The Feminine Mystique,* chaps. ii and x. New York: W. W. Norton & Company, Inc., 1963.

GOODE, WILLIAM J. "The Theoretical Importance of Love," *American Sociological Review,* Vol. 24, No. 1 (February, 1959), pp. 38–47.

HUNT, MORTON M. *The Natural History of Love.* New York: Alfred A Knopf, Inc., 1959.

——*Her Infinite Variety,* chaps iii and iv. New York: Harper and Row, Publishers, 1962.

KEPHART, WILLIAM. *The Family, Society and the Individual,* chap. xi. New York: Houghton Mifflin Co., 1961.

KIRKPATRICK, CLIFFORD. *The Family as Process and Institution,* chap. xii. New York: The Ronald Press Co., 1955.

LEWENSOHN, RICHARD. *A History of Sexual Customs.* New York: Harper & Brothers, 1958.

MACE, DAVID, and MACE, VERA. *Marriage East and West.* Garden City, New York: Doubleday and Company, Inc., 1960.

QUEEN, STUART A; ADAMS, JOHN B.; and HABENSTEIN, ROBERT W. *The Family in Various Cultures,* chap. xii. Philadelphia: J. B. Lippincott Co., 1961.

TAYLOR, G. RATTNAY. *Sex in History.* New York: The Vanguard Press, 1954.

THEODORSON, GEORGE A. "Romanticism and Motivation to Marry in the United States, Singapore, Burma and India," *Social Forces,* September, 1965, pp. 17–27.

MATE SELECTION

Most human beings reach a point in adolescence or in their adult years when they move into a marriage relationship. In all cultures, a number of persons of the opposite sex are theoretical marriage mates, yet in no culture is the selection of the marriage partner one of random choice. There are always restrictions that limit the final choice. All cultures have social restrictions and most cultures also have personal restrictions. The social restrictions can be such factors as the person being of the proper age, not already married, not too closely related to the chosen partner, and so forth. The personal factors involve the individual's satisfaction of his ego-needs—as in the United States where reciprocal love is of great importance.

In most cultures, the selection of a mate has not rested as much with the young people entering marriage as it does in the United States today. In a comparative study of 39 societies, Stephens found only five societies besides our own in which free choices were customarily permitted.[1] In most societies the possible mates are determined by the parents, usually the father, or other elder males connected with the family. Parents in other societies have limited the choice of a marriage mate for several reasons: (1) In the patriarchal society the father made most of the important decisions. (2) The choice of marriage partner was often related to economic factors important to the family. Through the use of bride price and a dowry system, marriage relationships were based in part on economic alignments between families. (3) When the young person selected a mate, limits of choice had usually already been set by the father. However, the final choice of a specific mate was, at least in part, that of the young person.

In the United States today, parents still have some influence on the selection of their offspring's mate. As previously discussed, the chief influence of parents is often through the passing on of values to the offspring. The findings of Burgess and Wallin (table 1) also

---

[1] William N. Stephens, *The Family in Cross-Cultural Perspective* (New York: Holt, Rinehart & Winston, Inc., 1963), p. 198.

indicate that parents influence mate selection because many young people discuss their choice of marriage partner with their parents. Today, in contrast to custom in the patriarchal system of the past, the mother is more apt to be consulted than the father. Table 1 shows that the mother was consulted by 62 percent of the men and by 70 percent of the women. The father was consulted by 44 percent

TABLE 6–1

INDIVIDUALS WITH WHOM THE CHOICE OF MARRIAGE MATE
WAS DISCUSSED, BY SEX

	Male	Female
Mother	62%	70%
Father	44	32
Friend (s)	43	42
Sibling	25	26
Doctor	8	3
Clergyman	7	3
Others	11	5

Adapted from: Ernest W. Burgess and Paul Wallin, *Engagement and Marriage* (Chicago: J. B. Lippincott Co., 1953), p. 178. Percentages are rounded off.

of the men and by 32 percent of the women. Discussion with a friend or friends by the male was as frequent (43 precent) as discussion with his father. The daughter was more apt to consult her friend or friends (42 percent) than her father.[2] The evidence indicates that parents continue to play a part in their offspring's mate selection, but it seems safe to assume that the young person is today more the ultimate mate selector than formerly. The Burgess and Wallin study found that 51 percent of the men and 42 percent of the women did not consult anyone on the wisdom of their choice of a marriage partner.[3]

Mate selection in American society is a gradual process that starts with dating and moves through the courtship process. It does not happen to an individual "all of a sudden," but rather it is the culmination of the young person's preparation over a number of years. Determined by his previous experiences and ego-needs, a person reaching the age of marriage starts to focus on a particular individual. His values have been pretty well established by the age of marriage, and the general type of person he will marry has, within reasonable limits, already been determined.

The experiences leading up to mate selection, and the values

---

[2]Ernest W. Burgess and Paul Wallin, *Engagement and Marriage* (Philadelphia: J. B. Lippincott Co., 1953), p. 178.

[3]*Ibid.*, p. 178.

involved, combine emotional with rational factors. As Waller and Hill write, "A man does not select the type of woman who will make a good wife, all things considered; he almost necessarily selects the sort of woman with whom he can fall in love, and women likewise select husbands on the same gloriously irrelevant basis."[4] Anthropological evidence indicates that when people are free to choose their own mates, individual and personal motives come into play. Some of these are "romantic love, sexual desire, loneliness, desire for children and full adult status, or more exotic motives. (One personal, "exotic" motive among the Siwai is the desire to raise one's own pigs.)"[5] The direction of choice, whether romantic or rational, will vary with different individuals. But regardless of variations by different individuals, the young person selecting his own mate today places far greater importance on the personal and emotional than did the parents of the past when they more actively helped select mates for their offspring.

From first acquaintance to marriage, the relationship of a couple often covers an extended period of time. In the Burgess and Cottrell sample of 526 marriages, only one in ten of the couples was acquainted less than six months before they married, whereas two thirds of them had been acquainted two years or more.[6] The indication is that even in a society in which the personal and emotional factors in mate selection prevail, considerable time continues to be devoted to the emergence of a relationship that continues to marriage.

Two general social changes in mate selection and marriage have developed over time in the United States: the percentage of Americans that marry has increased, and the age of marriage has lowered. About 92 percent of the population will be married at least once during their lifetime.[7] At the present time, the population of single persons is at its lowest point since 1890.[8] In 1963, 71 percent of all males and 68 percent of all females at age 14 and over were married.[9] The state of marriage has achieved a high popularity in the United States, and increasingly with younger people. In 1960 the

---

[4]Willard Waller and Reuben Hill, *The Family* (New York: The Dryden Press, 1951), p. 195.
[5]Stephens, *op. cit.*, p. 187.
[6]Ernest W. Burgess and Leonard Cottrell, *Predicting Success and Failure in Marriage* (Englewood Cliffs, N. J.: Prentice-Hall, Inc., 1939), p. 406.
[7]Paul C. Glick, *American Families* (New York: John Wiley & Sons, Inc., 1957), p. 198.
[8]Hyman Rodman, *Marriage, Family and Society* (New York: Random House, 1965), p. 290.
[9]*Ibid.*, p. 290.

median age for marriage in America was 22.8 years for males and 20.3 years for females, contrasted with the 1890 median of 26.1 years for males and 22.0 years for females. Table 2 shows that over the seventy-year period from 1890 to 1960, the median age at marriage for the male decreased by 3.3 years and for the female by 1.7 years.[10] (The greater decrease for the male reflects the tendency in the past for the male to postpone marriage until he had achieved some adult economic security. Today, many young men marry when they are just starting their occupational careers or while still in school.)

TABLE 6–2

MEDIAN AGE AT FIRST MARRIAGE, BY SEX, FOR THE UNITED STATES, 1890 TO 1960

	Male	Female	Age Difference (years)
1960	22.8	20.3	2.5
1950	22.8	20.3	2.5
1940	24.3	21.5	2.8
1930	24.3	21.3	3.0
1920	24.6	21.2	3.4
1910	25.1	21.6	3.5
1900	25.9	21.9	4.0
1890	26.1	22.0	4.1

Adapted from: Bureau of the Census, "Population Characteristics," *Current Population Reports*, Series P–20, No. 105, November 2, 1960, p. 3.

The discussion thus far has indicated some of the general marriage characteristics in the United States. Given the interest in marriage as reflected in our high national marriage rates, it is important to look at some of the variables that contribute to mate selection. The following discussion indicates the more important factors that help narrow the range of marital possibilities for the individual.

ENDOGAMY

Endogamy refers to the general norms of preferred or required mate selection within a particular group. It is used here to refer to the selection of a mate similar to the individual, in that they are both members of the same broad social grouping influenced by the same general norms.

Endogamy Factors

Propinquity. Propinquity means nearness. In its broadest sense it states the obvious—that people must meet if they are to select one

---

[10]Bureau of the Census, "Population Characteristics," *Current Population Reports*, Series P-20, No. 105, November 2, 1960, p. 3.

another as mates. In family research, however, propinquity also refers to certain social variables of similarity that tend to encourage the individuals to select each other for marriage. The most common of these are residential propinquity and occupational propinquity.

Strictly speaking, propinquity is not a category of endogamy. Propinquity often affects endogamy, but no "within-group" connotation is attached to it. Thus, propinquity does not imply norms or values, but it is included at this point because—just as endogamy does—it refers to "like marrying like."

Residential propinquity is a factor, of course, because two people who live close to each other have a better chance of meeting and deciding on marriage than if they live some distance apart. Bossard's early study of propinquity in 1931 covered 5,000 consecutive marriages in Philadelphia. He found that more than a third of these marriages were between people who lived within five blocks or less of each other and over half of them were between people who lived within twenty blocks of each other.[11] A more recent study done in Duluth, Minnesota, in 1952 found that residential propinquity continued to be a decisive factor. Marches and Turbeville found that 21 percent of the married couples they studied in Duluth had lived within five blocks of each other and 43 percent within twenty blocks.[12] These findings indicate that segments of the population continue to find their mates through or because of residential propinquity—nearness.

However, to say that people tend to marry those who live near them does not tell the whole story. In many cases, close residency is a reflection of other, more important endogamous factors. Residential areas in and around cities tend to be homogeneous. The people that live in such areas are often alike in race, religion, ethnic background, and general socioeconomic status. It is possible that if neighborhoods were more heterogeneous, high rates of residential propinquity in mate selection would be greatly reduced.

Occupational propinquity refers to the tendency of people working in the same occupational areas to marry one another; in other words—again to state the obvious—they are very apt to meet each other. But occupational propinquity is also influenced by other important social variables, particularly education. There is evidence that the higher the social class, the greater the degree of occupa-

[11]James Bossard, "Residential Propinquity as a Factor in Mate Selection," *American Journal of Sociology*, September, 1932, pp. 219–24.

[12]Joseph R. Marches and Gus Turbeville, "The Effect of Residential Propinquity on Marriage Selection," *American Journal of Sociology*, May, 1953, p. 594.

tional propinquity, a link that can be explained by the importance attached to educational similarity in the higher social classes. Further, in occupational propinquity, prospective mates are often in different but related occupations, with the male's educational level and prestige being higher than the female's; the physician and nurse, or the dentist and dental technician, for example.

Race. Of all the factors of endogamy, race exerts the strongest influence. The mores against interracial marriage are extremely strong in the United States. Thirty of the states have miscegenation statutes or laws prohibiting the marriage of whites to Negroes, Mongolians, Hindus, Malayans, Chinese, Japanese, or American Indians.[13] (The most common legal prohibitions are against Negrowhite interracial marriages.) But even in those states which do not by law prohibit interracial marriages, the rates of its incidence are very low. The belief held by many people, that without restrictive laws there would be a great increase in interracial marriages, is not supported by fact.[14]

It has been stated that the city of Los Angeles may have had the highest rates of interracial marriage of any city in the continental United States. In Los Angeles, the estimate for 1959 was that during that year interracial marriages made up about 1.6 percent of all marriages occurring.[15] For the entire United States, our own very rough estimate is that interracial marriages constitute somewhere between one in every five hundred to one thousand marriages during any given year. The overwhelming tendency for Americans, then, is to select a mate racially like themselves, and the available evidence indicates that race will probably continue to be the strongest type of endogamy practiced in the United States for many years in the future.[16]

In presenting data from various studies on interracial and interfaith marriages, sometimes rates of *marriage* are given, referring to the percentage of all marriages that are mixed according to some specific social category, and, sometimes rates of *individuals* in mixed marriages are given, referring to the percentage of all married indi-

---

[13]William M. Kephart, "Legal and Procedural Aspects of Marriage and Divorce," in Harold T. Christensen (ed.), *Handbook on Marriage and The Family* (Chicago: Rand McNally & Co., 1964), p. 947.

[14]George E. Simpson and J. Milton Yinger, *Racial and Cultural Minorities* (New York: Harper & Brothers, 1958), p. 559.

[15]See: Lee G. Burchinal, "The Premarital Dyad and Love Involvement," in Harold T Christensen (ed.) *Handbook of Marriage and The Family*, (Chicago: Rand McNally & Co., 1964), pp. 646–47.

[16]Simpson and Yinger, *op. cit.*, pp. 558–59.

viduals according to some specific social category.[17] How these two
differently based marriage rates can confuse may be illustrated as
follows: Suppose that of ten marriages there are six where both partners are Catholics and four where one partner is Catholic and his
spouse is a Protestant. We could say that 40 percent of the *marriages*
are religiously mixed. However, of the twenty individuals involved
in the ten marriages, sixteen are Catholics and four are Protestants.
Therefore, if our interest is in the number of non-Catholics in the
ten marriages, we have only four out of the twenty *individuals,* or
20 percent, half of the first percentage. It is useful to keep this distinction in mind when comparing different marriage rates.

Religion. Most Americans select mates of the same religious
background. No laws prohibit marriage across religious lines, but
few, if any, religions encourage marriage outside the religion, particularly if the person marrying, or his children, are lost to the
religious group. The belief in the norm of marrying within one's
religion is reflected in the dating patterns of young people, for the
evidence indicates that dating within the religion is the preferred
pattern of behavior. This appears to be true, even though there is
often a discrepancy between liberal views stated and the actual behavior followed.

A recent study on a midwestern campus asked "How important
is it to you that your date be a member of the same religion?" The
response given by 25 percent of the females and 42 percent of the
males was, "It makes little differences."[18] A similar, recent, nationwide study of adolescents found that only 35 percent said they
thought it very important to marry someone of the same religious
belief.[19] (The studies also indicate that boys are more liberal in
their stated attitudes than girls). But it seems that even after college
students state these liberal values they behaviorally tend to stay
within their religion, because of the possibility that the dating
relationship will move to a more serious relationship. By not dating
outside their religion, they do not allow this possibility. This writer
found, in a study of the dates of 124 college men and 133 college
women over a 28-day period, that for the males, by religion, 91 percent of the Jews, 81 percent of the Protestants, and 61 percent of

[17]Hyman Rodman, "Technical Note on Two Rates of Mixed Marriage," *American
Sociological Review,* October, 1965, pp. 776–78.
[18]Robert H. Coombs and William F. Kenkel, "Sex Differences in Dating Aspirations and Satisfaction with Computer-Selected Partners," *Journal of Marriage and
Family,* February, 1966, p. 63.
[19]*Newsweek,* "The Teenagers," March 21, 1966, p. 57.

the Catholics had dates with girls *within* their religion. For the females, religious endogamy in dating was 97 percent for Jews, 78 percent for Protestants, and 66 percent for Catholics.[20] However, even
those who do date outside their religion do not usually think of
marriage outside it. In a study of Jewish men, Kramer and Leventman found that while two thirds had once dated gentile girls, 87
percent preferred to marry a Jewish girl, and of those Jewish men
who were already married, 93 percent of them had Jewish wives.[21]

Because there is no central agency for the uniform collection of
data on religious endogamy, we are dependent upon the educated
estimates provided by experts. It is estimated that the percentage of
individuals entering an interfaith marriage is at least 24 percent for
Catholics, 9 percent for Protestants, and 7 percent for Jews.[22]

A similarity of religous background means a similarity in many
beliefs and patterns of life. Therefore, to say that people come from
the same religious background implies more than a similarity of
religious beliefs. Yet, even though the religious affiliation is the
same, the religious involvement of individuals can vary greatly. Individuals in all major religious groups range from the highly devout
to the nominally religious; therefore, religious intensity may be a
factor of similarity or difference in mate selection. Wide differences
in intensity of religion may indicate an area of conflict for the two
individuals. Though a quantitative comparison is impossible,
one could argue that the difference in religous intensity between an
Orthodox Jew and a Reformed Jew is greater than the difference
between a Reformed Jew and a Unitarian. However, social beliefs
of religious prejudice and discrimination cloud the issue and often
make the influence of religion more than one of theological differences.

Age. An individual usually selects a mate from a closely related
age grouping. Thus, a person is limited to the single members of
the opposite sex in his age group, rejecting the many that are either
too young or too old. Earlier in this chapter, the 1960 male-female
median ages of 22.8 and 20.3 years at the time of marriage were
mentioned. But averages tell us little about variations in age or factors related to those that marry at younger or older ages than the
average.

[20]Robert R. Bell, "Some Dating Characteristics of Students in a Large Urban University," unpublished.

[21]Judith R. Kramer and Seymour Leventman, *Children of the Gilded Ghetto* (New
Haven: Yale University Press, 1961), p. 180.

[22]Rodman, *Marriage, Family and Society, op. cit.,* p. 58.

Burchinal has done a great deal of research on young marriages. Young marriages are arbitrarily defined as those entered at under 19 years of age. "Youthful marriage rates among the white population are greater than pre-World War II, but have probably remained relatively stable during the past decade."[23] Individuals who select a mate in the younger age groups have certain characteristics that distinguish them from the older group. Burchinal found that early marriages:

1. Usually involve young girls and their slightly older husbands.
2. Involve premarital pregnancies in between approximately one third to one half of all cases.
3. Disproportionately involve persons with lower or working class backgrounds.[24]

Another study of young marriages indicates that girls who marry young are emotionally less stable than those who marry later and have less satisfactory relationships with their parental families.[25]

Burchinal suggests that the rates of young marriages may go down in the near future. He thinks it possible that the increasingly greater value attached to extending education will have an impact on young marriages: "Increased school and post-high school attendance should be associated with a reduction in young marriage rates. Among 17-year-olds, school dropout rates declined from 32 percent in 1950 to 24 percent in 1960."[26] But while marriage frequently leads to ending formal education if the individuals are in high school, it is much less apt to have the same negative affect when the couple are older and in college.

Those who marry at older ages, because they have lived as single adults for a long period, may find it difficult to adjust to the demands of the paired relationship of marriage. The fact that they have postponed marriage beyond the ordinary marriage period would indicate that they are different in some respects; possibly many had low marriage motivation. Glick suggests that marriages contracted at unusually advanced ages are of relatively short duration.[27]

Age endogamy is, specifically then, the selection of a mate within

---

[23]Lee G. Burchinal, "Research on Young Marriages: Implications for Family Life Education," *Family Life Coordinator*, September-December, 1960, p. 7.

[24]*Ibid.*, p. 11.

[25]J. J. Moss and Rudy Gingles, "The Relationship of Personality to the Incidence of Early Marriage," *Marriage and Family Living*, November, 1959, p. 377.

[26]Lee G. Burchinal, "Trends and Prospects for Young Marriages in the United States," *Journal of Marriage and Family*, May, 1965, p. 247.

[27]Glick, *op. cit.*, p. 111.

an age range close to the individual. Among couples who married between 1947 and 1954, the median difference in ages of the spouses was 3 years,[28] and the pattern in the United States is for the man to select a woman from a slightly younger age group than his own. The longer the man postpones marriage, the greater is his tendency to marry a woman in an extended younger age group. In other words, the older the man when he first marries, the greater the age difference between bride and groom. When the groom is 20 years old, the bride is only a year younger; when the groom is 26, the bride is 3.8 years younger; when the groom is 34, the bride is 6.5 years younger.[29]

The increasing age difference with older age at marriage has important consequences. It means that the older male desiring to marry—because he can marry down in age—has a wide market out of which to select a mate, while the older woman—because she must generally marry up in age—has a narrow market. Thus, while it is true that the longer each sex postpones marriage the less chance each has for marriage, the decrease of marriage probability with increased age is greater for the female than for the male.

Education. In the discussion thus far, the endogamous factors of mate selection have been treated independently. This approach should be recognized as an analytical device. In reality, of course, none of the variables remain or operate unaffected by the others. Thus, although the present section deals with educational levels, it is also necessary to relate a part of it to age factors.

Most Americans usually select a mate from the same general educational level. As a rule, men marry women of the same or a lower level of education, and women marry men of the same or a higher educational level. This is more apt to be true among the more highly educated. In the lower social classes, formal education is less important in separating the male from the female in mate selection. But, the higher the educational level, the greater the importance attached to education by both men and women and, therefore, at the higher levels, the greater importance attached to men having the same or higher levels of education than women.

Hollingshead and Redlich found the following educational differences between men and women by social class level. In class I (the highest social class), the median number of years of school completed by male heads of families was 17.8 and by their wives, 14.4;

---

[28]*Ibid.*, p. 125.
[29]*Ibid.*, p. 123.

in class II, the men, 15.5, and the women, 13.7 years; in class III, the men, 12.4, and the women, 12.1; in class IV, the men, 9.4, and the women, 10.5; in class V (the lowest social class), the men, 5, and the women, 8 years. Thus, in the highest social class the husband had 3.2 years more education than his wife, while in the lowest social class the husband had 3 years *less* education than his wife.[30]

For the total American population, Glick found that, on the average, among every 100 first marriages, the husbands and wives in 45 were in the same broad educational level; in 28, the wives were in a higher educational level; and in 27, the husbands were in a higher educational level.[31]

/For the male, educational level makes little difference in the percentage married. By years of education, the percentage of white males married, who are between 30 and 34 years of age is: eight years or less, 83 percent; high school graduates, 85.9 percent; and college graduates, 84.9 percent. Some variations exist in the percentage of married white women between the ages of 30 and 34 by education: eight years or less, 77.5 percent; high school graduates, 86.9 percent; and college graduates, 77.7 percent.[32] The statistics indicate a greater probability of being married for high school-educated females than for the other two educational groups. For the college-educated woman, the chances of marriage have increased; in 1940, only 62.9 percent between the ages of 30 and 34 were married, but by 1950 the number increased by 14.8 percent to reach 77.7 percent.[33]

The pattern in the past was one of postponing marriage with increased education, and while this tendency has been reduced, the college educated continue to marry at somewhat older ages than the rest of the population. Age at first marriage for those with eight or fewer years of education is 21.5 years; high school graduates, 21.1 years; and, college graduates, 23.9 years.[34] A trend to a lower marriage age for the college educated reflects attitudes about combining marriage and education which were probably influenced by the high marriage rate of GI's attending college after World War II.

Level of education has limited effect on age differences between husbands and wives. The husband with eight years of education or

---

[30]August B. Hollingshead and Fredrick C. Redlich, *Social Class and Mental Illness* (New York: John Wiley & Sons, Inc., 1958), pp. 75, 89, 98, 107, 120.

[31]Glick, *op. cit.*, p. 117.

[32]*Ibid.*, p. 107.

[33]*Ibid.*, p. 107.

[34]*Ibid.*, p. 116.

less marries a wife 3.7 years younger; the high school graduate male marries a wife 2.8 years younger; and the college graduate male, a wife 3.1 years younger.[35] The higher the male's level of education, the older his and his bride's age will be when they marry.

Educational level may have important implications for the woman who extends her formal education, particularly beyond the undergraduate degree. For the woman, extended education and increased age places her in a marriage market in which the number of available males meeting the requirements of as much or more education and an older age are very limited. In addition, the man can marry down both in age and education, which means increased competition by younger and less educated women for the available unmarried men. The unmarried male with a high level of education is in an optimum position for mate selection.

Social Class. Most of the variables already discussed are determinants of social class position. In social class analysis, education, occupation, and income are generally considered to be the most important variables. Therefore, social class may be considered a broad category of endogamy in mate selection. Because similarity of class often implies similarity of values and attitudes, social class factors are of prime importance in mate selection. For example, two middle-class individuals may share values about marriage roles, the having of children, adult ambitions, and so forth that make them alike in a very personal way.

In recent years, however, formal education has contributed to marriage between individuals of somewhat different social class backgrounds. This often implies upward social mobility through education for the individual coming from the lower social class background. The mate selection of individuals of different social class backgrounds has to a great extent developed since the end of World War II, and has centered on males moving up in the social system through education and marrying females from higher social class backgrounds.

On many college campuses, the coeds come from a higher social class background than do the men. Formal education is considered more important for men because of its direct relationship to the male's important adult occupational role. Therefore, males are often more personally motivated and socially encouraged to go to college if they have ambitions of upward mobility. Women are more apt to be sent to college because it is socially the thing to do, rather than

---

[35]*Ibid.*, p. 128.

for occupational preparation or intellectual development. If a family has limited economic means for assisting the college education of their offspring, the son will usually be given preference over the daughter. (Also, after World War II, the GI Bill sent many men to college who would not have otherwise attended, as well as sending them to schools they would not have been able to afford, even if they had gone on to college. It is possible that World War II veterans who went on to college had a high rate of marriage with females coming from a higher social class.)

Marriage of individuals from different social classes among college students is often seen more realistically by the young people than by their parents. The young person tends to place less emphasis on background and more on the assets of the other person, while the parents, who know less about the other person, place greater emphasis on his background. With the increase in the number of individuals going on to college, it seems safe to predict that college will continue to provide a setting for the mate selection of individuals from somewhat different social class backgrounds.

If a male does not marry while he is in college, his education provides him with an upward mobility into an occupational grouping that predisposes him to select a mate from his achieved social class level. His new social class level places his personal interests and behavior in a setting and market out of which usually comes his eventual selection of a mate.

Endogamy Deviations

None of the endogamy factors in mate selection are absolute. Some individuals marry persons from different residential or occupational areas, of different race or religion, or different age or education, or from different social class levels. In American society the two areas of endogamous deviation of greatest interest are interracial and interfaith mate selection.

Interracial Mate Selection. The American society's concern over mate selection across racial lines is often provoked by attitudes of prejudice and discrimination, rather than by the actual frequency of the event. The number of interracial marriages in the United States is not great. (The discussion in this section refers to the most commonly prohibited interracial marriage: Negro-white marriages, where the Negro background is known or openly presented.)

There is some evidence that when interracial marriage does occur, the tendency is greater for the Negro male to marry outside the racial group. A California study of interracial marriages indicates that in 78 percent of the instances it was the Negro male who married the white female.[36] There is also evidence that people who enter interracial marriages are somewhat older at the time of their marriages than those who marry within their race.[37] A study of 16,532 marriages performed in Hawaii found that in racially unmixed marriages the couples were usually about the same age or the groom was slightly older, while in interracial marriages the groom was often much older than his bride—although sometimes he was several years her junior.[38]

While feelings of racial prejudice probably account for a majority of individuals not marrying outside the racial group, other factors also operate. Because racial groups strongly circumscribe the social relationships of the individual, many persons have little or no contact with members of other races. When social interaction does occur, the relationship is often formalized and does not lead to the kinds of interpersonal involvement related to mate selection.

When individuals cross the lines of race in mate selection, they often encounter extreme difficulties in developing a satisfactory marriage relationship. Many times the individuals find themselves rejected by relatives and friends on both sides. The couple are often forced through social rejection into marginal groups. Many times they receive reassurance and support only if they seek out and interact with other couples like themselves. The individual from the majority group also undergoes a drastic role change if and when he is treated with prejudice for the first time. Because of his love for his spouse, the prejudiced treatment directed at them individually and together is often very painful because the loved one is the "cause" of the attack. The individual from the majority group has not been socialized to the nature of prejudice, either for himself or for his loved ones.

Very little is known about the "social types" who racially intermarry. A study in Chicago found that most of the intermarried couples fell into four broad groups: " (1) the intellectuals and 'Bohemians', (2) the religious and political radicals, (3) the 'sporting' world, and (4) the stable middle class. If the white spouse in a Negro-white marriage does not belong to one of these groups, that spouse is likely to be a foreign-born person who is incompletely as-

---

[36]Larry D. Barnett, "Interracial Marriage in California," *Marriage and Family Living*, November, 1963, 626.

[37]Quoted in: Burchinal, "The Premarital Dyad and Love Involvement," *op. cit.*, p. 647.

[38]Robert C. Schmitt, "Age Differences in Marriage in Hawaii," *Journal of Marriage and Family*, February, 1966, pp. 59–60.

similated into American life and does not fully realize what intermarriage means, or did not at the time of marriage."[39]

Together with evidence that it is more often the Negro male who marries the white female than it is the Negro female marrying the white male, there is some evidence that the first type of intermarriage is less characterized by divorce than the second type. That is, divorces of white husbands married to nonwhite wives are more numerous than are divorces of nonwhite husbands married to white wives.[40]

Often the most crucial problem of interracial marriage centers around the children. They will be treated as members of the minority group by the majority group, and may also be rejected in part by members of the minority group. The member coming from the majority group must face the frustration of seeing his children suffer indignities that he had not encountered. The realization that life will be difficult for the children may contribute to the low rate of interracial marriage. Some interracial couples have refrained from having children because of possible difficulties, but they seem to be the exception.[41]

Even though the problems are great in an interracial marriage, it may be that an increasing number of persons who enter such marriages are entering them with the motivations and abilities to make a success of the marriage. One recent study of 95 Negro-white marriages came to the following conclusion: "It would appear that such intermarriage now occurs between persons who are, by and large, economically, educationally, and culturally equal and have a strong emotional attachment, be it rationalization or real. The external pressures faced by interracial couples are often great but certainly do not appear to be overwhelming."[42]

Interfaith Mate Selection. Mate selection across religious lines differs from interracial marriage in that it is much more common, no laws prohibit it, and social criticism of it is much less severe. Most Americans identify with their religion and, in varying degrees, view other religious groups with suspicion. Therefore, religious prejudice often enters into the shaping of attitudes towards other religions, particularly when it is related to the intimate relationship of marriage.

---

[39]Simpson and Yinger, *op. cit.,* p. 562.

[40]Vital Statistics of the United States, 1961, Vol. 111, Sections 3, 4 and 7, "Divorces", U.S. Department of Health, Education and Welfare, p. 7.

[41]Simpson and Yinger, *op. cit.,* p. 564.

[42]Todd H. Pavela, "An Exploratory Study of Negro-White Intermarriage in Indiana," *Journal of Marriage and Family,* May, 1964, p. 211.

As stated earlier, people of the *same* religious faith may often vary greatly in the intensity of their religious beliefs, though such differences between husbands and wives can usually be resolved with little difficulty because religion is felt to be a part of the woman's role. The male can thus shift religous responsibility to the wife and thereby minimize their differences. And some similarity of religious intensity is probably common in mate selection. But the extremely religious person often views life in a way quite different from the person with limited religious interest, and a significant difference in religious intensity between husband and wife can have a negative influence on many areas of interaction.

Various studies show that the frequency of interfaith marriages has been increasing and that such mixed marriages are subject to a relatively high divorce rate.[43] It has sometimes been assumed that religious differences in a marriage would be a source of marital stress leading to mental health problems for one or both of the spouses. However, one study found that persons who marry a partner of a different religion show no greater mental health risk than those who marry a spouse of the same faith.[44]

A study of 1,167 Manhattan residents by Heiss provides some valuable insights into those who marry across religious lines. He found that Catholics who intermarry are characterized by: (1) nonreligious parents; (2) greater dissatisfaction with parents by the respondent when he was young; (3) greater early family strife; (4) less early family integration (or interdependency of roles); and (5) greater emancipation from the parents at the time of marriage. In the Protestant group, the two strongest characteristics were relatively weak ties to both the family and the religion. For the Jewish group, the only characteristic of any significance was the lower strength of family ties.[45]

Protestants. Because of the many and various subdivisions under the heading of Protestantism, there is no uniform Protestant statement in regard to interfaith marriage. While no Protestant denomination encourages marriage outside the religious group, the different denominations do not agree on the strength of the force they should exert on their members to stay within the religion, or how to treat those who do marry outside the religion. The Protestants

---

[43]John Thomas, "The Factor of Religion in the Selection of Marriage Mates," *American Sociological Review*, August, 1951, p. 16.

[44]Thomas S. Langner and Stanley T. Michael, *Life Stress and Mental Health* (New York: The Free Press of Glencoe, 1963), p. 327.

[45]Jerold S. Heiss, "Premarital Characteristics of the Religiously Intermarried in an Urban Area," *American Sociological Review*, February, 1960, pp. 53–54.

"lack of planned program to prevent or control interfaith marriages is due to the lack of organization among the many Protestant denominations."[46]

Most Protestant concern about interfaith marriage is directed at those who marry Catholics, and is a consequence of the long historical struggle of the Protestant movement in breaking away from the Roman Catholic church. The history of this struggle has been one of great bitterness and, as a result, each group often views the other with suspicion and mistrust. Protestants are also concerned with the loss of offspring to the Catholic church in a mixed marriage, because of the Catholic requirement that such offspring be reared as Catholics.

Estimates place the number of Protestants marrying outside their religion at about nine of every hundred. Of these, the overwhelming majority marry Catholics. It is estimated that only one fifth of 1 per cent of all Protestants who marry outside their religion marry Jews.[47] In fact, the only interfaith marriage with which a large number of Protestants are familiar is that of Protestant and Catholic.

One study indicates that the Protestant fear that children in a mixed marriage will always be reared as Catholics is not justified. Baber found in his sample of Protestant-Catholic marriages that the children were reared as Protestants in a ratio of three to one.[48] Other studies suggest that a higher rate of the children are reared as Catholics.[49] Unfortunately, reliable evidence about the religious rearing of children in interfaith marriages is lacking

Catholics. The Catholic Church takes a strong, unambiguous stand on mate selection outside the religion. The church prefers that the individual marry within the religion; however, it does allow marriage outside the faith. To be valid in the eyes of the church, a marriage between a Catholic and a non-Catholic must be performed by the Catholic Church. Prior to the marriage, the non-Catholic must sign an agreement or contract required by the Church. The non-Catholic, in signing the contract, agrees that:

1. The marriage bond contracted can be broken only by death.
2. The Catholic member shall be permitted the free exercise of

---

[46]Judson T. Landis and Mary G. Landis, *Building a Successful Marriage* (Englewood Cliffs, N.J.: Prentice-Hall, Inc., 1953), p. 150.

[47]Paul Landis, *Making the Most of Marriage,* (New York: Appleton-Century-Crofts, Inc., 1960), p. 231.

[48]Ray E. Baber, *Marriage and the Family* (New York: McGraw-Hill Book Co., 1953), p. 103.

[49]Landis and Landis, *op. cit.*, p. 156.

religion according to the Catholic faith without hindrance or adverse comment.

3. All children of either sex born of such marriage shall be baptized and educated only in the faith and according to the teachings of the Roman Catholic Church, even if the said (Catholic partner) shall die first.

4. No other marriage ceremony than that by the Catholic priest shall take place.

5. He realizes the holiness of the use of marriage according to the teaching of the Catholic Church which condemns birth control and similar abuses of marriage.

6. He will have due respect for the religious principles and convictions of the Catholic partner.

These conditions are a part of the Ante-Nuptial Agreement to be signed by applicants for dispensation from impediment of mixed religion or disparity of cult. Whether the non-Catholic signs the agreement is often determined by the strength of the Catholic partner's religion. Failure to sign the agreement means that the Catholic partner is not recognized as married by the Church—and Church recognition of the marriage would be very important to the Catholic partner with strong religious convictions.

While the Catholic position is very strong in regard to marriage outside the religion, more Catholics than Protestants or Jews enter interfaith marriages. Statistics on the frequency of Catholic mixed marriages are somewhat confusing. One study estimates that about 22 percent of all Catholics marry outside the religion, and indicates that the Catholic, in the vast majority of cases, marries a Protestant. The number of Catholics marrying Jews is less than one half of 1 per cent.[50] The best study of Catholic mixed marriages was done by Thomas, and his estimates are higher. Thomas suggests that between 1930 and 1950 about 30 percent of the marriages performed by priests in the United States were interfaith. "If mixed marriages involving a Catholic but performed outside the church were included, the proportion might be 50 percent."[51]

Evidence on the rearing of offspring indicates some sharp differences between the Catholic position (that all children of "recognized" mixed marriages shall be reared as Catholics) and what actually happens. In the Landis study of 192 mixed marriages, in which both the Catholic and the Protestant retained his faith, 50

---

[50]Landis, *op. cit.*, p. 231.
[51]Thomas, *op. cit.*, pp. 488–89.

percent of the children were reared as Protestants, 45 percent as Catholics, and 5 percent with no religious faith. The tendency was for the daughter to follow the faith of the mother and the son the faith of the father.[52]

Jewish. The Jewish faith has maintained an exceptionally high rate of religious endogamy for many years. Because of a long history of religious persecution and the development of a "ghetto" way of life, the pressures are extremely strong for the Jew to marry within his religion. It is estimated that in the United States about 93 of every 100 Jews marry within their religion. Of all the Jewish-gentile mixed marriages, it is estimated that in about 60 percent the non-Jewish spouse is Protestant and in about 40 percent, Roman Catholic.[53]

The Jewish religion recognizes two types of Jewish-gentile marriages. The first is *intermarriage* between a converted gentile and a Jew. This kind of couple can be married by Orthodox, Conservative, or Reformed rabbis. The second type, a *mixed marriage,* occurs when the gentile does not accept Judaism. No Orthodox and very few Conservative or Reformed rabbis can officiate at this type of marriage.[54] However, there is some evidence that a number of Reformed rabbis actually do perform mixed marriages.

In regard to marriage outside the faith, the Orthodox Jewish group takes the strongest position of any religious group. In this group, a Jew who marries outside the religion is considered dead, and the family goes through the bereavement ritual followed when a member actually dies. The Conservative and Reformed groups take a much less severe stand, though both groups emphatically discourage interfaith marriage.

In Jewish-gentile marriages, it is more common for the Jewish male to marry a gentile than it is for the Jewish female to marry outside her religion. In Los Angeles, in 1953, it was found that of all Jewish marriages, 7.4 percent were with non-Jews married to Jews and that almost 80 percent of the non-Jews were females.[55] In Washington, D.C., in 1957, there were 11.3 Jewish households classified as mixed married. Of that group of households, about 70

---

[52]Landis and Landis, *op. cit.,* p. 156.

[53]Bureau of the Census, "Population Characteristics," *Current Population Reports,* Series P-20, No. 79, February 2, 1958, p. 3.

[54]Landis and Landis, *op. cit.,* p. 161.

[55]Fred Massarik, *The Jewish Population of Los Angeles,* (Los Angeles: Los Angeles Jewish Community Council, 1953), p. 44.

percent had non-Jewish wives.[56] While both the Jewish male and female are often watched closely in reference to involved social interaction outside the religion, the female is guarded more closely than the male. The role of the male also permits him to get out from under family and community influence more often than does the role of the female. Therefore, it is comparatively less difficult for the male to become involved with gentiles.

There may also be a social-class influence on the tendency for Jews to marry outside their religion. Rosenthal, in his study of interfaith marriage in Washington, D.C., found that "those who engage in traditional Jewish activity, for the most part self-employed work, have a lower incidence of intermarriage. Those who were employed or who were college graduates tended to have a higher incidence of intermarriage."[57]

General Comments. Probably, only a limited number of individuals who enter mixed religious marriages do so deliberately from the start. In most cases, what begins as a relationship of a nonromantic nature moves over into romance and mate selection. Mayer, in his study of Jewish-gentile courtship, makes the following comments, which are applicable to many interfaith marriages. "The emotional vulnerability of the individual to others is not constant and will vary with different situations. At a particular time, a person may be in need of affection and support and, if someone offers him this, he may be strongly drawn to the donor."[58] When the donor has a different religion, the relationship that develops may be stronger than the negative force of the religious difference. In many relationships, as the emotional attachment intensifies, the two individuals spend more and more time with each other. As a result, they are increasingly cut off from other influences (or prospective marriage partners), which may lead them to become more and more dependent upon each other.[59] When their religions are different, they may seek out privacy to escape criticism. This leads to an increased interdependency and often results in greater emotional commitment.

---

[56]Stanley K. Bigman, *The Jewish Population of Greater Washington, in 1956* (Washington, D.C.: The Jewish Community Council of Greater Washington, 1957), p. 125.
[57]Erich Rosenthal, "Studies of Jewish Intermarriage in the U.S.," *American Jewish Yearbook,* LXIV, 1963, pp. 21–24.
[58]John E. Mayer, *Jewish-Gentile Courtship* (Glencoe, Illinois: The Free Press, 1961), pp. 83–84.
[59]*Ibid.,* p. 95.

Marriage success studies indicate that interfaith have higher divorce rates than intrafaith marriages,[60] though one caution may be suggested in interpreting the high interfaith divorce rates. A selective factor is operating on many who marry outside their religion that may make them more prone to divorce than those who marry within the religion. The factors that lead a person to marry outside the religion often indicate a tendency of rebellion toward cultural norms; this tendency may also operate in that the person feels less compulsion to continue a marriage if it does not meet his expectations. People who enter interfaith marriages are often less conservative than those who do not. When this characteristic is added to the negative social forces directed at those in interfaith marriages, the higher divorce rate becomes more understandable.

HOMOGAMY

The social influences of endogamy may be viewed as a funneling process for the individual. A person starts his life with a theoretically vast market for future mate selection, but as he is socialized and incorporates the value systems of his society, his market is drastically reduced. By the time he reaches marriageable age, he has, in effect, eliminated as potential mates those who, as a result of either social values or the low probability of acquaintance, are not like himself. Even at this point, however, the funnel still has a large spout and the number of potential mates is still fairly extensive. Out of the large number of different individuals still theoretically available to him, he must ultimately focus on one as his marriage choice.

The process of homogamy further limits his eventual choice of a marriage partner. By *homogamy* is meant the conscious or unconscious tendency of an individual to select a mate with personal characteristics similar to his own.

Homogamy Factors

Intelligence. People tend to select marriage partners who have a level of intelligence close to their own. Kuhn came to the conclusion, from his analysis of a number of studies of factors related to married partners, that the highest correlations were with respect to intelligence.[61] Intelligence overlaps some of the factors of endogamy that have been discussed. Higher intelligence is related to higher

---

[60]See: Landis and Landis, *op. cit.*, pp. 152–55, and Thomas, *op. cit.*, pp. 487–91.

[61]Manford H. Kuhn, "How Mates are Sorted," in Howard Becker and Reuben Hill, *Family, Marriage and Parenthood* (Boston: D. C. Heath & Co., 1955), p. 263.

education and more prestigeful occupations, as well as to social class. As with several of the endogamous variables, higher intelligence may be perceived as somewhat more important for the male than for the female. Some evidence indicates that girls tend to play down their basic intelligence while dating and going through courtship, if they believe it is regarded as threatening by the males with whom they are interacting.[62]

Physical Factors. As with intelligence, there is a tendency toward similarity of height in mate selection. One study found a coefficient of correlations of .31 for height. "This means that a man above the average height is likely to marry a woman taller than the average but that she will exceed the norm by only about one-third as much as her husband does."[63] In the United States, the taller man is probably more desirable to most women than the shorter man. A woman usually wants a man to be taller, and often he has to be significantly taller because, wearing high heels, she adds several inches to her own height. It is of interest to note that in the arrangement of "blind dates," the one "matching" variable that is almost always considered is that of height. In regard to weight, Burgess and Wallin found a correlation of .21; for health, .20; for physical appearance or "good looks," .20.[64] Homogamy for health is important because it affects many aspects of the relationship. If there are wide differences in health, the ability to enter into many shared activities will be limited. The physically active usually want a partner who is able to be active with them.

The factor of physical attractiveness is interesting and sometimes confusing. The concept of beauty is relative to cultural and personal values. What constitutes beauty in one society may not be recognized as such in another. In the American culture, the definition of beauty is wide and, except for individuals at the extreme, most people are not viewed as so unattractive they cannot find a mate. Thus, even though the person who most closely meets the ideal requirements of attractiveness generally has a wider market from which to choose, all one has to do is look around to realize that the physically unattractive do find mates—often their counterpart of the opposite sex. Furthermore, in contemporary American society, the sexual appeal of the individual may be as important as the more traditional concern with facial beauty.

---

[62]See: James S. Coleman, *Social Climates in High Schools* (U. S. Department of Health, Education, and Welfare, Monograph No. 4, 1961).

[63]Quoted in Baber, *op. cit.,* p. 80.

[64]Burgess and Wallin, *op. cit.,* pp. 80–81.

Because a young man often considers the attractiveness of girls he dates as reflecting on his prestige in the dating market, he may give this trait greater value than he does the girl herself. In a recent study of college students the only factor that was not rated higher by women than by men was physical attractiveness; "men were much more enthusiastic about having a 'good looking' partner than were women."[65]

Ideal Image. Many individuals tend to "carry in their head" an image of the person they would like to marry. The individuals they encounter are then measured against this ideal image. The image consists of both physical and personality qualities. Strauss found that "an overwhelming proportion of individuals (59 percent) judged that their mates came very close to, or were identical with, their physical ideal; and, an even larger proportion (73 percent) believed that their fiancés were close to or identical with their ideal of personality."[66] What no doubt happens in a number of cases is that after the mate is chosen and the commitment of love is given, the ideal image is altered or elements that once seemed important are discarded as no longer being important.

TABLE 6–3

CONSCIOUSNESS OF "IDEAL-MATE IMAGE" IN CHOOSING A
FIANCE(E), BY SEX

	Male	Female
Very conscious	31%	26%
Vaguely conscious	29	29
Mainly unconscious	16	10
Quite unconscious	8	20
None	4	6
Don't know	6	6
No answer	6	3
	100	100

Adapted from: Ernest W. Burgess and Paul Wallin, *Engagement and Marriage* (Chicago: J. B. Lippincott Co., 1953), p. 191.

Burgess and Wallin also studied the influence of the ideal-mate image in the choosing of a mate. They asked their respondents the degree of consciousness of the ideal-mate image they had when they chose their mate. Table 3 shows that only 31 percent of the men and 26 percent of the women were "very conscious" of the ideal

---

[65]Coombs and Kenkel, *op. cit.*, p. 65.

[66]Anselm Strauss, "Personality Needs and Marital Choice," *Social Forces*, March, 1947, p. 335.

image in choosing a mate.[67] Burgess and Wallin contend that the chief function of the ideal-mate image is negative. "It eliminates many persons with whom one may be in proximity from any consideration at all as matrimonial possibilities."[68] They further state that the "physical characteristics of the ideal mate function in the initial selection in courtship, but that the idealized personality traits have a more significant role in the final selection of a life partner."[69]

A common assumption about mate selection is that a person develops an ideal-mate image strongly influenced by his parent of the opposite sex. (This assumption is often presented in the guise of an Oedipus or an Electra complex.) These theories persist although there is little empirical data to support them. Generally, studies indicate that the ideal-mate image of *both* young men and women is one with qualities similar to those of their mother. Furthermore, the data indicates that both males and females show preferential affection for their mothers.[70] Mothers are generally more important in influencing both sons and daughters simply because they are more significant in their parental roles than are fathers.

With the different socialization experience of boys and girls, and with their different orientations to future adult roles, we would logically expect differences in their mate-selection values. The research evidence suggests these general sex differences: It is common for young men to place more importance than young women on the physical attractiveness, youthfulness, and popularity of their dates. Men also give high value to the woman's desire for a home and children, and to her housekeeping and cooking skills. In contrast, young women place greater importance on the ambition or industriousness of their dates. Women also see as important general intelligence, financial possibilities and similarity of backgrounds. And young women are more apt to stress the importance of chastity for themselves and the social skills or degree of the young man's refinement.[71]

COMPLEMENTARY NEEDS

The factors of endogamy help the individual focus on a potential market for mate selection, and the variables of homogamy aid him still further by narrowing the possible marriage partners within this

---

[67]Burgess and Wallin, *op. cit.*, p. 191.
[68]*Ibid.*, pp. 191–92.
[69]*Ibid.*, p. 194.
[70]Alfred J. Prince and Andrew R. Baggaley, "Personality Variables and the Ideal Mate," *Family Life Coordinator,* July, 1963, pp. 95–96.
[71]See: Burchinal, "The Premarital Dyad and Love Involvement," *op. cit.*, pp. 633–34.

market. Yet, even after individuals are sorted through endogamy and homogamy, a number of possibilities exist. Winch's theory of complementary needs attempts to explain how the range of marriage possibilities is further narrowed.

Winch argues that once the individual has determined the field of eligibles, he then seeks within that field the person who gives the greatest promise of providing him the maximum gratification.[72] Winch's major hypothesis is that in mate selection the need pattern of each spouse will be complementary rather than similar to the need-pattern of the other spouse.[73]

Winch developed a number of need-gratification areas and showed how they were related to one another through their complementarity. To illustrate, here are several combinations that might be found for two individuals in a marital relationship:

1. *Abasement-Dominance.* Abasement means the need to accept blame, criticism, or punishment; to blame or harm the self. Dominance refers to the need to influence and control the behavior of others.
2. *Recognition-Deference.* The need of recognition is to excite the admiration and approval of others, while the need of deference is to admire and praise another person.
3. *Nurturance-Succorance.* To give sympathy and aid to a weak, helpless, ill, or dejected person or animal is the need of nurturance. The need of succorance is to be helped by a sympathetic person; to be nursed, loved, protected, indulged.[74]

In testing the hypothesis of complementary needs, Winch found, after using five sets of data, that three supported the hypothesis and the other two, while they did not support the hypothesis, did not show a countertrend.[75]

Winch's theory of complementary needs, while interesting and provocative, is subject to criticism. First, the study sample was made up of only twenty-five white, middle-class, native-born married couples, and at least one person in each couple was an undergraduate student at Northwestern University.[76] The small size and highly selective nature of the sample raises questions as to the applicability of the theory to couples with different backgrounds. Second, the couples studied were married less than two years and were childless.[77] The study does not show or explain whether the need charac-

---

[72]Robert F. Winch, *Mate Selection* (New York: Harper & Brothers, 1958), p. 406.
[73]*Ibid.*, p. 96.
[74]*Ibid.*, p. 90.
[75]*Ibid.*, p. 119.
[76]*Ibid.*, p. 107.
[77]*Ibid.*, p. 107.

teristics of the couple after marriage are similar to what they were when the couple were in the process of mate selection. Once mate selection has taken place, the couple enter into close role relationships prior to their marriage, even closer after their marriage. Quite possibly, some couples at the time of mate selection had like needs, but through the interactional process of role relationships, one of them altered or modified his needs because the need similarity contributed to role conflict. Certainly we know that the intimacy of marriage role relationships often calls for the individual to redefine his needs. As Snyder has pointed out, "If attitude similarity among married pairs exists, as research seems to show, this similarity must be the result of the adjustive interaction shared by the couple and not necessarily an affinity at the onset of the relationship."[78]

Ktsanes, in a study of personality influences on mate selection, writes: "The findings of this study, based upon a sample of recently married, college-age, middle-class couples, indicate that for the population sampled the tendency for an individual to select a spouse unlike himself in a total emotional make-up far exceeds the tendency for him to select a spouse like himself in that respect."[79] Ktsanes, like Winch, used a sample of people already married. A study that would more accurately measure Winch's theory of complementary needs would be a longitudinal one, starting with dating and following the individual through dating-courtship, mate selection, and on into marriage.

Winch's theory of complementary needs is not without value. The selection of a mate is very possibly related to both like and unlike personality needs. Burgess and Wallin found that of 42 personality traits studied, 14 showed a greater than chance expectation for homogamous union of engaged couples.[80] For example, they found similarity of personality characteristics by engaged couples in such areas as daydreaming, loneliness, changing interests, and so forth. They also point out that the mating of like with like is much less for personality than for social characteristics.[81]

The theory of complementary needs provides some indication of how the potential market out of which the mate will be chosen is further limited. The process of mate selection can be summarized,

[78]Eloise C. Snyder, "Attitudes: A Study of Homogamy and Marital Selectivity," *Journal of Marriage and Family*, August, 1964, p. 336.

[79]Thomas Ktsanes, "Mate Selection on the Basis of Personality Type: A Study Utilizing an Empirical Typology of Personality," *American Sociological Review*, October, 1955, p. 551.

[80]Burgess and Wallin, *op. cit.*, p. 208.

[81]*Ibid.*, p. 208.

then, as a continuing process of elimination through endogamy, homogamy, and personality needs. The personality influences lead the individual to his final choice through the process of falling in love and having the love returned.

THOSE WHO NEVER MARRY

Even with this country's high marriage rate and great positive emphasis on marriage, about one out of every ten individuals never marries. An analysis of why some Americans never marry may shed added light on those who do.

As discussed earlier, the desire for love and marriage is a tremendous force in the United States, particularly for the woman. For example, this writer found in a study of unmarried coeds that only 2 percent of them had little or no interest in future marriage.[82] The number who never marry are much greater than those who desire not to marry, and for the former group the personal and social frustrations are often very severe. A number of the points that follow are taken from Manford Kuhn's insightful analysis of those who fail to marry.[83] In many cases, several of the reasons may account for an individual never marrying.

1. *Hostile marriage attitudes.* Some people, because of unpleasant childhood experiences in their family of orientation, grow up with a hostility to marriage or to members of the opposite sex. Example: In growing up, a girl develops a hatred for her father and projects the hatred to men in general, and specifically to men in the role of husband and father. Because of childhood experiences over which she had little control, she finds the idea of moving into marriage with a man in the husband-father role impossible.

2. *Homosexuality.* There are many levels of homosexuality, and a number of individuals who are either latent or manifest homosexuals enter marriage and achieve varying degrees of marital satisfaction. However, the individual whose overwhelming focus of love and sexual satisfaction is directed at members of the same sex often feels that marriage, with love and sex directed at a member of the opposite sex, is impossible. Example: The male, through socialization, may develop an image of members of his own sex as love objects and, in his adult years, cannot focus on members of the opposite

---

[82]Robert R. Bell, "Some Factors Related to Coed Marital Aspirations," *Family Life Coordinator*, October, 1962, p. 92.
[83]Kuhn, *op. cit.*, pp. 247–51.

sex; he therefore finds marriage, with its love and sexual demands, an undesirable role relationship.

3. *Parent fixations.* The individual may develop such an emotional identification with one or both of his parents that he cannot direct to another person the love necessary for marriage. In some cases, the possibility of loving someone else poses a threat to the exclusiveness of the love for the parent. Example: The young man is so fixated in his love for his mother that he cannot love a girl and, if he attempts to, he has feelings of guilt because he believed the love has been taken in part away from his mother. Because of his fixation, this removal of love from the mother becomes psychologically intolerable.

4. *Physical or health factors.* The person may deviate in physical characteristics to such an extent that very few are willing to marry him; or the health of the individual may be so poor that he cannot find a mate. Examples: the person may be "normal" in all respects except he is a dwarf and therefore finds it nearly impossible to find a mate. Or, a person may be in such poor health that he cannot enter into dating and courtship or, if he does, his health problems frighten away possible marriage partners.

5. *Unattractiveness.* As pointed out earlier, while the range of attractiveness adequate for finding a marriage mate is broad in America, individuals at the extremes may find it difficult to marry. As was also mentioned, attractiveness refers to both facial and body characteristics. Example: A girl may be excessively overweight and rarely asked for a date; she therefore has little opportunity for taking the initial step necessary for entering the dating-courtship process leading to mate selection. There are always a certain number of individuals who are never dated because they go beyond the minimum limits of attractiveness.

6. *Do not want responsibilities.* Mate selection implies a willingness on the part of each individual to take on some responsibility for the need satisfactions of the other, as well as for the relationship itself. Social responsibilities are also inherent in role rights and obligations of husband and wife. Examples: A person, in the first case, is not willing to give the love that the other person desires. In the second case, the man may not be willing to take on the responsibilities that go with the husband's role in marriage. He may not want to be socially responsible for the other person.

7. *Didn't get "the one."* A person may be so influenced by romantic love that he accepts the idea that only one person can really be loved. If the person feels he had found that "one" person

and then lost her, he may believe that the single chance has occurred and no others are possible. Example: A girl falls in love with a man and he rejects her for another. She may feel that no other man will do because the one lost was her only "real and true love." Having loved and lost, she must go through life without. Some individuals may desire to treasure the abstract love that ended, rather than face the reality of moving into a love relationship that actually exists.

8. *Inability to perform courtship needs.* Dating and courtship in the United States are complex and demanding. A person must develop some proficiencies in dealing with the opposite sex if he wants to achieve at least minimum dating-courtship success. Example: A young man may be socially inadequate when confronted with a young woman and unable to meet even the minimum requirements of communication. Thus, for him, nothing ever develops beyond the initial contact.

9. *Economic factors.* Some individuals are barely able to meet their own economic needs and cannot take on the financial responsibility of dating. Or, in some cases, a person may have financial responsibilities for others so that the added expense of marriage is impossible. Examples: A young man with a very limited income that barely meets his needs has little left for spending on the basic requirements of dating. In the second case, a man's total income is absorbed by the economic responsibility of caring for aged and dependent parents, leaving nothing for marriage.

10. *Career desires.* Some people have such high occupational motivation that they perceive marriage as a threat to occupational success. This factor may cause many to postpone marriage. Example: A woman who desires to be successful in pursuing a career may feel that marriage and motherhood will drastically curtail her chances of success or remove her from her career. This factor is probably applicable to women more often than to men, because career and marriage are not viewed as contradictory for men.

11. *No dating market.* Some individuals, because of geographical, educational, or occupational isolation find the chances of meeting eligible mates extremely limited. While they may desire marriage, they simply never have the opportunity to meet a person who meets even their basic requirements. Example: A woman who enters an occupation made up almost entirely of other women never has a chance to meet an eligible man in the work situation. If she has little or no social contacts outside the job, she finds herself isolated from her potential dating-courtship market and, as a result, her life is spent with women and uneligible men.

It should be reemphasized that any combination of the reasons suggested for failure to marry may operate for the individual. Ultimately, the individual who never marries is one who did not complete the mate selection process. Which factors are most responsible for an individual's failure to move successfully through mate selection is an important question. As a partial answer, for example, it may be that unattractiveness will hinder mate selection less than hostile marriage attitudes. Unattractiveness is a factor in *not being selected,* whereas hostile marriage attitudes refer to *not actively selecting.* Therefore, mate selection must ultimately be viewed as an interaction process wherein the selector and the selectee operate mutually upon one another. A person may select any number of different individuals as a mate but not be selected in return. On the other hand, a person who is not actively seeking a mate has, in effect, withdrawn from the mate selection process. In the long run, the person who has withdrawn from the process is more apt to remain unmarried than the person who is in the process but having problems in being selected.

It is striking that the never-married group—about 10 percent of the population—is almost completely overlooked in sociology-of-the-family literature. Yet, whether persons choose not to marry or are not chosen for marriage, they must make adaptations to a society where almost all major adult roles and related values are based on the assumption of marital experience. Therefore, a basic sociological question is how do those who never marry adapt to norms and roles generally based on the assumption of marriage?

A related assumption by society is that the norms influencing and determining unmarried behavior at age 18 will continue to be the same at ages 28 or 38, if the person does not marry. This point is illustrated by our sexual values which imply the same moral restrictions against non-marital (people who never marry) sexual behavior as against premarital sexual behavior. Obviously, people who never marry must make some adaptations to a value system that assumes categorical immaturity. This usually means that the *person* must make discreet adjustments—a social adjustment of values to fit the conditions is *not* implied, but rather the socially condescending view of, "Go ahead and do what you must, but don't get caught." We have no way of knowing to what extent this adjustment to the restrictive non-marital sexual values, especially for women, leads to feelings of guilt and shame.

However, the evidence we do have indicates that the female who does not marry is not the asexual individual she is often depicted as in various stereotypes. For example, while 96 percent of all married women by age 40 have achieved orgasm from any source, the rate for the never-married women at the same age is 73 percent.[84] When it is taken into account that some women never marry because of no sexual interest or even a very negative sexual interest, then the differences in orgasm experience between married and never-married women is not very great. The Kinsey data further suggests that active sexual incidence among single women is slightly related to education. For single women, in the age group 31 to 35, those with 9 to 12 years of education had an active sexual incidence of 65 percent, those with 13 to 16 years of education an incidence of 69 percent, and those with 17 or more years of education an incidence of 75 percent.[85]

It might be assumed that those who never marry and who must therefore follow some patterns of life contrary to general social values and norms would be characterized by a high rate of personal and social problems. However, one study of older unmarried subjects found that they did not suffer from the lack of companionship which marriage offers,[86] while another study found that single men had a much higher mental health impairment rate than did single women when age was held constant.[87] It is clear that we need comprehensive studies of the social patterns and role adaptations common to those who never marry.

The factors of mate selection discussed in this chapter refer to general patterns of behavior. They do not operate with equal or absolute force, and individuals do not "seek" and are not "selected" according to absolutes. If the factors of homogamy and complementary needs *were* absolutes, no one would ever get married. Relatively strong personal and social requirements for the individual indicate, however, why some never marry. For the vast majority who do marry, the requirements operate with flexibility and the individual is able to choose and be chosen for marriage.

---

[84]Alfred C. Kinsey, Wardell B. Pomeroy, Clyde E. Martin and Paul H. Gebhard, *Sexual Behavior in the Human Female* (Philadelphia: W. B. Saunders Co., 1953), p. 546.
[85]*Ibid,* p. 550.
[86]Gordon F. Streib, "Intergenerational Relations: Perspectives of the Two Generations on the Older Parent," *Journal of Marriage and Family,* November, 1965, p. 472
[87]Langner and Michael, *op. cit.,* p. 177.

SELECTED BIBLIOGRAPHY

BABER, RAY E. *Marriage and the Family,* chaps. iv and v. New York: McGraw-Hill Book Co., 1953.

BARNETT, LARRY D. "Interracial Marriage in California," *Marriage and Family Living,* November, 1963, pp. 624–27.

BELL, ROBERT R. "Some Factors Related to Coed Marital Aspirations," *Family Life Coordinator,* October, 1962, pp. 91–94.

BOSSARD, JAMES. "Residential Propinquity as a Factor in Marriage Selection," *American Journal of Sociology,* September, 1932, pp. 219–24.

BURCHINAL, LEE G. "Research on Young Marriages: Implications for Family Life Education," *Family Life Coordinator,* September-December, 1960, pp. 6–24.

BURGESS, ERNEST W., and COTTRELL, LEONARD. *Predicting Success and Failure in Marriage.* Englewood Cliffs, N. J.: Prentice-Hall, Inc., 1939.

BURGESS, ERNEST W., and WALLIN, PAUL. *Engagement and Marriage.* Philadelphia: J. B. Lippincott Co., 1953.

—— "Homogamy in Personality Characteristics," *Journal of Abnormal and Social Psychology,* October, 1944, pp. 475–81.

GLICK, PAUL C. *American Families.* New York: John Wiley & Sons, Inc., 1957.

HEISS, JEROLD S. "Premarital Characteristics of the Religiously Intermarried in an Urban Area," *American Sociological Review,* February, 1960, pp. 47–55.

KTSANES, THOMAS. "Mate Selection on the Basis of Personality Type: A Study Utilizing an Empirical Typology of Personality," *American Sociological Review,* October, 1955, pp. 547–51.

KUHN, MANFORD H. "How Mates are Sorted," in Becker, Howard, and Hill, Reuben, *Family, Marriage and Parenthood,* pp. 246–75. Boston: D. C. Heath & Co., 1955.

LANDIS, JUDSON T., and LANDIS, MARY G. *Building a Successful Marriage,* chap. ix. Englewood Cliffs, N. J.: Prentice-Hall, Inc., 1953.

MARCHES, JOSEPH R., and TURBEVILLE, GUS. "The Effect of Residential Propinquity on Marriage Selection," *American Journal of Sociology,* May, 1953, pp. 592–95.

MAYER, JOHN E. *Jewish-Gentile Courtship.* Glencoe, Illinois: The Free Press, 1961.

MOSS, J. J., and GINGLES, RUDY. "The Relationship of Personality to the Incidence of Early Marriage," *American Journal of Sociology,* May, 1953, pp. 592–95.

PAVELA, TODD H. "An Explanatory Study of Negro-White Intermarriage in Indiana," *Journal of Marriage and Family,* May, 1964, pp. 209–11.

PRINCE, ALFRED J. and ANDREW R. BAGGALEY. "Personality Variables and the Ideal Mate," *Family Life Coordinator,* July, 1963, pp. 93–96.

RODMAN, HYMAN. "Technical Note on Two Rates of Mixed Marriage," *American Sociological Review,* October, 1965, pp. 776–78.

SNYDER, ELOISE C. "Attitudes: A Study of Homogamy and Marital Selectivity," *Journal of Marriage and Family,* August, 1964, pp. 332–36.

STRAUSS, ANSELM. "Personality Needs and Marital Choice," *Social Forces,* March, 1947, pp. 332–35.

THOMAS, JOHN. "The Factor of Religion in the Selection of Marriage Mates," *American Sociological Review*, August, 1951, pp. 487–91.

WINCH, ROBERT F. *Mate Selection*. New York: Harper & Brothers, 1958.

CHAPTER 7

PREMARITAL SEXUAL ATTITUDES

Americans think and talk a great deal about sex. In the American society of the past, sexual attitudes and behavior were generally felt to be private, at least to the extent that they were not often discussed publicly or between the opposite sexes. Social historians generally regard World War I as the period when American sex attitudes and behavior increasingly came under the influence of forces leading to change. Since World War I, a large number of Americans have been increasingly interested in, if not preoccupied with, sexual matters.

One of man's universal culture characteristics has been his social control of sexual behavior. While societies vary a great deal in how they control sex and what they consider to be the areas of sexual behavior that need to be controlled, some social restrictions are always applied. "Possibly in man's long history there have been peoples who have failed to subject the sexual impulse to regulation. If so, none has survived, for the social control of sex is today a cultural universal."[1]

The relationship of marriage is an important factor in sexual control. Taboos on adultery are widespread; Murdock found they appeared in 120 of the 148 societies for which data were available. However, a substantial majority of societies permit extramarital relations with certain affinal relatives.[2] In most cultures, the control of sex does not center on the moral condemnation of sexual behavior, but rather on problems that often emerge from uncontrolled sexual behavior, as related to kinship, social stratification, marital status, and so forth.

Societies have tended to be more restrictive about marital than premarital sexual behavior. Murdock found that premarital license prevailed in 70 percent of the cultures for which he had information. "In the rest, the taboo falls primarily upon females and appears

---

[1]George P. Murdock, *Social Structure* (New York: The Macmillan Co., 1949), p. 260.
[2]*Ibid.*, p. 265.

to be largely a precaution against childbearing out of wedlock rather than a moral requirement."[3]

When a society does approve certain forms of adolescent sexual activity, it does not usually leave matters of behavior to chance. There are usually special social institutions that provide facilities for the young people to meet and spend time together. However, it is rare in the history of man to find a society like the American—where premarital sexual activity is prohibited but, at the same time, wide opportunity is allowed for private interaction to occur. Ford and Beach point out that in most restrictive societies there is a public conspiracy against the acquisition of any sexual knowledge by children.[4] In restrictive societies, the methods used during adolescence "include segregation of the sexes, strict chaperonage of girls, and threats of severe disgrace or physical punishment."[5] But as Ford and Beach go on to point out, there are probably no societies where any methods of control are completely effective in preventing premarital coitus among young unmarried couples.[6]

Christensen suggests a possible dilemma faced by societies who take *either* a restrictive or permissive view of premarital sexual relations. "There is a certain amount of evidence that the more permissive the culture regarding premarital sexual intimacy the higher will be the actual occurrence of such intimacy but the lower will be any negative effects deriving therefrom. And, conversely, the more restrictive the culture, the lower will be the actual occurrence but the higher will be the negative effects."[7]

The lesson to be learned from the rich storehouse of anthropological data is that man, through his social institutions, has developed a wide variety of attitudes and controls over sexual behavior. Waller and Hill in their characteristically vivid way write, "The sexual impulse can be conditioned to different forms of expression, modified to fit the social order, harnessed to do the work of the world, curbed and encouraged and frustrated and hammered out of shape. But it can never be completely eliminated, never wholly denied, nor can its essential character be destroyed.[8]

---

[3]*Ibid.*, p. 265.
[4]Clellan S. Ford and Frank A. Beach, *Patterns of Sexual Behavior*, (New York: Harper & Row, 1951), p. 180.
[5]*Ibid.*, p. 182.
[6]*Ibid.*, p. 182.
[7]Harold T. Christensen, "A Cross-Cultural Comparison of Attitudes Toward Marital Infidelity," *International Journal of Comparative Sociology*, September, 1962, p. 125.
[8]Willard Waller and Reuben Hill, *The Family* (New York: The Dryden Press, 1951), p. 58.

In an analysis of premarital sexual attitudes in the United States, two important considerations should be kept in mind. (1) Man, because of his social nature and because he is not biologically restricted in his sexual expression, has created a variety of sexual controls in general, and premarital sexual controls in particular. (2) The dynamic nature of society often leads to important and significant social changes—as has happened with American premarital sexual attitudes and behavior.

This chapter will focus on American premarital sexual attitudes; the next chapter on American premarital sexual behavior. While behavior is often determined by attitudes, it is also true that verbalized attitudes may be different from actual behavior patterns. In few areas is this better illustrated than with premarital sexual behavior. The commonly stated norms reflected in the attitudes of individuals are that premarital chastity, particularly for the female, is the ideal. However, behavioral studies show that chastity is frequently not the case for a large number of unmarried women. Also, publicly accepting the stated attitudes is often more important than whether or not one actually behaves according to them. A girl who states an acceptance of premarital chastity, but discreetly indulges in premarital sexual intercourse, will receive far less social criticism than the girl who states she does not *believe* in the norms of chastity, even though she does not herself enter into premarital sexual relations.

Many times the inconsistency between attitudes and behavior results from behavior being more subject to rapid social change than attitudes. When there is a general change in behavior patterns, the old attitudes usually continue to prevail, especially if they are a part of a larger value system. Largely as a result of the Kinsey findings, many Americans are concerned with what they see as the hypocrisy evident in the contrast between attitudes and behavior in premarital sexual relations. Kinsey forced many Americans to recognize that public verbalizations of approved sexual attitudes were not necessarily equivalent to strong individual behavioral controls. This leads to another consideration: The old norms and attitudes do not seem to be working in today's American society. Many Americans react to attitude-behavior differences with the belief that the norms must be strengthened so that behavior will be brought back into line. A minority argue that the norms should be redefined to fit the changes in behavior. The discussion that follows in this chapter will focus on the changing social nature of various premarital sexual attitudes in the United States.

Attitude as a Concept. Man's social behavior is learned. The newborn infant does not have attitudes, because he is not social. Through the process of socialization, he acquires the social characteristics made available to him by those already socialized. Therefore, all that is social is initially external to the human infant, but through social interaction with others he internalizes values, norms, and attitudes. Their intensity and significance for different individuals is not constant because of individual variations and differences in experience. In the following discussion of premarital sexual attitudes, the following concepts will be used: *Values*—Broad beliefs referring to the appropriateness of thought and action directed at individuals and objects. *Attitudes*—The more specific personal internalization of values referring to ideas, perceptions, and dispositions carried over from past experiences and directed at objects, persons, and groups. Attitudes may be general or specific. A woman expressing her attitudes about premarital sexual behavior for girls may state a general attitude for all girls or a more specific attitude if she relates the question to a teen-age daughter. *Norms*—Attitudes that are generally accepted as guidelines for conduct by social groups. Generally, the stronger the norms, the more closely behavior will conform to them—indicating that this country's norms against premarital sexual conduct are not very strong.

In this chapter and in the next chapter, then, we will be presenting data from a variety of research studies into premarital sexual attitudes and behavior. However, almost all research in the area of premarital sexual intimacy has taken place within the last 30 years.[9] In Chapter 8 we will discuss in some detail the Kinsey studies because they are our major source on premarital sexual behavior. We will also be referring to a variety of other studies. It should be kept in mind that most of the studies we will be citing apply to white, higher educated groups, and they have generally focused on sexual behavior rather than sexual attitudes.[10]

TRADITIONAL AMERICAN ATTITUDES

That sexual attitudes are in a state of change today can best be seen in light of attitudes of the past. But generalizations about the past run the same dangers as generalizations about present atti-

[9]See: Robert R. Bell, *Premarital Sex In A Changing Society*, (Englewood Cliffs, N.J.: Prentice-Hall, Inc., 1966), Ch. 1.
[10]Ira L. Reiss, *Premarital Sexual Standards in America* (Glencoe, Ill.: The Free Press, 1960), p. 74.

tudes. Human attitudes are never quite the same for all people or all groups. Therefore, our discussion centers around general traditional American sex attitudes, recognizing that there are many exceptions.

The American family of the past approximated the patriarchal model. (See Chapter 2.) The male was dominant in important areas of both marriage and the family, giving him both differential prestige and greater rights and obligations. It was generally assumed that the man had very different sexual needs and drives than the woman. While the male's sexual drive was sometimes seen as "animalistic," people generally believed that the drive had to be satisfied. Sex was expected to be of little or no personal interest to the woman, and was indulged in by her for purposes of reproduction and meeting her husband's sexual needs.

Woman's premarital chastity was very important for several reasons. First, in a patriarchal society the woman was often viewed by men as personal property, at least to the degree that marriages were arranged along economic lines. The worth of the woman was drastically reduced if she could not take chastity into marriage. Second, because the woman was assumed to have little personal interest in sex, any hint of premarital sexual experience might indicate that she was sexually susceptible, thereby threatening the male's image of the sexually pure role expected of the wife.

The sexual attitudes of men were contradictory. On the one hand, the man had strong sexual drives and the need to find a woman for sexual satisfaction. On the other hand, he wanted, for marriage, a woman sexually pure and little interested in personal sex satisfaction. To resolve this contradiction, men often divided women into two categories, the "good" and the "bad." "Good" women were those who were premaritally chaste and maritally restricted in their sexual interest. The "bad" were those women who were available in providing an outlet for the man's sexual needs. The patriarchal male rarely allowed the two female groupings to overlap, because he saw them as absolutes and not different by degree. The distinction had implications for both the man and the woman. The man could satisfy his sexual needs outside of marriage and still maintain belief in the purity of his wife. For the woman, however, any personal sexual satisfaction resulting from marriage could lead to guilt feelings. If she overtly displayed her sexual interests, the husband's suspicion might be aroused that she really was not "good." In many cases, the values effectively removed female sexual satisfaction from the marriage relationship.

Patiarchal beliefs were, in general, supported by religious beliefs in the United States. Early Protestantism, the dominant religion, placed a great emphasis on woman's constant struggle to resist evil and the "temptations of the flesh." While sex outside marriage was sinful for both sexes, it was far more sinful for the woman. In general, it may be said that the Protestant influence, because it included a religiously patriarchal definition of the family, supported the patriarchal family that prevailed.

Many characteristics of the patriarchal concept of sexual behavior still prevail in American society both in traditional, as well as in modified, forms. Thus, the changing patterns of sexual attitudes in the United States have been a matter of degree.

INFLUENCES ON CHANGING ATTITUDES

As previously noted, a shift from the institutional emphasis on the family as a group to the more personal emphasis on the ego-needs of the individual has occurred. This has meant that the impact of family influence on the attitudes of the individual has declined and, therefore, the traditional values of the family no longer have the same significance. Along with a contemporary emphasis on the individual seeking ego-need satisfaction, goes the middle-class concept of personal happiness as a measure of the individual's successful family relationships.

Of great importance to the changes in premarital sexual attitudes has been the increasing social equality of the American woman. Freedom and equality for the woman mean a weakening of the patriarchal traditions. Sex equality and patriarchal values are in contradiction and can rarely exist within the same social group. The emancipation of the American woman implies a number of important social changes. First, she is no longer as rigidly controlled by her family as in the past. Because of increased educational and occupational opportunities, she spends a great deal of time away from the parental home. Therefore, while the values of the parents are important, the young woman has the opportunity to come into contact with other values which may replace or modify the parental ones. This may have a cumulative effect—being out from under the influence of the parents often leads to attitudes that encourage her to move even further away from their control.

Second, increasing sexual equality leads to less female dependence on the male. In the past, the woman was almost totally dependent upon the male for her entire life, first to her father and then to her husband. But today, a woman may leave the influence of the father and not immediately move into a dependency relationship with a husband. While women desire and enter marriage at an extremely high rate today, it is much less a "forced" choice than it was in the past. Many young women also have a period of personal independence between leaving the parental home and entering marriage.

Third, to a great degree the female has broken away from parental influence over the selection of a marriage partner. Because the woman now has an equal role in dating and courtship, she has minimized parental influence and entered into a relationship of near equality with the male in mate selection.

Fourth, one of the most significant developments, particularly in the middle class, is the belief in sexual rights and privileges for the woman. Most young women believe that when they marry they have a right to expect personal sexual satisfaction and fulfillment. Attitudes about sexual rights in marriage have led to a new set of attitudes about sex in general. "Females today are less willing to accept the double standard and more likely to expect the same sexual pleasure as the male, or to apply to him the same restrictions."[11]

Yet while women have just about won the right to sexual equality in marriage, they continue to have far more restrictions placed on them in premarital sexual rights than do men. American values suggest that the American girl can be sexually *attractive* but not sexually *active*. As pointed out earlier, every society imposes some restrictions on sexual behavior, but what is most striking about American codes is a high level of permissiveness in most areas of premarital behavior with the exception of strong restrictions against premarital sex. Lerner writes, "The American girl, with wide leeway in choosing friends, clothes and schools, books and magazines, movies and plays, places to go and people to see, with freedom of movement, education and opinion, is nevertheless closely watched and admonished on everything affecting sexual relations."[12]

Secular Society

The American society over the past 50 years has been characterized by a shift away from the sacred values of a traditional society to the more secular ones of a society undergoing rapid social change. The American way of life today emphasizes the right of both sexes

---

[11]Thomas Poffenberger, "Individual Choice in Adolescent Premarital Sex Behavior," *Marriage and Family Living*, November, 1960, p. 326.

[12]Max Lerner, *America As A Civilization* (New York: Simon & Schuster, 1957), p. 677.

to seek personal pleasure and satisfactions out of life. "We have a hedonistic approach to living, not an ascetic one."[13] Reiss points out that "we are a nation of people who value rationality quite highly. And the inequality of our traditional sexual customs and the many inconsistencies in them make them a good target for rationalism. The asceticism of these sexual standards is opposed by our hedonism and secularism."[14]

A "religious revival" in the United States has been the subject of much current discussion. The evidence usually offered in behalf of such a revival is an increase in church membership. But greater church attendance does not mean that people's attitudes are being greatly affected by religious teachings. While a strong religious restriction in regard to premarital sexual behavior continues, it is questionable that it has a great impact. As Poffenberger points out, "Professional studies have reported that premarital coitus seldom has devastating results for those who indulge. In total, the society no longer takes the pious position that all premarital coitus is evil and the offender should be punished."[15]

Too, there may be some lessening of religious strictures against premarital sexual values as a result of changes internal to religion. For example, one of the most liberal Christian positions on premarital sexual behavior is that of the Quakers. The Quakers condemn as fundamentally immoral every sexual action that is not, as far as is humanly ascertainable, the result of a mutual decision.[16] Grunwald points out that "The implication is strong that, conversely, any act that *is* the result of a mutual, responsible decision may be considered moral. Hence, so continues the implication, only seduction, entrapment, or exploitation make an action immoral."[17] What the long range impact of this kind of religious view of premarital sexual morality will be is at present impossible to determine.

The traditional influence of religion as *the* determiner of premarital sexual values and behavior is at least in part being replaced by the influence of science and education. For example, the relative influence of the institutional forces of religion and science are reflected in a recent nationwide study of some attitudes of college students. The students were asked: "How much confidence do you have in these institutions?" With regard to the scientific community,

---

[13]Reiss, *op. cit.*, p. 220.
[14]*Ibid.*, p. 220.
[15]Poffenberger, *op. cit.*, p. 326.
[16]Henry A. Grunwald, *Sex In America* (New York: Bantam Books, 1964), pp. 150–51.
[17]*Ibid*, pp. 150–51.

the response, "a great deal," was given by 76 percent of the interviewees; to higher education, 64 percent; but, to organized religion only 34 percent.[18]

The study also found that those college students who maintained their religious faith while in college seemed to be far less certain of themselves than the non-believers.[19] As the number and proportion of young people going on to college increases, it would appear probable that the traditional influence of religion in areas of morality will continue to decline. In general, increased education is related to a decrease in the influence and significance of religion. One study found that "almost 40 percent of the students said their experiences in college had made them question their faith."[20]

It is not just that higher education reduces the influence of religion; institutions of higher education also themselves contribute to new and often different moral values. For example, a *Newsweek* study of college students found that two thirds of all those polled believed that prevailing campus standards encourage promiscuity; "and more than four out of five said their experience in college had made them take a more tolerant attitude toward those who defy traditional sexual morality."[21]

However, the importance of religion on many people's attitudes in regard to premarital sex can not be ignored. Kinsey vividly showed that the intensity of religious belief is of great significance in influencing sexual behavior. For those with a strong religious orientation, the secular nature of society has limited influence on their sexual attitudes. One study found that "when age, marital status, size of home town, fraternity membership, father's political inclination, and religious affiliation are each held constant, the relationship between sex attitudes and religiosity remains significant. These tests lead one to conclude that there is a relationship between the importance one attaches to religious matters and one's attitude toward premarital sexual relations, a relationship which cannot be accounted for by any of the background factors tested."[22]

Extended Adolescence

Adolescence is the period between leaving childhood and entering adulthood. Early in adolescence, the individual becomes biologically

---

[18]*Newsweek*, "Campus '65", March 22, 1965, p. 45.

[19]*Ibid.*, p. 57.

[20]*Ibid.*, p. 57.

[21]*Ibid.*, p. 58.

[22]Jean Dedman, "The Relationship Between Religious Attitude and Attitude Toward Premarital Sex Relations," *Marriage and Family Living*, May, 1959, p. 175.

capable of entering adult sexual relationships, but his—the American—society insists that such relationships should be postponed until adulthood and marriage. An important American social change has been the prolonging of adolescence and, therefore, the prolonging of premarital sexual restrictions. Adolescence has been prolonged by delaying the time when young people can earn their own living, a very important factor in assigning adult status. "But social adolescence is also being lengthened at the other end, by pushing the time of maturing down to an earlier age."[23] As a result of these two influences, the period of social adolescence may be twice as long today as it was 100 years ago. If the trend for younger ages at marriages continues, however, the time period may be somewhat shortened.

While the length of adolescence has increased, few socially approved changes in attitudes toward premarital sexual behavior have occurred. Premarital chastity continues to be the stated ideal. This leads to considerable conflict and strain for the adolescent. "The young person is permitted to associate closely with the opposite sex but is put on his honor to remain virtuous, is supposed to choose his mate independently but is in many ways still under the authority of the parents, and is forced to compete for love in a rating and dating system that interferes and gets entangled with his fortunes in the other competitive system, the occupational."[24]

During their extended social adolescence, the two sexes take different views of premarital sexual behavior. A very important part of the adolescent's social involvement is with members of his own sex, and this group influences the individual's attitudes about sexual behavior. The male group often encourages positive attitudes in regard to sexual conquests of females. While there are many variations, the prestige of the boy within the peer group may often be determined by the number of seductions he is able to persuade his peers he has achieved.

The adolescent girl's group values usually center around popularity, not sexual involvement. She often gains prestige from her female reference group if she has many different dates and if she can draw males into an overt emotional commitment. As the girl enters late adolescence, the emotional commitment of the male becomes even more important to her as a necessary prelule to mar-

---

    [23]Harold E. Jones, "Adolescence in Our Society," in Jerome M. Seidman, *The Adolescent* (New York: Holt, Rinehart & Winston, Inc., 1960), p. 55.
    [24]Kingsley, Davis, "Adolescence and the Social Structure," in Jerome M. Seidman, *The Adolescent* (New York: Holt, Rinehart, & Winston, Inc., 1960), p. 47.

riage. Built into adolescent boy-girl relationships are different attitudes that contribute to the struggle between the sexes as to premarital sexual behavior and emotional commitment.

Mass Media Influence

Many observers of contemporary America have commented on the contradiction of a society which holds the traditional sexual attitudes of chastity and asceticism, and simultaneously bombards individuals with sexual stimuli. While the great American interest in sexual behavior has complications for individuals at almost all ages, it has a particular impact on the adolescent and his sexual attitudes and behavior. Because he is in a position of role transition, and because the physical sex drives (particularly in the male) are strong, the adolescent is highly susceptible to the stimuli of an erotic culture. The impact of mass media also has a particular influence on the adolescent because of the insecurity of adolescent roles in reference to desired adult sex status. This insecurity can lead the young person to seek out sex symbols that he believes indicate adult sex status. The images of sexual attraction conveyed to the highly responsive adolescent through movies, television, and various reading materials emphasize the sexually attractive female. Thus, the adolescent girl often wears clothing, adopts hairdos, and plasters on the make-up used by the "sexy" female symbols of mass communication. This then makes her more erotically appealing to the male, who also has been influenced by the symbols of sex huckstered through mass media.

The girl, as a result, must maintain a delicate balance in her relationships with the highly sex-conscious boy. On the one hand, she wants as a female sex symbol, to stimulate the male, at least to the extent of being popular and desirable. On the other hand, she does not want to be so sexually obvious that she will no longer be defined as a "good" girl. The female's "sexiness" also contributes to the male-female struggles in which the girl tries to pull the boy in her direction of emotional commitment, and the boy struggles to pull the girl in his direction of sexual gratification.

EMERGENT PREMARITAL SEX ATTITUDES

The emerging sexual attitudes, in today's society are not clearly defined, and are often confused. A very important contribution to an understanding of different and often conflicting premarital sexual attitudes has been made by Ira Reiss. He suggests that there are two basic types of premarital sexual behavior, with their related attitudes, that may be seen as extremes on a continuum: (1) *body-centered*, with the emphasis on the physical nature of sex, and (2) *person-centered*, with the emphasis on the emotional relationship to a given individual with whom the sexual act is being performed.[25] Reiss suggests that individuals' premarital attitudes may usually be classified in one of four categories falling along a continuum.[26]

1. *Abstinence*—premarital intercourse is wrong for both the man and the woman, regardless of circumstances.

2. *Permissiveness with affection*—premarital intercourse is right for both men and women under certain conditions when a stable relationship with engagement, love, or strong affection is present.

3. *Permissiveness without affection*—premarital intercourse is right for both men and women regardless of the amount of affection or stability present, providing there is physical attraction.

4. *Double standard*—premarital intercourse is acceptable for men, but is wrong and unacceptable for women.

The traditional attitude, the double standard, continues to be accepted by many Americans of both sexes. The attitude of abstinence is often found along with the double standard. Historically, the double standard was applied to the male and the abstinence standard applied to the female. The two relatively new categories of permissiveness are the result of many factors of social change in the American culture. Permissiveness without affection places value on the sheer physical satisfaction derived from sex, although it is assumed that individuals will be sophisticated enough to control their pleasure in a careful way.[27] This attitude is probably less accepted than permissiveness with affection, which generally views sex not as an end in itself but as a means of expressing the end of affection.

The Age Factor

An often-heard stereotype suggests that sexual permissiveness is characteristic of most adolescents today. However, age differences among adolescents are clearly related to different attitudes regarding premarital sexual behavior. Reiss argues that "the vast majority of our approximately twenty million teenagers are not only not extreme but are quite conservative and restrained in the areas of pre-

---

[25]Reiss, *op. cit.*, p. 80.
[26]*Ibid.*, pp. 83–84.
[27]*Ibid.*, pp. 118–23.

marital sexual codes and behavior when we compare them to their older brothers and sisters."[28] Younger adolescents are often strongly under the influence of traditional values communicated to them by their parents. As they grow older and come increasingly under the influence of outside-the-family values, their traditional values are frequently altered. The shift from an age where sexual values are not behaviorally meaningful and only theoretically applied, to an age where the values are behaviorally meaningful and increasingly applied often results in new attitudes related to the new behavior. For example: "Teenage double standard males are often stricter than their older brothers who accept coitus for a girl when she is in love or engaged."[29] The older boys' experience of sexual behavior often leads them to redefine their premarital sexual attitudes.

The sexual act is almost always the end stage of a process of increasing sexual intimacy. Premarital intimacy interaction generally moves from kissing to necking to petting to intercourse. Changes in attitudes do not always center on greater liberality in regard to sexual intercourse, but often on a more intimate level of foreplay. Reiss suggests that the real increases in teen-age sexual behavior over the past generation have not been in the area of sexual intercourse, but rather in the area of petting.[30] This may represent a compromise in the sexual attitudes of the girls who continue to accept the ideal of virginity, but at the same time have an opportunity for some sexual involvement. When a girl has indulged in petting, she is still technically a virgin, but at the same time is sexually experienced.[31]

There may be problems for the "technical virgin." On some occasions, the intensity of petting may lead her across the final line to where she is no longer a virgin. Or by engaging in petting, she may find it difficult to stop the male from forcibly moving her across the line.[32] An accepted attitude that intimacy will stop at a certain point is often easier to state theoretically than to practice behaviorally.

It is also possible that for older unmarried girls the traditional attitudes of chastity are less meaningful and forceful. The role of "technical virgin" can be maintained as long as the girl believes that

---

[28]Ira L. Reiss, "Sexual Codes in Teen-age Culture," *The Annals*, November, 1961, p. 60.

[29]*Ibid.*, p. 57.

[30]*Ibid.*, p. 59.

[31]Reiss, *Premarital Sexual Standards in America, op. cit.*, p. 197.

[32]See: Clifford Kirkpatrick and Eugene Kanin, "Male Sex Aggression on a University Campus," *American Sociological Review*, February, 1957, pp. 52–58.

the distinction between petting and sexual intercourse is meaningful. The sharpness of the distinction may be dulled, however, by
increasing age and stage of emotional commitment, and the girl may
find it difficult to justify the distinction to herself or the boy.

DATING-COURTSHIP STAGES

If attitudes change as the unmarried person gets older, so does the
probability of being involved in more intense interpersonal relationships. Even when age is held constant, the different stages in the
dating-courtship process often imply different attitudes toward sexual intimacy. The interrelationship of intensity of emotional involvement and attitudes about premarital sexual behavior will,
therefore, be examined among the population for which some
empirical information is available.

Dating

Dating, it will be recalled, implies no commitment on the part of
either individual to the other; ego-fulfillment is the important value
in dating. Thus, dating often becomes a battle ground for the ego-
satisfaction of the two uncommitted individuals. Because the male
has no commitment, he frequently considers the female sexually
exploitable. The female wants popularity but often feels that if she
allows the male to go too far sexually, she may lose her reputation
and desirability as a romantic object, and become desirable primarily as a sex object. The situation might be simplified if the girl
took a rigid stand and discouraged *any* sexual overtures from the
boy. However, the girl may want the boy to indicate that he finds
her physically attractive. In fact, the girl often dresses to make herself as sexually attractive as possible. The girl often wants some
male aggression, but it must be restricted to her limits. Many girls
would probably be disappointed in their dating relationships if the
boys never overtly indicated a sexual interest, because the sexual
pass indicates sexual desirability, which is generally important to
the girl's self image.

It is clear that for many adolescents and young adults there is a
wide difference in sexual attitudes taken into the dating situation by
boys and girls. As discussed in Chapter 4, the differences are greatly
influenced by the lack of emotional commitment by either individual to the other. Ehrmann suggests that although both boys and
girls are profoundly affected by these matters, "females seem more

directly and overtly concerned with romanticism and males with eroticism."[33]

Several studies of college students' attitudes about sexual involvement at the various stages of dating and courtship indicate increasing levels of sexual intimacy associated with dating, going steady, and engagement. A recent study by Christensen and Carpenter provides some interesting contrasts in the attitudes of three cultures toward premarital sexual behavior.[34] One culture was predominantly Mormon and relatively conservative (Intermountain); the second group was in the midwestern part of the United States and believed to be somewhat typical of the country as a whole (Midwest); and, the third group was in Denmark, which has permissive premarital sex norms.[35] The findings on approval of premarital coitus on random or casual dates assuming mutual desire were, for the males: Intermountain, 6 percent; Midwest, 17 percent; and Denmark, 43 percent; for the females: Intermountain, 1 percent; Midwest, 3 percent; and Denmark, 34 percent.[36] Both of the U.S. populations indicate a low percentage of individuals accepting favorable attitudes toward premarital sexual behavior while dating. In all three groups the acceptance figures are lower for the females than for the males.

In their study of attitudes on premarital sexual behavior, Bell and Blumberg attempted to distinguish levels of sexual intimacy beyond which there were guilt feelings. "The level of guilt for females increases considerably when they go beyond necking during a dating relationship; while the level of guilt for males follows the female trend only beyond petting. Fifty-four percent of the females in contrast to twenty-five percent of the males said they had gone too far during a date when they had engaged in petting.[37] During dating, the level of approved sexual intimacy is much lower for the female than for the male, illustrating their differential sexual view of dating.

This study not only tried to get at the guilt feelings associated with sexual behavior that had "gone too far," but also at feelings

[33]Winston Ehrmann, *Premarital Dating Behavior* (New York: Henry Holt & Co., 1959), p. 270.

[34]See: Harold T. Christensen and George R. Carpenter, "Timing Patterns in the Development of Sexual Intimacy: An Attitudinal Report on Three Modern Western Societies," *Marriage and Family Living*, February, 1962, pp. 30–35.

[35]*Ibid.*, p. 30.

[36]*Ibid.*, p. 31.

[37]Robert R. Bell and Leonard Blumberg, "Courtship Stages and Intimacy Attitudes," *Family Life Coordinator*, March, 1960, p. 62.

that behavior had not "gone far enough." "About one-third of the females indicated that there were dating relationships in which they wished they had been more intimate than they were in fact. About three-fourths of the males indicated that they wished they had been more intimate."[38] The finding that a number of girls wished they had gone further, suggests for some a definition of sexual fulfillment at a higher level of intimacy in retrospect than that actually engaged in while dating. But the findings most vividly point out that dating implies sexual opportunities for the male, a majority of whom felt that sexual intimacy could have been greater. Thus, the male exhibits greater interest in sex than the female during dating, a time when he feels a limited emotional responsibility for the person dated.

The findings indicate that in a dating relationship petting and intercourse are the levels of intimacy the male would, if possible, like to reach. The female is interested in some intimacy, at least through necking. The different accepted levels of intimacy while dating clearly indicate the sexual struggle at this level of minimal pair-commitment.

Going Steady

The going-steady relationship is a mutual commitment by two individuals to exclude other members of the opposite sex as possible dates. In some cases, going steady means the individuals are in love and will eventually move into engagement and marriage. For others, particularly the younger, there may be no love involvement. This discussion will be limited to the older group and will assume that some affection or love is usual.

The Christensen-Carpenter and Bell-Blumberg studies examined attitudes on sexual involvement of couples going steady. In the Christensen and Carpenter study, the findings on approval of premarital intercourse for a couple in love and going steady, but not engaged, were for the males: Intermountain, 5 percent; Midwest, 19 percent; and Denmark, 73 percent; and for the females: Intermountain, 2 percent; Midwest, 4 percent; and Denmark, 59 percent.[39] Neither of the two American groups studied show a significant change for either the male or the female in stating approval of premarital coitus when going steady as compared with dating.

The Bell and Blumberg study found that "a little over one-third of the females and a little less than one-third of the males who had

---

[38]*Ibid.*, p. 62.
[39]Christensen and Carpenter, *op. cit.*, p. 31.

gone steady and who had done any petting, expressed guilt over their behavior. The differences between male and female are greater with respect to intercourse during the going steady period, although the differences are not statistically significant."[40] As with dating, the differences indicate more permissive behavior and attitudes on the part of the male. However, as intensity of relationship increases, the attitudes of the two sexes may converge. Going steady may be an intermediate point that allows fuller sexual expression, generally short of intercourse, and provides more emotional protection than dating, but not the strong commitment of engagement.[41] Reiss suggests that going steady has protective elements for the girl. It may reduce the conflict she may feel between a desire for sexual experience and a desire to maintain her reputation. "For many, sexual behavior is made respectable by going steady."[42]

Attitudes toward sexual behavior while going steady are also influenced by the previous sexual experiences of the individuals involved. We would expect that those with premarital sexual experience would be more liberal in their sexual views. In a study of college students by Prince and Shipman, respondents were asked if they would object to having premarital sexual relations with their "steady." For those with premarital sexual experience, 30 percent of the males and 64 percent of the females answered they *would* object. For those without premarital sexual relations, 63 percent of the males and 91 percent of the females said they would object.[43] Not only were those with experience more liberal, but the males in both categories of experience were more liberal than the females in the same category.

Going steady, when compared with dating, may mean greater liberality in the girls' attitudes on sexual intimacy. For some boys, going steady may mean a decrease in intimacy aspirations because of a commitment to the girl that they did not feel during the dating relationship. Petting, it is suggested, is a commonly accepted level of intimacy for both males and females while going steady.

Engagement

Engagement almost always means a mutual statement of love by two individuals and, usually, an agreement to enter into marriage at

[40]Bell and Blumberg, *op. cit.*, p. 62.

[41]Robert L. Karen, "Some Variables Affecting Sexual Attitudes, Behavior and Inconsistency," *Marriage and Family Living*, August, 1959, p. 239.

[42]Reiss, "Sexual Codes in Teen-Age Culture," *op. cit.*, p. 55.

[43]Alfred J. Prince and Gordon Shipman, "Attitudes of College Students Toward Premarital Sex Experience," *Family Life Coordinator*, June, 1958, p. 58.

some future date. As contrasted with dating and going steady, engagement means a greater commitment to, and a stronger sense of obligation and respect for, the other person.

The Christensen and Carpenter findings on approval of premarital coitus for those couples in love and engaged were for the males: Intermountain, 21 percent; Midwest, 54 percent; and Denmark, 87 percent; and for the females: Intermountain, 7 percent; Midwest, 27 percent; and Denmark, 74 percent.[44] For the conservative American group (Intermountain), the female's attitudes changed little between going steady and engagement, but the male's changed significantly. In the more typical American group (Midwest), both males and females changed significantly from going steady, with the change being greater for the male than for the female.

The Bell and Blumberg study found no significant differences between males and females in feelings of guilt during engagement for either petting or intercourse. When petting was the top limit of intimacy while engaged, 31 percent of the males and 26 percent of the females expressed feelings of guilt. However, 31 percent of the males and 20 percent of the females in the petting group had some regret they had not gone further. Of those who had intercourse during engagement, 41 percent of both males and females had some feelings of guilt.[45] The trend of convergence of male-female attitudes moves even closer during engagement because of the increased pair-commitment. Petting seems to be a generally accepted level of intimacy during engagement and, for a significant number, sexual intercourse may also be acceptable.

A study by Bell and Buerkle asked a group of college girls about intercourse during engagement. The question to be completed was: "Do you think sexual intercourse during engagement is - - - -?" The responses were: "very wrong," 35 percent; "generally wrong," 48 percent; and "right in many situations," 17 percent.[46] Thus, only one third of the respondents categorically rejected premarital sexual intercourse. The girl can take a more liberal attitude during engagement because a relationship of love, as well as a strong commitment on the male's part, exists. Engagement is the premarital relationship in which sexual intercourse probably has minimal psychological and social dangers.

---

[44]Christensen and Carpenter, op. cit., p. 31.
[45]Bell and Blumberg, op. cit., p. 62.
[46]Robert R. Bell and Jack V. Buerkle, "Mother and Daughter Attitudes To Premarital Sexual Behavior," Marriage and Family Living, November, 1961, p. 341.

Previous experience with premarital sex appears to influence attitudes about coitus during engagement. Prince and Shipman asked their respondents if they would object to having premarital sexual relations with their engagement partner. For those with premarital sexual experience, 17 percent of the males and 45 percent of the females responded that they *would* object. For those without premarital sexual experience, 47 percent of the males and 76 percent of the females said they would object to having sexual relations with their engaged partner.[47] The females in both experience categories are more conservative in their attitudes than are the males. It is worth noting that girls with premarital sexual experience were as liberal about sex with the engaged partner as were males with no premarital sexual experience.

The stages of interpersonal relationship clearly have a great influence on premarital sexual attitudes. The emergence of different attitudes at different stages of dating and courtship have been primarily the creation of young people, because the general attitudes of the adult population are of a uniform conservative bent. In Chapter 8, differences in sexual behavior at the different dating-courtship stages will be investigated in greater detail.

PREMARITAL CHASTITY OR NOT

The emergence of different attitudes and values regarding premarital sexual intercourse may often lead to conflict and confusion for many of the young unmarried. An attempt to assess the different attitudes and the supporting arguments that are often heard is therefore of value. This will *not* a statement of what to do, but rather a presentation of some of the factors worth considering in assessing attitudes both for and against premarital chastity.

Background

Before discussing some of the arguments, it is important to look at the background of sexual knowledge and experience the individual has in making a decision as to levels of premarital sexual intimacy. A relevant question is *when, how, and to what extent does the young person learn about sexual behavior?* In a study of urban middle-class boys between the ages of 12 and 16, Ramsey found that 90 percent of their first sex information was acquired from either male companions or from their own experience. He points

---

[47]Prince and Shipman, *op. cit.*, p. 58.

out that the most reliable sources are not the ones that contribute.[48] When the boys were asked to rate their parents' contribution to sex education, 60 percent said they had received none from their mothers, and 82 percent had received none from their fathers. Only 13 percent assessed the contribution of either parent as fair or adequate.[49]

No comparable studies for girls could be found, but it seems reasonable to assume that girls, who have a more limited concern with sex during adolescence, know even less than boys. Girls probably also acquire more information from their parents, particularly their mothers. By the time late adolescence is reached, it is assumed that both sexes have a fair amount of sexual knowledge, though it may be somewhat unreliable.

As individuals move into late adolescence and the early adult years, actual premarital sex experience increasingly occurs, though more often for the male than for the female. When individuals move into the relationships of going steady or engagement, previous sexual experiences are differentially viewed by the male and the female. While the male, especially the higher educated, may be less disturbed today than in the past if he discovers his loved one has had previous sexual experiences, he still prefers that she be a virgin. The girl has a somewhat different attitude in viewing her loved one's previous sex experience. Because premarital sexual conquest as a sign of masculinity is a stereotype accepted by a number of girls, as well as by boys, she may actually desire that he not be a virgin. Because she has been taught that sexual satisfaction is important to marriage, she may also feel that his experience will be a positive element in her achieving sexual satisfaction. Burgess and Wallin found that only about one third of the engaged women in their study reacted unfavorably to their engaged partner telling them of previous sexual experiences.[50] Kinsey also found that females are less inclined to demand that their husbands be virgins when they marry. "In our sample, something over 40 percent of the males wanted to marry virgins, while only 23 percent of the females expressed the same desire."[51]

---

[48]Glenn V. Ramsey, "The Sex Information of Younger Boys," in Jerome M. Seidman, *The Adolescent* (New York: Holt, Reinhart, & Winston, Inc., 1960), p. 337.

[49]*Ibid.*, p. 337.

[50]Ernest W. Burgess and Paul Wallin, *Engagement and Marriage* (Chicago: J. B. Lippincott Co., 1953), p. 350.

[51]Alfred C. Kinsey, Wardell B. Pomeroy, Clyde E. Martin, and Paul H. Gebhard, *Sexual Behavior in the Human Female* (Philadelphia: W. B. Saunders, 1953), p. 323.

Risks

For the male who has no emotional commitment to the female, premarital intercourse has limited risks. When the relationship is transitory, he indulges for the sake of sexual gratification, with little or no emotional involvement. The dangers related to paternity responsibilities in the case of pregnancy, or dangers of venereal disease, are minimal. If his behavior is found out, he is rarely subject to social criticism; in fact, he may gain prestige in the eyes of his male peer group.

When sexual intercourse results from a close emotional tie with a girl, there are more possible risks for the male. The risks tend to be psychological and often revolve around the double-standard attitudes which many males continue to hold. Since the male often wants the girl to whom he is committed to be "good," he may redefine her as "bad," if his relationship with her becomes sexual. "It is not unusual to find a relationship either broken up or its affectionate nature altered if a girl gives in to her double standard steady."[52] The male may become bothered by the fear that if *he* could seduce her, then so may others. The degree to which this fear prevails in the mind of the young man contributes to his tendency to define the girl as slipping out of the "good" category. As Reiss suggests, "One finds very often an inverse relation, in that boys prefer to have coitus with girls they do not care for, because they regard the girls they do care for as 'too good' for such behavior."[53] An inherent dilemma exists for many young men in their committed relationship with a girl. Because of the close relationship, they push for greater degrees of intimacy; but if they are successful in pushing the relationship to sexual intercourse, their very success may redefine the relationship and lead to its termination. It should be stressed that this dilemma has its greatest application to the double-standard male.

The girl has problems similar to those of the male, only more intensified. Social control over sexual behavior is often directed at the girl in terms of strong punishments if she deviates. Strong external social forces, as well as strong internal psychological forces, ensure the girl's conformity. One fear, which is not too important as a middle-class deterrent, is venereal disease. It is doubtful that many

---

[52]Reiss, "Sexual Codes in Teen-Age Culture," *op. cit.*, p. 57.
[53]*Ibid.*, p. 57.

middle-class girls consider this a strong reason for refraining from sexual intercourse. A more important deterrent for the female, though probably not as strong as it used to be, is the fear of pregnancy. One study that asked engaged couples their reasons for not having intercourse during engagement reported that 21 percent of the males and 19 percent of the females answered fear of pregnancy.[54] Another study of college students found fear of pregnancy as a reason for not having premarital coitus stated by only 7 percent of the men and 12 percent of the women.[55] Fear of pregnancy will probably be less of a deterrent in the future as contraceptive devices, particularly effective oral contraceptives, become more reliable and available.

One significant change is that the responsibility for control over premarital pregnancy may rest more and more with the girl. If this be true, it suggests a significant change for those girls who engage in premarital coitus with any regularity; they must be willing to anticipate the act and make the necessary preparations. That females are usually responsible for the contraceptive control is shown by the common usage of the diaphragm and increasingly through the various types of oral contraceptives used by the female. Today, it is relatively simple for a girl to go to a physician and say she is getting married and be fitted with a diaphragm or given a prescription for oral contraceptives.

Personal problems within a demanding social setting are a more important restriction on premarital intercourse for the female. If a girl is discovered as having engaged in premarital intercourse, she may be defined as "bad." Her reputation becomes highly suspect and this may curtail relationships with the type of boys and in the kind of emotional setting of commitment she desires. The social penalties for the girl who is found out continue to be severe in American society. She has been reared in a society that stresses the values of virginity, and to a great extent she internalizes the values so that their violation is often also an internal personality violation. Thus, the girl commonly has a high sense of guilt. Internalized values of chastity are probably the strongest female deterrents to premarital sexual intercourse. In the Burgess and Wallin study (Table 7-1) which asked engaged couples the reasons for not having intercourse, the response, "I don't consider it right" was given by 87 percent of the girls. The importance of the girls' values are also

[54]Burgess and Wallin, *op. cit.,* p. 344.
[55]Prince and Shipman, *op. cit.,* p. 59.

reflected in the engaged males' responses, 61 percent of whom gave "Fiancée doesn't consider it right" as their reason for not having coitus during engagement.[56]

TABLE 7-1

REASONS GIVEN FOR NOT HAVING SEXUAL INTERCOURSE
WITH ENGAGED PARTNER, BY SEX

	Male	Female
I don't consider it right	68%	87%
Fiancé(e) doesn't consider it right	61	40
Fear of pregnancy	21	19
Possibility of weakening relationship	21	16
Fear of hurting parents' feelings	16	20
Fear of social disapproval	13	14
Conditions did not permit	8	7
Other reasons	6	13

Adapted from: Ernest W. Burgess and Paul Wallin, *Engagement and Marriage* (Chicago: J. B. Lippincott Co., 1953), p. 344.

An internalized value that premarital sexual intercourse is wrong, and guilt feelings from its violation, continues to be important for a significant number of American girls. If we assume that some of the other restrictive forces are losing strength, then the moral attitudes of the girl take on increasing significance. It is possible that in the future the moral values restricting girls' premarital sexual expression are going to lose some of their force because the girl will have accepted countervalues such as those of secular and hedonistic satisfaction, a belief in marital sexual satisfaction as a right for women, lesser value attached to premarital virginity by the male, a belief in greater equality of the sexes, together with a decrease in adult control and influence.

The adult world generally continues to regard various types of premarital sexual intimacy as deviant behavior. A result of this perspective is that attention is directed to the risks, particularly for the female, who engages in premarital sexual intimacy. But there may also be "risks" for those who do not experience premarital necking, petting and coitus. For example, within the context of the subcultural setting, when some intimate experience appears to be common for most adolescents and young adults, LeMasters suggests that the "deviant girl or boy today is the one who does not neck, and they are the ones we have to explain."[57] With regard to the

[56]Burgess and Wallin, *op. cit.*, p. 344.
[57]E. E. LeMasters, *Modern Courtship and Marriage* (New York: The Macmillan Co., 1957), p. 191.

same point, Kinsey wrote that a great deal has been said about "the damage that may be done by premarital sexual activities, and particularly by petting; but relatively little has been said about the psychological disturbances and subsequent marital difficulties which may develop when there is such condemnation and constant belaboring of any type of behavior which has become so nearly universal, and which is likely to remain as universal, as petting is among American females and males."[58] It would appear that in a society changing as rapidly as ours, any single standard may have risks for the individual. Reiss points out that even the young woman who accepts the traditional abstinence standard may find she has problems in meeting dating expectations and that she may encounter role conflicts between "pure virgin" roles before marriage and "good sex partner" roles after marriage.[59]

ARGUMENTS

Because of the changing state of premarital sexual mores in the American culture, and because of a number of different attitudinal complexes, what the premarital standard *should be* is a matter of controversy. In many instances, the two sides of the argument are clearly divided into male and female arguments.

Popularity

Both male and female, although most often the female, are concerned with popularity. A reputation of being sexually aggressive may decrease the male's opportunities for dates, particularly with those girls who do not want to spend an evening refining their wrestling techniques. The more important popularity problem is for the girl and is often tied up with her emotional feelings about the boy. She has to decide how far she will go, considering her own, as well as his, needs. The girl who is more emotional than the boy in a relationship finds herself in a vulnerable position. She may feel that if she is not permissive enough, she will lose him; yet if she is too permissive, he may define her in a way that will not lead him to a greater emotional commitment.

One study indicates a high rejection of the idea that a girl must be permissive to be popular. The Landises asked if a girl must pet on dates if she is to be popular: 82 percent of the males and 92

---

[58]Kinsey, *op. cit.*, p. 261.

[59]Ira L. Reiss, "The Treatment of Premarital Coitus in Marriage and Family Texts," *Social Problems*, April, 1957, pp. 335–36.

percent of the females answered "No."[60] The question is loaded, however, because many girls react with indignation to the suggestion that their popularity is dependent on petting. However, behavioral studies indicate that a large number of young people do engage in petting because of either a conscious or an unconscious desire to be popular.

The most important danger of sexual permissiveness for the girl would seem to be that she may attain popularity through it—but, from her point of view, for the wrong reasons. Few girls probably want the phone to ring constantly with requests for dates because of a "sexual" reputation. The vast majority value a relationship with a boy for present and future emotional involvements, rather than for the physical sex.

It appears that the values of youth with regard to premarital sexual behavior are more permissive for others than for themselves. Ehrmann found that the peer group code of both males and females was more liberal than the personal codes. That is, both sexes were more liberal in their attitudes about what was permissive heterosexual behavior for their companions than for themselves.[61]

Testing

A frequent rhetorical gambit, almost always presented by the boy, is: *Sexual adjustment is extremely important to overall adjustment and happiness in marriage—therefore, we should find out if we are sexually compatible before we are married.* The first part of this argument is true enough. The second part makes the highly questionable assumption that sexual intercourse is psychologically and socially the same before marriage as after. The fact that the individuals are not married usually places the behavior in a different context than it will be in after they are married. For many girls, the role of wife gives the sexual relationship a great deal of its significance and satisfaction; not having that role may take something away from the meaning of a sexual relationship. Also, the setting in which the sexual act occurs will often be different. Sexual relations prior to marriage are often carried out in the backseat of a car, for example, or in the parents' home, in a motel, and so forth. The threat of discovery denies the relaxation and removal of apprehension generally important to satisfactory sexual relations, particularly for the girl. As long as social taboos about premarital

---

[60]Judson T. Landis and Mary G. Landis, *Building A Successful Marriage* (New York: Prentice-Hall, Inc., 1953), p. 69.

[61]Ehrman, *op. cit.*, p. 269.

intercourse exist and are incorporated into the attitudes of the individual, premarital intercourse will not usually be the same as marital intercourse.

The fallacy of the testing argument is its assumption that the sexual act is entirely physical and that therefore physical compatability can be measured. It ignores the important fact that human sexual relations have a highly important psychological and social context.

"Psychological Warfare"

The male and the female have different concerns with the sexual act. In arguing, the male often uses a "scientific" approach to persuade the female of the importance of their having sexual relations. Several variations of the same basic argument center around the assumption that sexual release is important to mental and physical health. The male may argue that the girl "owes it to herself" to have sexual intercourse, that she can't be a really "mature female" until she gives expression to the sexual facet of her personality, or that she is not being mature when she resists, because a sign of adult maturity is the willingness to develop and pursue all aspects of the personality. These arguments are difficult for the female to answer if she accepts the male's premise that sexual expression *per se* is a sign of social maturity.

Many adults believe the ability to give and receive in sexual relations is a sign of maturity, but in the American culture this ability defines maturity after marriage, not before. Psychological maturity in our culture often refers to the ability to fulfill the rights and obligations that go with adult roles. The female's ability to be mature in sexual expression is still defined as a part of marriage maturity. Once again the male's argument ignores the great importance attached to personal and social factors in defining appropriate physical behavior.

On some occasions the male may argue that "you owe it to me." This argument also centers on a physical approach to sex. The male emphasizes the great force of the sex drive (especially for himself, since individual males like to think of themselves as being well above average in sex drive) and how, if it is not satisfied, dire consequences will result for him. He sometimes goes so far as to suggest that if the girl does not provide him with sexual release, his physical health will be dangerously impaired. (There seem to be no records of males hospitalized on this account.) The physiological force of the male's sex drive does frequently build up to the point where semen release is necessary, but to argue that only the female can bring about this release is ridiculous. Most males are provided with a biological mechanism of sexual release, the nocturnal emission or "wet dream." The vast majority of males also use masturbation as a means of satisfying the sex drive, at least occasionally. The argument is again biological, and implies that sexual intercourse is the only means of satisfying the sex drive. Actually men can and do achieve sexual release through a variety of sexual outlets—other than the female—as will be discussed in Chapter 8.

THE PROFESSIONAL CONTROVERSY

Disagreement on premarital intercourse is not limited to the young unmarried; it is also found among those who professionally study the American family. Many academic studies, articles, and books have been presented on questions of premarital sexual behavior. With few exceptions, writers in the past took a conservative and often moralistic point of view. It is somewhat disconcerting to read marriage and family texts in which the writers draw logically upon research material related to areas of the family—until they get to their chapter on premarital sexual behavior. Then the empirical materials are presented, but they are defined and interpreted within a moralistic context.

For the person writing as a nonscientist, a moralistic approach is justifiable. But when the person approaching the study of marriage and the family as a social scientist shifts his frame of reference when he deals with sexual behavior, he violates a basic tenet of scientific inquiry: objectivity. He may point out how premarital sexual behavior is treated and perceived within the social context, but for him as a social scientist to be either for or against it is not justifiable. This writer therefore feels it is important to point out some areas of controversy which are not scientific disagreements, but rather disagreements between a moral interpretation and an objective presentation. The two conflicting interpretations will be referred to as the *conservative* and the *liberal*. Conservative is here used to refer to various arguments for the maintenance of traditional sex attitudes because they are believed to be right and proper; liberal, to refer to the arguments that traditional attitudes are subject to scientific investigation and any discovered social inconsistencies, conflicts, and inadequacies should be critically analyzed.[62]

---

[62]See: David R. Mace, "Chastity and Virginity: The Case For," and Rene Guyon, "Chastity and Virginity: The Case Against," in Albert Ellis and Albert Abarbanel, *The Encyclopedia of Sexual Behavior* (New York: Hawthorn Books, Inc., 1961), Vol. I, pp. 247–57.

The Conservative Arguments

Probably very few students of the family would adhere to all of the arguments presented in the professional writings, but they are pointed out because all of them have some advocates.

Some conservatives are so committed to the belief that premarital sexual intimacy is bad that they will exaggerate it in amount and consequences. They seem to believe that the United States is today experiencing a great sexual moral decay. For example, the rabbi and psychiatrist Max Levin writes, "Promiscuity we have always had, but where it used to be, in the main, surreptitious, it now has come into the open." He goes on to state that "the coed today will make no bones about the fact that she is no longer a virgin."[63] There is no evidence presented to support these assertions. The available evidence does suggest that virginity may no longer be viewed in the absolute sense it once was, but there is no evidence that premarital sexual promiscuity has increased over the past 40 years, or that girls take loss of virginity lightly. The statements are exaggerated, and verge on the irresponsible.

One conservative belief is that premarital sexual intercourse is almost exclusively a promiscuous and lustful physical relationship, with little or no affection and tenderness.[64] While this is true for many sexual relationships, particularly from the male's standpoint, it is clearly not true for all. Studies of sexual relations between those in love and/or engaged show that the relationships are often emotionally strong and the sexual act is far more than simply physical.[65] The logical fallacy is the projecting of characteristics of some premarital relationships to all.

Another conservative belief is that when a couple have premarital sexual relationships, they become sex-oriented rather than emotionally person-oriented. This argument, like the preceding, fails to see that in many premarital relationships the sexual act is only meaningful within broader emotional relationships. Reiss points out that this conservative view is not supported by empirical evidence. He suggests that in reality the opposite may be true. By abstaining from sexual relations one may think more about sex because it has not been attained.[66]

---

[63]Max Levin, "The American Sexual Tragedy: A Menace To Health," *Journal of Marriage and Family*, February, 1965, p. 108.

[64]Reiss, *Premarital Sexual Standards in America, op. cit.,* p. 73.

[65]See: Burgess and Wallin, *op. cit.,* and Bell and Blumberg, *op. cit.*

[66]Reiss, *Premarital Standards in America, op. cit.,* p. 183.

The third conservative argument shifts ground to criticize not the sexual relationship, but the possible consequences. Poffenberger argues that the "breakdown of premarital sex mores has damaged group welfare as evidenced by early marriage, premature parenthood, and early termination of education."[67] A vast body of evidence supports this argument as true in many cases; however, the dangers develop around the problem of pregnancy. This problem may be eliminated to a great extent in the future by the wide use of more effective contraceptives.

Poffenberger further argues that "the basic reason that societies control sex behavior at all levels is not fear of pregnancy but experience with the intensity and uncontrollability of sex and the resultant social disorganization when social sanctions are not imposed."[68] There is no reason to assume that premarital sexual behavior must be restricted or social disorganization will occur. As was pointed out at the start of this chapter, many societies have allowed premarital sexual relations; certainly no one would argue that all were socially disorganized.

A fourth conservative argument is that the need for sexual release during adolescence is overestimated and could be conditioned—at least to a degree. If this argument is used in reference to today's American society, it is sociologically näive. If anything, the American society continues to develop more and more erotic and sexually stimulating influences to titillate the adolescent. In addition, a vast body of psychiatric and psychoanalytic literature points out the possible dangers of sexual inhibition through social conditioning.

Conservatives also believe that the sex drive can be channelized in the direction of nonsexual gratification. A writer of advice to adolescents states, "Be glad if your sexual drives are powerful enough to torment you. This is the fuel you need to drive your way up the economic jungle to security and success. Instead of an illusory escape from poverty, through squandering it, you can win a permanent access to economic well being by conserving your sexual power and putting it to work for you."[69] This argument— that the sex drive is transferable to a nonsexual drive—is questionable. Even though the individual, through other involvement, may become less concerned with his sex drive, it continues to exist and, given meaningful personal sex stimulus, will probably come forth.

---

[67]Poffenberger, *op. cit.*, p. 300.

[68]*Ibid.*, p. 327.

[69]Shailer U. Lawton, *Sexual Behavior Among Teen Agers*, (New York: Wisdom House, 1964), p. 84.

So while the sex drive may be temporarily put aside because of other strong interests, the drive itself is not altered. It generally requires a sexual release and it is very doubtful that in an erotic society nonsexual forces can contain the young person's sex drive.

A final conservative argument is that premarital sexual control must be exerted or the prime motivation for marriage will be removed. This assumes that individuals get married primarily because marriage provides an opportunity for sexual gratification. The studies which show an increase of premarital intercourse over the past 50 years, over the same time that the marriage rate has been going up, indicate the fallacy of this argument.

The Liberal Arguments

Among professionals who study the family, the number who fall into the liberal category make up a minority. Some of the arguments that this group suggest have been presented—in the form of rebuttal—in the discussion of conservative beliefs.

The first rebuttal to the conservative point of view is that liberals maintain that in many relationships of sexual involvement, there are also deep personal and emotional involvements. This argument is best stated by quoting Kirkendall: "The ability to develop a relationship in which communication is free and honest has much to do with the success a couple has in coping with the stresses and strains that are often the consequences of premarital intercourse. The extent to which motives are mutual in nature and each-other centered, as against self-centered, divergent and opposing, provide important clues to how intercourse will affect a relationship."[70]

The second liberal argument is that an important value commitment made to young people in the American middle class is that they should be taught to think for themselves and that the responsibility of the adult world is to provide them with the necessary knowledge and insight for solving their own problems.[71] This means young people should think for themselves in *all* areas, including sexual behavior, and probably applies best to the unmarried of early adult years who are reaching social maturity. The argument would probably not apply to the adolescent who does not have the social maturity to make a decision on a matter as complex as premarital intercourse. Those who desire to see young people controlled in their sexual activity must work toward giving the young

---

[70]Lester A. Kirkendall, *Premarital Intercourse and Interpersonal Relationships* (New York: The Julian Press, Inc., 1961), p. 181.

[71]Lester A. Kirkendall, "Reply to Mowrer and Poffenberger," *Marriage and Family Living*, November, 1960, p. 331.

person ability to make decisions, because the constant face-to-face influence of adults will not always be possible. Kirkendall writes, "I think that when we [adults] have talked frankly and honestly, stated our position clearly, and laid our evidence on the line, we have gone about as far as possible."[72]

There is evidence to support the belief that the strongest behavioral limits placed on premarital sexual behavior tend to be internal to individuals, not those externally imposed. This belief suggests that controls are more apt to be on the "basis of what the individual *feels* is right rather than on the basis of what he has been *told* is right."[73] Nixon points out that the new mode of internal control "is difficult to achieve, costly, and dangerous: the individual may make mistakes." However, Nixon goes on to say that the old external method "was difficult to maintain, extremely costly, and far more dangerous."[74] The argument for internal controls implies that the young person's ability to make decisions is recognized by the adult world.

A third argument is in rebuttal to the view that because adults assume they are wise and know what is best for young people, they can therefore create wise prescriptions for the control of young people. The liberal criticism of this is that, in reality, adults have come up with few prescriptions to deal with the changing sex-role of the young person. If the present confusion over conflicting premarital sexual attitudes is to be eliminated, adults must, because of their maturity and experience, make a significant contribution. What they have done so far is to react with indignation at and disapproval of adolescent sexual behavior. As a result, adolescents have had to try to provide their own prescriptions.

Finally, the last liberal argument points out social inconsistencies. Many times, the punishment directed at the youngster who deviates from adult norms is excessive. Frequently, adult reaction is determined by the degree to which the sexual deviation is known to the community at large. The girl who has premarital sexual relations is much less condemned, particularly in the middle class, if she does not become pregnant. Pregnancy implies that her deviant behavior will be known to many; therefore, her punishment is great.[75] The excessiveness of the punishment, both psychologically

[72]*Ibid.*, p. 331.
[73]Robert E. Nixon, "Sex or Guilt," in Henry A. Grunwald (ed.), *Sex in America* (New York: Bantam Books, 1964), 136.
[74]*Ibid.*, p. 136.
[75]See: Clark Vincent, *Unmarried Mothers* (Glencoe, Illinois: The Free Press, 1961), chap. i.

and socially, may have long-range personal implications for the girl. The righteously indignant fail to realize that the punishment is often much more problem-creating than was the deviance.

It is important that the reader try to assess the logical and factual base of these professional disagreements. When he does so, he is prepared to arrive at a personal decision on premarital sexual behavior. One reaction that may have already occurred to you is that, factually and logically, no "right" answers are given in the foregoing presentation. Right and wrong answers are given by those who have a moral or ethical frame of reference. The social scientist can only try to provide information and some understanding of the social consequences of a given course of action.

SELECTED BIBLIOGRAPHY

BELL, ROBERT R. *Premarital Sex In A Changing Society* (Englewood Cliffs, N.J.: Prentice-Hall, Inc., 1966)

BELL, ROBERT R., and BLUMBERG, LEONARD. "Courtship Stages and Intimacy Attitudes," *Family Life Coordinator,* March, 1960, pp. 60–63.

BELL, ROBERT R., and BUERKLE, JACK V. "Mother and Daughter Attitudes to Premarital Sexual Behavior," *Marriage and Family Living,* November, 1961, pp. 340–42.

BURGESS, ERNEST W., and WALLIN, PAUL. *Engagement and Marriage,* chaps. xi and xii. Chicago: J. B. Lippincott Co., 1953.

CHRISTENSEN, HAROLD T. "A Cross-Cultural Comparison of Attitudes Toward Marital Infidelity," *International Journal of Comparative Sociology,* September, 1962, pp. 124–37.

CHRISTENSEN, HAROLD T., and CARPENTER, GEORGE R. "Timing Patterns in the Development of Sexual Intimacy: An Attitudinal Report on Three Modern Western Societies," *Marriage and Family Living,* February, 1962, pp. 30–35.

DAVIS, KINGSLEY. "Adolescence and the Social Structure," in Seidman, Jerome M., *The Adolescent,* pp. 42–50. New York: Holt, Rinehart, & Winston, Inc., 1960.

DEDMAN, JEAN. "The Relationship Between Religious Attitude and Attitude Toward Premarital Sex Relations," *Marriage and Family Living,* May, 1959, pp. 171–76.

ELLIS, ALBERT, and ABARBANEL, ALBERT. *The Encyclopedia of Sexual Behavior,* Vols. I and II. New York: Hawthorn Books, Inc., 1961.

GRUNWALD, HENRY A. (ed.), *Sex In America* (New York: Bantam Books, 1964).

JONES, HAROLD E. "Adolescence in our Society," in Seidman, Jerome M., *The Adolescent,* pp. 50–60. New York: Holt, Reinhart, & Winston, Inc., 1960.

KAREN, ROBERT L. "Some Variables Affecting Sexual Attitudes, Behavior and Inconsistency," *Marriage and Family Living,* August, 1959, pp. 235–39.

KIRKENDALL, LESTER A. "Reply to Mowrer and Poffenberger," *Marriage and Family Living,* November, 1960, pp. 330–32.

LANDIS, JUDSON T., and LANDIS, MARY G. *Building a Successful Marriage,* chap. viii. New York: Prentice-Hall, Inc., 1953.

POFFENBERGER, THOMAS. "Individual Choice in Adolescent Premarital Sex Behavior," *Marriage and Family Living,* November, 1960, pp. 324–30.

PRINCE, ALFRED J. and SHIPMAN, GORDON. "Attitudes of College Students toward Premarital Sex Experience," *Family Life Coordinator,* June, 1958, pp. 56–60.

RAMSEY, GLENN V. "The Sex Information of Younger Boys," in Seidman, Jerome M., *The Adolescent.* New York: Holt, Rinehart, & Winston, Inc., 1960, pp. 330–38.

REISS, IRA L. *Premarital Sexual Standards in America.* Glencoe, Illinois: The Free Press, 1960.

——— "Sexual Codes in Teen-Age Culture," *The Annals,* November, 1961, pp. 53–62.

WALLER, WILLARD, and HILL, REUBEN. *The Family,* chap. ix. New York: The Dryden Press, 1951.

CHAPTER **8**

PREMARITAL SEXUAL BEHAVIOR

Sex in all of its manifestations is of great interest to Americans. Almost all media of mass communications operate under the assumption that where sex is, public interest will be. The tabloid newspapers and confessional magazines provide "sex" for the lower social classes, and the novel, the Broadway play, and A movies, art movies, and foreign movies provide it for the more "sophisticated" middle and upper social classes, and *Playboy* magazine and the Playboy clubs provide it for all classes. "Sex" is a success in the commercial marketplace. Americans of all ages cluck their tongues in disapproval and then make bestsellers of such novels as *Peyton Place, The Carpetbaggers, Glover* and *Candy.*

Premarital sexual behavior is an area of human behavior that illustrates the "schizoid" nature of American society. Few will accept attitudes of premarital sexual freedom, but many find the actual behavior stimulating and fascinating. Of course, many adults have an honest concern with an attitude toward sexual behavior which they feel is both immoral and socially destructive. Some also feel that something should be done about the hypocrisy evident in the contrast between attitudes and behavior, though few offer any workable suggestions. But the reaction of a large number is either indifference or a kind of fatalism indicating that the younger generation has gone to seed or that youth must, as ever, "sow its wild oats." Some of the reasons for confused attitudes were discussed in Chapter 7. In this chapter, the discussion will center on what is known about premarital sexual behavior.

THE KINSEY STUDIES

No other study of human behavior in the present century seems to have had as great an impact on the American population as the Kinsey reports.[1] Other studies were made on American sexual be-

---

[1]Alfred C. Kinsey, Wardell B. Pomeroy, and Clyde E. Martin, *Sexual Behavior in the Human Male* (Philadelphia: W. B. Saunders Co., 1948), and Alfred C. Kinsey,

202

havior before the Kinsey studies,[2] and a number of studies have been made since,[3] but the Kinsey studies stand out from the others for two reasons: one, the size of the population studied (5,300 white males and 5,940 white females); and two, the vast range of human sexual behavior investigated.

The first Kinsey study—on the male—was published in 1948,[4] the second—on the female—in 1953.[5] In the decade following publication of the first volume, the name *Kinsey* became a household word, and the studies sold in huge numbers. (It is unlikely that very many of the copies were read through, however; they are very long, highly statistical, and written in a pedantic style.) This strong public interest was due in part to appearance of the books at a time when American society was highly receptive to the scientific and to the sexual. The prestige of science soared very high following World War II, and during the war many barriers to sexual behavior were let down; the more open interest developed and continued into the postwar period.

Many Americans reacted to Kinsey's findings with indignation, and many attempts were made to vilify him, his associates, and their work. Since the first appearance of the Kinsey studies, however, a general, if somewhat uneasy, acceptance of studies of human sexual behavior seems to have developed. Those who have engaged in sexual-behavior research since Kinsey owe him a great debt for establishing the right to do this kind of research.

One recent indication of change in the American public's view of sexual research was the reaction to the Masters and Johnson study, *Human Sexual Response*.[6] Four weeks after this study's publication, it made the *New York Times* general best-seller list. The Masters and Johnson book is essentially a medical study of coitus

---

Wardell B. Pomeroy, Clyde E. Martin, and Paul H. Gebhard, *Sexual Behavior in the Human Female* (Philadelphia: W. S. Saunders Co., 1953).

[2]See: K. B. Davis, *Factors in the Sex Life of Twenty-Two Hundred Women* (New York: Harper & Brothers, 1929); G. V. Hamilton, *A Research In Marriage* (New York: Albert & Charles Boni, Inc., 1929); L. M. Terman, *Psychological Factors in Marital Happiness* (New York: McGraw-Hill Book Co., 1938).

[3]See: Ernest W. Burgess and Paul Wallin, *Engagement and Marriage* (Chicago: J. B. Lippincott, 1953); Winston Ehrmann, *Premarital Dating Behavior* (New York: Henry Holt & Co., 1959); Eugne J. Kanin, "Premarital Sex Adjustments, Social Class and Associated Behaviors," *Marriage and Family Living*, August, 1960, pp. 258–62; Clifford Kirkpatrick and Eugene Kanin, "Male Sex Aggression on a University Campus," *American Sociological Review*, February, 1957, pp. 52–58; William R. Reevy, "Premarital Petting Behavior and Marital Happiness Prediction," *Marriage and Family Living*, November, 1959, pp. 349–55.

[4]Kinsey, *Sexual Behavior in the Human Male, op. cit.*

[5]Kinsey, *Sexual Behavior in the Human Female, op. cit.*

[6]William H. Masters and Virginia E. Johnson, *Human Sexual Response* (Boston: Little, Brown & Co., 1966).

and orgasm. It is based upon 11 years of research involving 694 men and women. The subjects were photographed, observed, measured and interviewed during and after coitus and masturbation. One news magazine observed that even more remarkable than the book's high sales was the minimal public hostility to it. In a short period after the book's publication, its authors had received about 1,000 letters, "10 per cent . . . favorable, 20 per cent hostile and 70 per cent pleas for help with sexual problems."[7] This public reaction is very different from that which greeted the work of Kinsey and his associates.

Techniques of Study

Kinsey and his associates used a combined interview-questionnaire approach in which the interviewer could follow formal questions, but could also elaborate or go back to previous questions if he felt it necessary. Interviewing was done only by the authors so, to a great degree, they were able to control variations that might result from using a number of different interviewers. Responses were recorded in a special shorthand that permitted the interview to proceed with a natural conversational flow. Recognizing the importance of social-group differences in vocabulary, the interviewers also attempted to use a level of language understandable to the interviewees. Checks for internal consistency allowed the interviewer to go back to previous questions to check for inconsistencies and to control honesty of response. Individual interviews lasted between one and one-half and two hours.

Professional Criticism

An important scientific control is the critical analysis of a study's methods and interpretations by other professionals. Because of the vast breadth of sexual behavior studied and the overall impact of the results, Kinsey's work was subjected to a very complete professional review.[8] Some of the major academic criticisms are considered here.

Sample. No other aspect of the study has been subjected to greater professional criticism than the nature of the sample used.

---

[7] *Newsweek*, "Response to '*Response*' ", May 23, 1966, p. 94.

[8] See: William C. Cochran, Frederick Mosteller, and John W. Tukey, *Statistical Problems of the Kinsey Report* (Washington, D. C.: The American Statistical Association, 1954); Albert Ellis, *Sex Life of the American Woman and the Kinsey Report* (New York: Greenberg, 1954); Seward Heltner, *Sex Ethics and the Kinsey Reports* (New York: Association Press, 1953); Jerome Himmelhock and Sylvia F. Fava, *Sexual Behavior in American Society* (New York: W. W. Norton & Co., Inc., 1955).

The Kinsey report was not based on probability sampling—in which each individual in the universe that is studied has an equal chance of appearing. Because of the impossible problems of acquiring a random sample, Kinsey and his associates attempted to substitute 100 percent participation of persons in various groups.[9] The assumption was that a group's members could persuade fellow members to volunteer for interviews. Through group pressures, this technique did bring in some interviews that would not otherwise have been obtained. However, the groups that participated were not made up of representative members of American society. The overall criticism of Kinsey's sample is that it is not a study of the American male or female, but rather a study of a population sample biased in the direction of individuals from the Northeast, from urban areas, and who were higher educated, and willing to be interviewed.

Physical Emphasis. Another criticism is that the Kinsey studies have too strong an organic or biological emphasis. The basic unit of sexual outlet used in the studies is the achievement of orgasm, and comparisons between various subdivisions are usually made on the basis of cumulation and frequency of orgasm. Orgasm was used as a measure because of the knowledge of almost all people as to this achievement of sexual release; that is, orgasm was believed to be a more objective measure than any emotional evaluation. Some critics argue that Kinsey's emphasis on the biological tends to rule out the significance of emotional elements. They illustrate their point with the question: Can you quantitatively equate an orgasm involving nothing more than purely physical release with one involving both physical and psychological aspects? The logic of the criticism is reasonable. However, the practical question arises of how one objectively gets at the emotional factors related to various types of sexual release. This is an extremely difficult methodological problem for which no one has come up with a research answer. Lerner points out it became fashionable to say that Kinsey's use of the frequency of sexual outlets "no more makes them moral than the frequency of the common cold makes it healthy—an equating of sex with disease which in turn sheds considerable light on the heritage of Puritan repression."[10]

Recall. Any study in which a human being is the source of information is limited by the human being's accuracy of recall. In

---

[9]Kinsey (Male), *op. cit.,* p. 93.
[10]Max Lerner, *America As A Civilization* (New York: Simon & Schuster, 1957), p. 680.

general, the further you probe back into the past of an individual, the more questionable becomes his recall. A middle-aged man asked to describe the frequency of some sexual outlet during his adolescence must go back over many years to give the answer; how much he will accurately recall is bound to be limited. It may be relatively easier to recall sexual events than many other events in one's life —they are generally significant and meaningful, and the individual often has reason to remember them—but there is a second problem related to recall. A person may honestly believe he is telling the truth, but in actual fact be distorting it. Over a period of time individuals may reach a point where they persuade themselves that something happened to them that is actually a figment of their imagination. This often occurs in the recall of sexual experience. Males are notorious liars in regard to their sexual behavior. If they tell stories long enough, to themselves or others, they may grow to believe the events actually happened. There are no doubt many middle-aged men who sincerely believe they were sexually active during their long past adolescence, when, in reality, they had very limited sexual experiences. An opposite distortion of recall may operate for some women. Women may conveniently "forget" certain sexual experiences of the past. This suggests that recall has a built-in psychological bias that makes the sexual experiences of men and women seem more different than they are in reality.

In the period following the publication of the Kinsey studies, there were some who contended that the data describing the nature and frequency of certain kinds of sexual behavior would serve to encourage many to try those activities. But in the decades that have passed since publication of the studies, there is no evidence to suggest that their readers have been particularly influenced in their sexual behavior. However, there is some evidence that the studies "have played an important part in the reduction of sexual anxiety and the dissemination of tolerance and understanding."[11]

Almost all professional critics do agree that, even with their limitations, the Kinsey studies are far superior to other sexual studies and certainly superior to "armchair speculation." Scientifically, the hope is that the Kinsey studies will be improved upon in future research and better studies will result. Until that happens, the Kinsey studies provide the most objective information on Ameican sexual behavior available.

---

[11]John Madge, *The Origins of Scientific Sociology* (New York: The Free Press of Glencoe, 1963), p. 376.

PREMARITAL SEXUAL BEHAVIOR

Man has developed a variety of methods for satisfying his sexual needs, and all of them are found among both the unmarried and the married. The physical sexual behavior of the unmarried and married is not different, but the social and psychological interpretations are. For the married population, some forms of sexual outlet are approved, but for the unmarried, no outlets receive complete social approval. Yet the sexual needs of the unmarried individual do not lie dormant until his wedding day; they exist, with some change over time and with wide individual variation, during the unmarried years as well as the married. Even though it is assumed that sexual needs can be ignored, conditioned, or transferred, in reality they often find expression. Table 8-1, from the Kinsey studies, provides information on various sexual outlets and frequencies up to the time of marriage.

TABLE 8-1

ACCUMULATIVE INCIDENCE TO ORGASM (PERCENT) RELATED TO
VARIOUS SEXUAL OUTLETS UP TO THE TIME OF MARRIAGE

	Male	Female
Masturbation	94	41
Nocturnal dreams	82	12
Petting	26	37
Coitus	80	27
Homosexual	30	5
Animal contacts	8	—
Total outlet	100	64

Adapted from: Alfred C. Kinsey, Wardell B. Pomeroy, Clyde E. Martin, and Paul H. Gebhard, *Sexual Behavior in the Human Female* (Philadelphia: W. B. Saunders, 1953), p. 520.

Masturbation

Masturbation is usually a solitary, conscious form of sex outlet. Because it does not involve a partner, it is less subject to moral condemnation than the paired types of premarital sexual outlet. The highly negative interpretation of masturbation that prevailed in the past has been softened a great deal, especially among the higher educated. No authority today accepts the old belief of great physical danger resulting from masturbation. Many authorities hedge, however, by saying masturbation has no biological dangers unless it is excessive; they then fail to say what *excessive* means or to provide evidence of the dangers. The one problem that continues to exist among adolescents is the feeling of guilt associated with masturbation. Many fears and taboos continue to be passed on and accepted by the young, and "folk" beliefs are that masturbation leads to "moral" degeneration, feeble-mindedness, and adult sterility. Masters and Johnson found that all the adult males they interviewed held to a theoretical concern for the imagined effects of excessive masturbation. In every case, "excessive levels," although not defined specifically, were considered to consist of a higher frequency than did the reported personal patterns.[12] For example, one man with a once-a-month masturbatory history felt once or twice a week to be excessive and that that rate might lead to mental illness. Another subject with a masturbatory history of several times a day thought that five or six times a day was excessive and that that rate might lead to a "case of nerves." There is no accepted medical standard for defining excessive masturbation.[13]

Kinsey found in his sample that, by the time of marriage, 41 percent of the females and 94 percent of the males had engaged in masturbation to the point of orgasm.[14] The range of variation in sexual activity is generally greater for the female than for the male. Kinsey found there were some women who had masturbated to orgasm as often as 100 times in a single hour.[15] In the unmarried groups, masturbation is the most common sexual outlet for many: in the female, it accounted for 27 to 85 percent of the total outlet; in the male, 31 to 70 percent.[16]

Among females, a significant change in the use of masturbation is related to higher educational levels, but this is only slightly indicated as true for men. "The accumulative incidence (masturbation at least once) ranged from about 34 per cent among the females who had never gone beyond grade school, and 59 per cent of the females of the high school level, to 63 per cent among the females who had gone beyond college into graduate work."[17] Among the males, 89 percent of the grade school group, 95 percent of the high school and 96 percent of the college group, had indulged in masturbation to the point of orgasm on at least one occasion.[18]

The increasing frequency of sexual experience, by education, is a pattern found in reference to several types of premarital sexual outlet. The higher-educated female is more apt to engage in sexual

[12]Masters and Johnson, *op. cit.*, p. 201.
[13]*Ibid.*, p. 202.
[14]Kinsey (Female), *op. cit.*, p. 520.
[15]*Ibid.*, p. 146.
[16]*Ibid.*, p. 173.
[17]*Ibid.*, p. 148.
[18]*Ibid.*, p. 174.

behavior for several reasons. First, she tends more often than the lower-educated female to accept the belief that women are equal to men in the area of sexual right. Second, she is less subject to social control through fear, superstition, and a belief in sin. Third, because she marries later, she has more opportunity to indulge in premarital sexual behavior than the lower-educated female. Education is one of the most significant social variables used by Kinsey in the analysis of differential female sexual behavior.

Nocturnal Dreams

Nocturnal dreams, erotic dreams that a person has while asleep, are solitary, uncontrolled sexual behavior. Simple eroticism in a dream is not a sexual outlet; for it to be a sexual outlet, orgasm must accompany the dream. Kinsey found that by the time of marriage, 12 percent of the females and 82 percent of the males had achieved orgasm during a nocturnal dream.[19] The reliability of this 12 percent figure for the female is questionable. If the female was asleep, one wonders how she knew she had an orgasm. After awakening, she may or may not recall an erotic dream, but she has no way of knowing whether or not it was accompanied by orgasm. The male has proof of orgasm—the ejaculated semen. No doubt women do achieve orgasm during nocturnal dreams, but the occurrence can not be reliably measured.

When nocturnal dreams are related to different levels of education, no differences in frequency are found for women, but a higher frequency among the college group is found for men.[20] This is probably due to the higher-educated male being more prone to fantasy and, therefore, more easily stimulated by his imagination.

Homosexuality

The use of a partner of the same sex for sexual gratification is very strongly condemned in American society for both sexes under all circumstances. Homosexuality may be considered paired, conscious sexual behavior. In the United States, a trend among some sexual experts is to accept homosexuality as a "natural" form of sexual behavior; the vast majority of the population, however, does not. One of the most significant changes over the past 50 years has been a reassessment of the causes of homosexuality. At one time, the causes were assumed to be biological or organic, but today it is be-

---

[19]*Ibid.*, p. 520.
[20]*Ibid.*, p. 215.

lieved that most cases of homosexuality have a complex causal explanation primarily of a psychological and social nature. In recent years, it has also been recognized that homosexuality and heterosexuality are not either/or patterns of sexual behavior. For example, of all those who ever engage in homosexuality only 1 to 3 percent of the females and 3 to 16 percent of the males are exclusively homosexual.[21]

Kinsey found that at the time of marriage about 5 per cent of the females and 30 percent of the males had engaged in homosexuality to the point of achieving orgasm.[22] Of those who engaged in homosexuality, 71 percent of the females had been involved with one or two partners while 51 percent of the males had one or two partners.[23] At the other extreme, only 4 percent of the women with homosexual experience, compared to 22 percent of the men, had been involved with 10 or more partners.[24] The homosexual male tends to be much more promiscuous than the homosexual female, which indicates that the notion of love and exclusiveness of the partner is more important for the female than the male, whether her partner be a man or another woman.

Homosexuality among women increased slightly by level of education. The figures, for females who ever had homosexual relationships to the point of orgasm, were: grade school, 6 percent; high school, 5 percent; college, 10 percent. For the males, a slightly lower rate was found at the lower level of education: grade school, 27 percent; high school, 39 percent; and college, 34 percent.[25] The figures on homosexuality, by sex, go counter to another popular myth that homosexuality is more frequent among women. The Kinsey figures clearly indicate that the male is much more prone to homosexuality than the female, which, to a great extent, is a result of the greater sexual interests and less restrictive sexual forces that operate on the male in the American society.

Premarital Petting

Petting is paired, conscious behavior that may be defined as physical contacts which involve a deliberate attempt to effect erotic arousal.[26] In marital and premarital coitus, some degree of petting as a means to the end of sexual intercourse is usual; however, in

---

[21]*Ibid.*, p. 488.
[22]*Ibid.*, p. 520.
[23]*Ibid.*, p. 488.
[24]*Ibid.*, p. 488.
[25]*Ibid.*, p. 488.
[26]*Ibid.*, p. 228.

petting, the "foreplay" becomes the sexual end. This form of pre-marital sexual outlet often allows the girl to achieve orgasm in the boy-girl relationship, and still remain a virgin. Kinsey provides information on the sexual experiences of the virgin at the time of marriage. For those females born after 1910, with between 13 and 16 years of education, 100 percent had been kissed, 70 percent had experienced manual stimulation of the breast, and 30 percent oral stimulation. Thirty-three percent had their genitalia manually stimulated, and 22 percent had manually stimulated the male genitalia.[27] Between one quarter and one third of these virgins may be considered highly experienced "technical virgins."

As the adolescent of both sexes became older, petting experience increased sharply: for the female, the percentage rose from 3 by age 15 to 81 by age 18; for the male, from 57 by age 15 to 84 by age 18. By the time the female reached age 20, about 23 percent had achieved orgasm while petting; the figure for the male of the same age is 32 percent. One important difference between the female and the male from the ages of 16 to 25 is that petting ac-counted for 18 percent of the girls', but only 3 percent of the boys' orgasms[28]

Whether the boy or girl reached puberty early or late was found to have some relationship to premarital petting experience. Those girls who had reached adolescence at earlier ages (by 11 or 12) were the first to start petting and petting to the point of orgasm.[29] However, Kinsey points out that there was a sharp contrast between the ages at which females and males started their petting experience. "In most instances the male's activity begins quite promptly with or immediately after the onset of adolescence. In the median female, on the other hand, petting did not begin until 15 or 16 years of age, which is three or four years after the average female turns adolescent."[30]

In premarital petting, as in all areas of sexual behavior, the male is sexually more promiscuous than the female. Of the females who had engaged in premarital petting, 42 percent were involved with 5 or fewer partners and 19 percent with 21 or more partners. Of the males, 26 percent had 5 or fewer partners and 37 percent had 21 or more partners.[31]

---

[27]*Ibid.*, pp. 280–81.
[28]*Ibid.*, p. 267.
[29]Kinsey, *op. cit.*, p. 246
[30]*Ibid.*, p. 246.
[31]*Ibid.*, p. 683.

Almost exactly the same percentage of the females at each educational level had engaged in petting to the point of orgasm before marriage,[32] while the percentage of males was highest in the high-school educated group.[33] One reason for the higher-educated male having greater experience with petting is that petting is probably more accepted by the higher- than the lower-educated females. The female usually determines the limits of intimacy, and, for many, petting is accepted in at least some relationships.

In most areas of female sexual behavior, there were significant differences among the Kinsey respondents by intensity of religion, with the more religious being the more restricted in behavior. But religious codes seem to have had little influence on the frequencies of petting to orgasm, even among the most devout females in the sample. "It is particularly significant to find that the devout female, after she has once achieved orgasm in a petting relationship, engages in such activity about as often as the average of the less devout female."[34]

Premarital Coitus

Because it sharply indicated the disparity between norms and behavior, no figure in either of the Kinsey reports was more shocking and upsetting to the American population than that which showed about 50 percent of all the women studied had had premarital coitus. This lack of virginity was viewed by many as categorically the same for all 50 percent, ignoring the variations in number of partners or the frequency of the sexual act. Kinsey pointed out that "a considerable proportion of the female premarital coitus had been in the year or two immediately preceding marriage, with a portion of it confined to the fiancé in a period just before marriage."[35] An important difference in the premarital sexual relations of the female and male continues; a modified double standard still exists. The important distinction between the unmarried male and female, at least for some groups, is no longer the virgin-nonvirgin double standard, but rather a double standard in which nonvirginity is found for both sexes, with the male often sexually promiscuous and the female generally restricted in number of sexual partners. The Kinsey findings offer evidence for this distinction in the premarital sexual experience of both males and

[32]*Ibid.*, p. 239.
[33]*Ibid.*, p. 267.
[34]*Ibid.*, pp. 248–49.
[35]*Ibid.*, p. 286.

females who were not virgins at the time of marriage. Fifty-three percent of the females, as contrasted with 27 percent of the males, had premarital coitus with only one partner; however, only 12 percent of the females, as contrasted with 40 percent of the males had premarital coitus with six or more partners.[36]

The variable of education is extremely important to the analysis of premarital coitus. It is important because there is an inverse relationship, by education, between male and female frequency of premarital coitus. By educational level, the percentages for the female are: grade school, 30; high school, 47; and college, 60.[37] The percentages for the male are: grade school, 98; high school, 85; and college, 68.[38] Frequency of premarital coitus for the girl goes up by education because of later age of marriage, more petting, and a less rigid notion as to the importance of virginity. The figures by education go down for the boy because of less coital opportunity and the use of other sexual outlets.

The higher-educated girl makes a less rigid distinction between virginity and nonvirginity. One important difference between high- and low-educated females is that while fewer low-educated girls have premarital coitus, those that do have a higher rate of promiscuity. For example, premarital coitus accounted for 38 percent of the grade-school educated female's active sexual experience, but only 18 percent of the college girls'.[39] If we assume that the male to female ratio is roughly equal at the different educational levels, it would mean that, in the grade-school group, there is one girl having premarital coitus for every three boys, while in the college group, the ratio is about one girl for every one boy. While a number of boys, particularly in the lower classes, have their premarital coitus with prostitutes, it must also be remembered that a number of the higher-educated boys have their sexual experiences with girls in lower social classes. When girls at all education levels are compared, the college-educated girls are least apt to be virgins at the time of marriage. However, when all girls who have ever had premarital coitus are compared, the "indulging" lower-educated girls are the most promiscuous.

The age factor also becomes important in understanding the higher probability of college-educated females having premarital coitus. Many of them have their sexual experiences at an age when

[36]*Ibid.*, p. 292.
[37]*Ibid.*, p. 293.
[38]*Ibid.*, p. 330.
[39]*Ibid.*, p. 331.

the lower-educated girl is already married. Of those girls who had premarital sexual experience, 18 percent of the grade-school group were having premarital coitus by age 15, as compared with 1 percent of the college-educated girls, and, respectively, between the ages of 16 and 20, 38 percent as compared with 18 percent. After age 20, the figures are about the same for all educational levels.[40] That 81 percent of the college-educated females who have premarital coitus have it past the age of 20, suggests premarital coitus is not usually an event of their adolescence, but rather of their young adult years.

Even if a number of girls are not effectively stopped from engaging in premarital coitus by the social attitudes, do they suffer any aftereffects from violating the norms? Moralists direct their indignation at those who violate the norms but do not seem to suffer remorse, and while many Americans are happy to take the errant back into the flock if they will say they are sorry and were wrong, they can become very vituperative toward those who violate the norms and are not penitent.

Kinsey found that "69 percent of the still unmarried females in the sample who had had premarital coitus insisted they did not regret their experience. Another 13 percent recorded some minor regrets."[41] Other studies offer evidence of low female negative reactions. One study found that the "immediate reaction of 77 percent of the girls to first experience with sexual intercourse was pleasurable."[42] A recent study of 49 middle-class college girls who had premarital coitus found that the predominate reaction was of enjoyment and satisfaction and guilt feelings were very little in evidence.[43] It may be argued that those girls who say they do not regret premarital coitus are rationalizing their behavior. Undoubtedly, many girls say they have no regrets because they feel they must justify their behavior to themselves and, in some cases, to others. However, the degree of rationalization is probably less than many people believe. Kinsey found that an even "larger proportion, some 77 percent of the married females, looking back from the vantage point of their more mature experience, saw no reason to regret their premarital coitus. Another 12 percent of the married females had some minor regret."[44]

[40]*Ibid.*, p. 295.

[41]*Ibid.*, p. 316.

[42]Gilbert Youth Research, "How Wild are College Students?" *Pageant*, 1951, pp. 7, 10–21.

[43]Marvin B. Freedman, "The Sexual Behavior of American College Women: An Empirical Study and An Historical Survey," *Merrill-Palmer Quarterly*, January, 1965, p. 41.

[44]Kinsey (Female) *op. cit.*, p. 316.

One very sharp difference between those unmarried females who did have premarital sexual relations and those who did not is found in their stated intent for the future. Among the unmarried females in the Kinsey study who had never had premarital coitus, 80 percent said that they did *not* intend to before marriage; in contrast, among those who had had such experience, only 30 percent said they did not intend to have more.[45]

As previously suggested, one of the strongest arguments made against premarital coitus in the United States centers on the danger of pregnancy. However, in Chapter 7 several studies were cited which indicated that fear of pregnancy was not a common reason given by young women for not engaging in premarital coitus. From the behavioral perspective, an important question is—To what extent does premarital pregnancy occur and what are some of its consequences? Obviously there is no way of knowing exactly how many conceptions occur among unmarried women (we will discuss premarital pregnancies that result in illegitimate births in Chapter 9), but examination of a variety of studies suggests that somewhere between 10 to 25 percent of all brides are pregnant at the time of their marriage.[46] When premarital pregnancy occurs, the engagement period is generally shortened. One study of premarital pregnancy found that for those girls who were not pregnant at marriage, the mean length of engagement was 12 months, but for those premaritally pregnant, the mean length of engagement was 7 months.[47]

Premarital pregnancy is often presented in the mass media as a problem most common among young and immature girls. Given the frequency of premarital pregnancy, what can be said sociologically about it? This: The evidence clearly indicates that even when girls have premarital coitus their chances of pregnancy are not nearly as great when they are in early adolescence as they will be during late adolescence or in the early adult years. This "adolescent sterility" means that coitus is less likely to result in pregnancy in the postpubescent girl than in the mature woman; the average age for full reproductive maturity in women has been estimated at about 23 years.[48] The reason for such relative sterility among girls appears to be that "the number of menstrual periods in which an egg is *not*

---

[45]*Ibid.*, p. 314.

[46]See: Paul H. Gebhard, Wardell B. Pomeroy, Clyde E. Martin and Cornelia V. Christenson, *Pregnancy, Birth and Abortion* (New York: Harper & Brothers, 1958), pp. 35–42.

[47]Samuel H. Lowrie, "Early Marriage: Premarital Pregnancy and Associated Factors," *Journal of Marriage and Family*, February, 1965, p. 52.

[48]Clellan S. Ford and Frank A. Beach, *Patterns of Sexual Behavior*, (New York: Harper & Row, 1952), p. 72.

released from the ovary is much higher among young adolescent females than in older females."[49]

The probability of pregnancy among unmarried girls having coitus is related *both* to "relative sterility" and to age at marriage. For example, if a girl starts having coitus during early adolescence and continues for a number of years without marriage she would have a relatively high probability of premarital pregnancy. The Kinsey data shows that for those girls who had premarital coitus before age 15, only 6 percent became pregnant. For those with premarital coitus by age 20, the pregnancy rate was 13 percent, and by age 30 it was up to 21 percent.[50] The point is that with increased age the sexually active unmarried girl's fertility potential increases *and* she has more years in which premarital pregnancy can occur.

A double-standard society directs most sexual restrictions at the female. When social controls on the female begin to lose some of their force, the change in behavior may become cumulative as the deviant behavior further weakens the norms. This would certainly seem to be the pattern for a number of American females for whom the norms no longer have the strength to function either as a deterrent or to punish through guilt feelings. The reader should be cautioned against assuming that the female has an indiscriminate sex orientation. Rather, many girls no longer consider the line between chastity and nonchastity as absolute, but as a matter of degree. For the vast majority of girls, love or affection must exist before they enter premarital sex relations.

MALE-FEMALE DIFFERENCES IN PREMARITAL SEXUAL BEHAVIOR

The boy-girl interactional patterns prior to marriage are often characterized by different motivations. The male role, as defined by both sexes, is to be the aggressor in areas of sexual activity; the female role is to determine the extent of sexual intimacy. The assumption made by both sexes is that the male will press for more intimate levels of intimacy unless he is stopped by the female.

There are some general sexual differences between males and females that appear common to most societies. For example, in most societies—as in the United States—men usually start sexual activity at younger ages and participate with greater frequency than women. Men also appear to be somewhat more responsive to psychological

---

[49]Gebhard, *op. cit.*, p. 32.
[50]*Ibid.*, p. 39.

and symbolic stimuli associated with sex; however, this difference may be becoming of decreasing significance in the United States. In most societies, men and women do not appear to differ in the initiative taken for starting sexual activity or in speed of achieving orgasm.[51]

Possibly, females are increasingly the initiators of sexual intimacy. The role of the male as aggressor is probably still dominant today, but is not as rigidly limited to him as it once was. Ehrmann found that "56 percent of the males and 54 percent of the females reported that the males always initiated the activity; and, 44 percent of both sexes stated that the female did on occasion; 10 percent of the males and 6 percent of the females said that the female started it as often as, or more often than, the male."[52] The male is probably the main aggressor in dating relationships, but as the level of interpersonal commitment increases, the female may play a more significant part in sexual initiation.

A study by Kirkpatrick and Kanin, among college students shows strong male sexual aggression as quite common. They found that of 291 responding girls, 56 percent reported having been offended at least once during the prior academic year at some level of sexual intimacy. "The experiences of being offended were not altogether associated with trivial situations as shown by the fact that 21 percent were offended by forceful attempts at intercourse and 6 percent by aggressively forceful attempts at sex intercourse in the course of which menacing threats or coercive infliction of physical pain were employed."[53]

The girls' feelings that the boy was excessively aggressive were not limited to the dating experience. Table 8-2 shows that offensiveness occurred as follows: first date, 26 percent; occasional date, 30 percent; and regular date, pinned, and engaged, 44 percent.[54] In dating, the girl often defines aggressive behavior by the boy as abrupt and unanticipated. On first-date occasions, 50 percent of the girls said there had been no prior sex play when the male aggression occurred. For the regular date, pinned, and engaged, 63 percent of the girls reported some prior sex play before the aggression occurred.[55] For all the offended girls, ignoring the dating-courtship

[51]Bernard Berelson and Gary A. Steiner, *Human Behavior*, (New York: Harcourt, Brace & World, 1964), p. 303.

[52]Ehrmann, *op. cit.*, pp. 63–64.

[53]Kirkpatrick and Kanin, *op. cit.*, p. 53.

[54]Eugene J. Kanin, "Male Aggression in Dating-Courtship Relationships," *American Journal of Sociology*, September, 1957, p. 200.

[55]*Ibid.*, p. 202.

level, the maximum number of erotic intimacy offenses defined as aggressive on at least one occasion was: necking and petting above the waist, 67 percent; petting below the waist, 14 percent; and attempted intercourse, both with and without violence, 30 percent.[56]

The emotional reactions of the girls to aggression varied: almost half reacted with anger, about one fifth with guilt, and one fifth with fear.[57] The reactions of the girls on how to deal with the problem varied: 31 percent ended the relationship; 23 percent kept it secret; 30 percent used discussion and warning; and 16 percent made an appeal to parents and other authorities.[58]

TABLE 8-2

PERCENT AT DATING RELATIONSHIP AND EROTIC INTIMACY
LEVEL AT WHICH OFFENSE OCCURRED, BY EPISODES

Date Relationship	Necking and Petting above the Waist	Petting below the Waist	Attempted Intercourse and Attempted Intercourse with Violence	Total
First date	30	16	14	26
Occasional date	31	27	26	30
Regular date, "pinned," and engaged	39	57	60	44
Total	100	100	100	100

Adapted from: Eugene J. Kanin, "Male Aggression in Dating-Courtship Relationships," *American Journal of Sociology*, September, 1957, p. 200.

Kanin also found evidence that sexual aggression among college males has some relationship to earlier experiences with women. For example, he found sexual aggression higher for those males who had unfavorable sentiments toward their mothers as well as for those males who had had unpleasant experiences with females during courtship.[59]

These findings indicate the nature of the male-female sex struggle. As long as the boy is the physical aggressor, he is not always going to allow the girl to stop the relationship when she chooses. A common belief among many young men is that a girl often says "no" when she really means "yes," that she must make some pretense of resisting intimacy as a kind of face-saving device. Sometimes a boy feels he can keep being aggressive until the girl really means "no."

[56]*Ibid.*, p. 198.
[57]Kirkpatrick and Kanin, *op. cit.*, p. 56.
[58]Kanin, *op. cit.*, p. 203.
[59]Eugene J. Kanin, "Male Sex Aggression and Three Psychiatric Hypotheses," *The Journal of Sex Research*, November, 1965, pp. 223–25.

Different reactions to aggression come because some girls say "no" and mean it, while others say "no" and really mean "go ahead." The girl who says "no" at one level and then allows the boy to go ahead may be in for trouble at the next level when she says "no" and really wants him to stop.

PREMARITAL INTIMACY AND DATING-COURTSHIP STAGES

In Chapter 7, different attitudes to premarital intimacy as related to dating, going steady, and engagement were pointed out. In general, the more intense the relationship, the greater the accepted level of sexual intimacy. It was also suggested that in the limited pair-commitment of dating, the sexual attitudes of the two sexes were most divergent, but, as the couple moved through going steady and engagement, their attitudes as to acceptable levels of intimacy converged. The discussion that follows is concerned with the sexual behavior of the unmarried at the dating and courtship stages and how their behavior relates to sexual attitudes.

Dating

The boy often perceives the girls he dates as falling into one of two categories that reflect a double standard of "good" and "bad" girls. He often thinks of the "bad" girls as "pick-ups," which implies that they are girls to whom he would not become committed, and with whom he can therefore pursue his sexual interests in a highly ego-oriented fashion. As Kirkendall points out, this "safeguards the male from the consequences of his actions, and at the same time leaves the females vulnerable."[60] The females are vulnerable if they feel committed to and desire a reciprocal commitment from a boy who has no intention of giving it. If the girl tries to force the boy to commit himself, she may find herself lined up against a cohesive male group. In sex-directed dating, the male frequently feels no commitment to protect the girl either personally or socially. If she has indulged in sexual relations with boys whose only interest in her was as a sex outlet, she may find that "some of the boys are spreading the word of her availability to others."[61]

Friendly dating contrasts with male sex-oriented dating. Friendly dating implies general equality between the sexes, particularly in

---

[60]Lester A. Kirkendall, *Premarital Intercourse and Interpersonal Relationships* (New York: The Julian Press, Inc., 1961), p. 75.

[61]*Ibid.*, p. 108.

broad social-class background, and from it generally grow the more committed relationships. The boy usually treats the girl with more respect than he does in sex-oriented dating, even though he may initially seek sexual fulfillment. In this type of relationship, there is a strong possibility that the boy's feelings for the girl will change if he does achieve sexual intercourse. Kirkendall found that 26 percent of the males he studied lost respect for their partner following intercourse.[62] The evidence indicates that in the dating relationship a far greater level of sexual intimacy is achieved by the boy than the girl. College girls, in particular, resist sexual intimacy without some emotional commitment from the boy. In a study of intimacy levels by courtship stages of college students, Bell and Blumberg found that the peak levels of intimacy while dating were, for girls, 49 percent petting and 10 percent intercourse, and, for boys, 37 percent petting and 46 percent intercourse.[63] Findings such as these, which indicate that petting was experienced by at least half the girls, suggest that the girls' actual behavior while dating is beyond the intimacy level they usually define as appropriate.

Going Steady

Though going steady normally implies a commitment to the other person in the paired relationship, commitments may vary for different couples, and generalizations are tenuous. In some college relationships, going steady involves some protection for the girl because the boy is emotionally committed enough to give her some consideration as a possible marriage partner. Kirkendall found that when there was considerable emotional involvement, but not engagement, the girl was protected by the boy's refusal to talk with other boys about their sexual relationship.[64]

Ehrmann found that a high *frequency* of both dating and going steady for males was related to greater sexual frequency and experience, but "for females greater sexual experience and frequency were related only to a high frequency for going steady.[65] If the girls felt the going-steady relationship involved an emotional commitment, these results would support the belief that a girl needs some feeling of emotional commitment from the boy before engaging in sexual intimacy.

In the Bell and Blumberg study, the peak levels of intimacy while

---

[62]*Ibid.*, pp. 127–28.
[63]Robert R. Bell and Leonard Blumberg, "Courtship Intimacy and Religious Background," *Marriage and Family Living*, November, 1959, p. 358.
[64]Kirkendall, *op. cit.*, p. 150.
[65]Ehrmann, *op. cit.*, pp. 168–69.

going steady were, for the females: petting, 57 percent, and intercourse, 15 percent; and for the males: petting, 45 percent, and intercourse, 40 percent.[66] These findings indicate very little change from the dating relationship for petting or intercourse for either the female or male. They do indicate that, for those girls studied who had ever gone steady, about three quarters had engaged in at least petting behavior.

Engagement

The greatest changes in premarital sexual behavior have probably occurred at the engagement stage of dating-courtship, particularly for the college-educated female whose marriage comes later and whose engagement often lasts for a year or more. For a large number of girls, a prerequisite to premarital sexual intercourse, that she have strong affection or love for the male, continues to prevail. In the past, both love and marriage were prerequisite to intercourse. Although love continues to be extremely important, marriage is less important for some girls than in the past. Ehrmann, in his extensive study of premarital dating behavior, found that female sexual expression is primarily and profoundly related to being in love, with a concomitant relationship of, at least, going steady.[67] The significance of the close relationship many girls deem necessary for sexual involvement has been well described by Kirkendall:

> Some deeply affectionate couples have, through the investment of time and mutual devotion, built a relationship which is significant to them, and in which they have developed a mutual respect. Some of these couples are relatively free from the customary inhibitions about sexual participation. Some couples with this kind of relationship and background can, and do, experience intercourse without damage to their total relationship.[68]

The interrelationship of love and sex is often very complicated for the girl. For example, she is often reared to believe that strong sexual desire on her part results *from* being in love. Hence, if she has strong sexual interests she may "explain" her feelings by defining herself as being in love. LeMasters suggests that "many girls, and especially 'nice' girls, have never been completely aroused sexually until they meet a certain boy, and then it has to be 'love'; otherwise, they are 'bad' girls; easily aroused by any man."[69]

---

[66]Bell and Blumberg, *op. cit.*, p. 358.
[67]Ehrmann, *op. cit.*, p. 269.
[68]Kirkendall, *op. cit.*, p. 199.
[69]E. E. LeMasters, *Modern Courtship and Marriage* (New York: The Macmillan Co., 1957), p. 194.

Various studies indicate that from one half to two thirds of the female respondents who had engaged in premarital sexual intercourse had the relationship only with the male they later married. Kinsey reported that 87 percent of the married females in his sample had at least a portion of their premarital coitus with the man they married and 46 percent exclusively with him.[70] Kinsey also found that premarital coitus with the future spouse was the least often regretted.[71] When coitus was only with the future spouse and during engagement, the Kinsey data indicate it was far more than an isolated experience or two. With two thirds of the engaged couples, premarital coitus occurred more than 10 times and in 25 percent of the cases occurred over a period of more than one year.[72]

In a study made by Davis in 1923 of 1000 women who were predominantly college graduates, only 7 percent reported premarital intercourse.[73] In 1929, Hamilton reported that 31 percent of the women he studied stated they had had premarital intercourse with the person they married.[74] Terman's findings in regard to date of birth point out changes over time for both sexes. Table 8–3 shows that for the males born before 1890, 51 percent had no premarital

TABLE 8–3

PREMARITAL SEX EXPERIENCE BY DATE OF BIRTH (PERCENT)

		Before 1890	Time of Birth 1890-1899	1900-1900	1910-Later
	Sex Experience				
Husbands:	None	50	42	33	14
	Spouse only	5	8	17	32
	Spouse and others	9	23	34	41
	Others only	36	27	16	13
Wives:	None	86	74	51	32
	Spouse only	9	18	33	45
	Spouse and others	3	6	14	20
	Others only	2	2	2	3

Adapted from: Lewis M. Terman, *Psychological Factors in Marital Happiness* (New York: McGraw-Hill, 1938), p. 41.

coitus, and 5 percent had coitus with "future spouse only"; for those born in 1910 and after, only 14 percent had no premarital coitus and 32 percent had coitus with "future spouse only." For females born before 1890, 86 percent were virgins at marriage, while 9 percent had coitus with "future husband only." For those born in 1910 or

[70]Kinsey (Female), *op. cit.*, p. 292.
[71]*Ibid.*, p. 318.
[72]*Ibid.*, p. 336.
[73]Davis, *op. cit.*, p. 178.
[74]Hamilton, *op. cit.*, p. 373.

later, only 32 percent were virgins at marriage, and 45 percent had coitus with "future husband only."[75]

When engagement is compared with dating and going steady, a convergence of male and female sexual attitudes and behavior is indicated. The Bell and Blumberg study found that for all the females and males who were or had been engaged, 31 and 46 percent, respectively, had had intercourse.[76] The convergence is generally a reflection of the increased pair-commitment found in engagement, especially for the male. He is often very conscious of what is "right" from his girl's point of view, because she is the one he plans to marry. Because the male is committed, he frequently will be less sexually aggressive, and the decision to have premarital coitus is very often a shared decision. Table 8–4 shows the changes in premarital coitus at the different dating-courtship stages.

TABLE 8–4

PERCENT HAVING PREMARITAL COITUS AT VARIOUS DATING-COURTSHIP STAGES

	Males	Females
Dating	46	10
Going steady	40	15
Engaged	46	31

Adapted from: Robert R. Bell and Leonard Blumberg, "Courtship Intimacy and Religious Background," *Marriage and Family Living*, November, 1959, pp. 358–60.

Some Social Correlates

Burgess and Wallin analyzed their respondents for possible differences in premarital coitus during engagement by age. They found no relationship for the women. When the man is in the older age groups, there is possibly less likelihood that the couple will have premarital sex relations during engagement. Of those pairs in which the male was over 26, coitus had occurred among 41 percent, as compared to 50 percent of the couples in which the male was under 23.[77]

Kanin and Howard found some relationship to religion. "Pairs in which neither spouse reported regular church attendance at the time of marriage were most apt to report intercourse." Premarital coitus was reported by 28 percent of the regular churchgoers, by 48 percent of the pairs made up of one regular and one nonregular attender, and by 61 percent of the pairs composed of two non-attenders.[78]

---

[75]Terman, *op. cit.*, p. 41.

[76]Bell and Blumberg, *op. cit.*, p. 360.

[77]Burgess and Wallin, *op. cit.*, p. 336.

[78]Eugene J. Kanin and David H. Howard, "Postmarital Consequences of Premarital Sex Adjustments," *American Sociological Review*, October, 1958, p. 557.

Kanin analyzed the rates of premarital coitus with the future spouse by social class. In his sample he found that upper middle-class women reported the smallest incidence of premarital coitus—31 percent; the middle-class female came next with 42 percent; and the highest incidence, 82 percent, was reported for the lower-class female.[79] As all of these women eventually married college men, there may be some indication that premarital coitus is significant to the lower-class female's relationship with the higher social class male she married.

Nature of Engagement

Length of engagement would logically seem—and is—related to a higher probability of premarital coitus. The longer the couple go together, the more they become sexually involved and the greater the tendency becomes to move to more intensive levels of intimacy. Burgess and Wallin found that premarital coitus was somewhat more common in longer engagements. For those couples engaged 8 months or less, 39 percent had premarital coitus, as compared to 48 percent for those couples engaged 28 months or longer.[80]

The discussion thus far has distinguished between those who have experienced coitus during engagement and those who have not. Burgess and Wallin provide information on the frequency with which the married couples had indulged in premarital intercourse. For all those who had premarital intercourse, it happened "once" with only 10 percent of the couples, "rarely" with 21 percent, "occasionally" with 40 percent, and "frequently" with 29 percent.[81] These findings indicate that premarital coitus becomes a fairly common occurrence for at least a third of the engaged couples.

Burgess and Wallin indicate that premarital sexual experience in prior relationships is related to a couple having intercourse during engagement. For those men who had coitus in a prior relationship, 56 percent had intercourse with their engaged partner, as contrasted with 35 percent of the men who had no prior coital experience. For the engaged women, the differences are even greater. For the women with a previous sex experience, 86 percent had intercourse with the engaged partner, while this was true of only 40 percent of the women who were virgins at the time of their engagement.[82]

Kanin studied the impact of the coming marriage on premarital

---

[79]Kanin, *op. cit.,* p. 259.
[80]Burgess and Wallin, *op. cit.,* p. 335.
[81]*Ibid.,* p. 330.
[82]*Ibid.,* p. 334.

coitus by investigating the sexual behavior of the couple in the last month prior to marriage. He found a slight decrease in activity during the last month for those involved in premarital coitus. Thirty-one percent indicated decrease, 22 percent, increase, and the rest reported their sexual activity unchanged.[83] Kanin's findings did not indicate a slackening off because the marriage was coming near; rather, the slackening off was largely dependent upon the female's failure to achieve orgasm.[84]

Finally, an evaluation of how premarital coitus affected the overall engagement relationship was sought. Burgess and Wallin report that 93 percent of the men and 91 percent of the women stated that sexual intercourse had strengthened their engagement relationship.[85] However, this sample is a select group in that they had premarital coitus and the relationship lasted; therefore, they were less apt to view the sexual activity as destructive. In those engagements that did not last, the act of coitus might be defined as a destructive factor, for the Burgess and Wallin study found that sexual intercourse during engagement was related to broken engagements. Coitus had occurred in 52 percent of the broken engagements, but in only 37 percent of the unbroken engagements.[86] An engagement may have difficulty surviving coitus, but when it does, the sexual aspect may be seen as contributing strongly to the overall relationship.

The various studies indicate several basic considerations in regard to engagement and coitus, though the nature of the cause-and-effect relationships is very complex. Sexual experience during some successful engagements is probably entered through mutual agreement and mutually defined as contributing to the relationship. The mutuality often means that a relatively high sense of security, particularly for the female, exists in the engagement relationship. The sex experience may then be felt to *add* to the relationship. By contrast, in broken engagements the relationship may not have been strong enough to accept the sexual experience, and it may, therefore, have been a highly disrupting influence.

PREMARITAL EXPERIENCE AS RELATED TO MARRIAGE

A common belief in the United States, based upon traditional attitudes, is that failure to conform to premarital sexual norms will

[83]Kanin, *op. cit.,* p. 260.
[84]*Ibid.,* p. 261.
[85]Burgess and Wallin, *op. cit.,* p. 372.
[86]*Ibid.,* p. 357.

contribute to postmarital problems. This attitude presumes that if sexual intercourse occurs before marriage, negative effects on both the sexual and the overall husband-wife adjustment will result. But behavior studies indicate that this assumption is much less true than many have believed. In the area of sexual adjustment in marriage, Burgess and Wallin point out that "the statistical findings on premarital intercourse and sexual success in marriage do not support the theory that coitus before marriage has an adverse effect on the sexual relationships after marriage."[87]

As to the broader question of adjustment in marriage, Kirkendall points out that "the negative effects on marital adjustments attributed to premarital intercourse *per se* have probably been greatly exaggerated in our culture."[88] The tendency in the past has been simply to view the act of premarital coitus as bad, without realizing that the act must be related to the social and psychological context of the individuals involved. Contributions of different personality characteristics and of variations in cultural values have been greatly underestimated, and often ignored.[89]

A number of studies have been specifically concerned with the relationship between premarital and postmarital coitus. Kanin and Howard found a relationship between premarital intercourse with spouse and full sex expression during the early weeks of marriage. "Sexual satisfaction was readily attained on the wedding night, by wives who had experienced premarital intercourse."[90] Of the females who had premarital intercourse with spouse, 71 percent reported wedding-night relations as "very satisfactory" or "satisfactory," in contrast to 47 percent of the females without premarital experience.[91] Of course the nonvirgins may have been less restricted biologically, psychologically, and socially in personal sex expression than the virgins.

It has also been found that the capacity for achieving orgasm in marriage is related to premarital sexual orgasm experience. "The type of premarital experience which correlates most specifically with the responses of the female in marital coitus is premarital coitus— *provided that that coitus leads to orgasm.*"[92] Kinsey found that among the females who had had even limited premarital sexual ex-

---

[87]*Ibid.*, p. 366.
[88]Kirkendall, *op. cit.*, p. 227.
[89]*Ibid.*, p. 277.
[90]Kanin and Howard, *op. cit.*, p. 560.
[91]*Ibid.*, p. 560.
[92]Kinsey, *op. cit.*, p. 386.

perience, only 19 percent had failed to reach orgasm in the first year of marriage. By contrast, among the females who had had premarital coitus but who had not reached orgasm in the coitus, 38 to 56 percent failed to reach orgasm in the first year of marriage."[93] Kanin and Howard found that of those women who had reached orgasm in premarital coitus, only 28 percent reported marital sexual difficulties, whereas difficulty was admitted by 47 percent of the women who had failed to achieve orgasm from premarital intercourse.[94] Thus, premarital sexual satisfaction seems to be important to marital sexual satisfaction. However, the higher orgasm frequency for the married women who had achieved orgasm in premarital coitus may also be attributable to the selecting out of those women who are most sexually responsive.

Burgess and Wallin found no significant differences in frequency of achieving orgasm in marriage when the woman had no premarital experiences or "with husband only," but in the virgin group, 71 percent usually or always achieved orgasm after marriage, and, for those who had premarital coitus "with husband and other men," 82 percent usually or always achieved orgasm after marriage.[95] These findings, too, would suggest a selectivity, in that women most able to achieve orgasm in marriage are more apt to have indulged in premarital sexual relations.

Burgess and Wallin also found some relationship between the frequency of achieving premarital orgasm with the future spouse and achievement of orgasm after marriage. For those women who frequently achieved premarital orgasm, 81 percent usually or always achieved it after marriage. For those women who had never achieved orgasm from premarital coitus with spouse, 71 percent usually or always achieved orgasm after marriage.[96] Kinsey, of course, has provided information on the broader area of premarital achievement of orgasm. First, he found "that there was a marked positive correlation between experience in orgasm obtained from premarital coitus, and the capacity to reach orgasm after marriage. Second, among those females who had never reached orgasm from any source prior to marriage, 44 percent had failed to reach orgasm in any of their coitus in the first year of marriage.[97] Kinsey also found that of those females who had reached orgasm at least 25 times in pre-

---

[93]*Ibid.*, pp. 385–86.
[94]Kanin and Howard, *op. cit.*, p. 560.
[95]Burgess and Wallin, *op. cit.*, p. 363.
[96]*Ibid.*, p. 362.
[97]Kinsey (Female), *op. cit.*, p. 328.

marital coitus, only 3 percent had failed to achieve at least some orgasm in marital coitus.[98]

Many women may achieve a state of sexual satisfaction in their marriage with limited or even no orgasm. If the love relationship is satisfactory, then the physical sex satisfaction may not be viewed as too important. However, it seems that the woman's personally felt need to achieve fulfillment in the sexual act, through orgasm, is becoming more important. The young woman of today, particularly the higher-educated, is being reared to believe that she has a "right" to expect sexual satisfaction in marriage. Today, many couples go into marriage believing they both can and should achieve sexual fulfillment. A reading of today's sex manuals for marriage shows great emphasis on the theme that both the husband and wife do everything they can to help the wife achieve orgasm as often as possible.

ADULT-YOUTH CONFLICT

In concluding our discussion about premarital sexual values and behavior, we will discuss some generational conflicts and bring together the main arguments both for and against premarital sexual intercourse. In the discussion of generational conflict, we will examine some of the premarital sexual values held by the younger generation and compare those values with those of their parents and other older adults.[99]

Given their different stages in the life cycle, parents and children are almost always going to show variations in how they define appropriate behavior for a given role. Values as to "proper" premarital sexual-role behavior from the perspective of the parents are greatly influenced by the strong emotional involvement of the parent with his child. On the other hand, the child is going through a life-cycle stage in which the actual behavior occurs, and must try to relate his parents' values to what he is doing or may do. There is an important difference between defining appropriate role conduct for others to follow and defining proper role conduct to be followed by one's self. What may be even more important to actual behavior is that often there is more than one significant group of role definers that the young person can turn to as guides for his sex-role behavior. We will examine some recent research

---

[98]*Ibid.*, p. 329.

[99]For a more extended discussion see: Robert R. Bell, "Parent-Child Conflict in Sexual Values," *Journal of Social Issues*, April, 1966, pp. 34–44.

that provides data on the attitudes of the younger generation as compared with the values of parents and other older adults.

A study by Bell and Buerkle compared the attitudes of 217 coeds with those of their mothers. Both mothers and daughters were asked to respond to the question, "How important do you think it is that a girl be a virgin when she marries?" Of the mothers, 88 percent said they thought it was "very wrong" not to be a virgin, while the remaining 12 percent thought it "generally wrong." Fifty-five percent of the daughters thought it "very wrong," 34 percent "generally wrong," and 13 percent "right in many situations."[100] Both mothers and daughters were also asked: "Do you think sexual intercourse during engagement is: very wrong; generally wrong; right in many situations?" The percentages for each response category were 83 percent, 15 percent and 2 percent for the mothers; and 35 percent, 48 percent, and 17 percent for the daughters.[101]

Responses to both questions show sharp differences between the attitudes of mothers and daughters toward premarital chastity. No doubt the responses of many of the mothers were influenced by their having a daughter in the age setting where the questions had an immediate and highly emotional application. Even so, the sharp differences between mother and daughter responses indicate that the area of premarital sexual behavior is one of potentially great conflict.

A common technique for minimizing conflict is for the daughter not to discuss her sexual attitudes or behavior with her mother. In the same study by Bell and Buerkle, it was found that only 37 percent of the daughters, in contrast with 83 percent of the mothers, felt that daughters should freely answer questions from their mothers about attitudes toward sexual intimacy.[102] The entire area of sexual attitudes appears to be highly influenced by emotion, especially for the mother as it concerns her daughter. The emotional reactions of some mothers may also be influenced by recollections of their own premarital sexual experiences. The Kinsey study, which provides data on the mother's generation in their younger years, indicates that the mothers were actually no more conservative in their premarital sexual attitudes and behavior than are their daughters.

However, it is problematic whether the liberal attitudes of the

---

[100]Robert R. Bell and Jack V. Buerkle, "Mother and Daughter Attitudes to Premarital Sexual Behavior," *Marriage and Family Living*, November, 1961, p. 391.

[101]*Ibid.*, p. 391.

[102]*Ibid.*, p. 392.

college daughters will continue for very long. A somewhat surprising finding in the Bell-Buerkle study was that differences in the educational background of the mothers *did not* produce differences in attitudes toward premarital virginity. It is possible that later in her life the college-educated daughter may be as conservative as her mother, when her attitudinal rationales are not related to herself or her age-peers, but rather to a daughter of her own. It is therefore possible that the "sexual emancipation" of the college girl exists only for a short time in her life span—the time of her own premarital love and/or engagement.

Reiss has done research with several large samples in an attempt to develop scales for the measuring of attitudes with regard to premarital sexual permissiveness, utilizing two major samples: (1) an adult sample of 1515 individuals aged 21 and older drawn randomly across the United States; and, (2) a high-school and college student probability sample of 903 students, ages 16-20, drawn from two high schools and two colleges in Virginia and one college in New York state.[103] This is the first study to draw on a large and randomly selected sample.

Reiss's respondents were asked to express their beliefs about different combinations of intimacy and degree of interpersonal commitment for both unmarried males and females. They were asked if they believed petting to be acceptable when the male or female was engaged. In the adult sample, the belief that petting during engagement was acceptable for the engaged male was the response of 61 percent, and for the engaged female it was the response of 56 percent. Of the student respondents, 85 percent approved for the engaged male and 82 percent for the engaged female.[104] Thus, not only are the adult attitudes about petting during engagement more conservative than those of the student population, but for both the adult and the student groups there is a single standard— that is, the acceptance rates are roughly the same for both males and females.

Reiss also asked his respondents if they believed that premarital petting was acceptable when the individual felt no particular affection toward his partner. To this item, "yes" was the response of 29 percent of the adult group with reference to the male, and of 20 percent for the female. In the student sample, "yes" was the

[103]Ira L. Reiss, "Premarital Sexual Permissiveness Among Negroes and Whites," *American Sociological Review*, October, 1964, pp. 688–89.

[104]Ira L. Reiss, "The Scaling of Premarital Sexual Permissiveness," *Journal of Marriage and Family*, May, 1964, pp. 190–91.

response for 34 percent of the males and 18 percent of the females.[105] (These responses provide some empirical evidence to validate Reiss's concept of permissiveness-without-affection.) Essentially the same rate of unacceptability for petting without affection is given by both the adult and the student samples. The adult responses suggest a single standard of rejecting this kind of behavior, however, while the student sample gives some indication of a double standard—a higher proportion suggesting approval for this behavior pattern for males than for females.

Reiss also asked his respondents if they believed full sexual relations to be acceptable if the male or female is engaged. Approval was the response given by 20 percent of the adult group for males and 17 percent for females. In the student group, acceptance was given by 52 percent for the male and 44 percent for the female.[106] Here, as with petting, there are significant differences between the adult and the student samples, and here both groups suggest a single standard of acceptance for both males and females.

Finally, Reiss's respondents were asked if they believed it acceptable for both males and females to have premarital coitus even if they felt no particular affection toward their partner. In the adult sample, 12 percent stated approval for the male and 7 percent for the female. In the student group, 21 percent approved for the male, 11 percent for the female.[107] As with petting with no particular affection, these data suggest that only a small number accept coitus without affection, and in the adult sample the acceptance difference for males and females is not significant. However, there is an indication that for the student population there may be a double standard, with somewhat greater acceptability for the male than for the female.

The data from Reiss's research, along with the data from smaller and more limited studies, clearly suggest important differences in attitudes about premarital sexual intimacy when young unmarried adults are compared with the general adult population.

The values of parents and the adult community in general may in time become more liberal and the conflict between generations reduced. (There seems little possibility that the opposite will occur). But until this happens—if it does—parents and their children will continue to live with somewhat different value systems with regard to premarital sexual values and related behavior. Parents will prob-

---

[105]*Ibid.*, pp. 190–91.
[106]*Ibid.*, pp. 190–91.
[107]*Ibid.*, pp. 190–91.

ably continue to hold to traditional values and assume that *their* child is conforming to those values unless his actions force them to admit otherwise. The youth generation will probably continue to develop their own modified value systems and keep those values to themselves, implicitly allowing their parents to believe they are behaving according to the traditional values. For many parents and their children, the conflict about premarital sex will continue to be characterized by the parent playing ostrich and the youth attempting to keep the sand from blowing away.

In Chapter 7, a number of conservative and liberal views were presented on the subject of premarital sexual freedom. It was not suggested that all of the arguments had equal weight, but that if an individual recognizes them as existing, he might be better equipped to make his own decisions. Although arguments are seldom presented that indicate possible values for premarital intercourse, the social scientist recognizes that they exist, even though those who are morally opposed to premarital sexual freedom may feel they would be better left unrecognized and unstated.[108] Here, to close this chapter, is a summary of Chapter 7's arguments:

Arguments for Premarital Sexual Freedom

1. A person may have a strong psychological need for sexual release that can only be satisfied through coitus.
2. A person may derive a high physical and psychological satisfaction from premarital sexual relations.
3. If little or no guilt exists, the sexual intimacy may intensify the emotional relationships between the two individuals.
4. Premarital coitus is probably more valuable in developing the emotional paired aspect of sexual interaction than the use of solitary forms of sexual release.
5. From premarital coitus, the individual may develop a capacity to make emotional interrelationships that are important to marriage.
6. It may provide an opportunity for learning sexual techniques that can be applied to marital coitus. (Many already assume this is important for the male.)
7. Emotional and physical adjustments are often easier to make at younger ages and therefore may be made with less difficulty before marriage.
8. Heterosexual experiences may prevent the development of homosexual patterns of sexual behavior.
9. Premarital sexual relations may in a positive way lead the couple into marriage.

---

[108]See: Kinsey (Female), pp. 308–9. Many of these suggestions were taken from Kinsey and his associates.

ARGUMENTS AGAINST PREMARITAL SEXUAL FREEDOM

1. The possibility of pregnancy.
2. Dangers of venereal disease.
3. The problem of a marriage brought about because of premarital pregnancy.
4. The personally disorganizing effects that premarital coitus may have because of the conditions under which it often occurs.
5. The personality dangers of guilt due to breaking the moral standards accepted by the individual. The feelings of guilt are related to the religious values of sin and immorality.
6. The possibility that guilt over the sexual act may end what was otherwise a very satisfactory relationship.
7. Premarital coitus may make some individuals feel obligated to marry the sexual partner.
8. The danger that the male will lose respect for the female and not want to enter marriage.
9. The fear (usually by the male) that his partner may be susceptible to extramarital relations after marriage.

SELECTED BIBLIOGRAPHY

BELL, ROBERT R. "Parent-Child Conflict in Sexual Values," *Journal of Social Issues,* April, 1966, pp. 34–44.

BELL, ROBERT R., and BLUMBERG, LEONARD. "Courtship Intimacy and Religious Background," *Marriage and Family Living,* November, 1959, pp. 356–60.

BELL, ROBERT R., and BUERKLE, JACK V. "Mother and Daughter Attitudes to Premarital Sexual Behavior," *Marriage and Family Living,* November, 1961, pp. 390–92.

BURGESS, ERNEST W., and WALLIN, PAUL. *Engagement and Marriage,* chaps. xi and xii. Chicago: J. B. Lippincott, 1953.

COCHRAN, WILLIAM C., MOSTELLER, FREDERICK, and TUKEY, JOHN W. *Statistical Problems of the Kinsey Report.* Washington, D. C.: The American Statistical Association, 1954.

DAVIS, K. B. *Factors in the Sex Life of Twenty-Two Hundred Women.* New York: Harper & Brothers, 1929.

EHRMANN, WINSTON. *Premarital Dating Behavior.* New York: Henry Holt & Co., 1959.

ELLIS, ALBERT. *Sex Life of the American Women and the Kinsey Report.* New York: Greenberg, 1954.

HAMILTON, G. V. *A Research in Marriage.* New York: Albert & Charles Boni, Inc., 1929.

HILTNER, SEWARD. *Sex Ethics and the Kinsey Report.* New York: Association Press, 1953.

HIMMELHOCK, JEROME, and FAVA, SYLVIA F. *Sexual Behavior in American Society.* New York: W. W. Norton & Co., Inc., 1955.

KANIN, EUGENE J. "Male Aggression in Dating-Courtship Relationships," *American Journal of Sociology*, September, 1957, pp. 197–204.

―――― "Premarital Sex Adjustments, Social Class and Associated Behaviors," *Marriage and Family Living*, August, 1960, pp. 258–62.

―――― "Male Sex Aggression and Three Psychiatric Hypotheses," *The Journal of Sex Research*, November, 1965, pp. 221–31.

KANIN, EUGENE J., and HOWARD, DAVID H. "Postmarital Consequences of Premarital Sex Adjustments," *American Sociological Review*, October, 1958, pp. 556–62.

KINSEY, ALFRED C., POMEROY, WARDELL B., and MARTIN, CLYDE E. *Sexual Behavior in the Human Male*. Philadelphia: W. B. Saunders Co., 1948.

KINSEY, ALFRED C., POMEROY, WARDELL B., MARTIN, CLYDE E., and GEBHARD, PAUL H. *Sexual Behavior in the Human Female*. Philadelphia: W. B. Saunders Co., 1953.

KIRKENDALL, LESTER A. *Premarital Intercourse and Interpersonal Relationships*. New York: The Julian Press, Inc., 1961.

KIRKPATRICK, CLIFFORD, and KANIN, EUGENE. "Male Sex Aggression on a University Campus," *American Sociological Review*, February, 1957, pp. 52–58.

REEVY, WILLIAM R. "Premarital Petting Behavior and Marital Happiness Prediction," *Marriage and Family Living*, November, 1959, pp. 349–55.

REISS, IRA L. "The Scaling of Premarital Sexual Permissiveness," *Journal of Marriage and Family*, May, 1964, pp. 188–96.

―――― "Premarital Sexual Permissiveness Among Negroes and Whites," *American Sociological Review*, October, 1964, pp. 688–98.

―――― "Social Class and Premarital Sexual Permissiveness: A Re-Examination," *American Sociological Review*, October, 1965, pp. 747–56.

TERMAN, L. M. *Psychological Factors in Marital Happiness*, chaps. x to xiv, appendices 1 to 3. New York: McGraw-Hill Book Co., 1938.

PART III

Marriage and Parenthood

SOME LEGAL ASPECTS
OF THE FAMILY

For most of man's history, the social control of human behavior has rested with the family, the clan, or the tribal unit. No society, past or present, simple or complex, has existed without controls over some areas of human behavior. Without some agreement as to rights and obligations for individuals within a group, there could be no society, only a collection of isolated, nonsocial individuals.

Historically, marriage and the family have been an important area of controlled social behavior. Societies have developed controls over the interactional relationship of marriage, the responsibility for meeting the needs of children, and the transmission of properties, rights, statuses, and knowledge from one generation to the next.

As complex and extended societies developed, social controls became more extensive and far-reaching. Extended social controls came to be vested in the society or its delegates through the emergence of political organization under various systems of government. Out of this development came formalized laws. An important difference between laws and social controls such as norms, or mores, or folkways is that laws are recorded. They therefore provide continuity as well as sanctions for controlling human behavior.

Laws provide formalized sets of controls available (at least in theory) to all members of a society, thus enabling individuals to know their rights and to anticipate the obligations their actions will entail. The human being is socialized to need and desire dependability and predictability in social interaction.[1] The legal system, along with the informal controls of society, provides a social order which allows the individual to proceed through the course of his day making generally accurate assumptions about the behavior of others and, thereby, to function with a sense of personal security in a wide variety of interactional settings.

Although people sometimes tend to perceive laws as being sacred

---

[1]Ray E. Baber, *Marriage and the Family* (New York: McGraw-Hill Book Co., 1953), p. 49.

and to attribute to them an intrinsic value of their own, laws are, nevertheless, created by man and are validated through their efficiency as a means of directing the behavior of individuals within the defined social group. Societies often incorporate punishments to ensure the social acceptance and usefulness of laws. But simply because laws exist with stated punishments for nonconformity does not mean that they will always be legally enforced. The vast majority of written laws in the United States is rarely or never applied. For example, in the area of sexual behavior, Kinsey and his associates concluded after initial preliminary analysis that "only a minute fraction of one per cent of the persons who are involved in sexual behavior which is contrary to the law are ever apprehended, prosecuted, or convicted."[2]

Generally, the enactment of new laws or the repeal of old ones is a very slow process. A dynamic legal system to fit the changing nature and needs of society is frequently an ideal, not a reality. Sometimes, too, the laws of a society no longer have their original meaningfulness because of changed social conditions, and they therefore create problems. In the discussion of law and the family that follows, some of the problems of legal and social conflict will be illustrated. The discussion centers on the laws related to entering the marriage role and to the legal role of the child. Some legal aspects relevant to the ending or modifying of the marriage relationship are discussed in Chapter 16. As there is no federal law in regard to marriage and the family, the discussion is general, with reference made to 53 different sets of laws. The 53 legal jurisdictions consist of the 50 states, the District of Columbia, the Virgin Islands, and Puerto Rico.

MARRIAGE LAWS

Legally there have been problems in defining marriage. The problem for courts and legislatures is that marriage can broadly be looked upon as a contract, a status, a relationship, or an institution.[3]

The concept of marriage as a contract has been handed down from English common law as the specific legal definition of marriage. The difficulty in this definition, however, is that while marriage is like the ordinary contract in many ways, it is also different. Clarke

---

[2]Alfred C. Kinsey, Wardell B. Pomeroy, Clyde E. Martin, and Paul H. Gebhard, *Sexual Behavior in the Human Female* (Philadelphia: W. B. Saunders Co., 1953), p. 18.
[3]Helen I. Clarke, *Social Legislation* (New York: Appleton-Century-Crofts, 1957), p. 73.

points out two ways in which a marriage contract differs from a private contract:[4] (1) Once the relationship of marriage has been legally established, the two members cannot through their own voluntary actions alter or break the contract. "It becomes a legal status that can be severed only by laws and acts of the state itself; whereas in the case of the private contract, the parties can modify or restrict it, enlarge it, or entirely release it by their mutual acts and consent."[5] (2) The requirements of legal capacity to enter into a marriage contract are different from those required for entering into an ordinary contract. For example, a person may contract a valid marriage at an age when he would not be old enough to make a binding contract in the business world.[6]

The laws relating to marriage that have emerged in the United States have basically met one or the other of two social needs, although sometimes the two needs are met within a single law. The two needs are: (1) "the fixing of financial responsibility so as to insure that the state will not have to bear the burden of supporting dependent women and children and (2) the encouragement of marital unions likely to produce acceptable offspring and the confinement of sexual activity within the boundaries of such a marriage."[7] It often appears that the laws with regard to marriage have a minimal social impact; their influence is apparent only when some of the common legal requirements for marriage are changed or introduced for the first time. In the late 1950's and early 1960's, for example, six states (Arizona, New Mexico, South Carolina, Indiana, Mississippi and Iowa) tightened up or introduced premarital legal requirements. When the combined marriage totals for the last calendar year before the reforms are compared with the marriage totals for the first calendar year after the new legal requirements, the six states show a marriage decline of 47 percent[8]

Legal Requirements

Age. Historically, the age of marriage was usually related to puberty, the biological age when reproduction is possible. While marriage at a very young age is still possible in some states, the

---

[4]*Ibid.*, p. 75.

[5]*Ibid.*, p. 75.

[6]*Ibid.*, p. 75.

[7]Harriet Pilpel and Theodora Zavin, "Laws on Marriage and Family," in Albert Ellis and Albert Abarbonel (eds.), *The Encyclopedia of Sexual Behavior* (New York: Hawthorn Books, Inc., 1961), p. 614.

[8]Alexander Plateris, "The Impact of the Amendment of Marriage Laws In Mississippi," *Journal of Marriage and Family*, May, 1966, p. 206.

general legal pattern has been to move the age for marriage into late adolescence and the early adult years. Furthermore, legal definitions have been made on differences in decision-making rights relative to different ages of marriage. The law has said that while some individuals may marry in late adolescence, legally the final decision is not theirs, but their parents'. Such legal control by the parents is a reflection of thinking handed down from the past, when parents were much more directly involved in controlling the marriages of their children than they are today.

Four legal ages for marriage exist in this country. The four ages are defined by sex and whether the individual may marry with or without the consent of the parents. "The most common age-with-consent is 18 for the male and 16 for the female, while the age-without-consent is most generally 21 for the male and 18 for the female."[9] The law recognizes age differences by sex as to physical and social maturity for entering marriage. Society, through its legal system, maintains marriage control until the minimum ages are reached, then gives the responsibility to the parents for the next few years, and finally gives the individual the right of legal decision-making. In effect, when all factors are taken into account, the legal range of minimum age for marriage in the United States is from 12 to 21.[10] It appears questionable that the consent of parents has much effect on the frequency of young marriages. For example, in 1957 for the first time, a girl in South Carolina had to show with her birth certificate that she was over age 18, or have the written permission of her parents to marry. But there is no evidence from the "data to support the hypothesis that the requirement of parental consent is deterrent to early marriage."[11] It may be that many of parents feel that when a girl is old enough to want to marry there is little reason to oppose her, or it may be that a young age at marriage is most common among the lower social classes (where there is greater tolerance of such marriages than in the middle class).

Parents also have certain other legally approved ways of influencing the marriage of their children, even if the children are old enough to marry without the parents' consent. The law supports

---

[9]William M. Kephart, The Family, Society and the Individual (Boston: Houghton Mifflin Co., 1961), p. 401.

[10]William M. Kephart, "Legal and Procedural Aspects of Marriage and Divorce," in Harold T. Christensen (ed.), Handbook of Marriage and The Family (Chicago: Rand McNally & Co., 1964), p. 945.

[11]David A. Gover and Dorothy G. Jones, "Requirement of Parental Consent: A Deterrent to Marriage," Journal of Marriage and Family, May, 1964, p. 206.

the idea that parents be given every opportunity short of slander and libel to advise their children on the selection of a mate.[12] Until children leave the parental home, their parents can use a wide variety of influences and pressures—in general, anything that is not specifically prohibited by law.

Family Restrictions. A number of individuals are legally excluded as marriage partners because they are defined as members of the family. Early in history, the church banned marriages of specifically related people, and the legal system gave early support to most of these restrictions. The legal prohibitions involve two categories of family relationships: *consanguinity,* a blood relationship or descent from a common ancestor; and *affinity,* a relationship resulting from marriage. All statutes in the United States prohibit consanguineous marriage with one's son or daughter, mother or father, grandmother or grandfather, sister or brother, aunt or uncle, niece or nephew. With other relationships of consanguinity, less agreement prevails, but over half the states prohibit the marriage of first cousins. Some examples of state affinity restrictions are that the male cannot marry the stepmother in 23 states, the stepdaughter in 22, the daughter-in-law in 17, and the mother-in-law in 13.[13]

Mental Deficiency. The mentally defective are generally unable to control their lives and meet the economic and social responsibilities of marriage. Thus, social concern over their marriage is a practical, economic one; mental inability may result in them and their children becoming the financial wards of the state. A number of states have specific statutes that prohibit the marriage of the mentally retarded. However, many states have no satisfactory method of preventing mentally deficient marriages because there is no generally accepted psychological definition of feeble-mindedness.[14]

Insanity. Most states have prohibitions against the marriage of the insane. Clarke points out that this restriction is derived from two theories, one legal and the other scientific.[15] The legal is based upon the fact that a marriage contract requires that the two individuals be capable of giving consent; the insane individual is in-

---

[12]John S. Bradway, "What Family Members Should Know About Law," in Howard Becker and Reuben Hill, *Family, Marriage and Parenthood* (Boston: D. C. Heath & Co., 1955), p. 566.

[13]Irving Mandell, *The Law of Marriage and Divorce* (New York: Oceana Publications, 1957), pp. 21–25.

[14]Clarke, *op. cit.,* p. 98.

[15]*Ibid.,* p. 97.

capable of doing so. The scientific reason is that the mentally incapable can create severe problems for both the family they procreate and society in general. The problem here, as with mental deficiency, is the legal establishment of an acceptable definition of insanity.

Miscegenation. Many states restrict marriage across racial lines. Miscegenation laws prohibit a white person from marrying someone of a different race. Originally, the prohibition was based on the belief that significant differences existed between races, and that marriage across racial lines would result in a "weakening" of the dominant race. These beliefs have been shown to have no scientific validity; a vast amount of research has failed to demonstrate any crucial differences in intelligence and general biological adaptability among racial groups. However, 31 states, mainly in the South and Southwest, still prohibit marriage between white and Negro. Seventeen states, primarily in the West, prohibit marriage between white and Oriental or Mongolian. Four states, all in the South, prohibit marriage of the white to the American Indian.[16] In those states which have no prohibitory statutes, persons of different races may legally intermarry.

Generally, individuals are legally defined as a member of a racial group not on the basis of being more of one race than of another, but rather on the basis of a limited part of their background. A common definition is that if the full-blooded ancestor was the third generation back, making the individual one quarter nonwhite, the person belongs to the minority racial group. In some southern states, a person is defined as Negro if any known ancestor anytime in the past was Negro. In those states with miscegenous marriage laws, the miscegenous marriage is usually considered void, the children illegitimate, and the relationship a crime, even a felony.[17]

Racial barriers to marriage are deeply imbedded in the thinking of many individuals, particularly the white Southerner. Because of geographical differences in racial discrimination, social and legal problems are sometimes created for individuals moving from one state to another. Generally, a marriage that is valid where contracted is valid everywhere, the only two exceptions being incestuous and polygamous marriages. However, many courts take an opposite view and may declare a valid marriage of another state void in their state.[18] For example, if a Negro and a white are married in

---

[16]Mandell, *op. cit.*, p. 26.

[17]Clarke, *op. cit.*, p. 104.

[18]Isabel Drummond, *The Sex Paradox* (New York: G. P. Putnam's Sons, 1953), pp. 271–72.

Pennsylvania, which has no miscegenation laws, their marriage is valid. But if they decide to move to any one of a number of southern states, and the authorities of that state become aware of their marriage, the marriage may be declared void and the couple may be arrested. Many legal experts believe that in the near future the United States Supreme Court will declare miscegenation laws an invasion of individual rights and, thus, unconstitutional.

Marriage Licenses. Marriage licenses are issued by the state. They serve the dual purposes of withholding legal permission for marriage from those who do not meet the legal requirements and as a means of acquiring marriage statistics. The license laws usually prescribe: (1) that a license shall be obtained for a valid marriage; (2) the form and content of the application, and by whom and where the license will be issued; and (3) the various regulations as to marriage qualifications that must be met by the parties desiring to marry.[19] The agent issuing the license is responsible for obtaining all necessary facts and ascertaining that the parties meet the legal requirements. The legal agent must acquire information in two broad areas. He must get the information that is needed for complete and accurate records, such as the names of the parties, residence and occupation, time of the proposed marriage, and parental names and addresses, and—of greatest importance—he must acquire the facts needed to establish the legality of the marriage, such as age, race, and the status of any former marriages.[20]

Blood tests are now a legal requirement for marriage in every state except Maryland, Minnesota, Nevada, South Carolina, and Washington, D.C. The usual purpose of the test is to determine whether either party has syphilis, or that the disease is not in the communicable stage.[21] These requirements operate much more effectively in theory than they do in actual practice. Clarke points out some of the problems connected with serological tests and what might be done to correct them:

1. Examinations are not required of women in some states. There is no sound reason why this should be.
2. Medical examinations are often perfunctory and superficial. Standardized laboratory tests should be required.
3. Statutory fee limitations encourage doctors to make hasty examinations. Public examiners might be designated for all examinations or for some defined classes of persons. Free Wassermanns might also be provided.

---

[19]Clarke, *op. cit.,* p. 88.
[20]*Ibid.,* p. 89.
[21]Kephart, *op. cit.,* pp. 948–49.

4. The laws are often evaded through out-of-state marriages. In those states already having laws forbidding certain kinds of out-of-state marriages, there should be an extension of the prohibition to include those persons seeking to evade the venereal disease provisions.[22]

One other legal requirement directly related to getting a marriage license are the "advance-notice" laws. These laws provide a period of time between when the person applies for or gets the license and when he can legally be married. This period of time is sometimes referred to as the "cooling-off" period. Without the time lag, a couple can marry immediately; with the waiting period, it has been estimated that as high as 20 percent of all applying couples never use the license or return to pick it up. The waiting period thus cuts down on the hasty marriages caused by sudden elopements, intoxication, or "temporary insanity," that have been correlated with high divorce rates.

Three kinds of advance-notice laws are in use in the legal jurisdictions of the United States. The most common is a period of time between the application for and the issuance of the license. The modal period of time between application and issuance is three days, but, in almost as many states, the waiting period is five days and in one state it is one day. This kind of law is generally considered to be more effective than the other two, one of which, found in only three states, requires a waiting period between the time the license is issued and when the marriage can take place. The waiting period ranges from one to five days. This method is less efficient than the first because the license is in the hands of the couple, and they may find someone who will marry them ahead of time and postdate the license. The third kind of advance-notice law, found only in New York, is a combination of the first two. The waiting period is three days between license application and issuance and then one more day before the marriage can legally be performed.[23]

The discussion thus far has pointed out a number of legal prerequisites for marriage. If all of the requirements are met, the marriage is considered to be *valid*. This does not mean that the legal requirements for marriage of all states must be met, because—with the exceptions already mentioned—a marriage valid where contracted is valid everywhere. For example, suppose a couple are too young to marry in their home state without the consent of their parents and they elope to another state where they are legally old

[22]Clarke, *op. cit.*, p. 103.
[23]Baber, *op. cit.*, pp. 60–61.

enough to marry without parental consent. They meet the other legal requirements of that state, are married, and return to their home state. This marriage is perfectly valid and will not be annulled or declared void by the home state.

If the legal requirements have not been met, the marriage may be defined as either *void* or *voidable*. In law, any act which is void is null and ineffectual; it has no legal force or binding effect. For example, suppose a woman gets married and later discovers that her husband is still legally married to a first wife. Her marriage is *void* as of the point of discovery of the previous marriage, and its dissolution does not normally call for any court action. A marriage void in its inception does not require the judgment of the court to restore the parties to their original rights.[24] A marriage which is *voidable* is one which may be declared void; it is not void in and of itself.[25] The marriage will be considered valid until it is nullified by the proper court proceedings. The couple cannot together seek to have the marriage voided, and the action must be brought during the lifetime of the two married individuals.[26] The most commonly used and accepted grounds for declaring a marriage void through the actions of the court are nonage and incapacity. For example, if a person marries under the statutory age of consent, the marriage may be annulled by judicial decree.

The distinction between the void and the voidable marriage is blurred in many states because their statutes do not always state clearly whether certain prohibited marriages are void or voidable. Distinctions between the two are necessary because a void marriage may be annulled after the death of the parties, but a voidable marriage may not be. Also, a voidable marriage can usually be ratified or affirmed, but a void marriage cannot be.[27]

Common-law Marriages

A common-law marriage is based entirely upon the mutual consent of the two individuals and is not solemnized by any particular form.[28] Common-law marriages were made legally acceptable in the United States as a result of certain historical factors. With only certain groups of people given the legal authority to perform a marriage, sometimes in the past no authority was available for long

---

[24]Clarke, *op. cit.*, p. 110.
[25]*Ibid.*, p. 109.
[26]*Ibid.*, p. 110.
[27]*Ibid.*, p. 111.
[28]Baber, *op. cit.*, p. 69.

periods of time. Under the assumption that it would be better for the individuals to be married if they so desired, they were given the legal right to enter into common-law marriage. But a corollary assumption was that they would be legally married when a person with authority to perform marriage was available. The legal right of the common-law marriage has been handed down from a frontier past, when it served a functional social need. Today, a lack of legal authorities to perform the marriage ceremony is rare. However, in the United States today, common-law marriage is recognized in about half the states and another six states recognize it if it occurred prior to a specific date.[29]

While legal definitions of what constitutes a common-law marriage vary, generally three conditions must be met. First, the couple must be legally marriageable. That is, they must be of the proper age, not already married, and so forth. Second, they must live together and hold themselves out to the community as husband and wife. Third, they must, mutually, intend to be legally married at some future date.[30] A popular myth, that has no basis in the law, is that the couple must live together seven years. Generally, no specifically mentioned length of time is needed to establish a common-law marriage.

Common-law marriages are frequently found in the lower socio-economic classes. Individuals enter this type of relationship for several reasons. They may be fearful of or hostile toward legal authority, or lack knowledge of marriage requirements. Possibly, many see the marriage relationship as tentative, or they plan on getting married, but just never get around to it. In the United States, persons are rarely called upon to give proof that they are married, and presenting themselves as husband and wife is almost always accepted without question by the community.

Problems sometimes develop in common-law marriages when one member attempts to have the marriage legally defined as valid. It is generally the woman who seeks to have the marriage validated, usually for reasons of financial help or inheritance questions. In attempting to establish the marriage's legality, the first two legal requirements are not usually difficult to prove, but the third one—of mutual intent to marry at some future date—is often legally difficult to prove, unless the proof of intent to wed is in writing,

[29]Mandell, *op. cit.*, p. 8.
[30]Kephart, *op. cit.*, pp. 405–18.

or very reliable witnesses are available. This is particularly true if one partner does not want the marriage declared valid and contends he never had any intention of legally marrying his partner.

The legal tendency in this country is to do away with common-law marriage, and it will probably be eliminated in many more states in the future. In modern American society, no logical reasons for its maintenance seem to exist, and it creates legal problems, such as legitimacy of children and property rights, that would not exist if the couple were officially married.

Breach of Promise

Breach of promise refers to a suit brought against a person who has agreed to enter into a marriage and then reneged. It is handled in court as a violation of contract. The logic of the action goes against much that is held to be important in engagement today, for example, the belief that engagement is a final testing prior to marriage and should be ended if important flaws in the relationship are discovered. In the past, the right to bring breach of promise actions was often abused—some of the cash awards made ran into hundreds of thousands of dollars. In some states, the breach of promise suit has been abolished and, in other states, its use is much less frequent than was the case in the past.

The policy of the law which allowed breach of promise suits has been condemned by a number of legal authorities. Clarke lists the following objections: (1) It was often used as a method of blackmail. A woman might sue a wealthy man as a source of income and not seek compensation for the loss suffered. (2) The considerable amount of publicity that was given to unhappy love affairs often had unfortunate consequences for the persons involved. (3) In reality, the use of breach of promise was available only to the woman. (4) The amount of damage awarded was often unjust, because the suit was heard by a jury, whose members are sometimes very gullible. (5) Engaged couples should be free to correct their mistakes without the fear of financial suit.[31]

When the woman had little choice of adult role other than marriage, a breach of promise was often viewed as depriving her of the chance to enter the marriage role. It was also based on the assumption of general female inferiority and was provided as special sex-role protection. However, many authorities feel that today the

---

[31]Clarke, *op. cit.*, pp. 86–87.

woman, with a wider choice of marriage partners, a choice of an adult role other than marriage, and increased social and legal equality, no longer needs such special protection.

Sometimes confused with the breach of promise suit is the right of the parties to keep gifts when a courtship relationship ends. Often the question is whether the girl should return the engagement ring. When these cases have been taken to court, the common decision has been that if the woman was not at fault in bringing about the end of the engagement, she can keep the ring.

Sex in Marriage

There are a number of ways in which legal controls are directed at the sexual aspects of marriage. It is important to recognize that the area of legal control has historically been greatly influenced by religion. While theoretically religion and the legal systems are separate in the United States, we know that in reality religion has greatly influenced American laws. Religious influence has been especially significant with reference to sexual behavior. In the United States, every type of sexual activity *in and of itself* is a crime or a sin. "Marriage removes the stigma of criminality from vaginal heterosexual congress, but many Christians believe that it does not mitigate its sinful quality, unless engaged in for the sole purpose of procreation."[32]

There is also some evidence on a cross-cultural level that during the emergence of the state with its complex and codified legal system, the moral imperatives of traditional values in regard to sexual behavior were influential. Stephens, in a cross-cultural analysis of sexual regulations, analyzed why civilized communities were relatively more strict about the regulation of sex than were primitive societies. He came to the conclusion that ultimately the answer rested in the development of the state.[33]

In an historical study of the emergence of common law in the Western world, Drummond comes to essentially the same conclusion about the significance of the state. She points out that in common law "all the sexual transgressions other than adultery were at first merely torts, or civil wrongs, whatever the punishment inflicted. They were classified as 'sins' and 'wrongs,' the former being offenses against God, the latter against one's neighbor."[34] Drummond further suggests that it was "only when the state became an entity

---

[32]Drummond, *op. cit.*, p. 3.
[33]William N. Stephens, *The Family In Cross-Cultural Perspective* (New York: Holt, Rinehart & Winston, Inc., 1963), p. 259.
[34]Drummond, *op. cit.*, p. 20.

that sins took on the aspect of crimes against the state and became indictable offenses."[35] One consequence has been that sexual laws have been altered very little over time. "Today, in twentieth-century America, formal sex restrictions are—in their general outline—much the same as they were in the times of Tertullian, St. Augustine, Martin Luther, or John Wesley."[36]

To say that sexual laws continue as a part of the formal legal system is not to say that the laws are generally applied. Pilpel points out that fornication—sexual intercourse between unmarried partners—is a crime but one that is rarely prosecuted in the United States.[37]

One important area of difference between legal definitions and some religious beliefs centers around the function of sex in marriage. All state laws agree that marriage is a sexual partnership and *not* an institution for reproduction. "Reproduction is desirable, but not a condition, whereas sexual cohabitation is a spouse's duty."[38] If a husband or wife refuses or is unable to fulfill sexual partnership in marriage, the partner has the right to contest the marriage or to seek divorce. On the other hand, childlessness does not give either party the right to have the marriage dissolved."[39] The final legal step of defining sex as only a part of monogamous marriage was reached in 1887, when the Mormons were forbidden to practice polygamy. "Thereafter there existed no State, no sect, no association entitled to depart publicly from the ruling norms of sex-life."[40]

Our legal systems do more than simply restrict sexual expression to marriage. They also attempt to legally define what is permissable sexual behavior *within* marriage. The laws basically assert in most states that all forms of sexual activity "are frowned upon except face-to-face intercourse by husband and wife."[41] Any variation by the couple, "despite the fact that such variation may be described and prescribed by the reputable sex authorities as a form of pre-coital behavior, is restricted in all states under one law or another."[42]

---

[35]*Ibid.*, p. 20.

[36]Stephens, *op. cit.*, p. 259.

[37]Harriet F. Pilpel, "Sex vs. The Law; A Study in Hypocrisy," *Harpers*, January, 1965, p. 36.

[38]Richard Lewinsohn, *A History of Sexual Customs* (New York: Harper & Brothers, 1958), p. 401.

[39]*Ibid.*, p. 401.

[40]*Ibid.*, p. 389.

[41]Pilpel, *op. cit.*, p. 36.

[42]Robert V. Sherwin, "Laws on Sex Crimes," in Albert Ellis and Albert Abarbanel (eds.), *The Encyclopedia of Sexual Behavior* (New York: Hawthorn Books, Inc., 1961), p. 620.

Furthermore, there is the requirement in two states that face-to-face sexual intercourse between the husband and wife must be without contraception. Pilpel points out that while these laws are rarely enforced, "their mere existence challenges a fundamental human right of privacy and their hypocrisy is no less pernicious for being absurd."[43]

Once two people are married, the law not only defines their sexual behavior but also restricts all sexual outlets to the marriage relationship. In the United States, adultery is defined by law and is the only legal ground recognized by all states as a basis for divorce. In most states, laws exist that could if applied call for a fine or imprisonment, or both, for those who commit adultery. Also, many state laws with regard to adultery are based on a double standard, with greater punishment directed at the wife. For example, in Texas, "a husband may secure a divorce for a single act of adultery by his wife, but a wife is only entitled to a divorce if her husband actually abandons her and lives with another woman."[44]

THE HAVING OF CHILDREN

Only in the very recent historical past has any consideration of the rational decisions as to whether or not to have children had any real meaning. While in a variety of societies, various devices were developed for controlling the number of births, the techniques were for the most part limited in both usage and reliability. The emergence of contraceptive knowledge and its usage by large numbers of Americans is a recent social development. Therefore, most of the legal statutes in the United States in regard to the sale and usage of contraception have been a development of the present century.[45] The various types of contraception are discussed in Chapter 14.

Contraception is often seen as only a negative force—the preventing of conception. While it is true that every time contraception is used effectively a theoretical conception does not take place, it can also be argued that, in the long run, the rational control of conception has a positive side. Medical opinion holds that both the mother's and the child's health are greatly aided by periods of time between births. Thus, the medical emphasis is frequently on the use of contraception as a means of spacing child birth.

---

[43]Pilpel, *op. cit.*, p. 36.
[44]Pilpel and Zavin, *op. cit.*, p. 618.
[45]John Hejno, "The Contraceptive Industry," *Eros*, Summer, 1962, pp. 13–16.

Religious points of view on contraception are not in agreement. Until very recently, the Catholic Church has taken the strongest position against it, prohibiting any mechanical, chemical, or physiological interference that will prevent the union of the ovum and the sperm. However, there are indications that the Catholic Church is modifying its position. The strength of the Catholic position rests in part on the central authority of the church, while the Protestants and Jews have no central religious authority. But the Committee on Marriage and Home of the Federal Council of Churches, which represents a large sector of United States Protestantism, has stated: "As to the necessity for some form of effective control of the sizes of the family and spacing of children, and consequently of control of conception, there can be no question."[46] In practice, the general position of the Protestant churches centers on the motivation for the use of contraception. If the motives are right, then the use is right. This position defines the sex act of marriage as being both for reproduction and for the exchange and expression of love between marriage partners. The Reformed Jewish position is similar to that of the Protestants, but the Orthodox Jewish position opposes contraception.[47]

Socially, the development of contraceptive knowledge has provided many individuals with a control over their lives rarely before achieved. The ability to determine the number and spacing of children has placed the question of parenthood more and more within the rational decision-making powers of the married couple. It has also removed for many women the dangers and health damages that may result from frequent pregnancies. This greater rational control over pregnancy has had an influence on the emancipation of American women, because the woman is less subject to the problems of "chance" pregnancy.

The Legal Tangle

The fact that contraceptive knowledge is available to the American population in theory does not mean it is always legally available. Many states have laws that prohibit the distribution of birth control knowledge. In 1955, only 19 states did not prohibit or restrict the dissemination of birth control information.[48] Both Massachusetts and Connecticut, through their state courts, have held that

---

[46]"Birth Control," *Encyclopaedia Britannica* (Chicago: Encyclopaedia Britannica, Inc., 1962), Vol. III, p. 650.
[47]*Ibid.*, p. 650.
[48]Clarke, *op. cit.*, p. 172.

birth control information and materials may not be dispensed, even by doctors for medical reasons.[49]

The legal tangle historically goes back to the lumping together of birth control information and laws on obscenity; consequently, contraceptive knowledge is identified with obscene writings and cannot be sent through the mails except to "qualified" individuals. The advertising of contraceptives is forbidden in nearly all states,[50] and some states also have statutes that prohibit the teaching of birth control in any school.[51] Because the usual social means for the communication of knowledge is closed to birth control methods, the knowledge is diffused informally and oftentimes haphazardly, cutting down on the basic efficiency of contraceptive knowledge and use. "It is estimated that of the $200,000,000 spent yearly in the United States for contraception, only about one-tenth of that sum pays for the kinds recommended as best by physicians and birth control clinics."[52]

The legal tangle may become more complicated in the near future with the further development of oral contraception. For many years birth control authorities have been seeking a method that would be efficient, cheap, and simple to use. Oral contraception may meet all of these requirements in the very near future, but one very important difference exists between the potential use of oral contraception and mechanical and chemical methods. The oral contraceptive *could* be given to people without their knowledge, because it can be mixed with food or liquids. It seems reasonable to assume that with the greater development and use of oral contraception, many legal questions will have to be resolved regarding its usage as a means of applied social control over the fertility of unaware individuals and groups.

Abortion

While contraception refers to the stopping of life before conception occurs, abortion refers to the stopping of life after conception but before live birth occurs. "Abortion is the ending of pregnancy at any time before the fetus or prospective child is large enough to have a fair chance for survival."[53] There is every evidence that

---

[49]*Ibid.*, p. 184.

[50]Drummond, *op. cit.*, p. 261.

[51]*Ibid.*, p. 261.

[52]*Ibid.*, p. 262.

[53]Alan F. Guttmacher, "Abortions," in Morris Fishbein and Ruby Jo R. Kennedy, *Modern Marriage and Family Living* (New York: Oxford University Press, 1957), p. 401.

abortion is and has been a cultural phenomenon found in almost all societies.[54] In Greece and during the greater part of the Roman Empire's existence, no laws prohibited abortion. But with the rise of Judaism and Christianity, the practice of abortion was prohibited.[55] The religious restrictions had an early influence on laws against abortion.

As with contraception, religious positions differ in regard to abortions. The Catholic Church regards directly induced abortion, as well as therapeutic abortion, as murder. Protestants are in general agreement in condemning abortion or any method which destroys human life except when the health or life of the mother is at stake. The Jewish faith has no official stand on abortion, although the Orthodox undoubtedly are strongly against it.[56]

Abortions are divided into three categories. *Spontaneous abortion* is caused by internal individual conditions and is estimated as occurring in about 10 percent of all pregnancies.[57] *Therapeutic abortion* is the "legal termination of pregnancy by artificial means before the baby is viable."[58] It is brought about by the physician because of some serious health complications for the pregnant mother which may threaten her life or impair her health. The need for therapeutic abortion is often difficult to determine medically, but may be necessary in about 1 out of every 200 pregnancies.[59] *Illegal abortion* is the unlawful termination of pregnancy. The individual may seek illegal abortion when, for many and varied reasons, she feels strongly against carrying the fetus full term and giving live birth. The actual number of illegal abortions that occur is unknown, but estimates suggest between 4 and 22 percent of all pregnancies are ended through illegal abortion.[60]

There is no abortion law of the land in the United States, and the prevailing law in most states is that abortions are illegal except when necessary to "save the life of the mother"[61] But even when abortion laws exist, "they have been only sporadically enforced with ambivalence by law enforcement officers and the public."[62]

---

[54]Lucy Freeman, *The Abortionist* (Garden City, New York: Doubleday & Co., Inc., 1962), p. 50.

[55]*Ibid.,* p. 46.

[56]See: *Ibid.,* p. 47.

[57]Guttmacher, *op. cit.,* p. 402.

[58]*Ibid.,* p. 410.

[59]*Ibid.,* p. 410.

[60]*Ibid.,* p. 410.

[61]Freeman, *op. cit.,* p. 52.

[62]Paul H. Gebhard, Wardell B. Pomeroy, Clyde E. Martin, and Cornelia V. Christenson, *Pregnancy, Birth and Abortion* (New York: Harper & Brothers, Publishers, 1958), p. 211.

In the extensive study of abortions made by Gebhard and his associates, no legal complications from securing illegal abortions were reported by any of their femal or male subjects.[63] In effect, the laws in the United States insist that once a pregnancy has occurred it must be carried full term. While the legal punishments against bastardy and illegitimacy are severe, they are not nearly as severe as the punishments against induced abortion.[64]

The social and legal problems in the United States center around therapeutic and illegal abortions. The therapeutic question is whether or not a woman's life is seriously endangered by her pregnancy. Because the medical doctor has an extreme degree of professional privacy, and because one physician does not commonly give legal testimony against another, the therapeutic abortion is rarely subject to a legal test of its medical necessity.

The more important social problem is the illegal abortion. One reason is simply the violation of the law, but a more important reason is the danger involved for the woman. One study estimates that of all illegal abortions in the United States, 50 percent are performed by medical doctors, 20 percent by midwives, and 30 percent by the patient herself.[65] Even for those 50 percent performed by physicians, the conditions, facilities, and medical skills are often limited and inadequate. The other 50 percent obviously involve an even greater danger for the patient.

Many argue that the illegal setting for abortion contributes to its nature as a problem. The argument is that women will have abortions anyway, and that the illegal definition forces them to have the operations performed in a dangerous setting; if abortions were legal, the argument goes, they could be performed under the advantages of full medical knowledge and facilities. A counterargument is that legal abortion would contribute to greater premarital sexual activity because the deterring fear of pregnancy would be removed. This argument assumes that the laws against abortion serve as effective deterrents to premarital sexual activities. The assumption itself is highly questionable; it also overlooks the fact that studies show the majority of illegal abortions are performed on married women. Often these women already have children but do not want any more for personal and social reasons. Even for unmarried girls who have an abortion, the experience

[63]*Ibid.*, p. 212.

[64]Paul H. Gebhard, Wardell B. Pomeroy, Clyde E. Martin, and Cornelia V. Christensen, *Pregnancy, Birth and Abortion* (New York: Harper & Bros., 1958), p. 31.

[65]Guttmacher, *op. cit.*, p. 410.

does not seem to greatly influence their sexual activity. Gebhard found that of 235 females studied who had had a premarital induced abortion, 90 percent continued premarital coitus after the abortion.[66] Furthermore, Gebhard found no evidence that a premarital induced abortion was sufficiently traumatic to lead to a breakup in a subsequent marriage.[67] This data would suggest that it might be more logical to be concerned with possible medical gains through legal abortion rather than how legal abortion may contribute to sexual permissiveness.

Basically, the question of legal abortion rights is an extension of the question of legal rights for birth control through contraception. Does the individual have the right to decide whether she will give birth to a child? In contraception, the "stopping" occurs before conception can take place while, with abortion, the halt comes after conception. There are very different social reactions to those two "rights." Only some of those who argue for the right of contraception will also argue for the right of abortion. Generally, the stated belief is that abortion halts a "life" while contraception does not. However, the end result is the same—no live birth. The legal interpretation tends to support the general public viewpoint, and a much greater acceptance of contraception than abortion exists in the law.

Illegitimacy

In the United States, illegitimacy has historically been viewed as morally wrong, as well as a social threat to the stability of the family institution. Both the unwed mother and her offspring have been subjected to strong moral and legal punishment. Historically, the two primary reasons for the harsh treatment of illegitimate children were the desire to protect property and inheritance rights, and the desire to preserve religious and moral precepts accepted by many as important.[68]

In recent years in the United States, the treatment of the illegitimate child has changed both legally and socially. "Legislation has been passed in every state tending to place the illegitimate child on an approximate legal equality with the legitimate child so far as his mother is concerned. Also, in many states he now has certain rights of maintenance, support, and inheritance from his father."[69] While

---

[66]Gebhard, *op. cit.*, p. 210.
[67]*Ibid.*, p. 211.
[68]Clarke, *op. cit.*, p. 365.
[69]*Ibid.*, p. 365.

some of the social stigma has been removed from the child, it still continues to exist for the unwed mother.[70] The new social attitude is that there are no illegitimate children, only illegitimate mothers.

Even though moral condemnation of the unwed mother continues, it seems to have limited influence on the behavior leading to unmarried pregnancy. In 1962 there were approximately 250,000 illegitimate births in the United States. From 1938 to 1958, the estimated number of illicit births per 1,000 live births in the United States increased slightly from 38.4 to 49.5,[71] though for the most part this rise in illegitimacy parallels the rise in all births. Herzog writes that it is "not that, suddenly and erratically, illegitimate births have shot up, and that this is an isolated aberration," but rather that this is a part of an evolution, not a revolution.[72]

It is commonly supposed that a large number of children are born to unmarried adolescent girls, and it is true that the proportion of all illicit births occurring to females under 15 years of age has remained about the same—2.3 percent in 1938 and 2.1 percent in 1963.[73] (In 1963, for those mothers between the ages of 15 and 19, about 39 percent of their births were out of wedlock.[74]) But while teen-agers do represent a large proportion of unwed mothers, they constitute an even larger proportion of *all* unmarried females. Thus, when teen-agers are considered as a proportion of *all* unmarried females, they actually represent a smaller proportion of unmarried mothers today than they did in the past.[75] While illegitimacy is a characteristic of fairly young women, it is not particularly common among young adolescent girls. Therefore, illegitimate babies are most often born during the years when their mothers are physically best able to bear a healthy child. This is important when it is realized that half or more of these children are placed out for adoption.

When the mother has an illegitimate child, she has several possible courses of action. She may give up the child by having it placed for adoption. Or, if she decides to keep the child, she may either take on complete responsibility for the child's rearing or seek financial help from the father by bringing a paternity suit against him. In

---

[70]Clark Vincent, *Unmarried Mothers* (Glencoe, Illinois: The Free Press, 1961), chap. 1.

[71]*Ibid.*, p. 1.

[72]Elizabeth Herzog, "The Chronic Revolution: Births Out of Wedlock," *Clinical Pediatrics,* February, 1966, p. 130.

[73]Vincent, *op. cit.*, p. 54 and *Ibid.*, p. 132.

[74]Herzog, *op. cit.*, p. 132.

[75]*Ibid.*, p. 131.

most paternity cases, the burden of proof rests with the accused to prove he is *not* the father. Generally, the courts will award a paternity responsibility to the male if he has great difficulty proving he is not the father. Blood tests are usually not legally accepted as evidence of nonpaternity. The old accused-male tactic of having a number of friends claim they had sexual relations with the girl no longer acquits the accused. Instead, what often happens is that the court makes *all* of the males financially responsible for the support of the child. In a paternity suit, the court is anxious to find someone who will be financially responsible, knowing that if it doesn't, the responsibility will rest with the state.

Since the burden of proof rests with the male in a paternity suit, males who are actually not the fathers may be exploited. There is nothing to stop a pregnant girl from selecting a male, claiming he is the father, and having the suit taken to court. In most cases, the accused can do very little about it and may be given financial responsibility for the child. (Some legal opinion holds that, while this could happen in theory, it does not occur very often in reality.)

CHILDLESSNESS*

If a married couple are unable to have a natural child of their own, they may, through legal procedures, go about attaining one. The number of couples who are unable to have biological offspring of their own is higher than many realize. One very extensive fertility study found that "approximately 10 percent of the couples with the wife 35-39 years old are childless *and* have a fecundity problem."[76] This suggests that 10 percent of these couples where the wife has almost completed the child-bearing years, are not biologically able to beget children. A discussion of two different ways in which the childlessness problem can be solved, and the legal aspects of the two procedures, follows.

Solutions to Childlessness

Adoption. In adoption, a child is taken bodily and completely from one family and legally made a part of another. This differs from custody, which shifts only the care and control of the child from one family to another.[77] The ultimate consequence of adop-

---

*The social-psychological implications of childlessness are discussed in Chapter 14.
[76]Ronald Freeman, Pascal K. Whelpton, and Arthur A. Campbell, *Family Planning, Sterility and Population Growth* (New York: McGraw-Hill Book Co., 1959), p. 47.
[77]Bradway, *op. cit.*, p. 587.

tion is that it creates reciprocal rights and duties between adoptive parents and child, and a number of states provide that the legal relationship shall be the same as between natural parents and child.[78]

The procedural features of adoption legislation usually include the following steps. First, the petition of the adopting parents or their substitutes. Second, notice to the child's parents or their substitutes and receipt of their consent. Third, the presence of the necessary parties in court, where the final judicial decree is handed down.[79]

While the procedure varies from one state to another, here is how these steps operate, for example, in Pennsylvania. Generally, the first step is the agreement of the natural parent or parents to place the child for adoption. Permission may be given by the parent or a legally delegated authority. After the adopting parents file a petition, there is a waiting period of six months before the final decree can be handed down. During that time, the adopting parents are usually investigated by a county social worker as to their fitness to be parents. Even though the adopting parents have the child during the waiting period, it is often a time of great anxiety for them because the child is not legally theirs. If the natural parent or parents should change their minds and want the child back, the adopting parents would in most cases have to give up the child. When the time for the final decree is reached, the natural parent or parents must be notified of the time and place of the legal hearing. They normally do not appear and the only ones present are the adopting parents with their lawyer and the child. Often the hearing is brief and held in the privacy of the judge's chambers. Once the decree is handed down, the child is then legally a member of the adopting family. The original birth certificate is impounded in the state capitol, and a new one is issued with the adopting parents' names. The new birth certificate is exactly like one issued to the parents of a natural born child.

In many states, the various social agencies have waged a legal battle for their complete control of all adoption and against the maintenance of legal rights of other specified individuals to place children for adoption. The trend has been to give the social agencies control over adoption under the assumption that they are best able to make an assessment of what will constitute a good home for the

---

[78]Clarke, *op. cit.,* p. 329.
[79]*Ibid.,* p. 317.

child. In 1963 there were 127,000 adoptions in the United States and almost half of the adoptions were made by other relatives, most often by step-parents. But of the remaining 67,000, the majority (44,000, or 66 percent) were arranged by adoption agencies.[80] Social workers seem to be in limited agreement on objective procedures for determing a good home, and many times their criteria are highly questionable. For example, some adoption agencies ask the prospective adopting parents to write essays on "Why I Think I Can be a Good Parent," or "Why I Want a Child." Even family authorities would disagree on what would be the "best" answers to these highly subjective questions. Very often the prospective parents write what they think the adoption agency wants to hear—not what they themselves really feel. Further techniques for screening out potential parents are often used, not because of meaningful differences between the various couples, but because the demand for white infants for adoption far exceeds the supply. It has been estimated that there are approximately 10 times as many applicants as there are children available for adoption.[81] (Two groupings of children sometimes lead to the impression that a large number of infants and children are available for adoption. One is the number of Negro infants and children up for adoption; but rarely are Negro children placed in white homes. The second is a common tendency to think of foster children as being available for adoption. There are about 175,000 children living in foster homes and 95,000 children in public institutions, but only about 5 percent of these are available for adoption.[82])

In making its final decision for placement, a social agency may not be so much objective as simply arbitrary. Too, the adopting parents rarely get the child before four to six months of age because the agencies want to keep the infants long enough to make a rather careful check on them. As a result, the adopting parents are not given the chance of rearing the very young infant. In acquiring a child for adoption through a legally qualified individual (often a physician or lawyer), the infant may be brought home six or seven days after birth.

It is estimated that about 100,000 petitions for adoption are made each year in the United States. It is further estimated that about 70

[80]Statistical Abstract of the U.S., *U.S. Bureau of the Census* (Washington, D.C.: Government Printing Office, 1964), p. 312.
[81]Hugo G. Beigel, "Illegitimacy," in Albert Ellis and Albert Abarbanel (eds.), *The Encyclopedia of Sexual Behavior* (New York: Hawthorn Books, Inc., 1961), p. 513.
[82]*Ibid.*, p. 513.

percent of all white illegitimate children are given up for adoption and that they constitute about 40 percent of the total adoption market.[83] The relationship between the two social problems of illegitimacy and childlessness is an interesting one. Illegitimacy is viewed as a social problem that should be eliminated; however, a significant decrease in illegitimacy would result in an increase in the number of marriages that would have to remain childless because of the lack of adoption opportunities. A marriage which is without children when they are desired is also viewed as a significant social problem. So one social problem (illegitimacy) helps to resolve another (childlessness). But there is a social-class difference in the two solutions. The higher the social-class level, as measured by education, the less the belief that the unwed mother should raise her child and the greater the belief that the child will be better off reared by adoptive parents. Kirk found that for those respondents with some high-school education or less, 73 percent thought the unwed mother should rear her own child and 27 percent that the child should be reared by adoptive parents; however, for college-educated respondents, only 27 percent said the unwed mother, while 73 percent said adoptive parents should rear the child—or exactly the reverse.[84]

The values reflected by legal and social agencies mean that children placed out for adoption most often go to upper middle-class couples. Furthermore, among childless couples there is a highly selective process operating. First, those couples are selected out of the total childless population by their decision to try to solve their problem through adoption. Second, once the decision to adopt is made, there is a further selection process determined by the ability of the couple to find and obtain a child for adoption, either independently or through agencies.

Usually the greatest pressure to adopt comes from the wife in a marriage. This seems logical, given the generally greater commitment to the parental role by the woman than by the man. Kirk found that 94 percent of his female respondents and 85 percent of his male respondents said they would adopt if they could have no children of their own.[85] Because many couples may spend several years trying to have natural children without success, and because they often have to wait some length of time before getting a baby for adoption, adopting parents become parents at older ages. Kirk

---

[83]Vincent, *op. cit.*, pp. 13, 195.
[84]H. David Kirk, *Shared Fate* (New York: The Free Press of Glencoe, 1964), p. 28.
[85]*Ibid.*, p. 134.

found that adopting parents were about seven years older than their biological counterparts when they received their first child.[86]

There is some evidence of a preference for sons by parents prior to the birth of their first natural child. However, Kirk suggests that there may be a tendency among adoptive parents to prefer girls,[87] arguing that with the wife feeling the most deprived in not being able to fill her parental role, and the husband often the hesitant spouse with regard to adoption, a girl may represent a compromise solution.[88] There may also be a belief that as a girl grows older, and begins to see the importance of her future mother role, she will have fewer concerns and anxieties about her own adoption than would a boy. It may also be that many times the adopted child had unwed natural parents, and being of illegitimate birth status may have less stigma for the girl than for the boy.

Often when a couple have made the important decision to adopt and have gone through all the demands necessary for adoption, they are not overly concerned with what may appear to be unimportant questions. For example, Kirk found that adoptive parents were fairly detached about matching their physical appearance to that of the child, with only 48 percent of the husbands and 50 percent of the wives saying they thought this factor important. There was even greater detachment with regard to the child's nationality background. Only on the question of racial background was the large majority of adopting parents in favor of a homogeneous family. Three quarters of all the respondents said that matching by race was very important.[89]

Artificial Insemination. For a number of childless couples, artificial insemination is the only way their problem may be biologically resolved. Artificial insemination was first attempted with a human in 1799 by the English physician Dr. John Hunter; the first recorded attempts in the United States were not made until 1866, by Dr. Marion Simms of North Carolina. She performed 55 inseminations with varying degrees of success.[90]

There are two types of artificial insemination. The first type, AIH or artificial insemination with sperm from the husband, is a medical procedure often used because of conception problems related to the sperm meeting the ovum through the natural method of sexual in-

[86]*Ibid.,* p. 9.
[87]*Ibid.,* pp. 126–28.
[88]*Ibid.,* p. 143.
[89]*Ibid.,* p. 60.
[90]Alan F. Guttmacher, *Planning Your Family* (New York: Macmillan, 1961), p. 254.

tercourse. This type of artificial insemination generates little social concern or legal interest. The second type is AID, artificial insemination with sperm from a donor. The donor is almost always anonymous. Much social and legal confusion has developed around AID.

Theoretically, AID could solve the childless problem of a large number of married couples. Conception inability among married couples is estimated to rest with the husband in about 40 percent of the cases. In many of these cases, the husband produces no sperm, or the sperm count is so low or the sperm are so sluggish that biologically fathering a child is impossible or extremely difficult for him. AID substitutes sperm from an anonymous donor so that the wife may become pregnant. When the sperm is contributed, some of the inheritable physical characteristics of the male donor are often recorded. The physician may then try to match the physical characteristics of the donor with those of the husband. The physician usually gets the sperm from a "sperm bank," so that neither he nor the couple know the identity of the contributor. Success of conception through AID has reportedly been achieved in 50 to 80 percent of the cases where it has been used.[91] Estimates suggest that there are about 20,000 persons in the United States who were conceived through AID.[92]

Clearly, AID is used in only a very small number of cases in which it theoretically could be applied. Of the several reasons for this, one is that probably only a limited number of Americans are aware of its possibilities. Second, it has had some religious opposition, particularly from the Catholic Church.[93] Third, two studies both indicate resistance to AID even when it is explained or known to the respondents, although the two studies show sharp disagreement in the stated approval of AID. In one study, 52 percent said they approved of AID, while in the other, only 17 percent approved. (In the second study, 27.5 percent were "undecided," while in the first, the respondents were forced to answer "yes" or "no.")[94] Vernon and Boadway found some difference in acceptance by sex. For the males, 22 percent indicated acceptance of AID, compared with 14 percent of the females.[95] The reasons given by the respondents for rejecting AID were: would prefer adoption, 40.6 percent; mor-

---

[91]Baber, *op. cit.*, p. 535.

[92]*Ibid.*, p. 534.

[93]Glenn A. Vernon and Jack A. Boadway, "Attitudes Toward Artificial Insemination and Some Variables Associated Therewith," *Marriage and Family Living*, February, 1959, p. 45.

[94]*Ibid.*, p. 44; and Joseph H. Greenberg, "Social Variables in Acceptance or Rejection of Artificial Insemination," *American Sociological Review*, February, 1951, p. 88.

[95]Vernon and Boadway, *op. cit.*, p. 46.

ally wrong, adultery, et cet., 16.6 percent; church disapproval, 16.6 percent; source of marital friction, 9.7 percent; others, 15.5 percent.[96]

The writer has many times presented the following question to his students: "If you were married and you both wanted children, and it was discovered that the husband was absolutely sterile, which method of resolving your childlessness would you prefer to use, adoption or AID?" About 90 percent of the students chose adoption. The main reason given is that if both husband and wife can't contribute to the genetic make-up of the child, then neither spouse should. When it is pointed out that if the inheritable traits of the wife are valued, it might make sense to transmit at least those, students may see the logic of AID argument, but they will still emotionally reject it; for them, half a genetic loaf is *not* better than no genetic loaf at all.

A legal judgment was not passed on AID in the United States until 1948, although at an earlier date the Canadian case of Oxford vs. Oxford in 1921 held that artificial insemination was adultery.[97] "In 1948 the New York courts established the legitimacy of a child born to a woman artificially impregnated with a donor's semen and with the husband's consent."[98] Drummond suggests that on the basis of legal principles, if AID were performed "without the husband's prior consent, it seems likely that he would have [a legal] action for damages against the doctor performing it."[99]

There are no federal or state laws in the United States that govern the use of artificial insemination. The only local ordinance is in New York city where "a section of the sanitary code imposes regulations for checking the health of a semen donor."[100] In six different states, bills have been introduced that deal specifically with artificial insemination; however, none of the bills have been enacted into law. In two states, "the bills were unfavorable and aimed at stigmatizing donor insemination as unlawful, the child illegitimate and the parties of the act subject to fine and imprisonment." In the other four states, "the bills were favorable with the objectives of legalizing the procedure, legitimizing the offspring and assuring their full rights of inheritance."[101] One student of society and the law suggests that "as in all other scientific achievements, the laws' response to

---

[96]*Ibid.*, p. 43.

[97]Clarke, *op. cit.*, p. 181.

[98]*Ibid.*, p. 181.

[99]Drummond, *op. cit.*, p. 252.

[100]Guttmacher, *op. cit.*, p. 269.

[101]Albert P. Massey, "Artificial Insemination: The Law's Illegitimate Child?", *Villanova Law Review*, Vol. 9, 1964, pp. 79–82.

artificial insemination has been, and will be, perfect horror; skepticism; curiosity; and then acceptance."[102]

As one would expect, there have been wife differences by organized religion with regard to both AIH and AID. Most Jewish and Protestant groups in the United States approve of AIH and AID. However, the Orthodox Jewish faith stipulates that AIH is permissable only after 10 years of a childless marriage and after other means of having children have failed. The Orthodox Jew believes that children born as a result of AID are legitimate, but the practice is forbidden. A woman who gives birth to a child as a result of AID, regardless of permission by the husband, may be sued by him for divorce.[103] The Catholic Church rejects both AIH and AID. On this subject, Pope Pius XII in 1956 said "Artificial Insemination is not within the rights acquired by a couple by virtue of the marriage contract, nor is the right to its use derived from the right of offspring as a primary objective of matrimony."[104]

LEGAL RIGHTS OF THE CHILD

From the earliest days of American colonization, the courts have set up certain legal rights for the child. The general principle is to allow the parents flexibility in handling their children unless certain treatments are felt to be detrimental to the child or to society. Today, the welfare of the child is of paramount legal consideration, and the mother has been given rights equal to the father in the custody of their children. The legal changes have corresponded roughly with the shift from patriarchal rights to the more democratic view of equal parental rights.

Usually only in "extreme" cases will the courts move in on the parents and take the custody of their children out of their hands. "Almost all cases where parents have been deprived of custody are those in which they were shown to be unfit or in which they had relinquished their right for a time and then sought the aid of the court to regain custody."[105]

Not only must parents legally meet basic requirements in the care of their children, but they must also provide for the children's education up to some legally specified age or grade or both. A system of

---

[102]S. B. Schatkin, "The Legal Aspects of Artificial Insemination," *Fertility and Sterility,* Vol. 5, 1954, p. 40.
[103]See: Guttmacher, *op. cit.,* p. 267.
[104]Quoted in: *Ibid.,* p. 266.
[105]Clarke, *op. cit.,* p. 224.

legal equity for the education of children beyond the basic requirements may also lead to extended educational responsibility for the parents. The courts "will exercise their discretion in civil suits to determine whether 'higher education' is necessary."[106]

In custody cases, most courts tend to follow the same legal reasoning in contests between the mother and father for the child. Courts generally award the mother custody of infants and young children, especially girls, "even where the mother's conduct has been such that if the children were older or of the other sex, their custody would be placed elsewhere."[107] The legal attitude reflects a general social belief that if there has to be a choice of one parent for the child, the mother is the more important one.

In the support of the child, the responsibility both in common law and by statute rests upon the father. During the father's lifetime, the mother has no obligation to support the children in the absence of statutory provisions.[108] The father's responsibility to his children remains even if the marriage is ended. "Today, the courts ordinarily hold that the father remains liable for the support of his minor children when he and his wife are divorced, legally separated, or living apart on an agreement, although there are circumstances when this is not true."[109] The courts' position is based upon the fact that if the father does not meet the economic needs of his children and the wife is unable to, then the costs would be the responsibility of the state.

Inheritance

The rights of inheritance in the United States have changed with the legal shift from a patriarchal to a more democratically oriented concept of the family. The change is reflected in the legal rights of inheritance for the wife and children. In a patriarchal society, the wife had few legal rights of inheritance. Inheritance followed the principle of *primogeniture,* in which inheritance or succession of authority was passed on to the first born, specifically the eldest son. The law of primogeniture as understood in England has been abolished throughout the United States, and male and female relatives inherit equally.[110]

---

[106]*Ibid.,* p. 251.
[107]*Ibid.,* p. 224.
[108]*Ibid.,* p. 242.
[109]*Ibid.,* p. 243.
[110]"Inheritance," *Encyclopaedia Britannica* (Chicago: Encyclopaedia Britannica, Inc., 1962), Vol. XII, p. 357.

As with all legal interpretations in the United States, no two states have identical rules of descent, although the passing on of real and personal property tend to be essentially the same. The usual form of statute gives the wife one half when there is but one child. When there is more than one child, the wife takes the same size share as each of the children.[111] These rights are legal rights provided by the state for cases in which the deceased has not made a formal designation for inheritance. There are two mutually exclusive legal procedures in reference to inheritance, absolute rights of *bequest* and *inheritance*. "In general, by an absolute right of bequest is meant the freedom to leave one's possessions exactly as one pleases, whereas an absolute right of inheritance is an unalienable right to possess what someone has left."[112]

In practice, when the individual has a fairly large amount of wealth, he makes his bequests through a will. Under a will, the person can "cut off" any member of his family he chooses, and if the will is legally valid it is very difficult to have it changed. But when no will exists, the inheritance statutes of the state determine the distribution of property and wealth.

The discussion of some legal and social aspects of marriage and the family suggest several generalizations: (1) Society, through the development of a legal system, sets up minimum requirements felt to be basic to the family. Because the legal framework is broad, the range of legally acceptable individual behavior is fairly wide. (2) The legal system tends to be resistant to social change and, as a result, a dysfunctional relationship often exists between the law and social attitudes and behavior. (3) Finally, a legal understanding of marriage and family laws is very difficult because there is no federal law, only the laws of 53 distinct legal jurisdictions.

SELECTED BIBLIOGRAPHY

Baber, Ray E. *Marriage and the Family,* chap. iii. New York: McGraw-Hill Book Co., 1953.

Bradway, John S. "What Family Members Should Know About Law," in Becker, Howard, and Hill, Reuben, *Family, Marriage and Parenthood,* pp. 558–95. Boston: D. C. Heath & Co., 1955.

Clarke, Helen I. *Social Legislation.* New York: Appleton-Century-Crofts, 1957.

Drummond, Isabel. *The Sex Paradox.* New York: G. P. Putnam's Sons, 1953.

---

[111]*Ibid.,* p. 357.
[112]*Ibid.,* p. 358.

GEBHARD, PAUL H., POMEROY, WARDELL B., MARTIN, CLYDE E., and CHRIS-TENSON, CORNELIA V. *Pregnancy, Birth and Abortion.* New York: Harper & Brothers, Publishers, 1958.

GREENBERG, JOSEPH H. "Social Variables in Acceptance or Rejection of Artificial Insemination," *American Sociological Review,* February, 1951, pp. 86-91.

GUTTMACHER, ALAN F. *Planning Your Family.* New York: Macmillan 1961.

KEPHART, WILLIAM M. "Legal and Procedural Aspects of Marriage and Divorce," in HAROLD T. CHRISTENSEN (ed.) *Handbook of Marriage and The Family,* (Chicago: Rand McNally & Co., 1964), pp. 944-68.

KIRK, H. DAVID. *Shared Fate.* New York: The Free Press of Glencoe, 1964.

MANDELL, IRVING. *The Law of Marriage and Divorce.* New York: Oceana Publications, 1957.

PILPEL, HARRIET F. "Sex vs. the Law: A Study in Hypocrisy," *Harpers,* January, 1965, pp. 35-40.

VERNON, GLENN A., and BOADWAY, JACK A. "Attitudes Toward Artificial Insemination and Some Variables Associated Therewith," *Marriage and Family Living,* February, 1959, pp. 43-47.

VINCENT, CLARK. *Unmarried Mothers.* Glencoe, Illinois: The Free Press, 1961.

THE NATURE OF MARRIAGE

Probably no other society in the world, past or present, has shown as great a social and personal concern with marriage as the United States today. All areas of mass communications devote time and energy to the question of marriage, and a great amount of their interest is directed at the "problem" areas of marriage: marital frustrations and unhappiness, sexual maladjustment, role confusion, and divorce. These areas, and many others, have also been of great interest to the social scientist studying the family institution.

Anthropological literature shows a wide range of social adaptations to the relationships of marriage and the family. It is important to keep in mind that the patterns of marriage common to other societies may be quite different from those found in the American middle class. While all societies, past and present, have had some form of marriage, they have not always been monogamous nor have they always even been assumed to be permanent. Nor in all societies has it been necessary for husband and wife to live together, "nor do necessarily they 'cleve together and forsake all others,' nor need they be the main source of either their own livelihood or the care, protection, discipline, and legal identification of their children."[1]

There is in the middle-class American family a strong belief in marriage being a relationship of togetherness. That is, in the United States, marriage generally involves a high degree of intimacy and sharing between husband and wife: "going together to parties, on visits, and to various recreations; jointly owning house, car, and other possessions: and so forth. This degree of togetherness is usually *not* found in other societies."[2] In some societies, the husband and wife do not "live" together in the sense that we use the word. In those societies, "the most common living arrangement is for each wife to have her own house (or hut); the husband either has another

---

[1] Conrad M. Arensberg, "The American Family In The Perspective of Other Cultures," in Eli Ginzberg (ed.) *The Nation's Children* (New York: Columbia University Press, 1960), p. 60.

[2] William N. Stephens, *The Family In Cross-Cultural Perspective* (New York: Holt, Rinehart & Winston, Inc., 1963) p. 270.

house of his own, or divides his time between the houses of his various wives."[3] And in many societies, characterized by the extended family, the young couple at the time of marriage usually move in with the husband's family of orientation. In the United States, on the other hand, the pattern has increasingly been that married couples will, as soon as they possibly can, have their own households. That this value is very strong is reflected in the statistic that in 1960, 98 percent of all married couples maintained their own households.[4]

One other important and almost special value placed on marriage in the American middle class is that the success of the marriage relationship generally determines the broader stability and success of that family of procreation. Our American ideals almost represent a cultural extreme, both in the reduction of the family in size and because of the major value placed on the success of the marriage relationship.[5] And even with the many changes in American marriage, and the increased availability of divorce, the institution of marriage appears to be stronger than ever in the United States.

Our interests in this chapter will be with the nature of marriage as it is found in the middle class today, and will focus on changes in patterns of marriage, the wedding and the honeymoon, reasons for entering marriage, and different marriage orientations. The next chapter, Chapter 11, will deal with marriage roles and marital adjustment.

PATTERNS OF MARRIAGE

American marriage rates are among the highest in the world. Over 90 percent of all Americans will be married at least once before they die. In 1900, two out of every three women in the total population of the United States had been married at some time in their lives, while at the present time this is true for four out of five women.[6] Currently, the proportion of single people in the United States is at its lowest point since the start of the 20th century.

Americans are now marrying at the youngest ages recorded over the past 70 years, and with a few exceptions over the years the pattern of movement has been steadily toward younger ages at

---

[3]*Ibid.*, pp. 270–71.

[4]U.S. Bureau of the Census, "Characteristics of the Population: Part I," *U.S. Census of Population*, 1960, Volume 1, Table 79.

[5]Arensberg, *op. cit.*, p. 60.

[6]Margaret Mead and Frances B. Kaplan (eds.) *American Women: The Report of The President's Commission*, (New York: Charles Scribner's Sons, 1965), p. 80.

marriage for *both* men and women. "Between 1890 and 1962 the median age of marriage dropped from 22.0 to 20.3 years for women and from 26.1 to 22.7 years for men."[7] These figures also show that the age difference between husband and wife has been decreasing—from 4.1 years in 1890 to 2.4 years in 1962. Another way of illustrating the increasing pattern of marrying at young ages is that during the 1950's and early 1960's about one half of all women entered their first marriage by the time they were 20 years of age; by contrast, in 1940, about half of all women had not entered their first marriage until they were about 21.5 years.[8] The evidence available at the present time suggests that the high marriage rate and the young marriage ages will continue into at least the near future.

While a great deal of criticism has been directed at elements of the dating-courtship process in the United States, the process must be recognized as being successful at least in respect to the large number of individuals who move from it into marriage. In several respects, the high marriage rate in the United States is surprising because of social and personal influences that might, on the surface, appear to reduce the desire for marriage. For example, it might be argued that any one of the following factors would reduce the interest in marriage:

High divorce rate. Because so many marriages end in divorce, some might choose not to marry because they are not willing to chance the psychological and social costs of having a marriage fail.

Marital adjustment. The image sometimes projected to young people is that in many cases marriage is a relationship of conflict and dissatisfaction. Individuals might feel they do not want a relationship that has a chance of going contrary to the values of personal happiness felt to be so important in the American society.

Freedom of women. In the past, women had little choice other than marriage for their adult role but, today, many occupational roles are open to them. Some might choose not to marry because the other alternatives provide more attractive adult role opportunities than does marriage.

Greater sexual freedom. The pleasures of sex were traditionally seen as something to be achieved from marriage. The evidence today clearly indicates that many achieve at least some sexual satisfaction

---

[7]Esther Peterson, "Working Women", *Daedalus,* Spring, 1964, p. 675.

[8]Paul C. Glick, "Demographic Analysis of Family Data," in Harold T. Christensen (ed.) *Handbook of Marriage and The Family* (Chicago: Rand McNally & Co., 1964), p. 301.

without marriage, so the sex inducement to marry has been reduced.

Familiarity with opposite sex. In the past, marriage often meant the first close personal contact with a "mysterious" member of the opposite sex. With today's long and intimate dating-courtship relationship, each sex learns a great deal about the other and is, therefore, less mysterious to the other.

While all of these factors might logically seem to be forces in reducing the desire to marry, they are not, in fact, marital deterrents of any great strength. The positive reasons for marriage seem to be overriding in their significance for the individual.

THE WEDDING

In all societies, the transition from single to married roles involves some ceremony—that is, some applied sanctions that are part of the social system. The individual also incurs new rights and obligations with his newly achieved status. The nature of the ceremony and rituals of marriage vary a great deal. Most societies celebrate marriage with extensive marriage ceremonies and in many societies marriage involves a series of wedding ceremonies. The marriage customs of the United States, when looked at in a cross-cultural perspective, are characterized by simplicity, informality, and cultural poverty.[9] In the United States the couple have a range of choices—from being married in a few minutes by a Justice of the Peace to a wedding ceremony and receptions that may last for several days.

At present, entering marriage means entering a role that will exist for a long period of time. The great attention and publicity that centers around the high divorce rates in the United States causes many to overlook the fact that most marriages last for long periods of time, and will be ended only through the death of one of the partners. Also, the years of marriage have been extended by the early age of marriage and the greater life expectancy of both sexes.

In the United States, the act of marriage has two important institutional focuses, the legal and the religious. All individuals must meet the legal requirements for marriage—those discussed in Chapter 9. Marriage, in the legal sense, is an act that places a man and woman under legal and social obligations to each other.[10] With

[9]Stephens, *op. cit.*, p. 239.
[10]Helen I. Clarke, *Social Legislation* (New York: Appleton-Century-Crofts, 1957), p. 27.

the exception of a few states, however, a religious ceremony is not a legal requirement. The couple have a choice as to type of ceremony because 47 out of the 50 states permit either a clergyman or a civil official to preside over the marriage ceremony.[11] (Most couples choose to be married in a religious ceremony. In 1961, 83 percent of all brides and grooms entering a first marriage were wed in a religious rather than civil ceremony.[12])

While all individuals have to meet certain legal requirements for marriage, many also choose to meet the religious requirements, because religious approval is of great importance to them. This is particularly true for the Catholic, because his church defines marriage as a sacrament. However, all clergymen perform the ceremony not in their capacity as ministers, but as civil officers constituted for that purpose by the state. The words and rituals of the religious ceremony do not make the couple legally married; the formal start of marriage begins with the signing of the marriage license by the delegated legal authority.

The religious as opposed to the nonreligious wedding ceremony has been of interest to a number of family researchers as it relates to success in marriage. Statistically, marriages with religious ceremonies have a higher rate of success than marriages without religious ceremonies—possibly for several reasons. First, the more conforming members of society, who would be less prone to ending their marriages through divorce, are more likely to have a religious ceremony. Second, starting marriage with an impressive ceremony may provide an added incentive for the couple to achieve success.[13] Third, religious group supports and sanctions add to the importance of maintaining the marriage.

Since the wedding ceremony differs in importance to different couples, their marriages take place in several different ways. They may elope or marry secretly, which means a minimum of social ritual. When persons choose to invite a number of guests, they may be married in a church, at home, or in a hired hall. Since both number of guests and site of wedding and reception can vary a great deal, the total cost of getting married ranges widely. For

---

[11]William M. Kephart, "Legal and Procedural Aspects of Marriage and Divorce," in Harold T. Christensen (ed.) *Handbook of Marriage and The Family* (Chicago: Rand McNally & Co., 1964), p. 949.

[12]Vital Statistics of the United States, 1961. Vol. III, Sections 1, 2 and 7, "Marriages" United States Department of Health, Education and Welfare, p. 4.

[13]Harold T. Christensen, *Marriage Analysis* (New York: The Ronald Press Co., 1958), pp. 349–50.

many middle-class families, the cost of launching a daughter on her marriage may be several thousand dollars.

The reception following the wedding publicly presents the couple as husband and wife for the first time. Their first acts as a married couple are frequently symbolic; their joined hands making the first cut in the wedding cake, for example. In the American culture, no single pattern socially defines the marriage ceremony. For some groups, marriage is a solemn and almost sad occasion, which may reflect an attitude that the young couple are leaving their carefree single years behind them and entering their responsible adult years. The traditional American wedding ceremony and reception often has this overtone. However, other groups view marriage as a time of great happiness, the start of a period of pleasure that now lies ahead for those who have acquired the privileges of marriage. This joyousness is often seen in the ceremonies and receptions of groups more recently transplanted to the American culture and it reflects "old country" values.

In Chapter 4, it was pointed out that engagement represents a period of high personal prestige and glamour for the girl, with her prestige reaching its peak on the wedding day. The folk cliché is that "all brides are beautiful." In American middle-class culture, the wedding, like the engagement, is female-centered, and usually the responsibility of the girl's family, with the planning generally done by the bride and her mother. The bride's central role in the wedding is symbolized by the time and expense devoted to her bridal gown, a gown that will be worn only once. By contrast, the groom may buy something new to wear, but it is put to use after marriage.

The groom is not necessarily the second most important figure at the wedding. Both domination and prestige tend to center on the female, and the glory spreads from the bride to her mother, the mothers, the matron or maid of honor, and the bridesmaids. The female's importance at weddings is related to several historical factors. First, the bride was traditionally given in marriage in the sense that she left the parental home for that of the husband. This is still true in many ways and is symbolized by the bride giving up her family name for that of the husband's. Second, marriage has been and continues to be entrance for the female into her most important adult status, wife-mother. Therefore, the marriage symbolizes the significance of role change for the woman getting married as well as for those women who have been or will be married.

Marriage is often seen as a "rite of passage" for the female into adult status.

The marriage ceremony also has a more extended social function related to prestige. For example, the dress and the overall material display associated with the wedding and the reception are often matters of social prestige. The family may desire to have an impressive wedding so as to launch the young couple into marriage with deserved fanfare. In other cases, the girl's family may have a costly wedding either in hopes of gaining prestige or out of fear of losing social face if they do not. The latter concern is illustrated by the success of business firms that completely take over the planning of a wedding and reception with the guarantee that it will be done "right" and family prestige will be retained or enhanced.

THE HONEYMOON

The honeymoon is increasingly accepted as a part of getting married. This is particularly true for middle-class couples, most of whom take a honeymoon that usually lasts for a period of a few days to a few weeks.

Honeymoon Functions

Recuperation. The period leading up to the wedding and ending after the ceremony and reception makes great demands on the physical and psychological stamina of the couple, particularly the bride. Once the day is over, the couple, who are often near exhaustion, need to go somewhere where they can relax. However, the tendency for some to take a long trip for a honeymoon, particularly if they are driving an automobile, often creates a situation in which rest and recuperation are extremely difficult. And being rested and relaxed is probably a contributing factor to the initial success of marital interaction.

Initial Adjustment. The honeymoon can provide favorable conditions in which to start filling the new roles of husband and wife. The couple can devote most of their attention to their new marriage roles and temporarily put aside other, possibly distracting, role demands. The honeymoon "removes the person from the environment in which his established habits function and encourages him to concentrate on the formation of new habits."[14] The newness of

[14]Willard Waller and Reuben Hill, *The Family* (New York: The Dryden Press, 1951), p. 257.

the honeymoon setting goes with the newness of the marriage roles.

While each partner has already made certain definitions of both his own and his spouse's marital roles, actual participation in the roles is, of course, new. Thus, one important element of adjustment in marriage is the individual's adjustment to the new role. While aspects of adjustment are discussed in Chapter 11, several factors may be pointed out here. First, the individuals rarely come back from their honeymoon fully adjusted either to their own new role or to the relationship between the husband and wife roles. The more common achievement may be some initial sense of ease with being a husband or a wife. Because adjustment in marriage is a dynamic process, a start in developing the facilities of adjustment would seem a reasonable expectation for the honeymoon. The negative influences of an unsatisfatory honeymoon may have unfortunate long range consequences. Because the honeymoon relationship is highly idealistic, an unsatisfactory initial adjustment may destroy the early idealism in marriage and lead to a feeling of great loss for the couple. One study estimates that 10 percent of all marriages start off married life with an unhappy honeymoon.[15]

Second, when the couple return to their everyday lives, other role demands will again be made and must be shared with the new marriage role demands. If very limited success results when full effort is directed at the marriage roles on the honeymoon, greater marriage role success may be even more difficult to achieve when some attention must be directed to other roles. Regardless of the honeymoon's success, when the couple leave it, they must move from an exclusive marriage-role orientation to one shared with other role demands.

Sexual Expression. Sexual adjustment in marriage is one subdivision of the total adjustment process, but it probably has an even more dynamic quality of change over time than most other areas. The sex needs and feelings of individuals are not constant and often change drastically with length of marriage. Therefore, the achievement of sexual adjustment on the honeymoon only means the couple have reached a point in their sexual relationship satisfactory at that time. This initial sexual adjustment makes no guarantee for the future. However, sex and the honeymoon are given great attention in American society because the folklore of the honeymoon equates it almost entirely with sexual behavior.

---

[15]George Gallup, "The Woman's Mind: America's Young Mothers," *Ladies Home Journal*, March, 1962, p. 96.

In the literature that gives sex advice to the newly married, great emphasis is placed on early sexual satisfaction for the bride. While the male usually enters marriage with great sexual anticipations, the female is probably more apt to enter marriage with some sexual anxiety and apprehension. Most of the professional advice given to the newly married couple for the honeymoon period stresses the need for the female to be encouraged and helped by an "understanding and skillful" husband.

Because the female is conditioned to believe that she must reserve her sexual expression for marriage, she may enter the honeymoon with some problems. To the extent that she accepts the belief that sexual relations go with being married, her entering into marital coitus with increasing degrees of freedom will be associated with her being accustomed to being married. As she comes to accept her new overall role as natural, she will also be increasingly apt to enter into marital sexual behavior with a minimum of inhibitions and anxieties.

The "romantic" nature of American sex training may also create problems for some girls on their honeymoon. A part of the rationale for abstaining from coitus before marriage is that sex after marriage will be worth waiting for. The girl may have developed an idealistic image or romanticized version of the marital sexual relationship that is behaviorally unobtainable. Some girls may have a feeling of letdown after their initial sexual experience in marriage—not because the experience was unpleasant, but because it did not reach the idealistic peaks they had imagined it would.

REASONS FOR MARRIAGE

As already indicated, some of the reasons for marriage have changed, and various combinations of old and new influences operate for different individuals. The following discussion will refer to some common influences that operate in today's American society.

Social Values

Since there are few clear-cut role definitions providing adult status for the young adult, the acquiring of what are believed to be particular adult roles takes on the added importance of providing meaning to the unclearly defined general role. The role distinction between the single and the married person is clear and unambiguous; the role distinction between adolescent and adult is not. Being single and adolescent are related roles filled by the same individual; being an adult and married are also generally seen as related. Therefore, a part of the desire to seek and achieve adult status is felt to be accomplished by getting married, and many young people are anxious for marriage for this reason.

The consideration of adulthood and marriage as related roles can also be seen in a common attitude toward the older single person. The bachelor is sometimes perceived as someone who will not "grow up" and take on responsibilities; that is, he won't get married. The spinster may be perceived as an unfortunate person unable to fill important adult roles. For example, people may consider her able to take care of someone's children but simultaneously believe that she does not *really* understand children because she has not personally experienced the roles of wife and mother.

Related to the above points is that marriage may be considered a means of sex-role fulfillment. This is probably much more important for the woman than the man, even today when the woman has a number of adult-role alternatives to marriage. The male has been socialized toward his important role of occupation, but, implied in his role indoctrination is that success in the occupational role will be given added significance when he uses it as the means of being a good provider as husband and father. Being a good provider contributes to his overall role as an adult male.

For the female, marriage is even more important. Generally speaking, no alternative adult roles are available to her that are of equal social value. A woman who pursues a career and never marries will normally be given less social recognition than the man who pursues a career and never marries. The reason, of course, is that marriage is still the female adult career most socially valued. Given the social pressure for the woman to marry, her personal motives become very strong and, for many women, a failure to marry indicates a failure to achieve the most important and significant female adult role. In American society, marriage provides a sex-role fulfillment for the woman greater than remaining single; however, the more complete fulfillment comes with the added role of mother. The woman who has become a wife and mother has, in most cases, achieved the highest adult status and sex role fulfillment available.

Another social pressure to marry is through the force of conformity. Because marriage is achieved by the vast majority, the unmarried individual stands out as being different and, as he grows older, he may find himself excluded from the world of paired-relationships. Americans believe strongly that social life across sex lines must be carried out by pairs. For example, the hostess who wants to invite a single man to a party finds herself trying to find a single woman with whom to match him off for the evening (and if possible forever after). The single person quickly learns that the pressure is on him. If he finds himself functioning extensively in the paired world, he may find the pressure to join those ranks increasingly difficult to resist.

Some married people view the single person as something of a threat to their paired commitment. If the married believe that their state is the natural one, they must develop a rationale to account for the unmarried. Some single persons may be defined as single for negative reasons such as immaturity, poor personality character- istics, other responsibilities, and so forth. If no rationalizations can be applied to account for the single person, his married friends very often feel he should join them as soon as possible. If he is a "normal" person (like the married), then he should get married, and if he does not marry, then he must be peculiar (unlike the married.)

The married couple's self-definition of their own marriage also influences their desire to see the single get married. They may feel that their marriage is so good and so satisfactory that they would like to see the single friend marry and achieve the same bliss. At the opposite extreme may be those who envy the single person's life and want him to join the ranks of marital misery. Those who have very unsuccessful marriages often make some of the strongest attempts to get single friends married.

Paired Relationship

When the couple are engaged, their private world takes on new significance and is projected to the time after marriage when it will become even more exclusive. The engaged couple who derive a great deal of pleasure and satisfaction from their exclusive re- lationship are often anxious to marry and extend the closed world even further.

It is generally during engagement that the middle-class couple move away from their involvement with unmarried friends and move more into their intense paired relationship. It has been sug- gested that the young woman begins to orient herself away from close friends during the period of engagement and to turn more and more to her partner for his determination of the kinds of activities they will pursue, and the people with whom they will associate.[16]

---

[16]Nicholas Babchuk, "Primary Friends and Kin: A Study of the Associations of Middle Class Couples," *Social Forces*, May, 1965, p. 486.

Out of this increasingly dependent paired interaction grows the feeling of belongingness.

Marriage is generally viewed as the *most* intimate relationship that can be achieved by two adults. The belongingness of marriage is very different from the belongingness of engagement because it is a continuous, rather than periodic, relationship. The male no longer takes the girl to her home and then goes to his; they go to their home together. The external world can be excluded for long periods of time and the couple can have extended privacy. Ego-satisfactions become of great significance in their private paired world; each individual realizes that the other wants only him most of the time. Hence one's sense of self-importance is affirmed by being important to the other. In a society often characterized by impersonal relationships, one in which a given individual is important to only a few, the most "significant other" takes on great importance in giving the individual a sense of personal value. Society helps contribute to the belief that the "significant other" of the spouse is special through the belief that the marriage relationship has something special in it that *can not* be found in any other relationship.[17] Martinson found in his study that "persons who marry demonstrate greater feelings of ego deficiency than do persons who remain single."[18] "It may be that it is the immature or not-so-well adjusted person for whom marriage has its strongest appeal."[19]

Social Relationships

As suggested above, one of the important role shifts from being single to being married is the increased involvement in social relationships as a pair rather than as an individual. While the male may see himself as an individual in pursuing his occupation and the female may see herself as an individual in taking care of the home, when two marriage partners enter a wide range of social activities in the extended community, they often do so as a pair. Babchuk, in his study of middle-class couples, found that couples constitute the basic unit with respect to primary friendship relations. "Not only is there a tendency for spouses to see themselves as a

---

[17]See: Jesse R. Pitts, "The Structural-Functional Approach," in Harold T. Christensen (ed.), *Handbook of Marriage and the Family* (Chicago: Rand McNally & Co., 1964), p. 97.

[18]Floyd M. Martinson, "Ego Deficiency as a Factor in Marriage," *American Sociological Review*, April, 1955, p. 163.

[19]*Ibid.*, p. 164.

unit in the friendship network but for their friends to see them as a unit."[20]

The development of friendship groups between married couples appears initially to be dependent more on the husband than on the wife. It was found that "husbands are likely to initiate friendships for the pair early in marriage and continue to exercise greater influence throughout the period of marriage."[21] Implied here may be that the men must first determine if they have anything in common; for example, occupation, sports, politics. If the men have something in common, it is assumed that the wives will find something in common because of their being wives, mothers and housekeepers.

Clearly implied in middle-class marriage friendships is that the husbands will be friends and the wives of the husbands will be friends. Babchuk writes that "many respondents stated explicitly that it would not be morally appropriate to be equally close to both married persons who were mutual friends, and a majority of subjects supported this position indirectly."[22] What seems to be clear in the social relationships of two married couples is that they may share things as two married couples, or as two individuals of the same sex, but not as two individuals of the opposite sex.[23]

In Chapter 3, it was stated that in the lower class the social life of the husband and wife was generally pursued separate from one another and in sex-peer groups. But in the middle class, the spouse often fills the role of being the mate's best friend. Babchuk found that middle-class couples do not maintain extensive friendship networks independently of each other. "Indeed, approximately half of the husbands and wives in our study claimed not to have a single primary friend independent of their spouses."[24]

Personality Relationships

An important part of marital-pair interaction centers around the relationships of the two as individual personalities. Prior to marriage, many young people probably feel that they understand both their own and their loved one's personality. However, the intensity and complexity of the marriage paired relationship brings forth for the couple new dimensions of each personality in the interactional relationship.

---

[20]Babchuk, *op. cit.*, p. 491.
[21]*Ibid.*, p. 492.
[22]*Ibid.*, p. 487.
[23]See: Chapter 5 for a discussion of platonic friends.
[24]Babchuk, *op. cit.*, p. 491.

The Landises point out that "before marriage, people in love have the tendency to emphasize the similarities in their ways of thinking rather than the differences."[25] The engaged couple discuss many areas, tending to put aside those that do not strike a responsive cord with the other, and to become thrilled over the things they have in common. After marriage, some of the areas passed over in the excitement of sharing begin to come forth. Because they are living together, without social restrictions, and because the "best foot forward" element of courtship is now past, new aspects of the personality emerge that may be received with feelings ranging from great pleasure to severe shock.

The marital partner's personality is important because in marriage, with its close paired relationship, personal abilities must be developed for predicting the personality of the other in many situations. As Kirkpatrick points out, "personality is never quite the same in each social situation and the partner has never been observed before in the situation of marriage."[26] Therefore, personality learning and adaptation is an ongoing process in marriage.

Sexual Satisfaction

Though probably very few individuals marry only to achieve a sexual outlet, the sexual nature of marriage is nevertheless a contributing factor to an interest in marriage. The importance attached to marital sex is generally different for the male and the female. Studies on premarital sexual intercourse show that marriage is often not the first time for sexual experience for either sex, but rather is the relationship in which social approval and personal ease of mind can be achieved in sexual experience.

Many males see marriage as an opportunity to satisfy sexual appetites that, in most cases, were at least partially starved during their single days. The single male often envies what he imagines to be the married man's always available sexual gratification. Many young men probably go into marriage perceiving the sexual relationship almost exclusively as a means of personal satisfaction, rather than as that and also a means of expression and love for the spouse. Sometimes it is assumed that males go into marriage with a highly idealistic version of marital sex. The single male has often experienced sex as a periodic event and thus may visualize sex in marriage as an unlimited series of events with a desirable sex partner. The

---

[25]Judson T. Landis and Mary G. Landis, *Building A Successful Marriage* (New York: Prentice-Hall, Inc., 1953), p. 253.

[26]Clifford Kirkpatrick, *The Family* (New York: The Ronald Press Co., 1955), p. 437.

young woman may look forward to the sexual relations of marriage with some degree of anticipation or apprehension. Sex is probably not initially viewed by most young women as a series of unlimited events to be entered into after marriage; rather, she may view the sexual experiences as a means of expressing love.

Economic Security

In the past, marriage was important to the female as a means of achieving economic independence from her father. Today, this is probably less of a motive for marriage because she has economic alternatives to marriage, though economic independence continues to be very important to the young woman in her desire to achieve adult status. Because of the alternatives, however, the economic force of marriage has decreased.

When a woman does agree to marry, she makes a great investment in her husband's ability to provide future economic security. This aspect of her decision may be more important today than in the past, because she often has the ability and opportunity to pursue a career of her own. When she chooses marriage, she is, therefore, by choice, placing her economic future in her husband's hands, placing an extra burden on the male for success because he not only must fulfill the traditional expectations that go with the bread winner role, but must also show his wife that her "sacrifice of career" was a wise decision.

Expectation of Success

Most people entering marriage are firmly convinced that it is what they want and that they will make a success of it. The stated beliefs indicate not just a relative lack of fear of marriage, but often the opposite—many individuals "know" they will be good at the relationship and cannot wait to marry. One study asked a group of unmarried college girls: "In thinking about marriage, how would you assess your chances of being a good wife and mother"; 87 percent answered "very good" and "good," 10 percent "average," 1 percent "poor" or "very poor," and 2 percent "don't know."[27]

While most couples go into marriage with the belief that they will be successful, they also believe that the marriage can be ended if it is not successful. Burgess and Wallin found a high proportion of the engaged couples they studied regarded divorce as justifiable on the grounds of temperamental or sexual incompatibility, or for

---

[27]Robert R. Bell, *Unpublished Research.*

repeated unfaithfulness.[28] The vast majority enter marriage with the notion that their individual marriage will be successful; and yet, by their belief that if it is not successful it can be ended by divorce, they imply the possibility of failure. Most individuals probably see themselves as being successful in marriage with divorce being available for "unsuccessful others."

As a summary of reasons for moving into marriage, probably no other human activity has a more perfect blending of Thomas' "four wishes": *The new experience* achieved through the new and different role relationships of marriage; *security* reached through the sense of belongingness inherent in the paired relationship of marriage; *response* brought about by the exclusive nature of the husband-wife relationship, and *the recognition* each gives to the other in being defined as important and meaningful.[29]

MARRIAGE ORIENTATIONS

The ensuing discussion of the different social orientations to the husband-wife relationship that exist in the United States today takes the changing nature of marriage roles into consideration. Different orientations place different emphases on the rights and obligations that go with the husband and wife roles. The orientations that are presented are not, however, completely distinct from each other and may, in fact, often overlap.

Patriarchal

Historically, the dominant marriage relationship was based on male authority and power. The traditional cultural values that determine the power relationships within the family appear to have been constructed by men. For example, deference customs are almost always wife-to-husband and rarely husband-to-wife.[30] Or as Jessie Bernard puts it, the Christian model of marriage is one in which, as Paul commanded, wives submit to their husbands, and as a result it is most likely to be the wife that does the adjusting to marriage.[31] Historically the common pattern of the patriarchal

[28]Ernest Burgess and Paul Wallin, *Engagement and Marriage* (Chicago: J. B. Lippincott, 1953), p. 411.

[29]Ray E. Baber, *Marriage and the Family* (New York: McGraw-Hill Book Co., 1953), p. 162.

[30]Stephens, *op. cit.*, p. 305.

[31]Jessie Bernard, "The Adjustments of Married Mates," in Harold T. Christensen (ed.) *Handbook of Marriage and The Family*, (Chicago: Rand McNally & Co., 1964), p. 681.

family has been that the husband is dominant in most areas; his wife's authority is in areas of childrearing, and caring for the home and is delegated to her by him. This pattern of marriage relationship is based upon a sharp distinction between the sexes and places a premium on masculinity and femininity that derive their meaning and significant difference by contrast to each other. Patriarchal marriages in a somewhat modified form are still found in some segments of American society, including some rural areas, immigrant families, and (as discussed in Chapter 3) the lower and upper social classes. The middle-class urban family represents the segment of American society from which the patriarchal family has, for the most part, disappeared.

Matriarchal

The matriarchal relationship vests authority and power in the wife-mother. Some observers have suggested that this pattern exists in the United States in the lower class, particularly for the Negro family. The wife-mother is the adult of responsibility in many lower-class families, because the husband-father is totally absent or may disappear for periods of time. But the woman gains her authority by default and not by agreement or consent. When a husband-father is in the home, the marriage is often patriarchal, and becomes matriarchal once again only if the male leaves. The lower-class male's role is often different from that of the traditional patriarch in that he frequently wants the authority but not the responsibility.

It has also been suggested by some writers that the suburban family of today tends to be matriarchal because the husband is away from home for long periods of time and the wife takes over many of the family responsibilities. But this, too, may be authority and responsibility by default; when the husband is home, the marriage authority may be shared by the husband and wife. A matriarchal marriage relationship does not seem to be common in contemporary America, for, in a true matriarchy, the wife-mother is the power figure with or without the husband's presence.

Companionship

Burgess and Locke have argued that, because of the impact of social changes on the family, a new form of relationship has emerged in the modern urban family. They suggest that the unity of the new marriage and family relationships are much less determined by community pressures and values, and more and more in "such inter-

personal relations as the mutual affection, the sympathetic understanding, and the comradeship of its members."[32] From the concept
of the companionship family, some have drawn the suggestion that
the husband and wife always make decisions as a democratic pair
and, as a result, their individual marriage roles are often essentially
the same.

Certainly many of the rights and obligations of marriage roles
have been drastically modified in the modern middle-class family.
These modifications have often had the effect of making the husband and wife increasingly alike in their attitudes and behavior.
Yet the husband and wife are not filling roles that are completely
interchangeable. Patterns of responsibility and decision making that
separate one role from the other in many otherwise democratically
oriented marriages, continue to operate.

Colleague

The colleague family provides a framework for taking the concept
of the companionship family with its emphasis on mutual, shared
behavior and adding the recognition of role differences. The colleague family is not drastically different from the companionship
family; the distinction is probably more important theoretically
than practically. In both types of families, decisions are partially
determined through the acceptance of other family members. Col-
league-family orientation indicates that the modern middle-class
family is *not* in reality an association of complete equals.

Miller and Swanson point out that, while women and men in
marriage are increasingly equal, they are also separate and different.
The development of specializations within marriage has led to new
relations between the married couple.[33] In different areas, both
recognize that authority is vested in the role or in the interests and
abilities of only one of them. This recognition allows each one to
defer to the other in different areas of competence, without loss of
prestige.[34] Furthermore, in most middle-class families, there is no
absolute equality between parents and children. The younger children are not given equal voice in decision-making with either older
siblings or parents, and the adolescent and young single adult often
continue to be partly under the authority and influence of the

---

[32]Ernest Burgess and Harvey J. Locke, *The Family* (New York: American Book
Co., 1953), p. 97.

[33]Daniel R. Miller and Guy E. Swanson, *The Changing American Parent* (New
York: John Wiley & Sons, Inc., 1958), p. 200.

[34]*Ibid.*, p. 200.

parents. The colleague family recognizes equality of rights in many areas, but differential rights and obligations in others.

Blood and Wolfe in their study found that "two decisions are primarily the husband's province (his job and the car), two the wife's (her work and food) while all the others are joint decisions."[35] In the more minor day-by-day decisions, a clear division of labor and authority exists in most middle-class marriages. However, the division of labor in the colleague marriage is not based on a belief of complete differences between the husband and wife roles and often, if conditions demand, one partner can temporarily take over the role of the other For example, not too many years ago many men would have been unwilling to do the family wash, and this chore is still generally assumed to be the role responsibility of the woman. However today, if the wife is indisposed, the male may do the wash and fear no personal loss of role prestige. But as soon as the wife is able to do the chore again, it is usually assumed that she will return to her role responsibility. Or, if the wife is working, the usual role responsibilites of the woman may be shared, but they generally revert back to her when she stops working.

The person socialized to any of the marriage orientations suggested may carry them into his own marriage. If the husband and wife come into marriage with different orientations because of differential socialization, they may have an adjustment problem. For adjustment to be achieved, they must arrive at some common orientation that is mutually acceptable and workable.

This discussion of marriage orientation has described some social patterns that operate in various ways and degrees on general social perspectives to marriage. The next chapter looks more specifically at marriage roles and adjustment in marriage. The discussion therefore moves from the general concern with the nature of marriage to the more specific interest in various aspects of marital adjustment.

SELECTED BIBLIOGRAPHY

BABCHUK, NICHOLAS. "Primary Friends and Kin: A Study of The Associations of Middle Class Couples," *Social Forces,* May, 1965, pp. 483–93.

BABER, RAY E. *Marriage and the Family,* chaps. x and xi. New York: McGraw-Hill Book Co., 1953.

BERNARD, JESSIE. *Social Problems at Midcentury,* chaps. xv, xvi and xvii. New York: The Dryden Press, 1957.

[35]Robert O. Blood and Donald M. Wolfe, *Husbands and Wives* (Glencoe, Illinois: The Free Press, 1960), p. 20.

BURGESS, ERNEST, and WALLIN, PAUL. *Engagement and Marriage,* chaps. i, xiii, and xiv. Chicago: J. B. Lippincott Co., 1953.

CHRISTENSEN, HAROLD T. *Marriage Analysis,* chap. xiv. New York: The Ronald Press, 1958.

FOOTE, NELSON N. "New Roles for Men and Women," *Marriage and Family Living,* November, 1961, pp. 325–27.

MARTINSON, FLOYD M. "Ego Deficiency as a Factor in Marriage," *American Sociological Review,* April, 1955, pp. 161–64.

MILLER, DANIEL R., and SWANSON, GUY E. *The Changing American Parent,* chap. viii. New York: John Wiley & Sons Inc., 1958.

WALLER, WILLARD, and HILL, REUBEN. *The Family,* chap. xiii. New York: The Dryden Press, 1951.

ADJUSTMENT IN MARRIAGE

In this chapter, the primary interest is marriage adjustment. Some aspects of marriage roles as related to adjustment, and various factors both within and outside of marriage related to possible problem areas for marriage interaction and adjustment will be discussed.

MARRIAGE ROLES

A person does not move into the role of husband or wife without at least some knowledge of marriage roles. For example, the young woman entering marriage generally has expectations on how she will perform as a wife. She must in her marriage achieve some basic agreement between her marital role expectations and her own personality needs. However, the wife's role expectations for herself may need to be altered if they are not congruent with what the husband believes is the appropriate wife role. Therefore, a second area of adjustment is betwen the role perceptions of the person filling the role and the spouse's beliefs about the role A third aspect is the interactional nature of the two roles; that is, whether the husband and wife roles, as filled by the two individuals, are mutually satisfactory and compatible.

Marital-role adjustment also has a dynamic quality because the needs of the individuals and their role relationships frequently change. For example, the bride may at first enjoy the role demands placed on her for taking care of the house, but later view them as unpleasant. Or, the wife may at first view her husband's solicitous actions as an expression of his love, but later as a lack of his recognition of her ability to do things for herself.

For many young single women there are romantic influences on their perceptions of the roles they will fill after marriage. This is reflected in the fact that while almost all girls want to marry, many of them do not want to fill all of the roles generally associated with marriage. One study found that while 90 percent of a group of high-school girls studied wanted to marry, only 15 percent of them said they wanted to be housewives. As Hunt points out, the

288

Mark4

modern girl "does not choose housekeeping as a role in life; she chooses marriage and motherhood, and has housekeeping thrust upon her."[1]

How the marital-role beliefs have been acquired is important. For most young people, the parents have served as important marriage role models. In the socialization of the individual, the relationship of the parents as husband and wife generally is the only marriage with which the person has had a lasting, intimate association. Because the learning has been going on all of one's life, this socialization to marriage roles is often deeply rooted in the marriage role expectations of the offspring.

Studies have shown that a person coming from a home in which the marriage of the parents was ended through divorce or bereavement has less statistical chance of success in his own marriage than does the individual coming from a home in which the parental marriage remained intact.[2] While the reasons for this are complex, one important factor is the influence on the youngster of the remaining parent's distorted role performance. If one parent is left with the main responsibility of rearing the child, the child no longer sees that parent in a marriage role. In effect, the parent no longer functions as a marriage model because one role is meaningless without a partner in the counter role. In addition, the parent is playing the role of both parents and therefore functioning differently than when a spouse is also available as a parent. For example, when a youngster sees his mother not only in the mother role, but also doing many things that are normally a part of the father role, he may get a distorted image of the combined parental role played by the mother.

The child socialized in the one-parent setting may take into his own marriage an exaggerated definition of the rights and obligations of that parent's role. If he marries a person who has been reared by two parents who were both active in their marriage and parent roles, strong differences in role definitions may be taken into marriage by each person. As a result, each may have a conflict in defining his own role and the role of his partner.

Another possible way that parents as marriage models influence the child is through their relationships to him. The most favorable relationship seems to occur when the child does not overidentify with one parent. To illustrate: "There is a convergence of evidence

[1]Morton Hunt, *Her Infinite Variety* (New York: Harper & Row Publishers, 1962), p. 144.

[2]Clifford Kirkpatrick, *The Family* (New York: The Ronald Press Co., 1955), p. 601.

to the effect that poorly adjusted wives tend to have experienced greater intimacy and perhaps affection with one parent."[3] Overinvolvement with one parent may lead to a role distortion, resulting in an exaggerated definition of the marriage role played by that parent. The distorted role image may be carried by the offspring into his own marriage, leading to possible problems with both his own role definition and that of his marriage mate.

The parents may also have influence after marriage, especially for the wife. While the young wife can compare herself with other women in the wife role, she often sees herself in contrast to her own mother and her mother-in-law. The mother-in-law becomes important as a wife-role model because of the young wife's emotional commitment to her husband. In a study by the writer, college-graduate wives were asked to compare themselves in their roles as wives with both their mothers and their mothers-in-law. In comparing themselves to their mothers as wives, 72 percent said they were about "the same or better"; 10 percent, "not as good"; and 18 percent, "can't answer." In comparing themselves with their mothers-in-law as wives, 58 percent said they were "the same or better"; 9 percent, "not as good"; and 33 percent, "cant' answer."[4] Although the daughters made little distinction between the mother and mother-in-law when comparing themselves as wives, only a few of the young wives defined themselves as not being at least equal to the two older important role models.

For many young women during the early years of marriage, their family of orientation has high significance. The young woman starting out in her roles of wife, mother and housekeeper can, with social approval and without loss of face, turn to her family (usually her mother) for some help and reassurance as to how she is filling her new roles. By contrast, the male's activities and interests are much more apt to be occupationally oriented and he has less reason to turn to his family of orientation. Stryker points out that the young wife is "more dependent upon family relationships in both a psychological and an economic sense. For her, more than for a male, the family represents a means through which directly utilitarian, as well as other, satisfactions are achieved."[5]

The individual enters marriage socialized by parents and other influences to the role he will play. One may wonder how accurate the premarriage role beliefs turns out to be. In the writer's study,

---

[3]*Ibid.*, p. 274.

[4]Robert R. Bell, unpublished data.

[5]Sheldon Stryker, "Conditions of Accurate Role-Taking," in Arnold Rose (Ed.), *Human Behavior and Social Processes*, (New York: Houghton Mifflin Co., 1961), p. 59.

wives were asked: "Would you say that your image of what is meant to be a wife before you were married has proved to be realistic?" Eighty percent of the respondents answered "yes," 20 percent "no."[6] There is bound to be some distortion between the actual premarriage beliefs and how they are recalled after moving through the experiences of marriage, but the findings indicate that many wives think their premarital beliefs proved realistic.

Since the two roles are interacting, it is obvious that one partner does not always play his role in the same way and cannot always choose that part of his role he wants most to play at a given time. An important quality of role playing is the ability to take the role of the other, so as to understand and predict the other's behavior and to relate it to one's own behavior—in short, having one's behavior influenced in part by the desires of the "significant other."

The ability and willingness to take the role of the other varies with different settings within the marriage relationship. In one study, husbands and wives were presented with problems to which solutions could be reached either by taking-the-role-of-the-other, or not doing so. The results of this study suggest that "variables frequently used to describe adjusted interaction in marriage must be qualified by observing their operation in a specific social system—the situation. How a given actor will act toward his spouse seems to be bound up in situation norms that dictate sex-role prerogatives,"[7] the important point being that even in very well-adjusted marriages, the altruism of the individual is not so great that he will always resolve a problem by looking at it from the perspective of the "significant other." He may weigh the other's desire against his own and choose his own. Too, the influence of the other's desires varies with different situations.

There is some evidence to suggest that women have a better understanding and grasp of their husband's views about his marriage roles than does the husband about his wife's perceptions of her roles.[8] Given our general assumption of greater involvement in marriage and family roles by the woman than by the man, we would expect this. There is also some evidence of changes in the importance of role expectations and behavior with length of marriage. The findings of one study suggest that "the husband's role definitions and expectations may be more important to the early success

---

[6]Bell, *op. cit.*

[7]Jack V. Buerkle, Theodore R. Anderson and Robin F. Badgley, "Altruism, Role Conflict and Marital Adjustment: A Factor Analysis of Marital Interaction," *Marriage and Family Living*, February, 1961, p. 22.

[8]See: Robert R. Stuckert, "Role Perception and Marital Satisfaction—A Configurational Approach," *Marriage and Family Living*, November, 1963, pp. 415–19.

292 MARRIAGE AND FAMILY INTERACTION

of a marriage than the wife's. Since our culture tends to define her role as centering around her family, there may be greater pressure on her to develop an accommodative pattern in relation to other members of the family."[9]

If an individual does not always sacrifice his own needs for the marriage partner, neither does he always ignore the needs of the other. In well-adjusted marriages, the two partners can probably meaningfully take the role of the other and pursue it as an end, even if it means some loss of personal role gratification. That there is a balance between the complete "other-" and complete "self-" orientation in successful marriage was shown in one study in which "the divorced couples were found to be four times as far apart in their views of correct roles for self and spouse as compared with the married couples."[10]

Ultimately, success in marriage roles depends upon the satisfaction achieved by the two individuals. The well-adjusted marriage is often one in which the roles for the two persons are not in significant conflict, when the desires of the individuals are given minimal satisfaction by both themselves and the other. The writer's study found some information on the interaction relationship through the wife's image of herself in the wife's role and her assessment of her husband in his role. When the wife was asked "How would you evaluate yourself as a wife?," 72 percent answered "good" or "very good"; 26 percent "average"; and 2 percent "poor" or "very poor." When they were asked "How would you evaluate your husband as a husband?," 82 percent answered "good" or "very good"; 15 percent "average"; and 3 percent "poor" or "very poor."[11] In regard to filling their respective roles, the wives gave their husbands somewhat higher evaluations than they gave themselves.

The complexity of marriage and family roles places a high significance on the difference in personalities brought into marriage. The abilities to meet and reach compatability between one's own needs and the roles filled both by one's self and by one's spouse are important. Jessie Bernard suggests that when the major importance is placed on the relational pattern between husband and wife, "the spouses adjust to one another primarily and to the role secondarily."[12] She goes on to stress that marital satisfaction is a team as

---

[9]Ibid., p. 419.

[10]Ray E. Baber, Marriage and the Family (New York: McGraw-Hill Book Co., p. 210.

[11]Bell, op. cit.

[12]Jessie Bernard, "The Adjustments of Married Mates," in Harold T. Christensen (Ed.) Handbook of Marriage and The Family, (Chicago: Rand McNally & Co., 1964), p. 688.

well as an individual or personality matter.[13] But it should also be recognized that there is no one marriage relationship that leads to better results for all husbands and wives. For example, Hurwitz found no evidence that couples who hold companionship values were any happier in their marriage than husbands and wives who held to traditional values.[14]

On the basis of this discussion of marriage roles, some general theoretical criteria of successful marriages will be suggested. These should not be thought of as universal to all adjusted marriages, but rather as patterns that are frequently found in marriages defined by the couples as successful. In various successful marriages, not all the criteria will have the same significance or be related in the same way.

1. *Satisfaction is achieved in one's own marriage role and that of the mate.* The individual entering marriage moves into a role that offers him a range of alternative courses of behavior within socially defined limits. He usually has no great problem in playing his role so long as his desired behavior falls within the defined limits. However, problems may emerge if his personal desires go outside of what he or his spouse define as appropriate role behavior.

In some cases, the individual who conforms to role expectations feels a sense of personal frustration. Few, if any, individuals will fill their marriage role for any length of time without some dissatisfaction; but for most, role dissatisfactions are not crucial enough to define the total marriage as unsatisfactory. For example, many women feel a sense of specific role frustration over the demands of housework, but do not usually find this basically disturbing to the total marriage satisfaction. By contrast, when a wife finds her role as a sexual partner very disturbing, her overall feelings about her mariage role may thereby be strongly influenced and may result in her negatively defining the marriage relationship.

As with one's own role, a person is also not always satisfied with how the spouse fills his role. Generally, the effects of this do not drastically disturb the total marriage relationship. A wife may feel that a part of her husband's role is to perform certain chores around the house. The fact that he does not always fill this role when she wants him to will not usually be seen as endangering the marriage relationship. However, if the husband in his role of provider gambles away his paycheck, the wife may consider this a role failure on his

---

[13]*Ibid.*, p. 729.

[14]Nathan Hurwitz, "Control Roles, Marital Strain, Role Deviation and Marital Adjustment," *Journal of Marriage and Family*, February, 1965, p. 31.

part that has serious implications for the total marriage relationship.

The congruence of role perception may be another problem. The partners may or may not essentially agree in their definition of whether one role is being filled satisfactorily. One of them may be quite satisfied that he is fulfilling his role, but the other person may not be. For example, the wife may feel that she is fulfilling the sexual role demands of the marriage very well, but the husband may perceive her as inadequate in her role of sex partner.

2. *Each partner in the marriage has some opportunity to express his own personality.* In some marriages, the role demands made by one's own role as well as that of the other may lead to a sense of personal frustration. The individual may feel that he never has the opportunity to develop personality interests of his own because the demands of the marriage roles are so overwhelming. Many times analysis of marriage interaction overlooks the need for individuality by placing all the emphasis on the paired role relationships. Mowrer writes that "assimilation is a process in which husband and wife become more and more nearly identical. Theoretically, the higher the degree of assimilation the higher the degree of marriage unity."[15] This argument is questionable because it does not take into account the need of many individuals to be themselves and hence be different from the spouse. While similarity and agreement are important in marriage, so too are individual differences. In many marriages, the relationship may actually be one of some accommodation—the couple agree to disagree and be different in some ways.

The opportunity for individual expression in marriage varies by sex and with time. The wife usually has less opportunity for individual expression than the husband because her life is more routinized and restricted. The demands made on the woman which restrict her individual expression often vary over time. For example, the young mother with preschool children may find that she must temporarily put aside most of her own personal desires; she may be able to accept this, because she knows that when the children get older her role demands will lessen and she will have more opportunity to pursue her individual interests.

In most marriages it is important to each of the spouses, and possibly to the marriage relationship itself, that each have or do some things *not* shared by the spouse. Because the spouse is often one's most important "significant other" it may help the adjustment of each mate if their spouse has some illusions about them that are not put to the test of reality. For example, the area of sports is in-

[15]Harriet R. Mowrer, "Getting Along in Marriage," in Howard Becker and Reuben Hill, *Family, Marriage and Parenthood* (Boston: D. C. Heath & Co., 1955), p. 353.

creasingly presented as an area of activity for the middle class husband and wife to share. Because we assume that men are (and should be) athletically superior to women, shared activity may place a strain on the husband to perform better than he can, and on the wife to urge him to. If there are activities that the couple can pursue independently, they are not faced with the need to compete. In sports this would allow one (usually the husband) to convey to his spouse the impression (real or exaggerated) of his masculine competency achieved in an all-masculine world.

There may also be some activities that the individual enjoys doing with others—but does not want that other to be his spouse. Once again sports may be used as an illustration. For example, one of the pleasures of playing golf for many husbands is to play the game with a group of male friends. It appears that pleasure for the individual through involvement with groups of his own sex is more common for men than for women. It seems quite possible that in the American middle class, women are psychologically and socially much more dependent on men than men are on women. And this appears to be true both in and out of marriage.

3. *Each marriage partner is an important focus of affection for the other.* Because love is an important reason for getting married and because it is important in giving the ongoing marriage a basic reason for existence, the partners usually must be reassured that love continues to exist. It is generally through the continuation of love and affection in marriage that the person maintains the feeling of being wanted and being important to the other. The reciprocal nature of the love relationship provides an important aspect of ego-need satisfaction for each partner. If one no longer sees the partner as the "significant other" of affection, a feeling of great loss in the marriage relationship may result.

In almost all marriages, the nature of the husband-wife affectional relationship changes and shifts with time. When children come, the parents direct affection at them, but this is not usually viewed as a threat to the affection given by the spouse to his partner. On occasion, a young father will perceive his child with some jealousy because his wife is directing a great deal of affection to the child and he may feel that, in a sense, this affection has been taken away from him. However, since people generally have no fixed limits of affection, they do not take from one relationship to give to another.

In a number of marriages, a partner may not substitute another person as an affectional recipient, but rather lose interest in his spouse because of various demands in life or change in personality needs. The partner's withdrawal of affection may represent a severe loss for the spouse who continues to desire the affection. This may be illustrated by the husband who, as he grows older, simply loses affectional interest in his wife and lives with her more out of habit than emotional feeling. For the wife who wants and needs his affection, this loss can be a severe shock. It also means that the relationship is continuing without the reciprocal affection so highly valued in middle-class marriage.

4. *Each partner derives some pleasures and satisfactions from the marriage role relationships.* Mutual satisfaction may be considered the opposite to the individuality stressed in the second point above. If some individual expression in marriage is needed, the couple also usually need to interact in their roles as husband and wife. If the individuals do not, their marriage roles will have little meaning because these roles derive their meaning and importance through the interrelationships.

The importance of the role relationship of marriage is related to different definitions of happy and unhappy marriages. One study found that those individuals who report very happy marriages tended to stress the relationship to the spouse as the major source of their happiness, "while those reporting less happiness in marriage tend to concentrate on the situational aspects of marriage (home, children, social life) as sources of their marital happiness."[16]

When two married people fill certain roles as a result of living together, but are not personally significant to each other, then an arrangement between two individuals, and not a marriage in terms of role interrelationship, exists. The husband and wife who live together, but do not participate together, are married in name only.

MARRIAGE ADJUSTMENT

Given the various ways in which modern middle-class marriage roles may be filled, the ultimate measurement of successful marriage is the degree of adjustment achieved by the individuals in their marriage roles and in interaction with one another. In the following discussion, adjustment and success are both used in essentially the same way to refer to the degree of satisfaction with marriage.

The concept of adjustment is applied to many aspects of social behavior. It may be used in reference to the individual being adjusted to external social expectations or to the internal relationship between personal desires and socially expected behavior. Because all human behavior is social, the patterns for adjustment either within

---

[16]Gerald Gurin, Joseph Veroff and Shiela Feld, *Americans View Their Mental Health,* (New York: Basic Books, 1960), p. 98.

or between individuals, which were originally external to the individual, had to be internalized through the process of socialization. Adjustment is of importance in both the social and psychological sense. *Social* refers to the interactional role relationships between individuals, and *psychological* to the relationship of internalized social roles and the personality desires operating for the individual.

Adjustment is a basic requirement of social participation and social organization. A society develops minimal requirements of adjustment in areas of social relevance and, if a given individual cannot meet them, he may be viewed as dangerous to himself and/or others and may be institutionalized or even eliminated. However, if he meets the minimum requirements, individual variations within the acceptable behavior range are generally permitted. All functioning members of a society are adjusted to at least a set of basic social requirements and maladjusted to the degree that no individual can accept and conform to all of the requirements. Social adjustment is not an either/or proposition, but a matter of degree.

Given the complexity of the roles and role relationships, as well as the personalities of different individuals, no marriage is absolutely adjusted or maladjusted. Even in marriages assessed as highly adjusted, some areas of conflict for or between the partners will exist. A marriage in which absolute personal and social acceptance and satisfaction always prevails is hard to imagine. Even in marriages that end in rapid divorce, some areas of adjustment for or between the couple existed.

Whether or not a marriage is successful is determined by the interaction between the two partners over the time span of their marriage. That is, a marriage is not simply the sum of the two individuals that make it up, but rather it is a unity of two interacting personalities, "neither one of which alone determines the success of the relationship. An outcome which has an extremely low value for the wife married to one may have a high value for her if married to another, and vice versa."[17] In other words, there is no type of personality that is a failure in marriage, but rather two individual personalities that have through interaction with one another failed in marriage. And while marital failure might not have occurred with a different mate, it is also true "that even happily married people might have been happier if married to someone else."[18]

Marital adjustment implies "that the individual or the pair has a good working arrangement with reality, adulthood, and expecta-

---

[17]Bernard, *op. cit.*, p. 730.
[18]*Ibid.*, p. 729.

tions of others."[19] The definition points out the individual and paired nature of marital adjustment. One may be adjusted in one area, but not the other; for example, a person may fill his role demands in his relationship to the role of the other, but feel personal frustration while filling the role. This dual stress on marital adjustment is more common in the United States today than it was in the past. When roles were clearly defined, marriage was more apt to be assessed on the basis of the ability of the two individuals to meet the rights and obligations of the role relationship. But with the development of the emphasis on the individual achieving ego-need satisfaction in marriage, and the confusion in marriage role definitions, an individual may increasingly find a conflict between the role demands made on him and his own desires and wishes.

Over the years, social scientists have attempted to develop techniques for determining success or adjustment in marriage.[20] The earliest attempts used a *single* criterion, such as happiness with marriage.[21] Ratings were achieved through self-evaluations of marriage or through evaluations by others who were familiar with the marriage. The limitations of single-criterion evaluation were that the criterion one person might use to make an assessment of a marriage might not be used by another and, even if the same criterion were used, the insight and ability of assessment would vary a great deal among different observers.

Later, a score system with several criteria was set up, under which a marriage's success rating was determined by responses of the married person to a number of items.[22] This led to the use of a *composite* index that recognized different facets of marital success. However, this technique was critized because the total score concealed the various contributions made by each of the criteria.[23] An overall success score tells little about the various parts that make up the whole.

Burgess and Wallin argue that the *multiple* criteria of marital success measurement meet the objections of the composite index, because each contributing criterion is composed of a number of

[19]Willard Waller and Reuben Hill, *The Family* (New York: The Dryden Press, 1951), p. 362.

[20]See: Ernest W. Burgess and Leonard S. Cottrell, *Predicting Success or Failure in Marriage* (New York: Prentice-Hall, Inc., 1939); Ernest W. Burgess and Paul Wallin, *Engagement and Marriage* (Chicago: J. B. Lippincott, 1953); Gilbert V. Hamilton, *A Research in Marriage* (New York: Albert & Charles Boni, Inc., 1929); Harvey J. Locke, *Predicting Adjustment in Marriage: A Comparison of a Divorced and a Happily Married Group* (New York: Henry Holt & Co., 1951); and Lewis M. Terman, *Psychological Factors in Marital Happiness* (New York: McGraw-Hill Book Co., 1938).

[21]See: Locke, *op. cit.*

[22]See: Burgess and Cottrell, *op. cit.*

[23]Burgess and Wallin, *op. cit.*, pp. 504–5.

items.[24] In their method, a total score for overall adjustment can be seen and used, as well as scores for the various categories that make up the total. Burgess and Wallin suggest that the "multiple criteria" method has been successful as an instrument in differentiating between successful and unsuccessful marriages by the practical test of validation, divorce.[25]

After a careful survey of the many research attempts to investigate marital relationships, Jessie Bernard distinguishes a variety of criteria that have been used. The criteria include: "(a) how well a marriage meets the needs and expectations of society; (b) its permanence or endurance; (c) the degree of unity and/or agreement or consensus developed between the members; (d) the degree to which it facilitates personality development; and, (e) the degree of marital satisfaction or happiness it achieves."[26]

One very important aim of all scientific disciplines is to expand the knowledge of an area so that a means of prediction may be developed. In the marriage and family field, prediction research and the development of reliable instruments has two major objectives. The first is the practical aim of gaining reliable prediction material which would be useful to the many individuals in positions of counseling the premarried as well as the married. The second is the general contribution which could be made to knowledge of human behavior in marriage.[27]

A vast body of research providing empirical information on factors related to success in marriage is available today.[28] The findings of the many studies are determined through statistical analysis and help explain the social influences of the variables tested. The research is not meant nor was it designed for individual application. Therefore, the reader must be cautioned against applying the findings to a given individual. Clifford Kirkpatrick has compiled the findings from a large number of empirical studies on different variables related to marriage.[29] A listing of selected variables that have been found in some research to have a relationship to success in marriage follows. An X in the first column indicates that research has provided some evidence that that variable is favorable to success in marriage, while an X in the second column indicates that that variable was found to be unfavorable.

---

[24]*Ibid.*, p. 505.

[25]*Ibid.*, p. 505.

[26]Bernard, *op. cit.*, p. 730.

[27]*Ibid.*, p. 555.

[28]See: Clifford Kirkpatrick, *What Science Says About Happiness in Marriage* (Minneapolis: Burgess Publishing Co., 1947).

[29]Kirkpatrick, *The Family, op. cit.*, pp. 346–54, 599–617.

Premarital Factors:	Favorable	Unfavorable
1. Happiness of parents' marriage (high):	X	
A. Parents divorced		X
B. Parent or parents deceased		X
2. Personal happiness in childhood	X	
3. Ease of premarital contact with the opposite sex	X	
4. Mild, but firm discipline by parents	X	
5. Lack of conflict with parents	X	
6. Courtship:		
A. Acquainted under one year		X
B. Acquainted over one year	X	
C. Approval of parents	X	
D. Similarity of age	X	
E. Satisfaction with affection of other	X	
7. Reason for marriage:		
A. Love	X	
B. Loneliness		X
C. Escape from one's own family		X
D. Common interests	X	

Postmarital Factors:	Favorable	Unfavorable
1. Attitudes:		
A. Husband more dominant..		X
B. Pair equalitarian	X	
C. Wife more dominant		X
D. Jealous of spouse		X
E. Feels superior to spouse ..		X
F. Feels more intelligent than spouse		X
2. Good relationships with in-laws	X	
3. Not living with in-laws	X	
4. Community of interest	X	
5. Desire for children	X	

The listing on the previous page gives an indication of some areas found through research to have a measurable relationship to success in marriage. The findings were based on a variety of different studies with a wide range of methods and samples. Furthermore, since scientific findings provide only evidence, not conclusive proof, future research may alter or invalidate the present findings. An unresolved, but very important problem is the interrelationship of the various items—that is, whether the existence of one variable influences or brings about the existence of others.

While many variables have been shown to have a statistical relationship with adjustment and success in marriage, none of them has been found to be absolute. The researcher must make a constant and concerted effort to distinguish the variables that make a successful or well-adjusted marriage. Few researchers would assume that all successful marriages will be made up of the same variables in the same relationships. While distinguishing variables in successful marriages is very important, it may also be suggested that adjustment in marriage is a "naming stage" for most married couples. The couple who feel that their marriage is good, and honestly see themselves as adjusted, are adjusted within their frame of reference. To say they are not is to imply a knowledge of what marital adjustment really *is* and of its application to all marriages. If the couple feel that their marriage is good and successful, their attitudes and behavior will generally reflect the belief. We would suggest that most couples who "name" their marriage as at least minimally satisfactory would meet two general criteria: first, a marriage is successful if the satisfaction is positive, "that is, if the rewards to both partners are greater than the costs"; and second, if the marriage relationship is preferable to any alternative.[30]

INTERACTION CHANGES WITH LENGTH OF MARRIAGE

One very important adjustment that has to be made by many couples early in marriage is the redefining of their inexperienced, premarital marriage role expectations on the basis of newly experienced reality. Waller and Hill write, "now gently, now with startling brutality, the real person and the reality of marriage pound at the portals of thought, and at length enter. One may struggle against disillusionment. As a hitherto unperceived facet of a personality reveals itself and destroys an illusion, one may build a mental bul-

---

[30]Bernard, *op. cit.,* p. 732.

wark around the old illusion or rationalize the new behavior into some sort of agreement with the old configuration."[31] Redefinition of the marriage roles is usually called for if the couple are to maintain a relationship that is satisfactory to them in light of their new experience. But very often marital adjustment over time is not a conscious or deliberate activity by either spouse. "People are sometimes surprised, in fact, when they become aware of the changes which have occurred in their relationship over a period of time; they have been adjusting to one another without even recognizing the fact."[32]

Disenchantment with the romantic relationship in marriage will vary over time. Pineo's study suggests that "men have apparently suffered more disenchantment in the early years than have the women. This is in sharp contrast to where the losses in adjustment from early marriage to the middle years were almost invariably larger for wives than for husbands."[33] This may be the result of the males' illusions being less realistic or the females' being slower to react to the reality of the marital relationship.

A positive development usually occurs as the disillusionment with the romantic idealism of premarriage unfolds—the increasing number of common experiences as husband and wife. New values are developed in the marriage relationship to replace the disappearing romantic illusions. The very fact of sharing experiences as a husband and wife provides a strong bond for many couples; they can derive satisfaction from the situations they have encountered and resolved. They may have developed a universe of discourse in which they can give and take in ways and areas they consider to be important. The increasing experience with the other also leads to the ability of many to predict the behavior of the spouse and, as a result, an intimacy of behavior develops not found in many other pair-relationships.

One of the realities of marriage is that the couple must face many problem areas, whereas in courtship the emphasis was generally on the pleasurable areas. The sharing of problems may lead to a closer tie between the pair because they can give aid and support to the other and gain satisfaction in successfully dealing with their problems. One study of husbands and wives found that only 28 percent

---

[31]Waller and Hill, *op. cit.*, pp. 258–59.
[32]Bernard, *op. cit.*, p. 680.
[33]Peter C. Pineo, "Disenchantment in the Later Years of Marriage," *Marriage and Family Living*, February, 1961, p. 10.

of the wives seldom or never told their husbands their troubles.[34] In many marriages, the husband and wife relationship will, with time, minimize personal pretense on the part of both partners. Each partner can therefore turn to the other for support and help with a minimum threat to his ego because of less need to "cover up."

It has been argued that even after marriage many of the romantic qualities of courtship and early marriage should continue. This argument overlooks the fact that romantic forms of expression frequently have their meaning only when the couple have no other shared areas for interaction with each other. If the marriage relationship brings a sense of security and satisfaction, the behavior patterns of the romantic stage are often no longer appropriate. They operated during a period of minimum interpersonal security and satisfaction. The wife who is upset because her husband does not bring home flowers every week may be reacting because she wants to hang on to the symbolism associated with the romantic courtship period. Or, if she wants the flowers as a sign of her husband's love, it might indicate that she doesn't feel other signs exist.

As time goes on, the husband-wife roles undergo change. Most family research has been directed at the early changes in the marriage relationship. The transfer from single to married roles offers the most dramatic change and, as a result, alterations later in marriage have usually been ignored. Foote suggests "it is about time that our writers consider the vast audiences that are waiting for relevant knowledge about marital relations during the years from 45 onwards."[35]

Earlier, we suggested some changes that occur in marriage over time. We know that with time, and as the married couple move through the various family-life stages, the importance of their marriage and family roles undergoes a variety of changes. One characteristic of most marriages is that with time the knowledge and predictability with regard to the spouse's feelings and behavior increases. The observation has been made that often the longer a couple are married, the less they verbally interact with each other. While this is no doubt true, it is also the case that the longer the couple are married, the less may be their dependency on conversation as their chief means of communication. The husband and wife often get to know each other so well over time that they can antici-

---

[34]Burgess and Wallin, *op. cit.,* p. 190.

[35]Nelson N. Foote, "New Roles for Men and Women," *Marriage and Family Living,* November, 1961, p. 326.

pate what the other will say, or a few words or gestures may be all the cue that is needed. Brownfield found that facial expressions and gestures were increasingly more important as means of communication as marriage interaction continued over the years.[36]

The evidence also suggests that over time the spouses' knowledge and assessment of each other is such that they may gradually turn less to each other. This may be an adaptation to an *over*-dependency that existed early in marriage. Blood and Wolfe found that young wives turned very often to their husbands both for sympathy as well as when they were angry. But they found that over time and with the involvement of children, "the husband assumes a less significant role as audience, being replaced by such alternatives as God, other people, and housework."[37]

It becomes clear that as time passes, new attitudes toward marriage develop. For many couples, the happiness ratings of their marriages go down with increasing age and with length of marriage. The happiest years of marriage may be the early years, even though it is generally during those years that most problems of marital adjustment occur. Gurin found that "feelings of inadequacy and problems progressively decrease with age. One might suspect that over time there tends to be an increasing adaptation to the marital partner and to the distresses in the marriage."[38] Or as Jessie Bernard suggests, the "marital relationship that comes with age may, therefore, reflect resignation rather than happiness."[39]

There is a very strong tendency to define marital happiness as it characterizes the early years of marriage and to hold to that definition for persons as they grow older and are married for longer periods of time. This bias is reflected in the common assumption that when a marriage relationship is described as "resigned" or "low in happiness," these descriptions refer to undesirable characteristics of a poor marital relationship. But with many years of marital interaction and the spouses' great familiarity with one another, it may be that most of the relationships in marriage must become routine and predictable. In fact, one might speculate that certain kinds of interaction that would end a marriage during the early years might become a reason for maintaining it in later years. For example, some older couples appear to detest each other. But this hostility may

[36]See: E. Dorothy Brownfield, "Communication—Key to Dynamics of Family Interaction," *Marriage and Family Living,* 1953, 15, pp. 316–19.

[37]Robert O. Blood and Donald M. Wolfe *Husbands and Wives* (Glencoe, Illinois: The Free Press, 1960), p. 189.

[38]Gurin, *op. cit.,* p. 102.

[39]Bernard, *op. cit.,* p. 732.

actually have a positive value because it indicates that the other is still "significant." While most of us would desire positive expressions directed at us by a "significant other," we might in their absence prefer negative expressions rather than none.

Because of the generally greater commitment of the woman to marriage, we will direct some attention to how she is affected and influenced with increasing length of marriage. When women enter their late 40's, their lives usually undergo drastic changes. First, since their children are growing up and leaving home, many women, especially those who have largely devoted themselves to their children, must make a difficult adjustment. The greater the degree to which the woman has involved and immersed herself in the rearing of her children, the greater the loss of function she suffers when they grow up. Some women may be able to adjust to this role loss by taking on other interests, but for the rest the role commitment to being mother has been so great that it is very difficult for them to move successfully into new roles.

Second, as the middle-class woman enters her middle years, her husband is often at his occupational peak and very often deeply involved in his career. Earlier in marriage, the wife might have been very helpful to the husband's career, but at this point her assistance is often limited. Thus, the husband's important occupational role may call for little involvement by the wife. A third important change is that the woman enters the menopause at about 47 years of age.[40] This change is associated with an ovarian-hormone decrease which leads to a variety of physical and functional changes. The psychological impact of the menopause is often very strong because it dramatically ends what many women believe to be their most important function—the having of children. It also forces the woman to realize her youth is now over and she is moving toward old age.

When these elements of change are combined, the impact on the middle-aged woman may be very great. As a result, she may seek roles outside the family to give new meaning to her life. The two prescriptions often offered as substitutes for the loss of the child-rearing role are volunteer activities and part-time employment. The real function of many social activities which suggest high social goals is often the attempt to provide the middle-aged, middle-class woman with a meaningful role. In Moore's comparison of the participation of middle-class and upper-class women in associations,

---

[40]M. Edward Davis, "Ovulation and Fertility," in Morris Fishbein and Ruby Jo Kennedy, *Modern Marriage and Family Living* (New York: Oxford University Press, 1957), p. 365.

she found that for the middle class the associations function "primarily to help adapt the woman herself to changes in the family life-cycle in a minimally disturbing way; for the upper class, it plays a role of significance to the entire social class."[41] One may wonder how long and to what degree the many "busywork" middle-class organizations can really delude the intelligent woman into believing she is filling a new and significant role. While some may believe that what they are doing is important, many others probably go along with the myth because they have nowhere else to turn. This may be the price many women pay for not maintaining and developing an individuality during their childrearing years.

The role changes are less severe for the middle-aged male, but exist to some degree. He has his occupational involvement, which may give him his most important role satisfaction. When a man has reached his late 40's, his occupational success has been pretty well determined. Some men are satisfied with their position and their expectations for the future, but many men may not be satisfied and a sense of occupational failure may force its way into their thinking.

Also at this time, a man's sexual interests and capabilities are often fading. If the male has associated his sense of masculinity with sexual behavior, he may undergo a drastic role shock. As a further complication, if the wife's sexual interests are still at a relatively high level, the husband may find himself in the highly disturbing position of being sexually inadequate. The sexual drive of the middle-class male may also be influenced by the occupational role. Foote raises the question of "what happens to sexual potency when the masculine ego is damaged by being occupationally conquered by a junior."[42]

MARRIAGE IN THE POST-PARENTAL YEARS

In Chapter 14 and Chapter 15 we will discuss various aspects of parent-child relationships. At this point we want to look at some aspects of marriage during the years after the children have grown up and left home. What is new and significant in the family life cycle after the children have left home has been the expansion of the period where the couple live together as husband and wife. The recent emergence and significance of the post-parental years is reflected in the statistics that in 1890 the average woman was a widow

[41]Joan W. Moore, "Patterns of Women's Participation in Voluntary Associations," *American Journal of Sociology*, May, 1961, p. 598.

[42]Foote, *op. cit.*, p. 326.

before her last child left home.[43] By contrast, today, the average woman can expect about 15 years of marriage after her youngest child has grown up and left home.[44] The large number of post-parental marriages may further be illustrated by the following statistics: In 1961 in the United States, there were 14.7 million husband-and-wife families with the male head in the age range of 45 to 64; of those families, 6.3 million (43 percent) had one or more children under 18 years of age at home, while 8.4 million (57 percent) had no children under 18 years of age at home.[45] In the discussion that follows, the age range of the post-parental marriages will be defined as 45 to 64, and old-age marriages as 65 years of age and older.

One might reasonably assume that when a couple have for many years participated minimally in their marital roles and maximally in their parental roles, problems might emerge when suddenly they find that most of their family-role involvement centers around their roles of husband and wife. Yet there is some evidence that the adjustment to post-parental marriage is not as great as has often been assumed, and that there are some available social means for adjusting to the new role demands. Deuscher, in the one major study of this area, suggests that "when urban middle-class post-parental couples describe their life, the hurdle does not appear to have been insurmountable and the adaptations are seldom pathological."[46]

Because of her generally greater involvement in the parental role, one would expect that the wife would be more concerned with post-parental adjustments than would the husband. Deutscher found that a larger percentage of wives assessed the post-parental period *both* more favorably and more unfavorably than did their husbands.[47] This would suggest that men were less influenced either negatively or positively than women because there were fewer adjustments and adaptations for them to make. With the relationship between higher social class and greater commitment and satisfaction

---

[43]Irwin Deutscher, "The Quality of Post-parental Life: Definitions of the Situation," *Journal of Marriage and Family*, February, 1964, p. 52.

[44]Margaret Mead and Frances B. Kaplan (Eds.) *American Women: The Report of the President's Commission* (New York: Charles Scribner's Sons, 1965), p. 89.

[45]Paul C. Glick, "Demographic Analysis of Family Data," in Harold T. Christensen (ed.) *Handbook of Marriage and The Family* (Chicago: Rand McNally and Co., 1964), p. 302.

[46]Irwin Deutscher, "Socialization for Postparental Life," in Arnold Rose (Ed.) *Human Behavior and Social Processes* (New York: Houghton Mifflin Co., 1961), p. 509.

[47]Deutscher, "The Quality of Post-parental Life: Definitions of the Situation," *op. cit.*, p. 58.

derived from marriage, it is not surprising that Deutscher found that upper middle-class spouses had a more favorable outlook with regard to their post-parental life than did their lower middle-class counterparts.[48]

There may be certain transitional learning experiences that directly contribute to the parents' adjustment to their children leaving home, and indirectly to their adjustment to the new demands placed on the marriage relationship. Deutscher suggests that adaptations to children leaving home are helped by the initial parental interpretation of it as a temporary phonomena, often with the parental expectation that the children will at some time again return to live at home. This means that the "temporary" can often change to a permanent separation without any traumatic transition.[49]

What may be most important to the post-parental marriage is how the couple define it and what they expect from their relationship. If for a number of years the marriage stayed together because of the children, then the couple must decide if they want to stay together now that they no longer fill active parental roles. Some couples who appear to have had a smooth marriage surprise their friends by suddenly getting a divorce. Yet as Hunt points out, "there is no mystery about it; they had simply been too busy to notice that they were no longer friends, until their aloneness made it obvious."[50] But it appears that most couples either make a satisfactory adjustment to the post-parental years or decide that staying married is the lesser of alternative evils.

By the time the couple reach old age (65 years of age and over), they constitute a family unit generally made up of only the husband and wife, and have for a number of years. In 1961 in the United States "only 4 percent of the 4.9 million husband-wife families with the head 65 years old and over had any children of their own under 18 still at home."[51]

One very important adjustment that often has to be made in old age and which has many implications for the marriage relationship is the occupational retirement of the husband. What is especially important in contemporary American society is that retirement is a new form of social life, in that it is different from previous patterns of old age, and has not achieved any specific institutional integration. "Past societies have had numbers of aged people, but these

---

[48]*Ibid.*, p. 58.
[49]Deutscher, "Socialization for Postparental Life," *op. cit.*, p. 515.
[50]Hunt, *op. cit.*, p. 219.
[51]Glick, *op. cit.*, p. 302.

were not *retired persons*. They remained integrated in traditional institutional orders through work and kinship roles and relationships."[52] Our interest here is with the impact of retirement on the marriage roles—the man retires from his occupation and spends most of his time at home with his wife.

Donahue suggests that in the normal life cycle a woman has often experienced two or three "retirements" by the time her husband is facing his first retirement. What Donahue means by "retirement" experiences of the woman are that many left jobs for child rearing and thus had experienced that retirement experience during early adulthood. Women also experience retirement in other activities; for example, "when their children grow up and leave the parental home, women experience another retirement from an essential function and have to make adjustments to the cessation of the maternal role."[53] Yet in some cases the woman may find it more difficult to accept her husband's retirement than it was to accept her own retirements. Several studies show that a significant proportion of women do not want their husbands to retire because they believe that they will have more housework to do, "that their daily routine will be disrupted, that they do not want their husbands home all day, and that they will have to live on a lower income."[54]

To suddenly have the husband around for long periods of time puts a strain on many marriages because the husband and wife must interact far more extensively than in the past. As Donahue and her associates describe it, the "daily absence from the home except over the week ends may have enabled many husbands to adjust to marital relationships which under conditions of closer contact they might have found explosive or intolerable."[55]

At present, most generalizations about marriage relationships for both the post-parental and old-age groups are based on limited empirical data and more research into husband and wife interaction during the older years is greatly needed. Not only do we need to know more about husband-wife interaction at different points in time, but also how the marital interactions at earlier points in time are related to the marriage at later time periods.

---

[52]Wilma Donahue, Harold L. Orbach and Otto Pollak, "Retirement: The Emerging Social Pattern," in Clark Tibbitts, *Handbook of Social Gerontology*, (Chicago: The University of Chicago Press, 1960), p. 334.

[53]*Ibid.*, p. 372.

[54]*Ibid.*, p. 371.

[55]*Ibid.*, p. 371.

SOME PROBLEM AREAS

Many individuals enter marriage roles and move through marital interaction encountering few significant problems. To some people, the concept of adjustment implies that individuals are making the best of a rather unpleasant situation. However, adjustment as it has been used in this discussion applies to the relationship of the individual to his marriage role and his role as related to the role of his spouse. For many, the search for adjustment is the search for the most workable and satisfying marital relationship. The characteristic of marital difficulties is common to all societies—at least to the extent that no society has found the means of achieving perfect marital harmony. In some societies, marital conflict is so great that the anthropologist devotes a great deal of space to explaining its nature. But, as Stephens points out, "I know of no case where marriage is so blissful, so free from strife, as to receive special comment from the ethnographer."[56] In the ongoing nature of marriage, some areas inevitably lead to problems.

Extent of Problems

Many couples feel their marriage involves no major problems. In the Burgess and Wallin study, fully half the husbands and wives report no major problems arising in marriage. "These couples, in the main, are those who had made their adjustments during engagement."[57] The Burgess and Wallin sample centered on the young married, many of whom will no doubt encounter major problems later in their marriage. Some further information on areas of adjustment is provided by Landis. He found that among couples who agreed they were adjusted from the start of their marriage, adjustment varied with different areas. For example, of the total number of couples, 76 percent felt they were adjusted in the area of mutual friends, 69 percent in the area of in-law relations and 53 percent in sex relations.[58] We have no way of knowing how a problem in one area affects other areas and the overall marriage relationship.

Consistent with the greater commitment to marriage of the woman, is a greater tendency for women to report problems in their marriages. This appears to be true at most educational and age

---

[56]William N. Stephens, *The Family in Cross-Cultural Perspective* (New York: Holt, Rinehart and Winston, Inc., 1963), p. 231.

[57]Burgess and Wallin, *op. cit.,* p. 618.

[58]Judson T. Landis, "Length of time Required to Achieve Adjustment in Marriage," *American Sociological Review*, December, 1946, p. 668.

levels. Furthermore, when "men do report marriage problems, they are less likely to attribute the cause of these problems to their wives than women are to attribute these problems to their husbands."[59]

For a few couples, a more basic marriage problem may be strong disillusionment with the person married. (A Gallup poll found that 70 percent of young married women said they would definitely marry the same man and 25 percent said they *probably* would.[60]) In this writer's study of the problem, the wives were asked a question which they answered, as follows: "If you had your life to live over, would you—"marry the same person," 85 percent; "marry a different person," 12 percent; "not marry at all," 3 percent.[61] Interestingly, very few wives, after the experience of marriage, view the alternative of remaining single as the more desirable role choice.

Many of the satisfactions as well as problems in marriage involve the ability of the couple to interact effectively. The nature of role interaction is not quantitative, but qualitative, and as such, definable by the couple. In marriage, the individual's ability to fulfill the marriage role for his own sake, as well as for the related personality and role filled by the spouse, is of central importance. This means the individual must not only be adaptable to his own personality and role needs, but to those of his spouse as well.

Burgess and Wallin find some evidence that the wife has a greater tendency to be adaptable to her husband's needs than he has to hers.[62] Given the wife's greater personal commitment to marriage, her greater willingness and ability to adapt is understandable. However, the Burgess and Wallin study also indicates that the wife is generally satisfied with her husband's understandings of *her* feelings and problems. They found that 86 percent of the wives defined their husbands' understanding as at least "all right."[63]

Blood and Wolfe found that the main satisfactions for wives in marriage were: (1) companionship in doing things together with the husband; (2) the chance to have children; (3) the husband's understanding of her problems and feelings; and (4) the husband's expression of love and affection.[64] The writer's study asked the re-

---

[59]Gurin, *op. cit.*, p. 110.
[60]George Gallup, "The Woman's Mind: America's Young Mothers," *Ladies Home Journal*, March, 1962, p. 96.
[61]Bell, *op. cit.*
[62]Burgess and Wallin, *op. cit.*, p. 437.
[63]*Ibid*, p. 214.
[64]Robert O. Blood and Donald M. Wolfe, *Husbands and Wives* (Glencoe, Illinois: The Free Press, 1960), p. 81.

spondents what the most satisfying part of being a wife was: companionship was for 35 percent; being needed and loved, for 28 percent; helping and making the husband happy, for 15 percent; and, all other satisfactions, 22 percent.

It may be estimated that roughly half of all married couples will encounter some important problems in their marriages. If the problems become very severe, many couples will end the marriage, but others will work out, ignore or live with the problems. The impact of problems on a marriage is evidenced by the number of couples that are or have been so dissatisfied with their marriages that they have thought about ending them. A Gallup poll found that 10 percent of the women interviewed had considered the possibility of divorce.[65] In the writer's study of college-educated wives, 14 percent said they had seriously considered divorce.

If needs to be stressed that the wife bears the greater burden or responsibility in marital adjustment. Burgess and Wallin state that "wives appear, on the average, to make the greater adjustment in marriage according to their own testimony and that of their husbands."[66] Some initial adjustment to marriage is probably greater for the wife than for the husband. Marriage, for many women, means a whole new daily routine of taking care of a home, while the occupational role for the man continues pretty much as it did before marriage. However, given the woman's greater commitment to marriage, she often has a greater personal and social investment in its being successful.

The woman's greater involvement in the family often means that she may be playing any one of several different role possibilities reflecting different views held toward her husband and toward her relationships to him. The following types of female role definitions of husband and family have been suggested in the work of Helena Lopata.[67] First, there is the wife who is *primarily husband oriented.* For this woman, even though she may be very involved in her role as mother, or in other roles, her major personal identification and life is built around her husband. A second role definition is the wife who is *sometimes husband oriented.* She may shift away from the husband as she devotes more time and energy to her children or when the husband becomes involved in his career. Third, is the woman who has a basic role identification and *orientation to her*

[65]Gallup, *op. cit.,* p. 96.
[66]Burgess and Wallin, *op. cit.,* p. 618.
[67]See: Helena Z. Lopata, "The Secondary Features of A Primary Relationship," *Human Organization,* Summer, 1965, pp. 116–23.

children. The husband is seen as outside this basic unit of mother and children, as someone who provides and performs tasks for the unit, or toward whom specific duties must be directed. Fourth, may be a *home orientation.* Here the woman's basic role commitment is not to husband or children, but to the home and her possessions in it.

Baber writes that women's two chief complaints are the isolation and monotony of housework, and the 24-hour-per-day care of small children.[68] The writer's study asked what the least satisfying part of being a wife was: 55 percent of the wives answered, "housework"; 14 percent, "boredom and isolation"; 13 percent, "relationships with the husband"; and 18 percent, "miscellaneous."[69]

Husband-Wife Disagreement

Couples can disagree about many things, but certain areas are most common. Blood and Wolfe found that the four most common were money, children, recreation, and personality.[70] As to disagreements and arguments in marriage, this writer asked his respondents two questions. To the first question—How would you estimate the amount of arguing in your marriage?—they answered: never, 1 percent; rarely, 34 percent; sometimes, 55 percent; often, 10 percent. The second question, and their answers were: when disagreements arise, do they usually result in—your (the wife) giving in, 20 percent; husband giving in, 5 percent; agreement by mutual give and take, 75 percent.[71]

Instead of arguing, some individuals may resort to pouting, icy or frozen treatment, or withholding privileges. But in general, these techniques are considered immature and unworthy of the married couple. The more common recourse is to vent disagreements in arguments; because the couple are also close and know each other well, they are usually uninhibited and tend to be frank in what they say.

Family specialists sometimes find themselves in a dilemma over marriage arguments because they are not sure whether they are for them or against them. They sometimes play with words and talk about *quarreling,* which is bad, and *constructive argument,* which is good. This writer suggests that in most marriages disagreements and arguments are going to occur. In fact, it seems probable that the

---

[68]Baber, *op. cit.,* p. 378.
[69]Bell, *op. cit.*
[70]Blood and Wolfe, *op. cit.,* p. 241.
[71]Bell, *op. cit.*

couples who go through married life with a normal amount of daily interaction without ever becoming irritated to the point of disagreement are very deviant social beings. When a couple never argues, it may mean that the persons have no individuality, that one does not recognize the other as being significant enough to disagree with, or that one may not disagree because of fear of the other. In these situations, the reasons for not arguing may be more detrimental to the marital relationship than arguments.

Many marriages develop a closeness of paired relationship never achieved with any other individual outside of marriage. When the relationship is open and unpretentious, the couple may be so frank with each other they are bound to disagree. Some married couples find that arguments can be stimulating and enjoyable. For the married couple who enjoy a give-and-take relationship, arguments can add an important positive dimension to marital interaction.

Along with the positive elements of arguing in marriage go, of course, some dangers. These arise when one of the individuals lets his emotions take over, gets mad and strikes out in every direction he can. The type of person who does this can endanger the marriage relationship. Some writers make a great deal out of this possibility, but whether or not it occurs in any significant number of marriages is not known. Furthermore, to project from the destructively arguing type to the generalization that all argument in marriage is bad is highly questionable. Individuals who randomly strike out at their mate may have severe marital limitations in other directions; their argumentativeness may be a manifestation of more important problems.

There appear to be some general patterns of reacting to marital problems and some general patterns of attempts to solve them that are common to middle-class couples. Though of course not all problems are of equal significance in various marriages, or in the same marriage over time, very often the problems defined as important are those close to the basic needs of the spouse doing the defining. One study found that the "two most important areas of disturbance in unhappy marriages concern the fulfillment of each other's needs and the kind of interaction which prevails between the spouses if basic needs are not satisfied."[72]

The belief that "talking out" is an important means of achieving some resolution to marriage problems is common, but it is most

---

[72]Vincent D. Mathews and Clement S. Mihanovich, "New Orientations on Marital Maladjustment," *Marriage and Family Living*, August, 1963, p. 304.

often found among higher educated and higher social class couples.[73] Some topics lend themselves to discussion more readily than others. For example, one study reports that "husbands say they talk openly about violations of expectations in the area of finances but not in the area of frequency of sexual intimacy."[74]

Also basic to problem-solving in marriage is the relative degree of commitment to the marriage by each of the partners. Here we have the principle of least interest, "namely that the one who cares more in any relationship is at a disadvantage vis-a-vis the one who cares less. The person who cannot tolerate quarreling and bickering will give more concessions than the spouse to whom it means less."[75]

One of the ironies of life is that solving one problem may result in a new problem. One partner, may effectively bring about changes in the behavior of the spouse only to find that the changed behavior creates new problems. For example, in studies of wives of alcoholics who had learned to control their problem, the wives were greatly disappointed by the results. Some women found "that they preferred the man who, however difficult he might have been intoxicated, was more lovable when sober than the man who is sober always."[76]

Parent and In-law Problems

The relationship of parents and in-laws to their young married children provides a logical point for concluding the discussion on marriage. The initial relationship is commonly a problem and involves both the couple who are starting marriage and their parents who are well along in the marriage relationship.

After marriage, the young couple have generally moved into adult statuses; however, for many, the movement is not sharp and distinct, but rather slow and evolving. Because the new roles of marriage are not always clearly distinguished from certain of the role aspects of being single, problems may emerge. One problem area develops from the fact that after marriage the couple do not always move completely away from the control and influence of their parents. A popular image in the United States is that in-law conflict is an expected consequence of marriage. Many young people think of

---

[73]See: Mirra Komarovsky, *Blue-Collar Marriage,* (New York: Random House, 1962), p. 195.

[74]Beverly R. Cutler and William G. Dyer, "Initial Adjustment Processes in Young Married Couples," *Social Forces,* December, 1965, p. 201.

[75]Bernard, *op. cit.,* p. 730.

[76]See: *Ibid.,* p. 695.

marriage and in-law conflict as being inevitable and, for them, it may turn out to be a "self-fulfilling prophecy." Of course, many times conflict with parents is due to more than simple anticipation. The nature of different family roles and their relationship to one another in the American middle class contribute to potential difficulties. The parents are faced with certain problems when their children marry. They see their young adult child not only in his present role, but also in all the roles he has filled from infancy on. The parents have taken the responsibility for rearing their child and making many of his decisions for him, and they often continue this to some degree right up until he marries. But once he marries, the parents often find that their child no longer listens, or that he no longer considers they have the right to instruct him. Some parents find this sudden shift in their role difficult to accept. In some cases, the role loss may lead to hostility directed at the offspring's spouse. Because of their emotional commitment to their own child, it may be difficult for the parents to recognize that the relationship has changed; the spouse may provide a convenient scapegoat.

The parents must also face the fact of "losing" their offspring to someone for marriage. The parents may have an exaggerated notion of their child's worth and they may view the person he marries as unworthy of him. "The father and mother of the newly married person necessarily overvalue their own child and cannot believe that anyone is quite good enough for him; they are thereafter highly critical of the newcomer in the group."[77] The parents' relationships to the offspring and his mate are complicated because each parent, in reference to the young married couple, is cast both in the role of parent and parent-in-law, and each member of the new marriage is cast as an offspring and an offspring-in-law.

The young married couple must also recognize that they have been through many roles in relationship to their parents, and that this may lead to difficulty when they marry and move into new role relationships with their parents and with their spouse. A long pattern of turning to parents for help has been established for many; it is not always easily ended with marriage. It may be viewed as threatening by the spouse in the new marriage. The young wife who feels her husband is turning to his mother when she feels he should be turning to her, will often see her wife role as being threatened.

Each of the newly married pair may also have a tendency to compare his spouse with his own parent of the same sex. This may have

---

[77]Waller and Hill, *op. cit.*, p. 290.

unfortunate consequences; the two compared are not role equals: one has been in the role for a long time and the other is just beginning it. The husband who compares his wife to his mother as a cook is comparing a novice to a woman with years of experience. He is also comparing what his mother, who has, in many cases, conditioned his tastes, thinks is "good cooking," to what his young wife, who may have very different tastes, thinks is "good cooking." The very fact that the young wife is in a new role often means role insecurity for her; comparing her to her mother-in-law may play upon this insecurity.

Another important element of the parent-married child relationship is that each has been a member of his family of orientation since birth. The cliché that at marriage "one doesn't lose a son (or daughter), but gains a daughter (or son)" is not wholly accurate. The son or daughter gained is an adult son or daughter, shaped and influenced by another family of orientation. When he enters into interaction with his in-laws, they enter with a limited knowledge of and experience with his family's background. Over the years, each family acquires a family culture both like and unlike other families. In the area of the unlike, the new in-law is a stranger. The wife and her family may talk about people and events of the past that mean nothing to the husband. While they may try to bring him into things by telling him about the past, he can never directly be a part of it.

Burgess and Wallin write that "in-laws constitute a problem of adjustment or unadjustment or even maladjustment in many marriages,"[78] and other studies indicate clearly that in-law problems are fairly common in the American middle class of today.[79] Yet there are very often contradictions with regard to the in-laws as problems. For example, one study found that the commonest complaint by young couples about their in-laws was that they were meddlesome and dominating. But the second most common complaint was that the in-laws were "distant, indifferent, thoughtless, and unappreciative."[80]

Mother-in-law and Daughter-in-law. The Landises, in their study of 116 husbands and 160 wives reporting various in-law conflict, found that 50 percent of the wives had a problem with their

---

[78]Burgess and Wallin, *op. cit.*, p. 603.
[79]See: *Ibid.;* Judson T. Landis and Mary G. Landis, *Building a Successful Marriage* (New York: Prentice-Hall, Inc., 1953); and Sheldon Stryker, "The Adjustment of Married Offspring to Their Parents," *American Sociological Review*, April, 1955, pp. 149–54.
[80]Quoted in: Bernard, *op. cit.*, p. 727.

mothers-in-law, making this the most frequent in-law conflict.[81] In the writer's study, college-educated wives estimated their relationships with the mother-in-law, when they could be assessed, as: very good and good, 75 percent; and fair or poor, 25 percent.[82] When the Landises computed the frequency of conflict with specific in-laws, the mother-in-law led the list and coming second, slightly ahead of the father-in-law, was the sister-in-law.[83] This indicates the female nature of in-law conflict. This is further supported in a study by Komarovsky who found that one third of the wives revealed serious dissatisfactions with their in-laws, whereas the husbands enjoyed fairly satisfactory in-law relationships.[84]

The adult roles of the mother-in-law and the daughter-in-law contribute to the frequency of conflict in their relationship. The important fact is that though their adult roles are essentially the same, they are two individuals with many differences in role experience. The young wife usually brings into marriage the training she received from her mother, and as a result may have ways of doing things different from her mother-in-law's ways. If the daughter-in-law rejects suggestions by the mother-in-law, she is questioning the way the mother-in-law has been doing things for many years; she is indirectly criticizing the mother-in-law's fulfillment of her role. On the other hand, for the daughter to accept the mother-in-law's way of doing things may indicate to her own mother a rejection of the way *she* has played her role. Thus, the young wife may be caught between two experienced women trying to show her how she should fill her new role. It is also important to note that many aspects of the woman's role and her efficiency and success are publicly available for assessment. How a woman manages her home or prepares a meal can be evaluated and compared, particularly by her relatives.

Competition between the mother-in-law and daughter-in-law for the son and husband may also occur. With the effective development of her marriage role, the daughter-in-law inevitably replaces her mother-in-law in many areas in which the mother-in-law in the past received her son's love and admiration.

Mother-in-law and Son-in-law. In more than half of the cultures of the world, a man and his mother-in-law are expected to avoid each other. Shlein points out that Americans have developed patterns of hostility and rejection that are never directed at the son

[81]Landis and Landis, *op. cit.*, p. 289.
[82]Bell, *op. cit.*
[83]Landis and Landis, *op. cit.*, p. 289.
[84]Komarovsky, *op. cit.*, p. 259.

or daughter-in-law, but only at the mother-in-law. This strong hostility is reflected in our humor. For example—Definition of conflicting emotions: You see your mother-in-law driving over a cliff in your new Cadillac.[85] The Landises found that 42 percent of the husbands in their study reported the mother-in-law as the main cause of in-law friction;[86] but on the other hand, "A mother is more likely to accept her son-in-law at par than her daughter-in-law."[87] The mother-in-law and son-in-law are of the opposite sexes in their role performances and cannot be personally compared. The mother-in-law may become critical of the son-in-law in his role of husband if he does not treat her daughter in the way she thinks he should. But because his world is so different from hers, possible areas for criticism are limited.

Probably the more important source of conflict comes from the feelings of the son-in-law. Because controls over behavior are usually longer and greater for the girl than the boy, the mother may have greater difficulty giving up the controls over her daughter when she marries. The son-in-law may feel that his mother-in-law is overstepping her rights and treading on his as husband if she continues to influence his wife.

Because of the mother's close emotional involvement with her daughter, and because she herself has been a wife for many years, she may feel that her daughter should listen to her advice on the role of the husband. Some mothers may want to shape their daughters' husbands into an image they have had for but not realized in their own husbands. Others may tell their daughters how to behave in the role of wife in a way that worked for them in their marriages, forgetting that the daughter's husband may be very different from their own. Komarovsky, in her study of the lower middle class found that the following conditions tended to be associated with an unsatisfactory relationship between the husband and his mother-in-law: "marriage to a better-educated wife; wife's hostility towards her mother; wife's emotional dependence upon her mother; and economic and social interdependence, including a joint household with in-laws."[88]

Father-in-law and Daughter-in-law. The Landises found only 11 percent of the young wives had a problem in this relationship, making it the one of least frequent conflict.[89] The father generally

[85]John M. Shlein, "Mother-in-Law: A Problem of Kinship Terminology," in Hyman Rodman (ed.) *Marriage, Family and Society* (New York: Random House, 1965), p. 199.
[86]Landis and Landis, *op. cit.*, p. 289.
[87]Baber, *op. cit.*, p. 221.
[88]Komarovsky, *op. cit.*, p. 261.
[89]Landis and Landis, *op. cit.*, p. 289.

has much less influence on the day-to-day rearing of his children and is therefore less involved after they marry. Also, because the daughter-in-law is filling an opposite adult sex role, he has little reason to compare her role with his.

The husband's father may see the daughter-in-law in a somewhat romantic light. Their relationship may be characterized by a kind of flirting very ego-satisfying to the father because of his older age and the youthfulness of his daughter-in-law. The daughter-in-law herself may be attracted, because many times the father-in-law has many of the same characteristics that her husband has. Hence, the role relationships between a father-in-law and daughter-in-law may provide a socially approved role relationship between a male and a female in which some degree of intimacy is acceptable.

Father-in-law and Son-in-law. Only 15 percent of the husbands in the Landis study named the fathers-in-law as the in-law causing friction.[90] Baber points out the jealousy of the father toward his son-in-law does not seem to exist, at least to the degree that is troublesome.[91] The important role difference, when compared with the mother-in-law and daughter-in-law relationship, is that, while the two males have the same primary role responsibilities, they are not usually subject to detailed and public comparison.

Both have the primary responsibility of earning a living, and if the father-in-law accepts the son-in-law's ability to do so, conflict is not apt to emerge. *How* the one fills his occupational role is not usually subject to observation by the other; the variety of occupations that a male can fill are almost endless, and most of them are known only in a very general way to persons not in them. It is probably important that the father-in-law respect the occupational role of the son-in-law, but he usually does, because of the social class similarity of individuals who marry.

Unlike the mother, the father is much less apt, even though experienced as a husband, to try to influence his son-in-law in that role. However, the father's concern may emerge if he feels the son-in-law is overstepping the rather broad limits of the husband's role. He may then feel called upon to perform as his daughter's protector. But generally, if the son-in-law is at least adequate in his important occupational role, his behavior in the husband's role is not of major importance to the father-in-law.

In-laws as Grandparents. One of the contradictions in stereo-

---

[90]*Ibid.*, p. 289.
[91]Baber, *op. cit.*, p. 221.

typed role images in the American society centers around the same person filling two different roles, the mother as mother-in-law and the mother as grandmother. Often the stereotype of the mother-in-law is of a hard, interfering battle-ax, while the stereotype of grandmother is a kindly lady handing out sugar cookies to her adoring grandchildren. The fact is that neither stereotype is very accurate.

In some situations of in-law conflict, the influence of grandchildren may be positive. They may provide a common focus of emotional and social involvement for both parents and grandparents. Many times the grandparents get a great deal of pleasure out of their grandchildren; they can deal with them pleasurably and without the responsibility of rearing them.

In other situations, grandchildren may provide an area of conflict. The dispute often involves the question of how the children should be reared, and it usually occurs between the mother-in-law and the daughter-in-law. Disputes arise because one has reared children in the past while the other is doing it in the present, and because of differences in training and attitudes. The mother-in-law has a rather devastating argument to use in support of her notions on childrearing if she chooses to use it. She can argue that her methods were obviously successful—the daughter-in-law chose to marry her son. To this argument, the wife has little recourse; she can hardly say that her husband grew up the way he did despite his mother.

While this discussion has pointed out possible in-law conflicts, it should not be assumed that they are inevitable. In most marriages, adjustments with the parents of both the husband and the wife will have to be made. But as Burgess and Wallin found, "in many cases little if any adjustment is necessary."[92] Perhaps, certain social changes are emerging in the American middle class that are or will decrease the extent of in-law conflict.

One factor of change, a decrease in the generational difference between the parents and their married children, has several causes. Two of these are the younger ages of marriage and the changes in "aging" resulting from increased knowledge in the medical and health areas. The young married couple and their parents are, therefore, much more apt to be closer age peers in a social and psychological sense than they were in the past. As a result, their pattern of life may be closer than has previously been the case.

A second factor is that in the middle class, with a high degree of

---

[92]Burgess and Wallin, *op. cit.,* p. 603.

geographical mobility for the younger generation, the parents and children often have limited contact after marriage. Increasingly, they are not living near each other and they may have to travel long distances to visit. Because they see less of each other, chances of strain that develop over long and continuous contact are reduced. When they do get together, it may be within a vacation setting rather than one of duty or obligation relationship. In some cases, however, this less frequent but more intense visiting may cause problems because the interactional demands are continuous.

SELECTED BIBLIOGRAPHY

BERNARD, JESSIE. "The Adjustments of Married Mates," in HERALD T. CHRISTENSEN (ed.) *Handbook of Marriage and The Family* (Chicago: Rand McNally & Co., 1964), pp. 675–739.

BLOOD, ROBERT O., and WOLFE, DONALD M. *Husbands and Wives.* Glencoe, Illinois: The Free Press, 1960.

BUERKLE, JACK V., ANDERSON, THEODORE R., and BADGLEY, ROBIN F. "Altruism, Role Conflict and Marital Adjustment: A Factor Analysis of Marital Interaction," *Marriage and Family Living,* February, 1961, pp. 20–26.

BURGESS, ERNEST W., and COTTRELL, LEONARD S. *Predicting Success or Failure in Marriage.* New York: Prentice-Hall, Inc., 1939.

BURGESS, ERNEST W., and WALLIN, PAUL. *Engagement and Marriage,* chaps. xv, xvi, xvii. Chicago: J. B. Lippincott Company, 1953.

CUTLER, BEVERLY R., and WILLIAM G. DYER. "Initial Adjustment Processes in Young Married Couples." *Social Forces,* December, 1965, pp. 195–201.

DEUTSCHER, IRWIN. "The Quality of Post-parental Life: Definitions of the Situation," *Journal of Marriage and Family,* February, 1964, pp. 52–59.

DONAHUE, WILMA, HAROLD L. ORBACH, and OTTE POLLAK. "Retirement: The Emerging Social Pattern," in CLARK TIBBITTS (ed.) *Handbook of Social Gerontology,* Chicago: The University of Chicago Press, 1960, pp. 330–406.

FOOTE, NELSON N. "New Roles for Men and Women," *Marriage and Family Living,* November, 1961, pp. 325–29.

HAMILTON, GILBERT V. *A Research in Marriage.* New York: Albert & Charles Boni, Inc., 1929.

HUNT, MORTON. *Her Infinite Variety.* New York: Harper & Row, Publishers, 1962.

KIRKPATRICK, CLIFFORD. *What Science Says About Happiness in Marriage.* Minneapolis: Burgess Publishing Co., 1947.

———— *The Family,* chaps. xv, xviii and appendix. New York: The Ronald Press Co., 1955.

LOPATA, HELENA Z. "The Secondary Features of A Primary Relationship," *Human Organization,* Summer, 1965, pp. 116–23.

LOCKE, HARVEY J. *Predicting Adjustment in Marriage: A Comparison of a Divorced and a Happily Married Group.* New York: Henry Holt & Co., 1951.

MOORE, JOAN W. "Patterns of Women's Participation in Voluntary Associations," *American Journal of Sociology,* May, 1961, pp. 592–98.

PINEO, PETER C. "Disenchantment in the Later Years of Marriage," *Marriage and Family Living,* February, 1961, pp. 3–11.

STRYKER, SHELDON. "The Adjustment of Married Offspring to Their Parents," *American Sociological Review,* April, 1955, pp. 149–54.

TERMAN, LEWIS M. *Psychological Factors in Marital Happiness.* New York: McGraw-Hill Book Co., 1938.

CHAPTER 12

MARRIAGE, FAMILY,
AND OCCUPATIONAL ROLES

In the American middle class, the most important adult role filled by the male is usually that of his occupation, and the most important adult role for the female is usually that of wife-mother. Nonetheless, the middle-class male's involvements in his family roles are often strong, and there are many women adding to their traditional adult roles of wife and mother by participation in occupational roles. However, the *relationships* between occupational roles and family roles have not been the subject of much study.[1] One pair of researchers has observed that the relationships between work and family life have seldom been studied explicitly by family sociologists and that other approaches—such as those of industrial sociology or occupational psychology—have usually treated each institution as a relatively closed system.[2]

In American society today, the work settings of men and women generally function separately; the man goes off to his place of work and the woman does her work at home. But this pattern of sex separation is of fairly recent origin. Before the industrial revolution, most men and women were co-workers on the land and in the home. "Women worked in the fields when the chores of the home and childrearing permitted, so that there was not only close association between work and home for both sexes, but even a certain amount of overlap in the sexual division of labor."[3] One of the most important historical changes in the family was the removal of the woman (and children) as contributors to economic production; and with increasing specialization of occupational roles, the man was increasingly removed physically and psychologically from the home.[4]

---

[1]Jesse R. Pitts, "The Structural-Functional Approach," in Harold T. Christensen (ed.) *Handbook of Marriage and the Family*, (Chicago: Rand McNally & Co., 1964), p. 102.

[2]Robert Rapoport and Rhona Rapoport, "Work and Family in Contemporary Society," *American Sociological Review*, June, 1965, p. 382.

[3]Carl N. Degler, "The Changing Place of Women in America," *Daedalus*, Spring, 1964, p. 654.

[4]*Ibid.*, p. 654.

At the same time that the man was being pulled out of the home to fill his occupational role, the family was becoming increasingly specialized in the functions of socialization and emotional support for its members. It was then that in those areas the woman took on her major role responsibilities.[5] The generally strong emotional commitment acquired by middle class wife-mothers continues to exist to the present day. Therefore, when they take on occupational roles, it is often to supplement their traditional roles rather than to replace them.

One important consequence of the man's great involvement in his occupational role and the woman's in her family roles is that a good part of their individual daily life occurs in quite different social settings. Hunt describes the different worlds for the upper middle-class man and woman as follows: "Between his twenties and his forties he spends about five thousand working days dealing with other human beings, acquiring knowledge in his field, experiencing something of the larger world he lives in, and attaining a measure of personal and professional stature."[6] By contrast, his wife during the same years, spends them with "her children, her housekeeping, and her fellow homemakers; she is very likely to emerge from motherhood in her forties with little more than the talents and stature she had in girlhood, somewhat faded from disuse."[7]

In the discussion that follows, we will first look at the changing nature of the American middle-class woman's roles—with particular stress on her family roles as related to her increasing involvement in occupational roles—and then we will examine the occupational roles of the middle-class male to see how those are related to his family roles. Conflicts and problems related to these roles and to middle-class marriage are best understood within a context of social change.

CHANGING ROLES OF THE WOMAN

Changes in women's roles also imply alterations in the related roles of husbands and children. In the past, the general, overall role for the woman was clear and relatively simple—her primary adult role was that of wife-mother. She met certain needs of the husband, had the main responsibility for the care and rearing of children, and maintained the home. While she might have frustrations and dissat-

---

[5]Hyman Rodman, "Talcott Parsons' View of the Changing American Family," *Merrill-Palmer Quarterly*, Volume 11, No. 3, 1965, pp. 217–18.

[6]Morton M. Hunt, *Her Infinite Variety*, (New York: Harper & Row, 1962), p. 220.

[7]*Ibid.*, p. 221.

isfactions in filling the traditional wife-mother role, the role was generally accepted as the "natural" behavior pattern for women. It was natural because it was what women had been doing for centuries, and few other significant adult roles were being filled by women to indicate any alternatives. The naturalness of the traditional wife-mother role is illustrated by the resistance of large numbers of women to the 19th Amendment; many women thought that giving women the right to vote would be to go against her nature, since she had not had that right in the past. But although the division of labor between husband and wife often appears natural the relationship is not necessarily due to inherent biological capabilities or limitations of the two sexes.[8]

Historically, many social factors led to changes in the woman's traditional role. Technological advances brought about alterations of the institutional family, as well as the specific roles within the family context, and led to increasing numbers of women in the work force, reduction of household chores, and the emergence of agencies taking over many traditional family functions. But the social forces that brought about significant changes in the actual roles available to American women were slow in development. For example, the first organized resistance to what had been accepted as natural roles for women did not occur until 1848—at Seneca Falls, New York. That convention came to the conclusion "that woman had too long rested content in the narrow limits worked out for her by corrupt customs and a perverted application of the scriptures" and that women should now secure their rights.[9] For many years after that first meeting the dominant view continued to be that the woman should remain in the home as a wife and mother. And well into the 20th century the woman who did not marry continued to be seen as a person to pity because she had failed in her basic adult role. As Peterson points out, if her family was not able to support her, she often had to try and find one of the few jobs available to women or move in with a married brother or sister and help them as a housekeeper and in the rearing of their children.[10]

By the 1920's the traditional roles assigned to women had been altered and they had established their rights to (if not always social acceptance of) a lack of restriction during their adult years. Degler

---

[8]William N. Stephens, *The Family in Cross-Cultural Perspective,* (New York: Holt, Rinehart & Winston, Inc., 1963), p. 281.

[9]Quoted in: Arthur W. Calhoun, *A Social History of the American Family,* Vol. II, (New York: Barnes & Noble, Inc., 1960), p. 119.

[10]Esther Peterson, "Working Women," *Daedalus,* Spring, 1964, p. 673.

points out that since the Twenties there have been few changes in the position of women that were not evident in that crucial decade, and that over the intervening years the "changes have penetrated more deeply and spread more widely through the social structure."[11] One illustration of basic change that occurred in the 1920's for women was in their styles of dress. The changes in dress represented —both symbolically and physically—a greater freedom. Women threw out "the corset and the numerous petticoats in favor of light under-garments, a single slip, silk or rayon stockings, short skirts and bobbed hair."[12] Except for a few minor variations, women of today dress about the same as did the women of the 1920's.[13]

Factors of Change

Education. Increased formal education is a characteristic of American young people. The number and percentage going on to college is constantly increasing. For example, in 1962, the median number of years of school completed was 12 for women and 11.6 for men. With entrance into college, the proportion of girls fall be-hind; the class entering college in 1962, for example, was made up of only 42 percent women,[14] and only one in three of the bachelor's and master's degrees conferred by universities and colleges go to women, only one in ten of the Ph.D.'s. These ratios represent a significant decrease since the 1930's, when two out of five bachelor's and master's degrees and one out of seven Ph.D.'s were earned by women.[15]

A higher level of education for more women has had a strong influence on both the definition and acceptance of the traditional wife-mother role. The college-educated female often moves directly from college into marriage and, for many, the college and the mar-riage roles overlap. In contrast to the male, a college education is not a serious career preparation for most young women. Even with-out career interests, however, the educational process creates for many women a sense of intellectual need and interest, which they find difficult to satisfy within the traditional female role setting.

The writer asked a sample of 196 college-educated women married 10 years or less the following question: "Do you ever feel that there should be something more to your life than being a wife (and

---

[11]Degler, *op. cit.*, p. 659.

[12]*Ibid.*, p. 657.

[13]*Ibid.*, p. 657.

[14]Margaret Mead and Frances B. Kaplan (eds.) *American Women: The Report of the President's Commission*, (New York: Charles Scribner's Sons, 1965), p. 27.

[15]Peterson, *op. cit.*, pp. 676–77.

mother) and taking care of a home?" The responses were: often, 43 percent; sometimes, 47 percent; and, never, 10 percent.[16] These findings do not mean that the women were unhappy with marriage, but rather they indicate agreement among college-educated wives that the traditional wife-mother role does not completely meet their personal needs.

It is of interest that the educated woman today does not see her education as detrimental to marriage. In the past, higher education was negatively correlated with the woman's chances for marriage. For example, around 1900 more than 25 percent of all women who graduated from college never married.[17] Today, the college-graduate coed has a high marriage probability, although she marries at age 22, about 2 years later than the national median.

Even though the highly educated college graduate has a high marriage rate, it is of interest to look at how they relate their education to marriage. One question in the study by this writer asked: "How do you feel your college education has contributed to your being a wife?" The responses were: helped, 84 percent; no influence, 14 percent; and hindered, 2 percent.[18] These data indicate a high positive assessment of extended education as a help for marriage. Of course, this may be a rationalization; the respondents were married college graduates.

For a woman to say that her education has contributed to the success of her marriage does not necessarily mean that she is completely satisfied with that marriage. For example, one study found that college-educated women were more apt to have feelings of inadequacy about their marriage than were women of lower educational levels.[19] It may be that higher-educated women have more critical and inquiring minds than women with less education and, as a result, may feel greater marital satisfaction at the same time that they recognize inadequacies or problems in their marriages.

Legal Rights. In the past, the woman's legal position in American society was basically that of a second-class citizen, and the term *emancipation* was used with reference to women as well as to slaves.[20] The emergence of the Woman's Rights Movement was primarily motivated by a desire to acquire legal rights and privileges. In the

[16]Robert R. Bell, unpublished research.

[17]Degler, *op. cit.*, p. 666.

[18]Bell, *op. cit.*

[19]Gerald Gurin, Joseph Veroff and Sheila Feld, *Americans View Their Mental Health*, (New York: Basic Books, 1960), p. 113.

[20]Jessie Bernard, *Social Problems at Midcentury*, (New York: The Dryden Press, 1957), p. 342.

present century, woman has achieved a closer approximation in legal equality to man, even though equality is not complete in a number of areas. The laws that discriminate against women generally do so for two reasons: first, she is still seen as not having the abilities or rights to do some things that men can do; and second, laws are made to "protect" her on the assumption that woman must, by the nature of her sex, be given special legal protection. An illustration of the first reason is that in three states women may not serve on juries of the state courts, and an illustration of the second reason is that in 26 states (and the District of Columbia) women called for jury duty may claim exemptions for reasons *not* available to men.[21]

One area of increasing legal equality has been in the realm of politics. However, women generally have not entered politics; when they have, it has been at the lower level of local politics. Women politicians are not common in state and national offices, but women have been influential in voting and in electing certain candidates, and it is generally assumed that there is a "woman's vote," at least in the broad sense that certain candidates and issues have a stronger appeal to women than to men.

Pregnancy Control. In the past, a woman had little control over pregnancy and, as a result, had a large number of children—often with disastrous effects on health and life expectancy. She also had to care for this large number of children. With the development and use of more effective means of controlling pregnancy, the middle-class woman has been freed to a great extent from unwanted pregnancies and this has contributed to her better health, longer life expectancy, and decreased time demands on her as a mother. Along with increased control of pregnancy have come technological changes contributing to a reduction of many household drudgeries, which has made the care of children somewhat easier.

Role Confusion

The loss of many of the traditional functions of the past has led to a .change in the woman's acceptance of appropriate behavior. However, the woman of today is still influenced in many ways by the traditional wife-mother role. As a result, she sometimes feels guilt. Since the traditional role was good enough for her mother, she wonders why it is not good enough for her. The young woman often fails to realize that she fills the wife-mother role in a social setting quite different from that of her mother. Therefore, what was socially ap-

---

[21]Mead, *op. cit.,* p. 67.

propriate for her mother may not, because of change, be socially appropriate for her. Many times the modern woman's problems of role adjustment are not due to personal inadequacy, but rather to social inadequacy. The old roles are no longer appropriate and new ones of equal social and personal acceptance have not been developed.

Role confusion is often a problem for the education woman because no new, intellectually satisfying role has been developed for her. Since the traditional wife-mother role has limited intellectual meaning, the modern woman may try to satisfy her needs through various agencies outside the home. She may enter the work force, return to school, participate in social and political activities, attend lectures and discussion groups, and so forth.

More personal factors are also related to the modern woman's role problems. Even the emancipated woman with many achievements may feel that the woman's role has special problems compared to the man's role, that the woman's role is inferior to that of the man and that her lot in life is second best. To the survey question, "If you could be born over again, would you rather be a man or a woman?", only 3 percent of the men said they would rather be women, but 25 percent of the women said they would rather be men.[22] A number of women imply a rejection of their biological sex because it forces them into social roles with many personal frustrations.

The changing rights and privileges of the modern female often lead to role confusion. The woman has achieved greater equality in some but not all ways. This more approximate equality has reduced male-female differences in many areas of behavior. As a result, the female is often neither meaningfully like nor unlike the male. Yet, a great deal of male-female role interaction continues to operate in the same way that it did when the sex roles were more sharply different.

One of the problems related to sex equality is the degree and type of equality. Rossi suggests a view of sex equality where the roles of men and women would be equal and similar "in such spheres as intellectual, artistic, political and occupational interests and participation, complementary only in those spheres dictated by physiological differences between the sexes."[23] This suggests a view which says: human being first, male or female second. This view is dif-

---

[22]Ray E. Baber, *Marriage and the Family*. (New York: McGraw-Hill Book Co., 1953), p. 378.
[23]Alice S. Rossi, "Equality Between the Sexes," *Daedalus*, Spring, 1964, p. 608.

ferent from that of the early feminists who wanted women to become completely equal by adapting a masculine stance in the world.[24]

The decreasing differences in sex roles lead to certain confusions in the perception of the opposite sex role and how one thinks his sex role is viewed by the opposite sex. Women may desire qualities in the male that he does not perceive as a part of the male sex role. When women describe their ideal man, they select favorable female characteristics as often as they select male characteristics. McKee and Sherrifs found "a pressure by women to have men more oriented to interpersonal relations and more expressive of human (feminine in the stereotype) feelings."[25] While the woman may want the man to be masculine in a traditional sense, she also wants him to possess what have been traditionally female qualities and, as a result, women often want in men qualities that have been traditionally contradictory.

Another related problem in male-female role interaction is how much equality the woman *really* wants. Most women want to maintain the important achieved rights of social equality: the right to vote, educational and occupational opportunities, and so forth. At the same time, many women still want the preferential treatment the female was accorded in the past when she was defined as the inferior sex. For example, the female still wants the male to hold doors for her and to help her into automobiles, and she rationalizes this by arguing that this behavior is not symbolic of inferiority but rather a matter of courtesy. Yet, courtesy is not limited by sex differences, while many of the traditional sex "courtesy" patterns are. As Baber writes "the same young women who vote emphatically for the maintenance of male gallantries insist upon equality in other areas of behavior."[26] Hunt writes that many of the patterns of male politeness that please and flatter the female are "symbolic of the frailty and inferiority she acquiesces in; when he takes her arm, holds her coat, orders the dinner, or pays the bill, she feels a pleasant little triumph in being taken care of, yet the triumph is gained only by accepting the tradition of her own passivity and weakness."[27] Women often argue for equality in areas where they feel exploited,

---

[24]*Ibid.*, p. 608.

[25]John P. McKee and Alex C. Sherrifs, "Men's and Women's Beliefs, Ideals and Self-Concepts," in Jerome M. Seidman, *The Adolescent* (New York: Holt, Rinehart & Winston, Inc., 1960), p. 291.

[26]Baber, *op. cit.*, p. 377.

[27]Hunt, *op. cit.*, p. 232.

but want to maintain inequality in the areas where they may do the exploiting.

The social and personal factors thus far discussed give some indication of the confused nature of what it means to be a middle-class woman today. The implication is that many of the modern middle-class woman's difficulties are due to a social role definition that does not adequately provide a framework for appropriate behavior. Many writers who deal with this problem suggest that the modern woman has a variety of available roles. They imply that her only real problem is one of role choice, and that once she makes the choice the behavior pattern is relatively well organized. This may be true in some cases as, for example, in the clear and unambiguous choice of pursuing a career to the point of excluding other role possibilities. But, for the majority of women, the choice is not so clear-cut because none of the possible role alternatives clearly defines a total set of behavior patterns. Both the elements of the general role and their application for a given woman change over time, which also adds to the confusion. What often results is the joining together of different behavioral definitions into a patchwork role. Basically, the problem is that women are caught between an impossible backward-looking definition of their role and a not-yet-established definition of new one.[28]

Most women want children and want to maintain a home of their own. In a large number of cases, the marriage will be felt to be lacking if the traditional expectations are not achieved. The difference today is that the woman often wants something more. This does not necessarily mean that she loves her husband, children, and home any less; but because of greater time and more greatly developed capacities for other interests, she has other strong desires that need fulfillment. Often the young women of today seems to view an accommodation of roles as her goal and this suggests that there is no inherent conflict between work and marriage. Rostow points out that women are only required to discover empirical compromises between the two roles and many women are in the process of doing so rather effectively and cheerfully.[29]

The confusion of modern woman's role can be further delineated by looking at some of her important activities and their related problems. Although specific areas of activity can be discussed separately, each area affects and is affected by the other.

---

[28]Bernard, *op. cit.*, p. 346.
[29]Edna G. Rostow, "Conflict and Accommodation," *Daedalus*, Spring, 1964, pp. 743–44.

THE WORKING WIFE AND MOTHER

The combining of marriage and parental roles with an occupational role is for large numbers of women something new. For example, in 1920, only 10 percent of all married women were in the work force.[30] By 1962 this proportion had increased to 32 percent and these married women comprised 56 percent of all working women.[31] The balance of the female work force was made up of 23 percent single women and 21 percent widowed, divorced or separated.[32]

Nye and Hoffman observe that over recent decades "a transition was made from a situation in which women were *forced* into employment with their labor the primary source of family income, to one in which women are *drawn* into employment to raise family living standards or for other reasons."[33] There are often social-class differences as to how women view or define their work participation. Lower-class women tend to see their jobs as labor and value them only for the money they earn. By comparison, upper middle-class women see their jobs as occupations to be valued not only for income but also because of the personal satisfactions derived from them. (This social-class difference is also generally true for how men view their occupations.)

Although women today enter occupations for many different reasons, they continue to enter those occupations that have been traditionally filled by women. Degler points out that "in 1950 almost three quarters of all employed women fell into twenty occupational categories, of which the largest was stenographers, typists and secretaries—a category that first became prominent as a woman's occupation over a half century ago."[34] Furthermore, if we look at occupations generally classified as professional, we find that about two thirds of all professional women are either nurses or teachers. And women are notoriously under-represented in the most prestigeful professions such as law and medicine. For example, in 1950 in the U.S. only 6 percent of all medical doctors and 4 percent of all lawyers and judges were women. "In contrast, almost three quarters of medical doctors

---

[30]Hyman Rodman, *Marriage, Family and Society* (New York: Random House, 1965), p. 291.

[31]Peterson, *op. cit.*, p. 674.

[32]*Ibid.*, p. 674.

[33]F. Ivan Nye and Lois W. Hoffman, *The Employed Mother In America*, (Chicago: Rand McNally & Co., 1963), p. 13.

[34]Degler, *op. cit.*, p. 661.

are women in the Soviet Union; in England the figure is 16 percent. In both France and Sweden women make up a high proportion of pharmacists and dentists; neither of these professions attracts many women in the U.S."[35]

The lower status of women's occupations is also reflected in the lower incomes they received when compared to men. In 1962, for full-time, year-'round workers, the median income of women was $3,458. For men it was $5,826. "This gap is partly the result of a difference in occupational patterns; the kind of work performed by women is traditionally low paid."[36]

There are several other social factors related to women working. An increasing number of women with higher levels of education are entering the work force. Forty-three percent of the married women who completed college are in the labor force, as against 32 percent of those who did not.[37] For the higher educated woman, this is not seen as a choice of working as against the traditional female roles. As Rostow points out, educated women want to enter the work world, "but principally in ways which do not imperil their fulfillment in traditional roles as wives and mothers."[38]

A look at the age distribution of women in the work force shows that the highest first peak is reached at about 19, then there is a falling off during the 20's and 30's, with a slow increase reaching the second high peak at about age 50. The big age change in recent years is the development of the second peak. But the overall increase of married women in the work force has occurred among two groups: young wives who have not yet had any children, and wives in later middle age whose children have grown up.[39]

￫ *Wife Role.* The relationship to the husband continues to be important, but the nature of the relationship has changed. In the traditional wife role, the woman was a helpmate to her husband, implying a secondary power and prestige relationship. The wife today is interested in a relationship of near equality and wants to be viewed not as a helpmate, but as a partner. The broader social change is an important factor underlying her partnership desires. When a woman believes in her general equality to the man, it is difficult for her to

[35]*Ibid.*, p. 661.
[36]Peterson, *op. cit.*, p. 682.
[37]Hunt, *op. cit.*, p. 290.
[38]Rostow, *op. cit.*, p. 746.
[39]Paul C. Glick, "Demographic Analysis of Family Data," in Harold T. Christensen (ed.) *Handbook of Marriage and the Family,* (Chicago: Rand McNally & Co., 1964), p. 302.

accept a traditional definition of marriage role based upon female inferiority.

One of the consequences of greater equality for the woman was a weakening of the old accepted belief that a woman's place was in the home. Because of many technological changes, she is no longer needed in the home for nearly the amount of time she was in the past. Furthermore, social agencies, which help relieve her of the traditional full-time function of caring for her children, have emerged. The woman now has fewer children and more outside-the-home agencies that can take care of them for at least part of the day. Finally, the economic needs of the American society have reached a point where many women are needed in the work force.

Large numbers of women have now left the home for either part-time or full-time entrance into the work force. The percentage that are in the work force is smallest when the traditional role demands are the greatest—during the childbearing and early childrearing years. The vast majority of both single and married women who enter the work force are thinking in terms of jobs, not careers. The job meets her economic and personal needs; she is not pursuing a career in the way that a man does.

The married women who enter the labor force are not limited to the lower income levels. One national study points out "the surprising proportion of 41 per cent of wives working in homes enjoying incomes of seven to ten thousand dollars annually, 42 per cent in homes from ten to fifteen thousand. The proportion of wives working drops off rapidly both after $15,000 and below $7,000."[40] So it is often the higher educated and less traditionally oriented woman who enters the work force.

The working wife also has significance for the husband's role. Traditionally, the male was the breadwinner and, in the past, his success as a provider was often taken as a direct indication of his success as husband, father, and male. But with women in the work force, the husband must give up the notion of breadwinning as an exclusively male role. In other words, the working wife many constitute a threat to some husbands' sense of masculinity. Burgess and Wallin found that engaged men were more conservative than engaged women in their conception of the wife's role, which included working. Almost two thirds of the men they studied subscribed to the

---

[40]Nelson N. Foote, "New Roles for Men and Women," *Marriage and Family Living,* November, 1961, p. 97.

traditional concept of the wife not working, compared to less than one half of the women.[41]

There is evidence that the husband's views about his wife working vary at different social-class levels. For example, in the decision to work, the lower-class wife overwhelmingly makes the decision by herself, while in the higher social-class marriages the husband takes an active part in the decision.[42] But what seems important to marital adjustment is that the husband approve of the wife's occupational decision, *whether or not* the wife is actually employed.[43] Blood and Wolfe found no difference in marital adjustment scores of working and non-working wives.[44] Another study found that the husbands of working wives showed a more liberal view with regard to their wife's employment, her economic equality and her privilege of indvidual sexual expresson than did husband's of non-working wives.[45]

While there appears to be an increasing acceptance by middle-class husbands of their wives working, this acceptance does not necessarily represent a view of complete occupational equality by either the wife or her husband. It may be that in many marriages there is an assumption that some male dominance will continue and this view may not be inconsistent with the wife working so long as "her position is lower than her husbands in the occupational hierarchy and yields a smaller portion of the family income."[46]

Mother Role. The question of what the working mother's added occupational role means in her mother-role relationships with her children becomes important as the number of married women with children continues to increase. In 1940, of all women married, husband present and with a child under 6 years of age, only 4 percent were in the work force. But by 1952 the rate had increased to 14 percent and by 1963 to 22 percent.[47] It is clear that the mothers' resistance to entering the work force—even with preschool-age children—is decreasing.

One area of investigation has been what impact working has on the mother herself. One study found no significant relationship between maternal employment and maternal attitudes toward child-

[41]Ernest W. Burgess and Paul Wallin, *Engagement and Marriage*, (New York: J. B. Lippincott Co., 1953), p. 407.

[42]*Ibid.*, p. 102.

[43]Nye, *op. cit.*, p. 280.

[44]Robert O. Blood and Donald M. Wolfe, *Husbands and Wives*, (The Free Press of Glencoe, Illinois, 1960), p. 101.

[45]Leland J. Axelson, "The Marital Adjustment and Marital Role Definitions of Husbands of Working and Nonworking Wives," *Marriage and Family Living*, May, 1963, p. 194.

[46]Nye, *op. cit.*, p. 5.

[47]Rodman, *op. cit.*, p. 291.

rearing or maternal rejection of the homemaking role, when the oldest child is of preschool, elementary school, or adolescent age.[48] Another study was made in referenec to the conflicting demands made on the working mother. The conclusion was that "while the employed mother may be under great physical strain and over-worked because of her dual roles, this apparently does not affect her performance of the material role."[49] The studies indicate that most working mothers are working by choice and that they reach a point of adjustment to the added role demands of the occupation. There seems little reason to believe that very many working mothers suffer from severe role conflict.

The role relationship between husband and wife is also an area worthy of investigation when the wife is a working mother. The traditional notion that the mother's place is in the home would indicate that marital conflict might arise because of a threat to the traditional husband's role in the family. However, Hoffman found that there "was no difference in husband-wife power between working and nonworking women."[50] This may indicate that the wives who work either have or gain acceptance from the husband. Certainly, the traditional values against the wife-mother working have been greatly altered. It may, however, be in exactly this area of marital interaction that the wife working presents the greatest potential danger. Nye and Hoffman, after extensive research, cautiously propose that the "relationship problems associated with maternal employment are more likely to be found in the husband-wife relationship than elsewhere."[51] But they also point out that even when employment of the mother increases conflict in the marriage relationship, this conflict may be counterbalanced by the satisfaction of employment for the mother.[52] It is also important to keep in mind that even in those studies that show lower marital adjustment in marriages where the wife works it has not been shown that "the poorer marital adjustment found in working wife families is not the cause rather than the effect of her entrance into the economic market place."[53]

A third important area for the working mother centers around

[48]Kathryn S. Powell, "Maternal Employment in Relation to Family Life," *Marriage and Family Living*, November, 1961, p. 354.
[49]Evan T. Peterson, "The Impact of Maternal Employment on the Mother-Daughter Relationship," *Marriage and Family Living*, November, 1961, p. 361.
[50]Lois W. Hoffman, "Effects of the Employment of Mothers on Parental Power Relations and the Division of Household Tasks," *Marriage and Family Living*, February, 1960, p. 35.
[51]Nye, *op. cit.*, p. 385.
[52]*Ibid.*, p. 272.
[53]Axelson, *op. cit.*, p. 195.

the impact of her working role on her children. Burchinal and Rossman write that "apparently maternal employment *per se* cannot be
considered as an index of maternal deprivation with consequent
detrimental effects on the development of children."[54] The same researchers write that "maternal employment during the specified periods of the children's lives had no apparent relationship with the
personality, school-related or social development characteristics of
the children selected as dependent variables in this study."[55] Still
another study reports that "school performance, psychosomatic symptoms, and affectional relationship to the mother appear unrelated to
the employment status of the mother."[56] Finally, it was found that
"the employment of the mother does not affect the amount of affection in a family as perceived by the sons and daughters."[57]

The employment of the mother does have some impact on the
day-to-day life of the children. Roy found that "a higher proportion
of the children of employed mothers perform household tasks than
the children of non-employed mothers."[58] The fact that the children
of employed mothers did more work around home; however, did
not affect their social life and spare time; they had as much as the
children of nonemployed mothers.[59]

These studies indicate that, while the daily life of the youngster
with an employed mother may be somewhat different from the
youngster with the nonemployed mother, the mother-child relationship does not suffer. One point often overlooked in regard to the
nonworking mother is that when her children are adolescents, they
are often away from home for about the same period of time during
the day as she would be, if employed. School and afterschool activities for the middle-class adolescent are often from "nine to five."
This frequently means that, whether the wife is working or not,
the family is together only during the evenings and on weekends.

One advantage that the nonworking mother does have is that she
can do her housework during the day when the children are not
around. But for many working mothers, housework is reduced by
family help or by the economic ability, through working, to hire

---

[54]Lee G. Burchinal and Jack E. Rossman, "Relations Among Maternal Employment
Indices and Developmental Characteristics of Children," *Marriage and Family Living*,
November, 1961, p. 339.

[55]*Ibid.*, p. 339.

[56]F. Ivan Nye, "Employment Status of Mothers and Adjustments of Adolescent
Children," *Marriage and Family Living*, August, 1959, p. 244.

[57]Prodipto Roy, "Maternal Employment and Adolescent Roles: Rural-Urban Differences," *Marriage and Family Living*, November, 1961, p. 345.

[58]*Ibid.*, p. 344.

[59]*Ibid.*, p. 345.

part-time help. It may also be true that a number of working mothers, by the very nature of filing the working role, are quite sensitive to fulfilling the mother role effectively. Those mothers who work by choice may also have a strong feeling of overall personal satisfaction, which has a positive influence on them in their role of mother.

What is most important is that no study has found any meaningful differences between the children of working mothers in general and the children of nonworking mothers.[60] Rossi points out that the "children of working mothers are no more likely than children of non-working mothers to become delinquent, to show neurotic symptoms, to feel deprived of maternal affection, to perform poorly in school, to lead narrower social lives, etc."[61] This lack of a problem relationship appears to be true for children of all ages with working mothers. For example, the number of years the mothers worked while the child was between ages 6 and 18 "does not seem to bear any consistent relationship to the respondents' mental health."[62]

Professionalization. Our discussion thus far has been about the relationship of woman's occupational roles to her roles of wife and mother. However, it is also important to look at the wife-mother who gives an almost total commitment to those traditional roles and at some of the new beliefs and rationales that have emerged around these traditional roles. By *professionalization* is meant the development of a set of rationales for an intellectual and emotional commitment to the functions of being a modern wife and mother. The new belief is that being a "good" wife and mother today calls for dedication, knowledge, and a sense of creativity similar to that found in the professions. To a great extent, the notion of professionalization of the wife-mother role has been developed by the mass media. Most women's magazines seek to give intellectual respectability and professional status to being a wife and mother. The woman is urged to be creative in furnishing her home and to achieve aesthetic self-fulfillment through her creations. The fact that most of the magazines show her how to be creative, and in what way, indicates that the illusion of creating, not actual creativity, is really the aim. The woman who is creative in the home has made a transition from the old "housekeeper" role to the new role of being a "homemaker." She is also presented with the means of being creative in the kitchen, where she no longer prepares meals, but creates and produces "culi-

---

[60]Nye, *op. cit.,* p. 191.
[61]Rossi, *op. cit.,* pp. 617–18.
[62]Thomas S. Langner and Stanley T. Michael, *Life Stress and Mental Health,* (New York: The Free Press of Glencoe, 1963), p. 185.

nary delights." The woman is provided with the rationale that she is no longer a servant in the home, but a productive and creative person pursuing a worthwhile professional career.

After all has been said and done, the role of housekeeper or homemaker is limited and carries low prestige in middle-class America. In fact, housekeeping is universally an activity for low-status groups and whenever possible has always been delegated to servants. When the modern woman lets it be known that she has a dislike for housekeeping, she is reflecting what she has been taught. "Thousands of advertisements and commercials show the happy housewife at her duties—while promoting the idea that housework is not something to revel in, but to get done with."[63]

It should also be kept in mind that whatever other roles the wife-mother fills she also has the responsibility for housekeeping. If she takes a job, she usually has to make sure the housework is done either by hiring someone to do it or by doing most of it herself during the evenings and over the weekends. Rostow points out that regardless of the cooperative relationship between the husband and wife, there is usually a tacit assumption that the household is primarily the woman's responsibility. "If she can cope with that and another job, fine, but the domestic burden is primarily hers."[64]

A negative definition of housekeeping appears to be much stronger among middle- and upper middle-class American women than among women in the lower classes. This may be a result of the lower-class woman seeing the role of housekeeper as "natural" for her and not defining other roles outside the home as desirable. Komarovsky, in her study of lower middle-class women found none who said they felt too good to do housework or that it was unchallenging manual labor.[65] Furthermore, only 2 out of 58 women "referred to the fear of 'mental stagnation' which college educated women frequently list among the frustrations of housewifery."[66]

Many changes can also be seen in the modern beliefs of caring for children. Children are often reared with a great deal of intellectual concern on the part of the middle-class woman (as illustrated by her study of the works of different experts on child rearing). And while the health of the child has always been of vital concern to the mother, she was usually anxious about the child's physical health; today she is more apt to be anxious about his psychological health.

[63]Hunt, op. cit., p. 144.
[64]Rostow, op. cit., p. 752.
[65]Mirra Komarovsky, Blue-Collar Marriage, (New York: Random House, 1962), p. 55.
[66]Ibid., p. 57.

In a world where we are constantly told we are all neurotic to some degree, the ambition of many women seems to be that their child will be a little less neurotic than the child next door. Concerning oneself with the psychological health of a child involves a greater intellectual commitment than simply worrying about his physical health.

Very often the middle-class woman has a busy and full day. This is particularly true for the mother of preschool youngsters, whose care is a full-time and demanding task. In recent years, however, greater numbers of young children—and at younger ages—have been placed in nursery schools. Many mothers do this because part of their "professional" orientation suggests that it is wise. The belief that young children need contacts and experience with a variety of other children for more "wholesome" personality development is commonly accepted by the "professional" mother.

Afterschool hours are often the busiest time for the mother because the children are then her responsibility. However, the main function of many young suburban mothers at this time is to serve as chauffeur. Many "professional" mothers are committed to the belief that they must develop many facets of their child's personality and must provide the best facilities for this development. Since the mother does not feel qualified to teach her child, she must find experts and see that the child is transported to them. The child may be given lessons in ballet, piano, and dancing, and, like his middle-class parents, he may join teams, clubs, and other activities. When medical and educational specialists are added, it is clear why the mother often spends a great deal of time transporting her children from place to place.

The problem with the "professional" wife-mother orientation is that the woman may lead a very busy day, but not necessarily one that is personally satisfying. At the end of the day she may feel physically tired, but intellectually untouched. She often feels that her skills and abilities are not really being utilized in a meaningful way; rather, her time is spent with "busy work." The "professional" wife-mother role is based partially on fact and partially on illusion. When the functions performed are useful and meaningful to the woman, few problems arise. But when "professionalization" only provides an illusion of significance, many intelligent women cannot delude themselves. As a result, they feel a sense of frustration.

Several general points can be made in conclusion. First, stability of roles belonged to societies less complex than today's American society. Role adaptability in many situations is necessary for social and personal satisfaction with marriage. Second, the modern woman's role has many facets and sometimes the dimensions are contradictory. A feeling of confusion and frustration often results. Third, a decrease in the traditional role distinctions between the male and female has emerged, which leads to problems of sex and marital role clarity.

OCCUPATIONAL AND FAMILY ROLES OF MEN

In the American middle-class family, the woman's primary role takes place *within* the family setting while the primary role of the man is performed *outside* the family setting. For example, Lopata found that of her female respondents 81 percent mentioned the mother role as the most important role of the woman and 87 percent gave the breadwinner role as the most important role for the man.[67] One variation in how the husband is seen as breadwinner is at different social-class levels. The higher social classes give him recognition according to how well he provides materially *and* also for the prestige of his occupation. However, in the lower classes, the important requirement is that he be a good provider; the nature of the occupation is often of little importance. Komarovsky found that lower middle-class women sometimes do not even know the specific occupations of their close relatives, and while they see a good job as the means to a good living, they do not see achivement in a specialized vocation as the measure of a person's worth.[68]

In the discussion that follows we will refer primarily to the upper middle-class male's involvement in his profession. The term *profession* is used simply to designate occupations that require a high level of formal education and generally imply high prestige and income. While we will be discussing some prestige aspects of professions for men, it should also be kept in mind that a part of his occupational prestige results from the material things that he gives his family. In this sense, his family directly translates his occupational prestige to the community through the material symbols his economic success provides.

Occupational Roles. The vast majority of American men leave their homes and their family members to pursue their occupations. This means that the adult male's life is often carried out in two

---

[67]Helena Z. Lopata, "The Secondary Features of a Primary Relationship," *Human Organization*, Summer, 1965, pp. 118–19.

[68]Komarovsky, *op. cit.*, p. 57.

separate worlds—the world of his family (and residential community), and his world of work. While occasionally his world of work may intrude on his family world—that is, working at home, moving his family, etc.—rarely does he physically bring his family into his work world—that is, take his wife or children to his place of work to interact with his occupational peers or work procedures.

The fact that a man spends many hours away from home in his occupational role has a number of implications for his family. It seems probable that many upper middle-class males strongly identify with and for the most part enjoy their professions. This kind of job involvement and satisfaction is generally not a characteristic of lower-class males. One study of factory workers found that only 24 percent of those studied could be labelled job-oriented in their life interests.[69]

It appears that given a choice between filling his occupational role or his family role, a professional man will choose his occupation. Yet the man is generally expected to put his family roles above all other roles *if* there is a choice. But if it appears necessary for him to pursue his occupational role over his family roles for the good of his family, then that is not only socially acceptable but often socially applauded. He may be defined as performing above and beyond the call of duty as a breadwinner and making special sacrifices for his family. We would suggest that often the professional man who says he doesn't want to work late or he doesn't want to make a trip is rationalizing his actions to his family (and possibly himself) by blaming his job.

What is of particular interest is that because the man does usually work away from his family, he is not subject to comparisons in those two role settings. And with those two roles filled in separate settings, the man may sometimes play off one role off against another. For example, at home he may play off his occupational role either because he *wants* to go to his place of work or to escape the family setting and its demands. And usually in leaving for his occupational setting he conveys the notion to his family (and even an extended community) that what he is doing is for the family's good.

On other occasions a man may play off his family role to escape from occupational role demands. For example, if he doesn't really want to work, he might say that his family is expecting him or that he promised them he would be home. This implies that he would like to stay on the job but has a responsibility to meet the demands

[69]Robert Dubin, "Industrial Workers' Worlds: A Study of the 'Central Life Interests' of Industrial Workers," in Irwin O. Smigel (ed.) *Work and Leisure*, (New Haven, Conn.: College & University Press, 1963), p. 60.

of his family role. This explanation allows him to meet the expectations of his occupational peers as to the primary importance of his professional role. It appears that it is rare for a man either in a professional setting or in any exclusively male setting to openly state that he would prefer to leave it and be with his family. That is, it is rare for a man to explain leaving his occupational world because he *wants* to join his family; he uses the explanation of being *expected* by his family.

The Family Setting. There is a great investment on the part of the wife and her children to their husband-father's success in his occupational role. This investment seems increasingly to imply a willingness by his family to do whatever they can to help him in his occupational role because they feel that the whole family stands to gain or lose by his performance in it.

For a woman, her commitment to marry a man implies at that time that she is betting on his future occupational role success. So in the long run the crucial economic decision made by most women occurs at the time they agree to marry. The wife may help or hinder her husband's occupational future, but ultimately what the wife can do is determined by the husband's particular abilities, motivations and opportunities.

Frequently in the American middle-class the young wife not only wants her husband to be occupationally successful for all the usual reasons, but also to justify for her the occupational future *she* gave up by marrying him. If the wife has a better background than her husband, she may feel a strong need to push him. One study found that when the wife had the superior education she was more apt to put achievement pressure on her husband and depreciate his ability to reach the goals she had set for him.[70] There is also some difference by social class as to wives defining their husbands as successful or unsuccessful. For example, lower-educated wives refer to "bad luck" when explaining the economic failure of their husbands, while higher-educated wives married to men they see as poor providers tend to accuse their husbands of a lack of drive.[71]

There are several different ways in which the middle-class wife is important to her husband in his occupational role. Blood and Wolfe suggest several categories in which wives may contribute to their husband's success in his occupation: (1) The *Collaborative* wife may be found where the couple own their own business (farm, store or

---

[70]Blood and Wolfe, *op. cit.*, p. 96.
[71]Komarovsky, *op. cit.*, p. 77.

office) and the wife works directly with the husband in running the business operation. (2) The *Working* wife is one who has as her primary function the supplementing of her husband's income so as to improve his occupational position. (3) The *Supportive* wife is generally young and in the upper middle class. She sees herself as providing emotional support as well as home entertaining as a means of helping her husband to get ahead. (4) The *Peripheral* wife is one who sees herself as minimally involved with her husband's occupation. This type of wife is most common to the lower social classes and among old couples, where the wife sees her main function as taking care of the house.[72]

There is sometimes a danger for the wife who helps her husband get ahead: he may "outgrow" her. If the husband greatly outdistances his wife intellectually, she is less able to function as his confidante and partner. Hunt points out that the "average top-level executive talks less to his wife about business than he did as a junior executive, not only because they spend less time together, but because she has fallen too far behind him to be an adequate listener."[73] So, ironically, the wife who is successful in driving her husband *ahead* occupationally may also drive him *away* as a partner.

Still another possible area of involvement by the wife with her husband's occupation may be in their social life. While this marital activity is common to the upper middle class, it is not nearly so common in the lower middle class. Komarovsky found that the great majority of wives in her study had no social contact with their husband's workmates. "The friendships husbands form on the job do not include their wives."[74] But in the upper middle class, the wife is very often intimately involved in a social world that pivots around her husband's occupational associates.

As we have mentioned, the wife of the professional man is often very strongly committed to his occupational success. This commitment is not only assumed by herself and by her husband, but may also be assumed at the place of the husband's work. A part of the expectation by both the couple and many business establishments is that the wife believe the company's demands to be of primary importance. Whyte found that most executive's wives agreed with the corporation view that "the good wife is the wife who adjusts graciously to the system, curbs open intellectualism or the desire to be

[72]Blood and Wolfe, *op. cit.*, p. 94.
[73]Hunt, *op. cit.*, p. 221.
[74]Komarovsky, *op. cit.*, p. 153.

alone."[75] Furthermore, it is generally assumed that, over time and if the husband is successful in his occupation, the wife will become even more actively involved. Rostow points out that the "job descriptions of many leading positions pre-suppose the active participation of a wife. No couple—ambassadorial or company president—is paid a double salary, although the wife may give as much in her part as her husband in his."[76]

The wife is generally expected to put up with social demands that her husband's occupation makes on them. If occupationally they see it as important to attend a dinner or party, even though it may not be what they really want to do, they are expected to attend. To absent themselves would be to run the risk of jeopardizing the husband's occupational future—and of course also the future of his wife and their children. This frequently means that social gatherings are not activities for relaxation and enjoyment, but rather social gatherings that function with a formal and clear-cut set of role relationships that the husband and his wife are expected to know and abide by.

With the husband's occupational future often significantly influenced by the success or failure of the wife in entertaining his occupational associates, she may often be conservative in what she does. For example, the wife may be very concerned with the image her home furnishings or her means of entertainment project to those who will be significant to her husband's occupational future. As a result of her apprehension, she may be conservative in how she decorates her home, the food and drink she serves, and even in the clothes she wears.

There are several other important consequences of a high occupational commitment by the husband. For example, often his great involvement with his occupation not only means that he may not be around the home very much, but that when he is he is less involved in the care and upkeep of the home than are other men. For example, higher-status men do less work around the house than lower-status men, and for everything that the successful man does less of, his wife does correspondingly more.[77]

Many men spend a good part of the time they are home working on matters related to their occupations. This is not only true about work directly related to their occupation—for example, bringing

[75]William H. Whyte, Jr., *The Organization Man*, (New York: Simon & Schuster, 1956), p. 258.
[76]Rostow, *op. cit.*, p. 752.
[77]Blood and Wolfe, *op. cit.*, p. 60.

home paper work from the office—but, it may also be seen in how some men use what they consider to be leisure time at home. Gerstl found these differences among three professional groups (admen, dentists and professors) on how they would use a hypothetical free two hours at home: 33 percent of the admen said they would use the time for a hobby or recreation and 24 percent said they would spend the time with their family; 32 percent of the dentists said a hobby or recreation and 29 percent said relaxation; among the professors, 50 percent said they would use the time for work or work-connected reading and 28 percent said for recreational reading.[78] We see in these three occupations a wide variation in spending leisure time, but for all three groups there is implied a belief that the home is in part a place for pursuing at least some individual interests that may have little to do with the rest of the family or the home.

Probably one of the most important consequences of the male's occupation for his family is its implications for his wife and children's mobility—both social and geographical. If the husband-father is economically successful, his family may move to a higher-priced home and community. Or the man may be asked to move to another part of the country. While this latter move is often presented to the man as something he may choose to do or not, a refusal may be defined as a lack of commitment to his occupation and be held against him in the future.

While there are still many complementary relationships between the male's occupational roles and those of his family roles, there are many situations where the two sets of role demands are in conflict. Increasingly it seems that for many middle-class males to become successful in their occupational roles, they must become less involved and committed to their family. Or, to put it another way, for the successful man, increasingly his occupational role setting functions more and more as his major reference group. His occupational role limits his direct family involvement, but represents greater indirect rewards economically and socially for his wife and children.

SELECTED BIBLIOGRAPHY

AXELSON, LELAND J. "The Marital Adjustment and Marital Role Definitions of Husbands of Working and Nonworking Wives," *Marriage and Family Living*, May, 1963, pp. 189–95.

---

[78]Joel E. Gerstl, "Leisure, Taste and Occupational Milieu," in Erwin O. Smigel (ed.) *Work and Leisure*, (New Haven, Conn.: College & University Press, 1963), p. 149.

DEGLER, CARL N. "The Changing Place of Women in America," *Daedalus,* Spring, 1964, pp. 653–70.

GRAY, ROBERT M., and SMITH, TED C. "Effect of Employment on Sex Differences in Attitudes Toward the Parental Family," *Marriage and Family Living,* February, 1960, pp. 36–38.

HOFFMAN, LOIS W. "Effects of the Employment of Mothers on Parental Power Relations and the Division of Household Tasks," *Marriage and Family Living,* February, 1960, pp. 27–35.

HUNT, MORTON M. *Her Infinite Variety,* (New York: Harper & Row, 1962)

KOMAROVSKY, MIRRA. *Blue-Collar Marriage,* (New York: Random House, 1962)

MEAD, MARGARET and KAPLAN, FRANCES B. (eds.), *American Women: The Report of the President's Commission,* (New York: Charles Scribner's Sons, 1965)

NYE, F. IVAN. "Employment Status of Mothers and Adjustment of Adolescent Children," *Marriage and Family Living,* August, 1959, pp. 240–44.

NYE, F. IVAN and HOFFMAN, LOIS W. *The Employed Mother in America* (Chicago: Rand McNally & Co., 1963)

PETERSON, ESTHER. "Working Women," *Daedalus,* Spring, 1964, pp. 671–99.

PETERSON, EVAN T. "The Impact of Maternal Employment on the Mother-Daughter Relationship," *Marriage and Family Living,* November, 1961, pp. 355–61.

POWELL, KATHRYN S. "Maternal Employment in Relation to Family Life," *Marriage and Family Living,* November, 1961, pp. 350–55.

RAPOPORT, ROBERT and RAPOPORT, RHONA. "Work and Family in Contemporary Society," *American Sociological Review,* June, 1965, pp. 381–94.

ROSSI, ALICE S. "Equality Between the Sexes," *Daedalus,* Spring, 1964, pp. 607–52.

ROSTOW, EDNA G. "Conflict and Accommodation," *Daedalus,* Spring, 1964, pp. 736–60.

ROY, PRODIPTO. "Maternal Employment and Adolescent Roles: Rural-Urban Differentials," *Marriage and Family Living,* November, 1961, pp. 340–49.

THE SEXUAL ASPECT OF MARRIAGE

Historically in the majority of cultures, marital sex has been important two ways: first, as the means of reproduction, and second, as a means of satisfying the sexual needs of the husband. With few effective methods of controlling conception, pregnancy frequently occurred as a consequence of marital coitus. This resulted in a large number of children, high rates of maternal mortality, and a short life span for the reproductive wife. In the past, while women could and did receive personal satisfaction from the sexual aspect of marriage, it was not usually an expected right. In the patriarchal system, sexual need was generally assumed to be a need of the man. The woman who also received sexual satisfaction was sometimes viewed by her husband (and herself) as somewhat "unnatural." "Good women," at least in terms of accepted social values, did not usually derive pleasure from the sexual act. Their role as sexual partner was one of duty to the husband.

In contemporary middle-class America, the traditional patriarchal beliefs about marital coitus have been altered and expanded. No longer is the relationship of the sexual act and conception viewed as beyond control of the individual. Through the development and use of birth-control methods, conception is increasingly controlled. A second change in the traditional beliefs about marital sex is today's assumption that the wife has as much right to expect sexual fulfillment in marriage as her husband. Thus, the two general social changes in regard to marital coitus have had their greatest impact on women. Because these two social changes are of importance, each is presented in some detail before discussing the broader area of sexual adjustment in marriage.

BIRTH CONTROL

Birth control, in a broad sense, refers to the various methods used to stop either pregnancy or live birth.[1] Sometimes birth control is

---

[1]See: Alan F. Guttmacher, *et al., The Complete Book of Birth Control* (New York: Ballantine Books, 1961).

used in reference to "positive" aspects of controlling family size through the spacing of children over time, but ultimately this means not having children except when desired. Birth control may be applied in a number of ways. First, *destruction* after conception; this may range from destroying the fetus by induced abortion or by giving birth to the child and then destroying it. Second, through *sterilization*, a process in which a person is made biologically incapable of producing or transmitting the ovum or the sperm. Third, the *processual* ways of controlling pregnancy. This may be through the withdrawal of the penis prior to ejaculation of sperm, or through a system where the sperm is present but no ovum is available for fertilization. Last, are the various *contraceptive* methods. The term contraception is generally applied to "mechanical or chemical barriers that prevent the access of spermatozoa to the uterus and Fallopian tubes at times when fertilizable ova are present."[2]

Historically, the techniques of abortion and infanticide were used much more widely than contraception to control family size.[3] This was true because knowledge of the reproductive nature of sexual relations and the means of controlling conception through the uses of contraceptive devices was limited. Only in recent years and particularly in the Western world, has the emergence of effective contraceptive devices used by large numbers of the population occurred. For example, Margaret Sanger opened the first birth control clinic in New York City in 1917—an act for which she served a prison sentence.[*]

During the past decade, as there has emerged an increasing concern with the rapid expansion of the world's population, birth control has become of increasing interest on an international level. It was not until 1830 that the world's population reached its first billion, but only one hundred years later, in 1930, the world's population was two billion and 30 years later, in 1960, it had reached three billion. It is estimated that the four-billion mark will be reached by 1975 and five billion by 1985. The United Nations estimates that world population is growing by 8,000 every hour or approximately 70,000,000 a year.[4] Given this population explosion, the development

---

[2]Edgar S. Gordon, "Taking Physical Factors into Account," in Howard Becker and Reuben Hill, *Family, Marriage and Parenthood* (Boston: D. C. Heath & Co., 1955), p. 337.

[3]Ronald Freedman, Pascal K. Whelpton, and Arthur A. Campbell, *Family Planning, Sterility and Population Growth* (New York: McGraw-Hill Book Co., 1959), p. 57.

[4]Elizabeth Ogg, *A New Chapter in Family Planning* (New York: Public Affairs Committee, Inc., 1964), p. 4.

[*]See Chapter 9 for a discussion of the legal and religious aspects of contraception.

of new, effective and inexpensive means of birth control is increasingly seen as important to all of mankind.

The use and effectiveness of controlling contraception in the United States has been documented through several extensive studies of large populations.[5] One of the studies, made with a probability sample of wives on a national level, found that 70 percent of the respondents had at some time used contraception and only 6 percent said "they did not intend to use preventive methods at some time."[6] Another study of couples in eight of the nation's nine largest metropolitan areas found that 53 percent of the couples first used contraception before the first birth, and 30 percent more before the second birth.[7] These two studies indicate both the frequency of use and the early starting point of pregnancy control in marriage.

Contraceptive Methods

Sterilization. Sterilization prevents parenthood without destroying the sexual abilities of the individual. The usual methods are the cutting of the *vas deferens* (vasectomy) of the male or the Fallopian tubes (salpingectomy) of the female.[8] Sterilization should not be confused with castration, which does destroy the sexual ability of the male. Other operations may also result in sterility, even though that is not their stated intent; for example, a female hysterectomy.

The "national" study found that 9 percent of all couples questioned controlled pregnancy by this method. Variations occur by education, with the college-educated representing only 6 percent and the grade school educated 13 percent, and by religion, with the Protestants representing 11 and the Catholics 5 percent.[9] While sterilization is the most reliable of all methods, it is also the most irrevocable; once sterilization has taken place, the person can rarely at some future date have the operation undone.

Rhythm System (Safe Period). The rhythm method of contraception is the refraining from sexual intercourse during that period when the female ovum is at the stage in the menstrual cycle

---

[5]See *Ibid.;* and Charles F. Westoff, Robert G. Potter, Jr., Philip C. Sagi, and Elliot G. Mishler, *Family Growth in Metropolitan America* (Princeton, N. J.: Princeton University Press, 1961).

[6]Freedman, Whelpton, and Campbell, *op. cit.*, pp. 61–62. This study will be referred to as the "national" study.

[7]Westoff, Potter, Sagi, and Mishler, *op. cit.*, p. 72. This study will be referred to as the "metropolitan" study.

[8]Helen I. Clarke, *Social Legislation* (New York: Appleton-Century-Crofts, Inc., 1957), p. 193.

[9]Freedman, Whelpton, and Campbell, *op. cit.*, p. 30.

when conception is possible. The fertility period during each menstrual period is determined by taking the midpoint of the cycle and subtracting two days and adding three to five days to give the period of greatest possible conception. This, then is the unsafe period, during which couples abstain from coitus if they do not desire pregnancy. Temperature charts are often used to determine the midpoint of a cycle; most commonly it is the 12th day. About 90 percent of the time, ovulation takes place between the 10th and 16th day.[10] The reason each woman determines her own midpoint (or ovulation) before adding and subtracting days for the period of sexual abstinence is that the midpoint varies among different women.

For the period 1938–39 until 1955, the "national" study found an increase in the usage of the rhythm system from 11 to 24 percent of the couples studied.[11] The "metropolitan" study found the rhythm system in current usage among 19 percent of the couples studied.[12]

Several problems are associated with the use of the rhythm system. First, extreme care must be exercised in the calculation of dates. This generally means that the more irregular a menstrual cycle, the less dependable the rhythm system. And absolute regularity of the menstrual cycle is a myth. "Eighty percent of women have cycles averaging 28.6 days, with a span between 26 and 34 days. The remaining 20 percent have either shorter or longer cycles, or exhibit considerable variation in cycle length. Variations of between 21 and 90 days occur in women who appear to be physiologically normal."[13]

The second problem is the enforced restriction placed upon sexual relations. The spontaneity of sexual satisfaction must be put aside for at least part of every month because of the dangers of conception, and sometimes human inability to restrict sexual desire leads to pregnancy. For those who accept these factors, however, the rhythm system can often be used with high efficiency. The "national" study points out that "rhythm is most likely to be used as an exclusive method by couples who have both the sophistication to understand and the special religious motivations that will compensate for the self-denial and risk in depending on it."[14] The effective use of the

---

[10]Edmund J. Ferris, *Human Ovulation and Fertility* (Philadelphia: J. B. Lippincott Co., 1955).

[11]Freedman, Whelpton, and Campbell, *op. cit.*, p. 174.

[12]Westoff, Potter, Sagi, and Mishler, *op. cit.*, p. 78.

[13]George W. Corner, Jr. "Menstrual Cycle," in Albert Ellis and Albert Abarbanel, (eds.) *The Encyclopedia of Sexual Behavior* (New York: Hawthorn Books, Inc., 1961), p. 729.

[14]Freedman, Whelpton, and Campbell, *op. cit.*, p. 192.

rhythm system by higher-educated Catholic women is an illustration.[15] However, the rhythm system is not to be used indiscriminately by Catholics. To be used without guilt by them, three conditions must be present: "(1) there must be a justifiable reason . . . (2) it must be agreed upon, and (3) the mutually agreed-upon abstinence must not be a proximate occasion of infidelity on the part of one or both spouses."[16]

Withdrawal (Coitus Interruptus). Like the rhythm system, withdrawal is a "processual" means of controlling conception in that it does not involve artificial impediments. Sexual intercourse is interrupted immediately before the male orgasm by withdrawal of the penis and ejaculation outside the vagina. Withdrawal is one of the least used methods in the United States today. In the "national" study, it was reported by 11 percent of the couples, and in the "metropolitan" study by even fewer, 5 percent.[17]

A number of problems are associated with this method. First, it demands very great will power on the part of the male. He must be willing to give up the final and often most satisfying stage of sexual intercourse. While the method does permit a physical release through orgasm, it may lead to a feeling of psychological incompletion for both the male and female. A second problem involves the ability of the male to anticipate accurately when he is ready to ejaculate. Sometimes ejaculation happens with little or no warning; or he may know it is coming but feel he can wait a little longer, and wait too long.[18] Third, even if the male withdraws ahead of ejaculation, some possibility of pregnancy still exists. The danger rests with the "sperm cells in the few drops of seminal fluid which often escapes from the penis before the orgasm is reached."[19]

Douche. Douching is the cleaning of the vagina with a mild acid, sperm-killing solution after sexual intercourse. In the 1930's, douching was the most common method of birth control used in the United States. But from 1938–39 to 1955, a strong shift away from its use occurred. In the "national" study, it was reported as used by 44 percent of the couples in 1938–39, but only by 11 percent in

---

[15]Westoff, Potter, Sagi, and Mishler, *op. cit.,* p. 215.

[16]Alphonse H. Clemens, "Catholicism and Sex," in Albert Ellis and Albert Abarbanel (eds.) *The Encyclopedia of Sexual Behavior* (New York: Hawthorn Books, Inc., 1961), p. 230.

[17]Freedman, Whelpton, and Campbell, *op. cit.,* p. 174; and Westoff, Potter, Sagi, and Mishler, *op. cit.,* p. 78.

[18]Gordon, *op. cit.,* p. 338.

[19]*Ibid.,* p. 338.

1955.[20] In the "metropolitan" study, douching was used by only 4 percent of the couples as an exclusive means of controlling conceptions.[21]

In many cases, a douche may be used to supplement other methods; for example, it may be used with the diaphragm. There are several difficulties in using the douche as the only means of controlling conception. It must be used immediately after intercourse, which may be psychologically upsetting to the woman, and there is no guarantee that all of the sperm will be reached and destroyed by it.

Condom. The condom is a sheath of rubber or animal membrane placed on the penis to catch the ejaculated sperm. The popularity of the condom has increased a great deal over the past 25 years. One reason for this is the wide publicity given the condom during World War II as a protection against venereal disease.[22] The "national" and "metropolitan" studies found the condom used, respectively, by 30 and 31 percent of the couples.[23]

One of the great advantages of the condom over most other methods of controlling conception is its simplicity. It can be placed on the penis quickly and it has little effect in influencing the natural development of the sexual act. However, it may dull the sensations of the nerve endings in the penis for some men (although this may have the positive effect of slowing down their orgasm) and it may be defective or broken so that sperm does escape.

Diaphragm. A diaphragm is a flexible rubber disc that is coated with a spermicidal jelly and covers the cervix, thereby preventing the sperm from reaching the ovum. It is left in place from 8 to 12 hours after coitus. The "national" study found 25 percent of the couples used this method; in the "metropolitan" sample, it was used by 18 percent.[24] Use of the diaphragm has increased, particularly among the higher-educated. In recent years, a great deal of medical stress has been placed on the use of the diaphragm, and it is often recommended by planned parenthood clinics.[25]

The diaphragm is generally considered to be one of the most reliable and efficient of all contraceptive methods in use today. Its advantage, besides efficiency if correctly fitted and inserted, is that

---

[20]Freedman, Whelpton, and Campbell, *op. cit.,* p. 176.

[21]Westoff, Potter, Sagi, and Mishler, *op. cit.,* p. 78.

[22]Freedman, Whelpton, and Campbell, *op. cit.,* p. 177.

[23]*Ibid.,* p. 174; and Westoff, Potter, Sagi, and Mishler, *op. cit.,* p. 78.

[24]*Ibid.,* pp. 174 and 78.

[25]Freedman, Whelpton, and Campbell, *op. cit.,* p. 177.

the woman may insert it long before intercourse occurs, precluding any need to destroy the continuity of the sexual act. However, if the diaphragm is not inserted ahead of time, a breakoff in sexual foreplay is required for its insertion. When it is not inserted prior to foreplay, some women find the squatting position usually needed for its insertion unromatic and destructive to their sexual interest.

Oral Contraception. Of increasing significance as a means of birth control, are the oral contraceptives. They work through: (1) the suppression of ovulation or spermatogenesis; (2) prevention of fertilization; or (3) preventing the implanting of the fertilized ovum in the uterus.[26] The so-called "steroids," pills that contain synthetic hormones, have been the most effective of the oral contraceptives. When they are taken daily from the 5th to the 25th day of the menstrual cycle, they halt conception by halting ovulation.

In November, 1959, the Federal Food and Drug Administration (FDA) approved for public sale the first pill to be used for purposes of birth control. Since that date, nine other oral contraceptives have been approved by FDA. Though the pills are for use only on a doctor's prescription, there are an estimated 4,000,000 women in the United States now taking some form of oral contraceptives.[27] The various pills are manufactured by a number of firms and are promoted through extensive advertising campaigns. Their sale is rapidly expanding.

One of the major problems resulting from the use of oral contraceptives is the control of undesired side effects. The most common of these are the same as those usually associated with pregnancy; that is, nausea, weight gain, breast discomfort, swelling of hands and feet, changes in skin and hair, vaginal spotting, and improvement of acne. In one study of a sample of more than 11,000 women who had used oral contraception for more than two years, about seven percent had experienced nausea and some swelling. The number dropped to about five percent for women who remained on the pills for 37 to 42 months. (Most of the women who stopped using the pills did so because of weight increase.[28])

There is no evidence that using the pills has a negative effect on those who desire a future pregnancy. "In every study so far, a high

---

[26]Hans Lehfeldt, "Contraception," in Albert Ellis and Albert Abarbanel, (eds.), *The Encyclopedia of Sexual Behavior* (New York: Hawthorn Books, Inc., 1961), Vol. I, p. 297.

[27]Winfield Best, "Birth Control Pills: An Up-to-Date Report," *Good Housekeeping*, September, 1965, p. 159.

[28]*Ibid.*, p. 160.

percentage of women who stopped taking the pills after one to 48 months of use promptly conceived—many in the very first cycle after stopping—and bore normal babies. The longer oral contraceptives had been used, the higher the pregnancy rate after women stopped taking the pills.[29]

The cost of oral contraception continues to be high enough that they are not economically feasible for use on any mass public health basis. At present, the most commonly used cost between $1.25 and $3.50 for a month's supply. If we average that to $2.50 and estimate that a couple have coitus on 10 different occasions in a month, then the contraceptive cost per coital protection would be about 25 cents. This would compare to the cost per coital protection of other methods as follows: foam, liquid and sponge, 4 cents; jelly and diaphragm, 6 cents; aerosel foam or foam tablets, 8 cents; and jelly or cream alone, 11 cents.[30] Of course, while the cost is greater for the oral contraceptive, its reliability is also greater.[31]

Oral contraception seems to be the contraceptive method of the future, though it will probably take some little time before it will be accepted and used with confidence by the majority of American women. Its advantages over older methods are that it offers a high degree of reliability—not only biologically but also psychologically, in that the human error often found with the use of the condom and diaphragm are minimized. Oral contraception can also contribute to greater spontaneity in the sexual act because the pill can be taken prior to sexual intercourse. Because of its great simplicity of use, it can also be taken by many not willing or able to correctly use the condom or diaphragm.

At the present time, there appears to be agreement among the officials of FDA, the pharmaceutical companies and physicians about the general assets and liabilities of oral contraceptives. The agreement is that: (1) the pills are at present the most effective means of birth control; (2) for most young women they are safe to take within the time limits set up by FDA; (3) there is no evidence that the pills are the cause of any disease; and, (4) the pills do produce certain side effects, or unpleasant reactions, in some women.[32] There will undoubtedly emerge in the near future great changes in oral contraceptives. At the present time, several drug companies are

---

[29]Ogg, op, cit., p. 6.
[30]Ibid., p. 13.
[31]Roy O. Greep, Human Fertility and Population Problems (Boston: Schenkman Publishing Co., 1963), p. 62.
[32]Best, op. cit., p. 160.

developing an injection that will prevent ovulation for from one to three months. "One compound produces its effect so gradually yet so powerfully that a single injection will suppress both ovulation and menstruation for six months to a year."[33]

These methods of birth control provide the means for controlling pregnancy. While they vary in their degrees of reliability, so do the individuals using them. The "national" study found that one pregnancy in eight was accidental, occurring in spite of preventive efforts.[34] The percentage of accidental pregnancies by type of birth-control methods used was also found to vary. For those using rhythm, 30 percent reported accidents; appliance methods, 20 percent; and withdrawal, 13 percent.[35]

In general, the most effective methods for controlling conception are the oral contraceptives, diaphragm and jelly, condom, and withdrawal; the least effective are the rhythm system and douche.[36] Many times the failure of contraception is attributed to the method, rather than the persons using it. The fact is that the most reliable methods used by careful individuals can and do effectively control pregnancy. From the point of view of significant social change, this fact has been revolutionary in affecting the married role of the woman. Today's middle-class wife now has the means of determining the number and spacing of her children.

THE SEXUAL "RIGHTS" OF THE WIFE

The second important change in the American middle class in regard to marital coitus has involved the "rights and expectations" of the wife. Today she is often taught that when she enters marriage she has a right to sexual fulfillment; in fact, some modern marriage manuals give this attainment the highest emphasis.[37] Such a change in expectations is closely related to the development of effective methods of birth control; these methods allow the wife to enter the sex act as an end in itself, rather than with the traditional belief that it can, on any given occasion, lead to pregnancy.

A brief look at some past professional attitudes provides a vivid contrast to marital coital attitudes for the female in today's society. Up to and well through the 19th century, both moral and "scien-

---

[33]Steven M. Spencer, "The Birth Control Revolution," *The Saturday Evening Post,* January 15, 1966, p. 25.

[34]Freedman, Whelpton, and Campbell, *op. cit.,* p. 70.

[35]*Ibid.,* p. 208.

[36]Westoff, Potter, Sagi, and Mishler, *op. cit.,* p. 77.

[37]See: Eustace Chesser, *Love Without Fear* (New York: Signet, 1949).

tific" criticism was directed at female sexual satisfaction. Dr. William Acton, in a standard text on the reproductive system, wrote "that the belief that women had a sexual appetite was a vile aspersion." William Hammond, surgeon-general of the United States, wrote "that nine-tenths of the time decent women felt not the slightest pleasure in intercourse"; and at the University of Basel, an eminent gynecologist named Fehling labeled "sexual desire in the young woman as pathological."[38]

Female sexual interest was even negatively tied in with the woman's reproductive function. "In 1839 a highly successful English marriage manual written by a physician named Michael Ryan warned that female sterility was due, among other causes, to an excessive ardor of desire or 'passion strongly excited.' . . . It is well known that compliance, tranquility, silence, and secrecy are necessary for a prolific coition."[39] Sexual satisfaction for the woman was to be achieved only by the prostitute—this attitude of the past was often voiced not only by the clergy, but also by poets and physicians.

Many sources could be drawn on to illustrate how historical attitudes about the sexual role of the woman have completely changed. In fact, it would be next to impossible to find any reputable writers in the United States today voicing the old beliefs. A common view today is that "it is necessary that she [the wife] share the grandeur of the topmost heights with him—orgasm, the sexual climax—or else the enterprise becomes meaningless for both."[40] To emphasize the great importance of sexual satisfaction for the woman, the same writer says, "to serve as the cornerstone of happy marriage, sexual intercourse must be welcome and delighting not to the husband alone but to the wife as well."[41] Sexual satisfaction as often viewed today not only is of prime importance for the personal satisfactions of the woman, but also for the overall marriage relationship.

Many of today's marriage manuals emphasize the sexual problems centering around the wife's achievement of orgasm. Attention is directed at the need for extended foreplay so that actual coitus does not start until the wife is near her sexual peak; the couple together may then reach "the ultimate summit of mutual orgasm." The assumption usually made is that the male should control his sexual

[38]Morton M. Hunt, *The Natural History of Love* (New York: Alfred A. Knopf, Inc., 1959), p. 319.

[39]*Ibid.*, p. 319.

[40]Maxine Davis, *The Sexual Responsibility of Women* (New York: Permabooks, 1959), p. 24.

[41]*Ibid.*, p. 95.

selfishness to make sure his wife reaches her sexual peak. Seldom is any attempt made to understand that prolongation by the male is not always susceptible to rational control. In addition, Himes and Taylor point out that "rarely do contemporary books have anything to say about the need of the woman's helping the man to prepare himself, especially when there is difficulty or slowness in erection."[42] The overall assumption is frequently that the husband is always sexually ready and all he must do is help his wife reach the same state.

The importance that is placed on the wife achieving sexual satisfaction is for the most part characteristic of the middle class. For example, Rainwater found in his lower lower-class sample that 67 percent of the respondents said the husband enjoyed coitus more, 7 percent said the wife and 26 percent about equal, as contrasted with the middle class where 33 percent said the husband enjoyed coitus more, 8 percent said the wife more and 59 percent about equal.[43] Masters and Johnson found that husbands with fear of sexual performance were confined primarily to the higher educated. They found that only 14 percent of those men with no college education expressed the slightest concern with responsibility for their partner's sexual satisfaction. "These men felt that it was the female's privilege to achieve satisfaction during active coition if she could, but certainly it was not the responsibility and really not the concern of the male partner to concentrate on satisfying the woman's sexual demands."[44] By contrast, of those males with college matriculation, 82 percent of them expressed concern with coital-partner satisfaction.[45]

One assumption that is rarely verbalized is that mutual orgasm is important and, as a corollary, that the interests, drives, and abilities of the two sexes are equal. This may well be a reaction to the second-class sexual rights allotted the woman in the past. Given the vast variations in sexual interests and abilities within *either* sex, however, the assumption that each partner can reach an optimum level of satisfaction is often unrealistic. Some writers confronted with this possible dilemma resolve it by stating that the couple's sexual differences are handled by working out a compromise. This may be far more difficult for many couples than is often recognized.

---

[42]Norman E. Himes and Donald L. Taylor, *Your Marriage* (New York: Rinehart & Co., Inc., 1955), p. 163.

[43]Lee Rainwater, *Family Design* (Chicago: Aldine Publishing Co., 1965), p. 68.

[44]William H. Masters and Virginia E. Johnson, *Human Sexual Response* (Boston: Little, Brown and Co., 1966), p. 202.

[45]*Ibid.*, p. 202.

The human female has a unique distinction among female animals. "As far as can be discovered, only the human female is capable of orgasm, or reaching a sexual climax."[46] Furthermore, "the anatomic structures which are most essential to sexual response and orgasm are nearly identical in the human female and male."[47] This means that, at least in theory, males and females, equally, have the capacity for achieving sexual satisfaction.

Masters and Johnson found that the female orgasm usually results in clearly recognizable physical changes and "the grimace and contortion of a woman's face graphically express the increment of myotonic tension throughout her entire body. The muscles of the neck and the long muscles of the arms and legs usually contract into involuntary spasm."[48] The potential range of difference in the female's experience of orgasm is great, and there are significant differences between different women, as well as marked variations in the individual female's orgasmic experience. Masters and Johnson write that "day to day, and week to week, she presents an entirely different picture of sexual activation for the observer."[49] They go on to point out that "there is great variation in both the intensity and the duration of the female orgasmic experience, while the male tends to follow standard patterns of ejaculatory variation."[50]

Masters and Johnson have through their research, for the first time, distinguished the female cycle of sexual response. During the cycle, many physiological, psychological and social influences are interrelated as the woman moves through the four phases, or stages, in the cycle. The first stage is the *excitement phase* which may be brought about by any physical or psychological sexual stimulation. If the source of sexual stimulation is maintained, the female enters the second or *plateau phase*. At this stage the degree of sexual feeling is intense and a state of complete tumescence of the breasts, perineum and vagina are reached. Third is the *orgasmic phase* which is brief and explosive and may erase for some women all other conscious stimuli. And finally is the *resolution phase,* in which the physiological residuals of sexual tension are slowly dissipated.[51]

---

[46]Ira L. Reiss, *Premarital Sexual Standards in America* (Glencoe, Illinois: The Free Press, 1960), p. 22.

[47]Alfred C. Kinsey, Wardell B. Pomeroy, Clyde E. Martin, and Paul H. Gebhard, *Sexual Behavior in the Human Female* (Philadelphia: W. B. Saunders Co., 1953), p. 593.

[48]Masters and Johnson, *op. cit.*, p. 128.

[49]*Ibid.*, pp. 57–58.

[50]*Ibid.*, p. 6.

[51]*Ibid.*, pp. 56–57.

Important differences exist in the development of sexual intensity for the male and the female. "The responsiveness of the human male develops earlier than that of the female. By 15 years of age, 92 percent of the human males have experienced orgasm, but the female population is 29 years of age before a similar percentage has experienced first orgasm."[52] The slower development of the woman is not attributed to biological reasons so much as to cultural and psychological influences. For example, males become aware of orgasm at a much younger age than females and they do not have to be taught how to bring it about. "Women more rarely experience orgasm spontaneously during waking hours; most of them have to learn how to bring themselves to climax. Many do not even know what they are supposed to be experiencing until they learn from observing their husband or male partners."[53]

The cultural values of American society have led to different sexual concerns and fears by men and women. Increasingly for middle-class women, fears of performance concern their ability to achieve orgasm. For the male, the fears are related to attaining and keeping a penile erection; his orgasmic capacity is assumed.[54] Beyond these fears there are two major areas of physiological difference between the orgasm experience of men and women. "First, the female is capable of rapid return to orgasm immediately following an orgasmic experience, if restimulated before tensions have dropped below plateau-phase response levels. Second, the female is capable of maintaining an orgasmic experience for a relatively long period of time."[55]

Another difference between the male and female involves sexual arousal and speed of achieving orgasm. Kinsey writes "there is a widespread belief that the female is slower than the male in her sexual responses, but the masturbatory data do not support that opinion. It is true that the average female responds more slowly than the average male in coitus but this seems to be due to the ineffectiveness of the usual coital techniques."[56] After intensive study, Kinsey and his associates concluded that "in spite of the widespread and

[52]Alfred C. Kinsey, "Sex Behavior in the Human Male: Physiological and Psychological Factors in Sex Behavior," *Annals of the New York Academy of Sciences,* May, 1947, p. 636.

[53]Jessie Bernard, "The Adjustments of Married Males," in Harold T. Christensen (ed.) *Handbook of Marriage and the Family* (Chicago: Rand McNally & Co., 1964), p. 713.

[54]Masters and Johnson, *op. cit.,* p. 218.

[55]*Ibid.,* p. 131.

[56]Kinsey, Pomeroy, Martin, and Gebhard, *op. cit.,* p. 164.

oft-repeated emphasis on the supposed differences between female and male sexuality, we fail to find any anatomic or physiological basis for such differences."[57] Therefore, differences in sexual behavior between the male and female "appears to be the product of learning and conditioning."[58]

Some comparison of the psychological differences between males and females illustrate their differences in susceptibility to erotic influence. The following percentages refer to the percentages of females and males that reported definite and/or frequent erotic response to observing various stimuli.[59]

		Percent Females	Percent Males
1.	Portrayals of nude figures	3	8
2.	Genitalia of opposite sex	21	many
3.	Own genitalia	1	25
4.	Moving pictures	9	6
5.	Burlesque and floor shows	4	28
6.	Portrayals of sexual action	14	42
7.	Animals in coitus	5	11
8.	Fantasies of opposite sex	22	37
9.	Fantasies during masturbation	50	72
10.	Stimulation by erotic stories	2	16

These findings indicate a higher erotic response by males to almost all sexual stimuli. The male and female are closest together on those items involving some "love" and furthest apart on those items related to "pure sex." It is possible that the difference in male and female responses to erotic stimulation are either becoming less or may have always been less than was generally believed. For example, Masters and Johnson found that 75 percent of the women they studied showed a reaction of the clitoral glands when they were exposed to pornographic literature.[60]

"Our sexual behavior is essentially the result of our attitudes toward sex; and these attitudes, in turn, are a product of how we have been brought up."[61] Given the emergent middle-class assumption of sexual rights in marriage for the wife, a new kind of social conditioning is taking place. The woman enters marriage expecting sexual

---

[57]Ibid., p. 164.
[58]Ibid., p. 644.
[59]Ibid., pp. 652–71.
[60]Masters and Johnson, op. cit., p. 102.
[61]Allan Fromme, Sex and Marriage (New York: Barnes and Noble, Inc., 1955), p. 95.

satisfaction; if she does not achieve it, she may feel that something very important to marriage is missing. The implications of this assumption for the husband-wife relationship will be discussed later in the chapter.

Differential Reproductive Burden

The significant reproductive difference between the male and female is the absolute biological requirements of sex. The woman must carry the fetus from time of conception until she gives birth; the male need only provide the sperm. Even in "emancipated" contemporary American society, the woman may find that her greater reproductive burden leads to various kinds of sexual discrimination. If married, she may not get the kind of a job she wants or a promotion in a job she has because it is assumed that if she becomes pregnant, she must leave the job for at least several months.

Historically, the reproductive load on the woman has been viewed as inevitable. Yet there is a possibility that, in the future, this could be reduced a great deal. Suppose that a woman could have her own natural child, but not have to go through pregnancy and the giving of birth. Could a woman have a child through a "proxy mother"? Winchester feels there is reason to believe that it is possible.[62] "An egg from the wife, fertilized by a sperm from the husband, could safely develop in the body of another woman with young, healthy reproductive organs and the couple could have a child which was entirely their own—just as much so from the standpoint of heredity as if the wife had borne it."[63] While the proposal is probably of little appeal for the vast majority of women, it does offer a startling means of reducing the traditional reproductive burden of women. As Winchester points out, "For thousands of years, women have often depended on the so-called 'wet nurse' to feed their babies after birth. Why not then carry the process a step further and have prenatal 'wet nurses'?"[64]

SEXUAL ADJUSTMENT

Because of the great interest and attention directed at sexual adjustment in marriage, sexual and overall adjustment in marriage are sometimes thought of as being synonymous. But while the sexual

[62]A. M. Winchester, *Heredity and Your Life* (New York: Dover Publications, Inc., 1960), p. 52.

[63]*Ibid.*, p. 52.

[64]*Ibid.*, p. 53.

aspect is of great importance, it is not the same as overall marital adjustment. To assume that good sexual adjustment will make a marriage, or that poor sexual adjustment will destroy it, does not seem to be the usual case. Burgess and Wallin came to the conclusion in their study that "although good sexual adjustment increases the chances of high marital success, poor sexual adjustment by no means precludes it."[65] Terman found that, of those he studied, intercourse was almost as frequent in the most unhappily married group as in the happily married group.[66]

As discussed in Chapter 10, the honeymoon and early stages of marriage are of great importance for developing the paired abilities related to the changing nature of sexual adjustment in marriage. Marriage provides the setting for sexual expression but, as Kirkpatrick points out, marriage has a dual influence on sexual behavior. "On the one hand, a more favorable environment for love is usually provided, with privacy, social approval, freedom from guilt feelings, and a more exclusive direction of erotic responses to the marriage partner. On the other hand, there is some extinction of sex responses with loss of novelty and with intimate association."[67] The initially exciting novelty of sex in marriage may quickly move into the realm of marital routine. If it does, the ability to redefine the sexual situation becomes important for many couples.

The Changing Nature of Sexual Adjustment

Sexual adjustment in marriage calls for at least minimum satisfaction for the self and the other in sexual interaction. The sexual-role relationship is less often than other areas of interaction in marriage guided by open verbal communication. Frequently, each partner may have to try and "read" the sexual desires of the partner. Because of the failure to communicate, one partner may mistakenly believe that the techniques and frequency of marital coitus are satisfactory to the other. Role-relationship efficiency is based on the assumption of symbolic interaction and if it does not exist, the persons may feel a sense of role frustration. Because the sex act and the marriage role are new to the young married woman, and because taboos against open sex verbalization—even after marriage—still exist, the woman may not be able psychologically to free herself for

[65]Ernest Burgess and Paul Wallin, *Engagement and Marriage* (Chicago: J. B. Lippincott Co., 1953), p. 692.

[66]L. M. Terman, *Psychological Factors in Marital Happiness* (New York: McGraw-Hill, 1938), p. 277.

[67]Clifford Kirkpatrick, *The Family* (New York: The Ronald Press Co., 1955), p. 439.

open communication. The young wife may desire greater frequency of intercourse, different methods of foreplay, or different techniques of sexual expression, but be too inhibited to let her husband know it, either by action or word. As time goes along and the wife's role as a sexual partner becomes more internally a part of her self concept, many of her inhibitions may be dropped. Over the years, most females become less inhibited and develop an interest in sexual relations which they may then maintain until they are in their 50's or even 60's.[68]

The importance of sexual communication in marriage is stressed by Masters and Johnson. They suggest that "rather than following any preconceived plan for stimulating his sex partner, the male will be infinitely more effective if he encourages vocalization on her part. The individual woman knows best the areas of her strongest sensual focus and the rapidity and intensity of manipulative technique that provides her with the greatest degree of sexual stimulation."[69] The above suggestion helps to get away from the idea that the male, in some intuitive way, is an expert on the female's sexual feelings and desires. Because of the different sexual needs of males and females, as well as variations for either sex at different times, the achievement of sexual expertise will be the result of the effective interaction between the two individuals, rather than resting only on the skills of the male partner. What often happens is that the man thinks himself an expert and the female is reluctant to point out otherwise. The woman is always faced with the problem of the male wondering how she acquired her knowledge "and arousing his anxiety about her ability to make invidious comparisons. Consequently, the sexual relation is learned by and large through the exchange of cues and gestures rather than through discussion or direct experimentation."[70]

A majority of young women are probably able to achieve at least some degree of sexual satisfaction early in marriage. Kinsey found that 49 percent of the females in his sample had experienced orgasm in their coitus within the first month of marriage. By the end of the first year, 75 percent had experienced orgasm in at least some of their coitus.[71] Later in marriage, sexual satisfaction decreases for both the male and female. By the time the wife reaches her late 50's, about 65 percent were reaching orgasm. In a study of husbands, it

---

[68]Kinsey, (Female), *op. cit.*, p. 353.
[69]Masters and Johnson, *op. cit.*, p. 66.
[70]John H. Gagnon, "Sexuality and Sexual Learning in the Child," *Psychiatry*, August, 1965, p. 214.
[71]Kinsey, (Female), *op. cit.*, p. 383.

was found that, over a 10-year period, 25 percent changed their level
of sexual adjustment. The writers felt it was impressive that 75 percent retained their early levels of sexual adjustment.[72]

Frequency of sexual relations is closely related to length of marriage. The average frequency of marital coitus in the Kinsey sample
had started at 2.8 per week for the females who were married in
their late teens.[73] This coital frequency dropped to 2.2 per week by
30 years of age, to 1.5 per week by 40, to 1.0 per week by 50, and
to 0.6 per week by age 60.[74] While 99 percent of all the married females in the younger age groups had an active incidence of marital
coitus, the number dropped to 80 percent of the women after 55
years of age.[75]

Frequency of marital coitus may or may not correspond with the
desires of different couples or individuals in any given marriage.
Burgess and Wallin asked their couples the number of times per
month they preferred intercourse. Only 17 percent of the husbands
and 25 percent of the wives said four or fewer times per month. At
the other extreme, 46 percent of the husbands and 37 percent of
the wives said nine or more times per month.[76] These data indicate
some differences between men and women, with the men desiring
greater sexual frequency than the women. A contrast with desires
in the past, as stated by husbands and wives, can be seen by comparing the responses of Burgess and Wallin with the earlier study by
Terman. The Terman study found that only 29 percent of the husbands and 20 percent of the wives said they would like to have coitus
nine or more times per month.[77]

The degree of satisfaction with sexual intercourse is also important. One common measurement used is the achievement of orgasm,
though this is a measurement of satisfaction with given sexual acts
and not a measurement of whether or not the person feels his sexual
needs are being satisfied over the long run. In reference to the sexual
act itself, the male almost always achieves orgasm but the married
female reaches orgasm in only a portion of her coitus; and some percentage of all the females in the Kinsey sample had never reached
orgasm at any time, in any of their marital coitus.[78] Of all those

[72]Robert A. Dentler and Peter Pineo, "Sexual Adjustment and Personal Growth of
Husbands: A Panel Analysis," Marriage and Family Living, February, 1960, p. 46.
[73]Kinsey, (Female), op. cit., p. 348.
[74]Ibid., p. 349.
[75]Ibid., p. 348.
[76]Burgess and Wallin, op. cit., p. 663.
[77]Terman, op. cit., p. 287.
[78]Kinsey, (Female), op. cit., p. 352.

women who achieved orgasm in marital coitus, Kinsey estimates the average female in the sample had reached orgasm in something between 70 and 77 percent of her marital coitus.[79]

The second aspect of sexual satisfaction is whether the marriage partner satisfies the individual's overall sexual desires. Burgess and Wallin found in their sample that complete relief of sexual desires was given by the marital partner for 73 percent of the husbands and 61 percent of the wives.[80] One psychiatrist writes that "conservative estimates report that less than half of all marriages show sexual compatibility. Less conservative ones indicate that not one marriage in ten has a satisfactory sexual relationship."[81] While these studies and estimates show wide variations, it seems safe to assume that at least one partner in from one quarter to one half of all marriages finds the sexual relationship to some degree inadequate.

It is of interest to note that Kinsey found the higher-educated female had a distinctly higher frequency of achieving orgasm in marriage than the lower-educated female. Rainwater, in his study, found that 50 percent of the middle-class wives stated a very positive gratification about their sexual relations as compared to 20 percent of the lower lower-class wives.[82] He also found that 78 percent of the middle-class husbands were "very interested" in marital coitus as compared to only 35 percent of the lower-class husbands.[83] Contributing to the higher-educated woman's greater sexual satisfaction is the fact that she is less restricted by fear and ignorance, and that there is also probably more extended foreplay and general sexual sophistication on both her part and the part of her husband.

MALE-FEMALE COMPARISONS

Because of the differential socialization process, young men and women enter marriage with different attitudes in regard to marital coitus. Burgess and Wallin found that 10 percent of the husbands and 26 percent of the wives entered marriage with sex attitudes of disgust, aversion or indifference.[84] But what is of greatest importance is that while some sex differences continue, the differences are not

[79]*Ibid.*, p. 375.
[80]Burgess and Wallin, *op. cit.*, p. 669.
[81]O. Spurgeon English, "Sexual Adjustment in Marriage," in Morris Fishbein and Ruby Jo R. Kennedy, *Modern Marriage and Family Living* (New York: Oxford University Press, 1957), p. 215.
[82]Rainwater, *op. cit.*, p. 64.
[83]*Ibid.*, p. 67.
[84]Burgess and Wallin, *op. cit.*, p. 660.

great. That 90 percent of the husbands and 74 percent of the wives entered marriage with sex attitudes of interest, anticipation, or eager longing shows the overall high interest for both males and females.

This writer in a study of college-educated wives asked: "Looking back to before you were married, in light of your married experience, how would you assess your estimate at that time as to the importance of sex in marriage?" The responses were 29 percent, "overestimated"; 58 percent, "about what was estimated"; and 13 percent, "underestimated."[85] The fact that 3 out of 10 wives made a downward reassessment of the importance of sex in marriage is of interest. Further, a relationship existed between the assessment of the importance of sex in marriage and the overall evaluation of happiness with marriage. The importance of sex in marriage was about what they had estimated, for 67 percent of those who rated their marriage "very happy," as contrasted to only 36 percent of those who rated their marriage happiness as "average" or less.[86]

In the same study, the wives were asked to estimate their own and their husband's feelings about the sexual adjustment of their marriage. Seventy-nine percent of the wives rated their sexual adjustment as "very good" or "good" and 78 percent rated their husband's feelings at the same level. Of those women who rated their marriages as "very happy," 95 percent rated their own sexual adjustment and 94 percent their husband's sexual adjustment as "very good" or "good." This is in contrast to 51 and 46 percent ratings of self and husband's sexual adjustment as "very good" or "good" by those women who assessed their marriage as "average" or less.[87] The general sexual satisfaction of the husband and wife, at least as seen by the wife, seems to be the same at different levels of marital happiness.

Burgess and Wallin provide some figures on the comparative degree of passion between husband and wives. Of the husbands, 47 percent said they were more passionate and 17 percent said that their wives were. The wives said the husbands were more passionate in 59 percent of the cases and that they were in 8 percent.[88] These findings indicate some tendency for both husbands and wives to overestimate the passion of the other. It is important to recognize that

[85]Robert R. Bell, "Some Factors Related to the Sexual Satisfaction of the College Educated Wife," *Family Life Coordinator,* April 1964, p. 44.
[86]*Ibid.,* p. 44.
[87]*Ibid.,* p. 44.
[88]Burgess and Wallin, *op. cit.,* p. 662.

roughly half of both husbands and wives see the wife as equally or more passionate than the husband.

The purpose of these figures is to indicate that the wife in marriage has not as yet reached the same level of sexual interest and anticipation as the husband. However, very great changes have occurred, so that in possibly half of all marriages the wife will, on some occasions, show a sexual interest equal to or greater than that of the husband. This writer contends that these figures indicate a drastic change in the cultural conditioning of sexual expectations for the female in marriage. The important question is raised of just how far the changes in social conditioning may go and what the implications for the sexual nature of marriage may be in the future, if the woman should achieve even greater sexual emancipation.

Experts today generally believe that, no matter how high or low the incidence of intercourse may be, the frequency of sexual relationships is not the question; rather, the question is how the couple define the relationship, and that is a matter of agreement between them.[89] As one writer puts it "happiness in sexual relationships comes most readily to the couple who have been able to adjust their desires so that approximately the same amount and type of sexual intimacy satisfies both."[90]

Some writers believe that sexual satisfaction can be reached through the will and desire to do so. They base this belief on the assumption that the couple can and will articulate their sexual needs to one another, and act on them. However, if needs are different, an agreement on a sexual relationship may be reached that does not meet the needs of one of the individuals. Too often, the implication of some writers is that simply by reaching agreement the basic sexual needs are changed. This assumption is illustrated by the statement of one writer that "the two share intercourse just as they share dancing, picnics, or music."[91] If the sexual needs of the couple are quite different, they may reach a point of compromise which is workable for their relationship, but which may not meet their individual sexual needs. To say that you will have intercourse less, because your partner wants it less, does not mean that you will no longer continue to wish it were more frequent. Frequency of marital coitus is a more complex and interpersonally meaningful decision than whether to take hard-boiled or deviled eggs on a picnic.

---

[89]Fromme, *op. cit.*, p. 99.
[90]Ruth S. Cavan, *The American Family* (New York: Appleton-Century-Crofts, Inc., 1957), p. 261.
[91]*Ibid.*, p. 261.

Given the importance of need satisfaction in the sexual nature of marriage, contemporary emphasis on the interests of the woman adds an increasingly important dimension to the problem of sexual adjustment in marriage. One implication of this change is that not only are women increasingly achieving sexual satisfaction, but they are also increasingly conscious of *lack of achievement*. An implied assumption has been that once restrictions on marital sex are removed, the wife will catch up to the husband in sexual desire and will then be his sexual equal. What generally has not been recognized is that some women may pass their husbands in sexual interest. In the writer's study, when the wives were asked to assess the frequency of sexual relations in their marriages, 25 percent said that it was "too infrequent."[92] One out of four wives were saying that, for a variety of reasons, there was not enough coitus in their marriage to satisfy them. This is a recent and generally unanticipated sexual response for wives.

As more and more restrictions are removed from the woman and she is encouraged to achieve sexual satisfaction, it seems logical that the change in her sexual desires will include the desire for greater frequency of sexual intercourse. Theoretically, the woman's ability to indulge in sexual intercourse is not biologically restricted. In other words, she continues to be sexually limited by social and psychological influences, but as these are altered or removed, the biological restrictions remain few. It is suggested that through the loss or modification of inhibiting values, women are moving in a less inhibited direction. If this be true, then the biological differences between the male and female in regard to sexual frequency become of increasing significance. In illustration of male-female differences, "actively masturbating women controlling their own sexual response levels will experience five to twenty recurrent orgasmic experiences with sexual tension never allowed to drop below a plateau phase maintenance level until physical exhaustion terminates the session."[93]

Thus, a number of married couples may find themselves in a situation where the sexual interests of the wife have increased past those of the husband. But because of the biological limitations on the man, he, unlike the woman, cannot normally, without some interest, function as a sex partner. While this difference is probably not an important problem early in marriage, it may become one as

---

[92]Bell, *op. cit.*, p. 45.
[93]Masters and Johnson, *op. cit.*, p. 109.

the couple grow older, with the sexual interest of the woman often increasing and many of her early inhibitions removed. As the male grows older, his sexual drive—as well as, in some cases, his sexual interests—are often decreasing. Thus, the older wife may desire more frequent coitus, while her husband is neither physically nor psychologically capable of satisfying her need. This can be extremely important to the male who makes a close association between his sexual potency and his sense of masculinity.

A somewhat extreme case will illustrate the implications of this situation for the male. Suppose that the wife for some reason hates her husband and wants to hurt him. She could do this sexually by insisting on intercourse until he is no longer able to have an erection, and then accuse him of not being a man. It is the male who must always quit; no equivalent of erection is required for the woman to indulge in sexual intercourse.

In the future, the number of marital sexual problems involving a lack of satisfaction for the woman may possibly increase. While this would be an ironic switch from the past, the results may be far more serious for the inadequate or uninterested male than they were for the restricted female.

SEXUAL PROBLEMS IN MARRIAGE

The nature of the problems related to both personal and paired sexual satisfaction in marriage are complex, because in varying degrees they are causally related to biological, psychological, and social influences. The discussion that follows focuses on several important sexual problem areas in marriage.

Frigidity

Generally, frigidity is defined as the failure of the woman to be sexually aroused or to reach orgasm in sexual relations. The definition implies several possible dimensions. One indicates an incapacity to function sexually, which is sometimes attributed to biological causes. But most of the evidence today indicates that the causes of frigidity are primarily psychological, rather than physical. To illustrate, the causes may be due to early negative socialization in regard to sex, or may be a result of the female's feelings for her sex partner. For example, some women become frigid if they develop a dislike for their husbands; for them the necessary condition of love has been destroyed. In most instances frigidity seems to have been caused by "irrational guilt and shame—invoking ideas which have been inculcated in the frigid woman early in her life and which she has been unconsciously reiterating to herself for many years."[94] The frequency of frigidity is difficult to estimate. In the Kinsey study of the female, it was found that ultimately 10 percent of the wives never achieved orgasm in marital coitus.[95] However, the failure to achieve orgasm does not necessarily mean that the woman is frigid; some women may achieve sexual satisfaction in marriage without orgasm. They may find the act pleasurable to themselves and their husbands because of psychological satisfactions. The woman who honestly defines her sexual activity as satisfactory, with or without orgasm, has from her point of view achieved sexual satisfaction. In some cases, she may feel some sense of sexual frustration but still perform the sexual act so that her husband believes she is achieving complete satisfaction. The husband will rarely do this.

Impotency

As a sexual problem, impotency for the man is quite different from frigidity in the woman. The most common type of impotency is *erectal* impotence, which means the inability to have an erection sufficient for sexual intercourse. A second type, called *ejaculatory* impotence, is the incapacity to ejaculate even when aroused and in erection. This second type is very rare; Kinsey and his associates found it in only 6 out of 4,108 males they studied.[96]

The Kinsey study found that impotency in the male was less common than many experts have believed. They found erectal impotence in less than 1 percent of the males under 35 years of age and of this group, only a small number had lifelong impotency.[97] Impotency increases as the male ages, but not at a rapid rate; of males 70 years of age, only 27 percent have become totally impotent.[98]

Impotency for the male has generally far more important implications than frigidity for the female. The impotent male cannot usually indulge in sexual relations, while the frigid female can, and sexual potency is usually more closely linked to masculinity than sexual desire in the woman is to feminity. As suggested earlier, a decrease in the husband's sexual interest and ability may have implications for the wife with strong sexual interests and unrestricted ability.

---

[94]Ellis and Abarbanel, *op. cit.*, p. 455.
[95]Kinsey, (Female), *op. cit.*, p. 392.
[96]Alfred C. Kinsey, Wardell Pomeroy, and Clyde E. Martin, *Sexual Behavior in the Human Male* (Philadelphia: W. B. Saunders Co., 1948), p. 237.
[97]*Ibid.*, p. 237.
[98]*Ibid.*, p. 237.

Aging

With few exceptions, the approach to marital sex has traditionally been presented by family textbook writers as something peculiar to the young and newly married, with discussion centering around the early stages of sexual expression and adjustment in marriage. The implication seems to be that with time the married couple will either achieve some sexual adjustment or that sex will become of lesser importance to them. That marital sex for middle-aged and elderly married couples has generally been ignored by text writers has been in part due to there being little research knowledge to draw upon. One of the major contributions of the research of Masters and Johnson has been their findings with regard to sex and the aging.

For the woman, the first strong feeling of aging usually occurs at the time of the menopause. But while this represents the end of her childbearing years, it does not mean the end of her sexual interests or abilities. The menopause does not occur all at once, but may represent a transition over many months. The menopause may start as early as age 35, but it more commonly begins at 45 to 47 and it may not occur until the early or even the middle 50's.[99] The majority of women, "about four-fifths in fact, pass through this period without any ill effects whatever and, so far as regular health is concerned, without even being aware of it."[100] Masters and Johnson found no reason why the menopause should be expected to slow down the female's sexual capacity, performance or drive. "The healthy aging woman normally has sex drives that demand resolution—there is no time limit drawn by the advancing years to female sexuality."[101]

As the woman moves into older age, her sexual activity shows some decrease, usually due to two main causes. One, her own decrease in sexual interest and two, the fact that a large number of older women have no spouse or have a spouse with little or no sexual interest and/or ability. Christenson and Gagnon found that for married women at age 55, 89 percent were coitally active; by age 60 the rate was 70 percent and by age 65 the rate was 50 percent.[102] Also at age 65, of the married women, 25 percent were actively in-

[99]G. Lombard Kelly, "Menopause" in Albert Ellis and Albert Abarbanel, (eds.) *The Encyclopedia of Sexual Behavior* (New York: Hawthorn Books, Inc., 1961), p. 719.

[100]*Ibid.*, p. 718.

[101]Masters and Johnson, *op. cit.*, pp. 246–47.

[102]Cornelia Christenson and John H. Gagnon, "Sexual Behavior in a Group of Older Women," *Journal of Gerontology*, July 1965, p. 352.

volved in masturbation; and of women of the same age no longer married, 33 percent were engaging in masturbation.[103]

The major limiting factor on the older woman is not lack of sexual interest but rather the lack of a sexually active partner. Christenson and Gagnon found that "in terms of both incidence and frequency of coitus the relative age of the husband was a strongly determining factor: the wives with husbands younger than they showed higher figures and those with older husbands considerably lower ones, at successive ages for the females."[104] Masters and Johnson came to essentially the same conclusion—that the sexual activity of women at 70 year of age and over was greatly influenced by male attrition.[105] In the Christenson and Gagnon sample, there was not a single case of a woman at 65 or over involved in post-marital coitus.[106]

For the male, the central problem of aging is the fear of impotency. A male at any age may have temporary impotency. It may occur only on occasion, or for varying periods of time. In almost all cases, impotency is believed to be caused by psychological factors such as overwork, anxiety, fear, and fatigue. For the male in a temporary state of impotency, the inability may contribute to his problems and intensify his impotency. He worries about his inability to have an erection and, as a result, the worry contributes to even greater difficulty. Generally, the cure for impotency is rest and mental relaxation—which for many men may be easier said than done.

Generally speaking, as the male grows older his fear of impotency becomes increasingly important. Masters and Johnson state that there is no way to overemphasize the importance that "fear of failure" plays in the aging males withdrawal from sexual performance. "Once impotent under any circumstances, many males withdraw voluntarily from any coital activity rather than face the ego-shattering experience of repeated episodes of sexual inadequacy."[107]

As suggested, the fear of impotency is not something that waits for old age, but it is often a characteristic of middle age. Fears of impotence, "were expressed under interrogation, by every male study subject beyond forty years of age, irrespective of reported levels of formal education."[108] As the male reaches middle age, there are often many concerns on his part that repress his sexual interests for long

---

[103]*Ibid.*, p. 352.
[104]*Ibid.*, p. 355.
[105]Masters and Johnson, *op. cit.*, p. 245.
[106]Christenson and Gagnon, *op. cit.*, p. 352.
[107]Masters and Johnson, *op. cit.*, pp. 269–70.
[108]*Ibid.*, p. 202.

periods of time. "This sensitivity of male sexuality to mental fatigue is one of the greatest differences between the responsiveness of the middle-aged and the younger male."[109]

As the male moves into old age, there are other factors that restrict his sexual interest and/or sexual ability. Masters and Johnson state that "loss of coital interest engendered by monotony in a sexual relationship is probably the most constant factor in the loss of an aging male's interest in sexual performance with his partner."[110] At the same time, many of these men may be married to women who have little or no sexual interest and many of the women "by their own admission . . . no longer showed either sexual interest or sexual concern for their husbands."[111]

What appears to be most significantly related to active marital sexual expression in old age is whether there has been an overall pattern of active sexual interaction during the marriage. "When the male is stimulated to high sexual output during his formative years and a similar tenor of activity is established for the 31–40 year age range, his middle-aged and involutional years usually are marked by constantly recurring physiologic evidence of maintained sexuality."[112] But what is of great importance in the research of Masters and Johnson is that the "male over 50 years old can be trained out of his secondarily acquired impotence in a high percentage of cases. If he is in adequate health, little is needed to support adequacy of sexual performance in a 70- or even 80-year-old male other than some physiologic outlet or psychologic reason for a reactivated sexual interest."[113]

Adultery

In the United States, the stated attitudes and values are that sexual outlet after marriage will be restricted to the marriage partner. In the past, the male might discreetly indulge in sexual relations outside of his marriage. Sometimes he was expected to, because of sexual needs that could not be met by the good, nonsexual woman he married. But only under rare circumstances was the wife expected to have a sexual outlet outside of marriage. The traditional double-standard attitudes have changed to the extent that both partners are expected to restrict their sex needs to marriage and any extramarital

---

[109]*Ibid.*, p. 267.
[110]*Ibid.*, p. 264.
[111]*Ibid.*, p. 265.
[112]*Ibid.*, p. 262.
[113]*Ibid.*, p. 263.

"rights" of the husband are not much greater than those of the wife.

Anthropologists find that, in some societies, a need is recognized for some extramarital coitus for the male. Generally, this permission is given to relieve for him the pressures of society's insistence on stable marital partnerships. These same societies, however, less often permit it for the female.[114] Some primitive societies reflect the same patriarchal distinctions of sexual outlet for the husband and wife as did the American society of the past. But there have been some societies where adultery for the female was an accepted pattern of sexual behavior and did not result in any undue conflict.

Compared to many other societies, the United States takes a strong position against adultery. Hunt points out that various American studies suggest that roughly 80 percent of American women do not expect or intend to seek extramarital relations, "while 36 percent of a sample of French and Belgian women—though not asked exactly the same question—said that a wife's fidelity is unimportant to the marriage, and another 37 percent termed it desirable but not necessary."[115] Christensen, in comparing the responses of a midwestern American sample with one from Denmark, found several important differences. He found that 41 percent of the Danish males and 36 percent of the females indicated approval of sexual infidelity if the need arose during a long absence from the spouse. Approval was stated by only 12 percent of the American males and 5 percent of the females.[116] Christensen also asked for reactions to infidelity if one was in love with another married person. Approval for sexual relations under this condition was stated by 27 percent of the males and 29 percent of the females in the Danish sample, but only 7 percent of the males and 2 percent of the females in the midwest American sample.[117]

Adultery is used here to refer to sexual intercourse with a partner outside the marriage. Adultery is legally punishable in the United States, but actual prosecution is rare. Adultery has its greatest legal importance as grounds for divorce. The traditional taboos against adultery are reflected in the fact that adultery is the only legal ground for divorce recognized by all legal jurisdictions in the United States.

The attitude in this country is that, after marriage, one will want

[114]Kinsey, (Female), *op. cit.,* p. 413.

[115]Hunt, *op. cit.,* p. 127.

[116]Harold T. Christensen, "A Cross-Cultural Comparison of Attitudes Toward Marital Infidelity," *International Journal of Comparative Sociology,* September, 1962, p. 130.

[117]*Ibid.,* p. 130.

to concentrate his sexual drive exclusively on the marriage partner. Implied in discussions of marital sexual adjustment is that the adjustment is between the two married individuals. Rarely is it argued that a married couple might turn to other partners to achieve sexual adjustment, or that, if the needs are different, one might use masturbation, or manual or oral means of achieving a greater sexual outlet without the partner's outlet also increasing. The fact that these possibilities are rarely seriously presented indicates the great influence the legal, religious, and moral values of monogamous coitus have in the United States.

Monogamous sexual values are further implemented by the personalized attitudes that individuals have in regard to sex. The female is generally conditioned to believe that love is a precondition for sexual behavior. If a woman is in love, she gets married if at all possible, and then the relationships of marriage, love, and sexual outlet are usually seen by her as inseparable. The male often views his wife as his exclusive sexual property; any tampering with her is viewed as a severe threat to that which he feels very possessive about. And for both partners, the exclusive, ego-centered nature of the love relationship implies the spouse is not interested in any other age-peer of the opposite sex in any romantic or sexual way. If one shows a romantic or sexual interest in someone else, this may be viewed as catastrophic to the ego-relationship of marriage. But even in this area, male and female differences continue. Many men feel that adultery on the part of the woman is an irreparable blow to their marriage. Women are less inclined to see male adultery in the same extreme way. The husband who has what is seen by the wife as a single sexual encounter may be forgiven; however, if he has an affair of some length, the wife is much more threatened because, to her, a lengthy affair implies that her husband must care about the other woman—thus the "other" woman becomes an emotional threat.

Yet one often gets the impression through the mass media, that adultery is very common to the American middle class. Hunt suggests that, if one accepts the view of mass media, "the major reason for the prevalence of adultery is that it no longer poses moral problems to women, but only tactical ones—the choice of how and when, and the avoidance of detection."[118] But adultery is certainly not common to the vast majority of American middle-class women. "She does not view sexual straying as one of her rights, not adulterous love as a pleasure she deserves to enjoy in addition to those of her married

---

[118]Hunt, *op. cit.*, p. 118.

life. In our society adultery does not coexist with marriage, but combats it; the affair rarely achieves balance and equilibrium, but nearly always is a cause of change and upheaval which ends in its own termination or in marriage."[119]

The stated attitudes against extramarital coitus are extremely strong; yet the behavior patterns indicate that a number of individuals deviate from the norms. The extent to which behavior deviates from the stated values indicates the weakness of the values in effectively influencing behavior. The deviancy also raises questions about the total acceptance of monogamy with exclusive and total sexual satisfaction being achieved through the marital partner.

As suggested, one element of marital sex is the extent to which the partner serves as the exclusive sexual outlet. While it is almost always believed that the total sexual outlet of the married person will be achieved through the marriage partner, many realize that some seek out other sex partners. However, some who do not use the marriage partner as the total sexual outlet do not find other partners. Kinsey estimated that, in the married population studied, the woman achieved about 10 percent of her total sexual outlet through masturbation, and the man 4 to 6 percent.[120] He further estimated that about 89 percent of the married woman's total sexual outlet was with her husband and 81 percent of the husband's with his wife.[121]

When the Kinsey study on the female was first published, several statistics startled the American public, including those on extramarital coitus. Kinsey found in his sample that by age 40, 26 percent of the married women and 50 percent of the married men had had an extramarital coital experience.[122] He found important age differences for men and women; for the men, the highest percentage was in the very young married group, with a gradual decrease with increased age. For the women, the highest percentage was in the age group 36 to 40, but was low for the very young and the older women.[123] The peak rates for extramarital coitus correspond to the different stages of greatest sexual interest and drive for the male and female.

The number of different partners for extramarital coitus is also of importance. Kinsey writes, "Up to the time at which they contributed their histories, some 41 per cent of the females in the active

---

[119]*Ibid.*, p. 119.
[120]Kinsey, (Female), *op. cit.*, p. 173.
[121]*Ibid.*, p. 393.
[122]*Ibid.*, p. 437.
[123]*Ibid.*, p. 416.

sample had confined their extramarital coitus to a single partner; another 40 percent had had contacts with somewhere between two and five partners. This means that 19 per cent had had more than five partners and some 3 per cent had had more than twenty partners in their extramarital relationships."[124] No corresponding figures are in the Kinsey studies on the male.

One should not underestimate the great importance of love to sexual involvement for most women. (This was discussed in some detail with regard to premarital sexual attitudes and behavior, and the variable of emotional feeling is important to all female sexual relationships, including the homosexual. For example, one study found that "the majority of female jail house turnouts have genuine love affairs with their sexual partners, and have repeated contact with the same person."[125] A second study found that the woman who "terminates affairs too quickly is held in scorn by the inmates, as her behavior is held to be promiscuous. This behavior draws forth words of scorn from the inmates because the ideal cultural pattern in the prison is to establish a permanent relationship."[126]

For the female, the Kinsey studies found no overall relationship between frequency of extramarital coitus and educational level, but for the male, the rates were higher in the less educated.[127] By religion for women, the active incidence of extramarital experience was highest among the less devout and was true of all the Protestants, Jewish, and Catholics in the sample.[128] The same general relationship to devoutness of religion was also found for the male.[129]

As pointed out earlier, Kinsey also found a relationship between premarital and extramarital coitus for the female. For example, by age 40, 20 percent of the females without premarital coitus and 39 percent with premarital coitus had experienced extramarital coitus.[130]

Kinsey found that, in the available sample, about 85 percent of all those females engaging in extramarital activity were responding at least on occasion to orgasm. However, as Kinsey points out selective factors may have been involved, and the more responsive fe-

[124]*Ibid.*, p. 425.
[125]David A. Ward and Gene G. Kassebaum, *Women's Prison* (Chicago: Aldine Publishing Co., 1965), p. 193.
[126]Rose Giallombardo, "Social Roles In A Prison for Women," *Social Problems*, Winter, 1966, p. 284.
[127]Kinsey, (Female), *op. cit.*, p. 437.
[128]*Ibid.*, pp. 424, 437.
[129]*Ibid.*, p. 437.
[130]*Ibid.*, p. 427.

males may have been the ones who had most often engaged in extra-marital coitus.[131] Of greater importance than the women's physical response to extramarital coitus—given the strong social taboos against it—are their psychological reactions. If the norm and values of society were fully accepted and incorporated into the personality structure of the individual, then one might expect strong feelings of remorse and guilt by the adulterous females. Kinsey found that "among the married females in the sample who had not had extra-marital experience, some 83 percent indicated that they did not intend to have it, but in a sample of those who had extramarital ex-periences, only 44 per cent indicated that they did not intend to renew their experiences."[132] These findings indicate that a number of women did not have strong enough feelings about their past ex-periences to be deterred from future experiences.

Given the traditional importance attached to the husband's ex-clusive sexual rights to his wife, it might be assumed that a husband who found his wife guilty of adultery would either end or drastically alter the nature of the marriage. But Kinsey found that, of the fe-males who had extramarital coitus, about 49 percent believed that the husband knew or suspected.[133] And in those marriages where the husband suspected or learned of the wife's extramarital activities, 42 percent of the women stated they had no difficulty.[134] While some of the women may have been reading their husbands' reactions in a distorted way, it is also possible that many were not. If they were not, it indicates a very drastic change for at least some husbands from the traditional notion of the wife's sexual exclusiveness. Cer-tainly the feeling of jealousy would be common to the spouse who finds that his partner has been engaging in adultery. But as Steph-ens points out, in some societies that allow adultery, "the jealousy problem still exists; some people are still hurt when their spouses engage in perfectly proper and virtuous adultery."[135]

Realizing the limitations of the Kinsey studies, they nevertheless offer important suggestions about the changing nature of adultery and the influence of traditional attitudes in the United States today. It seems clear that a significant number of both husbands and wives seek and find sexual partners outside of marriage. It also seems clear that this cannot be attributed in all cases to a series of chance cir-

[131]*Ibid.*, p. 418.
[132]*Ibid.*, p. 431.
[133]*Ibid.*, p. 434.
[134]*Ibid.*, p. 434.
[135]William N. Stephens, *The Family in Cross-Cultural Perspective* (New York: Holt, Rinehart & Winston, Inc., 1963), p. 252.

cumstances, especially in the case of the woman who has more than one partner and plans on continuing her extramarital coitus experience in the future. While no stated changes in the attitudes toward extramarital coitus have been made, it is obvious that the old norms no longer exert effective control over a number of husbands and wives. Most significant is the indicated behavioral change in the sexual experience of wives; the philandering of husbands has generally had latent acceptance, but the philandering of wives has not, past or present.

The increase in extramarital coitus is no doubt due to many factors. A brief discussion of a number of variables that may enter into extramarital coitus follows. It should be recognized that, for any given individual, the suggested variables may operate in various combinations with various degrees of intensity.[136]

1. *Variation of sexual experience.* As suggested earlier, the monogamous sexual relationship of man and woman is culturally conditioned, and the conditioning may not be as strong for some individuals as for others. In some cases, the sexual relationship of marriage become routinized and boring and the idea of a new partner suggests the different, new, and exciting. In others, the person may feel his marriage partner is inadequate in meeting his sexual needs and, consequently, seek out a person believed to be a superior sexual partner. The basic motivation may be the desire for new experience.

2. *Retaliation.* If one person in the marriage discovers that his partner has had an extramarital affair, his reaction may be, "If he can, so can I." The motivation is not one of sexual desire for another partner, but of revenge. An affair by the husband of a woman who believes in sexual equality may be interpreted by her as something she too must have to show her sexual equality. In these situations, getting even is a greater factor than sexual interest.

3. *Rebellion.* Some may feel the monogamous nature of marriage is placing an undesired restriction on them and, through extramarital coitus, show their independence. The rebellion may be directed at the spouse, whom they feel restricts them, or against social codes. Some who may feel that the social norms are unreasonable show their objection and contempt by entering a sexual liaison. Here, too, the motivating factor is not the extramarital sex partner, but "showing" the spouse or society in general.

---

[136]*Ibid.,* pp. 432–35. The following list of variables is in part drawn from those compiled by Kinsey and his associates.

4. *New emotional satisfaction.*   Many individuals obviously do not feel their personal ego-needs are being met in the marriage relationship. This may lead some to seek satisfaction from a partner outside the marriage. If the wife feels that the extramarital partner is satisfying her emotional needs, sex often enters the picture. It may also enter as a result of the man meeting other needs she has. The primary motivation here is the search for emotional and/or sexual needs outside of the marriage relationship.

5. *Development from friendship.*   It has been suggested that one reason why cross-sexual friendships among adults are very difficult is the possibility of their moving into romantic or sexual intimacy. In some cases, the man and woman may be friends, and if they spend time together, they may find themselves developing an emotional and sexual interest in each other. Here the motivations may not all be conscious and are possibly related to increased interest and feeling for the person, which ultimately includes sex.

6. *Spouse encouragement.*   In some cases in the Kinsey sample, the husbands had encouraged their wives to engage in extramarital activities. The motive of a number of husbands originated with their desire to find an excuse for their own extramarital activity.[137] What is sometimes referred to as "wife swapping" usually involves this kind of situation. Kinsey found that "most of the husbands who accepted or encouraged their wives' extramarital activity had done so in an honest attempt to give them the opportunity for additional sexual satisfaction."[138]

7. *The aging factor.*   As mentioned earlier, the highest rate of extramarital coitus for women occurs in the age group 36 to 40. Several factors may operate for women in this age group. First, their sexual desires and interests are high as a result of a strong sex drive and the loss of many sexual inhibitions that operated when they were younger. At the same time, many of their husbands have had a decrease in sexual drive and interest. Second, the woman is entering middle age and leaving her youth behind. She may want to prove to herself (and sometimes others) that she is still a desirable female; extramarital affairs may be seen as one way of doing so.

When adultery does occur, whatever the reasons, it tends to be of short duration, because the sexual act is not usually treated separately from the general values of love and interpersonal commitment by the woman. Hunt writes that "the adulteress in Ameria generally

---

[137]*Ibid.*, p. 435.
[138]*Ibid.*, p. 435.

makes a rather poor mistress, even when she is sexually responsive and suitably flattering to a man's ego, because she wants too much of her lover—she wants him to be her mainstay in life, her be-all and end-all, and, inevitably, her legal mate. It is enough to frighten any sensible philanderer away."[139]

Many other variables are related to extramarital coitus, but the ones suggested point out some of the ways in which this kind of behavior may be influenced. When we relate our discussion of extramarital sexual behavior to premarital sexual behavior, it becomes clear that the stated attitudes and actual behavior are often in conflict in today's American society. More important, it indicates to the social scientist that the attitudes are not effective deterrents of nonmarital coitus and are not incorporated by a number of individuals to the extent that their violation leads to any great guilt or remorse. The question of whether individuals "really" feel guilt is a problem for the psychiatrist to study. The lack of agreement between the moral sexual norms and the sexual behavior of many individuals points up the "schizoid" nature of sex in America.

SELECTED BIBLIOGRAPHY

BELL, ROBERT R. "Some Factors Related to the Sexual Satisfaction of the College Educated Wife," *Family Life Coordinator,* April 1964, pp. 43–47.

CHRISTENSON, CORNELIA and JOHN H. GAGNON. "Sexual Behavior In A Group of Older Women," *Journal of Gerontology,* July 1965, pp. 351–56.

CLARKE, HELEN I. *Social Legislation,* chaps. vii and viii. New York: Appleton-Century-Crofts, Inc., 1957.

DENTLER, ROBERT A., and PINEO, PETER. "Sexual Adjustment, Marital Adjustment and Personal Growth of Husbands: A Panel Analysis," *Marriage and Family Living,* February, 1960, pp. 45–48.

FARRIS, EDMUND J. *Human Ovulation and Fertility.* Philadelphia: J. B. Lippincott Co., 1956.

FREEDMAN, RONALD, WHELPTON, PASCAL K., and CAMPBELL, ARTHUR A. *Family Planning, Sterility and Population Growth.* New York: McGraw-Hill Book Co., 1959.

FROMME, ALLAN. *Sex and Marriage.* New York: Barnes & Noble, Inc., 1955.

GORDON, EDGAR S. "Taking Physical Factors into Account," in Becker, Howard, and Hill, Reuben, *Family, Marriage and Parenthood.* Boston: D. C. Heath & Co., 1955.

---

[139]Hunt, *op. cit.,* p. 139.

GUTTMACHER, ALAN F., *et al. The Complete Book of Birth Control.* New York: Ballantine Books, 1961.

HUNT, MORTON M. *The Natural History of Love,* chaps. ix and x. New York: Alfred A. Knopf, Inc., 1959.

KINSEY, ALFRED C., POMEROY, WARDELL B., MARTIN, CLYDE E., and GEBHARD, PAUL H. *Sexual Behavior in the Human Female.* Philadelphia: W. B. Saunders, 1953.

MASTERS, WILLIAM H. and VIRGINIA E. JOHNSON. *Human Sexual Response,* (Boston: Little, Brown and Co., 1966).

OGG, ELIZABETH. *A New Chapter in Family Planning.* New York: Public Affairs Committee, Inc., 1964.

TERMAN, L. M. *Psychological Factors in Marital Happiness,* chaps. x to xiii, and xiv. New York: McGraw-Hill Book Co., 1938.

WESTOFF, CHARLES F., POTTER, ROBERT G., SAGI, PHILIP C., and MISHLER, ELLIOT G. *Family Growth in Metropolitan America.* Princeton, N. J.: Princeton University Press, 1961.

WINCHESTER, A. M. *Heredity and Your Life.* New York: Dover Publications, Inc., 1960.

14

PARENT-CHILD INTERACTION: INFANCY AND CHILDHOOD

In all societies, marriage is generally expected to be followed by parenthood. Positive values about children are basic to societies because the birth of infants is an obvious necessity for their continuation. Murdock points out, "even if the burdens of reproduction and child care outweigh the selfish gains to the parents, the society as a whole has so heavy a stake in the maintenance of its members, as a source of strength and security, that it will insist that parents fulfill these obligations."[1]

Historically, parents have had a variety of personal and social obligations in childbearing and childrearing. The first function of parents is simply that of reproduction. Societies have generally accepted the belief that reproduction should be a function of marriage, and taboos of varying strengths against birth outside of marriage have been developed to keep the reproductive function within marriage. Second, societies have almost always delegated the responsibility for meeting the needs of the totally dependent infant to the parents, especially the mother. The parents continue to meet the child's needs until he reaches the social age of independence. Third, the parents are expected to make the child a functioning member of society. "Parents are society's representatives, and they are expected to bring the child into conformity with the socially approved patterns."[2]

It is through society that the agencies and the agents of socialization are brought to bear on each newborn infant. Socialization is not only basic to the social development of each individual, but it is also necessary to the future of any society. For a society to continue, there must be institutionalized means through which the young are trained to take on a positive orientation to significant cultural

---

[1]George P. Murdock, *Social Structure* (New York: The Macmillan Co., 1949), p. 9.
[2]Ray E. Baber, *Marriage and the Family* (New York: McGraw-Hill Book Co., 1953), p. 252.

values. "This socialization is not only basic to personality develop-ment, but also has manifest implications for and is requisite to social organization."[3]

The three basic functions of parent-child relationship could and have been met by other agencies of society, but usually they have been fulfilled by the parents. Because the parent-child relationship has been in existence so long and in all societies, many view it as "natural," rather than socially determined. Historically, it has been assumed that if adults were capable of having children they were capable of rearing them. The fact that many adults in all societies are poor parents, by any criteria, is generally ignored. In most cul-tures of the world, including the United States, society is so "loath to interfere with the ultimate primary relationships of the family that only in extreme cases will it take the child from its parents."[4]

THE HAVING OF CHILDREN

The having of children sometimes seems to many Americans to be inevitable. Yet a number of American couples will have problems or be completely unable to become biological parents. In the "na-tional" fertility study, it was found that, according to the criteria the investigators used, about one couple in three had a fecundity impairment.[5] Fecundity refers to the capacity of a couple to have children in the future.[6] Ultimately 10 percent of all couples in the "national" study will have no children.[7] In their study of couples in Detroit, Blood and Wolfe found that 11 percent were childless.[8] The "national" study found that less than 1 percent of the couples studied intended to have no children,[9] and the "Detroit" study found that of all the couples, with or without children, only 3 per-cent "wouldn't want any children if they had their life to live over again."[10] It is estimated that about 10 percent of all married couples will be childless, but only 1 to 3 percent are personally satisfied with their childlessness. Therefore, about one out of every 12 couples are

[3]Edward Z. Dager, "Socialization and Personality Development in the Child," in Harold T. Christensen (ed.) Handbook of Marriage and The Family (Chicago: Rand McNally & Co., 1964), p. 747.

[4]Ibid., pp. 252–53.

[5]Ronald Freedman, Pascal K. Whelpton, and Arthur A. Campbell, Family Planning, Sterility and Population Growth (New York: McGraw-Hill Book Co., 1959), p. 26.

[6]Ibid., p. 17.

[7]Ibid., p. 26.

[8]Robert O. Blood and Donald M. Wolfe, Husbands and Wives (Glencoe, Illinois: The Free Press, 1960), p. 137.

[9]Freedman, Whelpton, and Campbell, op. cit., p. 48.

[10]Blood and Wolfe, op. cit., p. 137.

childless even though they desire children. High positive values about having children are accepted by the vast majority of Americans, and the majority of childless couples are not that way by choice.

Fertility problems, and the possibility of childlessness, are generally seen as more personally serious by women than by men. For example, Kirk found that involuntary childlessness represented a serious problem for women: "The terms used by wives have an emergency quality about them. Men, although they may be disappointed by childlessness, appear to feel less deprived. However real their loss, it is probably more readily compensated for by occupational activity."[11]

In recent years, the number of childless couples has been decreasing in the United States. The percentage childless among women married, ages 15 to 44, was in 1910, 16.2 percent; in 1950, 22.8 percent; and in 1959, 14.8 percent.[12] The "national" study points out that "among native born white wives aged 45–49 in 1950, 17 percent had not borne a child. But among those who will be 45–49 in 1965, fewer than 10 percent were childless in 1955."[13] The decrease in childlessness has particular relevance for the middle class, because it is that group which has most drastically increased its birth rate since the end of World War II.[14] A contributing factor has been the high state of economic prosperity during that period, for it may be predicted that the number of middle-class wives having children and the number of children born per wife would be effectively reduced if the American economy should go into an extended depression. A birth rate decrease for the middle class is suggested because of this group's relatively high rational and controlled birth rate.

The "national" study found some relationships between childlessness and social variables. For example, there was "relatively more subfecundity found among the twice-married wives than the others when the comparisons are restricted to wives of the same age or duration of marriage."[15] Perhaps those women who did not have children may have been more prone to divorce than those who did have children. It was also found that working wives had higher incidence of fecundity impairments than those who did not work.[16]

[11]H. David Kirk, *Shared Fate*, (New York: The Free Press of Glencoe, 1964), pp. 2–3.
[12]United States Department of Commerce, Bureau of the Census, *Statistical Abstract of the United States, 1961*, 82d Annual Edition, p. 54.
[13]Freedman, Whelpton, and Campbell, *op. cit.*, p. 46.
[14]*Ibid.*, p. 7.
[15]*Ibid.*, p. 43.
[16]*Ibid.*, p. 53.

(This, however, reflects the fact that a woman without children is more apt to enter the work force than a woman with children.)

In marriage, two crude dimensions of sterility or infertility are made. *Relative* sterility refers to a couple who are having problems of conception, but whose problems may be treated and corrected medically or in some cases are resolved with time. *Absolute* sterility refers to those couples who, on the basis of present knowledge, are incapable of having biological children of their own. One reason for a decrease in the number of childless couples in recent years has been some shift of diagnosis and treatment from absolute to relative sterility. Some infertility problems defined as hopeless a few years ago are susceptible to corrective medical treatment today, because of increased scientific knowledge.

To say that a marriage is sterile says, of course, that the two people cannot be natural parents, even though in most cases the responsibility rests with just one of them. Until recent years, it was generally assumed in most cultures that a childless marriage was the "fault" of the wife. In recent years, the role of the sterile husband has come to be increasingly recognized. Today it is estimated that, in about one third to one half of all infertile marriages, the inability to conceive rests with the husband.

Sterility

Male. Sterility is more easily diagnosed in the male than in the female, though he is not always more easily treated. Farris found that, in 80 percent of the male sterility cases with which he worked, the problem was physiological in origin, not psychological.[17] Sterility in the male is related to number, vigor, and structure of the spermatozoa. The medical assessment of male fertility focuses primarily on an analysis of the cellular components of the ejaculate to determine: (1) if a large number of spermatoza are present and (2) if a large enough number of those spermatozoa have a degree of motile activity sufficient for them to move through the uterus and Fallopian tubes to the ovum.[18]

Farris on the basis of his research findings set up three levels of fertility in the male: "1. *High fertility,* indicated by a count of above 185 million active spermatozoa on the first day and above 80 million on the next day; 2. *Relative fertility,* with a range of 80 to 185 million on the first day, but less than 80 million on the next day;

[17]Edmond J. Farris, "Male Fertility," in Marvin Sussman, *Sourcebook in Marriage and the Family* (Boston: Houghton Mifflin Co., 1955), p. 135.

[18]John Macloed, "Fertility in Men," in Albert Ellis and Albert Abarbanel, (eds.) *Encyclopedia of Sexual Behavior* (New York: Hawthorn Books, Inc., 1961), p. 428.

3. *Subfertility*, with a count of less than 80 million in the majority of semen examinations."[19] On the basis of his studies, Farris suggests that "about 40 percent of the males were highly fertile, about 35 to 40 percent relatively fertile, about 15 percent subfertile, and the rest sterile."[20]

Female. Because the reproductive system of the woman is so much more complex than that of the man, her sterility is often more difficult to diagnose and treat. Some of the most common problems of infertility in the woman are: (1) failure to ovulate; (2) the egg cannot or does not pass through the tubes into the uterus; (3) sperm cannot get through the cervix; (4) vaginal or cervical secretions are hostile to sperm; and (5) the ovum cannot be developed and maintained after fertilization.[21] Many times the diagnosis and treatment of the woman extends over long periods of time, because the use of various corrective measures is ultimately tested by the result of pregnancy. Each new medical approach must normally be tried in a new menstrual cycle; therefore, medically, it may not be possible to work with the patient more than once a month. In many cases, the woman may undergo medical treatment for years.

There is also the fact that the fertility potential of the woman is not the same at all periods during her theoretical childrearing years. As discussed earlier, the fertility of a girl at age 15 is not as great as it will be when she reaches age 20. The greatest fertility age period for women is in the age range of 21 to 25.[22] From then on the woman's fertility potential decreases and by age 35 to 39 the average conception rate is estimated to be about 50 to 75 percent of what it was at the ages of 21 to 25.[23] Only about 1 out of every 1,000 births is to a woman 45 years of age and over.[24]

While pregnancy impairments may emerge after the birth of one or several children, probably the greatest degree of dissatisfaction exists among those couples who are unable to have any children. The existence of fertility problems often takes time to become known and be recognized by married couples. Most people when they marry never think about the possibility of infertility—they simply assume their own fertility potential. Kirk found that with

---

[19]Farris, *op. cit.*, p. 136.

[20]*Ibid.*, p. 139.

[21]James A. Rosen, *Fertility in Men and Women* (New York: Coward McCann, Inc., 1952), pp. 51–52.

[22]Paul H. Gebhard, Wardell B. Pomeroy, Clyde E. Martin, and Cornelia V. Christenson, *Pregnancy, Birth and Abortion* (New York: Harper & Brothers, 1958), p. 81.

[23]Charles F. Westoff, Robert G. Potter, Jr., and Philip C. Sagi, *The Third Child* (Princeton N. J.: Princeton University Press, 1963), p. 23.

[24]Gebhard, *op. cit.*, p. 82.

only 9 out of 70 couples adopting a child could either spouse recall ever considering the possibility that they might not be able to have a child until they were actually faced with the problem.[25] Another study found that women did not become seriously upset about their slowness to conceive until they had been trying for about a year.[26]

For couples who want children, the difference between none and one is usually much greater and important than between one and two. The different degrees of desire for children have not been studied. At one level, couples go through a number of years of marriage without children, but do nothing medically. At another level are those who find they cannot have natural children of their own and stop at that point. Finally, some couples who find out they cannot have biological children of their own seek out a child through adoption. Yet, couples on all of these levels may say and honestly believe they want children.

In childless marriages, the wives are probably more ready to take the necessary steps to try to resolve the problem than are husbands. Because of sex differentials in socialization, the wife sees the child as a greater necessity to her adult role than the husband does to his. Husbands often put up a strong resistance to medical checkups because of a fear that they will be found infertile, a possibility viewed by some men as threatening to their personal sense of masculinity. Husbands may also be more resistant to the possibilities of adoption because they feel less compulsion to be a father and are more threatened than the wife by the idea that the child "would not really be their own."

Mortality

Maternal Mortality. Maternal mortality refers to the death of the mother at the time of childbirth. Over the years, maternal mortality rates have been steadily decreasing and they have continued to decrease through recent years. For example, in 1952, the maternal mortality rate was 6.8 deaths per 10,000 live births while in 1961 it had dropped to 3.2 per 10,000 live births.[27] Or, described in another way the maternal mortality rates dropped an amazing nine tenths in the two decades between 1940 and 1960.[28] But one population group

---

[25]Kirk, *op. cit.,* p. 6.

[26]Westoff, *op. cit.,* p. 31.

[27]*Vital Statistics Report,* Vol. 10, No. 13 (July 31, 1962) (United States Department of Health, Education and Welfare), p. 17.

[28]Paul C. Glick, "Demographic Analysis of Family Data," in Harold T. Christensen (ed.) *Handbook of Marriage and the Family* (Chicago: Rand McNally & Co., 1964), p. 301.

that still has a relatively high maternal death rate are nonwhite women. In 1960, the maternal mortality rate was 2.8 per 10,000 live births for white women as compared to 10 per 10,000 for nonwhite women.[29]

One important reason for the decrease has been the greater tendency for women to have their babies in hospitals—over 90 percent of all births today take place in hospitals. This has taken many births out of the hands of midwives and placed them where medical facilities are available should complications arise. Maternal mortality rates could be still lowered, particularly in the lower social classes and in rural areas.

A relationship exists between maternal mortality and the age of the mother at the time of birth. In 1959, for white women ages 20 to 24, the maternal mortality rate was 1.4 per 10,000 live births; for women age 30 to 34, it increased to 3.3; and for women 45 and over to 14.0.[30]

Infant Mortality. Before discussing infant mortality, some mention must be made of *fetal deaths,* which refer to deaths during pregnancy. Many fetal deaths occur too early in pregnancy to be recognized. "It has been estimated that the complete reporting of fetal deaths in the United States might bring the fetal death rate to 150 or even 200 per 1,000 fetuses."[31] The "national" study found that "one in four of the wives in their sample who were ever pregnant had at least one fetal death."[32]

For many women who experience fetal death, it occurs once or twice and is interspersed with other pregnancies that are healthy and successful. But some childless women also fall into this category; they have no trouble conceiving, but cannot carry a fetus full term and give live birth. Some in this category can be helped by proper medical attention and are eventually able to give live birth.

In the past, the chances of an infant surviving the first year of birth were often limited. As recently as 1940, there were 47.4 deaths per 10,000 live births in the United States, but this dropped to 26 per 10,000 by 1960.[33] Generally, the older the infant the greater his chances for survival. "Twice as many babies die in the first month

[29]"Mortality Analysis and Summary," *Vital Statistics of the United States, 1961,* Vol. 2, Section 1 (United States Department of Health, Education and Welfare), p. 11.
[30]Metropolitan Life Insurance Company, *Statistical Bulletin,* Vol. 42, August, 1961, p. 6.
[31]Freedman, Whelpton, and Campbell, *op. cit.,* p. 35.
[32]*Ibid.,* p. 31.
[33]"Infant Mortality," *Vital Statistics of the United States, 1961,* Vol. 2, Section 3 (United States Department of Health, Education and Welfare), p. 7.

as in all the other months of the first year. Premature babies account for almost half of all infant deaths within the first month after birth."[34] There are several other social factors related to different fetal and infant mortality rates. There is a higher probability of fetal deaths when there are plural births, when the fetus is male and when the pregnancy is among nonwhites.[35] Infant mortality is higher for males as well as nonwhites.[36]

Child spacing is also related to infant mortality. "When births are one year apart, the loss of babies is nearly 50 percent higher than when the births are two years apart."[37] As with maternal mortality, the rate of infant mortality has decreased with greater use of medical facilities. Here, too, improvements can be made in the lower social classes and in rural areas. Both maternal and infant mortality rates could be lowered by earlier medical attention during pregnancy. For example, in many lower-class areas, the mother receives her first medical attention at the time of birth. Problems discovered at that time might not have developed, or could have been medically planned for, if the mother had been under medical supervision earlier in pregnancy.

Pregnancy Fears

One final problem, though probably not as severe as the others discussed, is the apprehension among some women about pregnancy and birth. While the girl in the American culture is socially conditioned for the day when she will become a mother, her first pregnancy is usually an impressive personal experience and she is forced to think about its culmination while it is still months away. Because she is *the* pregnant woman and because she has heard many stories about pregnancy and childbirth, she may face the future birth with some concern. In a study by the Poffenbergers of first pregnancies of a college group, they found that 41 percent worried about the normality of children and 63 percent feared childbirth itself.[38]

A part of the mythology of the American culture is that when a young married woman discovers she is pregnant for the first time she

---

[34]Baber, *op. cit.*, p. 542.

[35]"Fetal Mortality," *Vital Statistics of the United States, 1960*, Vol. 2, Section 4 (United States Department of Health, Education and Welfare), p. 8.

[36]"Infant Mortality," *Vital Statistics of the United States, 1961*, Vol. 2, Section 3 (United States Department of Health, Education and Welfare), p. 4.

[37]Baber, *op. cit.*, p. 546.

[38]Shirley Poffenberger, Thomas Poffenberger and Judson T. Landis, "Intent Toward Conception and Pregnancy Experience," *American Sociological Review*, October, 1952, p. 620.

becomes flushed, coy and radiant; "in actual fact, she is very likely to be frightened and depressed, masking these feelings in order not to be considered contemptible."[39] The belief that pregnant women live in a euphoric state is as misleading as the idea that pregnant women are characteristically anxiety-ridden. Brodsky found that while some expectant mothers fall in the categories of euphoria and anxiety there was no tendency in either direction among pregnant women significantly different from control groups of non-pregnant women with children and married women never pregnant.[40] While pregnant women do not show a deep antagonism to motherhood, it does sometimes happen that "the arrival of pregnancy interrupts a pleasant dream of motherhood and awakens them to the realization that they have too little money, or not enough space, or unresolved marital problems, or have not yet acquired the skills of house-keeping, and so on."[41]

Some women pregnant for the first time probably also tend to make the most out of their pregnancy. When this is added to the common human fear of the unknown and unexperienced, the pregnant woman may build up a state of anxiety. If the first birth turns out to be not too difficult, the second one is usually viewed with much less apprehension.

There is in American society a certain romanticism centered around the birth experience and its significance for the mother. A part of the romantic belief is that giving birth to the first child symbolizes achieving "complete" female role fulfillment. Yet today the birth experience has increasingly become a technical event where the administrative and technical needs of the hospital have top priority and the emotional needs and personalities of the mothers often get in the way of efficiency. "Birth itself may be subordinated to the schedule: some doctors schedule their deliveries, and induce labor to keep them on time. Even 'natural' labor may be slowed down or speeded up by drugs for convenience."[42]

Sexual Relations and Pregnancy. There is often confusion as to what is sexually appropriate when the woman is pregnant, especially for the first time. One common belief has been that the pregnant woman loses interest in sex and her husband finds her sexually

---

[39]Morton M. Hunt, *Her Infinite Variety* (New York: Harper & Row, 1962), p. 174.
[40]Stanley L. Brodsky, "Self-Acceptance in Pregnant Woman," *Marriage and Family Living,* November, 1963, p. 484.
[41]Hunt, *op. cit.,* pp. 174–75.
[42]Marian G. Morris, "Psychological Miscarriage: An End to Mother Love," *Transaction,* January-February, 1966, p. 9.

less attractive as she moves through pregnancy. If there is any question of possible danger, either physical or psychological, to the pregnant mother or her unborn child through sexual relations, then the sexual aspect of the marriage is almost always put aside. This, when it occurs, symbolizes a role decision for the married couple that will prevail for many years—that is, the role demands of being parents will generally take precedence over the role desires of being husband or wife.

Through the research of Masters and Johnson, we now have some data on changes in sexual tensions and effectiveness of sexual performance through the stages of pregnancy.[43] The nine months of pregnancy are divided into three three-month periods, referred to as the first, second and third trimesters. The women studied were divided into two groups, those going through a first full-term pregnancy (Nulliparous) and those attempting a second or more, full-term pregnancy (Parous).

During the first trimester (first three months) of pregnancy, 77 percent of the nulliparous women reported a reduction in sexual tensions or effectiveness in their sexual performance, while 14 percent reported no change and 9 percent an increase. Many of these women were suffering from nausea, and all of them were affected by sleepiness and symptoms of chronic fatigue.[44] Probably because of being pregnant for the first time and unsure of themselves, 60 percent of the nulliparous women reported "fear of injury to the conceptus (frequently not vocalized to their partner) as affecting the freedom of their physical response in coital activity during the first trimester."[45] Possibly due to their previous experiences with pregnancy, very few of the parous women noted any sexual changes during the first trimester; 84 percent reported no change, 10 percent reduction, and 6 percent increase in their levels of sexual interest or effectiveness in sexual performance.[46]

During the second trimester (middle three months), "sexual patterns generally reflected a marked increase in eroticism and effectiveness of performance regardless of parity or ages of the women interrogated."[47] Only 26 percent of the nulliparous and 12 percent of the parous stated no improvement in sexual interest or performance.[48]

---

[43]William H. Masters and Virginia E. Johnson, *Human Sexual Response* (Boston: Little, Brown & Co., 1966), pp. 156–60.
[44]*Ibid.*, pp. 156–57.
[45]*Ibid.*, p. 157.
[46]*Ibid.*, p. 158.
[47]*Ibid.*, p. 158.
[48]*Ibid.*, p. 158.

In the third trimester (last three months) of pregnancy, there was a significant reduction in coital frequency. About three quarters of the women studied had been advised by their doctors to sexually abstain for periods of time varying from four weeks to three months prior to delivery.[49] Although strongly influenced by medical restrictions, 82 percent of the "nulliparous women reported that they personally gradually lost interest in sexual activity during the third trimester."[50] Among the parous women, 75 percent were medically restricted from coitus for various periods of time during the third trimester, and 67 percent of this group reported "a significant reduction in eroticism and frequency of sexual performance as the estimated date of confinement approached."[51]

Masters and Johnson also found that 88 percent of those women "for whom coition was interdicted medically expressed concern with the prescribed period of sexual continence and its possible effect upon their husbands' sexual requirements."[52] Fifty-five percent of the medically restricted nulliparous and 70 percent of the parous women "reported that they made deliberate attempts to relieve their husbands during the period of prescribed continence."[53]

Once the mother has given birth to her child, there is often confusion as to how long the couple should wait before reactivating their sexual life. In many societies there are *post partum* sex taboos and in many societies the sex taboos last for several years.[54] In the Masters and Johnson study, 47 percent of the women described themselves as having low or essentially negligible levels of sexuality during the interviews conducted early in the third post partum month. However, the highest level of postpartum sexual interest in the first three months after delivery was reported by this group of nursing mothers. Not only did they report sexual stimulation induced by suckling their infants, but as a group they also described interest in as rapid return as possible to active coition with their husbands."[55]

THE PLANNING OF FAMILIES

In Chapter 13, the means available today for the planning of families in regard to number and spacing of children was discussed. It

---

[49]*Ibid.*, p. 159.
[50]*Ibid.*, p. 159.
[51]*Ibid.*, p. 160.
[52]*Ibid.*, p. 160.
[53]*Ibid.*, pp. 159–60.
[54]William N. Stephens, *The Family in Cross-Cultural Perspective* (New York: Holt, Rinehart & Winston, Inc., 1963), pp. 348–49.
[55]Masters and Johnson, *op. cit.*, pp. 161–62.

was suggested that along with the rise of contraceptive knowledge has emerged the belief by the married couple that childbearing is a matter of choice rather than fate. However, a number of couples exert little or no control over pregnancy for a variety of personal and social reasons. The "national" study found that, of the couples they studied, 85 percent either completely or partially planned their pregnancies.[56] It is also pointed out that completely planned families are small families. "Not one of the 86 families with six or more births was completely planned."[57] Personal motivation and interest on the part of the wife is also related to child planning. "Among fecund couples, working wives are much more likely than non-working wives to have completely planned fertility."[58]

The ideal number of children in the United States ranges from two to four. Very few women state that they want one or no children and few say they want more than four. There is some evidence that the ideal number of children has shifted upward from the early 1940's. Rainwater found that "almost half the women interviewed think the ideal family should have at least four children. In 1941 only 26 percent thought so."[59] Blood and Wolfe found that 83 percent of the women they studied preferred from two to four children.[60] They also point out that, in the older generation they studied, the higher the social status, the smaller the family, but in the younger generation exactly the opposite was true.[61]

The question might be raised as to why the vast majority of adults want children. Many of the reasons that existed in the past for having children no longer seem important. The economic motive has not only disappeared for the middle class, but in some respects reversed itself. In the past, children made an economic contribution to the family from a rather early age, and also gave economic security and aid to the parents in their old age. When children work today, they do it primarily as a "valuable learning experience," or for "spending money" and not usually to contribute to the total family income. Few middle-class parents expect their children to take care of them in their old age. In fact, in middle-class families, many parents continue to help their children financially long after the

[56]Freedman, Whelpton, and Campbell, op. cit., p. 79.
[57]Ibid., p. 81.
[58]Ibid., p. 137.
[59]Lee Rainwater, And The Poor Get Children (Chicago: Quadrangle Books, 1960), p. 24.
[60]Blood and Wolfe, op. cit., p. 118.
[61]Ibid., p. 131.

children are married.[62] Blood and Wolfe found that only 2 percent of the parents in their study mentioned "children provide security" as one of the good things about having children.[63]

The old motive of having children to carry on the family name also has much less middle-class relevance today than in the past, as a result of the shift in importance from the family unit to the individual. In a society that stresses and rewards individual achievement, family ties and background have lost most of their past significance, except for a few ancestor worshippers. No doubt many couples today see their children as extensions of themselves who will be living after they are gone, but, for most, this does not have the significance it did in the old patriarchal society. Blood and Wolfe found that 16 percent of the couples they studied said that one of the good things about having children was "they gave to life purpose and meaning."[64] However, this probably reflects the children's importance in the present rather than in the future.

Because of the highly emotional and personal emphasis placed on the individual within the family setting today, the most important reason for having children probably centers around the ego-needs of the parent. This does not imply a selfish motive, but rather that the parents want to give and receive love in relationship to their children. Because the infant is totally dependent, the parents are of great importance to the child. Blood and Wolfe found that, heading the list of good things about having children, "pleasure and emotional satisfaction" was given as the reason by 48 percent of the mothers.[65] An adventurous and challenging aspect to childrearing may operate for many future parents. Many adults without children look at those with children and are sure they can do a better job of childrearing; many married couples anticipate the kind of child they can help create and develop.

Problems may accompany the positive factors of having children. Some parents are surprised to find that the reality of childrearing may be quite different from the idealized beliefs they had prior to becoming parents. Parents must constantly reconcile their idealized images of their child with the reality of the child's personality. Parents may encounter problems with their children in many different

---

[62]See: Marvin B. Sussman, "The Help Pattern in the Middle Class Family, *American Sociological Review*, February, 1953, pp. 22–28.
[63]Blood and Wolfe, *op. cit.*, p. 138.
[64]*Ibid.*, p. 138.
[65]*Ibid.*, p. 138.

areas, from birth on through the years. Blood and Wolfe write that 29 percent of the parents reported they felt their children presented no real problems, but for those with problems, the areas were: financial, 17 percent; illness, 15 percent; childrearing burdens, 15 percent; and other problems, 24 percent.[66]

There are several variables that appear to be related to the probability of parents defining themselves as having problems with their children. One study found 72 percent of the parents reporting that they had some problems with their children and this rate was about the same for all social class levels.[67] However, in the same study, only 4 percent of the high-status parents said their children gave them more trouble than pleasure, as compared to 21 percent of the lower-status parents.[68] Another study found that the greater the number of children, the higher the rate of parents saying they had problems in raising their children, but at the same time there was "no relationship between number of children and feelings of inadequacy."[69]

Given the historical changes in the importance of children, and the emergence of many new considerations that parents must take into account in rearing children, the motives for having children are somewhat confusing. Dager raises the question of what functions children serve and points out that: "They are strictly economic liabilities; they keep parents awake; they prevent parents from going anywhere of any significance for several years; they create continuous anxiety in parents lest they not grow up in accordance with 'established' psychological principles, break a leg, fail a grade, get pregnant; *ad infinitum.*"[70] Dager then goes on to suggest that it is no wonder that many parents are ambivalent about having and rearing children.

The average-size family in the United States in 1960 was 3.68 individuals, which was somewhat greater than in 1950 when it was 3.54.[71] To put it another way, in 1960, 67.7 percent of all families had from three to six persons and 32.3 percent had only two persons.[72] The two-person families were predominantly the young married couple prior to their childbearing years and the older married

---

[66]*Ibid.,* p. 142.

[67]Thomas S. Langner and Stanley T. Michael, *Life Stress and Mental Health* (New York: The Free Press of Glencoe, 1963), p. 335.

[68]*Ibid.,* p. 338.

[69]Gerald Gurin, Joseph Veroff, and Sheila Feld, *Americans View Their Mental Health* (New York: Basic Books, 1960), p. 134.

[70]Dager, *op. cit.,* p. 775.

[71]United States Department of Commerce, Bureau of the Census, *Population Characteristics,* Current Population Reports, Series P-20, November 2, 1960, p. 4.

[72]*Statistical Abstracts, op. cit.,* p. 39.

couple after the children had grown up and left the parental home. That many American families have very young children is illustrated by the fact that, in 1960, almost one third (30.5 percent) of all families in the United States had one or more children under six years of age.[73]

The actual number of years in her life that the wife is bearing children is quite limited. In 1950, the median age of marriage for the wife was 20.1 years and she gave birth to her last child at the median age of 26.1 years.[74] That means that the median childbearing years cover a period of six years. Glick estimates that, on the average, women today are through their childbearing years about six years younger than were their grandmothers.[75] When the average woman today reaches 45, about the period when her biological capacity for childbearing ends, she often finds her youngest "baby" is about 18.

The statistical material indicates that parent-child interaction involves parents in their 20's and early 30's. In the following discussion of parent roles, it should be kept in mind that the middle-class parent of today is younger and usually is closer in age to his children than parents were in the past.

FATHER-MOTHER ROLES

As discussed in previous chapters, adjustment to marriage roles develops and changes over time. Because the role relationships of marriage are dynamic, it was suggested that in many successful marriages the couple are able to reach general satisfaction with the demands of their own role and the role of their partner. Therefore, couples who enter the parent roles shortly after marriage have had very little time to develop exclusively the new roles of marriage. Glick found that half of the women 30 to 35 had their first child less than 1.7 years after marriage.[76] This means that half the couples had less than a year in the husband-wife roles before moving into "expectant parents" roles.

Limited time spent in nonparental husband-wife roles may have both long- and short-range implications for marriage. In the long run, it may mean that the demands of being parents influence the

---

[73]*Ibid.*, p. 39.
[74]Paul C. Glick, *American Families* (New York: John Wiley and Sons, Inc., 1957), p. 54.
[75]*Ibid.*, p. 195.
[76]*Ibid.*, p. 64.

marriage relationship before the couple have had time to develop their husband and wife roles. After children enter, the couple have much less time or opportunity to function exclusively as husband and wife. Later in their marriage, after the children grow up and the couple revert back to the exclusive husband and wife roles, they may have little to return to in the way of a husband-wife relationship. Blood and Wolfe found that, during the childbearing years, husbands and wives often cease doing things together and grow apart from each other. "When they are left with each other again for company, their losses are only partially recouped. For many couples, the estrangement is permanent and the second opportunity comes too late to catch fire."[77]

The short-run problems center around the couple's ability to relate their new parental roles to their marriage roles. The success of the husband and wife role relationships is often related to the maintaining of some autonomy in the face of the new parental roles. However, it is doubtful if any marriage role development is going to be unaffected by parental roles. While individuals are husbands and wives both before and after parenthood, being a husband-father or wife-mother is bound to be different because the roles are not mutually exclusive.

The interrelationship of marriage and parent roles may be illustrated in a number of ways. Since the relationship of marriage is between two individuals assumed to be mature adults, and the relationship of the parents to the infant and child is between the mature adult and the immature child, the element of adult responsibility enters. The young child in real need of his mother must normally be given preference over the need of the husband for his wife.

Together, the couple are also bound to meet many cases of role conflict between their marriage and parent roles. For example, the couple who plan on going out as husband and wife, but discover they have a child who is ill, must usually put aside their husband-wife roles and stay home as parents. As the child grows older, they may, in a role-conflict situation, choose to pursue the marriage roles, because the demands of the child become less pressing.

The specific nature of later acquired parental roles will be examined with the realization that the parents are first husband and wife. As indicated above, becoming parents for the first time is probably the most significant and demanding new role that most individuals encounter during their lifetime, and the new experience demands

---

[77]Blood and Wolfe, *op. cit.,* p. 174.

an extended emotional involvement. New parenthood is somewhat different for the mother role and the father role, though it should be emphasized that these roles derive an important part of their meaning in relationship to one another. The interactional importance of the parent roles has two interrelated dimensions: parent-child and mother-father. The mother-father relationship is important as a division of labor and responsibility, as well as a buttressing paired role relationship in interacting with the children. For example, a mother and father not supporting each other in their role relationships as parents may create confusion for the children or set up a situation in which the children play one parent off against the other.

Mother Role

The mother role as filled in the American middle class is very different from that of most other cultures. Cross-cultural studies show that many societies do not have the kind of mother-child role relationships that are seen as "natural" in the United States.[78] In traditional societies, the mother and father roles were most sharply defined because the father had an authoritarian and exulted position with regard to his children. But in present middle-class American society, the contrast between father and mother roles insofar as control and influence over the children is concerned has for the most part disappeared.[79]

In the United States, the role of mother is important but also characterized by contradictions as to its significance. On the one hand, most studies show that American women rate "children and the joys of motherhood high on the list of marital values, far above economic security, sexual satisfaction, understanding, and so on."[80] On the other hand, the view of motherhood is not pure and simple, "but impure and complex; it is symbolic that our country was the first to make a great to-do about Mother's Day, and the first to make 'mom' a dirty word."[81]

On the social signficance attached to the mother role, Alice Rossi writes that "for the first time in the history of any known society motherhood has become a full-time occupation for adult women."[82] She goes on to suggest from her studies that full-time motherhood is

[78]Dager, *op. cit.*, p. 770.
[79]Stephens, *op. cit.*, p. 320.
[80]Hunt, *op. cit.*, p. 167.
[81]*Ibid.*, p. 168.
[82]Alice S. Rossi, "Equality Between the Sexes," *Daedalus*, Spring, 1964, p. 615.

not sufficiently absorbing (nor beneficial to the children) to justify today's woman devoting 15 or more years to it as an exclusive occupation. "Sooner or later—and I think it should be sooner—women have to face the question of who they are besides their children's mother."[83]

But it seems clear that the role of wife-mother continues to be the basic role aspiration and achievement for most middle-class women. One study found that for the wife, marriage was not as great a role transition as becoming a mother.[84] This is true because greater demands are placed on the woman as mother than as wife. The young mother finds herself moving into the new role when, because of the total dependency of the newborn infant, the demands of that role are the greatest. Moving from the nonmother role to the mother role is not transitional, but abrupt, and demands an extensive revision of her daily life.

Becoming a mother calls for important changes in a wife's behavior and often over time calls for highly important adaptations. One study asked a sample of mothers "How is a woman's life changed by having children? By far the most common response was that children meant less freedom, particularly that they restricted the mother's freedom of movement."[85] Also, the greater adaptability to crisis by the mother than by the father has been shown in a study of families with a severely retarded child. It was found that fathers were less adaptable than mothers and were more vulnerable to social stigma and extrafamilial influences such as children's physical appearance and sex.[86]

Because the role is so demanding and entails such extreme responsibility, the new mother often feels anxious and apprehensive. In the day-to-day care of the infant and child, she must make constant decisions and, because of her inexperience, the decisions can be dangerous to the infant. Some women may also have conflicting feelings about the mother role. The female is socialized to want to be a mother, but she is given little direct preparation for the role; on the other hand, she wants and loves the child, but is faced with some role insecurity. Therefore, the idealized image of wanting children may be altered by the reality of having and caring for them. A Gallup poll of young mothers found that 1 in 5 said motherhood was

---

[83]*Ibid.*, p. 624.
[84]Blood and Wolfe, *op. cit.*, p. 43.
[85]Gurin, *op. cit.*, p. 30.
[86]Irving Tallman, "Spousal Role Differientiation and The Socialization of Severely Retarded Children," *Journal of Marriage and Family*, February, 1965, p. 42.

dissapointing at first, and 4 in 10 said there were times after the birth of the first child when they felt they did not want any more children.[87] In a study by Miller and Swanson, mothers were asked about their reactions and feelings to the period of their children's infancy. In that sample, 66 percent reported "very pleasant experiences," 19 percent "mildly pleasant experiences," and 14 percent "unpleasant experiences."[88]

That some mothers severely reject their children either psychologically or physically is often overlooked, but the truth is that many American women do not love or want their babies. And though few mothers actually kill their infants, "the crippling effects of early maternal rejection on children can hardly be exaggerated—or glossed over."[89] The following statistics give an indication of the extent of this problem: There are about 50,000 to 70,000 children neglected, battered or exploited annually and there are about 150,000 children placed in foster homes for these reasons. There are over 300,000 children in foster care altogether. Eight to 10 percent of all school children in one 20-county study were found to be in need of psychiatric examination and some type of treatment for their problem.[90]

Role satisfaction for the mother is learned experience. While most mothers probably derive a sense of role fulfillment from parenthood, a number clearly do not. As with many roles in the American society, the problem may be the conflict between the idealized image of the role and its realities. The image of the cuddly, happy infant may be quite different from the reality of a messy, screaming infant demanding immediate attention.

Father Role

The transition to the father role is probably not as great as the transition to the mother role. This would seem to be true if for no other reason that that the father role is usually not nearly so demanding and time consuming. Because the male's occupational role is performed in a setting different from his family roles, the child often has only an indirect influence on this role. Even when many new fathers are at home, the new child may have less influence on their new father role than on the longer-established husband-wife

---

[87]George Gallup, "The Woman's Mind: America's Young Mothers," *Ladies Home Journal,* March, 1962, p. 72.

[88]Daniel R. Miller and Guy E. Swanson, *The Changing American Parent* (New York: John Wiley & Sons, Inc., 1958), p. 216.

[89]Morris, *op. cit.,* p. 8.

[90]*Ibid.,* p. 8.

roles. The husband may find he has to make a more drastic readjustment to his wife as mother than to his new role as father.

The male in his occupational role is affected by the obligations of his new role as father. Because the male through his occupation must provide his wife and children with their material needs, children place a greater financial responsibility on him. In middle-class occupations, the male's income gradually increases over the years. Yet, at the time when the children are young and the financial demands may be the greatest, he is at a relatively low point in his lifetime income level. The husband may feel frustrated if increases in income seem inadequate to meet the increasing costs of the children. Children may also mean a loss of occupational mobility because the male, aware of his financial responsibilities, may be very hesitant to leave his job with its security for a more risky new job with more potential. The basic contrast between the mother role and the father role is that, for the wife, procreation may be either the acme of self-expression or the anonymity of motherhood, while, for the male, the significance of parenthood is painted in less vivid hues.[91]

In addition to the relationship of marriage and parent roles, the parents' view of the children's impact on their marriages is also important. The Gallup poll found that 9 out of every 10 young mothers said they loved their husbands more after the arrival of the first child, and 54 percent considered their marriage improved.[92] Burgess and Wallin also provide information on the reported effect of children on the happiness of marriage partners. Seventy-nine percent of the husbands and 83 percent of the wives reported that children "added very much" to their happiness in marriage.[93]

The acceptance of parental roles and their impact on marriage roles will vary a great deal for different couples. Satisfaction is theoretically related to the ability of the individuals to perceive their new roles as parents in relationship to themselves, each other, and the children. The parent who feels a basic role conflict involving his parental role is bound to feel some dissatisfaction with both that role and the one it is frustrating. Therefore, the ability to fill parental roles calls for adaptability to the new role needs and a redefinition, where necessary, of other role requirements.

---

[91]Robert F. Winch, The Modern Family (New York: Henry Holt & Co., 1952), p. 224.

[92]Gallup, op. cit., p. 72.

[93]Ernest W. Burgess and Paul Wallin, Engagement and Marriage (Chicago: J. B. Lippincott Co., 1953), p. 707.

CHILDREARING

Historically, childrearing had a strong parental orientation. That is, parents tended to rear their children according to their own needs and values. But over time in the United States, a transition from the parental to the child orientation has been made. The following quotation briefly describes the major historical emphases in childrearing in the United States:

It is convenient to divide this history of American child training into four broad periods. The first extends from the middle of the 1700's to about the time of the Civil War. Those years saw the decline of techniques for "breaking the child's will" and the beginning of attacks on corporal punishment. In the second period, roughly from 1869 to the First World War, corporal punishment and the arbitrary use of parental authority drew less and less support. The 1920's and 1930's represent a third phase in rearing children. The great theme of those decades is the training of children who would be highly independent. Finally, in the fourth period, a span of years from about 1945 to the present, there occurred many drastic changes in ideas about child care. For the first time in American history, it became proper to let the child set the age at which he was ready to be disciplined, weaned, and trained to use the toilet. Thumbsucking and genital play were tolerated.[94]

The changes in childrearing and child care have been so great in the American middle class that often there are very significant differences in beliefs from one generation to another. In a study by Kell and Aldous, it was found that in "comparisons of the mothers' childrearing values with their mothers . . . only in the area of discipline were the two generations significantly more likely to have values alike than unlike."[95]

Childrearing practices have undergone such rapid change in recent years that mothers sometimes feel frustration not over whether what they are doing *is* basically right, but whether it is still *believed* to be right. One can almost choose at random his beliefs in childrearing and then, by looking around, find various experts to support them. The concern here is not with the pros and cons of various schools of childrearing, but with the social context in which the child is currently perceived and how social values shape rearing practices.

---

[94]Miller and Swanson, *op. cit.*, pp. 5–6.
[95]Leone Kell and Joan Aldous, "Trends in Child Care Over Three Generations," *Marriage and Family Living*, May, 1960, p. 176.

As has been pointed out, the modern, urban, middle-class family is no longer strongly bound together by traditional family ties. Without the strong kinship supports and the related dependency of women on men, new family ties had to be developed. The new ties center around the emotional setting of the family in meeting the ego-needs of its members; but the nature of the need relationships within the family setting are influenced by social values outside the family.

Miller and Swanson suggest that the middle-class family of today is increasingly bureaucratic because there is a complex relationship between a society that stresses bureaucratic values and the family that prepares its children to move into this kind of social setting. "The adult, as the child, must be warm, friendly, and supportive of others. The powerful ambitions and desires for independence cherished by our middle classes for two centuries would unfit a youngster for participation in a society that requires him to be relaxed and cooperative."[96] This theme is one that has been developed by other writers such as Riesman and Whyte.[97] The middle-class family, in rearing its children, is faced with the basic problem of teaching the children to be competitive enough to stand out to some degree, but not to be so different they will be viewed as threatening to generally accepted social values. In the "bureaucratic" middle-class family, the child "increasingly meets his peers as colleagues whose favor he must court and whose respect he must win."[98] In a society where being liked is important, the child is often taught not to select one or two close friends and ignore the others, but to learn to fit in smoothly with all of his age peers. "He must learn to be a 'nice guy'—affable, unthreatening, responsible, competent and adaptive."[99]

This picture of the basic values implied in middle-class childrearing today seems to be sociologically accurate; a society where many of the new and prestigeful adult occupations stress the facility of relating to others, getting along, and not being an "odd ball" will stress the same values in the rearing of children. In many ways, today's parents want their children to fall within a more restricted behavioral spread than did parents of the past. The parent may want the child to learn the rudiments of playing the piano but not be a pianist, to be bright but not brilliant, to be attractive but not hand-

---

[96]Miller and Swanson, op. cit., pp. 55–56.
[97]See: David Riesman, Nathan Glazer, and Reuel Denney, The Lonely Crowd (New York: Doubleday Anchor Books, 1953); and William H. Whyte, Jr., The Organization Man (New York: Doubleday Anchor Books, 1956).
[98]Miller and Swanson, op. cit., p. 202.
[99]Ibid., p. 203.

some or beautiful, and to be a good student but not an excellent one. It may be that, given an American society increasingly dominated by middle-class values, parents are preparing their children in the most socially efficient manner. But the long-range social implications of a society oriented to the mediocre, conforming middle range is frightening to many social observers.

THE NATURE OF THE CHILD

The discussion thus far has concerned the parents' roles and child-rearing. A further understanding of the relationship of parents to their children necessitates some discussion of the nature of the child. The question of how the child emerges from the stage of total infant dependency to a social being able to function independently has interested observers for many centuries, and many theories of human development have been put forth. One theory or way of looking at the social development of the infant and child is presented here. Most experts today assume that the infant's development as a social being is a result of internal factors such as inheritance and physiological make-up and the initially external social factors. At one time there was great controversy as to which of these two areas was the most important, but today it is recognized that a biological and social interrelationship is needed to explain human development. Generally speaking the infant *inherits* his original nature and *acquires* his human nature.[100]

Biological

Each child enters life having received half of his genetic make-up at the time of conception from his father and half from his mother. The factors of inheritance are passed on through 23 chromosomes from each of the parents, and each chromosome is made up of many genes related to specific inherited characteristics. Because of the vast number of genes and possible combinations, "the chance that any two human beings, now living or having lived, having identical sets of genes is practically zero, identical twins always excepted. The hereditary endowment which each of us have is strictly our own."[101]

At the time of conception, the genetic structure determines one fact about the individual which is of greatest importance in deter-

---

[100]Baber, *op. cit.*, p. 253.
[101]L. C. Dunn and Th. Dobzhansky, *Heredity, Race and Society* (New York: The New American Library, 1952), p. 56.

mining his social development—that is, the sex of the individual. Genetically, the structure of inheritance differs between the male and female. The male like the female has 46 chromosomes, but the male has only 22 matched pairs; the 23rd pair consists of one large and one small chromosome. The father determines the sex of the child. If a sperm carrying the X chromosome (the large one) fertilizes the egg, there will be 23 matched pairs and a girl will result. If a sperm carrying a Y chromosome (the small one) fertilizes the egg, there will be only 22 matched pairs, plus the unequal pair, and the result is a boy.[102]

The original inheritance places limits on many aspects of future personal and social development. For example, one inherits from his parents a range of possible height and, given the most favorable environmental conditions in the world, the individual will not grow beyond the upper limits set genetically. How many human qualities of development are limited in this way is unknown, but, in general, the inherited factors set a variety of limits within which social factors enable the ultimate achievement.

An important biological factor in the development of the child is *maturation*. This term is generally defined in biological terms, though it has a direct relationship to human functions of a social nature. Maturation is coming to be defined as the personal and social behavior that becomes possible through changes in the physical characteristics of any part of the human organism.[103] Some understanding of maturation is important in knowing what the child can achieve socially. For example, before a child can walk he must have matured enough so that he has the motor skills needed for walking. Many parents attempt to train their child to an activity before the child is biologically capable of performing the activity. This often happens with toilet training and, in some instances, explains why the child who has developed some skills in toilet training "regresses." He may not have developed adequately to anticipate his needs, or not have been completely socialized as to the function of the toilet. In some cases, the child may be old enough biologically to be toilet trained but not socialized enough to accept its use.

Social Learning

In addition to biological factors, the process of acquiring social characteristics is also significant. It should be remembered that no

[102]A. M. Winchester, *Heredity and Your Life* (New York: Dover Publications, Inc., 1960), p. 108.

[103]Arthur T. Jersild, "Redevelopment as a Product of Learning and Growth," in Jerome M. Seidman, *The Child* (New York: Holt-Dryden, 1958), p. 26.

one is born social, but that he must acquire social characteristics from others and incorporate them into his own personality. Social learning or socialization is the process by which someone learns the ways of a given society or social group so that he can function within it.[104] Because he starts life with no social experience, socialization is most crucial to the infant and child although, because it is never completed, the process continues during the total life span of the individual.

For a child to become socialized, three conditions must operate.[105] First, there must be an ongoing society. Society provides the necessary background of social factors to be transmitted to the child. Second, the child must have the basic genetic and biological background for the acquisition of social factors. For example, the mentally defective infant can only be partially socialized, because he falls below the minimum level of the basic requirements for learning. Third, "a child requires 'human nature,' defined as the ability to establish emotional relationships with others and to experience such sentiments as love, sympathy, shame, envy, pity, and awe."[106] It is through these sentiments that many social relationships are learned and developed.

Given the necessary conditions and background for socialization, the process of social development in the infant occurs. The child is taught the realities of his society not in the abstract, but by encountering his culture through already socialized individuals. In most cases, the important agency for transmitting the culture is the immediate family of the child. The family is important because it "gets him first, keeps him longest, is his major source of cultural imperatives, and proscribes them with emotional finality. It is important because it not only satisfies the wishes of the individual but it is instrumental in shaping those wishes into a form which only the family can satisfy."[107] The family initially sets up goals and many times offers the means of achieving them. Furthermore, the role-models the family provides for the child provide directions for his developing attitudes and behavior.

As the young child starts to explore avenues of action, his behavior has to some degree been predetermined by the family and, with future action, the family helps him to refine his roles. In this pro-

---

[104]Frederick Elkin, *The Child and Society* (New York: Random House, Inc., 1960), p. 4.

[105]See: *Ibid.*, p. 7.

[106]*Ibid.*, p. 7.

[107]Willard Waller and Reuben Hill, *The Family* (New York: The Dryden Press, 1951), p. 33.

cess, the child defines the meaning of his own acts by the behavior which these acts evoke in adults.[108] For example, the child who throws his food on the floor elicits forms of disapproval from the mother, showing him that his behavior is wrong. While the mother's disapproval may have little influence on a single occasion, over the long run her reactions will usually channelize the child's behavior in the approved direction.

From a broader point of view, the parents in setting up controls and direction over the child's social development are communicating the values of society. This provides the high agreement in the socialization of most children in the same society. The meanings communicated by the parents are, for the most part, not arbitrary, but a part of the culture in which the process takes place.[109] Because the parents have been through essentially the same socialization process, a basic continuity is provided for individuals to relate with each other in meaningful ways.

Initially, the child's learning moves from the broad to the more narrow, the general to the specific. This is particularly true in the acquisition of language. To be social, the individual must be able to communicate, and all human communication ultimately rests on the ability to use language. While the newborn infant has the capacity for learning a language, the specific language must be provided for him through experiences with members of society already capable of using the accepted language forms. The socially meaningful vocabulary of the child is acquired gradually, and then over time develops more rapidly. The child initially gives only a general meaning to the words he uses. For example, at first "doll" may be applied to all toys and, only later, to a specific type of toy.

Along with learning a more specific application of language, a more specific definition and understanding of role behavior generally develops. The role is a primary means of social growth for the child. The child adds to his understanding of the roles he plays by learning from others in the roles they play. One important function of role learning is through "playing the role of another." The child who plays the role of the mother may project himself into the mother role in reference to himself, thus seeing himself, in part, as his mother does. For example, the child playing the role of the mother in relationship to a doll may say to the doll "don't do that." The importance of this kind of behavior is that the child is developing an

---

[108]*Ibid.*, p. 39.
[109]*Ibid.*, p. 39.

awareness of how his actions are perceived by others. It is through these various experiences that the child develops a generalized concept of himself. The generalized concept of how others view him becomes a meaningful determinant of action. In other words, the child is becoming social by being influenced by others and internalizing those values.

"As the child develops, the 'generalized other' becomes an internalized model consisting of the standards from which he views and judges his own behavior, the perspective which determines whether he is pleased or displeased with himself."[110] This may be illustrated by the child who starts some behavior and then, realizing that the behavior has been defined as wrong and having accepted, as a part of his own internal structure, that it is wrong, refrains from the action. "Since we grow into favorable roles, we tend to become what we imagine that we are, or rather, what we imagine that others imagine that we are. We grow away from unfavorable roles and elaborately avoid imagined unfavorable judgments."[111]

The initial stages of socialization, then, are provided the child through the primary influence of family models and controls in his role development. Socialization is not smooth and many times it involves conflict, refusal to accept presented roles, and regression into earlier socialized behavior. But ultimately socialization wins because the child reaches a point where his behavior and self-image fall within the limits defined as acceptable by society. Because the individual accepts the values the family transmitted as socially important, he may think they were a matter of choice or are peculiar to him as an individual. However, society determines not only the "things the child thinks about but also what he thinks about the things he thinks about."[112]

In the middle class, the parents are not only concerned that the child learn from others to develop his self-awareness but also that he learn how to relate and get along with others. To be able to interact effectively with others is a highly valued middle-class skill. One study found that the highest social-class level respondents showed the greatest concern for the interpersonal relations of their children and they point out that the "higher status child gets pushed in the direction of caring what the other fellow thinks."[113]

After initial socialization, as the child's experiences and capacities

---

[110]Elkin, *op. cit.*, p. 35.
[111]Waller and Hill, *op. cit.*, p. 48.
[112]*Ibid.*, pp. 42–43.
[113]Langner, *op. cit.*, p. 336.

increase and as he becomes more familiar and proficient with his roles, the rights and obligations that go with his roles change.[114] The complexity of the child's roles increase for a variety of reasons. First, he comes into contact with new role models that have significance for him. The child entering the playgroup is encountering a new kind of model, a model close to himself in age and without the emotional commitment to him that his parents have. When he was in his own home with his parents, the toys he played with were often his own; but now he has to learn the attitudes and behavior related to possessiveness. A three-year-old joining the playgroup for the first time may grab the toy of another child. The other child may grab the toy back and hit him over the head with it: the three-year-old is being socialized in reference to peer-group behavior.

Second, the child finds that he no more than reaches a level of proficiency in filling a role than the role may no longer be appropriate for him. What may have been viewed as acceptacle role performance at four years of age may not be at six years of age. Adults constantly force the child to recognize different role behavior for different ages. The six-year-old is told to quit acting like a baby. He is also presented with contrasts between his present age role and future roles he will fill. He may be told that he cannot do something because he is not old enough. This often has the important influence of moving the child along in new age roles because the future roles are frequently presented as including rights that seem desirable. Thus, future roles sometimes function as a dangling carrot to lead the child into new age roles. As a result, many children live in anticipation of the future because of the greater rights that go with older age roles. Often adults do not show the child that along with the rights of older age roles also go greater obligations.

Another important factor associated with the social development of the child is his love relationship to his parents. Kirkpatrick writes "it seems justifiable to conclude that the infant in our culture has a love need in the sense that denied love response from parents or parent-substitutes, he will be handicapped in his emotional development. It should not be forgotten, however, that a hypothetical love need is probably a matter of aspiration and expectation based on past experience."[115]

It should also be pointed out that the world of the child is quite different from the world of the adult. Although the child achieves

---

[114]Elkin, op. cit., p. 23.
[115]Clifford Kirkpatrick, The Family (New York: The Ronald Press Co., 1955), p. 201.

socialization from adults, he translates this into a world determined by his own immaturity and influenced by other chilen. In one important way, the world of the child is different from both the infant and adult worlds: The child often develops a fantasy world and dreams his way out of conflicts and defeats.[116] His fantasy world sometimes provides him with an opportunity to experiment emotionally with role possibilities. The young boy may dream he is another Willie Mays; while this is an unrealistic role expectation, it gives him an experience with the process of role identification that becomes valuable in identifying with roles he will ultimately seek to achieve. The fantasy world of the child often makes an important contribution to his breadth of social knowledge and understanding and, therefore, contributes to socialization.

REWARDS AND PUNISHMENTS

The child may be coerced, encouraged, and indoctrinated in many different ways, but with few exceptions the methods are based on a reward and punishment system. For example, even the child who emotionally and intellectually responds to social demands is often doing so because he sees some personal gain or reward. Or, put the opposite way, a child will not usually change voluntarily if he anticipates little or no gain for himself.

Discipline for the child must always originate externally, because it is related to social expectations he must learn. Baber points out that "at first, discipline seems to come entirely from the parent's side, and obedience to be wholly the function of the child. But as development takes place, discipline shifts from its position of outward authority to an inner position of self-control, there blending with obedience until the two are indistinguishable. Obedience becomes then not a yielding to superior force but the spontaneous expression of self-discipline."[117]

Discipline or obedience is a requirement made by all societies. The individual must conform and accept at least a minimum set of social requirements; if he did not, social relationships would have no order or predictability. The question is not discipline or no discipline, but rather what degree and type of discipline. Even in the most "permissive" upbringing of a child, some adult social discipline must be exerted on the young child or he would not survive.

As to type of discipline, experts disagree. Some argue for spank-

[116]*Ibid.*, p. 220.
[117]Baber, *op. cit.*, p. 298.

ing and others against it. One type of discipline will probably work with some children and not others. It seems important, whatever the form of punishment, to relate the punishment to the act and not to give the child the feeling of rejection or loss of love. Because the love of the parents is socially important, punishing through withdrawal of love may create for the child a situation more harmful than the behavior that led to the punishment.

Parents sometimes use excessive love as a means of controlling their children. In some middle-class families, the parents saturate their children with love and, as a result the love of the parent means little. The child may feel he can do anything because the love of his parents is not altered by his behavior. Or the child may be convinced that his parents love him so much that not meeting their expectations means letting them down, which may result in strong feelings of guilt when he does not meet their expectations.

The types of reward and punishment used in the American society vary greatly; no single system is used by all parents. The Miller and Swanson study indicates some of the types of punishments used by mothers for a child 10 years of age "who had done something with which the mother was extremely upset or angered." The most common punishments were "restrict behavior and withdraw privileges," 44 percent; "scolds and threatens," 25 percent; and, "physical punishment," 22 percent. A much higher agreement was found in rewards for a 10-year-old: "psychic reward or other verbal praise," 68 percent, and "material reward, money, gifts, etc.," 19 percent.[118]

These are some of the patterns of socialization frequently found in the American middle class. While actual procedure varies widely, the variations normally fall within an acceptable social range. In all aspects of socializing the child, parents are given alternative courses of action, and it is only if they go beyond the accepted limits that society steps in and takes responsibility for childrearing out of their hands.

When compared to the rest of American society, the middle class has certain values that it stresses with regard to child care and rearing. For example, one study reports that "middle class parents train their children earlier, are more affectionate, and employ 'conditional love' techniques of discipline to a greater extent than lower class parents."[119] Middle-class parents are more concerned with "de-

[118]Miller and Swanson, op. cit., p. 221.
[119]Bernard C. Rosen, "Family Structure and Value Transmission," Merrill-Palmer Quarterly, January, 1964, p. 74.

veloping internalization of self control by the child, and in this sense are future oriented, while lower-class parents are more concerned about immediate consequences of child behavior and maintaining order and obedience."[120] Lenski found that among upper-middle class Protestants 90 percent valued intellectual autonomy above simple obedience, as compared to 48 percent of the lower-working class.[121]

Ultimately the test of socialization is the end product. The fact that some children turn out to be inadequate in a social and/or personal way is a reflection on society, as well as the adults who were responsible for the socializing. With so many children and adolescents (as well as adults) experiencing severe psychological problems, the American system of childrearing often seems to be inadequate. In most of these cases, the responsibility probably rests with those who did the childrearing, rather than society in general. This is suggested because so many individuals *are* reared to emerge as well-socialized individuals in reference to both social and personal criteria. It is difficult to define a good or effective personality in psychological terms; however, it is possible to make some suggestions within a social context. To say a person has a "good" personality in the American middle class usually means that the person is able to make the social adjustments required of him and, at the same time, maintain enough individual flexibility to deal effectively with new situations.[122] Another way of saying essentially the same thing is in terms of social and psychological maturity: that is, the individual is able to function as an adult in society. Baber suggests that probably the best single index of maturity is "the extent to which a person has progressed from the utter self-centeredness of childhood toward full acceptance of the responsibilities of social living."[123]

Implied in the above discussion is that some balance should exist between the demands of society and individual desires. Some degree of conformity is needed for the individual to function in society; however, an opportunity for expression of individual desires must also be given. The social and personal demands will not always balance and, in many instances, the individual may go counter to

---

[120]Dager, *op. cit.*, p. 750.
[121]Gerhard Lenski, *The Religious Factor* (New York: Anchor Books, 1963) p. 223.
[122]Read Bain, "Producing Marriageable Personalities," in Howard Becker and Reuben Hill, *Family, Marriage and Parenthood* (Boston: D. C. Heath & Co., 1955), p. 192.
[123]Baber, *op. cit.*, p. 144.

social demands and expectations. Deviancy from social norms leads to degrees of individual personality variations as well as possible social change.

THE FAMILY SETTING AND INTERACTION

The parents provide the children with direction not only in the roles they are playing at a given point in time, but also in reference to their future roles. As indicated earlier, the childrens' experiences in learning from their parents the roles of husband and wife have long-range implications for their own future marriage. This is also true in regard to the future roles of the children as parents.

One very important role the parents play during the growth of the child is as sex-role models. The children learn to a great extent, at least in their early years, role conceptions of adult masculinity and femininity from their parents. This is important not only in learning the sex-role that the child will play, but also in learning something of the opposite sex-role. The middle-class child has limited experiences with adult males, and therefore the influence of the father as a male role model is important to both sons and daughters. Because the role of the father is generally less developed in relation to the child than is the role of the mother, the children may be influenced more by male role models provided through the mass media than by their own father. A study by Lynn found that "males tend to identify with a cultural stereotype of the masculine role, whereas females tend to identify with aspects of their own mothers' role specifically."[124]

A stated ideal that may not always be easy to carry out is that parents have equal feelings for all of their children, or at least show no overt preference. Even if their emotional commitment to their children is essentially the same, their treatment of each child will be different because of personality and age-sex differences. When this happens, the child may "see" the brother or sister receiving different treatment and define it as preferential treatment. The older child may feel that the parents let the younger one get away with more, not realizing the younger is given greater leeway because he is less mature. On the other hand, the younger child may feel that the older sibling has more privileges, not realizing that that is a result of the parents recognizing greater maturity.

---

[124]David B. Lynn, "A Note on Sex Differences in Development of Masculine and Feminine Identification," in Jerome M. Seidman, *The Adolescent* (New York: Holt-Dryden, 1960), pp. 271–72.

In any family the personalities of the children differ, and because their age and sex differ too, the parents must treat them differently. Some children are very cooperative and are not subjected to parental control to the same degree as a sibling who is not cooperative. To the child, the reason and the logic for variations in parental treatment are usually difficult to understand.

Finally, many parents do, in fact, have a preference for one of their children. A great deal of research has been done on birth order and sex of children in relationship with their parents, but it has not established any definite tendency for a specific type of child to be selected as a favorite.[125] As examples, one might argue that a mother would feel closer to her oldest child because he was her first-born, or one might equally argue that she will feel closer to her youngest because he continues to be her "baby." It might be argued that a father would feel closest to a son because the son is an extension of himself or, in contrast, that he would feel closest to the daughter because of the attractiveness of the child of the opposite sex. What evidence there is would seem to indicate that the choice of a favorite child will be determined by the peculiar personality factors of both the parents and the children.

The Relation of Mother and Child

The mother will generally be perceived by the children in a different light than the father because the "mother role tends to be anchored between family and mother-child systems, the father role between family and extra-familial systems."[126] The fact that the mother spends time in a variety of role activities means that her children see her role as more extended than that of the father.

A study of children between the ages of 6 and 12 found that a majority of both boys and girls perceived their mothers as friendlier, less punitive, less dominant, and less threatening than fathers.[127] Winch suggests that in the "middle class American society there is a tendency for: (a) the mother to be the preferred parent, (b) the son to be the preferred child, and (c) for the mother-son relationship to be the strongest of the four parent child relationships."[128] While

[125]See: James H. S. Bossard, *The Sociology of Child Development* (New York: Harper and Brothers, 1948).

[126]Talcott Parsons and Robert F. Bales, *Family, Socialization and Interaction Process* (Glencoe, Illinois: The Free Press, 1955), p. 81.

[127]Jerome Kagan, "The Child's Perception of the Parent," in Jerome M. Seidman, *The Child* (New York: Holt-Dryden, 1958), p. 139.

[128]Winch, *op. cit.*, p. 299.

a good deal of evidence supports the first two suggestions, the third seems questionable. The mother-son relationship is the Freudian Oedipus tie that seems to perpetuate itself in family writing, but has very little empirical support. The evidence appears to clearly illustrate that the mother is the major parental influence for both sons *and* daughters. For example, Langner found that a "worrying mother" was somewhat more harmful with respect to the offspring's mental health than a worrying father. "A third of the [disturbed subjects'] mothers were worriers, but only a tenth of the fathers."[129]

The Relation of Father and Child

In middle-class American society, children see much less of their father than their mother. The period of time between when the husband returns home in the evening and when the children go to bed may be short and not particularly centered around father and children interaction, and on the weekend, many middle-class fathers are involved in personal activities and have limited time to spend with their children. The children also have interests of their own and often want to pursue them on the weekend. The father who "gives" Saturday morning to his son may really be "taking" the son from something he would rather be doing.

Some fathers see in their sons an opportunity to project their own ambitions. (This may also be true for mothers.) The father's projection to his son may be in the area of physical success through athletics. The father may play games with his son not so much for the pleasure of playing the games, but rather to help the boy become more athletically proficient. This is illustrated by the middle-class "little league syndrome." Anyone who believes that little league baseball is always performed for the pleasure that the boy will derive from the game should attend a few little league practices or games.

For many a father, relationships with his son are to help him be a "real boy" according to the definitions accepted by the father. The father's control over the daughter tends to be much less direct and concentrates more on the pleasurable aspect of the relationship than on a responsibility of her rearing. While many fathers are concerned that the son is not meeting their expectations, they are inclined to leave the setting of daughter expectations and behavior to the mother. Many parents assume that because the father was a boy and the mother a girl they are qualified to understand, diagnose, and prescribe behavior for the child of the same sex. Though the father

---

[129]Langner, *op. cit.*, p. 221.

assumes that the mother can take care of the son in the everyday requirements of childrearing, he also believes that he should move in and give the son the masculine direction he needs. While it is important that the parent of the same sex perform as a sex-role model, it does not necessarily mean that simply because they are the same sex they are best qualified to know what is appropriate for the child.

In most texts about the family, the assumption is made that two parents, with positive role relations, are needed for successful socialization of their children. It seems highly probable that the most favorable family socialization occurs for children when they do have a positive and ongoing relationship with both their parents, but simply having both parents present and actively interacting with their children does not necessarily lead to positive patterns of parent-child relationships. More relevant is the corollary assumption that *not* having a parent (almost always the father) present is highly negative to the process of socialization. If the assumption is true, one would expect a strong body of evidence showing negative consequences for children reared in fatherless families.

In a study by Nye, broken (one-parent) and remarried homes were compared with intact but unhappy homes. Nye found that the broken homes were somewhat superior to the intact unhappy homes, but, in general, no evidence of more adjustment problems for children in any one of the three types.[130] Burchinal, in a study of homes similar to Nye's types, found no significant differences in most aspects of adolescent adjustment.[131] Perry and Pfuhl, in comparing one-parent homes to remarried homes, found among the children studied no differences in delinquency, psychosomatic complaints or school grades.[132] Crain and Stamm used two groups of second-grade children to test the hypothesis that regular prolonged absence of the father affected the child's perceptions of both the mother and the father. "The results did not support the hypothesis. Generally, non-significant differences are found between father-present and father-absent children in the child's perception of father and mother as sources of authority and love."[133]

---

[130]F. Ivan Nye, "Child Adjustment in Broken and in Unhappy Unbroken Homes," *Marriage and Family Living,* November, 1957, pp. 356–61.

[131]Lee G. Burchinal, "Characteristics of Adolescents from Unbroken, Broken, and Reconstituted Families," *Journal of Marriage and Family,* February, 1964, pp. 44–51.

[132]Joseph B. Parry and Erdwin H. Pfuhl, "Adjustment of Children in 'Sole' and 'Remarriage' Homes," *Marriage and Family Living,* May, 1963, pp. 221–23.

[133]Alan J. Crain and Caroline S. Stamm, "Intermittent Absence of Fathers and Children's Perceptions of Parents," *Journal of Marriage and Family,* August, 1965, pp. 344–47.

The studies raise serious questions about the general assumption as to the absolute need of the father. The point is not that a father makes no significant contribution, but rather that absence of the father (the one-parent family without a father) may not, in fact, be *the* cause of almost all personal and social problems. (The one-parent family *has* been used to "explain" delinquency, mental illness, crime, sex-role and sexual inadequacies, school problems and poverty.)

The assumption has been that the presence of the father is needed to serve as a sex-role model in the socialization of his children. But as we have decreased the amount of time and degree of involvement of the father—even in an "ideal" family—the influence of the father as a sex-role model may have become greatly diminished. Children often find sex-role models outside the family to supplement or replace the father, as Lynn found, that is, males tending to identify with a cultural stereotype of the male role.[134] The stress placed on the great importance of sex-role models also implies a society where there are important sex-roles differences, but there is a good deal of evidence to suggest that masculinity-femininity differences are decreasing in America.

In brief, in today's American middle-class family, parents are less involved in the socialization of their children than they were in the past. The father role is primarily supportive and the functions he performs are often minor and replaceable either by the wife or by outside-the-family agencies—without evidence of significant negative costs to the child. The mother role is comparatively more important than formerly—when compared to the father role—because increasingly the mother includes in her role combined parental functions.

Sibling Relationships

When the sex differences of children are analyzed, it is clear that the socialization process has many areas of difference. Parents in most cases rear daughters differently than they do sons. (Sex differences in the socialization of children are not peculiar to the American society. A survey of 110 cultures showed that "in childhood there is, as in our society, a widespread pattern of greater pressure toward nurturance, obedience, and responsibility in girls, and toward self-reliance and achievement striving in boys."[135]

---

[134]Lynn, *op. cit.*, pp. 271–72.

[135]Herbert Barry III, Margaret K. Baron, and Irvin L. Child, "A Cross-Cultural Survey of Some Sex Differences in Socialization," in Robert F. Winch, Robert Mc-

Many parents start to stress sex distinctions long before the infant is aware of his own sex. The dressing of boys in blue and girls in pink, or the sex-differentiated toys given to infants are examples. As boys and girls grow up, the whole family is consciously aware of their sex differences and, as a result, sibling conflict and competition may be minimized. Because the boy and girl are often reared within somewhat different frames of reference, they are less compelled to make comparisons with each other than are sibilngs of the same sex.

When the siblings are of the same sex, they are developing with essentially the same socialization emphases and are apt to view each other and be viewed in a competitive light. But the younger sibling may also have the advantage of using the older brother (or sister) as a role model. The older sibling, who is further along in the socialization process but still relatively close in age actions to the younger sibling, may be a more effective agent of model expectations than the much older adult parents.

Many younger children view their older siblings with mixed feelings. On one hand, the older siblings may do things that the younger would like to do but can not because he is not old enough; on the other hand, they are perceived as helpful by the younger because of their greater experience and prestige.

As Kirkpatrick points out, if "siblings are simliar in age, there is companionship at the price of possible rivalry. If they are widely separated in birth order, there is lack of competition but sacrifice of companionship."[136] This indicates that there is no ideal relationship in age for siblings. Research has shown by its inconclusiveness that little of a reliable nature can be said about any particular birth position, age, or sex sibling relationship making a greater positive contribution than any other.

Brim found that through interaction and taking the role of the other, cross-sex sibling relationships lead to some differences in the acquiring of masculine and feminine traits. For example, a girl with an older brother is more masculine than her counterpart with an older sister, and the boy with an older sister is more feminine than this counterpart with an older brother.[137] Research on the two-sibling family indicates some important differences in the learning

Ginnis, and Herbert R. Barringer, *Selected Studies in Marriage and the Family* (New York: Holt, Rinehart & Winston, 1962), p. 274.

[136]Kirkpatrick, *op. cit.*, p. 233.

[137]Orville G. Brim, Jr., "Family Structure and Sex Role Learning by Children: A Further Analysis of Helen Koch's Data," in Robert F. Winch, Robert McGinnis, and Herbert R. Barringer, *Selected Studies in Marriage and the Family* (New York: Holt, Rinehart & Winston, 1962), p. 286.

of sex roles. "While the younger, as contrasted with the older, girl with a brother manifests only a slightly greater degree of masculinity, this difference for boys is quite striking: the younger, as contrasted with the older, boy with a sister is substantially more feminine."[138]

There are some advantages of having siblings.[139] First, the child is usually provided with age peers, which means that he has someone of about the same age with whom to interact, and who generally contribute to his overall socialization. Second, the siblings help bring him into contact with other children. His siblings will have their friends who will be around him, and this will extend his experiences. In some cases, this may have unpleasant implications if the older sibling's friends are the younger child's primary reference group and they reject him. Third, the sibling functions as a role model in teaching the younger sibling his future role behavior. Fourth, because children other than himself are in the family, the child must learn to share with them the rights and privileges of the family. This is important in the social sense that a child must learn that his wishes cannot always be satisfied or must sometimes remain unsatisfied because of the needs of others.

Some general problems related to family siblings also exist. First, the personalities of the different children may conflict. The very fact that they are different in age and personality structure will lead to some differences. In many families, sibling relationships seem to be one long series of conflicts. Second, there will be some sibling rivalry. The fact that what the child wants is not always available to him just when and to the degree he wants it may be due to the competition of a sibling. Therefore, the child often perceives the sibling as a threat and a rival. Many experts have suggested that sibling rivalry is inevitable in the family, and there seems good reason to believe this is true. A third problem may be the development of family cliques. While this sometimes happens with a parent and child, it is probably more common among the children themselves. For example, two children of the same sex may organize against a child of the opposite sex, or two older siblings against a younger. Some kinds of alignments among siblings seem inevitable, though in many families these may be shifting and temporary.

The family relationships among children and with the parents are a pattern of complex interaction in the middle class. This is true

---

[138]*Ibid.*, p. 287.
[139]See: Kirkpatrick, *op. cit.*, pp. 230–32.

because of the numbers as well as the demands made in learning to fill appropriate age-sex roles. With the entrance of an added child, the family takes on greater numerical complexity. When only the two parents and one child are in the family, only three interactional relationships exist. The addition of the second child increases the interactional relationships to 6, the addition of a third child to 10, and so forth. It has been argued that large families in the past had fewer problems than today; however, if this was true, it may have been because the social and psychological demands made on both parents and children in the past were probably fewer and simpler than in today's American middle class.

SELECTED BIBLIOGRAPHY

BLOOD, ROBERT O., and WOLFE, DONALD M. *Husbands and Wives.* Glencoe, Illinois: The Free Press, 1960.

BRIM, ORVILLE G., JR. Family Structure and Sex Role Learning by Children: A Further Analysis of Helen Koch's Data," in Winch, Robert F., McGinnis, Robert, and Barringer, Herbert R., *Selected Studies in Marriage and the Family*, pp. 275–90. New York: Holt, Rinehart & Winston, 1962.

BRODSKY, STANLEY L. "Self-Acceptance in Pregnant Women," *Marriage and Family Living*, November, 1963, pp. 483–84.

DAGER, EDWARD Z. "Socialization and Personality Development in the Child," in HAROLD T. CHRISTENSEN (ed.) *Handbook of Marriage and The Family*. Chicago: Rand McNally & Co., 1964, pp. 740–81.

DUNN, L. C., and DOBZHANSKY, TH. *Heredity, Race and Society.* New York: The New American Library, 1952.

ELKIN, FREDERICK. *The Child and Society.* New York: Random House, Inc., 1960.

FARRIS, EDMOND J. "Male Fertility," in Sussman, Marvin B., *Sourcebook in Marriage and the Family.* Boston: Houghton Mifflin Co., 1955.

GALLUP, GEORGE. "The Woman's Mind: America's Young Mothers," *Ladies Home Journal*, March, 1962, pp. 72, 96–97.

GLICK, PAUL. "The Family Cycle," *American Sociological Review*, April, 1947, pp. 164–74.

JERSILD, ARTHUR T. "Redevelopment as a Product of Learning and Growth," in Seidman, Jerome M., *The Child*, pp. 25–31. New York: Holt-Dryden, 1958.

KAGAN, JEROME. "The Child's Perception of the Parent," in Seidman, Jerome M., *The Child*, pp. 138–40. New York: Holt-Dryden, 1958.

KELL, LEONE and ALDOUS, JOAN. "Trends in Child Care Over Three Generations," *Marriage and Family Living*, May, 1960, pp. 176–77.

LYNN, DAVID B. "A Note on Sex Differences in the Development of

Masculine and Feminine Identification," in Seidman, Jerome M., *The Adolescent*, pp. 260–72. New York: Holt-Dryden, 1960.

MASTERS, WILLIAM H. and JOHNSON, VIRGINIA E. *Human Sexual Response*. Boston: Little, Brown & Co., 1966.

MILLER, DANIEL R., and SWANSON, GUY E. *The Changing American Parent*. New York: John Wiley & Sons, Inc., 1958.

POFFENBERGER, SHIRLEY, POFFENBERGER, THOMAS, and LANDIS, JUDSON T. "Intent Toward Conception and the Pregnancy Experience," *American Sociological Review*, October, 1952, pp. 616–20.

ROSEN, JAMES A. *Fertility in Men and Women*. New York: Coward McCann, Inc., 1952.

WINCHESTER, A. M. *Heredity and Your Life*. New York: Dover Publications, 1960.

PARENT-CHILD INTERACTION: ADOLESCENCE AND LAUNCHING YEARS

As pointed out in the previous chapter, the first few years of the young child's life are centered almost completely within his family of orientation. As the child grows older, other agencies and influences in society take on relevance for him. The influence of the playgroup and the school start early in the life of the child and take on greater and greater significance as the child grows older. This generally means that the influence of the family decreases. It is important to recognize that the family is "helped" to give up some of its influences over the child by the other agencies becoming increasingly important to the child. This "help" normally occurs whether the parents want it or not.

In the American middle class, adolescence is a transition stage in which the youngster is no longer socially defined as a child but is not yet an adult. The period of adolescence roughly corresponds to the teen-age years; the young person is neither "fish nor fowl" in filling child or adult roles. Many primitive societies had no similar period of role confusion in moving from child to adult status because the individual was treated as a child until he qualified for adult status and underwent the "puberty rites" of his society. From that point on, he was recognized as an adult.

That the American society has no clear-cut age when adult status is reached is illustrated by the different legal ages giving rights and obligations to the young person in the United States. Over time and in different states a variety of ages may be set for marriage, voting, going into the armed forces, and so forth. For purposes of discussion, it is suggested that, in the middle class, adolescence corresponds with the teen-ages and the "launching" years run from about 18 into the early 20's. Of course individual exceptions will occur; some persons may be socially recognized as adults at 18 or 19. Before discussing the social nature of adolescence, however, it is necessary to say something of the biological influences during this period.

EARLY ADOLESCENCE

Pubescence taken in its literal sense refers to the period of time during which the pubic hair is developing. This means that the youngsters are moving physically through changes that make them sexually mature males and females. Pubescence is a stage or period of development for the youngster, and while the duration varies to some degree, it is rarely less than two years and may be considerably longer. By the time pubescence is ended, the boy has completed the development of pubic hairs, facial hair, voice change, and enlargement of the genitals. For the girl, the physical changes are growth of pubic hair, rounding of the hips, enlargement of the breasts, some vaginal changes, and the first menstrual period.[1]

During the 20th century, many physical characteristics of the American population have undergone change. With the development of new knowledge in medicine, nutrition, sanitation and disease control, the younger generations are somewhat more physically advanced at earlier ages than previous generations. For example, in 1888 the average Yale freshman was 5 feet 7½ inches tall and weighed 136 pounds, as compared to the freshman of 1957 who was 3 inches taller and 20 pounds heavier. And coeds at Vassar and Smith in 1957 were almost 2 inches taller and 10 pounds heavier in the 1950's than were their counterparts at the start of this century.[2]

Puberty occurs in girls at an average age of 12, in boys at an average age of 14. Girls start out ahead of boys in physically maturing and maintain the lead through adolescence; they reach physical maturity at about the age of 18, 2 or 3 years ahead of their male contemporaries.[3] The important phenomena of menstruation occurs about a year after the girl enters the period of pubescence. The average age of first menstrual period for girls in the United States is about 13. The range of usual occurrence is between 11 and 15, with about 3 percent falling below and 3 percent above the limits.[4] "It appears that this average has become somewhat earlier in recent

[1]Harold C. Stuart, "Normal Growth and Development During Adolescence," in Jerome M. Seidman, *The Adolescent* (New York: Holt-Dryden, 1960), pp. 100–102.

[2]*Newsweek*, "The Teenagers," March 21, 1966, p. 64.

[3]Robert Bierstedt, *The Social Order* (New York: McGraw-Hill Book Co., 1957), p. 317.

[4]Stuart, *op. cit.*, p. 102.

years and that girls reach the menarche on the average a few months earlier than did their mothers."[5]

The reaching of puberty, and particularly the menarche, does not mean that girls are completely adult females in reproductive ability. "The evidence suggests that conception is extremely unlikely to occur during the first year following the menarche, and that for a period of four to six years it is less likely than after full maturity. Conception can occur very early, but it seldom does so before the age of sixteen, regardless of the age at the menarche."[6]

There are important differences in the physical growth of boys and girls around the time of puberty. Girls gain in height at an accelerating rate from 9 to 12 years, whereas boys do so from 11 to 14 years.[7] Thus, in the age group 11 to 13, the girls are frequently taller than the boys. Relationships are often difficult for youngsters in this age group because of the reversed physical differences in height and the general awkwardness of the social relationships.

The age range for reaching pubescence has different implications for girls than it does for boys. While early or late pubescence is a biological fact, its occurrence is treated within a variety of social definitions. Harold Jones did a study of the physically most precocious 20 percent and the physically most retarded 20 percent in a random sample of girls from a public school. The two groups were matched according to intelligence, social class, race, and childhood health records.[8] His general findings were that "the early-maturing (girls) were below the average in prestige, sociability, and leadership; below the average in popularity; below the average in cheerfulness, poise, and expressiveness."[9]

The Jones study indicates that the girl who goes through pubescence at a later age has definite advantages over the early bloomer, and suggests several reasons for this advantage. The first is a physical advantage. Those girls who are later in sexual maturing have less sudden physical growth, which involves fewer hazards of physiological imbalance and physical distortion for them than for the early maturing girls. Jones writes that the longer period of growth "affects particularly the legs, and the late maturing girl is therefore longlegged, and tends to conform closely to our American standards of

[5]*Ibid.*, p. 102.
[6]*Ibid.*, p. 104.
[7]*Ibid.*, p. 90.
[8]Harold E. Jones, "Adolescence in Our Society," in Jerome M. Seidman, *The Adolescent* (New York: Holt-Dryden, 1960), pp. 50–51.
[9]*Ibid.*, p. 56.

beauty of figure, which in the present code of commercial advertising must always be long-legged and usually a bit hypo-feminine."[10]

A second important factor is that the early-maturing girl moves abruptly into being physically a young woman, but her age and social abilities do not keep pace with the sudden change. With a later maturation, the parents and the girl herself have a longer time in which to get used to the new interests, new impulses, and new requirements as to behavior.[11] A third factor is that the late-maturing girl is more nearly in step with the boys in her age group than is the early-maturing girl. The two-year lag in the average maturity patterns of boys as compared with girls is reduced or eliminated among those girls who mature late and, as a result, various social activities are more immediately satisfied.[12]

For the boy, the consequences of early maturing are just the opposite. "The early-maturing boy enters adolescence at a time when girls in his age group are appreciative of male acquaintances who no longer insist upon being children. He also acquires traits of strength and athletic ability which give him prestige with his own sex."[13] By contrast, the boy who matures late is out of step with all the others in his age group and is often treated by them as a little boy.[14] It was found that those boys who were physically accelerated had little need to strive for status and from their ranks come the outstanding leaders in senior high school.[15]

The variations in achieving physical maturity, by sex, provide a contrast in the social definition of early adolescent roles. For the boy, early physical maturity if accompanied by appropriate coordination provides him with an advantage in the valued activities of boys. Being nearer to male adult physical development provides him with an advantage over other boys. But socially just the opposite is often true for the girl. The early-adolescent girl who stands out from most of her age peers in physical development is, like the early-developing boy, closer to female adult physical growth. She is often viewed by adults as a little girl with a woman's body and it is often feared that her social and psychological immaturity will get her into trouble. (However, her physical development may provide her with advantages in acquiring dates.)

---

[10]*Ibid.*, p. 58.
[11]*Ibid.*, p. 58.
[12]*Ibid.*, p. 58.
[13]*Ibid.*, p. 58.
[14]*Ibid.*, p. 59.
[15]*Ibid.*, p. 59.

In many groups of girls, there is a tendency to conform in physical appearance. The girl with greater physical development may try to hide it, or the underdeveloped girl may try to give the impression of being more developed. The second is probably a more common trait in today's American society. For example, in the past the girl with early breast development might wear loose clothing or become stoop shouldered to hide her "deformity." In contrast, the slower-developing girl today may buy "falsies" to catch up with the "honest" girl who reflects the norms of the group.

Because early adolescence signals the period of rapidly developing interest in the opposite sex, general physical attractiveness becomes of great importance. One study found that 57 percent of both sexes were concerned about blackheads and pimples—a concern that led all other concerns about attractiveness.[16] Also at this age, girls tend to be greatly concerned with weight. "Almost one third of the girls see themselves as heavy, with more than half of them expressing some concern. Only 3 percent of the boys describe themselves in this manner, and little concern is expressed by them."[17]

Clearly, physical characteristics become important for the early adolescent within the context of social definitions. Physical maturity continues to emerge fairly rapidly for the adolescent; however, he is not necessarily attaining social maturity at the same rate. "In terms of growth, strength, fecundity, and mental capacity, full maturity tends to be attained only a short time after puberty; but socially the adolescent still has a long way to go, in most cases, before full status is reached."[18] This is particularly significant for the middle-class girl who may achieve physical maturity at about 17, but is still 4 or 5 years away from achieving adult role recognition.

The description of the teenager as being neither child nor adult during adolescence is generally accurate in terms of both appearance and behavior. Kirkpatrick writes "A significant and baffling aspect of adolescence is the fact that there is often an erratic, inconsistent, and shifting pattern of maturity. The girl is half child and half woman and the male adolescent is half boy and half man, each capable of unpredictable behavior which violates expectations. The baffled parent does not quite know whether to spank or trust, and either course may have its dangers."[19] Consequently, both the par-

---

[16]Alexander Frazier and Lorenzo K. Kisonbee, "Adolescent Concerns with Physique," in Jerome M. Seidman, *The Adolescent* (New York: Holt-Dryden, 1960), p. 145.

[17]*Ibid.*, p. 142.

[18]Kingsley Davis, "Adolescence and the Social Structure," in Jerome M. Seidman, *The Adolescent* (New York: Holt-Dryden, 1960), p. 42.

[19]Clifford Kirkpatrick, *The Family* (New York: The Ronald Press Co., 1955), p. 241.

ents and the adolescent are often erratic in their interactions, so that sometimes when the youngster wants to be an adult the parent treats him as a child and, on other occasions, just the opposite occurs.

Teenagers are not only of physiological and sociological importance, but also represent a numerically large part of the American population. This is a result of the consistently high birth rate in the United States since the end of World War II. The medium age of the American population has been declining and is at present 28 years; there are about 18 million Americans in the age range of 13 to 17.[20]

THE ADOLESCENT AND HIS PARENTS

The relationships of parents to their adolescent children are in part affected by the stage of the parents' adulthood. One important fact is that, when their children are in adolescence, many parents have left their young adult years behind and are moving into the middle-age years. The adolescent period is thus made more difficult for both parents and children, because the parents' adjustment problems to middle age are often occurring at the same time. As Kingsley Davis aptly puts it, "At the time of adolescence the contrast is between an organism which is reaching its full powers and one which is just losing them."[21]

In the youth-oriented culture that characterizes the American middle class, the problems of the adolescent are often stressed to the point of ignoring the personal problems of the parents. Leaving the young adult years behind is not easy for many parents and when they are faced with the youthful images of themselves presented by their children, the problem may be further intensified. Some parents react by doing everything possible to keep from moving into the middle-age category. The mother who is mistaken for the older sister of her adolescent daughter often feels that she has achieved the ultimate in compliments. One common middle-class belief is that the parents who successfully stay close to their children in "psychological age" are to be admired. This belief reflects a lack of social value and prestige associated with being older psychologically—and is questionable in terms of an ongoing socialization process. The parents may "regress" to the psychological and social level of the adolescent rather than performing at their own age level and serving as adult role models for their children as they grow older.

---

[20]*Newsweek, op. cit.,* p. 57.
[21]Kingsley Davis, "The Sociology of Parent-Youth Conflict," in Jerome M. Seidman, *The Adolescent* (New York: Holt-Dryden, 1960), p. 374.

The middle-class belief that a parent should be a "pal" to his children reflects a social value which gives importance to a common world for parents and children. The belief in a common world has developed around notions of democracy between parents and children and implies they are equals socially, psychologically, and intellectually. If this is true, it is a devastating picture of the parents because it implies they are still essentially teenagers. The fact is that a mature adult is usually superior to his children in almost every way and, as a role model, this superiority is very important.

It might be added that moving down to the level of the young person is reflected in many kinds of adult-young person relationships in American society. For example, some college professors feel that their students should determine the level of intellectual interaction, and many times those so persuaded will go into the classroom and present a topic to the students for their discussion. While this may have some social advantages, it is a moot point whether intellectual development can emerge from a common base of student ignorance.

It may be that the adult's belief in being a "pal" to the teenager has little relationship to what the adolescent wants. The adults, whether parents, teachers or youth activity leaders, are almost always in a position of power and the adolescent may find it to his advantage to pretend an enthusiasm for adults in the "pal" role. There are many adults who serve as youth leaders and believe they are "reaching" the adolescent, when in reality the adolescent contemptuously sees them as "jerks, creeps and squares" to be conned in the "pal" relationship so long as it is advantageous to do so. There is a certain arrogance and lack of perception in the adult belief that an adolescent wants him for a pal. We tend to feel most comfortable with peers who share our interests and have no strong power over us and these are two characteristics generally missing from adult-adolescent "pal" role relationships. At any rate, there is evidence that adolescents don't really think of an adult as pals. For example, in one study of teenagers, two thirds of the girls interviewed said they felt closest to another girl or a sister, and only one tenth felt closest to their mothers.[22]

While some of the problems of parent-adolescent relations rest with the parents' personal problems and their effect on the adolescent, others result from a lack of social clarity in the treatment of the adolescent. One basic problem for parent and adolescent alike is the degree of freedom and independence the youngster should ex-

---

[22]Quoted in: Morton M. Hunt, *Her Infinite Variety* (New York: Harper & Row, 1963), p. 55.

432   MARRIAGE AND FAMILY INTERACTION

pect or be encouraged to take. All societies must develop procedures for moving their youth into adult roles. Stephens has examined a number of cultures with regard to the emancipation process; that is, the transition from the childhood dependence on parents to the freedom and autonomy of adulthood.[23] "In this area our society also appears to be unusual, but in this case it is not because we are 'late.' Rather, it is because emancipation is so sudden, radical, and early in our society."[24] Because the parents have the child from the early age of total dependency, it is sometimes very difficult for them to assess the adolescent's ability to handle independency. The Miller and Swanson study found that the start of adolescence was a period of important change in the central relationship of mothers to their children. In the 13th or 14th year, the median mother no longer keeps track of what he (the youngster) is doing most of the time.[25] However, almost a third (28 percent) of the mothers felt that close supervision should go on for 17 years or more.[26]

Entering high school is also of importance at this age. It not only implies a social definition of greater independency for the adolescent, but may also alter his daily life patterns to the extent that the mother is less able to keep track of him even if she wants to. The fact that about one third of the mothers believe that close supervision should go on until 17 years of age means that for a number of adolescents conflicts will arise between the demands of the mother and the individual freedom of adolescent behavior associated with the high-school ages.

The Miller and Swanson findings also point out another area of possible conflict between young adolescents and their parents. Since different mothers give freedom at different ages, adolescents sometimes run into difficulty with their age peers. The fact that his mother is still watching him closely can be very disturbing to a youngster. This is especially true for the boy, because his untactful peers point out to him that he is tied to "mother's apron strings." The problem is not so much which of the mothers is right as it is their lack of agreement in the treatment of children; and the lack of agreement reflects the lack of clearly defined social norms. Because adolescents are often strong conformists, they may use any differential treatment as a weapon in trying to "con" their mothers. The

---

[23]William N. Stephens, *The Family in Cross-Cultural Perspective* (New York: Holt, Rinehart & Winston, Inc., 1963), p. 393.
[24]*Ibid.*, p. 393.
[25]Daniel R. Miller and Guy E. Swanson, *The Changing American Parent* (New York: John Wiley and Sons, Inc., 1958), p. 224.
[26]*Ibid.*, p. 224.

mother (and sometimes the father) is constantly asked, "Why can't I do (have) something all the other kids do (have)?" The mother who believes what her child tells her may change if she feels that she is wrong, or if she does not want her child to be too different. Through this process, youngsters probably manipulate their parents far more than many parents realize.

Because the interaction of parent and adolescent in many middle-class families is based upon some different values and ends, conflict seems inevitable. From the conflict, certain changes in the relationship develop. "When the child's will collides with that of the parent, the relation begins to be pervaded by ambivalence."[27] Through conflict and ambivalence, independency may emerge. If nothing else, the changed feelings indicate that the child no longer accepts the parent as the final arbiter and begins to question what he once accepted as absolute authority. And until parental authority is questioned, the youngster is not achieving independence. Ideally, this conflict can have a great deal of psychological and social value because it allows the youngster to reach for independence at a time when the parents can partially control the reaching. However, a balance between the reaching of the youngster and the controls of the parents is often difficult to achieve.

Probably every generation views the adolescent as a problem, but this view seems to be even more intense among the present adult generation, if for no other reason than the greater attention directed at the adolescent. As mass media often "makes" a crime wave, they may also "make" an upsurge in adolescent "problems." It is interesting that while most of the mass media presents the adolescent as the cause of problems, there are a number of professional "adolescent experts" who see the adolescent as suffering from problems created by the adult world. This position—one taken by some educators and psychologists—is that the adolescent "instead of riding roughshod over helpless adults, is actually being segregated, shunned, manipulated, discriminated against and forced to live in a deluxe ghetto where tastes and mores of a distinct subculture flourish only for lack of meaningful integration into a stable adult society."[28] It is quite probable that the adolescent as the cause of many social problems *or* as the object of destructive manipulation by adults are both exaggerations.

The evidence suggests that the amount of conflict and disagree-

---

[27]Willard Waller and Reuben Hill, *The Family* (New York: The Dryden Press, 1951), p. 390.
[28]*Newsweek, op. cit.*, p. 62.

ment between the adolescent and his parent is not very great. One study on the extent of teenage disagreement with parents found that 13 percent said they disagreed often; 31 percent, occasionally; and the rest, rarely or never.[29] A *Newsweek* national survey found that a vast majority of adolescents say they get along well with their parents. Only 12 percent think their parents try to run their lives and 86 percent said that "the folks at home mind their own business."[30] *Newsweek*, in another study of a national sample of college students, found that 80 percent of the students thought the parent's permissiveness had been "about right," 11 percent thought their parents had been "too strict," and 8 percent thought they had been too permissive."[31]

While to some degree conflict between parents and children is inevitable, in most cases it is not severe enough to lead to breakdown in either the interactional relationships or the personality of the individual. However, the vast body of psychiatric literature indicates that the relationships of the child to his family is an important causal factor in mental illness. Some of the problems that may emerge and some family variables related to psychological difficulties have been demonstrated in a study by Myers and Roberts, a sociologist and a psychiatrist. They made an extensive study of 50 patients diagnosed as neurotics and schizophrenics in class III (middle class) and class V (lower class) families.[32]

In class III, the home and children were the mother's domain, and the father's participation in the childrearing process was limited to handling extreme tension situations.[33] Myers and Roberts found that most of the male patients were close to their mothers, but hostile to their fathers. The males were dependent upon their mothers after whom they modeled much of their behavior.[34] By contrast, female patients were close to their fathers, but hostile to their mothers. The females were unwilling to accept the traditional feminine role and had serious conflicts about the role they should assume.[35]

When Myers and Roberts compared the families in class III, they found *more* often among families with schizophrenics than neurotics

---

[29]Thomas S. Langner and Stanley T. Michael, *Life Stress and Mental Health* (New York: The Free Press of Glencoe, 1963), p. 255.

[30]*Newsweek, op. cit.*, pp. 58–9.

[31]*Newsweek*, "Campus '65," March 22, 1965, pp. 44–5.

[32]Jerome K. Myers and Bertram H. Roberts, *Family and Class Dynamics in Mental Illness* (New York: John Wiley and Sons, Inc., 1959), chaps. iv and v.

[33]*Ibid.*, p. 61.

[34]*Ibid.*, p. 104.

[35]*Ibid.*, p. 114.

that: (1) The mothers had more power in the family. (2) The mothers were more apt to be rigid perfectionists in their requirements for their children. (3) The mothers had frustrated mobility aspirations and projected the need for mobility to their children. (4) The wives dominated the husbands. (5) The mothers withheld affection as a means of controlling the offspring's behavior.[36] One implication for the middle-class family from this study is the danger of high social aspirations by the mother for the son. The son who accepts his mother's expectations and is not successful in achieving them has failed for both himself and his mother.

The Myers and Roberts study should not be taken as an absolute statement on middle-class family relationships and potential psychological problems. Rather, it should be viewed as an indication of what can happen, given certain social and personal qualities. Many individuals may accept the mobility aspirations projected by their parents and satisfactorily meet them or, through personal experience, redefine their own expectations. Nevertheless, the emphasis is that the relationships of the offspring to his parents from infancy on may have important implications for many of the mental health problems found in the United States today.

THE ADOLESCENT SUBCULTURE

In sociology, the concept of subculture refers to a fairly cohesive cultural system within the larger system of the total culture.[37] The adolescent subculture in the American middle class is, basically, a system created over time by adolescents themselves. The adolescent, being neither child nor adult, and having no clearly defined role made available to him by the overall culture, has created a loose cultural system to provide some role meaning for his adolescence. Adolescents accept *most* values of the adult world (often, unquestioningly), but the emphasis here is on those areas in which adolescent values differ from those of the adult world.

Because the adolescent subculture is to some degree self-developing, it has certain conflict points with the dominant adult cultural system. However, the inconsistency of adult definitions of adolescent behavior has also contributed to the emergence of subcultural values. The very fact that the adult views the adolescent with inde-

---

[36]*Ibid.*, p. 64.
[37]See: *The Annals*, November, 1961. The entire issue is devoted to the teen-age subculture. Also see: James S. Coleman, *Social Climates in High Schools*, U. S. Department of Health, Education, and Welfare, Monograph No. 4, 1961.

cision as to appropriate behavior means that the adolescent is treated one way on one occasion and in a different way on another. Since the adolescent often desires decisiveness and some precision in role definitions, he consequently tries to create his own. When he does, he often demands a high degree of conformity by other adolescents as "proof" of the rightness of his definitions. It is ironical that the adolescent often thinks of himself as a social deviant. What he fails to realize is that his adolescent group deviates from the adult world, but that the requirements for conformity within his subculture are extremely strong.

It appears that the group nature of adolescent subcultures has different meanings and significance for boys and girls. Henry argues that different sex patterns develop before adolescence and subcultural involvement. He suggests that in boys' groups most of the games they play require teams and it would be very difficult for a boy to avoid group life and teamwork with his age and sex peers.[38] By contrast, "little girls play with their dolls, their sewing, their cut-outs, or their jacks. Boys flock; girls seldom get together in groups above four whereas for boys a group of four is almost useless. In boys' groups the emphasis is on masculine unity; in girls' cliques the purpose is to shut out other girls."[39] The sex differences described by Henry carry over into adolescence, with boys generally interested in sports with their own sex and in dating, the latter often for the prestige it will give them with their male peers. On the other hand, the adolescent girl is generally not interested in large female group activities. She would rather be with one or two girl friends to talk to about boys. And increasingly the girl's orientation is to herself and a boy, with decreasing interest in age peers.

In addition to parents, other adults have been partially responsible for the development of the adolescent subculture. The school is of particular importance because, during weekday hours, the teacher and other school adults are responsible for placing adult limitations on the adolescent's behavior. The primary historical function of the school was to educate the child. However, the adolescent finds that many times the adults at school want to be democratic in defining adolescent roles, and, like his parents, they treat him in a contradictory fashion. As a result, the adolescent often perceives the school adults as having the same lack of clarity in providing him with role definitions as do his own parents, and again turns to his own subcultural values.

<hr/>

[38]Jules Henry, *Culture Against Man* (New York: Random House, 1965), p. 150.
[39]*Ibid.*, p. 150.

The school functions as the main location for the development of the subcultural values—large numbers of youngsters are in the school and interacting with one another, and so the school provides the physical setting for adolescent value development. The far-reaching influence of both the formal and informal impact of the school is shown by the fact that, in 1959, 85 percent of all males and 81 percent of all females, ages 16 and 17 were in school.[40]

In part, the adult world of parents, teachers, and others contributes negatively to the development of the adolescent subculture. In the middle class, they make few role demands on the adolescent and as a result he has a great amount of free time. Jessie Bernard points out that "our teenage culture—in contradistinction to the teen-age culture of the past or of other societies—is a product of affluence."[41] This means that the middle-class adolescent has both the time and the money to develop patterns of behavior and values peculiar to himself. The adolescent subculture partly results because we can afford a "large leisure class of youngsters not in the labor force but yet consumers on a vast scale, or, if in the labor force, free to spend their earnings on themselves."[42] Because they have money to spend and do spend it on specific goods, they become recognized by at least one segment of the adult world—the businessman who produces the goods that adolescents buy. And because the businessman caters to him, the adolescent gains a sense of adult recognition in some areas he has defined as important. Teenage spending—on clothes, cars, record players, cosmetics, and so forth—reached an estimated $10 billion in 1959 and is expected to reach twice that by 1970.[43] *Newsweek* found that most studies estimated that rising allowances and increasing income from part-time and summer jobs would in 1966 "put a whopping 12 billion dollars into the jean pockets of the nation's high-school boys and girls. This about equals the total income of South Africa and adds up to an income of $670 per teen per year."[44] This money is spent on luxury and recreation goods. The automobile is the bicycle of the 1960s, rebuilt hot rods are passé and sport cars are in.[45] The importance of "wheels" is reflected in the finding that 18 percent of all the boys interviewed said they had a car, 20 percent of the boys owned motor bikes, and the

---

[40]Jessie Bernard, "Teen-Age Culture: An Overview," *The Annals*, November, 1961, p. 2.
[41]*Ibid.*, p. 3.
[42]*Ibid.*, p. 3.
[43]*Ibid.*, p. 4.
[44]*Newsweek*, "The Teenagers," *op. cit.*, p. 71.
[45]*Ibid.*, p. 61.

next thing that 44 percent of the boys wanted was a car, 9 percent a motor bike.[46] With both the number and percentage of the population falling into the adolescent years increasing as a result of the high birth rate since the end of World War II, the adult world of business will continue to give strong recognition to the adolescent's material demands.

When looking at general characteristics and interests of adolescents, one must keep in mind that among adolescents are many individuals who are exceptions and whose values may be in complete opposition to the more common teenage values. While some individuals deviate as individuals from the common adolescent pattern, there are also some deviant subgroups within the overall adolescent subculture. For example, because of the selectiveness of its student population, a high school may have group values that place high prestige on outstanding academic achievement. When this subgroup pattern exists, the factor of conformity to group norms is often just as strong as in those schools where the values are just the opposite. The following discussion, however, concentrates on the more general subcultural values of middle-class adolescents in today's society.

One way in which adolescents make themselves different from the adult world is through a special language. This language serves to maintain barriers between themselves and the world of adults. A youngster may speak over the phone with his age peer in a jargon that leaves the parents wondering what he is talking about.

Another element of the adolescent subculture is the development of special heroes, particularly in the area of music. The very fact that most adults reject "rock and roll" makes clear to the adolescent that it is something that belongs to him.[47]

The adolescent often goes along with peer values, not because he likes them, but because he fears negative consequences if he rejects his peer group's values. The negative consequences may not only be directed at him by his peers, but may also result from his own fear of threatening what have become personal, internalized values. The *Newsweek* study found that more than half of the boys and girls "confessed they disapproved of boys' wearing long hair; yet when their parents criticized long hair, the majority defended it. In other words, nothing can solidify a fad faster than adult opposition."[48]

Two important factors contributing to the loose ties of the adolescent subculture across the United States have been the teenage

[46]*Ibid.*, p. 72.
[47]Robert R. Bell, "The Adolescent Subculture," *Education*, March, 1961, p. 3.
[48]*Newsweek, op. cit.*, p. 74.

music programs on television and radio, and teenage-specialized magazines. One study points out that the specialized magazines usually use the word "teen" in combination with some other word for the title and that the basic format is double-barreled: it has both a confessional and a cultic aspect.[49] The confessional centers around relationships with the opposite sex and such personal problems as how to be attractive and popular. The cultic centers around rock-and-roll entertainers, and movie and television players. "The articles deal with the most intimate of matters to such an extent as to constitute an almost morbid preoccupation."[50]

Over a 17-year period, two social scientists at Purdue University have carried out a series of polls with about 3,000 high-school students across the United States. Their findings provide a picture of teenage interests and values.[51] These researchers write that the "passion for popularity translates itself into an almost universal tendency to conformity among our younger generation. It runs through all social classes. . . . This is the most striking and most consistent fact that has emerged from our polls through the 17 years."[52] They further point out that "38 percent declare that the worst of all calamities is to be considered an 'oddball.' "[53]

The Purdue researchers draw attention to the adolescent's basic anti-intellectualism: "Almost three quarters of the high school students believe that the most important thing they can learn in school is 'how to get along with people.' Only 14 percent place academic learning first."[54] They also found in a poll of a representative sample of college students that the same attitudes prevail. "Sixty percent would rather be popular than brilliant; 51 percent believe that students with low grades are more likely to be popular than those who get good marks; 72 percent believe that development of a well-rounded personality is the main purpose of education; 71 percent feel that personality counts more than grades when it comes to looking for a job."[55]

It should be emphasized that these values of the personality cult and anti-intellectualism are not at variance with those of the adult

---

[49]Charles H. Brown, "Self-Portrait: The Teen-Type Magazine," *The Annals*, November, 1961, p. 15.

[50]*Ibid.*, p. 15.

[51]H. H. Remmers and D. H. Radler, "Teenage Attitudes," in Jerome M. Seidman, *The Adolescent* (New York: Holt-Dryden, 1960), p. 600.

[52]*Ibid.*, p. 600.

[53]*Ibid.*, p. 600.

[54]*Ibid.*, p. 601.

[55]*Ibid.*, pp. 601–602.

culture. What is of particular social relevance is that, historically, youth have usually been those with the least commitment to tradition and the *status quos* and therfore rebellious. However, today adolescents and young adults have created a subcultural value system different from that of the adult world only in areas of what are essentially social irrelevancy. Being different from adults in dress, music, and aspects of language is not of great social significance. Especially relevant when both youth and adults tend to be alike in the acceptance of such social values as personal conformity and intellectual mediocrity. An important result of these likenesses is a limitation on social change and a restriction of individual expression.

In one other respect, the adolescent value system reflects the shift in middle-class values from a commitment to others to a commitment of self. The fact of high social conformity does not necessarily mean a high identification with others, but rather that the "significant others" provide security for the individual's behavior because the others do not question it. Thus, the person who is really different is defined as an "oddball," implying that something is wrong with him. Defining *his* behavior as wrong implies that *your* behavior is right; therefore his behavior is much less threatening. For the adolescent, with his age and social insecurities, the need to account for the nonconformist often takes on great significance.

As suggested, the adolescent in most areas of behavior is not very different from his parents. Teenagers and young adults for the most part want what the adult world wants them to want, and they are essentially content with their way of life. Furthermore, they have little doubt that their tomorrows will be even better than their todays.[56] This suggests that the compatibility between most adolescent peer group values and those of the adult community is very high and that for the most part the peer group of adolescents has assumed a position that is complementary to both the school and the family.[57]

While the world of the adolescent seems removed in many respects from the adult world, there comes a time before reaching adult status when the young person must make certain decisions that will have a very important influence on his future. In today's Amer-

---

[56]*Newsweek, op. cit.*, p. 58.
[57]Talcott Parsons and W. White, "The Link Between Character and Society," in S. M. Lipset and Leo Lowenthal, (eds.) *Culture and Social Character* (New York: Free Press of Glencoe, 1961), p. 122.

ican middle class, probably the most important decision that the boy must make is whether to continue his education after high school. If he does not go on educationally, his occupational future will be increasingly limited; if he does pursue education, he must often simultaneously make his occupational choice by deciding what he is going to study in college. Yet, in the American middle-class society it is questionable that the 18-year-old has the background for making an occupational choice on any extended rational basis. Whether or not to go on to college is probably becoming less of a choice for the middle-class boy because he is being socialized with parental values that simply assume that he will go on to college. He unconsciously assimilates this assumption into his own value system.

With the increae in population of college age, plus the percentage increase in that age group going on to college, new anxieties are created for both the high-school graduate and his parents. Will he get into the college of his choice or even get into any reputable college? In recent years, new attitudes about higher education may have developed for both adolescents and their parents. One possible change may be a reduction in anti-intellectualism and greater social recognition given to those with intellectual ability. If the colleges and universities, with their great increases in enrollments, force students to come up to higher academic standards, there may be even more drastic changes in the intellectual values and attitudes of the middle class over the next 25 years. And when today's adolescents become the parents of tomorrow's generation, the parent-adolescent relationship may be quite different from what it is today.

The schools are important for the adolescent and the young adult in that they take up a great part of the young person's time and activity. Home life has been preempted by the high school because adolescents spend most of their week days there. When after-school activities are added to classroom time (plus, often, the time involved in bus rides to and from school), the adolescent's day may run from 8 A.M. to 6 P.M. In the schools, adolescents "make most of their friends, learn most of their lessons and are advised, encouraged, analyzed, consoled and profoundly influenced by specialists in surrogated parenthood, the guidance counselors."[58] Our economic system increasingly is demanding specialized training of youth for their adult futures. The kind of training needed for their futures in-

---

[58]*Newsweek, op. cit.*, p. 59.

dicates that "children are increasingly dependent on agencies other than the family for the fuctional means of fitting themselves for their future roles."[59]

THE LAUNCHING STAGE

At various points, the preceding discussion of adolescence has overlapped with what may be called the "launching stage"—the period when children are ending adolescence and starting to leave the parental home for college, occupations, and marriage. "During the 'launching stage' the family is variable in size, expanding on holidays and vacation periods and contracting quickly thereafter. It is an unpredictable family, spasmodically familistic and individualistic."[60] In effect, the launching stage in the family is the transitional stage between the family of orientation and the establishment of the offspring's family of procreation.

As with adolescence, the young adult years are often seen as years of great rebellion from parents and other adults. The mass media give the impression that many college students are "protesting" something or other most of the time. But it appears that the vast majority of college students are not rebels and are little concerned with social problems—except as those problems affect them personally. For example, most college students are not so much concerned with the rightness or wrongness of American foreign policy as they are with how they can avoid the military draft. Nor are they for the most part concerned with continued graduate education because of strong intellectual motives, but rather because extended formal education leads to greater economic rewards. Most college students have no strong feelings about wanting to change the social system; they seem quite satisfied with the *status quo*. The *Newsweek* study of college students found that 85 percent were satisfied with college and only 12 percent dissatisfied. The students were also asked how much confidence they had in other social institutions. Seventy-six percent said they had a "great deal" of confidence in the scientific community and 64 percent gave the same positive response for higher education. At the other extreme, only 34 percent of the student respondents stated a "great deal" of confidence in organized religion and only 13 percent in television.[61]

---

[59]Edward Z. Dager, "Socialization and Personality Development in the Child," in Harold T. Christensen (ed.), *Handbook of Marriage and The Family* (Chicago: Rand McNally & Co., 1964), p. 774.

[60]Waller and Hill, *op. cit.*, p. 431.

[61]*Newsweek*, "Campus '65," *op. cit.*, p. 45.

The launching stage is also important because in many situations, it symbolizes the period of role transition from adolescent to adult. It is at this time that independence for the young person becomes very important, because increasing independence is a major criterion in his being socially recognized as an adult. Yet independence must mean a breakdown of the long existing dependency ties with the parents. While both parents and children may have been leading up to this role change, it is not always easily accepted by all involved. Often the "launching stage" provides a setting in which the expectations of parents and their young adult children are incompatible. As Waller and Hill point out, "the wishes of the young for independence clash with the need for the parents to be needed."[62]

One basic problem during the launching stage centers around the parents being able to let go of their offspring. A part of the problem is that there is no cultural preparation for those parents who want to give up control and guidance. In the past, "the task of socialization was to prepare the child to remain with the family rather than depart from the family for an independent existence."[63] When the time for independence is reached, the parents are expected to let go, but since this must occur after many years of interacting with a dependent child, letting go may be very difficult to carry out in actuality. The situation is sometimes further complicated because some young adults do not want or are not ready for independence when their parents want them to have it. For "letting go" to be successful, the parents and the offspring must both be willing and able.

Because the offspring has reached the young adult years does not mean that the parents no longer have a strong emotional and vested interest in his future. Davis points out how this situation may lead to a conflict of interests for many parents. "Because his [the child's] acquisition of independence will free the parents of many obligations, they [the parents] are willing to relinquish their authority; yet, precisely because their own status is socially identified with that of their offspring, they wish to insure satisfactory conduct on the child's part and are tempted to prolong their authority by making the decisions themselves."[64]

One other problem for parents during the launching stage, is that, the move of the young person is often not to complete independence. The young person is not leaving his parents behind; in fact,

[62]*Ibid.*, p. 430.
[63]*Ibid.*, p. 426.
[64]Davis, *op. cit.*, p. 381.

he often continues to live at home, although it may be for specific periods of time rather than consistently as at younger ages. And with the extension of formal education, a common pattern in middle-class society is the continued economic dependence of the son or daughter on the family. Nevertheless, the offspring are at the same time "biologically mature, psychologically capable of making individual and independent decisions, and socially competent to fit into an adult society."[65]

A closer look at some of the role relationships at the time of the launching stage will be useful in distinguishing some of the differences during this period for the mother and father, as well as the son and daughter.

The Mother. The findings of some studies presented earlier indicate that the mother role is the one laden with the greatest emotional significance of all family roles. In American society, pathos and sentimentality are often attached to the image of the mother. When her children grow old enough to leave her, she is often seen as coming to the end of her most important adult role. If the mother then has nothing to turn to with some role significance, she often experiences severe personal frustrations. Even when she has other interests, she may have a period of difficult adjustment to the loss of the mother role; maternal roles do not taper off gradually, as they did when families had more children more widely spread in age. Furthermore, today's mothers are physically and psychologically "not nearly so ready as their grandmothers were to retire to their knitting in the easy chair by the fireplace as their children leave home."[66]

As we have previously discussed, some of the consequences of the mother role in American society have led to unfortunate results both for the mother and for her children. Because the mother is more involved in the parent role than the father, it is not surprising that she has the greater number of parental problems. One study found that while only 19 percent of the sample of adolescents said they had disagreements with their fathers, 33 percent said they had disagreements with their mothers.[67] When mothers and fathers are each linked to daughters and sons, the most common relationship for disagreement between an adolescent child and one of his parents is that of mother and daughter. One study found disagreement problems for 36 percent of the mothers and daughters and 29 percent of

[65]Waller and Hill, *op. cit.,* p. 436.
[66]*Ibid.,* p. 427.
[67]Langner, *op. cit.,* p. 258.

the mothers and sons, and for 24 percent of the fathers and sons and 16 percent of the fathers and daughters.[68]

There also appears to be a strong body of evidence that links many problems manifested in the adult years to inadequacies in the earlier mother-child relationship. When the son is the one with the problems (the "failure"), he is often visible to the broader community. Female failures are not as socially visible. But as Rossi suggests, "It is a short-sighted view indeed to consider the immature wife, dominating mother or interfering mother-in-law as a less serious problem to the larger society than the male homosexual, psychoneurotic soldier or ineffectual worker, for it is the failure of the mother which perpetuates the cycle from one generation to the next, affecting sons and daughters alike."[69]

Recognizing the problems that face the mother, it is not surprising that many of them consciously or unconsciously resist the growing independence of their children during the launching stage. Many parents, and especially mothers, maintain a new and modified parental role with their children even after the children have left home and are married. In the middle class has emerged what Sussman calls the "help pattern": the parents continue to be involved with their children even after the children are married, which often allows the mother to play at least a modified mother role.[70]

Sussman found in about 80 percent of the cases he studied that parents had established a pattern of giving moderate help and service to their married child's family. "In return for this assistance parents expected their children's continual attention."[71] In a more recent study, Adams found that all types of aid to the married couple were the greatest during the first 10 years of marriage and that financial aid was little influenced by differences in residential distance between the couple and the parents. Adams also found that in both middle-class and working-class marriages the parents of the wife gave more frequent total help than did the parents of the husband.[72] These patterns represent some modification from the traditional role of parents and their married children. The continuation of help after the children's marriages makes the behavior similar to some aspects of the interactional relationship that existed when the chil-

---

[68]*Ibid.*, p. 259.
[69]Alice S. Rossi, "Equality Between the Sexes," *Daedalus*, Spring, 1964, p. 621.
[70]Marvin B. Sussman, "The Help Pattern in the Middle Class Family," *American Sociological Review*, February, 1953, pp. 22–28.
[71]*Ibid.*, p. 23.
[72]Bert N. Adams, "Structural Factors Affecting Parental Aid to Married Children," *Journal of Marriage and Family*, August, 1964, p. 330.

dren were younger and, from the married children's side, is a change from the traditional pattern of the independency of the male after marriage. Often, the children may accept financial help as well as some influence in decision-making from the parents. In the majority of cases, this help pattern is probably between the parents and the married daughter, since the daughter tends to maintain closer relationships to her parents after marriage than does the son. If this is the case, the young husband is not only accepting help *for* his family of procreation, but that help is coming *from* his in-laws. It appears that the young middle-class husband and father is increasingly willing to accept help after he is married and does not feel his role threatened, even when the help comes from his in-laws. One study found that "more males than females feel that their spouse's families have strengthened their marriage."[73]

The Father. Some of the comments above on the middle-class "help pattern" also have application to the father in and after the launching stage. Because the father's commitment to his role is usually not as great as the mother's to hers, when the children grow up and leave home, he is usually not so greatly affected as his wife. "Usually the adjustment that the father makes is relatively less painful, since he often continues secure in his earner role and in his more detached position as representative of the family in the business community. His paternal roles in father-child activities are frequently more peripheral than central to his life organization, and the departure of the children to college and later to jobs and marriage does not threaten his way of living drastically."[74] However, because the loss of children may mean a great deal to his wife, he may be greatly needed to help her adjust to her loss of the mother role; thus, in some situations he becomes involved—not directly in his father role, but indirectly in his husband role.

Some of the father's problems at the launching stage may involve the age period they are going through, rather than the actual loss of their children from home. About the time his children are growing up, the man must face certain facts that may be personally disturbing. He may find that he is not going to reach his earlier occupational expectations and must try to adjust to occupational reality, and as mentioned in an earlier chapter, the middle-aged man is often faced with decreased sexual interest and ability. The combination

---

[73]Robert M. Gray and Ted C. Smith, "Effect of Employment on Sex Differences in Attitudes Toward the Parental Family," *Marriage and Family Living*, February, 1960, p. 37.

[74]Waller and Hill, *op. cit.*, p. 429.

may result in a feeling of threatened masculinity. Finally, the father is often forced to contrast himself with the youthful vigor of his sons and daughters, and their friends.

The Daughter. Generally, daughters have a closer attachment to their parents both before and after marriage than do sons. One study points out that "the female tends to be more attached to the parental family in that the wives reported being homesick more frequently and seeing their parents more often than did the males."[75] Because girls are generally given less personal freedom and are thus reared in a close association with their parents, ties to their parents often continue to be strong after they marry.

Winch suggests there is "some evidence to support the impression that the girls who are not emancipated have a greater than average probability of becoming engaged in marriage."[76] Perhaps the girl who is more emancipated from her parents has less interest in marriage. But even if this is true, it is important that the girl can remain to some degree dependent on her family without jeopardizing her possibilities of achieving the wife role. For this kind of daughter-parent relationship, the transition from family of orientation to family of procreation is often relatively smooth.

There is evidence that educational level of the parents is related to the image and degree of closeness by daughters to their parents. In a study which compared a variety of attitudes and images by college daughters of their parents, analysis was made by the educational level of the mothers. In this study, the daughters were divided into three groups by mother's education: "college graduate," "some college," and "no college." Where differences existed between the daughters, those with "college graduate" mothers had a higher and more positive relationship to their mothers. The "college graduate" group also had the highest positive image of the father and the closest relationship to him.[77] One important factor was that because the daughter was in college and both parents had college educations, parents and daughters tended to have fewer areas of disagreement; they accepted the same general values.

A study by this writer attempted to analyze the daughter's role during the launching stage.[78] In this study, 229 daughters and their

---

[75]Gray and Smith, *op. cit.,* p. 37.
[76]Robert F. Winch, *The Modern Family* (New York: Henry Holt and Co., 1952), p. 303.
[77]Robert R. Bell, unpublished research.
[78]Robert R. Bell and Jack V. Buerkle, "Mother-Daughter Conflicts During the 'Launching Stage,'" *Marriage and Family Living,* November, 1962, p. 384–88.

mothers responded to questions in reference to the daughter's role. The findings indicate a number of areas of conflict between mothers and daughters in defining the daughter's role. A summary of the overall mother and daughter findings were: "In the area of mate selection, mothers were less influenced by the 'romantic' attitudes when thinking of husbands for their daughters, and the mother's values lead her to believe that her daughter should place greater stress on 'rationality' in selecting a mate. Added to this was the belief by the mothers that they should have a greater veto power, if they feel it necessary, over their daughter's mate selection than the daughters feel they should have. These different attitudes suggest that during the 'launching stage' mate selection is a potential source of conflict between mothers and daughters. The fact that daughters placed a greater importance on establishing some close ties with a girl friend, as well as attributing greater importance to the father, indicates a second possible area of conflict. Financial aid from the parents may constitute a third area of conflict. Daughters feel less willing to accept financial help and have a greater suspicion of it when given, than do the mothers."[79]

The findings indicate that the launching stage as perceived by mothers and their in-college daughters has a number of potential areas of disagreement and conflct. The daughter is in the process of making the break away from her parental home. "She lives in a society that both encourages and demands that she increasingly be her own decision maker. Yet, the daughter is often torn between her love for and obligations to her mother and her increasing desire for independence. Many of the mothers still adhere to the traditional belief that the parents are the important, right and ultimate decision makers."[80]

A part of the conflict between the mother and daughter centers around defining of appropriate role behavior for the daughter. In her younger years, the daughter's role is defined to a great degree by her mother. As she grows older, she is influenced by other definitions, which she internalizes and applies to herself in her movement toward self-determination. However, the mother often continues to visualize the daughter's role as it was defined in the past and assigns the same importance to her function as mother in defining her daughter's role. "But given the rapid social change associated with the family roles the definer, as well as the definitions, may no longer be institutionally appropriate. Therefore, the daughter's concept of

---

[79]*Ibid.*, p. 386.
[80]*Ibid.*, p. 388.

her role during the 'launching stage' will differ at least in some degree from that of the mother, because the function of role definition is changing."[81]

The middle-class daughter in a "launching" relationship to her parents will be influenced by several factors. First, the need for a high degree of emancipation is probably less for those girls who still accept many of the values and role functions that their parents accept. Second, those girls who find the greatest conflict are often those who are operating within a role concept of self which is different from that of the parents, particularly the mother. This often happens when the daughter is strongly influenced by a value system different from that of the parents. Third, for many daughters conflict occurs during the launching stage, but once she is fairly well established with her own family of procreation, the conflict will probably decrease.

The Son. The son entering the launching ·stage probably has a greater need for emancipation from the family of orientation than the daughter. The pressures from society in general are very strong for him to express his independency, which is often taken as the sign of his having achieved adulthood. Independence is probably more readily attained by the son than the daughter, because male emancipation from the family will usually be more clear-cut. One indication of the need for the male to attain emancipation, particularly from the mother, is that "a close relationship with the mother is correlated with low courtship progress."[82] However, it is possible for the son not to make a strong break with his father and still achieve his adult occupational role. This situation often arises when the son goes into the father's business or into the same, or a related, occupation. The need for the son's independence from the father may occur when the son's occupation is the father's choice, not that of the son.

It also seems likely that the family helps and encourages the son's independence more than they do the daughter's. His earlier and more distinct emancipation may be brought about as the result of several factors: (1) the parents provide the sons with earlier and more frequent opportunities for independent action; (2) the parents give boys more privacy in their personal affairs; and (3) the son is held to a less exacting code of filial and kinship obligations than is the daughter.[83]

---

[81]*Ibid.*, p. 388.

[82]Winch, *op. cit.*, p. 303.

[83]Mirra Komarovsky, quoted in Ray E. Baber, *Marriage and the Family* (New York: McGraw-Hill Book Company, 1953), p. 384.

Once the children have been launched into their adult roles, the relationships with the parents undergo change as the parents move into the roles of grandparents and, as the parents grow older, in relationship to their adult children. Eventually, roles may be reversed, with the aged parents dependent upon their adult children. A more extended set of family relationships may be emerging in the middle class. When the middle-age parents are launching their children into independency, they may simultaneously be developing a relationship with *their* parents of an increasingly dependent nature. This series of separate, but interrelated families, probably will become more and more common with increasingly greater life expectancy and earlier ages at marriage; in the future, a whole new series of family relationships may develop. For example, a married couple in their early 20's with young children could have both of their parental families in their 40's and up to four pairs of grandparents in their 60's. Such a situation would alter many aspects of family living. For instance, the young couple's children would grow up not only with grandparents, but also with various great-grandparents during childhood and adolescence. What the implications of these sets of related families would be remains to be determined.

One other possibility may also be mentioned. A point that has been made on several occasions is that when the children grow up and leave the parental home, the demands on the husband-wife role relationship become very important. Because many couples end the launching years of their children while still in their 40's, they have 20 or 30 years of life expectancy left to them. In the near future, perhaps more couples who reach this age period will realize little is left in the husband-wife relationship, and decide that the years ahead with the partner seem intolerable. As a result, it is possible that the divorce rate for couples in their 40's will increase in the future.

SELECTED BIBLIOGRAPHY

Bell, Robert R., and Buerkle, Jack V. "Mother-Daughter Conflict During the 'Launching Stage'," *Marriage and Family Living*, November, 1962, pp. 384–88.

Bernard, Jessie. "Teen-Age Culture: An Overview," *The Annals*, November, 1961, pp. 1–12.

Brown, Charles H. "Self Portrait: The Teen-Type Magazine," *The Annals*, November, 1961, pp. 13–21.

Burchinal, Lee G., and Rossman, Jack E. "Relations Among Maternal Employment Indices and Developmental Characteristics of Children," *Marriage and Family Living*, November, 1961, pp. 334–39.

COLEMAN, JAMES S. *Social Climates in High Schools.* U. S. Department of Health, Education, and Welfare, Monograph No. 4, 1961.

DAVIS, KINGSLEY. "The Sociology of Parent-Child Conflict," *American Sociological Review,* August, 1950, pp. 523–35.

FRAZIER, ALEXANDER, and KISONBEE, LORENZO K. "Adolescent Concerns with Physique," in Seidman, Jerome M., *The Adolescent,* pp. 140–50. New York: Holt-Dryden, 1960.

JONES, HAROLD E. "Adolescence in Our Society," in Seidman, Jerome M., *The Adolescent,* pp. 50–60. New York: Holt-Dryden, 1960.

JONES, MARY C., and BAYLEY, NANCY. "Physical Maturing Among Boys as Related to Behavior," in Seidman, Jerome M., *The Adolescent,* pp. 150–68. New York: Holt-Dryden, 1960.

MILLER, DANIEL R., and SWANSON, GUY E. *The Changing American Parent.* New York: John Wiley and Sons, Inc., 1958.

MYERS, JEROME K., and ROBERTS, BERTRAM H. *Family and Class Dynamics in Mental Illness,* chaps. iv and v. New York: John Wiley & Sons, Inc., 1959.

STUART, HAROLD C. "Normal Growth and Development During Adolescence," in Seidman, Jerome M., *The Adolescent,* pp. 86–115. New York: Holt-Dryden, 1960.

SUSSMAN, MARVIN B. "The Help Pattern in the Middle Class Family," *American Sociological Review,* February, 1953, pp. 22–28.

PART V

Marriage Breakdown and Alteration

THE ENDING OF MARRIAGE

The divorce rate in the United States has climbed over past decades, and as a result there has developed an increasing concern with the ending of marriage—through divorce. In addition to the greater number of marriages ended by divorce, the number in which death ends the marriage has also increased. (Because of the increasingly greater life expectancy of the woman, an increasing proportion of the latter are terminated by the death of the husband). However, the ending of marriage through death does not elicit the same social concern as the ending through divorce. Divorce implies the failure of a marriage, and while all marriages, successful or unsuccessful, must ultimately end, the greatest social concern is directed at those marriages ended through the deliberate choice of the individuals involved. Implied in this reaction is the continued acceptance by our society's members of the belief that marriage should continue until ended by death.

Sometimes the mass media give the impression that today's American marriages are of short duration. But a couple marrying today can statistically expect about 35 years of marriage before the relationship ends either through divorce or with the death of one spouse. That is, because of greater life expectancy and younger age of marriage, the young couple of today enters marriage and remains in the marital relationship longer than did their grandparents. And even with today's high divorce rate, the average couple spend about half their life with one marital partner. The essential stability of marriage is illustrated by the following statement by Glick:

> Among women who entered their first marriages during the 1920's and who had, by 1954, already passed through about 30 years of exposure to the risk of losing their husbands by divorce or death, four out of every five had married only once. Moreover, among those in this group who had been above the age of 21 at the time of first marriage, fully nine out of every ten had not remarried by 1954. These facts point to the essential stability of marriages in the United States, especially of those contracted after the woman had passed her teens.[1]

---

[1] Paul C. Glick, *American Families* (New York: John Wiley & Sons, Inc., 1957), p. 112.

This chapter focuses on social and legal factors related to the different ways in which marriages may be altered or ended. Chapter 17 concentrates on social-psychological factors related to divorce and remarriage.

BEREAVEMENT

All marriages not dissolved in some other manner eventually end with the death of one marriage partner; and bereavement accounts for the ending of well over half of all first marriages. The legal start, and eventual finish, of marriage coincides with the social view of start and finish. The marriage has its legal and social start at the time of marriage and is terminated at the death of one of the partners. When the partner dies, the surviving spouse takes on the new legal and social role of widow or widower.

When bereavement is compared with divorce in the ending of marriages, the death of the spouse accounts for about twice as many terminations as does divorce. Divorces are most common as a means of ending marriages of short duration, but as the couple are married longer, divorce becomes less common and the chances of bereavement increase.

In one important sense, the comparison of marital termination through divorce with bereavement is misleading. Divorce must occur through the deliberate actions of the married couple, while death occurs without choice. Therefore, many individuals have experience with marriages ending through more than one means. Even the divorced person who remarries, and stays married, ultimately has the second marriage end through death.

In all types of marital termination, one area of great interest is the impact and consequences of the ending of a marriage on its children. The significance for the child is of importance because of the psychological, social, and economic factors related to the rearing of the child by the single responsible parent. The differential effects of bereavement and divorce on the child are discussed in Chapter 17.

The greater life expectancy of the woman, plus the fact that the father is statistically about three years older than the mother, means that it is the death of the father that most often ends the marriage. Of all orphans under 18 in the United States, about two thirds were orphaned as the result of the death of their fathers. But when compared with divorce, bereavement less often affects children under 18 years of age because it occurs later in the parental marriage than does divorce. Also, the chances of the child being orphaned before he is 18 are less today than they were in the past because of the earlier age of marriage and greater life expectancy of the parents.

DESERTION

While desertion is frequently used as a legal ground for divorce, it is considered here as an informal means of altering or ending marriage. Marriage starts at the same point in time socially and legally; however, when one of the marital partners deserts, the marriage ends only socially, not legally. The fact that a marriage altered by desertion is not legally recorded means that the estimates of desertion in the United States are very crude. Only those that reach the courts are recorded.

Baber gives a conservative estimate of the number of desertions per year at about 100,000 and points out that this would be roughly one desertion for every four divorces.[2] A study by Kephart of desertion and divorce in Philadelphia indicates that for that city, the ratio of desertion to divorce has been about one to one.[3]

Desertion is typically a male phenomenon, though it is possible for the woman to desert. When the woman deserts, it is often used as a ground for divorce. For example, in many states the wife must move with the husband if he must change residence for occupational reasons, and if she refuses she may be legally defined as guilty of desertion. When the man walks out on his family, he often returns after a period of time although he will then often desert again at a later date.[4]

Kephart has provided valuable information on some social characteristics related to desertion in his Philadelphia studies. In family literature, desertion has often been characterized as "the poor man's divorce," the implication being that, in the lower social classes, individuals desert rather than get divorces. Kephart, after careful study, writes: "When Philadelphia desertion cases were analyzed by occupational level, the idea of the 'poor man's divorce' failed to materialize, at least to the degree that had been expected."[5] Kephart found that 43.6 percent of the white desertions are derived from the upper half of the occupational ladder.[6]

---

[2]Ray E. Baber, *Marriage and the Family* (New York: McGraw-Hill Book Co., 1953), pp. 493–94.

[3]William M. Kephart, "Occupational Level and Marital Disruption," *American Sociological Review*, August, 1955, p. 460.

[4]Baber, *op. cit.*, pp. 493–94.

[5]Kephart, *op. cit.*, p. 464.

[6]*Ibid.*, p. 461.

Table 16–1 provides a comparison for occupational level of divorce and desertion in Philadelphia. The findings indicate that with slight variations the rates of desertion and divorce are just about the same for the different occupational levels. The most important factor to be derived from this study is that both desertion *and* divorce rates increase with a decrease in occupational level. The lower social classes, as measured by lower occupational level, are characterized by the highest rates of marital breakdown through *both* divorce and desertion.

TABLE 16–1

PERCENTAGE DISTRIBUTION OF MALE DESERTERS AND DIVORCEES, BY
OCCUPATION: FIRST MARRIAGES, PHILADELPHIA, 1950

Occupational Category	Divorce Sample (N=939)	Desertion Cases (N=922)	Divorces Minus Desertions (Percent Differences)
Professional	4.9	3.1	+1.8
Proprietors	4.4	8.7	−4.3
Clerical and sales	20.4	14.8	+5.6
Skilled	20.0	21.6	−1.6
Semi-skilled	38.6	37.0	+1.6
Labor-service	11.7	14.8	−3.1
Total	100.0	100.0	

Adapted from: William M. Kephart, "Occupational Level and Marital Disruption," *American Sociological Review*, August, 1955, p. 462.

Race is also a social variable related to higher desertion rates. In Philadelphia in 1950, Kephart found that nonwhite married males constituted 17.1 percent of the total married male population but accounted for 40.3 percent of the desertions for that year.[7] High desertion rates among Negro husbands have been attributed by some writers to a family system that is more transitory than that found among the white population. Yet there is evidence that higher desertion rates among Negroes are rather a reflection of social-class level. This is indicated in the Kephart study by a comparison between white and nonwhite males when occupational level is held constant. Taking the upper half of the occupation categories (professional, proprietors, clerical, and sales and skilled), 60 percent of the white males fall within this grouping and acount for 47.3 percent of the desertions. For the nonwhite population, 23.1 percent fall into the same occupational category and account for 17.1 percent of the nonwhite desertions.[8] Thus, desertion may be more influenced

[7] *Ibid.,* p. 461.
[8] *Ibid.,* p. 462.

by occupational level and social class than by different family patterns related to supposed racial characteristics.

Monahan and Kephart did research on desertion and divorce in Philadelphia as related to religious background. Their statistics were compiled from records kept by the Philadelphia Municipal Court. Having religious information available for analysis is rare because "except in Iowa, marriage records in this country contain no information on the religious preference of the parties."[9] Monahan and Kephart found that "in the white desertion and non-support cases which came to court, the Catholic group, with reference to their proportion in the population, is overrepresented by nearly 40 percent. On the other hand, the Jewish group is underrepresented to somewhat the same degree. The white Protestant class is about 25 percent underrepresented."[10] The high rate of desertion among Catholic males is probably due to the religious restrictions against divorce, and the disproportionate number of Catholics in the lower social classes. The low rates for the Jewish males may be explained by the strength of the combined religious-ethnic values in reference

TABLE 16–2

DESERTION CASES BY RELIGION: PHILADELPHIA, WHITES, 1950

Religion	Percent of 1950 White Population	Percent of Philadelphia Desertions		
		Both Same Religion	Husband's Religion	Wife's Religion
Jewish	16	9.6	10.5	10.5
Catholic	40	44.4	54.9	55.8
Protestant	44	22.9	33.9	33.0
Total	100	76.9	99.3	99.3

Adapted from: Thomas P. Monahan and William M. Kephart, "Divorce and Desertion by Religious and Mixed Religious Groups," *American Journal of Sociology*, March, 1954, p. 463.

to the stability of the family, and their higher social class position. Table 16–2 provides a comparison of desertion rates by the religion of both husband and wife.

Monahan and Kephart conclude that the "Philadelphia data show clearly that Jewish desertions are found primarily in the upper occupational brackets, in contrast to the Catholic, Protestant, and mixed Catholic-Protestant groups. It is evident also that Protestant desertions, on the whole, derive from a higher occupational level

---

[9]Thomas P. Monahan and William M. Kephart, "Divorce and Desertion by Religious and Mixed Religious Groups," *American Journal of Sociology*, March, 1954, p. 456.

[10]*Ibid.*, p. 462.

than Catholic cases. However, with the exception of the professional category, the differences between the Protestant and Catholic occupational hierarchies are only moderate, albeit consistent."[11]

Finally, Kephart's extensive research indicates an important relationship to drunkenness on the part of the husband. In 1949, in 2,937 new cases of desertion and nonsupport, 28 percent involved drunkenness as an alleged causal factor in desertion.[12] Drunkenness is important because it may be both the result and the cause of other marital problems.

When the research of Kephart and Monahan is combined with other empirical findings, the picture of desertion in the United States indicates the following: Desertion is usually a male pattern of behavior with a high degree of recidivism. Baber suggests that the median age of first desertion for the male is 33 and that two thirds of desertions occur within the first 10 years of marriage.[13] The average age of the husband and the length of marriage appear to be about the same for desertion as for divorce. The belief that desertion is "the poor man's divorce" is only partially true. It is more common in the lower classes, but is not necessarily a substitute for divorce; the divorce rates are equally high. Kephart's findings indicate that at all social levels the probability of desertion is about the same as the probability of divorce.

Children are involved more often in desertion than divorce cases. Monahan and Kephart found that "for the native white primary marriages in the *divorce* sample all religious groups showed between 57 and 61 percent to be childless couples. In the same type of desertion cases only 19 percent were childless, and the average number of children was 1.32 per family."[14] The higher number of children involved in desertion cases is due to several factors. (1) There is a selective factor, because women with dependent children are often placed on the records as having a deserting husband. The fact that she has children means she is more apt to seek financial help than is the childless woman whose husband has deserted. (2) Because the deserting husband often returns to his wife, the probability of their continuing to have children increases. (3) There is some evidence that the overall social length of marriage is shorter in divorce than in desertion, thereby increasing the probability of the deserted family having more children. (4) It is possible that the children are

[11]*Ibid.*, p. 464.
[12]William M. Kephart, "Drinking and Marital Disruption," *Quarterly Journal of Studies on Alcohol*, March, 1954, p. 71.
[13]Baber, *op. cit.*, pp. 494–95.
[14]Monahan and Kephart, *op. cit.*, p. 463.

responsible for some husband-fathers deserting because the fathers feel unable to cope with the demands of the family, feel personally inadequate, or desire to escape responsibility.

Of great concern to the courts is the financial responsibility for the children in desertion cases. As discussed in Chapter 9, the court knows that if the father does not assume the financial responsibility, then costs must often be met with tax dollars. Monahan points out that a "basic revolution has taken place in the field of family law and social control over deserting spouses. Family fugitives can no longer flee to the frontier or the anonymity of the metropolis, as they have done before."[15] Many states now have working agreements with other states in returning the deserting spouse to his home state and financial responsibility for his family. The legal concern is not so much with the stability of the family as it is that the husband-father meet his economic responsibilities. So long as he meets them, the court has little interest in whether or not he lives with his family.

Even with the tightening of laws in regard to the deserting husband-father, many husbands are still able to escape their financial responsibilities. Monahan further points out that authorities "remain reluctant to confront a man with his marital responsibilities and to energetically insist that he be responsible for the wife or children he has abandoned, or suffer imprisonment."[16]

An important contrast between desertion and divorce is that in the majority of desertion cases it is the husband who "rejects" his wife by leaving her, while, in a majority of divorce cases, it is the wife who "rejects" the husband by bringing suit against him for divorce. With the great importance that most women attach to the wife-mother role, their husbands' rejecting them by walking out may be psychologically very upsetting. Although this is probably most true in the middle class, the middle-class woman may reverse the "stigma" by bringing a divorce suit against the husband for desertion, thereby "rejecting" *him*. In the lower class, desertion is often viewed with some indifference while, in the middle class, the social reactions are usually those of pity or even scorn.

LEGAL SEPARATION

Legal separation (*divorce a mensa et thoro*) is a partial or qualified divorce for cause by the judgment of a court, which forbids the parties to cohabit. It does not affect the basic obligations of the

---

[15]Thomas P. Monahan, "Family Fugitives," *Marriage and Family Living*, May, 1958, p. 150.
[16]*Ibid.*, p. 150.

marriage, and under it there is no right to remarry.[17] Limited divorces (or legal separations) are granted in about half of the legal jurisdictions of the United States. Of the total number of marital dissolutions in the United States, limited divorce or legal separation probably account for no more than 2 to 3 percent of the total.[18]

Because the husband and wife cannot live together, the marriage socially ends with legal separation. Legally, however, the marriage is altered, not ended. From the male's point of view, a legal separation means that he continues to have the responsibilities of marriage, but not the rights. If the couple should decide to live together again, they would have to go back through the courts; if they should decide to get an absolute divorce, they would have to go through the usual divorce proceedings.

Legal separation is not a popular means of resolving marital problems. It is used if there are strong reasons for not getting a divorce, or as a means of economic protection for the wife. Suits are generally brought by the wife for permanent maintenance and support. Since most decrees are concerned with questions of property settlement and custody of the children, a majority are contested. This is in contrast with divorce, where very few are contested.

ANNULMENT

A decree of annulment means that no marriage ever legally occurred. Hence, neither party ever acquired any marital rights and upon the issuance of the decree, the parties returned to the *status in quo* at the time of marriage. No property rights accrue, and in the absence of a statute to the contrary, children are illegitimate.[19] It is estimated that annulments account for about 3.5 percent of the total marital dissolutions in the United States.[20]

A marriage ended through annulment has a very different meaning when viewed legally and socially. Legally the marriage never had a starting point and therefore cannot be legally ended. However, socially the marriage started at the time the couple were married and ended when the couple stopped living together as husband and wife. While an annuled marriage may never have existed

---

[17]Helen I. Clarke, *Social Legislation* (New York: Appleton-Century-Crofts, Inc., 1957), p. 119.

[18]William M. Kephart, *The Family, Society and the Individual* (Boston: Houghton Mifflin Co., 1961), p. 584.

[19]Clarke, *op. cit.*, p. 120.

[20]Kephart, *The Family, Society and the Individual, op. cit.*, p. 587.

legally, it usually had a social meaning in marital role relationships for the couple.

Annulment of a marriage is based upon fraud committed prior to the marriage. It is based upon the legal definition that the couple were not eligible for marriage for such reasons as duress, bigamy, nonage, and insanity. The term fraud is a broad term and is the most popular cause for annulment; it covers a number of specific causes generally related to some premarital disrepresentation.

In 1961, California reported 5,643 annulments and New York reported 2,310. The 7,953 annulments granted by these two states constituted over two thirds of all reported annulments in the United States during 1961.[21] It is common knowledge that annulments in these two states generally serve to circumvent certain aspects of their divorce laws. (In New York, divorce may be granted only for adultery, so that annulment is frequently used as an alternative to divorce.)

DIVORCE

Most writers, both academic and nonacademic, view divorce as a social problem. Frequently, the assumption is that divorce is evil or destructive to both the personal and social make-up of the American population. In Chapter 17, the use of divorce will be discussed as a part of contemporary American society.

It should be emphasized that divorce is not new or peculiar to the American society. Some kind of divorce arrangements are universal in all the cultures of the world, both past and present. Historically, the right of divorce in most cultures was given to the husband. Two common historical grounds used by the male in divorcing his wife were "barrenness" and adultery. Generally, if the wife did not bear children the fault was assumed to be hers. In many societies where great value was attached to the continuity of the family line through offspring, the failure to reproduce was viewed with great concern; therefore, the husband often had the right to divorce his wife and acquire a new one. In patriarchal societies, the dual sex standards operated around adultery. The husband was not usually punished for adultery but the wife was often subject to severe criticism, and this many times took the form of divorce. Divorce in the past provides a sharp contrast with divorce in the United States today, for the

---

[21]United States Department of Health, Education and Welfare, Public Health Service, National Office of Vital Statistics, "Divorce," *Vital Statistics of the United States, 1961,* Vol. III, Sections 3, 4 & 7, p. 6.

legal grounds today are more favorable for the wife than for the husband, and the wife more often than the husband gets the divorce. In the United States "absolute divorce, or *divorce a vinculo matrimonii*, is the legal separation of man and wife effected for cause by the judgment of a court totally dissolving the marriage relation."[22] Socially and legally the marriage started at the same point in time, but in many cases the social relationship of the marriage ends before the marriage is legally terminated. This is true because the couple often cease living together as husband and wife before the final decree of divorce is granted.

It has sometimes been argued that the increase in divorce rates in the United States represents an increase in unhappiness or maladjustment in marriage. But there is no way of knowing whether or not married couples are more or less happy in marriage today than they were in the past. Divorce is more socially and personally acceptable today than it was in the past; therefore, the increase in divorce may be influenced by a growing unwillingness to *endure* unhappiness in marriage.[23] Also, divorce is legally more available today than it was in the past. All legal jurisdictions of the United States grant absolute divorce, South Carolina in 1949 being the last to do so.

Unquestionably, divorce rates have been increasing in the United States. At about the time of the Civil War the divorce rate per 1,000 population was 0.3, but by 1920 the rate had reached 1.6 and by 1945 the rate was 3.5.[24] "The divorce rate hit an all-time peak in 1946, as an aftermath of World War II, when many marriages deteriorated. It then declined steadily until the late 1950's, at which time the number of divorces per 1,000 married persons under 55 years of age reached approximately the same level as that for 1940. By 1961, the divorce rate had risen again slightly, to about the 1950 level."[25] The number of divorces increased in the United States from less than 10,000 in 1867 to about 400,000 in 1961. Thus, within roughly a century, "with almost one out of every four marriages ending in divorce, it was evident that one of two things would happen: (a) the divorce laws would be made more liberal, or (b) the enforcement of the laws—the divorce procedure itself—would become more lenient. As it turned out, it was the latter practice which came to the fore, hence the development of the American divorce

---

[22]Clarke, *op. cit.*, p. 119.

[23]Baber, *op. cit.*, p. 509.

[24]Hyman Rodman, *Marriage, Family and Society* (New York: Random House, 1965), p. 290.

[25]Paul C. Glick, "Demographic Analysis of Family Data," in Harold T. Christensen (ed.), *Handbook of Marriage and The Family* (Chicago: Rand McNally and Co., 1964), pp. 301–2.

paradox: relatively stiff laws on the one hand versus lax law enforcement on the other."[26]

Rates of divorce often vary when related to different social conditions or variables. For example, the divorce rate varies somewhat by geographical region. During 1960 1 married couple out of every 104 was divorced. However, the rate was lowest in the Northeast with 0.8 divorces for every 100 marriages, 2.2 in the North Central states, 2.8 in the South and 3.5 in the West. "Thus the divorce rate in the West was more than four times as high as that in the Northeast."[27] The high divorce rate of the West reflects a large number of people from the Northeast, particularly from New York, going to Nevada for their divorces.

There is also some relationship between divorce rates and economic conditions. Divorce, like marriage, closely follows the business cycle. It is low in periods of depression and correspondingly high during periods of prosperity. One primary reason for the decrease in divorce during periods of economic depression may be the cost; when money is limited, divorce may be temporarily postponed. This would also explain in part why divorces goes up with increased prosperity. With greater affluency, there are not only those who have reached the point of wanting a divorce, but also those who have postponed it because of the cost in the past, but are now able to afford it.

In the United States today, divorce is a common means of ending marriage. Glick estimates that "under current conditions, close to one out of every five marriages is likely to end in divorce."[28] However, one point that is often overlooked is the high rate of remarriage among those who get divorces. Glick points out "that about two thirds of the divorced women and three fourths of the divorced men will eventually remarry."[29] For the majority, divorce does not indicate disillusionment with marriage in general, but rather with a specific marriage. (An extended discussion of remarriage is presented in Chapter 17.)

THE LEGAL NATURE OF DIVORCE

Anyone who studies the legal nature of divorce in the United States is forced to the conclusion that little relationship exists be-

---

[26]William M. Kephart, "Legal and Procedural Aspects of Marriage and Divorce," in Harold T. Christensen (ed.) *Handbook of Marriage and The Family* (Chicago: Rand McNally & Co., 1964), p. 952.

[27]United States Department of Health, Education and Welfare, *op. cit.*, p. 3.

[28]Glick, *American Families, op. cit.*, p. 198.

[29]*Ibid.*, p. 199.

tween the legal approach to and the social reality of divorce. As
stated before, the United States has no federal divorce law, but
rather the various laws of 53 different legal jurisdictions. Therefore,
the laws vary from state to state and, even when agreement seems to
exist on certain legal points, in reality disagreement prevails between
states and even on interpretation of a specific point within a given
state. The historian Blake writes that "Nevada with its quickie
decrees represents one extreme of the American divorce spectrum;
New York with its antiquated law and consequent abuses represents
the other."[30] Several of the more important legal considerations related to divorce are presented in the following discussion.

Legal Considerations

Collusion. Suppose that a couple have been married for a few
years and reach a point of mutual agreement that their marriage is
miserable and they would both like to end it with a divorce. They
might go to court and ask for a divorce on the grounds that they
have conscientiously tried marriage but theirs has failed, they are
unhappy, and after careful consideration have mutually agreed they
would be better off not married to each other. The court's response
would be to tell the couple they cannot have a divorce for the legal
reason that they are guilty of collusion. "Collusion is any agreement
between the parties by which they endeavor to obtain a divorce by
an imposition on the court."[31] A number of courts have held that
"any agreement between the husband and wife whereby they attempt to obtain a divorce by imposing upon the court is collusion."[32]

Legally speaking, any couple who mutually decide they want a
divorce cannot have it. Yet, in a vast number of cases, divorce is
sought because the marriage partners find they are incompatible.
Except in one state, however, incompatibility is not a legal ground
for divorce; therefore, one party must find some legal ground he
can use to divorce his partner. While legally there can be no collusion, in reality the spouse's agreeing to divorce does occur. Baber
points out that the "amount of collusion is enormous. Judges in
various cities report that 85 to 90 percent of their cases are uncon-
tested."[33] The law insists on the myth of noncollusion although in
reality collusion exists in the majority of divorce cases.

Contest. The legal restriction against collusion is based upon

---

[30]Nelson M. Blake, *The Road to Reno* (New York: The Macmillan Co., 1962), p. 7.
[31]Clarke, *op. cit.,* p. 128.
[32]*Ibid.,* p. 129.
[33]Baber, *op. cit.,* p. 479.

the assumption that divorce is a contest between the innocent and guilty (referred to legally as the plaintiff and defendant). However, suppose that our couple go to court and the wife states a number of charges against the husband and asks for a divorce. After her charges are presented, the husband stands up and admits that what she said is true but then makes a number of charges against her. In almost all cases, the divorce would not be granted because the husband has engaged in *recrimination.* "The doctrine of recrimination is grounded on the old equity theory that one who asks relief must come into court with clean hands and that divorce laws are made to give relief to the innocent and not to the guilty party."[34] When recrimination is used, then there is no longer an innocent and guilty party but rather two guilty parties, and the general rule is no divorce granted to either party.[35]

Two other legal factors are important in the contest for divorce. Suppose that the wife is asking for a divorce on the grounds that her husband committed adultery. But when the charge of adultery is brought out, the wife states that it really was not her husband's fault, that he was the victim of an immoral, unscrupulous woman and she, the wife, forgives him. Legally this is known as *condonation,* the forgiveness of a marital offense constituting a ground for divorce.[36] In a situation of this type, a divorce would not usually be granted because a person can use an act for divorce only so long as he has not forgiven the act.[37]

Suppose that the wife is suing her husband for divorce on the grounds of adultery but it comes out in the testimony that the wife had little sexual interest and that she both knew and consented to her husband having sexual relations with another woman. This is legally an illustration of *connivance,* the consenting by one married person to the marital offenses and acts of the other.[38] The legal theory is that if an individual consented to an act or a wrong, they cannot be injured by it and therefore it cannot be used as a ground for divorce.[39]

Usually the plaintiff must be present in person at the divorce trial, but in most divorce actions the defendant does not put in an appearance. Because the defendant is not present, it is assumed that he is guilty. He has been notified as to the time and place of the

---

[34]Clarke, *op. cit.,* p. 132.
[35]*Ibid.,* p. 132.
[36]*Ibid.,* p. 131.
[37]*Ibid.,* p. 131.
[38]*Ibid.,* p. 130.
[39]*Ibid.,* p. 130.

hearing, and therefore his absence creates the legal fiction that he must be guilty as charged or he would be there to defend himself. Because the defendant wants the divorce, he has usually been told to stay away from the court. As a result, over three quarters of all applications for divorce decrees are granted.

The legal procedure is clear. The plaintiff must go into court as the wronged party in the marriage and the defendant must be the villain. Any variation from these clearly defined legal roles leads to difficulty in obtaining a divorce. The fact that the legal picture has little to do with the realities of the divorce situation is often beside the point so far as the courts are concerned.

The legal contradictions are obvious. With collusion or agreement making divorce legally unobtainable, the implication is that one partner wants the divorce and the other does not and that the one has been wronged by the other. Yet, if the involved parties are not in agreement and the defendant recriminates, the divorce will not usually be granted. Therefore, in many divorce cases collusion must in fact occur to eliminate the possibility of recrimination in order that the divorce be granted. In most divorce cases, the parties are probably guilty of some legal violation although it is generally ig-nored—as shown by the fact that divorce is granted.

Another factor indicative of the manipulation of divorce laws is that the wife is the plaintiff in over three out of every four divorce suits.[40] There is no reason to believe that within the social and psychological context of marriage wives should be the wronged party three times as often as husbands. The probability of the wife being the plaintiff in divorce cases has increased over the past 100 years in the United States. In the 1860's, when the first divorce statistics were gathered, the Census Bureau figures show that the husband was the plaintiff in about one third of the cases.[41] Kephart also points out that there are variations from state to state, "56 per-cent being wife-plaintiff cases in Georgia, as compared to a figure of 82 percent in Wisconsin."[42] But in general the wife is the plaintiff more often than the husband for three important reasons: (1) more legal grounds for divorce are available to the wife than the husband; (2) out-of-state divorces are easier for the wife to obtain because the husband's occupation ties him closer to home; and (3) less social criticism is directed at the woman if she sues for divorce than if she is sued for divorce.

---

[40]Kephart, *op. cit.,* pp. 956–57.
[41]*Ibid.,* p. 956.
[42]*Ibid.,* p. 957.

Legal Grounds

Over the past 100 years, cruelty has been steadily increasing in relative importance as a ground for divorce. At the same time that cruelty has been increasingly used as a grounds for divorce, its meaning has been changing and cruelty has come more and more to be a catchall legal category. It is probably safe to assume that about two thirds of the divorce suits in this country at the present time use cruelty as the legal grounds.[43]

TABLE 16–3
THE NUMBER OF THE 53 LEGAL JURISDICTIONS LEGALLY RECOGNIZING
SPECIFIC GROUNDS FOR DIVORCE

Adultery	53	Alcoholism	44
Desertion	50	Impotence	37
Imprisonment or		Nonsupport	31
conviction of crime	48	Insanity	30
Cruelty	47		

Adapted from: Ray E. Baber, *Marriage and the Family* (New York: McGraw-Hill Book Co., 1953), p. 450.

Table 16–3 shows the total usage of legal grounds in the 53 different legal jurisdictions. Adultery is the only ground recognized in all legal jurisdictions. The number of grounds that may be used varies among different states. Nearly a third of all legal jurisdictions grant divorces on 10 or more different legal grounds, but New York on only the single ground of adultery. However, legal grounds that sound the same may be defined very differently in the various legal jurisdictions. For example, desertion as a legal period for divorce ranges from six months in Hawaii to five years in Rhode Island.

That the legal grounds used for divorce bear little relation to the actual causes underlying marital breakdown is generally accepted. The lawyer often has to ignore what appears to be the actual reason for the couple's seeking a divorce and look for the available legal grounds that he may advise them to use. One study asked a sample of Idaho lawyers to classify the "real" causes, as opposed to the legal causes actually used, in 282 divorce cases. The major "real" causes were, in declining order: "Financial problems (including support), infidelity, drunkenness, and basic incompatibility."[44] But in most cases these were not the causes the lawyers could advise their clients to use in the divorce procedures.

[43]*Ibid.*, p. 953.
[44]Harry C. Harmsworth and Mhyra S. Minnis, "Non-Statutory Causes of Divorce: The Lawyer's Point of View," *Marriage and Family Living*, 17, 1955, pp. 316–21.

Kephart, in his extensive study of marital disruption, came to the conclusion that "while in most of the divorce suits, but, in no means all, the relationship between real and alleged cause is nebulous, specific incidents as a rule are not fabricated. They are usually exaggerated, both in frequency and intensity, and are sometimes distorted beyond reasonable recognition."[45] He found that, in general, the incidents reported by the plaintiff were not made up and did seem to have some basis in fact. "The inflation and distortion that exist appear to be in degree rather than kind."[46] For example, some cruelty may have occurred, but not to the extent presented at the divorce hearings.

Alimony

Alimony generally refers to the continued support of the wife by the husband after divorce. It is possible in 12 states for the husband to receive alimony from the wife, but such awards are rare. On the other hand, it is not unusual for alimony to be granted to the wife in cases in which the husband petitions for and obtains the divorce. In theory, the amount of alimony is to be determined by the standard of living that existed during the marriage, but usually the woman actually receives only a small amount of alimony.

Because of the great publicity given to large cash settlements in a few divorce cases, the impression often is that large amounts of money are involved in many cases. Cash settlements at the time of divorce may result from two different situations. One, the husband may make a total settlement rather than pay alimony over time. Second, a form of blackmail may be involved. A cash settlement may be a payoff for agreeing not to protest the divorce. This second situation sometimes leads to large cash settlements which receive a great deal of publicity, leading people to believe they are much more common than they are.

Alimony payments should not be confused with child support. With rare exceptions, the father is responsible for the economic support of his children after a divorce. This paternal responsibility usually continues until the father is no longer legally responsible for the youngsters, either because the children have grown up or, as in some cases, he has given up legal responsibility to an adopting father. Even when the father pays for the support of his children, the amount may not realistically meet the economic costs of rearing the

---

[45]Kephart, "Drinking and Marital Disruption," *op. cit.,* p. 65.
[46]*Ibid.,* p. 65.

child. Goode in his study of divorced mothers found that the median amount of support payments per child by the husband was only $8.90 a week.[47]

Migratory Divorces

As with large alimony payments, the amount of mass media attention given migratory divorces leads to a belief that they are more common than they actually are. Migratory divorce probably accounts for less than 5 percent of the total divorces granted annually. There seems little evidence that people seek migratory divorces because of easier grounds; rather, they seek it for personally favorable grounds and speed in having the divorce granted. (An illustration of seeking more favorable grounds for divorce through migration would be in the case of New Yorkers who have only adultery as a ground for divorce.)

The popularity of some states for migratory divorces is due to the speed in which divorces are processed in them and the short length of time needed to acquire legal residency within the state. The migratory divorce is valid in the United States because of reciprocity agreements between the states, meaning that the laws of one state are recognized by the other states. However, if it can be proved that the individual went to the other state to gain advantage from more liberal divorce laws but had no intention of establishing permanent residence in that state, the divorce may be declared invalid. In reality, almost always the individual does go to another state to gain advantage of the law; however, no legal action will be taken in the home state unless someone brings suit, and this rarely occurs.

THE SOCIAL NATURE OF DIVORCE

The findings clearly show that divorce is a characteristic of the relatively young with a short marital duration. In 1959, in 12 reporting states, the median age at divorce was 34.2 for the husband and 30.9 for the wife.[48] In 1959, in 16 reporting states, 38.6 percent of all divorces were granted to couples married less than 5 years and 62.9 percent to couples married less than 10 years.[49] There is some indication that divorce is occurring a little later in marriage than it

---

[47]William J. Goode, *After Divorce* (Glencoe, Illinois: The Free Press, 1956), p. 221.

[48]United States Department of Health, Education and Welfare, Public Health Service, National Office of Vital Statistics, "Marriage and Divorce Statistics," *Vital Statistics of the United States, 1959*, Section 2, p. 13.

[49]*Ibid.*, p. 29.

did in the past. In 1950, the median duration of marriages ended by divorce and annulment was 5.8 years but had increased to 7.0 years in 1959.[50] In general, the frequency of divorce rises rapidly after the first few months of marriage, reaches a maximum during the first three years of marriage and then declines with increasing length of marriage. There is also a relationship between legal causes used for divorce and the length of marriage. For example, the marriages with the greatest duration by legal cause is 9.5 years for desertion, followed next by 7.2 years for nonsupport and then 6.8 years for cruelty.[51]

As was mentioned, a marriage ends in a social sense in many cases well before it is legally ended through divorce. Kephart, in his study of the duration of marriage, found that "the recorded time period between marriage and divorce is, in good part, a legal fiction." He found in his sample of 1,434 divorce cases a difference in medians of 4.6 years between the legal duration of marriage and the actual duration.[52] "More than 40 percent of the couples in our sample had separated within the first three years of married life! Within the same period divorces had been granted to but 16 percent of the couples."[53] The peak year for separations lies within the *first* year of marriage, and with each succeeding year the percentage decreases. Using the divorce rate, the peak period lies within the second and fourth year, with a subsequent yearly decline."[54] Kephart's study indicates that, for many couples who end their marriages with divorce, the process of alienation leading to separation and ultimate divorce begins shortly after the marriage takes place.

Premarital Factors

Chapter 11 discussed factors of dating and courtship related to success in marriage. In this section, the concern is with several social variables rooted in the premarital stage which show some statistical relationship to divorce. There is evidence that a very young age at marriage is related to young age at divorce. Glick writes that "the youngest women at separation or divorce are those who left high school before graduation. These women are eight or

---

[50]United States Department of Commerce, Bureau of the Census, *Statistical Abstract of the United States, 1961*, 82nd Annual Edition, p. 68.

[51]United States Department of Health, Education and Welfare, "Divorces," *op. cit.*, p. 11.

[52]William M. Kephart, "The Duration of Marriage," *American Sociological Review*, June, 1954, p. 290.

[53]*Ibid.*, p. 290.

[54]*Ibid.*, p. 290.

nine years younger at the time when their marriages are broken, on the average, than college graduates who become separated or divorced."[55] The combination of a very young age at marriage and low education level characterizes a social group with a high divorce rate.

The evidence from Goode's study indicates that a short engagement is also related to a greater tendency toward divorce. He found that 71 percent of the divorced women in his sample had never been engaged or had been engaged less than six months.[56] As pointed out earlier, this may represent a more unconventional group, as illustrated by the short engagement, and therefore they may be more prone to turn to divorce if dissatisfied with their marriage.

Christensen found a relationship between premarital pregnancy and divorce. He found that of all the women who gave birth to their first child in less than 139 days after their marriage, 19.7 percent had divorces. For those who gave birth between 140 and 265 days after marriage, the divorce percentage was 14.1 The first group and many in the second group indicate premarital pregnancy. By contrast, of those women who gave birth to their first child between 266 and 391 days after marriage, 9.1 percent had been divorced.[57] This indicates that marriage brought about because of pregnancy has a greater probability of ending in divorce than does marriage in which pregnancy was not involved.

TABLE 16–4

ATTITUDES TOWARD THEIR MARRIAGES AS GIVEN BY DIVORCED WOMEN, PERCENT

Group	Approval	Disapproval	Indifference	Don't Know or No Answer
Husband's family	55	25	11	9
Wife's family	46	40	11	3
Husband's friends	51	5	20	24
Wife's friends	56	16	20	8
Mutual friends	45	8	22	25

Adapted from: William J. Goode, *After Divorce* (Glencoe, Illinois: The Free Press, 1956), p. 82.

Goode's study also indicates some possibility of a relationship between the feelings of relatives and friends to the marriage and eventual divorce. Table 16–4 shows the feelings toward the marriage as stated by divorced women and indicates that disapproval from the

[55]Glick, *op. cit.,* p. 152.
[56]Goode, *op. cit.,* p. 78.
[57]Harold T. Christensen, *Marriage Analysis* (New York: The Ronald Press Co., 1958), p. 207.

wife's family was more significant than from the husband's family.[58] But probably of greater importance is that both families and friends in about half of the cases approved of the marriage, indicating that their positive attitudes toward the marriage were not particularly significant in those cases of divorce.

Religion

No religious groups encourage divorce, although they differ in tolerance and acceptance of divorce. In their study of divorce and desertion in Philadelphia, Monahan and Kephart found that "Jews account for about their expected share of divorces (but no more than that); that the Catholics account for one half to two thirds the number of divorces which one might expect from their proportion in the population; and conversely, that the Protestants account for a relatively greater part of Philadelphia's divorces."[59]

TABLE 16–5

PERCENT OF FAMILIES BROKEN BY DIVORCE, OR DIVORCE AND SEPARATION, BY RELIGION, FOUND IN THREE STUDIES

	Percent of Broken Marriages		
Religion	*Bell (Maryland)*	*Weeks (Washington)*	*Landis (Michigan)*
Both Catholic	6.4	3.8	4.4
Both Jewish	4.6	10.1	5.2
Both Protestant	6.8	—	6.0
Mixed Catholic-Protestant ...	15.2	17.4	14.1
Both no religion	16.7	23.9 ·	17.9

Adapted from Thomas P. Monahan and William M. Kephart, "Divorce and Desertion By Religious and Mixed Religious Groups," *American Journal of Sociology*, March, 1954, p. 457.

Table 16–5 shows the percentage of broken families by religion, found in three different studies. It may be noted that separation and divorce are higher among mixed marriages and couples with no religion than for any of the three religious groups when the partners are of the same religion. This too may be a reflection of less conventional behavior, as reflected by the mixed marriage or no religion, that would make the couple more apt to turn to divorce.

CHILDREN AND DIVORCE

The impact of divorce on children causes a great amount of the social concern directed at American divorce. The implication is

---

[58]Goode, *op. cit.*, p. 82.
[59]Monahan and Kephart, *op. cit.*, p. 460.

that when the disruption of the parental roles is added to those of the marriage roles, divorce becomes a greater problem. The impact of divorce on the child will be discussed in Chapter 17. The interest here involves some of the social characteristics with respect to children and the divorce of their parents.

The length of marriage prior to divorce is related to whether or not children are involved. For example, in 1961, "the median duration of marriages with no children under 18 years of age was 4.7 years, those with one child 5.9 years, those with two children 8.9 years, and those with three children or more 12.1 years."[60] The fact that a majority of divorces do not involve children is due to the heavy concentration of divorces in the early years of marriage. It is also probable that many couples, who would get a divorce if they did not have children, remain married because of the children. Finally, some couples may get a divorce because they do not have children and their childlessness is an important reason for defining their marriages as a failure.

In recent years, an upswing in the proportion of divorce decrees involving children has occurred. In 1953 less than half (45.5 percent) of all divorce decrees involved children, but by 1957 the rate was 50.9 percent and by 1961 the rate had reached the level of three fifths (60.3 percent) of all divorce decrees.[61] This means that the number of children affected by divorce has increased more rapidly than has the number of divorces and may reflect some changes in attitudes about divorce and children. While social criticism continues to be directed at the couple getting a divorce when children are involved, it is probably less severe than it was in the past.

In a study of divorced women, Goode found no significant difference between the religion of the mothers and the number of children. The number of children per divorced mother was: Protestant, 1.92; Catholic, 1.80; and "other or none" 1.81.[62] Goode did find some differences in number of children per divorced mother by education. Of those mothers with a high school education or more, 32 percent had two or more children, whereas 68 percent of those mothers with some high school or less had two or more children.[63]

Because divorce tends to occur early in marriage, it means that when children are involved they are often very young. The indications are that about two thirds of the children affected by divorce

---

[60]United States Department of Health, Education and Welfare, *op. cit.*, p. 11.
[61]*Ibid.*, p. 14.
[62]Goode, *op. cit.*, p. 108.
[63]*Ibid.*, p. 109.

are under 10 years of age. It is clear that the presence of children is not necessarily a deterrent to divorce, although some couples do stay together "for the sake of the children" and as a result some unhappy or unsuccessful marriages are not ended until after the children grow up. It seems probable that when couples postpone divorce for the sake of the children, or for other reasons, they will be less apt to actually get a divorce when the time of postponement ends. This may be because they have worked out their problems or it may be that after putting up with their marriage until the children grew up, many reach a point of accommodation where they no longer feel divorce is necessary.

Custody of Children

In the great majority of divorce cases (about 90 percent) which involve minor children, the mother is given custody.[64] Custody of the child is almost universal for the mother when she is the plaintiff in the divorce action and also in about half the cases when the husband is the plaintiff.[65] It might seem logical to assume that in a divorce case—with an innocent party and a guilty party—the innocent party would almost always be given the custody of the children. This is almost always true when the mother initiates the action for divorce (when she is the innocent party). On the other hand, when the father is the plaintiff, the children are as likely to be assigned to the mother as to the father. Basically, this reflects the attitude that the children should be reared by the mother. Even if she is guilty of certain indiscretions that lead to the divorce, it is still assumed that she is better able than the husband to rear the children. Most divorced fathers, whether plaintiff or defendant, probably accept the notion that the mother is best able to care for the child.

The custody of the child and questions of child support are often handled by the courts in an offhand and—some would say—irresponsible fashion. "Usually the judge merely ratifies the separation agreement that has been drawn up by the lawyers representing the husband and wife. Yet those documents are rarely the products of sensible thinking, usually they are merely treaties with provision determined by the relative bargaining power of the two sides."[66]

Over the years, a great deal of criticism has been directed at divorce laws in the United States. One common complaint has been that

---

[64]Morris Ploscowe, *The Truth About Divorce* (New York: Hawthorne Books, 1955), p. 219.
[65]*Ibid.*, p. 220.
[66]Blake, *op. cit.*, p. 237.

there is a need for uniform, federal divorce laws. Yet there seems little reason to expect any significant change in divorce laws or the emergence of federal divorce laws in the near future. In all probability, the legal system of divorce will continue to have little connection with reality, and it will continue to be true that any couple desiring a divorce and having the time and the money to get it will be able to do so. While many Americans become righteously indignant about some social aspects of divorce, few are bothered by the hypocrisy of divorce laws. Given the desire for divorce, individuals will probably continue to use the divorce laws in the most beneficial personal manner, and the fact that the laws are being distorted and circumvented will continue for the most part to be socially and legally ignored.

SELECTED BIBLIOGRAPHY

CLARKE, HELEN I. *Social Legislation.* New York: Appleton-Century-Crofts, Inc., 1957.

GLICK, PAUL C. *American Families.* New York: John Wiley & Sons, Inc., 1957.

GOODE, WILLIAM J. *After Divorce.* Glencoe, Illinois: The Free Press, 1956.

KEPHART, WILLIAM M. *The Family, Society and the Individual,* chaps. xix to xxii. Boston: Houghton Mifflin Co., 1961.

————. "Drinking and Marital Disruption," *Quarterly Journal of Studies on Alcohol,* March, 1954, pp. 63–73.

————. "The Duration of Marriage," *American Sociological Review,* August, 1955, pp. 456–65.

KEPHART, WILLIAM M., and MONAHAN, THOMAS P. "Desertion and Divorce in Philadelphia," *American Sociological Review,* December, 1952, pp. 719–27.

MANDELL, IRVING. *The Law of Marriage and Divorce,* chaps. ii, iii, iv and v. New York: Oceana Publications, 1957.

MONAHAN, THOMAS P. "Family Fugitives," *Marriage and Family Living,* May, 1958, pp. 146–51.

————. "The Duration of Marriage to Divorce: Second Marriages and Migratory Types," *Marriage and Family Living,* May, 1959, pp. 134–38.

MONAHAN, THOMAS P., and KEPHART, WILLIAM M. "Divorce and Desertion by Religious and Mixed Religious Groups," *American Journal of Sociology,* March, 1954, pp. 454–65.

WIDOWHOOD, DIVORCE, AND REMARRIAGE

In Chapter 16, some of the social and legal aspects of ending a marriage were discussed. This chapter focuses on the social and personal setting of marriages that end through the death of one of the marriage partners and through divorce, as well as the remarriage of widows and divorcees. Some factors leading to divorce are treated in this chapter because of their relationship to both divorce roles and remarriage.

BEREAVEMENT

All cultures have recognized the inevitability of death and all have developed various social procedures and rituals for dealing with it. While the death of any individual in any family role may alter the family configuration, only the impact of the spouse's death and its significance for the surviving partner is considered here. In the broadest sense, death of the spouse means that the surviving partner is immediately provided with a new social role that conveys to other members of society the person's new social position. The new role definitions of widow for the surviving wife and widower for the surviving husband provide fairly clear social prescriptions to guide behavior.

The new roles of widow and widower are in some respects different because of sex differences. For several reasons, the new role of widow may be more socially and psychologically difficult to adjust to than the role of widower. First, because marriage is usually more important for the woman than for the man in American society, the ending of marriage means the ending of a role more basic to the wife than may be the case for a surviving husband. Second, the widow is given less personal and social encouragement to remarry and, therefore, she is more apt than the widower never to remarry. Third, related to the second point, are the widow's problems in taking on financial responsibility for herself and her children, because her financial potential will usually be less than that of the widower. Fourth, because the woman must be less socially aggressive, she often finds her social life more restricted than does the widower. Finally, because there are far more widows than widowers, the chances for changing status through remarriage is much more difficult for the widow than for the widower. This last point is shown by the fact that, in 1954, in the distribution of the American population 14 years of age and over, only 3.2 percent of the males were classified as widowers, while 9.8 percent of the females were widows,[1] a statistic that reflects both the greater proportion of widows than widowers at time of bereavement and their lower rate of remarriage.

Widowhood occurs for a number of women who are still relatively young. The average age at which women become widows is in their middle 50's. The significance of the years after widowhood is illustrated by the fact that for women 45 years of age, 48 percent can expect 25 more years of life and, for women 46 years of age, 76 percent can expect 25 more years of life.[2] The younger the age of the widow with years of life expectancy ahead, the more often she changes her status of widow through remarriage. This remarriage probability also reflects less interest and less chance for the older widow to remarry.

While a woman may be widowed at a young age, the greater numerical concentration is within the older population. This is an important part of the overall change related to an aging population in the United States. "Persons 65 and older in the United States quadrupled between 1900 and 1950. It is anticipated that nine percent of the population will soon be over 65 and that the percentage will level off at about ten percent by 1975."[3] One important consequence of an aging population is the large number of older women who have the status of widow. For the population 65 years of age and over, 66 percent of the men are married as contrasted with only 37 percent of the women, while only 24 percent of the men are widowed as contrasted with 54 percent of the women.[4] The greater proportion of women to men also reflects the greater life expectancy of

---

[1]Paul C. Glick, *American Families* (New York: John Wiley & Sons, Inc., 1957), p. 104.

[2]*Statistical Bulletin* (Metropolitan Life Insurance Company, Vol. 39, November, 1958), p. 2.

[3]Quoted in Paul H. Glasser and Lois N. Glasser, "Role Reversal and Conflict Between Aged Parents and Their Children," *Marriage and Family Living*, February, 1962, p. 46.

[4]Ernest W. Burgess and Paul Wallin, *Engagement and Marriage* (Chicago: J. B. Lippincott Co., 1953), p. 319.

women over men at all ages. For example, between the ages of 40 to 45, the male has an average life expectancy of 31.5 years and the female of 36.9 years. In the 70 to 75 age range the male has 10.5 years while the female has 12.6 years of life expectancy.[5]

With an aging population disproportionately represented with widows, one further family impact may be on their children's families. Because the marriage has been ended, the survivor may both need and desire to live with the adult children. In a sample obtained by the United States Census Bureau in 1952, it was found, among those 65 years of age and over, that almost one third of the widowed, divorced, and separated males and almost one half of the widowed, divorced, and separate females lived with their children.[6] Because there are more widows, and because these figures show a somewhat greater tendency for the widow than the widower to turn to the children, important effects on the way of life for the widow and her adult children may follow. A greater financial dependency on adult children by widows and widowers is one implied effect. Frequent need for family financial aid during the older years is due to the low financial benefits available to older people. The primary benefits of retired workers are currently about 76 dollars per month. A widow becomes eligible at age 62 to receive a benefit equal to 82.5 percent of her husband's primary benefit; this averages out to about 66 dollars per month.[7]

THE SOCIAL-PSYCHOLOGICAL SETTING OF WIDOWHOOD

In a patriarchal society, becoming a widow meant a continued reliance on the social position given by the deceased husband and, possibly, the attainment of a new social position through remarriage. In modern American society, the continued influence of the deceased husband is probably of less importance. The widow is less apt to live in the community today as the "Widow Jones," but rather as Mrs. Jones with the responsibility of caring for herself and her children and attaining social recognition primarily on her own or through remarriage.

Important crises in the life of the individual call for a process of

---

[5]"Life Tables," *Vital Statistics of the United States, 1961,* Volume 11, Section 2 (United States Deparement of Health, Education, and Welfare, Public Health Service, National Office of Vital Statistics), p. 7.

[6]Quoted from John Kosa, Leo D. Rachiele, and Cyril O. Schommer, S.J., "Sharing the Home with Relatives," *Marriage and Family Living,* May, 1960, p. 129.

[7]Margaret Mead and Frances B. Kaplan (eds.), *American Women: The Report of the President's Commission* (New York: Charles Scribner's Sons, 1965), p. 61.

adjustment, with the initial adjustment to the loss of a significant role often more difficult than adjustment to a new role. However, society provides the bereaved individual with the means of easing some of the problems of adjustment. As Waller and Hill point out, bereavement is a personal crisis for which society "provides the individuals with models of every phase of the process: it tells him how he shall react to death, how he shall arrange for burial, and what he shall say and think, and it provides hints as to how long he shall mourn."[8] The social patterns often help the individual to adjust but, because of the strong ego-involvement in the death of the spouse, many highly personal adjustments must also be made.

When a marriage ends with the death of one partner, the general assumption is that without the death the marriage would have continued. Therefore, the surviving partner is seen as an individual not only having lost a loved one, but also having had a successful marital relationship ended. Often with death, no gradual transition from having a marriage partner to not having one occurs—in contrast to divorce, which often involves an extended period of alienation before the marriage is dissolved. The bereaved person is often a husband or wife one day, with a satisfactory marital role relationship, and a widower or a widow the next day, with the marital relationship completely ended. The marriage may have been an unhappy one in reality; but so long as this was not generally known, the death of the spouse is assumed to have ended a satisfactory marriage, thereby providing the survivor with sympathy for the loss of a loved spouse. Thus, for some, bereavement may lead to an image of marriage (sometimes even for the surviving partner) quite different from what the marriage was in reality.

One of the important initial adjustments the surviving partner must make is that of being without a spouse in a world of paired relationships. One common tendency for older people is to seek out others like themselves as, for example, the interacting groups of elderly widows who all have the same marital status and live in a specialized "single" world. This world is different from that of the unmarried or divorced because, being widows, they can interact on many occasions in reference to their late husbands. In addition, they are recognzed as not being a part of the "paired world" for reasons beyond their control. As Eliot points out, the "widowed, like the divorced, must reorganize their friendship groups on a single basis,

---

[8]Willard Waller and Reuben Hill, *The Family* (New York: The Dryden Press, 1951), p. 489.

but for the former there are no estrangements nor is their status rendered ambiguous."[9]

Those who are younger may have more difficulty accepting the new "single" world of the widowed, because they are not willing to live simply with memories of the ended marriage relationship. Even holding constant the decreasing marriage market available to the older widow, the younger widow probably has a greater personal motivation to remarry. The very fact that many older widows find that many of their age-sex peers have the same marital status probably makes it easier for them than for the younger widow, most of whose are peers are still married. Some of these factors will be further developed later in this chapter when some factors of remarriage for the widowed are discussed.

DIVORCE

Unlike bereavement, divorce does not just suddenly happen. It is the termination of a process that may have developed over a long period of time. The background leading to the ending of marriage through divorce is very different from that of ending a marriage through bereavement. This difference in prior experience makes the new roles of the divorced and the widowed different.

Goode in his extensive study of divorced women found that divorces were preceded by a long period of conflict, "and the final action is the result of a decision and action process that lasts on the average about two years."[10] Goode goes on to point out that "40 percent of the separations occurred over one year prior to the decree, and 50 percent occurred over 10 months prior to the decree. In the social sense then, adjustment to divorce has begun before the decree for perhaps most divorces."[11] In this process, many divorced persons have filled the vaguely defined role of a person who has decided to end his marriage and therefore may be no longer actively functioning as a husband or wife, but has not yet legally and socially moved into the divorced status.

The decision to end a marriage through divorce results from a vast variety of experiences when related to the range of differences among the involved couples. It may be assumed that most marriages

---

[9]Thomas D. Eliot, "The Bereaved Family," in Howard Becker and Reuben Hill, *Family, Marriage and Parenthood* (Boston: D. C. Heath & Co., 1955), p. 666.
[10]William J. Goode, *After Divorce* (Glencoe, Illinois: The Free Press, 1956), p. 137. Also see: William M. Kephart, "The Duration of Marriage," *American Sociological Review*, June, 1954, p. 290.
[11]Goode, *op. cit.*, p. 179.

start out with a high degree of personal satisfaction and that the extent to which the marital satisfaction becomes altered varies greatly with different marriages. The marriage that is defined as successful by its members is often one in which the couple accept the changing nature of their marriage relationship and are basically satisfied. In other marriages, the couple may feel with time that the marriage is becoming an unpleasant relationship and, as a result of experiences defined as unpleasant by the individuals, the process of marital alienation occurs. Each new crisis of unpleasantness in the marriage may more negatively define the marital relationship. One consequence may be even greater alienation and greater instability in the relationship, ultimately leading to the belief that the marriage relationship is no longer tolerable. However, this is not an inevitable process, because the degree of alienation may stop at any point. That is, the couple may not continue to be driven further apart or may with time return to a greater marital closeness. Furthermore, there is no set degree of alienation that means that the marriage is finished. Kirkpatrick points out that "divorce is not a simple, inevitable consequence of extreme maladjustment. There may be maladjustment without divorce, and persons may walk out an open door without extreme maladjustment."[12]

It would seem that, in a society in which the woman has a greater commitment and investment in marriage than the man, she would be less willing to see her marriage ended through divorce. The fact that three quarters of all plaintiffs in divorce suits are wives says little about the initial desire to end a marriage. Goode suggests that "although the wife will have fairly serious charges to make against her husband, we believe that in our generation it is more often the husband who first wishes to escape from marriage."[13] Goode further points out that, while 60 percent of the divorced women he studied first suggested the divorce, the husbands may have forced their hand.[14]

Considering the strong middle-class stress on ego-need satisfaction in marriage, any knowledge that the partner "wants out" may lead the individual to feel he has no choice but to end the marriage. The very fact that one partner wants to end the marriage means that the other is often seen as no longer satisfying his ego-needs. For the person to say he will continue the marriage when the partner wants

[12]Clifford Kirkpatrick, *The Family* (New York: The Ronald Press Co., 1955), p. 518.
[13]Goode, *op. cit.*, p. 135.
[14]*Ibid.*, p. 135.

to end it, often indicates he is willing to do without that which most middle-class Americans have accepted as a basic reason for marriage, being the love object. For example, the woman who says she will stay married for the sake of the children, even though her husband no longer loves her, may be commended for her sacrifice for the children but at the same time be viewed with some contempt for staying with a husband who no longer loves her.

In American society, it may be ironically true that the women with the greater commitment to marriage finds herself in a position of being forced to end the marriage if the husband so desires. Behavior indicating rejection by her husband is often so disturbing to her ego that she may feel compelled to end the marriage as soon as possible. Goode found that "when the husband was admitted to have been the first to suggest divorce, the median time was 5.4 months (to filing decree), but when the wife claims that she first suggested the divorce, the time was 12.9 months, and when there was mutual suggestion, the median time was 18.5 months."[15] His findings indicate that the husband feels less compulsion to formally end the marriage when the wife suggests it, perhaps reflecting less commitment to marriage on his part and therefore less feeling of personal threat when his wife no longer wants to continue the marriage.

The reactions of individuals to divorce are to a great extent determined by existing cultural values. "All family systems have some kinds of escape mechanisms built into them to permit individuals to survive the pressures of the system, and one of these is divorce."[16] In some societies divorce has been viewed with a very casual social interest, while in others it is viewed with great concern. In the American society, the social values in regard to divorce are in a stage of transition from the restrictive to a more permissive social acceptance. The very fact of transition in social attitudes toward divorce leads to confusion and contradiction in American middle-class response and behavior.

Divorce Prejudice

With very few exceptions, any discussion of divorce in this country, either of a professional or nonprofessional nature, states or implies that divorce is bad or undesirable. Waller ad Hill point out that divorce prejudice, like other prejudices, shows itself in the

---

[15]*Ibid.*, p. 144.
[16]*Ibid.*, p. 9.

unconsidered parts of one's speech; for example, such common expressions as "alarming rise in the tide of divorce," "divorce evil," and "the unhappy children of the divorced."[17] Implied in a great deal of the thinking about divorce is that it is a personal and social problem and should be alleviated or eliminated for the betterment of the individual and society.

Sometimes the concern is the fear that divorce is destroying the American marriage and family system. Yet, this fear is hard to support in reference to marriage when it is realized that the United States marriage rate is at a near record high and, even more important, that the remarriage rate of those who get divorces is very high. Very often divorce implies disillusionment with a specific marriage, but not marriage in general. Divorced persons have not emerged as a statistically significant new marital group when the remarriage factors are considered. For example, the marital distribution of persons 14 years of age and over show that, in 1890, 0.2 percent of the men and 0.4 percent of the women were classified as divorced (and not remarried), and, by 1954, this had increased to only 1.8 and 2.2 respectively.[18]

Many of the contemporary values against divorce reflect traditional family values that have limited application to modern middle-class marriage. Often implied in negative attitudes toward divorce is the assumption that marriage is secondary to the greater family unit and functions. However middle-class marriage is based to a great extent on the ego-needs of the individual, and the individual may feel that his marriage is not successful unless these needs are satisfied. The attitude many have today about divorce is that, as Koos suggests, if the needs, expectations, and values "cannot be met, realized, and adjusted, there seems—for those who can accept the idea of divorce—little reason to continue the marriage."[19] The ego-need factor related to divorce is logically consistent with the ego-need factor that leads to marriage.

Mable Elliot writes "divorce is part of the American way of life. In our country permanent monogamy constitutes the most desirable form of marriage relation; but for those, especially urban residents, who can no longer find an endurable satisfaction in marriage and for whom a continued relationship offers only frustration, hypocrisy, and deterioration of both personalities, divorce has become a respect-

---

[17]See: Waller and Hill, *op. cit.*, p. 537.
[18]Glick, *op. cit.*, p. 104.
[19]Earl L. Koos, *Marriage* (New York: Henry Holt & Co., 1957), p. 309.

able solution."[20] Divorce is probably not yet as respectable as Elliot indicates, for many still believe that a miserable marriage is more commendable than a more satisfying divorce, particularly if children are involved.

One point about divorce in the American middle class which needs to be emphasized is that divorce is causally related to the social framework of mate selection. The whole complex of romantic love, idealization, and ego-need satisfaction places a high premium on the personal nature of marriage; when these expectations are not achieved or are frustrated, marriage has not met the expectations held by the individual or society. Interestingly, the great bulk of social criticism is directed at divorce as if it were a decision made by the couple without a causal background related to social values. It would be socially naive to expect that with the system of courtship and marital expectations that prevail in today's American society a low divorce rate would prevail.

Some people also hold the view that divorce is due to some kind of "mental sickness" and that something is psychologically wrong with those who get divorces. But as Davis writes, "certainly the divorce itself does not constitute evidence of neurosis without independent confirmation."[21] The "sickness" approach to divorce suggests that those who remain married are mentally healthy, and thereby has the convenient supportive facility of negatively defining those who deviate from the traditional norms of marital stability. It also ignores the fact that divorces are a part of the American folkways and mores and, therefore, cannot be regarded as socially abnormal.[22] In theory one might argue just the opposite—that in today's American society, many individuals who are unhappy in their marriage and do not get a divorce are resistant to the social means available for at least partially resolving their marital difficulty and regaining some degree of personal happiness.

Finally, some professional and lay people believe that when a couple want a divorce they should be given counseling which will help resolve their marital problems so that divorce will no longer be necessary. Kingsley Davis writes that "those who believe that the incidence of divorce can be greatly reduced through the counseling of couples after they have already sought divorce are probably mis-

---

[20]Mable Elliot, "The Scope and Meaning of Divorce," in Becker and Hill, op. cit., p. 684.

[21]Kingsley Davis, "Divorce and Its Effects," in Morris Fishbein and Ruby Jo R. Kennedy, Modern Marriage and Family Living (New York: Oxford University Press, 1957), p. 111.

[22]See: Ibid., p. 111.

taken. By that time marital discord or ennui has usually grown too deep to be banished by verbal discussion."[23] Marriage counseling probably has its greatest potential in the early stages of alienation before the marriage has reached a point of no return. The very fact that a couple have reached a stage in their relationship where divorce has been discussed and seen as a means of resolving their difficulty means that even if they remain married their marriage will often have been altered. Certainly some marriages return from the brink of divorce and become reasonably satisfactory to the individuals, but it is questionable that this happens in a large number of cases. Some couples are probably misled into maintaining their marriages when they might in the long run be better off divorced.

The overall picture appears to be that divorce in the United States is not yet institutionally accepted, but is in a process of becoming so.

THE ROLE OF THE DIVORCED

Social confusion prevails in the treatment of the divorced person. The general social view of divorce tends to reflect the legal one, that there is a guilty and an innocent party involved. To be the guilty party often means to be viewed with social criticism and so, frequently, both parties attempt to place the blame for the divorce on the partner. Waller and Hill write that "he [the divorced] can set himself right only by putting the divorced mate in the wrong, and by so doing he incurs at least a minimum amount of shame for having placed his heart so badly."[24] The point of personal error in mate selection is an important one because, with mate selection being for the most part the province of the individual, he must assume the responsibility of error when his choice proves to be so poor that divorce occurs.

Another aspect of the social confusion, the reaction to the divorced person, is illustrated by the problem faced by many when they come into contact with someone recently divorced—they don't know whether to extend condolences or congratulations. To say to a person recently divorced, "It's too bad," or "I'm sorry to hear it," may imply to the divorced person that he shouldn't have gotten the divorce. On the other hand, to congratulate the divorced person does not seem appropriate either, in light of the personal trauma usually found in divorce.

---

[23]*Ibid.*, p. 101.
[24]Waller and Hill, *op. cit.*, p. 555.

The Personal Setting

One realization with which all divorced persons are faced is that they have failed in their marriage and in their role as husband or wife. What may make this particularly difficult for some to accept is that the majority of people do not end their marriage through divorce; therefore, the divorced person may feel that he has not been able to make a success of what has been achieved by the majority. Many divorced persons probably do not view their divorce as a basic personal failure, but honestly feel that they made a mistake in the selection of a mate. Others may attempt to rationalize their failure by arguing that most marriages that remain intact are really unhappy and unsatisfactory. Because of the high American divorce rate, the sizable minority of divorced persons will probably provide an increasingly significant reference group of self-justification for those entering divorce. Both the increasing number of divorces and the related changing attitudes may make the role of the divorced person somewhat easier and subject to less social stigma in the future.

Even with more liberal divorce attitudes, the individual divorcee tends to see his marriage in a highly personal way: the sense of failure in not having a successful marriage can only be partially eased by the fact that many others are also divorced. But, as Goode found in his study, the trauma of divorce is not so overwhelming for the individual as to lead to personality disorganization.[25] In part, this may be so because of the process nature of divorce: by the time the actual divorce occurs, the individual has psychologically accepted it. Goode found that the greatest personal disturbance appeared at the time of the final separation rather than at the time of formal divorce.[26] Therefore, the period leading to divorce may demand greater readjustment for the individual than entering the new divorced or remarriage roles.

In adjustment to divorce, Goode found a number of social factors related to the degree in which divorced women felt trauma over their divorce. Higher trauma was associated with the five following factors. (1) Longer duration of marriage. The longer the woman was married the more difficulty she had adjusting to divorce because of her greater personal and social commitment to the marriage. (2) Older age. For the older woman, her personal patterns of life based

---

[25]Goode, op. cit., p. 187.
[26]Ibid., p. 187.

upon marriage have often become such an important part of her personality that their loss through divorce may be psychologically very disturbing. Facing life as a divorcee may also seem much more hazardous for her than for the younger divorcee. (3) Having two or more children. The overall responsibilities of caring for and rearing a number of childen by herself often seem frightening to the divorced woman. Because of the number of children, she may also have an extended fear about their being personally affected by the divorce. (4) The husband suggested divorce. The husband's suggesting divorce leads to the personal trauma for the woman of reconciling herself to being "rejected." (5) Unsteadiness in the decision about divorce. The "on again, off again" nature of divorce makes great demands on the psychological equilibrium of the individual and may create a constant state of anxiety and insecurity for many.[27]

The divorced woman is, in part, aided in her adjustment to divorce by her relatives and friends. Evidence indicates that the divorced woman is more apt to be viewed with sympathy and approval than is the divorced man. Goode found that over twice as high a percentage of the wife's families stated attitudes of strong approval for the divorce as husband's families (44 vs 21 percent).[28] Goode also found stronger approval among her friends (40 percent) compared to his friends (16 percent).[29] This may be a reflection of the previously mentioned point that, when divorce seems inevitable, the woman has little choice but to get the divorce and, therefore, sympathy will often be for her. This distinction is further indicated in the common point of view which sees the divorced woman as "losing" and the divorced man as "escaping" from marriage.

Goode also presented some findings in regard to desertion, a "love triangle," and time lapse before application for divorce, all of which offer further evidence of the greater significance of divorce for the woman. When the complaint involved both a "triangle" and desertion, the median time for consideration before filing for divorce was 18.5 months. When the complaint involved a "triangle" but no desertion, the median time for consideration before filing for divorce was only 2.2 months.[30] The husband with a girl friend who is not living with his wife is not nearly the threat that the husband is who is involved with another woman but continues to live with his wife.

---

[27]See: *Ibid.*, pp. 191–94.
[28]*Ibid.*, p. 167.
[29]*Ibid.*, p. 167.
[30]*Ibid.*, p. 143.

A wife in the second situation is faced with a husband who philanders while continuing in his role as a husband. In this situation, the wife has little "choice" but to file for divorce as soon as possible, because the husband is emotionally rejecting her.

Children

Probably the greatest area of social concern about divorce is its effects on children. While children are not involved in a majority of divorces, they are involved in a large enough number to justify the interest. The basic question often raised but never empirically answered is: Is it better for the child when the parents remain together in an unsuccessful marriage, or when they end the marriage and alter their personal marital frustrations? A variety of attitudes prevail in the United States in regard to divorce and children. One common belief is that the couple should put aside their marriage role problems for the maintenance of parental roles. Implied in this belief is that the marriage roles are secondary to the parental roles. Yet in a society that places great emphasis on personal ego-need satisfaction in marriage, the placing of marriage in a secondary position may be difficult for the married person to accept. The crucial question again is whether children "gain" by having their parents remain married. A couple who are unhappy in their husband and wife roles are usually going to reflect their feelings for each other in ways which will influence their relationship to the children. One may also question whether a person dissatisfied with one basic role can stop that from negatively influencing another of his basic roles. Can an unhappy wife be a good mother? These role questions are only beginning to be adequately researched. While studies indicate the many problems that children face when their parents get a divorce, few studies have dealt specifically with the children in marriages when the parents have stayed together "for the children's sake."

The existing evidence suggests that the chances of psychological damage to children resulting from the divorce of their parents is no greater than that for children in unbroken homes marked by continual marital tension.[31] The evidence further suggests that the causes for ending marital relationships are not related to significant differences in problems for their children. For example, one study found that homes broken by parents' divorce, desertion, or separa-

---

[31]See: Judson T. Landis, "The Trauma of Children When Parents Divorce," *Marriage and Family Living*, February, 1960, pp. 7–13 and F. Ivan Nye, "Child Adjustment in Broken and In Unhappy Unbroken Homes," *Marriage and Family Living*, November, 1957, pp. 356–61.

tion seem to involve about the same mental health risk as homes broken by the death of one parent.[32] In a study of adolescents in the 7th and 11th grades in a metropolitan area, Burchinal states that "inimical effects associated with divorce or separation and, for some youth, with the remarriage of their parents with whom they were living, were almost uniformly absent in the populations studied. Acceptance of this conclusion requires the revision of widely held beliefs about the detrimental effects of divorce upon children."[33]

Obviously the child must make important adjustments to the loss of a parent—usually the father—in his day-to-day life. In some ways, this is more difficult after divorce than after the death of a parent, because with the death of a parent the relationship is cleanly broken, whereas after divorce the relationship, particularly with the father, is greatly altered but not ended. The child may see his father for one day each week or month; thus, a new type of parent-child interaction emerges in which the child interacts with his parents one at a time in different settings for different periods of time. Because the parents are divorced, the child may also be caught in the middle of parental conflict and suffer a strong conflict of loyalty and emotional commitment to them. This may be particularly true if one of the divorced parents criticizes the other and the child feels it necessary either to argue or disagree with one parent's position.

However, the usual tendency is to see the parent-child relationship as either one where the parents are both present or where one parent is absent. This tendency often results in a failure to recognize that while a marriage may remain legally and sometimes even socially intact, the two parents may not both be actively functioning as parents. Generally the actual presence of a father is believed to be of crucial importance, even though he may have very little significant involvement in his parental role. It seems reasonable to suggest that there are many legally intact paired-parent families where the father has little more significant influence on his children than does the father who is divorced from his wife and not living with her and their children. In reality there are several family types where the father as an influential parent for his children may fall somewhere between the ideal paired-parent family and the one-parent family. To illustrate, several categories are suggested, although they have not been examined through research.

---

[32]Thomas S. Langner and Stanley T. Michael, *Life Stress and Mental Health* (New York: The Free Press of Glencoe, 1963), p. 169.

[33]Lee G. Burchinal, "Characteristics of Adolescents from Unbroken, Broken, and Reconstituted Families," *Journal of Marriage and Family,* February, 1964, p. 50.

(1) *Altered Families—External.* There are some families that for
periods of time must function as one-parent families due to causes
outside the family unit. For example, the occupation of the husband-
father may call for long separations from his family. Or alterations
may be due to one of the parents being institutionalized. These
kinds of families would be legally intact, but socially non-intact for
various periods of time.

(2) *Altered Families—Internal Voluntary.* Some families may remain legally intact but function for varying lengths of time as one-
parent families because one parent has voluntarily left his family
roles. A common type would be the husband-father who deserts his
family. This kind of family would be legally intact but socially one-
parent as long as the father stays away.

(3) *Altered Family—Internal Involuntary.* Some families may remain both legally and socially intact, but one of the adult members
suffers a drastic loss in his family role functioning. Included here
would be familes where restrictive illness occurs, where the father
is unable to work, where there is family role impairment due to alco-
holism, and so forth. Here the parent would be physically present
but would not be able to meet the minimal requirements of his parental role.

A final distinction should be made between the divorced man and
woman when children are involved. While divorce means the ending of the specific marriage roles, it usually means the maintenance
of the mother role for the wife, but a drastic alteration of the father
role for the husband. In fact, in many cases, the divorced father
loses most of the social functions of being a father. As the children
grow older, and if the mother remarries, the father may find his contact with his children increasingly limited. In this respect, divorce
may have more long-range trauma for the man in his role of father
than for the woman in her role as mother.

Personal Feelings about Divorce

Not only does social confusion exist in regard to divorce, but also
in many cases there may be a personal ambiguity of feelings. The
fact that both the loss of the marriage partner and the ending of the
marriage relationship are essentially personal means that the individual after divorce is often confused in reference to his divorce. As
a result the individual may be affected by both the social confusion
in regard to divorce and his own mixed feelings. This is illustrated
by Goode's findings that the feelings of the wife toward her divorce

were negative in 52 percent of the cases, positive in 31 percent, and ambivalent or "other" in 17 percent.[34]

The feelings that the individual has in regard to his divorced status will often have a strong influence on how he will fill his new role of divorcee. For example, if the woman is extremely bitter toward her ex-husband, this may influence her attitudes and relationships with other males and thereby restrict or inhibit her heterosexual relationships. On the other hand, defining one's divorced status as better than the past marital status may have a positive influence on adjustment to the new divorce role. Goode found that 50 percent of the women he studied felt that if there had been no divorce, things would have been worse.[35] The stated belief of at least half the divorced women was that their divorce was a personal improvement over their marriage.

The feelings in regard to the ex-husband are often influenced by the woman's ability to adjust to her divorced status. If she is unhappy and frustrated, she is apt to have strong negative attitudes about the ex-husband. Goode found that "an increasing proportion of ex-wives who are neither married nor going steady feel negatively toward the former husband, because of the position in which they find themselves over time."[36] The development of new relationships with men is of great importance because it is in this way that the divorced woman can re-enter marriage, which is often seen as the best way of regaining that which was lost. By regaining "face" through remarriage, the hostility directed at the first spouse will often be reduced because the failure of the first marriage becomes less important.

Sexual Activity

Because some individuals view the divorced woman as "sinful," she is sometime faced with special sex problems. The divorcee, like the widow, had extensive personal sexual experience in her marriage, and some males view the ex-married woman as an experienced sex object who must desire sexual activity because of her marital experiences. She is older and sexually experinced, and the male may view her as a possible sexual partner with whom a minimum of commitment is called for on his part. Another attitude that sometimes enters the male's thinking is that if a woman divorced her husband, he

---

[34]Goode, *op. cit.*, p. 183.
[35]*Ibid.*, p. 342.
[36]*Ibid.*, p. 298.

may have been sexually inadequate in meeting her needs and she is therefore interested in a new sex partner. The writer has found from talks with divorced women that the most persistent sexual aggression often comes not from single or divorced men, but from married men. As one divorcee put it, "The minute a married man says, 'My wife doesn't understand me,' get ready for a proposition." Possibly, the married man perceives the divorced woman as one who will make few demands on him because he is already married.

A number of divorced women are probably faced with a personal conflict over the desire for sexual relationships and their lack of marital status. The divorced woman is probably much less inhibited in satisfying her sexual needs than a younger, less experienced, and never-married female. This suggestion gains some support from Bernard's findings. She writes: "The previously married woman is more likely than her unmarried sister to be sexually exploited by casual suitors and to have had premarital sexual relations with her future (second) spouse."[37] Bernard's use of the word "exploitation" may be somewhat of an exaggeration because many divorcees probably enter sexual relations with at least some degree of willingness.

Sexual attitudes and behavior during courtship are bound to be different for the divorced than for the single woman. First, since the divorcee is not a virgin, she does not have to concern herself with conveying the notion of virginity. Second, the divorcee's sexual activity will probably be more influenced by her personal interest in sex than by general social values. Third, the male may be less apt to define the divorcee as "bad" and unworthy of marriage because of premarital sexual activity.

Implied in society's general sexual values, as related to those persons in postmarital roles (those after the death of the spouse or because of divorce), is that they are assumed to behave within the same framework as they were expected to in their premarital days—that is, they must abstain from sexual activity. But of course the values, as well as the controls over the sexual behavior of the young and the inexperienced, cannot realistically function in the same way for those who are older and sexually experienced. Rarely in studies of or textbooks about the American family is there a discussion of the sexual adaptations of the postmarital. It seems to be assumed that most postmarital persons, epecially the women, will give up all active sexual behavior once their marriage relationship has ended. Yet the available evidence indicates that postmarital women do not

---

[37]Jessie Bernard, *Remarriage* (New York: The Dryden Press, 1956), p. 155.

return to their premarital levels of sexual abstinence. Kinsey wrote that "the most notable aspect of the histories of these previously married females was the fact that their frequencies of activity had not dropped to the levels which they had known as single females, before they had ever married."[38] For example, Kinsey found that for women in the age range of 41–45, of those single (never married), 68 percent had some sexual outlet as compared to 93 percent of the married and 84 percent of the previously married.[39]

One recent study indicates that an important factor in the desire of women to continue coitus after their marriage has ended was their capacity to achieve orgasm. Christenson and Gagnon point out that once the capacity for sexual orgasm is achieved by women, they are likely to have coitus after the end of their marriages.[40] As to types of sexual outlet, obviously married women have a higher frequency of heterosexual contact than do previously married women. However, the previously married women are more apt to turn to other sexual outlets. For example, the Kinsey data shows that for women in the age range 41 to 45, only 13 percent of the married as contrasted to 32 percent of the previously married women were using solitary sexual outlets. And while none of the married women were using homosexual outlets, 6 percent of the previously married women were.[41]

Also, as has been pointed out for other patterns of sexual behavior, the higher-educated postmarital females have a greater frequency of involvement. Gebhard found that almost three quarters of the previously married women studied had some postmarital coitus.[42] By levels of education, the coital rates for females were 56 percent for those with eight years or less education, 76 percent for those with 9 to 12 years and 73 percent for those with 13 to 16 years of education.[43] Gebhard further found that the highest educated (post graduate) white women had had longer periods of time involved in postmarital coitus as well as greater frequency.[44]

The divorced and the widowed find themselves in a position of having functioned for various lengths of time in the paired world

---

[38]Alfred C. Kinsey, Wardell B. Pomeroy, Clyde E. Martin, and Paul H. Gebhard, *Sexual Behavior in the Human Female* (Philadelphia: W. B. Saunders, 1953), p. 533.

[39]*Ibid.*, p. 549.

[40]Cornelia Christenson and John H. Gagnon, "Sexual Behavior in a Group of Older Women," *Journal of Gerontology*, July, 1965, p. 356.

[41]Kinsey, *op. cit.*, p. 562.

[42]Paul H. Gebhard, Wardell B. Pomeroy, Clyde E. Martin, and Cornelia V. Christenson, *Pregnancy, Birth, and Abortion*, (New York: Harper & Brothers, 1958), p. 144.

[43]*Ibid.*, p. 145.

[44]*Ibid.*, p. 147.

with their past spouse and then being required to function in it without the necessary partner. This is particularly difficult in the middle class in which the number and importance of social relations is often great. The unmarried often find that if they do not have a "social" partner, their hostesses will go to great lengths to provide one. This pairing may have a positive function for the unmarried person in that it provides him with the opportunity for meetng members of the opposite sex and the possibility of finding a new mate. It is probably more important for the female than for the male because she has less opportunity to seek out and meet members of the opposite sex. Another reason for pairing off the divorcee may be the desire to remove a "threat" to married couples. The divorced possess some degree of glamour in the eyes of many; in addition, they are often felt to be seeking a new mate. Thus it is feared that they might even steal someone's spouse if given the chance—and it is therefore good sense to render them harmless by providing a partner for them.

Remarriage

Before discussing some of the factors related to remarriage of the divorced, it is of value to look at those divorced persons who do not choose or are not selected for remarriage. Some suggestions of psychological types who remain in the divorced status follow.

The first may be called *the bitter*. The bitter would include persons who have defined their relationship with their first spouse as so unsatisfactory that they believe the past type of relationship would prevail in any marriage. It is also possible that the hostility to the ex-spouse is so great that it is projected to all in reference to that marriage role. For this group then, marriage is a rejected relationship based on hostility to the opposite sex in the marriage role. The second group may be called *the frightened*. The important point here is the individual's fear about himself in marriage. The failure of his first marriage may make him feel he will not be able to make a success of marriage with another partner; or, if the breakup of the first marriage was very unpleasant, he may not want to face the possibility of going through the same experience again. Therefore, the remarriage has risks the individual is not willing to take. Third might be *the overdemanding*. The person may feel he has learned from the first experience of marriage and before entering a second marriage will make sure that the mate selected will have qualities ensuring its success. As a result, the demands for the second mate may be so great the individual never finds a person who can meet them.

The fourth group may be called *the rejected*. They may never have an opportunity to enter a second marriage because of social or psychological factors which make them undesirable as a marriage mate. The fact that they were successful in finding a first mate is no guarantee that they will be successful in being chosen a second time. This has particular relevance for the woman because the older her age bracket, the greater her competition in the decreasingly available male market. One final group may be called *the adjusted*. These are individuals who accept the role of the divorced person and are satisfied to remain in it. Individuals in this group have generally rejected remarriage. The difference between them and the others is that they accept the divorce status, while the individuals in the other groups are more or less forced into it.

None of the suggested groups is autonomous and the influences probably overlap in the failure of many to remarry. As with those who never marry, those who do not remarry may do so by not choosing to or by not being chosen.

The best possible adjustment that many can make to divorce is remarriage. This provides the individual with an opportunity personally and socially to "right the wrong" of the previous marriage failure. The same strong remarriage desire does not usually exist for the widowed because their first marriage was not a failure. Table 17–1 shows the great importance of remarriage in the United States: about one quarter of all brides and grooms are persons marrying for at least the second time. It may also be noted that almost three out of every four marrying for the second time had their first marriage end through divorce. Therefore, the divorced are involved in the majority of remarriages.

TABLE 17–1

THE PERCENTAGE DISTRIBUTION OF ALL MARRIAGES PERFORMED IN 28 REPORTING STATES, BY MARITAL STATUS

Marital Status	Brides	Grooms
Single	76.1	77.2
Widowed	6.2	5.5
Divorced	16.6	16.4

Adapted from: "Marriage and Divorce Statistics," *Vital Statistics of the United States*, 1959, Section 2 (United States Department of Health, Education, and Welfare, National Office of Vital Statistics), p. 8.

No legal restrictions are placed on the widowed as to remarriage, but some minor restrictions are put on the divorced. "In 24 jurisdictions both plaintiff and defendant must wait 2 months to 1 year before remarrying; in five states the period is one year or more."[45] But ultimately both the plaintiff and the defendant have the legal right to remarry.

Social Factors

Before looking at some of the social psychological factors related to remarriage for the widowed and the divorced, some of the general social characteristics of remarriage will be considered. One obvious fact is that those who enter remarriage are older than those entering first marriage. In the United States in 1959, the median age at first marriage was 20.3 for brides and 22.8 for grooms; at second marriage, 34.0 for brides and 38.3 for grooms; and at third or later marriage, 41.4 for brides and 46.9 for grooms.[46] The vast majority of remarriages refer to second marriages as only 3 percent of the brides or grooms were marrying for the third time, and 0.5 percent entering a fourth or later marriage in 1959.[47] There is no evidence that in recent years the percentage of marriages involving a partner with a previous marriage has increased or decreased.[48] As a general statement it may be useful to keep in mind that "one in four marriages ends in divorce; two out of three divorced persons remarry; more than nine out of ten of the remarried stay married."[49]

Not only are those who remarry older than those entering first marriage, but the age difference between the spouses is also greater. In 1959, the median ages of all first marriage brides and grooms was 20.3 and 22.8 years, with an age difference of 2.5 years.[50] For the same year for all remarriages, the median age of the bride was 35.4 years and the groom 39.8 years, with an age difference of 4.4 years.[51] Spouses are about two years further apart in age if either or both are remarrying than if neither partner was previously married.

The divorced tend to enter remarriage after a shorter lapse of time from the end of their first marriage than do the widowed. "During the early 1950's among those who had remarried the median length of time which had elapsed since their previous marriage had been

---

[45]Ray E. Baber, *Marriage and the Family* (New York: McGraw-Hill Book Co., 1953), p. 488.

[46]"Marriage and Divorce Statistics," *Vital Statistics of the United States*, 1959, Section 2 (United States Department of Health, Education, and Welfare, Public Health Service, National Office of Vital Statistics), p. 9.

[47]*Ibid.*, p. 9.

[48]"Marriages," *Vital Statistics of the United States, 1961*, Volume III, Sections 1, 2 and 7 (United States Department of Health, Education and Welfare, Public Health Service, National Office of Vital Statistics), p. 3.

[49]Ben J. Wattenberg and Richard M. Scammon, *This U.S.A.* (Garden City, New York: Doubleday & Co., Inc., 1965), p. 36.

[50]*Vital Statistics of the United States, op. cit.*, p. 7.

[51]*Ibid.*, p. 7.

dissolved was 2.7 years for those who had been divorced and 3.5 years for those who had been widowed."[52] Several reasons exist for this difference. First, the widowed have a longer period of "mourning" over the loss of the first spouse. Second, the widowed are less strongly motivated to rectify the ending of the first marriage by entering a second one. Third, the basic reason some attained a divorce was the involvement with the person who is to be the next spouse, so that courtship had begun before the divorce actually occurred. Fourth, the divorced are younger and have a greater and earlier chance for remarriage than the widowed. In point of fact, a large number of the divorced have a short period of time in the divorce role. Furthermore, whether the woman has children or not does not appear to significantly influence her probabilities of remarriage. Glick found that, when standardized by age, a woman with three or more children has about the same chance of remarriage as a childless woman.[53]

TABLE 17-2

WHO MARRIES WHOM? TWENTY-NINE REPORTING STATES, 1959

(PERCENTS)

Previous Marital Status of:	Previous Marital Status of Spouse			
	Single	Widowed	Divorced	Total
Bride:				
Single	91.0	1.5	7.6	100
Widowed	23.8	43.8	32.4	100
Divorced	38.9	9.7	51.4	100
Total	78.1	5.5	16.4	100
Groom:				
Single	89.9	1.9	8.2	100
Widowed	20.6	50.0	29.3	100
Divorced	35.7	12.4	51.9	100
Total	77.2	6.3	16.6	100

Adapted from: "Marriage and Divorce Statistics," *Vital Statistics of the United States*, 1959, Section 2 (United States Department of Health, Education and Welfare, National Office of Vital Statistics), p. 9.

In marriage choice the individual may select a mate from one of the three general marital categories—single, widowed, or divorced. Table 17-2 provides a statistical picture of mate selection by the marital status of both the bride and the groom. About 9 out of every 10 individuals entering a first marriage selects a mate who is also entering a first marriage. About one half of all divorced women marry divorced men and about 4 in 10 marry a single man. The pattern for the divorced man is essentially the same as for the divorced

---

[52]Glick, *op. cit.*, p. 138.
[53]*Ibid.*, p. 138.

woman. Among the widowed population, there is a slightly greater tendency for the widower to select a widow, but for the widow to select a single or a divorced man. Taking the largest categories of choice for each of the three groups, like tend to select like—the single, widowed, and divorced marry each other.

Bowerman's research into remarriage found several general social patterns. First, single persons selected as mates were younger than were those selected mates who had been previously married. And the median age of selected mates who had been previously widowed was higher than for those mates previously divorced. Second, as men grew older, they married women increasingly younger than themselves and the age differences were the greatest for men who married single women and the least for men who married widows. Third, as women increased in age they tended to marry men closer to their own age. Fourth, there was a greater range in the ages of mates selected by older people than by younger ones. Finally, the variability in age differences between spouses was greater for males than for females.[54]

Because a single marriage relationship is the generally assumed pattern in American society, people who experience more than one marriage are sometimes viewed as having psychological problems. While we will discuss later in the chapter the divorce-prone—who often do suggest some particular psychological problems that make marriage difficult—it cannot be assumed that most of those who divorce and remarry have any special psychological problems that separate them from the once-married population. One national study of mental health found little difference in the mental health risk of men and women who have remarried and "among neither men nor women is remarriage associated with a great increase in mental health risk."[55]

By age 30 for both men and women, the divorced and widowed have a better chance for remarriage than the single person has for making a first marriage. It may be recalled that roughly 10 percent of the population will never marry. In the younger age groups, the group that will never marry constitutes a small percentage of the total; but as age increases and more have entered marriage, the number of "marital rejects" accounts for an increasingly greater percentage of the "never married." By contrast, the widowed and divorced

---

[54]Charles E. Bowerman, "Age Relationships at Marriage, By Marital Status, and Age at Marriage," *Marriage and Family Living*, Vol. 18, 1956, pp. 231–33.
[55]Langner, *op. cit.*, p. 333.

have shown their success on the marriage market by their previous marriage.

SOME SOCIAL-PSYCHOLOGICAL FACTORS IN REMARRIAGE

Widowed

The widowed person contemplating remarriage must reconcile his feelings for his first spouse in relationship to a second spouse. In a first marriage the individual of course has no other marriage experience with which to compare the spouse. In remarriage after divorce, the second spouse may be favorably compared with the first mate who was not successful as a marriage partner; but the widowed person contemplating a second marriage may feel a sense of personal conflict between the first and the second mate. If the widowed person felt close to his first mate, the idea of a second marriage partner may lead him to some confusion and conflict about his feelings. If he feels he really loved the first mate, he may wonder how he can also love the second one; or loving the second mate may suggest he really did not love the first, resulting in feelings of guilt. This ambiguity is often a reflection of the romantic notion of one and only one true love during a lifetime. In such cases, the widow and others sometimes rationalize by stating that the second love is different—more mature and rational—thereby minimizing conflict and leaving the romantic image of the first marriage intact. The belief in a single great love is probably becoming less important in the middle class; increasingly, people who remarry may feel less personal conflict in having loved two spouses.

It sometimes happens the the widowed person recalls his first mate in an idealized way. This idealization may even stop some from remarrying because no second mate could come close to the first mate's image. If such a person does remarry, the idealized image may create problems in the remarriage because of an unrealistic comparison of the two spouses. In successful remarriage of the widowed, the recollections of the first spouse are probably favorable, but realistic. Bernard found that about two thirds of the remarried widows and widowers held friendly attitudes toward their first marriage partners, and about one third were indifferent, unfriendly, or had "no attitude."[56] By contrast, the spouses of the widowed had somewhat less favorable attitudes in regard to their spouse's first mate. Bernard found that 39 percent of the husbands and 47 percent of

---

[56]Bernard, *op. cit.*, p. 206.

the wives felt friendly to the spouse's deceased first partner.[57] Table 17-3 indicates that the husbands were more apt to feel indifferent toward the first spouse than were wives. Once again this is probably due to the greater personal involvement with marriage by the woman.

TABLE 17-3
ATTITUDES TOWARD THE SPOUSE'S FIRST MARRIAGE PARTNER

	Friendly	Indifferent	Jealous or Resentful	Other	Total
Husbands of widows ...	38.7%	44.8%	8.0%	8.5%	100%
Husbands of divorced women	21.7	59.5	14.8	4.0	100
Wives of widowers	46.6	36.4	5.1	11.9	100
Wives of divorced men	27.6	46.6	19.8	6.0	100

Adapted from: Jessie Bernard, *Remarriage* (New York: The Dryden Press, Inc., 1956), p. 206.

Bernard suggests that when at least one partner in a remarriage is a widowed person, there are several important areas of potential difficulty in which the couple must adjust.[58] First is the tendency of the widowed spouse to idealize the deceased mate. Second, the knowledge that the partner's first marriage was not terminated voluntarily may imply to the second spouse that if the first partner were still alive, the mate would still be with him and that he is thus a second choice. Third, friends and relatives may feel that the new spouse is an intruder. Patterns of behavior were established in the past with the deceased person in the role of spouse. The second marriage partner is not only bound to be at least somewhat different, but is also moving into already established relationships; hence, the new spouse may feel or be treated as an intruder. Friends and relatives may also compare the second spouse to the first, leading to problems for the second mate. Fourth, an expansion of the family relationships often occurs with the addition of a new set of in-laws resulting from remarriage. As Bernard points out, "a remarried widow not only must adjust to her new in-laws but may have to appease her old ones as well."[59] The family of the deceased partner usually has a strong emotional commitment to his memory; remarriage of his spouse may lead to a feeling on their part that he is not being adequately respected. If children are involved, they may

---

[57]*Ibid.*, p. 206.
[58]*Ibid.*, p. 199.
[59]*Ibid.*, p. 196.

also fear that their relationship will be replaced by the new in-laws established through the remarriage.

Finally, a variety of problems may exist when children are involved. The children must adjust to a stepparent, and the mother or father must adjust to someone new in the counter parental role. The latter may be a problem for some individuals who first shared the parent role with their first spouse, then played a combined parental role when widowed, and finally, through remarriage, moved back into sharing the parental roles with a new marriage partner. The widowed person with young children may be faced with a dilemma in contemplating remarriage. On the one hand, he may feel that remarriage will once again provide the children with someone in the needed parental role. On the other hand, someone new in the parental role may be seen as disturbing to the memory and influence of the natural parent. Sometimes after remarriage, the children are faced with two persons in the same parental role, the memory of the first and the reality of the second. With or without remarriage, the influence of the deceased parent may continue to be strong for the children. The surviving parent may attribute to the deceased parent a variety of expectations for the children. The children may be told "your father would have wanted you to do this or that" and the attributing of expectations to the respected and idealized departed sometimes makes honest disagreement seem like an attack on the deceased parent's memory. The surviving parent functions in the role of interpreter and spokesman of the departed and what he attributes to the departed may or may not be true. In some cases, a deceased parent may actually become more of a force dead than he was when alive.

In the American society, the role of the widowed person is generally a respectable one. Little stigma is attached to the widowed and there is no strong taboo against remarriage. Remarriage for the widowed is often the respectable and even expected course, and if it is a widower with children, the social pressures for remarriage are often very great. This reflects the common belief that children need a woman in the role of mother. The widow is not subject to the same social pressures to find a new father for her children, because the father role is viewed as less important in its significance for children. It may also be that the widow is expected a little more than the widower to "treasure" the memory of the departed spouse by not remarrying.

The success of remarriages of the widowed seems to be reasonably good.[60] Because the widowed enter second marriages at older ages than do the divorced or the single, they probably enter with less romantic expectations. Their successful first marriage may have provided the satisfaction of their romantic needs, and the second marriage may be entered for more rational reasons. "Older persons may have less exacting standards; they may be willing to settle for less than when they were younger. The contrast between the loneliness of life without a spouse and the companionship and security of married status may tip the scales in favor of marriage, even if it is not a success by any other measure."[61]

Table 17-4 shows the relative success in remarriage of the widowed and the divorced. About two thirds of the widows and widowers are recorded as having "very happy" or "happy" remarriages. These figures indicate a somewhat higher level of success in remarriage for the bereaved than for the divorced. The evidence seems to indicate that the remarriage of the widowed has about the same probabilities of success as do first marriages.

TABLE 17-4
RELATIVE SUCCESS IN REMARRIAGE OF WIDOWED AND DIVORCED

	Divorced Men	Widowers	Divorced Women	Widows
Very happy	25.3	32.3	25.1	34.0
Happy	28.8	29.0	25.5	30.0
Average	32.6	25.9	33.2	24.0
Unhappy	8.5	7.8	9.9	5.0
Very unhappy	4.8	5.0	6.3	7.0
Totals	100.0	100.0	100.0	100.0

Adapted from: Jessie Bernard, *Remarriage* (New York: The Dryden Press Inc., 1956), p. 111.

Divorced

As previously suggested, the role of the divorced in the United States continues to be somewhat ambiguous, but the high remarriage rates of the divorced indicate both the desire and ability to enter a second marriage. Because the divorced are younger than the widowed, they probably face less difficulty moving back into the dating-courtship process necessary for finding a second mate The fact that they are *divorced* in many cases makes their courtship experience prior to a second marriage different than it was prior to their first marriage. Bernard found that "in general, courtship in second marriages was simpler than in first marriages. The dating and engage-

---

[60]*Ibid.*, p. 111.
[61]*Ibid.*, p. 279.

ment periods were shorter; the proportion of brides who had received an engagement ring was smaller, and the ring was less valuable; fewer remarrying women had had showers given for them, and there were fewer showers per bride."[62]

The fact that a high percentage of divorcees remarry indicates that courtship opportunities are adequate. Yet we have no way of knowing if the choice of the second mate was "forced"; given the strong motivation for remarriage, the individual may make a quick decision within a limited set of choices. Goode in his study of divorced women found a wide variation in their dating opportunities. The chances appear to be far from adequate for many. "Of our 188 divorcees who were not remarried and were not going steady, 18 per cent had more than one date weekly, 20 per cent had one date each week, 14 per cent had 1 or 2 dates monthly, and 48 per cent almost never had a date.' "[63] However, this group is somewhat biased because many of the more "desirable" divorcees had already been selected out and were remarried, engaged, or going steady.

The age of the divorcee also influences her dating opportunities. Goode writes "whether or not the young respondents (20–24) are positively motivated toward love and marriage, about two thirds of them have many or some opportunities. However, almost two thirds of the older respondents (30 and over) who do not want to remarry also fail to report having opportunities to meet people."[64] In the older group, the lack of interest in remarriage may be a rationalization for the lack of opportunity, or the lack of interest in remarriage may greatly reduce the chances of meeting eligible males.

In the discussion of mate selection in Chapter 6, it was pointed out that the middle-class family today plays a rather insignificant part in helping the young person meet potential marriage mates. According to Goode's findings, the same may also be true for the divorcee meeting potential marriage partners. Goode found that "the peer group is more effective than the family in producing men with whom the divorcee would consider marriage."[65] This is due to the greater circle of acquaintanceships with eligible age peers of the divorcee and their friends. Many divorcees are helped in finding a new mate by friends who have emotional identifications with the divorced person and desire to help them rectify the failure of the first marriage through a successful second one.

---

[62]*Ibid.*, p. 39.
[63]Goode, *op. cit.*, p. 258.
[64]*Ibid.*, p. 251.
[65]*Ibid.*, p. 275.

Regardless of the desire of friends and relatives to help the divorcee find a second mate, Goode found that 56 percent of the divorcees he studied stated they had not received help from either friends
or family in meeting eligible men.[66] Goode did find a difference in
help received by the age of the divorcee. For those in the age groups
20 to 29, 50 percent said they had received help from either friends
or relatives, compared to 37 percent of the divorcees 30 and over.[67]
This may simply be a reflection of the fact that, in the younger age
group, more eligible men are available than in the older group and
the divorcee's age peers have more contacts.

Children

When age is held constant, the fact of having or not having children does not seem to have any significant influence on the chances
of remarriage. Furthermore, Goode found that among divorced
mothers the number of children seems to have almost no significant
effect on the activities leading to remarriage.[68] This point is often
ignored in the criticism directed at divorce which involves children
and implies that after divorce the child will live in a personal world
of separated parents. The fact is that a large number of the mothers,
who usually have custody of the children, remarry not long after
the divorce. Therefore, the child usually comes into a new relationship with the second husband as a stepfather. This relationship may
be one of conflict and insecurity for the child, but in many cases it
means that with time the divorce is compensated for at least in part
by a new set of family relationships.

The fact that the family situation in a remarriage after divorce
is more likely to involve a new father than a new mother is significant. The role of the mother is generally the most significant one
in an involvement with the children; therefore, the individual as
mother is constant in the relationship with the children in the first
marriage, during divorce, and in remarriage. While the children
have many adjustments to make, they almost always have available
to them the parent of greatest significance and emotional involvement.

It may also be argued that, over the long run, children may be
better off when an unsuccessful marriage has been ended and replaced by one that is successful. The two important roles of marriage
partner and parent are interrelated, and dissatisfaction and frustra-

---

[66]*Ibid.*, p. 257.
[67]*Ibid.*, p. 257.
[68]*Ibid.*, p. 272.

tion in one role often influences the other. Couples who keep an unsuccessful marriage intact for the sake of the children may often function as inefficient and unsuccessful parents, because the frustration and unhappiness of the marriage role may rub off on the parental role. The parents may also, consciously or unconsciously, blame the children for their remaining in a marriage that is unsuccessful, with this having an effect on their relationship with their children. By contrast, if the remarriage is successful, the parent is satisfied with the marital role, and this may positively influence him in his role as parent.

There is some evidence as to a possible relationship between parent's remarriage and the mental health consequences for their children. Langner found that the mental health risk was greater for those children whose parent remarried than for those children with a remaining parent who did not remarry.[69] This would suggest that some children found their emotional involvement with their remaining parent threatened by the entrance of their parent's new spouse.

Stepparents. Persons with children contemplating remarriage must usually consider the implications for their two interrelated roles of marriage partner and of parent. Until recently there had been little research into the possible impact of remarriage on parental roles. Some recent research, especially that of Bowerman and Irish, is starting to fill in the research gap in this area of family relationships.[70]

The impact of remarriage on children appears to be related to the age of the child. "The general consensus among remarried parents seems to be that very young or quite grown-up children tend to assimilate a new parent more easily than do adolescents."[71] There may also be a social class difference related to children and their getting along with stepparents. For example, one study found a larger proportion of low social class respondents (31 percent) than high social class respondents (20 percent) not getting along with their stepparents.[72]

Remarriage of the parent the child lives with of course places the child in new parental relationships. If his parents' marriage ended through divorce, he may find himself with a father he has little contact with and a stepfather with whom he has day-to-day inter-

---

[69]Langner, *op. cit.*, p. 169.
[70]Charles E. Bowerman and Donald P. Irish, "Some Relationships of Stepchildren to Their Parents," *Marriage and Family Living*, May, 1962, pp. 113–21.
[71]Bernard, *op. cit.*, p. 216.
[72]Langner, *op. cit.*, p. 174.

action. If his parent's marriage ended through the death of a parent (most often the father), and his mother remarries, he finds himself with memories of a father and day-to-day interaction with a stepfather. Bowerman and Irish found that a greater proportion of children of divorce adjusted to stepparents than did the children of bereavement.[73] They suggest that this difference may be because the child of a divorce acquires a stepparent "more promptly after the event, at an earlier age, and in fewer numbers (per family) than do those who have experienced the death of a mother or father."[74]

When the child has a live natural parent and a stepparent of their own sex, the adjustment is poorer toward the stepparent. But in most of the "parent-child and age-sex combinations the stepfather appears to fare better in comparison with the real father than do stepmothers in contrast with mothers in normal homes."[75] The level of affection by children toward stepfathers is usually much lower than toward real fathers,[76] but the lowest level of affection was found to be by children to their natural father and a stepmother.[77]

Often a child with both natural parents alive and caring for him does not and cannot state a choice of preference for one parent over the other. However, a child living with a natural parent and stepparent is more likely to express a preference for one parent to the other. Bowerman and Irish found that "girls and adolescents are more apt to express a preference than are the boys and our younger respondents. Stepchildren more often prefer the real parent over the stepparent."[78]

The difficulties that may be created because of a new marital partner as a stepparent may also contribute to some problems in the remarriage. That is, strains in the parental roles are often related to strains in the marital roles. Bowerman and Irish found this to be true in that the level of marital discord was higher in stepparent homes than in first marriages.[79]

Remarriage Success

Monahan, after careful study of divorce and remarriage, found that "with respect to remarriage the evidence is quite consistent and strong. Not only do second marriages ending in divorce show a

---

[73]Bowerman, *op. cit.*, p. 117.
[74]*Ibid.*, p. 118.
[75]*Ibid.*, p. 117.
[76]*Ibid.*, p. 116.
[77]*Ibid.*, p. 117.
[78]*Ibid.*, p. 119.
[79]*Ibid.*, p. 117.

shorter duration than first marriages, the duration also diminished with each successive remarriage. When the data are arranged to show the factors of divorce versus widowhood, it becomes apparent that it is the divorce group which exerts a major influence on the result. With each prior experience with divorce, the duration of the remarriage ending in divorce becomes shorter."[80] Using divorce as a means of comparing the success of first and second marriage is very crude. First, the length of remarriage is bound to be shorter than in a first marriage because the person is older when he enters a second marriage. Second, the divorced person who remarries has been selected out of the total first married population as one who *has shown* he will turn to divorce. As divorces occur, the continued first-married population proportionately increases in being composed of individuals who would probably *not* turn to divorce under any conditions. While the remarried-divorce population clearly has a higher divorce rate than the first-married population, this indicates a greater tendency for the once-divorced to divorce again, but says little about the relative marital adjustment of the two groups.

The above suggestions are not meant to indicate that remarriage after divorce is necessarily equal to or better than first marriages, but rather to point out the inadequacy of divorce as a measurement of relative marital success. Table 17–5 provides a comparison of success of remarriage for the divorced and the widowed. It may be noted that 54.1 percent of the divorced men as compared with 61.3 percent of the widowers have remarriages rated as "very happy" or "happy." For the women, 50.6 percent of the divorcees and 64 percent of the widows have marriages rated as "very happy" or "happy."[81] These data indicate that the widowed have a slightly higher rate of happy remarriages than the divorced, and the difference in the two groups is somewhat greater for the women than the men. The latter offers some support for Baber's contention that divorced women are about 10 percent poorer marital risks than are divorced men.[82] The possible higher divorce tendency of the divorced woman over the divorced man may be due to the woman's greater personal involvement in marriage, making her more negatively influenced by the experience of the first marriage. It may also reflect the possibility that remarriage is more of a "forced choice" for the

---

[80]Thomas P. Monahan, "The Duration of Marriage to Divorce: Second Marriages and Migratory Types," *Marriage and Family Living*, May, 1959, p. 136.

[81]Bernard, *op. cit.*, p. 111.

[82]Baber, *op. cit.*, p. 190.

divorced woman than for the divorced man, leading to a poorer second marriage choice.

Table 17–5, taken from Locke's research, provides a comparison of marital adjustment between the "once married" and the "divorced-remarried," and indicates that no significant difference exists between the two groups in the rating of "fair" adjustment, but that the "once married" are slightly more apt to have a marriage rated as "good" than the "divorced-remarried" and somewhat less apt to have one rated as "poor." The evidence presented for both the divorce rate and ratings of marital success suggest a somewhat lower success rate in remarriage than in first marriage. However, it may also be argued that most remarriages of divorced persons are successful if they are compared with the individual's first marriage. All of their first marriages were failures (in that they ended in divorce), whereas the majority of divorcees who remarry have entered a new marriage that lasts. Therefore, when compared with their first marriages, most of the second marriages are successful. Goode points out that 87 percent of his remarried-divorced sample stated that their present marriage was much better than the first.[83]

TABLE 17–5

MARITAL ADJUSTMENT OF MARRIED-ONCE AND DIVORCED-REMARRIED

| | Marital Adjustment (Percent) | | | |
	Good	Fair	Poor	Total
Married once	50.0	39.1	10.9	100
Divorced-remarried	44.7	38.3	17.0	100

Adapted from: Harvey J. Locke, *Predicting Adjustment in Marriage: A Comparison of a Divorced and a Happily Married Group* (New York: Henry Holt and Co., 1951), p. 307.

There is some evidence of a slight decline in the proportion of remarriages ending in divorce. In 1958, for six reporting States, 31 percent of the divorcing husbands and 32 percent of the wives were ending a remarriage. By 1961, as indicated from 18 reporting States, the percentages were 26 for husbands and 27 for wives.[84]

When we look at all divorcees and see that 97 percent of the men and 96 percent of the women have been divorced only once, it becomes clear that divorce is not an experience that any one person has very often. As one observer points out, "Divorce is working best

---

[83]Goode, *op. cit.*, p. 131.

[84]"Divorces," *Vital Statistics of the United States, 1961*, Volume III, Sections 3, 4 and 7 (United States Department of Health, Education and Welfare, Public Health Service, National Office of Vital Statistics), p. 9.

not for those who marry promiscuously but for those who have made a mistake and are not inclined to repeat it."[85]

The Divorce-Prone

Divorce-proneness may result from a variety of social and psychological factors. Jessie Bernard suggests that the "concept of divorce-proneness is supported by the fact that the divorce rate increases with each subsequent divorce."[86] As an example, the writer once talked to an attractive and intelligent woman in her middle 30's who had been divorced from three husbands. She stated that her three husbands were essentially alike in personality and that their personalities in relationship with hers made a successful marriage impossible. Furthermore, she had enough insight into herself to say that if she married again, she would probably marry a man like the first three, implying that a fourth marriage would also end with divorce.

It is very probable that some persons who do not, for any number of reasons, have much chance of making a go of marriage are selected out of the remarriage market. Bernard suggests that "divorce may weed out of the once-married population a good many of the marital misfits; the exigencies of finding a second mate may select them out of the remarried population also. The result, so far as the unremarried widowed and divorced are concerned, is a population with adverse social characteristics; so far as remarried widowed and divorced are concerned, it may be a population with superior social characteristics."[87] If Bernard's suggestion is true, it indicates that the rate of successful remarriage would be much less if all who were eligible for remarriage had an equal chance of finding a second mate. While it seems clear that some of the obvious marital misfits are weeded out, it is also evident that a number who will prove with future marriages to be divorce-prone are not.

It may also be suggested that the divorce-prone constitute an internal bias in the comparison of both the divorce frequency and marital adjustment of first marriages with remarriages. Here is a hypothetical illustration: If we take all first marriages that occur in any given year, we know that out of that group at least one partner in a number of the marriages will prove with time to be divorce-prone. For the sake of illustration, it is suggested that such will prove to be the case in 5 percent of the first marriages. Suppose that for the

[85]Wattenberg, *op. cit.*, p. 36.
[86]Bernard, *op. cit.*, p. 90.
[87]*Ibid.*, p. 167.

same year, we take all second marriages in which at least one of the partners has been previously married and divorced. The very fact that all of these remarriages involve at least one divorced person means that the percentage of marriages with a divorce-prone partner will have greatly increased. Once again for the sake of illustration, suppose that 25 percent of the second marriages involve at least one partner who is divorce-prone. The illustration may be continued by taking for that same year all third marriages in which at least one of the partners is entering his third marriage after two prior divorces. It is now suggested that 50 percent of all third marriages have a partner who is divorce-prone. This might be projected to sixth or seventh marriages in which close to 100 percent would include a divorce-prone person. Thus, the probability of these marriages also ending in divorce would be very high.

Using the above illustration, it may be argued that if some way were found to control the divorce-prone group and then compare the "non-prone" in first marriages and remarriages, the divorce frequency and adjustment differences would no longer exist. Of course at the present time, no such controls are available, but the divorce-prone bias should be recognized. One further point of bias is that, because the divorced tend to marry divorced persons, their remarriage relationship has a greater probability of having at least one divorce-prone partner than when the divorced marries the single or widowed, or when the widowed marries the single or widowed.

The questions raised about the "success" of the divorced in remarriage are emphasized for this reason: Given the high divorce rate in the United States today and the great social concern directed at it, more careful analysis of what happens to the divorced is greatly needed. This is important both sociologically and psychologically, because there is no indication that divorce is going to decrease significantly in the foreseeable future. The vast bulk of research is directed at the predivorce and divorce states, rather than the extended area of postdivorce adjustment to the divorced or remarried roles. Greater attention also needs to be directed at remarriage as a social force reducing some of the conditions often assumed to be problems of divorce. Increasingly, remarriage may emerge as a force of equilibrium in relationship to what is often called the divorce "problem."

SELECTED BIBLIOGRAPHY

BERNARD, JESSIE. *Remarriage*. New York: The Dryden Press, Inc., 1956.
BOWERMAN, CHARLES and IRISH, DONALD P. "Some Relationships of Step-

children to Their Parents," *Marriage and Family Living,* May, 1962, pp. 113–21.

BURCHINAL, LEE G. "Characteristics of Adolescents from Unbroken, Broken, and Reconstituted Families," *Journal of Marriage and Family,* February, 1964, pp. 44–51.

DESPERT, J. LOUISE. *Children of Divorce.* New York: Doubleday & Co., Inc., 1953.

GLICK, PAUL C. *American Families.* New York: John Wiley & Sons, Inc., 1957.

GOODE, WILLIAM J. *After Divorce.* Glencoe, Illinois: The Free Press, 1956.

KIRKPATRICK, CLIFFORD. *The Family,* chaps. xxi and xxii. New York: The Ronald Press Co., 1955.

LANDIS, JUDSON T. "The Trauma of Children When Parents Divorce," *Marriage and Family Living,* February, 1960, pp. 7–13.

LOCKE, HARVEY J. *Predicting Adjustment in Marriage.* New York: Henry Holt & Co., Inc., 1951.

MONAHAN, THOMAS P. "The Duration of Marriage to Divorce: Second Marriages and Migratory Types," *Marriage and Family Living,* May, 1959, pp. 134–38.

NYE, F. IVAN. "Child Adjustment in Broken and in Unhappy Unbroken Homes," *Marriage and Family Living,* November, 1957, pp. 356–61.

Indexes

AUTHOR INDEX

517

SUBJECT INDEX

Pregnancy—*Cont.*
  sexual relations and—*Cont.*
    second pregnancy, 394–95
    trimesters and, 394–95
Puritans
  bundling, 34–35
  children, 41–43
    idleness, 42
    religion, 42–43
    subservience, 42
  colonists, 29
  courtship, 30–32
  divorce, 43–44
  marriage, 35–41
    adultery, 41
    husband role, 36, 37–38
    religious values, 35–36
    secular nature, 36
    sex, and, 40–41
    wife role, 35, 38–40
      childbearing, 38–39
      personal life, 39
  premarital sexual behavior, 32–35
    male chastity, 32
    prostitution, 33
    punishments, 33–34
  "Puritanism" and, 46
  religious beliefs, 28–30
    history of, 28
    significance of, 29–30
    sovereignty of God, 28
  remarriage, 44–45
  romantic love, 31
  significance of, 27–28, 45–46

R

Remarriage
  adjustment, 497
  divorce prone, 511–12
    factors, 411
    failure bias, 411–12
    marital misfits, 511
    "nonprone," 512
  divorced, 504–6
    age, 505
    children, 506–7
    courtship, 504–5
    family, 505–6
    motivations of, 504
    "no help," 505
    opportunities, 505
    peer group, 505–6
  ego-need satisfaction, 10
  market, 499–500
    divorced, 499–500
    single, 499–500
    widowed, 499–500
  rates, 465, 497

Remarriage—*Cont.*
  social factors, 498–501
    age, 498
    spouse age difference, 498–99
  success, 508–11
    adjustment, 508–10
    divorced, 508–9
    personal assessments, 510
    sex differences, 510–11
    widowed, 509–10
  time from first marriage, 498–99
    divorced, 498–99
    sex differences, 498
    widowed, 499
  types, never remarry, 496–97
    adjusted, 496
    bitter, 496
    frightened, 496
    overdemanding, 496
    rejected, 496
  widowed, 501–4
    children, and, 502–3
      deceased parent influence, 503
      stepparent, 503, 507–8
    conflict about spouse, 501–2
    friends, 502
    "idealized" first spouse, 501–2
    in-laws, 502
    relatives, 502
    sex differences, 501–2
    success, 503–4

S

Sex, marital
  adjustment, 363–67
    coital frequency, 366
    communication, 365
    education, 367
    orgasm success, 365–67
    over time, 364–67
    satisfaction, 366
  aging, 373–75
    frequency, 373–74
      husband's age, 374
      no partner, 374
    life patterns, 375
    menopause influences, 373
  birth control; *see* Birth control
  male-female comparisons, 367–71
    different needs, 369–70
    different socialization, 367
    frequency, 368–69
    importance, 368
  past beliefs, 357–58
  problems
    frigidity, 371–72
      causes, 371
      defined, 371
      frequency, 372
      significance of, 372

This book was set in 11 point Baskerville, leaded 2 points and 10 point Baskerville, leaded 1 point. The chapter numbers are in 30 point Spartan Medium; chapter titles in 18 point Bernard Modern italic. The part numbers are in 36 point Futura Medium; part titles in 30 point Bernard Modern italic. The size of the type page is 27 by 46½ picas.